A HISTORY OF KOREA

A HISTORY OF

KOREA

FROM
"LAND OF THE MORNING CALM"
TO STATES IN CONFLICT

JINWUNG KIM

INDIANA UNIVERSITY PRESS   *Bloomington and Indianapolis*

This book is a publication of

Indiana University Press
601 North Morton Street
Bloomington, Indiana 47404-3797 USA

iupress.indiana.edu

Telephone orders 800-842-6796
Fax orders 812-855-7931

Library of Congress Cataloging-in-Publication Data

Kim, Jinwung.
  A history of Korea : from "Land of the Morning Calm" to states in conflict /
Jinwung Kim.
    pages cm
  Includes bibliographical references and index.
  ISBN 978-0-253-00024-8 (cloth : alkaline paper) — ISBN 978-0-253-00078-1
(ebook) 1. Korea—History. 2. Korea (South)—History. 3. Korea (North)—
History. I. Title.
  DS907.18.K53296 2012
  951.9—dc23

                            2012032989

1 2 3 4 5 16 15 14 13 12

Contents

Acknowledgments

I DEEPLY THANK MY PATRON, Spencer C. Tucker, former John Biggs Chair of Military History at Virginia Military Institute and currently Senior Fellow of Military History at ABC-CLIO. Dr. Tucker helped me find a publisher for my work on the history of Korea and offered many suggestions and constructive criticism on my manuscript, all the while expressing endless enthusiasm for its publication. This book would never have been completed without his help and reassurance.

I also thank Robert J. Sloan and Sarah Wyatt Swanson, editorial director and assistant sponsoring editor, respectively, at Indiana University Press, for their excellent suggestions for improving the quality of the book. I also thank the anonymous reviewer of my manuscript for valuable suggestions and comments that further improved this work.

Finally, this book could not have been completed without the love and sacrifice of my daughter, Hyungeun Grace Kim. Her love for her father and endless encouragement helped make all this possible.

Jinwung Kim
Taegu, Republic of Korea

Introduction

KOREANS, A BRANCH OF THE Ural-Altaic family, began their long, rich history as small tribes entering Manchuria (Manzhou) and the Korean peninsula from the Asian mainland hundreds of thousands of years ago. The vast plains of Manchuria, which now belong to China, had been the main arena of activity for Koreans until AD 926, when the Korean kingdom of Parhae fell to Qidan (Khitan) Liao. At first the Korean people came together into a cluster of villages and tribal states, termed "walled-town states." As stronger walled-town states subjugated weaker ones under their dominion, these walled-town states grew into confederated kingdoms, including Old Chosŏn, Puyŏ, Koguryŏ, Paekche, and Silla, as well as the Kaya confederation. Among these, the kingdoms of Koguryŏ, Paekche, and Silla developed into centralized kingdoms, opening the period of the Three Kingdoms. When Silla unified two rival kingdoms in 676, or certainly when Koryŏ ended the period of the Later Three Kingdoms in 936, Koreans finally came together into a single homogeneous nation that has kept its identity despite repeated invasions by surrounding countries and peoples.

During the Koryŏ and Chosŏn dynasties, Korea was an autonomous, unified state with a sophisticated central government for a millennium. When Japan annexed the Chosŏn kingdom in 1910, Koreans lost their independence and came under Japanese colonial rule. Koreans tenaciously resisted unrelenting pressure from the Japanese to annihilate their way of life, and they succeeded in preserving their own culture intact. Since liberation from the Japanese in 1945, and as a result of the Cold War, Korea came to be divided into two states, North and South. Despite this division, Koreans in each state have regarded those in the other as their brethren and have aspired to reunification.

In short, throughout their long history, Koreans have endured all kinds of trials to maintain an ethnic and cultural identity quite separate from that of China or Japan. Koreans all speak the same language and share the same culture, and clearly their language, alphabet (*han'gŭl*), arts, and customs are distinct from those of the Chinese and the Japanese.

Although it began as a small nation on the eastern tip of the Asian continent, Korea has had a long, important civilization. Korea's extensive history has been characterized both by the persistent assertion of a distinctive Korean identity and by military, political, and cultural assaults from external sources. Korean historians note that, throughout its history, Korea has been invaded by foreign aggressors once every two years on average. Given Korea's strategic location and the much greater power of its neighbors, first China, and then Japan and Russia, it is remarkable that the Korean nation has survived.

While establishing its national identity, the Korean nation has produced remarkable cultural achievements. Recently South Korea (Republic of Korea) has excelled from the standpoints of political and economic development. Indeed, it has been universally acclaimed as a political and economic success story. An internationally recognized middle power, South Korea is marked not only by a fully functioning modern democracy but also by a high-tech modern world economy. It has raised itself from the depths of devastation and poverty following the Korean War (1950–1953) and shaken off the shackles of authoritarian rule to become a fully democratic nation committed to human rights, the rule of law, and economic prosperity for its people. The history of South Korea is also one of the fastest socioeconomic growth stories in the world during the past six decades.[1] As of 2008 it was the 15th largest economy and the 12th most active trading nation among 186 countries. It has become a much more dynamic and creative society than it was 20 years ago. The country is now a leader in information technology, and its popular culture, known as *hallyu*, or the Korean wave, dominates much of Asia. South Korea's full-fledged democracy and internationally oriented, prospering economy has earned it recognition as the legitimate government on the Korean peninsula.

Throughout its history the Korean nation has been influenced by the immense power and culture of China. Historically the Chinese were far more numerous and more powerful militarily than Koreans; their technology and culture were also more advanced. Before 1895 successive Chinese dynasties from the Han to the Qing empires exerted great power and influence on Korea. Koreans drew from the Chinese model in organizing its political institutions, and the Korean adoption of the Chinese political system extended to society and culture. But this adoption of Chinese institutions and culture was not an expression of submission. Rather, it was the indispensable condition of being civilized in the East Asian context. It did not obliterate the identity of the Korean people.

After 1895, following its military defeat of China (the First Sino-Japanese War of 1894–1895), Japan made political and economic inroads into Korea, which led to Korea's 35 years of subjugation. No sooner was Korea liberated from Japan's imperialistic rule at the end of World War II than Western influence arrived in two conflicting forms—the capitalistic, liberal-democratic tradition of the United States and the communism of the Soviet Union. Conflicting ideologies and a rivalry for power in what came to be known as the Cold War split the Korean nation into two hostile states.[2] Despite these formidable outside influences, it was the blood, sweat, and passion of its own people that basically shaped Korea's long history and made Koreans stand out as the masters of their own history.

In the premodern era Korea suffered from a major problem. Compared to other nations, each of Korea's dynasties lasted too long, much longer than in China or any other country, and fell into chronic corruption, stagnation, inertia, and lethargy. The dynastic cycle was so long in Korea that the reforms needed to meet changing domestic and international situations were absent. One reason may have been that Korea was a relatively small and culturally uniform country with fewer variables to bring about a rapid dynastic change. Another reason may have been Koreans' unflagging adherence to the Confucian concepts of loyalty, which led them to cling to a dynasty, once it was established, much more faithfully than other peoples.

This book aims to provide foreign readers with a general survey of Korea's long, rich history from ancient times to the present. To achieve this goal, it discusses Korea's major political, economic, social, and cultural developments, as well as the dynamics underlying them. In history, the closer the past is to the present, the more important it seems to us. This book therefore devotes a great deal of space to the description of the post-Chosŏn period. In particular, it treats in detail the most recent developments, including the Hwang U-sŏk scandal and the spreading Korean wave of pop culture throughout Asia.

Like that of many other countries, Korean history is also full of different interpretations by individual historians. This work endeavors to suggest the most recent interpretations on every controversial issue in Korean history. The account in this book also generally reflects a coherent consensus of varying schools. For instance, on the origins of *yangban* ("two orders" or "two sectors"), the aristocratic class of the Chosŏn dynasty (1392–1910), this book takes the view that, from the beginning of the kingdom, the yangban and commoner classes were strictly differentiated.

New historical facts are also revealed in these chapters. Here I list just a few examples. First, the rank of the six ministries, *yuk-pu* in the Koryŏ dynasty and *yuk-cho* in the Chosŏn dynasty, was actually arranged in the order of Yi (Personnel), Pyŏng (Military), Ho (Taxation), Hyŏng (Punishment), Ye (Rites), and Kong (Engineering), instead of Yi, Ho, Ye, Pyŏng, Hyŏng, and Kong following the account in the *Kyŏngguk taejŏn,* or the Great Code of State Administration, which was perfected in 1470. Second, the Three Kingdoms of Koguryŏ, Paekche, and Silla all accepted Buddhism as a result of the proselytizing efforts of Indian Buddhist monks, some of whom suffered martyrdom in Korea. Third, in the late Chosŏn period, when the kingdom was the focus of a fierce power struggle between neighboring powers, it was not Hermann Budler, the German vice-consul to Chosŏn, but rather Paul Georg von Möllendorf, who came to Chosŏn in late 1882 as one of the special advisers on foreign affairs, who proposed that it become a neutral, unaligned nation. And finally, in 1895 Queen Min, the consort of the Chosŏn king Kojong, was not murdered in her bedroom. She was dragged to the courtyard of the Kyŏngbok-kung palace and then publicly hacked to death by the Japanese.

Character assessment occupies a prominent place in the study of history. This book endeavors to assess the major leaders in Korean history, especially those in post–World War II Korea, North as well as South, that is, Syngman Rhee and his successors in South Korea as well as North Korean leaders Kim Il-sung and Kim Jong-il.

This book stresses, in particular, a "history war," South Korea's long-standing battle with China and Japan over historical records and territorial disputes. The Republic of Korea is now at odds with the People's Republic of China over the recent Chinese attempt to include the histories of Korea's ancient kingdoms of Old Chosŏn, Puyŏ, Koguryŏ, and Parhae into its own history. Specifically China has been making systematic attempts to portray the once mighty Koguryŏ kingdom, which ruled the northern part of the Korean peninsula and parts of present-day Manchuria between the first and seventh centuries, as ethnic Chinese rather than an independent Korean nation. Korea has also been at loggerheads with Japan over that country's attempts to revise its secondary-school textbooks to omit discussions of the atrocities committed during its colonial rule (1910–1945) and the conflicting sovereignty claims over the Tok-to islets, known as Takeshima in Japan, in the East Sea.

THE McCUNE-REISCHAUER SYSTEM

Regarding the form of the Korean names, this book generally follows the McCune-Reischauer system now internationally used, with the exception of such well-known names as Seoul (Sŏul), Pyongyang (P'yŏngyang), Syngman Rhee (Yi Sŭng-man), Kim Il-sung (Kim Il-sŏng), Park Chung-hee (Pak Chŏng-hŭi), and Kim Jong-il (Kim Chŏng-il). Family names precede personal names, which usually consist of two syllables and are hyphenated. This book also uses the *pinyin* rather than Wade-Giles spelling for Chinese names.

GEOGRAPHY

As with most other states, geography and climate have played key roles in Korean history. Korea is a peninsula situated at the northeastern rim of the Asian continent. The Korean peninsula and its adjacent islands, which have sustained the Korean people for hundreds of thousands of years, lie within the latitude range of 33° to 43° north and the longitude range of 124° to 131° east. This is almost equal to the distance between the states of South Carolina (Columbia) and Massachusetts (Boston). The Korean peninsula is 600 miles in length, but in width it varies from 200 miles at the broadest point to 90 miles at its narrow waist.

Shaped somewhat like a rabbit or a tiger and comprising a landed area about the size of the state of Minnesota, the total area of the Korean peninsula is some 85,000 square miles (221,000 square kilometers). Of this total, the part under administrative control of the Republic of Korea (ROK) takes up 38,000 square miles (99,000 square kilometers), or about 45 percent of the whole. The Korean peninsula is about two-thirds the size of the Japanese home islands and equal to the island of Great Britain. South Korea (ROK) is slightly larger than Portugal and Hungary or the state of Indiana. The shortest distance from the Korean peninsula's west coast to the Chinese Shandong peninsula is about 119 miles (190 kilometers), and 129 miles (206 kilometers) from the east coast to the Japanese islands.

In far northern Korea, the Yalu (Amnok) and the Tumen (Tuman) rivers separate the Korean peninsula from China and Russia. The historic rivers have their sources on the slopes of Paektu-san, a border-straddling extinct volcano which, at 9,000 feet (2,744 meters), is Korea's tallest peak and whose crater contains Lake Ch'ŏnji, or Heavenly Lake. Koreans have historically regarded this mountain as a sacred place. Thus Kim Il-sung, North Korea's "Great Leader," and his guerrilla band claimed an association with this mountain as part of the founding myth of North Korea. Also, the personality cult of its "Dear Leader," Kim Jong-il, holds that he was born in a humble log cabin on the slope of the mountain (he was actually born in the village of Vyatskoye, near Khabarovsk, then in the Soviet Union). The upper reaches of the two rivers are usually shallow and completely frozen over during the winter months, allowing movement of human and animal cargoes over their icy surface. In the past the Korean people could easily wade across these frozen rivers to Manchuria, where they migrated in large numbers and established pioneer settlements. These gradually evolved into prosperous agricultural settlements, where their descendents have maintained a coherent ethnic and cultural unity up until the present.

Three bodies of water—the East Sea (Sea of Japan), the Yellow Sea, and the South Sea—enclose the Korean peninsula on three sides. Compared to the smooth coastline of the east coast, the west and south coasts are marked by an endless succession of bays, inlets, and peninsulas and have good natural harbors, including Pusan and Inch'ŏn.

Approximately 70 percent of the Korean peninsula is mountainous. Of the total land mass, elevations of more than 1,000 meters (3,300 feet) above sea level account for 10 percent. The higher mountains are located mostly in the northern and eastern parts of Korea. The peninsula is crisscrossed by several ranges of mountains; the dominant feature is the Nangnim and T'aebaek mountain ranges, which run down the east coast like a spine and cause most of Korea's rivers to flow westward. These mountain ranges have historically inhibited communication and cultural homogeneity between various parts of the country. Regional isolation has also led to conflict throughout the country's history, particularly between the Chŏlla and Kyŏngsang provinces in southern Korea and between the P'yŏngan and Hamgyŏng provinces in northern Korea. Mountains, steep hills, and streams command Korea's landscape, which appears to have been a factor in shaping what is said to be one of Koreans' peculiar characteristics, that of a quick temper.

Although relatively short and shallow, Korea's rivers have played an important part in the nation's history. The rivers running in an east-west direction have provided physical barriers against foreign invaders. More important, they have functioned as arteries of commerce, provided water for the irrigation of farm-lands, and, in the twentieth century, served as sources of hydroelectric power. Stretches of plains appear intermittently along the rivers and streams, essentially isolated from one another by mountains and hills. Although comprising only 20 percent of the land area, these plains, which provide the bulk of the country's agricultural products, have been essential, throughout the country's history, in providing a means of livelihood for the majority of the Korean people. But because of the low fertility of Korea's soil, life has never been easy for those untold millions who have toiled over the centuries on Korea's plains and elsewhere in the country's rural areas.

The Korean peninsula as a whole is only moderately endowed with natural resources. Most of the farm products, especially rice, have historically come from the southern part of the peninsula. Southern Korea, in fact, is considered the rice bowl of Korea. Throughout Korea's history, rice has been the staple diet and has also functioned as currency. For these reasons, South Korea has always had a much greater population density than other parts of the country. On the other hand, the northern mountain ranges contain concentrations of mineral deposits. In fact, North Korea has most of the mineral resources of the peninsula. As of 2008 North Korea had $6.2 trillion worth of ample mineral resources, 24.1 times more than South Korea's $257 billion. In addition, North Korea has 6 billion tons of magnesite (South Korea has none), 20.5 billion tons of coal, and 2,000 tons of gold, as well as important deposits of iron ore, lead, zinc, tungsten, barite, graphite, molybdenum, limestone, mica, fluorite, copper, nickel, silver, aluminum, and uranium. South Korea has overcome this disadvantage by producing a highly educated and motivated populace that has made that country one of the ten largest industrialized nations in the world. As of 2009 South Korea's economy was 37.4 times larger than that of North Korea. Its nominal GNI stood at $837.2 billion in stark contrast to North Korea's $22.4 billion. South Korea's per-capita GNI, at $17,175, was 17.9 times larger than North Korea's $960. Its total trade volume of $686.6 billion was 201.9 times greater than North Korea's $3.4 billion.

Korea's looming mountains are unevenly distributed in the eastern part of the peninsula, as are Japan's highest mountains in the western part of the main island of Honshu. Therefore, whereas the Korean peninsula faces China, the Japanese islands face the Pacific, although the East Sea provides a few natural havens for ships. As a result, Korea has had a geographical affinity with China but, figuratively, turns its back on Japan.

In mountainous Korea the settlements that formed had mountains or hills in the rear and rivers or streams at the front. According to traditional geomantic theories, these areas were considered propitious sites. The Korean peninsula had many such favorable places where villages and cities were formed.

The Korean peninsula served as a land bridge over which Chinese culture was diffused from China to Japan. At first Ural-Altaic tribes migrated eastward from Siberia toward the Korean peninsula and carried with them Neolithic culture and, later, Bronze Age skills. Through their intimate cultural contact with China, Koreans brought Buddhism and Confucianism into the peninsula and transmitted these to Japan. On the other hand, the peninsula has proved vulnerable to foreign invasion both from the sea and the continental mainland, having been invaded by the Chinese in the seventh century, Mongols in the thirteenth century, the Japanese in the sixteenth century, and Manchus in the seventeenth century. Korea's geographical position also made it the focus of regional conflict in the Far East. At the turn of the twentieth century Korea was the object of two wars, as China and Japan in turn fought to maintain footholds on the peninsula, and then Japan fought to exclude a Russia keenly interested in Korea's ice-free ports. Taking note of its contours and strategic locations, some Western observers have likened the Korean peninsula to a dagger or pistol pointed at the heart of the Japanese archipelago.

Like its landscape, Korea's climate has also influenced the course of its history considerably. In Korea seasonal differences are striking, with the annual rainfall varying around 40 inches (1,000 millimeters) overall and concentrated in the summertime; indeed, two-thirds of Korea's precipitation falls between June and September. This climatic condition is highly favorable for rice farming. Droughts appear one every eight years on average. Summers are hotter and winters colder in the Korean peninsula than along the western coast of the Eurasian continent at the same latitude. Although it has four distinct seasons, the Korean peninsula, reaching across a latitude of nearly 10°, experiences considerable variations in climate, particularly in winter. The climate at Korea's extreme south is essentially a marine climate, and that at the extreme north is essentially continental. In spring, a powerful sandstorm, known as "yellow dust," often hits the Korean peninsula from China.

TOK-TO

In the East Sea, about 47 nautical miles east of Ullŭng-do (Dagelet), stands the Korean island of Tok-to, formerly called Liancourt Rocks by the Occidentals. In the nineteenth century European sailors who explored the seas around Korea gave Western names to many Korean islands, including Tok-to, as their Korean names were unknown to the Europeans.

Tok-to, formed from volcanic rocks and composed of two main islets, is Korea's easternmost island, situated in the middle of the East Sea, at latitude 37° north and longitude 131° east. In 512 the ancient Korean kingdom of Silla conquered Usan-guk (state), of which the main part was Ullŭng-do. Thereafter the Korean people have considered Tok-to to be part of Ullŭng-do and therefore their territory. Historically the subsequent Korean kingdoms of Koryŏ (918–1392) and Chosŏn (1392–1910), as well as the Republic of Korea (since 1948), have exercised sovereignty over Tok-to.[3]

PEOPLE

As of July 2008 the Korean peninsula sustains a population of about 72 million, compared to approximately 20 million at the end of the nineteenth century and 28 million in 1945, at the end of World War II. Some 49 million of the peninsula's population live in the Republic of Korea, and indeed South Korea is one of the most densely populated areas of the world.

In terms of race, Koreans are predominantly of Mongoloid stock. They trace their ancient origin to the Central Asian area. Although they bear some physical resemblance to the Chinese, their language is totally unlike Chinese; it has similarities, however, with Turkish, Mongolian, Japanese, and other Central Asian languages. Koreans are taller, on average, than most other East Asians and are distinctive in appearance.

Whereas the United States is a nation of immigrants, represented by multiculturalism and diversity, foreign observers tend to characterize Korea as a more uniform nation whose people are overtly nationalistic and patriotic. In fact, nationalism has historically been a dominant ideology in Korean society and has inspired the Korean people to strongly resist foreign intervention and the influx of foreign cultures.

Culturally and genetically Koreans are one of the most homogeneous peoples in the world. Many branches of the Tungusic people in Manchuria and Mongolia are racially mixed with one other and culturally assimilated with the Chinese, but Koreans have succeeded in maintaining their own ethnic and cultural identity. Despite frequent cultural exchanges, Koreans have rarely intermarried with the Chinese. Koreans all share a sense of destiny and a perception of themselves as a unique people, bound together by a common language, culture, and religion. The peninsula's geographical conditions, including its remoteness from the Chinese mainland, enhanced a feeling of uniqueness among Koreans and encouraged strong nationalism and a desire to resist foreign domination. Indeed, Korean nationalism was strengthened because of successive foreign invasions. Korea, as a small country in a strategic location, has a deep sense of injustice about being manipulated by the great powers around it.

For most Koreans, the notion of "motherland," and patriotism, overrides virtually everything. Since they have to defend their motherland as well as their own culture from the continent, Koreans have traditionally emphasized the importance of unity rather than diversity, to the point of sometimes antagonizing others. That explains, in part, why Koreans are rather poor at mingling with outsiders and are angry when insolvent Korean enterprises are taken over by foreign capital.

Besides being ultra-nationalistic and excessively patriotic, the Korean people are said to be quick-tempered, even impulsive. Instead of calculating possible outcomes calmly and rationally, Koreans are prone to emotional actions, reactions, and interactions. Occasionally they go to extremes, but consider such actions as demonstrations of "manliness." The average Korean is often aroused to a state of sustained passion if the issue is an emotional one. The Korean idea of *uri nara,* or our country, exemplifies Koreans' strong patriotism and nationalism, which may be demonstrated in such varied circumstances as a soccer game against Japan or during an anti-American flare-up.

A HISTORY OF KOREA

1

DAWN OF THE KOREAN NATION

The Paleolithic Age

AS A NATION, Korea has a long history. The archeological finds suggest that, at some point in the misty past, tiny bands of tribesmen inhabiting the lands along the Altai Mountains of Central Asia began making their way eastward in the eternal quest for the "land of life" (the East), moving into Manchuria and the Korean peninsula. The habitation of early men in the Korean peninsula started as early as 700,000 years ago. Some North Koreans claim that the peninsula may have been inhabited for a million years. Until now Paleolithic remains, dating about 700,000 to 8,000 years ago, have been excavated in various parts of the Korean peninsula, from the Tumen River basin to the north to Cheju-do Island to the south. The most important Paleolithic sites, amounting to more than a hundred, are mostly found at the sides of big rivers.

The best-known sites of the Early Paleolithic Age, which ended approximately 100,000 years ago, include those at Sangwŏn county (Kŏmŭnmoru cave and Yonggok-ni) in the Taedong River basin, at Yŏnch'ŏn county (Chŏn'gok-ni) in the Hant'an River basin, at Chech'ŏn city (Chŏmmal cave of P'ojŏn-ni) and Tanyang city (Kŭmgul cave) in the South Han River basin, and at P'aju county (Chuwŏl-ri and Kawŏl-ri) in the Imjin River basin. The sites of the Mid-

1

dle Paleolithic Age, dating about 100,000 to 40,000 years ago, include those at Unggi county (Kulp'o-ri) in the Tumen River basin, at Sangwŏn county (Yonggok-ni) and the Yŏkp'o area of Pyongyang in the Taedong River basin, at Tŏkch'ŏn county (Sŭngni-san) in the Ch'ŏngch'ŏn River basin, at Yanggu county (Sangmuryŏng-ni) in the North Han River basin, at Yŏnch'ŏn county (Namgye-ri), Yangp'yŏng county (Pyŏngsan-ni), Chech'ŏn city (Myŏngo-ri), and Tanyang city (Suyanggae cave) in the South Han River basin, and on Chejudo (Pile-mot pond). The sites of the Late Paleolithic Age, dating about 40,000 to 8,000 years ago, include those at Unggi county (Kulp'o-ri [the upper layer] and Pup'o-ri), Pyongyang (Mandal-ri) in the Taedong River basin, Kongju city (Sŏkchang-ni) and Ch'ŏngwŏn county (Turubong cave) in the Kŭm River basin, Hwasun county (Taejŏn-ni), Koksŏng county (Chewŏl-ri), and Sunch'ŏn city (Chungnae-ri) in the Sŏmjin River basin. Given the wide distribution of these sites, it is presumed that Paleolithic men lived in virtually every part of the Korean peninsula.

At the remains mentioned above, Paleolithic stone tools such as choppers, scrappers, hand axes, and cleavers have been unearthed. Choppers and scrappers were mainly used to take animal meat off the bones. Hand axes and cleavers were later produced for many purposes. At Sangwŏn county and Yonggok-ni, fossilized human bones were uncovered. Although North Koreans argue that these bones may date back to 500,000 to 1,000,000 years ago, interpretations have varied on the estimated dating.

In the Paleolithic Age the implements needed for hunting were fashioned by chipping stone. At first a lump of rock, flint stone in particular, was struck until a usable tool with sharp edges or points was produced. Later a number of pieces that had been broken off were also given additional edge or sharpness by chipping or flaking and then were utilized as implements. This improvement in tool-making methods allowed access to a wide range and amount of food sources, and was essential to the invention of bows and spear throwers. Bone implements made of animal bones and horns were also used for fishing.

Paleolithic men at first lived in caves, and later they began to build dugouts on level ground. Instances of the former are found at the Kŏmŭnmoru cave (Sangwŏn county) and at the Chŏmmal cave (P'ojŏn-ni, Chech'ŏn city), and the latter is illustrated by a dwelling site at Sŏkchang-ni. A hearth, together with animal figures of a bear, a dog, and a tortoise, radiocarbon-dated to 20,000 years old, has been unearthed at Sŏkchang-ni. The existence of a hearth demonstrates that fire was used both for heating and for cooking food.

These Paleolithic men were grouped together in small-scale societies such as bands and gained their subsistence from hunting wild animals as well as gathering fruit, berries, and edible plant roots. They also gathered firewood and materials for their tools, clothes, and shelters. The invention of harpoons allowed fish to become part of human diets. At Sangwŏn county, many fossilized fauna remains from the diet of early humans have been discovered. By the late Paleolithic period, beginning about 40,000 years ago, Paleolithic people had begun to carve animal images on the walls of caves, demonstrating their simple artistic activity.

Whether these Paleolithic people were the ancestors of present-day Koreans is difficult to know. The Paleolithic Age lasted for an extensive period, and presumably, upon experiencing a succession of glacial eras, Paleolithic men periodically perished and were replaced by newcomers or survivors migrated to other warmer areas.

The Neolithic Age

About 6,000 BC the tribes on the Korean peninsula began to pass from the Paleolithic to the Neolithic Age. It is presumed that the late Paleolithic people on the Korean peninsula evolved into the early Neolithic people, because when the Paleolithic evolved into the Neolithic Age the Korean peninsula experienced no rapid increase in population and pottery found in some areas of Korea predated pottery discovered in Siberia and Mongolia. These original natives were supplemented by Neolithic newcomers who migrated from Siberia. Numerous sites of the Neolithic period have been found on the Korean peninsula, particularly along the Taedong River near Pyongyang and the Han River near Seoul, and in the Naktong River estuary near Pusan. The best-known sites include those at Tongsam-dong on Yŏng-do Island off Pusan, Amsa-dong in Seoul, and Misa-ri in Kwangju city, in the Han River basin; Kulp'o-ri at Unggi county, in the Tumen River basin; and Kŭmt'an-ni and Ch'ŏngho-ri near Pyongyang, in the Taedong River basin.

Neolithic men were characterized by their ability to make polished stone tools and to manufacture and use pottery. By polishing stone, they produced sharp knives, spears, and arrowheads. They also manufactured a range of stone tools for farming. The polished stone axe, above all other tools, made forest clearance feasible on a large scale. As a result, Neolithic people were able to enjoy more conveniences in their lives than their Paleolithic predecessors. Their greatest technical invention was the use of pottery. At first they manufactured plain, round-bottomed pottery, and then, from sometime around 4000 BC, a new type of pottery called *chŭlmun t'ogi* (comb-pattern pottery) appeared on the Korean peninsula and became characteristic of Korea's Neolithic Age. Comb-pattern pottery was gray in color with a V-shaped pointed bottom, and was distinguished by designs on the entire outer surface of parallel lines (comb-patterning, cord-wrapping decorations) that resembled markings made by a comb. The comb-pattern design was added to prevent cracks on the surface. Mainly used to store grains, this pottery has been found at numerous Neolithic sites throughout the Korean peninsula. The wide distribution of the pottery in Manchuria, Siberia, and Mongolia indicates that Neolithic men on the Korean peninsula bore cultural ties with the Ural-Altaic regions.

Around 2000 BC a third pottery culture, originating in central China, spread into the Korean peninsula from Manchuria, and was characterized by painted designs marked by waves, lightning, and skeins on the outer surface and the flat bottom. Much of this newly introduced pottery has been found in the western and southern coastal regions and the river basins. Stone plowshares, stone sickles, and stone hoes have been discovered with carbonated millet at the remains of this new pottery culture, indicating that stone implements and harvested grains were stored in pottery.

Like previous Paleolithic settlers, these Neolithic people first lived by hunting, fishing, and gathering. By about 4000 BC, however, people had learned to plant grains, especially millet, using horn or stone hoes to dig and stone sickles to harvest. An incipient farming culture appeared in which small-scale shifting ("slash-and-burn") cultivation was practiced in addition to various other subsistence strategies. Carbonated millet found at the remain at Chit'am-ni (Pongsan county in Hwanghae province) attests to this early farming culture. These Neolithic people practiced agriculture in a settled communal life, organized into familial clans. They also domesticated and raised livestock such as dogs and pigs. They used nets to catch fish and learned to fish with hook and line.

These Neolithic people turned animal skins to good account for clothing. They scraped away flesh for food with stone knives and then sewed skins together using bone needles made of deer horns. People later wove cloth from animal fur or plant fibers, especially hemp, with primitive spindles, and their clothes were often adorned with shells or beads.[1]

Once they began farming, the growing need to spend more time and labor tending crops required more localized dwellings, and so Neolithic men increasingly moved from a nomadic to a sedentary existence. As a result, permanent or seasonally inhabited settlements appeared. Mainly living in pit dwellings, they built huts in round or rectangular dugouts, with posts set up to support a straw thatch covering to protect against the wind and the rain. The rough ground was covered by platforms, mats, and skins on which residents slept. One to several hearths were placed in the center of the floor of the dwelling and used for cooking and heating. Storage pits for storing grains and instruments were located beside the hearth or near the entrance, which faced south to benefit from the sunlight. Five or six family members inhabited a dwelling pit.

The basic unit of Neolithic society was the clan, which was bound together by its distinct bloodline. Economically independent and self-sufficient, each clan formed its own village. Economic activities within territories claimed by other clans were prohibited, and such a violation would incur either punishment or compensation. Despite this tight-knit economic life, exogamous marriage was common, and spouses were invariably sought from other clans. Neolithic society, in a word, was relatively simple and egalitarian.

Neolithic clans held totemic beliefs in which they worshiped objects in the natural world, namely certain animals or plants, as their ancestors. In its worship of a specific totemic object with which it closely identified, a clan differentiated itself from others. Neolithic men also had animistic beliefs, as they were convinced that every object in the natural world possessed a soul. They therefore worshiped mountains, rivers, and trees. Foremost among natural objects to be worshiped was the sun, considered the greatest being in the universe, which they called *hanŭnim*, or heavenly god. Man, too, was believed to have an immortal soul which would ultimately return to heaven where God resided. Thus, when a man died, he was said to "return" to nature and, in burying the man's body, his corpse was laid with its head facing eastward, in the direction of the sunrise.

The cult of heaven and the spirits caused Neolithic men to look upon a shaman, who was believed to have the ability to link human beings with heavenly god and the spirits, as the greatest figure. Neolithic people believed that, by virtue of his authority and on behalf of God, a shaman could drive off evil spirits and evoke good spirits so as to produce positive results, such as fecundity, longevity, and the complete cure of diseases. It was these shamans who filled the roles of clan and tribal leader in the Neolithic and Bronze Ages. The Neolithic Age is worthy of examination, since men of this early period were the ancestors of present-day Koreans.

THE ORIGINS OF THE KOREAN PEOPLE

The Bronze Age

In the first millennium BC the tribal peoples of Korea passed from the Neolithic to the Bronze Age. The Bronze Age began in Manchuria between approximately the fifteenth and thirteenth centuries BC and on the Korean peninsula in the tenth century BC. Because Korea's Bronze culture was closely linked to the founding of Old Chosŏn, whose territory included southern Manchuria, the Bronze culture in Manchuria must be examined along with that on the Korean peninsula. By the tenth century BC people in Manchuria and the Korean peninsula had learned to fashion tools, utensils, and weapons of bronze. They also learned to cultivate rice, developed new forms of political and social organization, and constructed great tombs of stone. These were initiated by new settlers, who were differentiated from the native Neolithic people.

Toward the end of the Neolithic Age a new wave of migration from the north arrived in Manchuria and the Korean peninsula, increasing the region's population and bringing with them Bronze Age technology and undecorated pottery. Numerous Bronze sites have been found in southern Manchuria and throughout the Korean peninsula, particularly in the southern tip of the Liaodong peninsula and the river basins of the Tumen, Taedong, Imjin, Han, Kŭm, Yŏngsan, and Naktong rivers.

Two typical instruments representing Korea's Bronze culture are the mandolin-shaped copper dagger and the multi-knobbed coarse-patterned mirror, neither of which have not been discovered outside southern Manchuria and the Korean peninsula. In the fourth century BC the mandolin-shaped copper dagger, used mainly for rites, evolved into a more sophisticated finely wrought bronze dagger, and the multi-knobbed coarse-patterned mirror, also used in rituals, developed into a more polished multi-knobbed fine-patterned mirror. Still using comb-pattern pottery, Bronze Age men also manufactured a new type of pottery, *mumun t'ogi,* or undecorated pottery. Far more refined than comb-pattern pottery, this type of pottery has thicker walls and displays a wider variety of shapes, indicating improvements in kiln technology. This new undecorated pottery represents Korea's Bronze Age pottery. It has been unearthed only in southern Manchuria and the Korean peninsula.

Remains of Korea's Bronze culture are predominantly found on higher ground overlooking wide and fertile flatlands along river courses, which suggests that the Bronze Age settlers mainly engaged in agriculture. These people plowed fields with stone plowshares, hoes, and wooden plows, cultivating millet, Indian millet, barnyard millet, barley, and beans. By the eighth century BC rice cultivation had begun in some warm regions. A large amount of carbonated rice, excavated at Hunam-ni in Yŏju city in the South Han River basin, at Songgung-ni in Puyŏ county in the Kŭm River basin, and in shell heaps in Kimhae city in the lower reaches of the Naktong River, suggests that rice was brought into Korea's southern and western coastal areas from China's Yangtze River valley. Crescent-shaped stone knives seem to have been used at harvest time to cut rice stalks, and grooved stone axes served to cut down trees and turn over the soil preparatory to planting.

In the Bronze Age round pit dwellings, or dugouts, gradually went out of use and were replaced by huts. The huts, rectangular in shape and built on stone foundations with supporting pillars, were partitioned into rooms serving different purposes. Dwelling sites were grouped into settlements. A cluster of dwelling sites has been found in a single location, suggesting that settlements increasingly grew.

Bronze Age men used delicately polished stone swords and arrowheads as well as bronze swords and spears to hunt animals or conduct wars. The existence of these bronze weapons implies that conquest by warfare was common in this period and that Bronze Age people could presumably gain easy ascendancy over Neolithic men who were armed with stone weapons. At the same time, as a small number of influential individuals monopolized bronze farming implements and weapons, they were able to produce more plentiful agricultural products and seize greater spoils from war. In these ways they commanded greater power and wealth, and gradually emerged as chieftains. These chieftains were armed with bronze spears and mounted horses decorated with bronze ornaments. To demonstrate their authority, these privileged individuals were ornamented with mandolin-shaped copper daggers, multi-knobbed coarse-patterned mirrors, and bronze bells. These articles, which lent prestige and authority to the personages who wielded great power, were used as ritual symbols of authority for the chieftains, who fancied themselves as the sons of heaven.

When these chieftains died, their bodies were buried in megalithic tombs such as dolmens or in stone cists, which were underground burial chambers lined with stones. Because these tombs were reserved for the ruling class, burial practices reflected increasing social stratification. Dolmens, which have been found in great numbers in almost every part of the Korean peninsula, are mainly constructed in two basic forms—the table style and the board style. The table style, often called the northern style because of its distribution predominantly in the areas north of the Han River, was constructed by placing several upright stones in a rough square to support a flat capstone. The board style, often known as the southern style because of its widespread discovery in areas south of the Han River, employed a large boulder as a capstone placed atop several smaller rocks. A third type of dolmen tomb, distributed throughout the Korean peninsula in larger numbers, has no supporting stones, and the capstone is placed directly atop the underground burial chamber. Corpses were buried in dolmen tombs together with bronze daggers and pottery that the men had used during their lifetime.

Along with numerous menhir, or large upright stone monuments, these dolmen tombs represent the megalithic culture in Korea. Some dolmen tombs weigh dozens or even hundreds of tons. The individuals who were buried in these gigantic tombs clearly wielded great authority to command the labor services of vast numbers of people to construct the tombs, and are therefore considered to have been tribal chieftains.

The appearance of dolmen tombs is unique. The round, flat capstone presumably symbolized heaven and the square upright stones represented the earth; people at the time believed that the souls of their chieftains reposed where heaven and earth met. The Bronze Age chieftains, who, as noted, believed they were the sons of heaven, dominated their people with the mandate of heaven.

Small-scale states, dominated by these chieftains, emerged in various parts of the Korean peninsula and southern Manchuria during the Bronze Age. The rulers of these petty states built the earthen fortifications begirded with moats on hillside plateaus and controlled the agricultural population that farmed the plains beyond the fortifications. Because of their physical appearance, these political units have been generally termed *sŏngŭp kukka,* or walled-town states. Although the states were tribal in character, they were also territorial in that they controlled populations beyond their own tribal domains. Walled-town states were the earliest form of state structure in Korea. The Bronze Age may be considered particularly important in Korean history, as the Korean people, during this period, developed more advanced technology and implements, practiced rice farming, and witnessed the appearance of the first political units.

Korean Roots

The possibility of a biological link between Paleolithic people and present-day Koreans has not yet been clearly explored, partly because both archeological and anthropological evidence is lacking. Scholars do agree, however, that modern Koreans do not descend directly from Paleolithic men but instead from the Neolithic people who succeeded them. The ethnic stock of these Neolithic men has continued unbroken to form one element of the later Korean race. It is believed that in the course of a long historical process these Neolithic people merged with one another and, together with new ethnic settlers of Korea's Bronze Age, eventually constituted Koreans of today.

Because the population increased so rapidly at the point when the Neolithic Age became the Bronze Age, Bronze Age settlers in southern Manchuria and the Korean peninsula are also believed to have constituted the Korean race. In fact, these Bronze Age men, who had migrated on a large scale and subjugated Neolithic natives, were to become the mainstream of the Korean people.

The ancient Chinese thought that these Korean ancestors belonged to *dongyi* (*tongi* in Korean), or eastern barbarians, and often divided them into two groups: the northern people, called *Ye, Maek,* or *Yemaek,* and the southern people, called *Han.* This classification is meaningless, however, as these two branches of the Korean people all spoke the same language, Korean, and shared the same culture and customs. For several thousand years they joined forces to create unified Korean kingdoms.

The Bronze culture on the Korean peninsula shared many things in common with the cultures of southern Manchuria and eastern China. For example, the dolmen tombs, the undecorated pottery, and the mandolin-shaped copper dagger have been unearthed only in these areas. It is not accidental, therefore, that from ancient times the Chinese have called the populations of these regions dongyi and distinguished these people from themselves. According to tradition, the Chinese and the dongyi people had fiercely competed for supremacy in central China before the Qin and Han empires unified China in the late third century BC. China's Yin (Shang) dynasty (1751–1122 BC) is known to have been founded and ruled by the dongyi people. As the Zhou dynasty, founded in the Wei River valley, began to wield influence over eastern China in the twelfth century BC, the dongyi people in the region massively migrated eastward to southern Manchuria and the Korean peninsula. When Yin fell to Zhou in 1122 BC, a group of the dynasty's ruling class came to the east and became the ruling elite because of their advanced culture. Thus the legend of Jizi, in which Jizi, a member of royalty of the Yin dynasty, came to Old Chosŏn to found Jizi Chosŏn, has been handed down through the generations.

When China proper was unified by the Qin and Han empires in the late third century BC, a majority of the dongyi people in eastern China had become assimilated and converted to Chinese. But many among the ruling classes chose to go into exile in southern Manchuria and the Korean peninsula. For instance, Wiman, a refugee from the Yan dynasty, which then existed around present-day Beijing, led his band of more than 1,000 followers into exile in Old Chosŏn in the early second century BC. To summarize, in the course of China's unification, the dongyi people were squeezed out of their territories in eastern China and forced to move to southern Manchuria east of the Liao River and the Korean peninsula. Thus Korea's Bronze Age people, Neolithic natives, and the dongyi who had migrated from eastern China all merged together to become the ancestors of the Korean race.

OLD CHOSŎN

The Myth of Tan'gun

According to legend, Korea received its birth as a nation-state in 2333 BC, when a king named Tan'gun, "the Lord of the Pakdal [sandalwood] tree," founded "(Old) Chosŏn," usually translated as "Land of the Morning Calm." As the legend goes, a divine spirit named Hwanung, a son of Hwanin, the sun god, who yearned to live on the earth among the people, descended from heaven to Mount T'aebaek (present-day Paektu-san), with 3 divine stamps and 3,000 followers, and proclaimed himself king of the universe. Hwanung constructed a holy city just below the divine sandalwood tree at the summit of the mountain and administered 360-odd human affairs, including crops, diseases, punishments, and good and evil, with the help of his vassals *p'ungbaek,* or god of the wind; *ubaek,* or god of the rain; and *unsa,* or god of the clouds. He instituted laws and moral codes, and taught the people arts, medicine, and agriculture. His son was Tan'gun. The story of Tan'gun's birth appears in one of the oldest extant history texts, *Samguk yusa,* or Memorabilia of the Three Kingdoms, written by the Buddhist monk Iryŏn in 1285:

> In those days there lived a she-bear and a tigress in the same cave. They prayed to Hwanung to be blessed with incarnation as human beings. The king took pity

on them and gave each a bunch of mugwort and 20 pieces of garlic, saying, "If you eat this holy food and do not see the sunlight for 100 days, you will become human beings."

The she-bear and tigress took the food and retired into the cave. There, eating the food, they were to spend 100 days. In 21 days, the she-bear, who had faithfully observed the king's instructions, became a woman. But the tigress, who had disobeyed them and stepped out of the cave in a few days, remained in her original form.

The bear-woman could find no husband, so she prayed under the divine sandalwood tree to be blessed with a child. Hwanung heard her pray and took her for his wife. She conceived and bore a son who was called Tan'gun Wanggŏm.[2]

Every year, on 3 October, the day that Tan'gun ("Lord of Sandalwood") founded Chosŏn in 2333, is celebrated in South Korea as *Kaech'ŏnjŏl*, or Foundation Day. Holding his court at Asadal (Pyongyang), Tan'gun reigned with unparalleled wisdom until 1122 BC. In present-day South Korea, one may observe shrines to his memory. Another legend holds that a noted sage named Kija (Jizi in Chinese) became disheartened with the lawless state of China and migrated to Tan'gun's Chosŏn with 5,000 followers. In 1122 BC Tan'gun abdicated the throne in favor of Kija to become a mountain god.

The myth of Tan'gun is symbolic on several levels. First, Hwanung and his followers, numbering 3,000, who descended from heaven, symbolize newcomers with a highly advanced Bronze culture. The animals, the she-bear and the tigress, represent ancient tribal totem symbols. Early Korean or Tungusic tribes were usually represented by totem symbols of animals. Specifically a bear was worshiped throughout Northeast Asia, and a tiger frequently figured in Korean folklore and art. The tribes represented by the she-bear and tigress were probably native settlers with a Neolithic culture. The bear-woman's marriage to Hwanung thus signifies the union of two large tribes in Korea. In other words, the Hwanung tribe, believing itself to be descendants of the king of heaven, became the "king tribe," and the bear tribe defeated the tiger tribe to become the "queen tribe." Tan'gun's birth between Hwanung and *"ungnyŏ,"* or the bearwoman, suggests that a migrant tribe with a Bronze culture united with a native tribe with a Neolithic culture to form a walled-town state named "Chosŏn."

The mugwort, the 20 pieces of garlic, and the gods p'ungbaek, ubaek, and unsa all suggest that Old Chosŏn was an agricultural society. The term tan'gun means shaman, or religious leader, and wanggŏm means political leader, and so the name Ta'gun Wanggŏm implies that Old Chosŏn was a theocratic society. Thus Old Chosŏn was an agricultural theocracy.

Tan'gun Chosŏn and Kija Chosŏn

There is no archeological or anthropological evidence to support the legend that Tan'gun Chosŏn (Old Chosŏn) was founded in 2333 BC, but archeological finds suggest that because Bronze culture appeared in southern Manchuria in the fifteenth century BC, small-scale walled-town states, or tribal states, such as Tan'gun Chosŏn, probably did come into existence. Some Chinese documents, written in the early seventh century BC, recorded that a Chinese kingdom of Qi (Che in Korean) traded with Chosŏn, suggesting that Old Chosŏn was an internationally known, commanding state. Then, in the sixth century BC, Chosŏn was so well known among the Chinese that the famous sage Confucius was said to have wished to go to Chosŏn to lead a life there. This tale indicates that the ancient Chinese saw Chosŏn as a "utopia," where life was far better than in China, a place infested with constant warfare and turmoil.

After the Han empire was founded in 206 BC, references to the existence of Chosŏn became more obvious in Chinese records. For instance, the Chinese historian Sima Qian's *Shiji,* or Historical Records, described that when the Yin dynasty fell to the Zhou dynasty in 1122 BC, Jizi (Kija), a member of Yin royalty, with 5,000 intellectuals and technicians in tow, migrated into Chosŏn to ascend the nation's throne. Considering that the first Chinese historical documents describing Jizi, such as *Zhushu jinian,* or the Bamboo Annals, and *Lunyu,* or the Analects, made no mention of Jizi's supposed migration to Chosŏn, this legend of "Kija Chosŏn" suggests that not Jizi himself but his descendants might have come to Chosŏn in succession in the fifth and fourth centuries BC. Wielding highly advanced iron implements, these people became the new ruling class in Chosŏn, which was still then in the Bronze culture. These Yin people also migrated to Chosŏn, as Chosŏn was considered the native state of the dongyi people. Because their own country was also founded by the dongyi people, they may well have felt that the Zhou, established by the Chinese, might not suit them well. When the Han dynasty was later at war with Chosŏn, Chinese historians embellished Jizi as the progenitor of Old Chosŏn.

Kija's descendants succeeded the throne until the early second century BC, when, as mentioned above, Wiman, a political exile from the Yan dynasty, usurped the throne. King Chun, the last king of Kija Chosŏn, is said to have fled southward to the state of Chin, where he called himself the "Han King." Since the period of the Three Kingdoms, Chun's descendants seem to have had such family names as "Han," "Ki," and "Sŏnu."

With the advent of Bronze culture, several walled-town states began to appear in Manchuria and the Korean peninsula. Around 450 BC Puyŏ arose in the upper reaches of the Songhua River in Manchuria, Ye (Yemaek) along the middle reaches of the Yalu, Imdun in the Hamhŭng plain on the northeast seacoast of the Korean peninsula, and Chinbŏn in today's Hwanghae province in North Korea. Chin emerged in the region south of the Han River around 430 BC, and at about the same time some people of Chin found their way into western Japan.

Among these walled-town states the most advanced was Old Chosŏn, established before the eighth century BC at the latest. Originally Old Chosŏn appears to have been just a small political entity dominating a minor portion of the Liao River plains, but by the early fourth century BC it had entered the Iron Age and proceeded to incorporate, by alliance or military conquest, other walled-town states scattered throughout the vast region between the Liao and the Taedong rivers to form a large confederation. At this stage Old Chosŏn was entitled to be called a confederated kingdom.

Old Chosŏn held its court at Pyongyang. At the time there were three different sites called "Pyongyang" (meaning "flatland"): one west of the Liao River, a second east of the river, and the third in northwestern Korea. One can surmise that the first capital of Old Chosŏn was located west of the Liao River, was then transferred east of the river as the Chinese forced Old Chosŏn out of the region, and finally, with the decline of its power, was relocated in present-day Pyongyang in its last years.

By the late fourth century BC the northern Chinese state of Yan had begun to use the term *wang*, or king, upon the decline of the suzerain Zhou kingdom. Old Chosŏn assumed the same title for its ruler and firmly maintained equal relations with China's regional lords in the Warring States Period (403–221 BC). In about 320 BC, when Yan attempted to invade its territory, Old Chosŏn planned a counterattack. As the two states confronted each other, Old Chosŏn's commanding posture caused the Yan people to criticize the Korean nation as "arrogant and cruel." There is no doubt, in short, that Old Chosŏn exhibited formidable strength at that time as an independent power in Northeast Asia.

The Coming of the Iron Age

During the Old Chosŏn period the Bronze Age was fated to pass. In the early fourth century BC commodities fashioned from iron began to enter southern

Manchuria and the Korean peninsula from China, and by 300 BC iron implements had widely come into use.

Iron culture was first introduced to southern Manchuria and northwestern
Korea, Old Chosŏn's territory, and from there it soon spread in all directions.
At the same time another Bronze culture of Scytho-Siberian origin took root
in Manchuria and the Korean peninsula. As iron implements came into use, the
mode of life in Korea underwent profound changes. First of all, with the use
of hoeing implements made of iron and sophisticated iron farming tools such
as plowshares and sickles, agriculture experienced remarkable development.
Food production markedly increased compared to that of the Bronze Age. The
increased output, however, was not shared equally by the whole society but was
monopolized by a ruling class. Thus the rulers wielded even greater authority
than before.

Iron culture also influenced weaponry. Iron weapons such as daggers and
spear points as well as bronze daggers, spear points, and spears have been excavated from Iron Age remains in large numbers. These sharp weapons fashioned
from hard metal were monopolized by a small number among the ruling elite.
Members of the ruling class also mounted on horseback or rode horse-drawn
vehicles in imposing their authority on the rest of the people. These horse-
riding warriors were the undisputed masters of Iron Age society.

People in the Iron Age who lived in pit dwellings or huts began to use *ondol,*
the traditional Korean underground heating device in which the stone that
constituted the room floor was heated by hot air circulating beneath it. This
unique heating system led Koreans to adopt a "sitting culture." The prevailing forms of burial at the time were earthen tombs, into which corpses were
directly placed, and jar-coffin interments which utilized two large urns laid
mouth to mouth to contain the body. A new type of pottery, a hard, iron-rich,
and more highly fired Chinese-style gray stoneware, appeared, characterized
by a smooth, lustrous surface.

China's deep influence on this new development of Iron culture in Korea
is apparent, attested by the discovery of the Chinese coins *mingdaoqian,* or
crescent knife coins, at many Iron Age excavation sites. But the transmission
of Chinese Iron culture to Korea (Old Chosŏn) did not lead to the extension
of Chinese political domination over the Korean people.[3] The introduction
of Chinese Iron culture only contributed to the rapid development of the Korean nation.

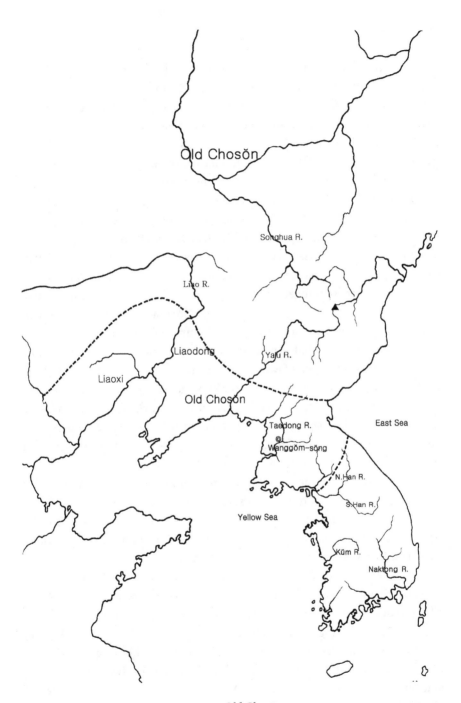

MAP 1.1. Old Chosŏn

Wiman Chosŏn

In the fourth century BC Old Chosŏn was bordered on the west, far beyond the Liao River, by the northern Chinese dynasty of Yan. Thereafter, under heavy pressure from the Yan, it entered a period of gradual decline. In the early third century BC Old Chosŏn was invaded by Yan forces, commanded by their general Qinkai, and lost its territory in the Liao River basin to the Chinese kingdom. At the same time, Old Chosŏn may have transferred its capital to Pyongyang, called Wanggŏm-sŏng at the time, in northern Korea.

From the mid-third century BC Old Chosŏn experienced a long period of civil turbulence in neighboring China, having gone through the late Warring States Period. By the late third century BC China had become a unified empire under the Qin and Han dynasties. As opposing dynasties wrestled for supremacy in China, small bands of refugees periodically made their way into Old Chosŏn. Leading one of these refugee bands was a warrior known as Wiman, a native of Yan. Wiman and his followers, numbering more than 1,000, submitted themselves to King Chun of Old Chosŏn, who in turn assigned them to guard the state's western frontier. But Wiman gathered additional refugees from China, armed them with weapons fashioned from iron, and, after marching to the capital under the pretext of protecting the king against Chinese invaders, seized the throne in 194 BC. At the time relations between Old Chosŏn and Han were strained because of a struggle for suzerainty over Korean states and populations. The dethroned king Chun is said to have taken a ship to the southern state of Chin to become its king ("Han King").

Although Wiman came from the former Chinese Yan dynasty, when he sought refuge in Old Chosŏn, he is said to have styled his hair in a topknot resembling that of the Old Chosŏn people and to have dressed in the Chosŏn style. He also continued to use "Chosŏn" for the name of his kingdom. These considerations suggest that Wiman might be a dongyi man.

For the next 86 years (194–108 BC), under Wiman and his heirs, Chosŏn enjoyed peace and prosperity. Wiman Chosŏn embraced the native elite of Old Chosŏn society, and some members of that elite were given the highest government position of "sang." Possessed of highly advanced Iron culture, Wiman Chosŏn expanded its territory and subjugated its neighboring states to the north, east, and south. In about 190 BC Chinbŏn in today's Hwanghae province and Imdun in present-day South Hamgyŏng province, both now situated in North Korea, were forced to submit to Wiman Chosŏn. China's Han empire was concerned about the threat posed by a possible alliance between Wiman Chosŏn and the nomadic Xiongnu people, then rapidly expanding into Manchuria from their heartland in Mongolia. From early times the nomadic peoples beyond the Great Wall were a constant challenge to China, and several Korean states, including Wiman Chosŏn, forged close ties with these powerful nomads. At this point, in 128 BC, Namnyŏ, the ruler of Ye, who had been forced to yield to Wiman Chosŏn, defected to Han with his people, numbering 280,000. Taking advantage of this opportunity, Han sought to outflank Wiman Chosŏn by establishing the Canghai (Ch'anghae in Korean) Commandery in the Ye territory, located in the mid-Yalu and the Tongjia (present-day Hon) river basin. Two years later, in 126 BC, however, the fierce resistance of the Ye people dismantled the Chinese commandery, and the Han empire's ambitious designs to weaken Wiman Chosŏn ended in failure. Around 110 BC King Ugŏ of Wiman Chosŏn, who sought to profit as an intermediary in trade between Korean states and Han China, prevented the state of Chin, located south of the Han River, from direct contact with the Han empire.

Bilateral negotiations failed to heal the breach between Wiman Chosŏn and the Han empire. At this critical moment a major crisis occurred. A Chinese envoy named Shehe, who had earlier been rewarded after killing a Wiman Chosŏn commander and fleeing back to China, was killed in retaliation by Chosŏn soldiers in 109 BC. The Han emperor Wudi, who had already engaged in aggressive military campaigns to crush Xiongnu's threat, used this incident as an excuse to launch an armed attack on Wiman Chosŏn.[4] Wudi sought to neutralize Xiongnu's power by conquering the Korean nation. In 109 BC he sent out 50,000 army troops and 7,000 naval forces to destroy Wiman Chosŏn. After suffering defeat at the beginning of the war, the Chinese sought to provoke internal strife within the Chosŏn ruling class. As a result, although Wiman Chosŏn fought hard against the Chinese invaders for a year, its resistance was weakened by internal dissension. Many high-ranking pacifists surrendered to Han, and one of them, Nigye-sang Sam, assassinated King Ugŏ in 108 BC. Led by the high-level official Sŏnggi, a hard-liner on the Chinese, the struggle continued for a time but could not be maintained indefinitely. Finally, after pacifists killed Sŏnggi, Wanggŏm-sŏng was taken by the Chinese. Wiman Chosŏn was devastated and replaced by four Chinese commanderies. For the first time in their history Koreans were placed under foreign domination. After Wiman Chosŏn was conquered by the Han empire, many members of its ruling class went south, greatly encouraging the development of the three Han federations. It appears that these refugees from Wiman Chosŏn established the Chinhan federation.

The Four Han Commanderies

Immediately after destroying Wiman Chosŏn, the Han empire established administrative units to rule large territories in the northern Korean peninsula and southern Manchuria. In 108 BC it built three commanderies—Nangnang (Lelang in Chinese), Chinbŏn (Zhenfan in Chinese), and Imdun (Lintun in Chinese)—within the former domain of Wiman Chosŏn, and the next year it created Hyŏndo (Xuantu in Chinese) in the former territory of Ye. The locations of these four Chinese commanderies have been interpreted differently, but one widely accepted version places them as follows: Nangnang in the Taedong River basin around Pyongyang; Chinbŏn in present-day Hwanghae province north of the Han River (the old Chinbŏn region); Imdun in today's South Hamgyŏng province (the former Imdun area); and Hyŏndo in the middle reaches of the Yalu River.

In the face of continuing hostility and stiff opposition on the part of the native Korean population, however, the Chinese conquerors soon found themselves overextended. A generation later the original four commanderies were reduced to just one, that of Nangnang. In 82 BC local opposition expelled Chinbŏn and Imdun, and the Han empire abolished both commanderies, attaching the areas under their jurisdiction to Nangnang and Hyŏndo, respectively. Seven years later, in 75 BC, the newly emerging Korean kingdom of Koguryŏ attacked the Hyŏndo Commandery, expelling it far to the northwest, out of the former Ye territory. Soon the Chinese commandery ceased to exist.

Controlling the northwestern part of the Korean peninsula, Nangnang endured for more than four centuries, outlasting its father Han empire by 100 years. But Nangnang also experienced a succession of serious crises both internally and externally. In AD 24 Wang Diao, a powerful member of the Nangnang gentry, rebelled against its governor and proclaimed himself the new governor. This coup was suppressed in AD 30 by Wang Zun, the newly arrived governor from China, but it had a significant impact on the indigenous Korean people, who had been pushed down to the southern part of the Korean peninsula when the Han empire expanded into Korea. As the once domineering Nangnang weakened, these native Korean societies recovered their earlier strength. To cope with the growing power of the Korean population, in AD 205 the Gongsun clan, then in control of the Liaodong region, established a new commandery,

Daifang (Taebang in Korean) in the area south of Nangnang, formerly administered by Chinbŏn. Since the first century BC Nangnang felt heavy pressure from
the northern Korean kingdom of Koguryŏ, established in the north of the commandery and expanded into Manchuria. Nangnang finally fell to Koguryŏ in
313, and in 314 its neighboring commandery of Taebang was also overwhelmed
by the native Korean kingdom.

A rich and prosperous outpost of Han civilization, Nangnang was a replica
of the Han empire proper, particularly its culture. Chinese civilization flowed
into the Korean peninsula through Nangnang. The Chinese introduced their
customs, their writing system, and their literature to Koreans. Nangnang also
functioned as the international trade center of East Asia. Trade was conducted
between China and the rest of Korea and even Japan through the Chinese commandery. Many Chinese merchants migrated into Nangnang to engage in commerce. They imported timber, salt, and iron from the indigenous tribal states
south of the Han River. To strengthen business ties with native Korean societies, the Chinese granted their leaders ceremonial offices and ranks, official
seals, and ceremonial attire. These served as formal tokens of their submission
to Nangnang's authority as well as Chinese recognition of their independent
status.

Although Nangnang was the core area for Chinese colonial policy in Korea, severe political repression did not occur. The native populace rigidly opposed China's colonial administration, and, as a result, the Chinese were forced
to grant substantial political freedom to the populace whom they governed.
Pyongyang, the center of Nangnang's colonial administration, was transformed into a sumptuous, international city, and Chinese officials, merchants,
and many others came to live there. The luxurious lifestyle of these Chinese,
who boasted that they were colonial overlords, is evident in the burial objects
found in the tombs in Pyongyang's environs, items such as gold filigree work
and superb pieces of lacquer.

The indigenous Korean society was heavily influenced by the Chinese. Some
natives became rich and grew accustomed to the Chinese way of life, which
prompted class divisions. The class division in Old Chosŏn society is evident
from its burial system in which living slaves are entombed with their dead
masters. In Old Chosŏn's two tombs, apparently built sometime between the
eighth and seventh centuries BC, more than 140 slaves were buried alive with
their dead masters in one, and more than 100 slaves were buried alive with their
dead masters in the other.

The presence of wealthy natives also prompted the need for the rich to protect their property. Thievery greatly increased, committed largely by Chinese merchants. The original code of law in Old Chosŏn consisted of eight articles, but, of these, only three stipulations are presently known. As in many other states in the ancient world, Old Chosŏn's code of law followed the talion principle: a murderer was put to death; someone who caused bodily injury was required to pay compensation in grain; and a thief was made the slave of his victim but could be exempted from that penalty by paying each victim "500,000 coppers." Other legal articles may have included provisions on adultery, jealousy, blasphemy, and so forth. Because of the heavy Chinese presence in Old Chosŏn, the original body of law was eventually expanded to include more than 60 provisions. The legal structure of the indigenous society thus became extremely complicated and crimes rapidly increased. On the other hand, the advanced Chinese culture encouraged the development of the Korean indigenous culture. Koguryŏ, for example, took over Pyongyang and inherited a well-established, rich Chinese civilization. In sum, after the fall of Wiman Chosŏn and the establishment of Chinese commanderies, Chinese inroads into native Korean societies exerted tremendous effects upon Koreans both positively and negatively.

CONFEDERATED KINGDOMS

Puyŏ

Puyŏ, along with Old Chosŏn, was the source of the Korean nations. Chumong, the founder of Koguryŏ, moved south from Puyŏ. When King Sŏng of Paekche relocated his capital from Ungjin (present-day Kongju, South Ch'ungch'ŏng province) to Sabi (present-day Puyŏ, South Ch'ungch'ŏng province) in 538, he renamed his kingdom "South Puyŏ." Puyŏ (meaning "deer" or "wide flatland") emerged in the vast plains of the upper and middle reaches of the Songhua River in Manchuria, and thus the people of Puyŏ engaged in farming and raising livestock. Puyŏ's nation building as a walled-town state seems to have begun in the mid-fifth century BC. From the first century AD on, the name "Puyŏ" appeared frequently in Chinese historical records, and by this time Puyŏ had grown into a confederated kingdom. In AD 49 the Puyŏ ruler was using the Chinese title *wang*. Puyŏ was founded by the Yemaek branch of Koreans. Since people of Puyŏ origin later founded the Korean kingdoms of Koguryŏ and Paekche, Puyŏ deserves a great deal of weight in Korean history.

Puyŏ had existed for almost 1,000 years before Koguryŏ finally annexed it in 494. In its heyday Puyŏ extended its territory to the Heilong (Amur) River to the north, the Maritime Province of Russia to the east, Paektu-san to the south, and the upper reaches of the Liao River to the west. Since around the third century AD, however, it was reduced to a small state with a population of 80,000 households.

Puyŏ not only had existed for an extended time but had long maintained friendly relations with China's successive Han, Wei, and Jin dynasties. Because it lay between the nomadic Xianbei people on China's northern frontier and Koguryŏ to China's northeast, both of whom posed a serious threat to China, Puyŏ and China shared in common the need to check the expansion of these two powerful peoples. Unlike its good-neighbor relationship with China, Puyŏ's relations with Koguryŏ to its south, as well as with the Xianbei people to the north, had long been antagonistic. China's close, friendly ties with Puyŏ had convinced the Chinese of the peaceful inclinations of the Puyŏ people. The converging interests of the two nations revealed itself in a series of events.

Puyŏ sent its first envoy to China in AD 49, during the Later Han dynasty, and thereafter sent emissaries almost every year. At the end of the Later Han, the Gongsun clan, who as Chinese warlords controlled the Liadong region, forged marriage ties with Puyŏ's royal house. When Guanqiu Jian, a general of the Wei dynasty that succeeded the Later Han, invaded Koguryŏ in 244, Puyŏ supplied provisions to the invading Wei army, cementing its friendship with China. Such pro-China policy was fruitfully rewarded. When the Xianbei ruler Murong Wei invaded Puyŏ in 285, its king Ŭiryŏ committed suicide and the king's sons and brothers fled to Okchŏ in the northeastern part of the Korean peninsula. Upon realizing that Puyŏ's existence was in serious jeopardy, the Chinese state of Jin, which had succeeded Wei, seated Ŭira, a member of Puyŏ royalty, on the empty throne. Thereafter, with the help of the Chinese, Puyŏ barely remained in existence.

Because successive Chinese states served as patrons of Puyŏ against the incursions of the nomadic Xianbei people and Koguryŏ, the decline of Chinese strength imperiled Puyŏ's survival. When Jin was driven south by the nomadic tribes from northern China in 316, Puyŏ was completely isolated and exposed to foreign threats. When Puyŏ was invaded in 347 by Murong Huang, the ruler of the Xianbei kingdom of the Earlier Yan, its king Hyŏn and more than 50,000 of his people were taken prisoner. Upon the extinction of the Xianbei kingdom by another nomadic state of the Earlier Jin in 370, Puyŏ came under the influence of Koguryŏ. Finally, Puyŏ was destroyed by the nomadic Mulgil (Malgal; Mohe in Chinese) people in January 494, and the next month its king voluntarily surrendered to the Koguryŏ king Munja and his territory was annexed to Koguryŏ. Puyŏ, which had had a long history and was the root of several subsequent Korean states, finally left the scene of history.

In the confederated kingdom of Puyŏ, the king was first among equals in his relations with powerful tribal heads called *ka*, or governor. The king ruled only the central part of his nation, and four governors controlled the eastern, western, southern, and northern parts of the kingdom. Their domains were termed *sa ch'ulto*, or four outlying provinces, which, along with the territory administered by the king, formed the "five-section system." The king had his own officials called *taesaja*, or great retainer, and *saja*, or retainer. Local governors were also served by saja household retainers. This system demonstrates that original walled-town states united to form the confederated kingdom of Puyŏ.

At first a council, which was comprised of ka governors and decided important national affairs, elected the king or dethroned him, greatly limiting the king's authority. Later, however, with the introduction of the hereditary monarch system, royal authority grew increasingly strong.

Puyŏ encompassed the vast plains of the Songhua River basin and was a heavily agricultural and livestock-raising country. The raising of livestock was such a thriving practice that the names of domestic animals such as the horse (*ma-ga*), ox (*u-ga*), pig (*chŏ-ga*), and dog (*ku-ga*) were used to designate the four powerful governors of the kingdom. The wealth gained from the farming and livestock enterprises presumably led to peaceful inclinations among the Puyŏ people, who were known to be skilled archers (called *chumong*) and horseback riders. Puyŏ exported its special products such as horses, jewels, and furs to China.

Puyŏ's social strata included ka, *homin*, or wealthy people; *min*, or common people; and *haho*, or low households. The min and haho strata included mostly the farming population, and below them were a small number of slaves. These slaves, who were war prisoners, debtors, and the family members of murderers, were the possessions of the ka and homin people. When their masters died, slaves were buried alive with the dead, as noted earlier, sometimes as many as 100-plus slaves. When war came, it was members of the homin and min who took up arms to fight the enemy. The haho people were not allowed to take part in combat operations but supplied provisions to the combatants.

Puyŏ had four legal provisions to protect the lives and property of the privileged and to ensure patriarchy and polygamy. In Puyŏ a murderer was put to death and members of the murderer's family became slaves; a robber had to compensate his victim 12 times the amount stolen; a woman adulterer was put to death; and a jealous wife was also put to death, and the corpse was left to rot in the mountains south of the capital (the family of such a woman might claim the body by making a suitable payment in cattle or horses).

In the 12th lunar month of the year, a thanksgiving festival called *yŏnggo* or spirit evoking drums, was held in Puyŏ, where the entire populace would throng together to perform a thanksgiving service to heaven, enjoy food and drink, and sing and dance. There the four ka governors would discuss important state affairs and would judge prisoners guilty or innocent. Also oracle bones, specifically oxen hooves, would be used to foretell a person's good or ill fortune. The festival, presumably a survival of a tradition practiced in the primitive hunting society out of which Puyŏ evolved, was a shamanic event celebrated on a national scale. The other Korean states of Koguryŏ, Okchŏ, Tongye, and Chin had similar thanksgiving festivals. For this reason, a third-century Chinese historian described Koreans as a people who loved singing and dancing.

Koguryŏ

According to legend, Koguryŏ (meaning "head walled-town") was founded in 37 BC by Chumong and a band of his followers who fled south from Puyŏ. Because there had been a prefecture named "Koguryŏ" within the territory of the Chinese Hyŏndo Commandery which was established in 107 BC, one may infer that a small state of Koguryŏ had already existed in the second century BC. Let us call it "Old Koguryŏ." Viewed in this light, Koguryŏ was the first of the Three Kingdoms to be established.

This Old Koguryŏ consolidated its strength in the mountainous region centered in the middle reaches of the Yalu River and the upper reaches of the Tongjia (Hon) River, a branch of the Yalu, in Manchuria. The Yemaek people in this region are believed to have already established their own political entity in the fourth century BC. In 128 BC the Ye "lord" Namnyŏ, who exercised dominion over a population of 280,000, defected to the Han empire, seeking its support in his effort to resist domination by Wiman Chosŏn. This Yemaek society formed the basis of Koguryŏ, and, in 75 BC, the Koguryŏ people were strong enough to expel the Hyŏndo Commandery far to northwestern Manchuria.

After ousting the Chinese commandery, the Koguryŏ people established a confederated kingdom consisting of walled-town states named *na* or *no*. In this confederation, these small na (no) states were increasingly integrated into five larger entities: Sono-bu (enclave), Chŏllo-bu, Sunno-bu, Kwanno-bu, and Kyeru-bu. At first the Sono-bu people, natives of the region, were the leaders of the confederated kingdom, and their chieftains claimed the throne. Later, however, the Kyeru-bu people, who had moved south from Puyŏ, grew powerful and replaced the Sono-bu people as leaders of the confederation. The legend of Chumong, in which he was defeated in the struggle for power in Puyŏ by Taeso, the son of the Puyŏ king Kŭmwa, and escaped the country for fear of being killed, suggests that the Kyeru-bu men wrested political leadership in the confederated kingdom of Koguryŏ away from the Sono-bu men. Thus emerged the beginning of "New Koguryŏ."[5]

Based on their outstanding skills at horseback riding and archery, the people of Chumong and Kyeru-bu integrated neighboring walled-town states into Koguryŏ and constructed fortresses, royal chambers, and shrines at Cholbon (Hwanin), their capital. In AD 3 Koguryŏ transferred its capital to Kungnae-sŏng on the Yalu, not far from and south of Hwanin. By the beginning of the first century AD Koguryŏ had adopted the Chinese title *wang* for its ruler.

Koguryŏ, because of its location in a mountainous region with narrow plains, endured economic hardship and could only compensate for its inadequate resources through warfare. To enrich themselves, the Koguryŏ people had to rely on tributes of grain and other necessities of life from their conquered territories. Simply put, Kogyryŏ was an economy based on plunder and the spoils of war. Thus, unlike the people of Puyŏ, the Koguryŏ people frequently conflicted with the Chinese and impressed them as vigorous and warlike, eager to attack their neighbors.

Despite poor agricultural production, the Koguryŏ people held a thanksgiving service to heaven called *tongmaeng* or *tongmyŏng*, or worship of Chumong. At this harvest festival held in the tenth lunar month of the year, all the Koguryŏ people came together to eat, drink, and dance. Koguryŏ had an unusual custom called *sŏok*, or son-in-law chamber. According to the custom, the groom went to the bride's home after marriage and lived with his wife in the son-in-law chamber until receiving the formal consent of her parents to bring her back to his clan. Permission to do so was given only after the couple's children had reached a certain age. This Koguryŏ custom of matriarchy dated back to the Neolithic period.

In the course of armed struggle with the Chinese, Koguryŏ became a powerful kingdom. It directed its territorial expansion toward the Liao River basin to the southwest, the Songhua River basin to the northwest, the Taedong River basin to the south, and the plains along the northeast coast of the Korean peninsula. Because all these areas were either directly administered by the Chinese or within their sphere of influence, warfare between Koguryŏ and China was inevitable. In the early first century A D, in particular, Koguryŏ came into violent conflict with Wang Mang's Xin (A D 8–23). When Wang Mang enlisted Koguryŏ forces in a campaign against the Xiongnu people in A D 12, the Koguryŏ contingents refused to join the battle and killed the commander of the Chinese Xin forces. Wang Mang, who was enraged by the action but could not retaliate against Koguryŏ, had to console himself with his extraordinary decree that the king of Ko ("high") guryŏ was to be degraded to the title lord of Ha ("low") guryŏ. Thereafter Koguryŏ forces frequently violated Xin's frontiers.

In the reign of King T'aejo (A D 53–146?) Koguryŏ territory included present-day Hamgyŏng province in northeastern Korea, regions north of the Ch'ŏngch'ŏn River on the Korean peninsula, the Maritime Province of Russia, and the upper reaches of the Tongjia (Hon) River in Manchuria. In extending its territory, Koguryŏ annexed more than ten walled-town states including Haengin-guk (state), Okchŏ, Sŏnbi, Yangmaek, Kaema-guk, Kuda-guk, Nangnang-guk, Kalsa-guk, and Chuna-guk. Koguryŏ under King T'aejo and his successors continued to mount attacks on the Chinese in the Liao River basin. Thus the history of Koguryŏ's territorial expansion was characterized by ceaseless struggles with the Chinese. Koguryŏ's growth depended, in particular, on the expulsion of Chinese commanderies from Korean territory. Already in this early period Koguryŏ's standing in Korean history was marked by its resistance to Chinese expansionism into Korea.

Okchŏ and Tongye (East Ye)

Located in the northeast coastal areas of the Korean peninsula were two loosely organized "states," Okchŏ and Tongye. Geographical conditions apparently prevented them from developing into full-fledged confederated kingdoms. Though cut off almost entirely from the outside world by rugged mountain ranges, the language, food, clothing, and customs of these two "states" nevertheless resembled those of Koguryŏ.

The small state of Okchŏ, situated in today's Hamgyŏng province and consisting of some 5,000 households, had long remained a confederation of tribes, with tribal chieftains called *hu, ŭpgun,* and *samno* independently administering their own domains. Originally Okchŏ was controlled by Old Chosŏn (Wiman

Chosŏn). Then, with the establishment of Chinese Han commanderies, it fell under the rule of the Imdun Commandery and later the Nangnang Commandery. Since the first century A D Koguryŏ brought Okchŏ under its dominion and levied tributes from the small state. It is said that the Okchŏ people carried salt, fish, "Maek cloth," and other local products on their backs to Koguryŏ over a distance of "1,000 li," or 200 to 300 miles. In the early fifth century Okchŏ was completely under the command of the Koguryŏ king Kwanggaet'o.

In Okchŏ young girls were often taken into other families as future daughters-in-law. When people died in Okchŏ, they were temporarily buried and their bones were later laid in wooden coffins with the bones of other family members. An entire family, in other words, was buried together in a single large coffin.

Tongye, located in today's northern Kangwŏn province, had more than 20,000 households. Though bigger than Okchŏ, it also never evolved into a confederated kingdom. Like Okchŏ, Tongye had also been controlled by Old Chosŏn and Chinese Han commanderies, later to be annexed to Koguryŏ.

Geographical isolation virtually relieved Tongye of outside interference and influence. Thus its hereditary customs were long maintained, handed down through the successive clan societies. Each clan was required to remain within its own territory, where it engaged in such economic activities as hunting, fishing, and farming. Should this prohibition be violated, slaves, oxen, and horses had to be given in compensation. This custom was known as *ch'aekhwa*, or responsibility for damages. The Tongye people worshiped the tiger as a deity.

Tongye possessed fertile farmland and was rich in marine products. It produced fine silk and hemp cloth, horses called *kwahama*, and seal furs. A thanksgiving service to heaven known as *much'ŏn*, or a dance to heaven, was also performed there in the tenth lunar month of the year. Because the Tongye people's livelihood depended on agriculture and fishery, the national thanksgiving event functioned as a festival to celebrate both a good harvest and a large catch. Failing to become confederated kingdoms because of their geography and their more powerful neighbors, Okchŏ and Tongye ultimately disappeared from the landscape of history.

The State of Chin and the Three Han Federations

About the time when the confederated kingdoms of Old Chosŏn, Puyŏ, and Koguryŏ were established by the Yemaek people, a culturally homogeneous political entity had also taken shape at the hands of the Han people in the region south of the Han River. Nation building progressed more quickly in the west-

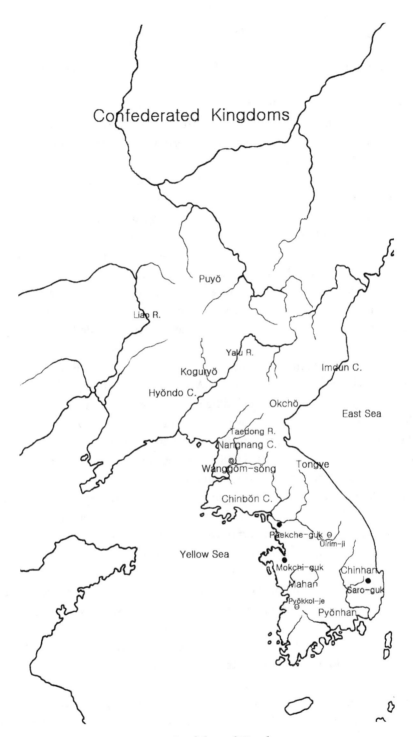

Confederated Kingdoms

Puyŏ

Liao R.

Yalu R.

Imdun C.

Koguryŏ

Hyŏndo C.

Okchŏ

East Sea

Taedong R.

Nangnang C.

Wanggŏm-sŏng

Tongye

Chinbŏn C.

Paekche-guk ⊖
Ŭirim-ji

Yellow Sea

Mokchi-guk

Chinhan

Mahan

Saro-guk

Pyŏkkol-je ⊖

Pyŏnhan

MAP 1.2. Confederated Kingdoms

ern part of the region, in the basins of the Han, Kŭm, and Yŏngsan rivers, than in the eastern part, the Naktong River basin. Because of easy access to China, vast fertile farmland, and abundant products, people in the western region, later called Mahan, enjoyed a superior lifestyle to people in the east. Therefore, after the fall of Old Chosŏn, refugees from the north settled in this region.

Around the eighth century BC the Han people, a branch of the dongyi who had migrated from northeastern China, already used high-level mandolin-shaped bronze daggers and refined polished stone daggers, and constructed gigantic board-style dolmen tombs. Presumably, from early times on, a large number of walled-town states had already been established in this southern region, as evidenced by the use of finely wrought bronze daggers since the fourth century BC. A Chinese historical record from the third century AD notes that as many as 70 to 80 states had belonged to the *Sam-han,* or three Han, federations. These "states," the larger ones controlling more than 10,000 households and the smaller ones just 600 to 700 households, were all walled-town states.

Chin, a loosely organized union of "states," was established in the late fifth century BC and was centered on the southwest coastal areas of the Korean peninsula. Since the fall of Old Chosŏn to Wiman in 194 BC, many refugees from the territory of Old Chosŏn, including its last king, Chun, swarmed into the Chin domain. Again, with the downfall of Wiman Chosŏn in 108 BC, a number of refugees also fled south, settling in Chin territory. The immigration of these refugees from the north enabled Chin to adopt a more advanced iron culture. As a result, Chin society rapidly experienced a profound transformation, which eventually resulted in the restructuring of the Chin territory into three new political entities, known collectively as the three Han federations—Mahan, situated in the southwestern part of the Korean peninsula; Chinhan, located east of the Naktong River; and Pyŏnhan, positioned west of the Naktong River.

It is said that the Mahan federation was made up of 54 states and more than 100,000 households. Among the numerous states, the ruler of the Mokchi state, situated in today's Chiksan, South Ch'ungch'ŏng province, was elevated to the "Chin King" to assert nominal lordship over the three Han states. Later, however, the state of Paekche in the lower reaches of the Han River became increasingly powerful and competed for dominance over the Mahan federation with the state of Mokchi. The later Paekche kingdom developed out of the state and acquired predominance in the Mahan region. Paekche was founded by immigrant people from the north, and its founder-king is said to have been Onjo, a son of Chumong, the legendary founder-king of Koguryŏ.

The Chinhan federation, consisting of 12 states, was established by the Wiman Chosŏn people who had migrated south into the Naktong River basin and today's Kyŏngju region. An outstanding example from this migration was Chosŏn-sang Yŏkkyegyŏng, who fled south immediately before the fall of Wiman Chosŏn leading more than 2,000 households. These migrants from the north may have wanted to settle in the Mahan area but, upon meeting resistance from the existing inhabitants, they moved down to the present-day Kyŏngsang region along the Naktong River. The later Silla kingdom emerged from the walled-town state of Saro, one of the 12 Chinhan states.

In the southeast coastal region of Kimhae and Masan, in present-day South Kyŏngsang province, a federation of 12 maritime states known as Pyŏnhan was established. The Pyŏnhan people engaged in vigorous maritime activities and produced high-quality iron in large quantities. They exported iron wares to Japan and Nangnang through the "iron road." Later, six Kaya kingdoms emerged from the Pyŏnhan region.

From the late third century BC the influence of refugees from the north brought the state of Chin and the three Han federations solidly into the Iron Age. The introduction of iron technology enabled the widespread manufacture of iron artifacts for daily use. A variety of farming implements such as hoes, plowshares, sickles, and mattocks were fashioned from iron. With the extensive use of iron appliances, rice agriculture developed in the rich alluvial valleys and plains to the point where reservoirs for irrigation were established. The famous Pyŏkkol-je (reservoir) at Kimje, North Chŏlla province, and Ŭirim-ji (reservoir) at Chech'ŏn, North Ch'ungch'ŏng province, were built in the Mahan region.

Rulers of the three Han federations were called *sinji, hŏmch'ŭk, pŏnye, salhae, kyŏnji,* and *pŏrye,* and *ŭpch'a.* These indigenous titles are all interpreted as having meant "chief" or "head." These political leaders had secular powers only, while religious ceremonies were performed exclusively by masters of ritual called *ch'ŏn'gun,* or heavenly lord. Functioning as shamans, they are said to have had authority over separate settlements known as *sodo* or *sottae.* It is recorded that a tall wooden pole was erected in the sodo on which were hung bells and a drum, believed to be the instruments for invoking spirits. The sodo was regarded as a sanctuary; if a criminal entered the precincts of the sacred sodo, he could not be apprehended there. Because religion and politics had already been separated in the three Han federations under this standard, the society there was considered more advanced than in Old Chosŏn and Puyŏ, where church and state were united.

The three Han people also performed ceremonies dedicated to heaven, similar to those celebrated in Puyŏ's yŏnggo, Koguryŏ's tongmaeng, and Tongye's much'ŏn. The harvest thanksgiving festival took place in the tenth lunar month, at the conclusion of the harvest. No less important was the ceremony held in the spring to pray for a bounteous year, observed in the fifth lunar month, after seeds had been sown. The entire populace, without class distinctions, celebrated these festivals, eating, drinking, singing, and dancing for several days on end. The three Han people engaged in communal farming using the system of *ture,* or mutual help, in which the labor supply worked all the farms in turn.

People of the three Han federations actively engaged in heaven worship. A traditional Korean belief dates back to the era of the three Han federations that all generations of men are born into the world from heaven and return to heaven when they die. An ancestral rite was identified as a sacrificial rite to heaven and was considered one of the most important moral virtues of filial piety. Burying tomb furnishings in a grave together with the corpse derived from the belief that a man returned to heaven to enjoy ultimate immortality.

Heaven worship was well illustrated through drawings incised on rocks. One such drawing at Yangjŏn-dong (village), in Koryŏng county, North Kyŏngsang province, consists of a number of concentric circles symbolizing heaven (the sun). Another at Ch'ŏnjŏn-ni, in Ulchu county, Ulsan metropolitan city, includes a variety of geometric designs—circles, triangles, and diamonds—as well as sketches of animals, suggesting that heaven (circles), the earth (diamonds), and human beings (triangles) coexisted harmoniously. An incised rock drawing at Pan'gudae (cliff) near Ch'ŏnjŏn-ni, created in the Bronze Age, depicts hunting scenes on land and at sea, and includes pictures of whales, tortoises, and other marine life, of wild animals such as deer, tigers, bears, boars, and rabbits, and of human beings, suggesting a prayer that the people of that age might live together peacefully with all of Mother Nature. The hunting and fishing scenes also imply a supplication that these essential economic activities would be accomplished successfully.[6] As these drawings make clear, the art created by the three Han people was closely related to heaven worship.

The era of the Chin and three Han federations has been considered "forgotten history," mainly because of the near absence of historical records. But this period occupies an eminent place in Korean history not only as a unique historical entity in itself but also as preparation for the advent of a new historical period, that of the Three Kingdoms of Koguryŏ, Paekche, and Silla.

The period ranging from the Paleolithic Age to the rise and development of confederated kingdoms, Old Chosŏn in particular, represents the "dawn" of the Korean nation. This early age witnessed the formation of the Korean race, the acceptance of advanced Bronze and Iron cultures, and the emergence of important Korean states, including Old Chosŏn, Puyŏ, and Koguryŏ. In a word, this era laid the groundwork for the development of all future Korean history.

2

THE PERIOD OF THE THREE KINGDOMS
(57 BC–AD 676)

THE GROWTH OF KOGURYŎ

The Early Development of Koguryŏ

BEGINNING AS A SMALL WALLED-TOWN STATE before the second century BC, Koguryŏ grew increasingly into a confederated kingdom after its expulsion of the Chinese commandery of Hyŏndo in 75 BC. At around that time there were five large tribal enclaves: Sono-bu (or Piryu-bu), Chŏllo-bu (or Yŏnna-bu), Sunno-bu (or Hwanna-bu), Kwanno-bu (or Kwanna-bu), and Kyeru-bu. In 37 BC Chumong and his Kyeru-bu people, the so-called horse-riding warriors, took political leadership in the confederated kingdom, heralding the beginning of "New Koguryŏ."

At first the Koguryŏ people were a hunting tribe that had settled in the mountainous regions of southern Manchuria. Thus Koguryŏ had to break out of these regions and make inroads into the south, with its vast stretches of plains. In AD 3 Koguryŏ transferred its capital from Cholbon (Hwanin) to Kungnae-sŏng on the Yalu. Defended by Hwando-sŏng in the rear and fronted by the Yalu River, the new capital was a natural stronghold.

By the first century AD Koguryŏ was firmly established as a state power. King T'aejo (53–146?) vigorously expanded the Koguryŏ territory through aggressive military activities allowing Koguryŏ to exact tribute from its neighbors. T'aejo subjugated Okchŏ to secure a base in the rear and consolidate the material foundations by acquiring a tributary state. He also actively took the offensive against the Chinese, attacking the Liaodong region east of the Liao River and the Chinese commandery of Nangnang. T'aejo and his successors then absorbed the newly won resources and manpower into Koguryŏ, thus continuing Koguryŏ's territorial expansion. Domestically T'aejo established the permanent right to the throne by the Ko house (clan) of the Kyeru-bu lineage, and thus he came to be called T'aejo, or the founder-king.

During the reign of King Kogukch'ŏn (179–197) the monarch's authority became further consolidated and the kingdom's political structure became increasingly centralized. First, the five original tribal enclaves from the earlier, traditional society were reorganized into five centrally ruled districts termed *pu*, or provinces, and given names connoting the directions north, south, east, west, and center; these were the administrative units of the capital and its neighboring areas. Chieftains of the former enclaves were integrated into the central aristocracy. Second, royal succession changed from a brother-to-brother pattern to one of father to son, representing a growth in monarchical power. Third, it became established practice for queens to be taken from the Myŏngnim house of the Chŏllo-bu (or Yŏnna-bu) lineage, which allowed the king to secure a permanent ally against potential political centers that might oppose the strengthening of royal power. Fourth, King Kogukch'ŏn appointed as prime minister an obscure individual named Ŭlp'aso to enforce the *chindaepŏp*, or relief loan law, which prevented poor peasants from becoming slaves of the aristocracy and enabled them to borrow grain from the state during the spring famine season and repay it at low interest after the autumn harvest.

As Koguryŏ achieved domestic stability, it gained great momentum for waging military campaigns against the Chinese. Repeated Chinese counterattacks failed to crush the elusive warriors of Koguryŏ, who were well protected in their mountainous habitat and highly mobile as a result of long experience with a hunting economy. In the first such campaign, in 242 King Tongch'ŏn (227–248) attacked Xianping(Sŏanp'yŏng in Korean), a Chinese strategic county at the estuary of the Yalu, in order to cut off the land route linking China proper with its Nangnang Commandery. The Chinese Wei dynasty immediately retaliated. The Wei (222–280) was one of three dynasties that had been established in China after the Han empire fell in 220 and was the closest to Koguryŏ. In 244, with the intention of succeeding the Han empire in Nangnang, Wei sent an invading force led by Guanqiu Jian to Koguryŏ, capturing Hwando-sŏng near the capital of Kungnae-sŏng. When Wei's military forces, led by Wang Qi, invaded Koguryŏ again the next year, King Tongch'ŏn had to flee and seek refuge in Okchŏ.

Wei's attempt to punish Koguryŏ was short-lived, however, as Wei itself was destroyed by the subsequent dynasty, the Jin, in 265. Jin was only able to achieve a brief reunification of China, as it, too, was soon overtaken by the nomadic peoples in 316. China was divided into the Northern and Southern dynasties until the Sui empire under Wendi achieved its unification in 589. Seizing upon the opportunity of China's division and internal struggles, Koguryŏ renewed its offensive against the Chinese territory east of the Liao River. Finally, in 313, King Mich'ŏn (300–331) drove out the Chinese from their Nangnang Commandery in 313. Koguryŏ's control of the former domain of Old Chosŏn in the Taedong River valley laid the groundwork for its future growth.

With the Jin driven south into the Yangtze River valley, five "barbarians"— Xiongnu, Xianbei, Di, Jie, and Qiang—established 16 ephemeral kingdoms in northern China. Among the five nomadic peoples, the Xianbei people became firmly predominant. As their state of Earlier Yan, founded by the Murong tribe, advanced into Manchuria, Koguryŏ was forced to engage in a fierce struggle with it for control of the Liao River basin. Koguryŏ, under King Kogukwŏn (331–371), met with disaster when it was invaded by Murong Huang, king of the Earlier Yan, in 342. His forces stormed into the Koguryŏ capital of Kungnae-sŏng, burned the royal palace to the ground, dug up the corpse of the previous king (Mich'ŏn), and seized the queen mother and 50,000 other Koguryŏ captives. A generation later, in 371, the Paekche king Kŭnch'ogo, who pursued a policy to go north, sacked Pyongyang-sŏng and killed King Kogukwŏn in battle.

Kogukwŏn's successor, King Sosurim (371–384), to save his nation from a great crisis, embarked on reshaping the pattern of the nation's institutions. He accepted Buddhism and established the T'aehak, or National Academy, for the teaching of Confucianism, in 372, and the next year drew up and promulgated the *yulyŏng*, or code of administrative law. Buddhism would function as the instrument to spiritually unite the kingdom; the T'aehak would create a new officialdom loyal to the king; and the yulyŏng would provide a systematic, legal structure for the state. Because of the defeats Koguryŏ had suffered under the Earlier Yan and Paekche dynasties, King Sosurim also initiated military reform. With the aim of molding Koguryŏ into a more advanced aristocratic nation, the king also reorganized national institutions based on China's advanced culture. These steps laid the groundwork for Koguryŏ's great territorial expansion that would ensue under King Kwanggaet'o (391–413).

Koguryŏ Flourishes

Koguryŏ reached its zenith in the fifth century, when King Kwanggaet'o and his son, King Changsu, expanded its territory into almost all of Manchuria and part of Inner Mongolia, and took the strategic Han River basin to the south from Paekche. During their reign the two kings virtually subdued Paekche and Silla, loosely unifying Korea.

Achieving the greatest expansion of Koguryŏ territory, King Kwanggaet'o built and consolidated a great empire in Northeast Asia. As his name, which means "broad expander of domain," implied, under his leadership Koguryŏ grew in all directions. His exploits are recorded in detail on the huge memorial stele that today stands near Kungnae-sŏng. According to the inscription, consisting of 1,775 Chinese characters, King Kwanggaet'o, in 397, occupied Later Yan's important stronghold in Manchuria, the Liaodong fortress. From 400 to 406 Koguryŏ ceaselessly struggled with Later Yan to take the Liaodong region and finally succeeded in integrating the whole Liaodong area into its territory. In 398 he subjugated the Sushen people, a Tungusic tribe on Koguryŏ's northeastern frontier. From 392 on, he attacked Paekche to the south, extending Koguryŏ's frontier into the Han River valley. In 396, he captured the Paekche capital of Hansŏng (present-day Songp'a district of Seoul or Hanam city, Kyŏnggi province) and brought the Paekche king Asin to his knees. The Paekche king gave him 1,000 Paekche people and 1,000 bolts of silk cloth as a sign of submission and asked him to make peace with his kingdom. In 400, extending a helping hand to Silla, he sent 50,000 infantry and cavalry troops to crush an allied force comprised of Paekche, Kaya, and Wae (Wa) Japanese that had attacked Silla. The Koguryŏ army completely annihilated the Paekche-Kaya-Wae forces in the Naktong River basin. In the entire course of his life he conquered a total of 64 fortress domains and some 1,400 villages. He created a great kingdom extending over two-thirds of the Korean peninsula and much of Manchuria. In particular, by conquering the Liaodong region, he recovered the former territory of Old Chosŏn, which had been lost to the Chinese Yan 700 years earlier. Based on his great confidence in his kingdom, he instituted his own era name, Yŏngnak, or Eternal Rejoicing, thus heralding Koguryŏ's status of equality with the major Chinese dynasties.

In 413 King Kwanggaet'o was succeeded by his son, King Changsu (413–491), meaning "long-lived." During his long reign he continued his father's campaign of conquest, and, under his rule, Koguryŏ's national strength attained its climax. China's split into the Northern and Southern dynasties afforded him an opportunity to diplomatically maneuver these two bitterly contending forces to Koguryŏ's advantage. While continuing a fierce struggle with the nearby Northern dynasties, he sought diplomatic contact across the Yellow Sea with the Southern dynasties. In 427 King Changsu moved Koguryŏ's capital from Kungnae-sŏng to Pyongyang, creating a new epicenter for the kingdom in the Taedong River basin. It was there that he built the Anhak-kung palace for his court. Because Pyongyang was located in the vast, fertile Taedong River basin and had been the center of advanced culture of Old Chosŏn and Nangnang, this move led Koguryŏ to attain a high level of economic and cultural prosperity. But with this relocation of the capital from a region of narrow mountain valleys to a wide riverine plain, the Koguryŏ people lost their inherent spirit of toughness, simplicity, and martial spirit, and increasingly indulged in luxury and pleasure.

Meanwhile, the transfer of Koguryŏ's capital far southward to Pyongyang posed a grave threat to its southern neighbors, Paekche and Silla. Thus Paekche forged an alliance with Silla in 433, and, in 472, sent an envoy to the Chinese Northern Wei dynasty to appeal for military assistance against Koguryŏ's southward advance. In 475, however, Koguryŏ seized the Paekche capital, capturing King Kaero and beheading him in retaliation for the death of King Kogukwŏn a century earlier. Paekche was forced to move its capital south to Ungjin on the Kŭm River, barely managing to preserve its national existence. Now Koguryŏ embraced a vast new territory stretching far into Manchuria and the Korean peninsula. Its frontiers reached the Liao River to the west, the Maritime Province of Russia to the east, the Songhua River in Manchuria to the north, and the Sobaek and Ch'aryŏng mountain ranges on the Korean peninsula to the south. In its heyday from the late fifth to the early sixth century, Koguryŏ occupied some 90 percent of the entire territory of the Three Kingdoms. The Koguryŏ people took pride in their country as a great kingdom and despised Silla, then their protectorate, as a state of the "eastern barbarians." In short, Koguryŏ established a great "empire" in Northeast Asia and, taking advantage of the division and confusion in China, held sway over vast territory in the region.

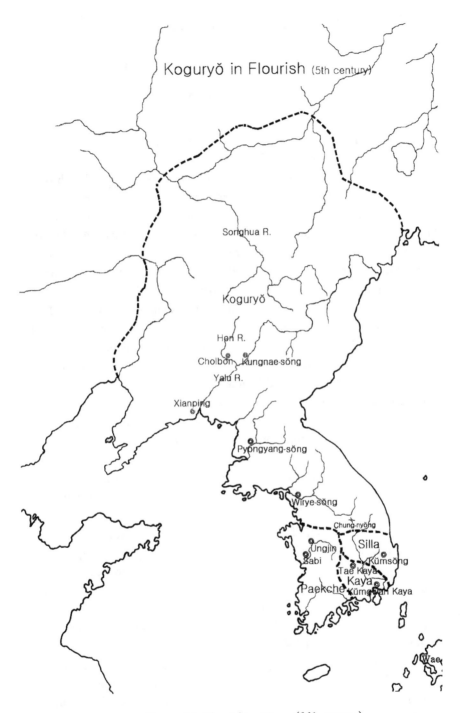

MAP 2.1. Koguryŏ in Flourishing Times (fifth century)

THE RISE AND DECLINE OF PAEKCHE

The Growth of Paekche

According to an old Korean historical record, *Samguk sagi,* or History of the Three Kingdoms, Paekche was established in 18 BC by Onjo, who was said to be a son of Chumong, the founder of Koguryŏ.[1] When his eldest half-brother, Yuri, became heir apparent to the throne of Koguryŏ, Onjo and his elder brother, Piryu, migrated south to the Mahan territory with their followers and set up tribal domains. Piryu settled in Mich'uhol, present-day Inch'ŏn and the Asan Bay region on the west coast, and Onjo founded the state of Paekche at Wiryesŏng, today's Seoul. Because it was located just south of the Han River, it was called Hanam ("south of the river") Wiryesŏng. Whereas the Onjo people at Wirye-sŏng made a comfortable living, Piryu, who settled in the soppy, salty seashore region, failed to develop his domain. Ashamed of his failure, Piryu committed suicide, and his people submitted to Onjo. This story suggests that a branch of the Puyŏ people moved south to the Han River basin, and two groups competed for dominance over the people. It is surmised that the Onjo group finally became predominant and founded Paekche.

Immediately after its founding, Paekche transferred its capital of Wirye-sŏng to north of the Han River, and it was renamed Habuk ("north of the river") Wirye-sŏng. As the occasion required, Paekche moved its court between Habuk and Hanam Wirye-sŏng. A royal palace and a shrine to memorialize the mother of the state (Onjo's mother) were constructed there, and a mud rampart and fence was built around it to strengthen the defense of Wirye-sŏng (later renamed Hansŏng).

Paekche developed out of one of the 54 walled-town states that comprised the Mahan federation. At first it was weak, frequently invaded by forces from Nangnang and by the Malgal people, and forced to pay tribute to the "Chin King" of the Mahan federation. Taking advantage of its location in the fertile Han River basin, however, it finally grew into a confederated kingdom by integrating the territory settled by the Piryu people into its domain and conquering other walled-town states of Mahan.

In the mid-third century King Koi (234–286) expanded Paekche territory by pushing the Chinese commanderies of Nangnang and Taebang and the Malgal people to the north. In 246 he drove back a large force of Nangnang and Taebang commanderies, and also proceeded to shape national institutions. In 260 he appointed six ministers, called *chwap'yŏng,* to conduct affairs of state along appropriate functional lines. He created 16 grades of office rank and prescribed colors for the attire of each rank. By transforming locally scattered tribal chieftains into king's subjects in the central government, Paekche became a well-established, centralized kingdom. Later the Paekche people were to honor King Koi as its founder-king with commemorating ceremonies that were performed four times annually.

Based on King Koi's efforts to transform his state into a centralized, aristocratic kingdom, during the reign of King Kŭnch'ogo (346–375) Paekche embarked on a large-scale campaign of conquest. In 369 Kŭnch'ogo destroyed the Mahan federation, acquiring all its territory. In 371 Paekche struck northward into the Koguryŏ territory as far as Pyongyang-sŏng, killing the Koguryŏ king Kogukwŏn in battle. Paekche thus dominated the entire southwestern part of the Korean peninsula, including all the modern provinces of Kyŏnggi, Ch'ungch'ŏng, and Chŏlla, as well as some portions of Kyŏngsang, Hwanghae, and Kangwŏn provinces.

At this time Paekche grew into a prosperous, cultured kingdom, as it occupied the most densely populated and agriculturally richest part of Korea. Cut off from northern China by Koguryŏ, it maintained close maritime contact with the Southern dynasties of China. In the fourth century Paekche forged friendly ties with Chinese East Jin in the Yangtze River basin and the Wa (Wae) people in Japan. It acquired China's advanced culture and technology, and then transmitted its own cultural developments to Japan. Having the command of the Yellow Sea and the South Sea, Paekche established a trade base in the region west of the Liao River and sent its merchants to the Shandong peninsula across the Yellow Sea. Exerting great influence on the Japanese, Paekche made them its ally against its northern neighbor, Koguryŏ. In a word, Paekche developed into a powerful, internationally well-known trading nation, and its advanced shipping technology was inherited by the later Koryŏ kingdom.

King Kŭnch'ogo virtually completed Paekche's state system as a centralized kingdom, and, with the establishment of the father-to-son succession to the kingship, monarchical authority was firmly established. Also during his reign there began the "age of Chin family queens,"as the king's immediate successors continued to choose their consorts from this single aristocratic clan. Paekche had eight different aristocratic clans with the family names of Chin, Hae, Sa, Yŏn, Kuk, Hyŏp, Mok, and Paek. They seem to have been inherited from those who migrated south from Puyŏ and Koguryŏ as well as from native Mahan chieftains. King Kŭnch'ogo ordered the scholar Kohŭng to compile

Sŏgi, a history of Paekche, to show off his consolidated kingly authority and the firmly established national institutions of Paekche. *Nihon shogi,* or History of Japan, believed to have been compiled in 720, was modeled on this *Sŏgi.* King Kŭnch'ogo was succeeded by King Kŭn'gusu (375–384), who in turn was followed by King Ch'imnyu (384–385). In the first year of King Ch'imnyu's reign, in 384, Paekche accepted Buddhism from Chinese East Jin as a new religious faith. In the second half of the fourth century Paekche attained its highest level of prosperity.

The Decline of Paekche

In the fifth century the once prosperous Paekche increasingly declined following the invasion of its territory by the mighty Koguryŏ king Changsu, who, in 475, captured Paekche's capital of Hansŏng and killed its king, Kaero. The next Paekche king, Munju (475–477), was forced to move his capital southward to Ungjin on the Kŭm River to preserve its very existence. He chose Ungjin as the new capital because it provided easy access to southern China and Japan. But Paekche's loss of the Han River basin struck a fatal blow to the kingdom.

Paekche was restored later on, however, following the efforts of kings Tongsŏng (479–501) and Muryŏng (501–523) to rehabilitate the kingdom. To gain an ally against Koguryŏ, King Tongsŏng forged a "marriage alliance" with Silla in which he married the daughter of a high-ranking Silla official in 493. King Muryŏng formed a friendship with the Chinese Liang dynasty, then the most developed nation among China's Northern and Southern dynasties. Because of Koguryŏ's continued southward expansion into Paekche's territory, Paekche also forged close relations with Japan, and its royal house maintained marital ties with the Japanese royal house. At crucial moments, Paekche always asked Japan for military aid. In return for Japanese military assistance, Paekche dispatched many scholars and artists to Japan, introducing its highly advanced culture to the island country. After transferring its capital to Ungjin, Paekche, in order to further centralize its government, reorganized its administration into 22 districts, or *tamno,* in the regions outside the capital; a prince or other member of the royal family was invested with a fiefdom in each tamno.

Ungjin's isolation in mountainous terrain, while securing it against northern aggression, also cut it off from the outside world. In need of a more favorably located capital, King Sŏng (523–554), in 538, despite stiff opposition on the part of the Ungjin aristocracy, moved his capital to Sabi on the broad plain on the Kŭm River. The location of Sabi on the navigable Kŭm allowed for easier

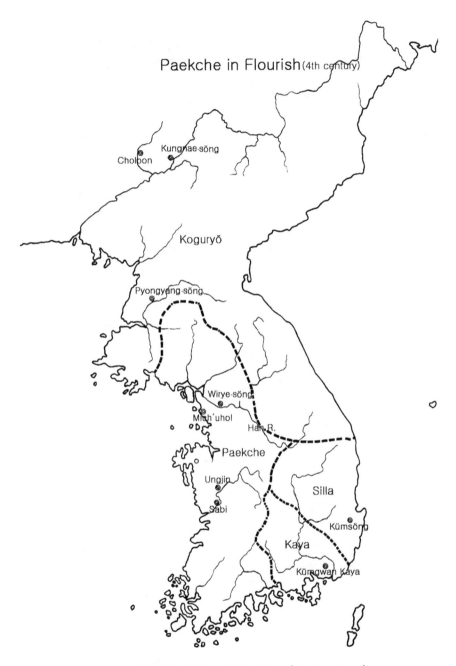

Paekche in Flourish (4th century)

Cholbon
Kungnae-söng
Koguryŏ
Pyongyang-söng
Wirye-söng
Mich'uhol
Han R.
Paekche
Ungjin
Sabi
Silla
Kümsŏng
Kaya
Kŭmgwan Kaya

MAP 2.2. Paekche in Flourishing Times (fourth century)

41

contact with China and Japan. At the same time the king renamed his kingdom "South Puyŏ." After the capital was transferred to Puyŏ, the system of 22 central government offices, 5 capital districts (*pu*), and 5 provinces (*pang*), was established.[2] Also, King Sŏng further strengthened Paekche's ties with the Liang dynasty in southern China.

Having restructured his kingdom and built up its strength, King Sŏng devoted himself to recovering Paekche's former territory in the Han River basin. To this end, he made a military pact with the Silla king, Chinhŭng (540–576), and struck northward against Koguryŏ. In 551 he succeeded in recovering the lower reaches of the Han River, and Silla took the upper reaches of the river.[3] In 553, however, Silla unexpectedly seized the strategically important lower region from Paekche. The enraged King Sŏng, with an army of 30,000-strong comprising Paekche, *Wa* Japanese, and Kaya forces, struck back at Silla, but, in 554, the king himself was killed in battle at Kwansan-sŏng (present-day Okch'ŏn, North Ch'ungch'ŏng province). Thereafter Paekche, though making peace with its former foe Koguryŏ, looked upon Silla as its sworn enemy and delivered one attack after another against that kingdom. In the "Sabi period" (538–660), six kings succeeded one another for some 120 years: King Sŏng (523–554), King Widŏk (554–598), King Hye (598–599), King Pŏp (599–600), King Mu (600–641), and King Ŭija (641–660).In this era Paekche continued to decline, whereas Silla was emerging more strongly.

THE RISE AND GROWTH OF SILLA

The Rise of Silla

The Silla kingdom, which evolved from the walled-town state of Saro, is said to have been founded by Pak Hyŏkkŏse. Situated in the Kyŏngju plain, Saro was one of the 12 "states" constituting the Chinhan federation in southeastern Korea. Although *Samguk sagi* records that Silla was the first of the Three Kingdoms to be established, other written and archeological records indicate that it was the last of the three to do so. The author of *Samguk sagi*, Kim Pu-sik, a man of Silla lineage, probably attempted to legitimate Silla rule by giving it historical seniority over its rival kingdoms, Paekche and Koguryŏ.

According to legend, in 57 BC Pak Hyŏkkŏse, at the age of 12, was enthroned as the first ruler of Saro by the headmen of six villages who named his state "Sŏrabŏl" or "Saro." Thus Saro was initially made up of six clan groupings. Legend has it that in 69 BC six village headmen approached a white horse and found a bright red egg; the egg immediately hatched, and out sprang a shining boy. The boy was named Pak ("bright") Hyŏkkŏse. Soon he married a girl named Aryŏng, who was said to have been born from the rib bone of a chicken. This myth suggests that immigrants from the north joined forces with native tribes to establish the walled-town state of Saro. Pak Hyŏkkŏse apparently was a member of horsemen that came down from the north, took leadership of Saro, and represented themselves by the horse totem. A powerful native clan that had come to the Saro region earlier than the Pak clan, and was represented by the chicken totem, appears to have been chosen as the "queen clan." The six villages seem to have been native tribes that were inferior in strength to these two groupings.

Subsequently leadership of Saro (Sŏrabŏl) was seized by the clan of Sŏk ("old") T'arhae, who was said to come from the coastal region east of Saro. T'arhae possessed the attributes of both a skilled metalworker and a shaman. It is surmised that the T'aehae clan immigrated from the north, bringing a highly advanced iron culture. By this time Saro had broken out of the confines of the narrow Kyŏngju plain and forged a federation with other walled-town states in the region east of the Naktong River. The terms used to designate Saro's rulers during this period were, first, *kŏsŏgan*, or chief, and then *ch'ach'aung*, or shaman; later the term *isagŭm*, or successor prince, was adopted. These titles were not considered to represent kings of a centralized state such as later Silla.

In addition to the Pak and Sŏk clans, another clan in Saro named Kim ("gold" or "metal") also came to the fore. With Kim Archi, who was said to have sprung from a golden box when a white chicken crowed in the grove of Kyerim, as its progenitor, the Kim family appears to have been a native clan that worshiped gold and was represented by the chicken totem. At first, these Pak, Sŏk, and Kim clans shared the kingship on a rotational basis. This governmental system was unique in the Three Kingdoms but ultimately, from the mid-fourth century on, the Kim family monopolized the kingship.

Silla was less affected than other major Korean states by Chinese culture or outside conquest because of its geographical isolation. Several centuries passed before Silla, initially weak and backward compared to Koguryŏ and Paekche, adopted a centralized government system. It was in the second half of the fourth century that Silla was then able to occupy most of the 12 Chinhan states.

By the time of King Naemul (356–402), Saro (Sŏrabŏl) had grown into a confederated kingdom and controlled the region east of the Naktong River in present-day North Kyŏngsang province. Naemul adopted a title befitting his new position as the ruler of a confederated kingdom. Instead of *isagŭm*, the term used by his predecessors, he took the title *maripkan* ("ridge," "elevation," implying "great chief"). From the time of King Naemul, the kingship no longer alternated among the three clans of Pak, Sŏk, and Kim but instead was monopolized on a hereditary basis by the Kim family. Since the reign of King Nulchi (417–458) the father-to-son pattern of succession to the throne was established. In the latter half of the fifth century, as a step toward the centralization of governmental authority, Saro's original six clan communities were reorganized into 6 administrative districts (*pu*) of the capital. As part of the efforts to establish a centralized kingdom, King Soji (458–500) built post stations throughout the nation in 487.

In the latter half of the fourth century, Silla had to seek help from Koguryŏ to defend itself from a much stronger Paekche, which won both Kaya and the Wae Japanese over to its side. This Silla effort was successful in 400, when Koguryŏ forces crushed an allied force of Paekche, Kaya, and Japan. With this military assistance, however, Silla was reduced to being Koguryŏ's protectorate. Threatened by powerful Koguryŏ, Silla increasingly strengthened its ties of friendship with Paekche. In 493 it forged a marriage alliance with King Tongsŏng of Paekche.

Silla Flourishes

Silla entered its flourishing era in the early sixth century. As it matured as a centralized kingdom, Chinese influence increased and became an important factor in Silla's growing power. In 503, in the reign of King Chijŭng (500–514), the nation's name was declared to be "Silla" and the Chinese term "wang" replaced the native title of "maripkan." Originally Silla's name was not spelled with Chinese characters, and the state was simply called "Sŏrabŏl" or "Saro," meaning the "eastern land." Then, in 503, Chinese characters that, when pronounced, sounded like "Saro" were chosen for the state's name, and it became "Silla."[4] By this time the Silla people had already been accustomed to Chinese writing, so the use of Chinese terminology reflected Silla's preparedness to actively accept China's advanced political institutions.

As part of consolidating royal authority, the Pak family emerged as the "queen clan." Important advances in agricultural technology, such as the introduction of ox-plowing and extensive irrigation works, increased agricultural production. In 512, King Chijŭng gave Isabu an order to conquer the "state" of Usan at Ullŭng-do in the East Sea.

In the reign of King Pŏphŭng (514–540), Silla grew into a centralized aristocratic kingdom. In 520 the yulyŏng was promulgated, and proper attire for the officialdom was instituted. The provisions of the yulyŏng may have included such basic regulations as delineating the 17-grade office-rank structure and installing the kolp'um, or bone rank, system. Already in 517 the king established the Pyŏng-bu, or Ministry of the Military, through which he could assume military command of the kingdom. In 536 Silla adopted an independent era name, Kŏnwŏn, or Initiated Beginning, to make a show of the firm establishment of royal authority within the country and its equal standing with China in the international community. After a man named Yich'adon martyred himself, Buddhism was officially adopted in 527 and would serve as an ideology to bring national unity and solidarity to the newly centralized kingdom. Taking the offensive in his relations with neighboring countries, King Pŏphŭng, in 532, conquered the once powerful Kŭmgwan Kaya in the present-day Kimhae region in South Kyŏngsang province, making it a stepping stone for advancing into the entire lower Naktong River basin. This was surprising, considering that Silla had originally been weaker than Kaya, not to mention Koguryŏ and Paekche.

Silla flourished the most during the reign of King Chinhŭng (540–576), who promoted the hwarang, or flowering youth, bands as a national warrior organization. He pushed ahead most vigorously with Silla's territorial expansion at the expense of Koguryŏ, Paekche, and Kaya. In 551, in concert with King Sŏng of Paekche, Silla attacked the Koguryŏ domain in the Han River basin. The upper reaches of the Han River fell to Silla, and Paekche occupied the lower Han River region, which was far more important strategically and economically than the zone taken by Silla. In 553 Silla drove Paekche out of the lower reaches of the river and took possession of the entire Han River basin. Incensed by this betrayal, King Sŏng launched a retaliatory attack on Silla in 554 but was killed in battle at Kwansan-sŏng. Silla's occupation of the Han River basin, a fertile and populous region, brought the kingdom enormous human and material resources. It also gave Silla an outlet to the Yellow Sea, opening up trade and diplomatic access to China. Now Silla's advancement both culturally and technologically would come directly from China. In 562 King Chinhŭng annexed Tae, or Great, Kaya in the present-day Koryŏng area in North Kyŏngsang province, thus acquiring all of the Naktong River basin. Silla also extended its territory up to the northeastern coast of the Korean peninsula into the old Okchŏ and Tongye regions. In the year 561 a stone monument was erected and given the name Chŏksŏng-bi (monument) at Tanyang in North Ch'ungch'ŏng province;

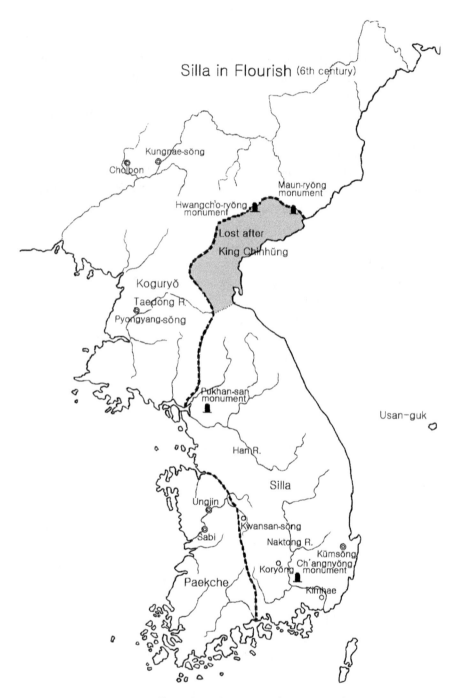

MAP 2.3. Silla in Flourishing Times (sixth century)

four other stone monuments were also built: at Pukhan-san in Seoul (555), at Ch'angnyŏng in South Kyŏngsang province (561), and at Maun-nyŏng (pass) (568) and Hwangch'o-ryŏng (pass) (568), both in South Hamgyŏng province. They bore witness to the king's brilliant achievements in Silla's territorial expansion. As Silla rapidly grew in strength, the Three Kingdoms competed more fiercely for dominance over the Korean peninsula.

THE RISE AND FALL OF KAYA

The Emergence of the Kaya Confederation

By the first century AD 12 "states" of the Pyŏnhan federation in the lower reaches of the Naktong River had developed into the Kaya confederation that included six "kingdoms"—Kŭmgwan Kaya at Kimhae, Tae Kaya at Koryŏng, Ara Kaya at Haman, So Kaya at Kosŏng, Koryŏng Kaya at Hamch'ang, and Sŏngsan Kaya at Sŏngju.[5] Among the 12 Pyŏnhan states, Kuya honored Suro as its first king and developed into the kingdom of Kŭmgwan Kaya, or Pon ("original") Kaya. Initially Kŭmgwan Kaya led the Kaya confederation, but in the late fifth century, Tae Kaya replaced Kŭmgwan Kaya as leader of the Kaya states.

According to legend, in AD, 42 nine village headmen, called *kan*, climbed up Kuji-bong (hill) at Kimhae and sang the "turtle song," upon which they found six golden eggs that had descended from heaven. The eggs soon hatched, and Suro, the first to emerge, ascended the throne in Kŭmgwan Kaya; the five others who sprang from the eggs became rulers of the five other Kaya states. This myth suggests that Kŭmgwan Kaya, which produced large quantities of high-quality iron, engaged in rice farming, and was actively involved in maritime activities, became the leader of the Kaya confederation.

Because of geographical proximity, large-scale migration took place from Kaya (later called Imna) to the Japanese islands. Until the fourth century the Kaya people established settlements on the Japanese islands of northern Kyushu and the southern tip of Honshu. Gradually the Kaya domain extended from the southeastern part of the Korean peninsula to the southwestern region of the Japanese islands. Contemporary Chinese historians called these people *Wo* (*Wae* in Korean, *Wa* in Japanese). After the seventh and eighth centuries the word "Wa" was used to indicate only the Japanese. Before the seventh century, it also referred to the Kaya people who lived in the southern part of the Japanese islands. These Kaya people in this region of Japan vigorously engaged in maritime activities with Kaya kingdoms on the Korean peninsula.

The Decline and Fall of Kaya

Kaya's development was impeded by Paekche and Silla, and the struggle between these two rival kingdoms rendered it impossible for Kaya to fully advance
politically and socially in order to become a centralized kingdom. Since the second half of the fourth century the Paekche king Kŭnch'ogo undertook a large-
scale campaign of conquest, and consequently Kaya submitted to Paekche.
Since the descendants of the Paekche general Mok Nakŭnja, who subjugated
Kaya, went over to Japan, *Nihon shogi* recorded, erroneously, that Japan conquered Kaya and created the Mimana Nihon-fu, or Japanese Office at Imna,
in that region. After it reduced Kaya into submission, Paekche established a
center in Kaya for trading with Japan, which the Japanese later distorted as a
mechanism for Japan's colonial administration of Kaya.

Beginning in the sixth century Silla actively expanded its territory at the
expense of Kaya and other neighboring states. In 532, taking advantage
of Paekche's preoccupation with its transfer of capital from Ungjin to Sabi,
King Pŏphŭng annexed Kŭmgwan Kaya at Kimhae. In the late fifth century
Tae Kaya took Kŭmgwan Kaya's place to lead the Kaya confederation. Taking advantage of the growing momentum to defeat King Sŏng of Paekche at
Kwansan-sŏng in 554, the Silla king Chinhŭng destroyed Tae Kaya, which had
allied with Paekche, in 562, thus gaining control of the entire Kaya region. The
other four petty Kaya states had already suffered the same fate. The history
of Kaya, which had achieved a high level of civilization, finally came to an end.

SILLA'S UNIFICATION

Koguryŏ's Struggle with Chinese Sui and Tang

About the time that Silla occupied the Han River basin in the mid-sixth century,
the international situation in Northeast Asia had developed to the kingdom's
advantage. After some 300 years of internal division, China was once again
reunited under the Sui dynasty (581–618) in 589. The reunification of China
by the Sui dynasty, and subsequently by the Tang, had a profound impact on
Korea's strategic position.

Whenever China, in previous times, became united and was able to exert
great power, the Korean kingdoms felt its weight. The Han empire was the best
example of this. But after the Chinese Han collapsed in 220, China was divided into several parts, dynasties rose and fell rapidly over three centuries, and

China was so disunited and overrun by "barbarians" that it exercised little direct military influence on Korea. Until the late sixth century Koguryŏ enjoyed relative peace with the Chinese, but then the Korean kingdom, which bordered China at the time, grew uneasy about Sui's successful unification of China. To counterbalance that pressure, Koguryŏ sought to forge friendly ties with the Tujue people (Turks), then a newly rising power in the steppe region of north-central Asia. As in previous periods of Chinese strength, however, the Sui empire launched military campaigns to subjugate the Tujue people. Determined to crush the Tujue threat, Sui planned to outflank them by conquering Koguryŏ.

In response to this crisis, Koguryŏ carried out a preemptive strike against the Chinese region west of the Liao River in 598. The Sui emperor, Wendi (581–604), sent out an expeditionary force, some 300,000 men, to launch a retaliatory attack on Koguryŏ in the same year. But the Koguryŏ forces held firm against the invading Chinese forces and defeated them. In 612, however, Yangdi (604–617), the next Sui emperor, mobilized some 1,130,000 troops and mounted an enormous invasion of Koguryŏ.

Koguryŏ stood up to the Chinese invasion with a force, said to be some 300,000, much inferior in number but better trained and more battle-experienced than the Chinese. Sui forces failed to take the Liaodong fortress, the anchor of Koguryŏ's line of fortifications on the Liao River. Yangdi then developed a new strategy to conquer Koguryŏ, which was to keep Koguryŏ fortresses in Manchuria at bay and meanwhile send a contingent army to take the Koguryŏ capital of Pyongyang. But an estimated 300,000 Sui troops could not occupy Pyongyang. The retreating Sui forces were lured into an ambush by the Koguryŏ commander Ŭlchi Mun-dŏk, one of the most celebrated generals in Korean history, and suffered a crushing defeat at Salsu (present-day Ch'ŏngch'ŏn River). It is said that only 2,700 of the 300,000 Chinese soldiers escaped alive. Yangdi was forced to withdraw his forces to China proper. The Koguryŏ general now has a street (Ŭlchi-ro) named for him in downtown Seoul. Again Yangdi sent his armies into Koguryŏ in 613 and 614, once more without success. The great defeat of the Sui empire in part caused the downfall of the dynasty itself in 618.

When the Tang dynasty succeeded the fallen Sui dynasty, Koguryŏ anticipated further Chinese invasions and therefore strengthened its defenses, including, in 628, the construction of its "Great Wall," a thousand *li* (about 300 miles) in length across its northwestern frontier. At first the Tang emperor

Taizong sought to subjugate Koguryŏ by diplomatic means, including sending envoys to urge Koguryŏ to come to terms with Paekche and Silla, but to no avail. Koguryŏ had no intention of recognizing China's suzerainty over the state.

At about the same time an internal power struggle developed among Koguryŏ's ruling elite. In 642 Yŏn Kae-somun emerged as a military strongman by staging a coup. He slaughtered King Yŏngnyu, who had attempted to kill him, and others who had opposed him. He enthroned King Yŏngnyu's nephew as King Pojang, but he himself retained absolute power. Yŏn Kae-somun took an increasingly provocative stance against Tang and Silla. When the Silla envoy Kim Ch'un-ch'u asked him for help in repelling attacks from Paekche, he demanded that Silla return the Han River basin to Koguryŏ. In 643 Koguryŏ assisted Paekche in occupying Tanghang-sŏng in the Namyang Bay, Silla's gateway to China. Exposed to the menace of both Paekche and Koguryŏ, Silla asked Tang for military assistance. Yŏn Kae-somun rejected a Tang demand that Koguryŏ halt its military operations against Silla, and the enraged Tang Taizong responded by launching a huge invasion of Koguryŏ in 645, marshaling more than 300,000 men.

Taizong and his Chinese forces crushed almost all of Koguryŏ's network of defenses in the Liaodong region, and Tang forces took the Liaodong fortress, turning it into an advanced base. But they suffered a massive defeat at the Anshi fortress, the last link in the defense chain. The Anshi fortress withstood a siege of almost three months, during which Tang forces threw all their strength into as many as six or seven assaults in a single day. But the stubborn Koguryŏ defenders, under the command of the legendary Koguryŏ general Yang Man-ch'un, drove back each new attack and, in the end, won a striking victory. Taizong finally withdrew his troops with heavy losses, but he observed military courtesy by leaving behind 100 bolts of silk cloth for the Koguryŏ commander. In 647 and 648 Taizong again dispatched expeditionary forces to invade Koguryŏ, but these attacks, too, were repulsed by Koguryŏ. Taizong never accomplished his ambition to conquer Koguryŏ in his lifetime.

Koreans ever since have seen these victories against the Sui and Tang empires as sterling examples of resistance against foreign aggression. Koguryŏ's victories did not end in triumphs for the state alone, since the conquest of the Korean kingdom was just one stage in the grand imperial design of both Sui and Tang to dominate all of East Asia, including Paekche and Silla. Koguryŏ served as a strong bulwark against repeated Chinese invasions, and, as a result, all the

Korean people were saved from the grave peril of Chinese conquest. Successive wars between Koguryŏ and the Sui and Tang, however, exhausted Koguryŏ's national strength and increased animosity between the kingdom and China. Combined with an internal schism among the three sons of Yŏn Kae-somun, these wars against China led to Koguryŏ's final collapse in 668.

The Downfall of Paekche

While Koguryŏ was preoccupied with its life-and-death struggle against Sui and Tang, Paekche conducted a ruthless offensive against Silla. In 642 King Ŭija captured Taeya-sŏng (present-day Hapch'ŏn, South Kyŏngsang province) and some 40 other strongholds in the fortified zone on the contested border between the two kingdoms. When Paekche forces took Taeya-sŏng, they killed the daughter and son-in-law of Kim Ch'un-ch'u, who later became King Muyŏl of Silla, incurring his grudge. Silla was forced to retreat east of the Naktong River, and in 643 Paekche occupied Tanghang-sŏng, Silla's important outlet leading to China. The desperate Silla sent Kim Ch'un-ch'u to Koguryŏ, asking for military aid. But Yŏn Kae-somun, who held power as *mangriji*, or prime minister, demanded the return of the Han River basin as the price for Koguryŏ's help. Silla then sought an alliance with Chinese Tang, offering Tang the opportunity to accomplish its failed ambition to conquer Koguryŏ. The Chinese empire acceded to Silla's request for a military alliance and settled on the strategy of first destroying the weaker Paekche and then striking out against the stronger Koguryŏ.

Silla and Tang planned a joint military invasion of Paekche. In 660 the Tang emperor Gaozong sent 130,000 troops under the command of Su Dingfang over the Yellow Sea, while 50,000 Silla forces led by General Kim Yu-sin marched to attack Paekche. The Tang forces landed on the south bank at the estuary of the Paek River (present-day Kŭm River), by which time the Silla army had already crossed the T'anhyŏn pass, east of present-day Taejŏn. King Ŭija, who had fought many wars against Silla and had taken hundreds of its towns and castles, gave little heed to military and government affairs. Having ignored the advice given him some time earlier by Sŏngch'ung, a high-level official, and now repeated by Hŭngsu, another loyal official, the Paekche king belatedly sent General Kyebaek to halt the Silla advance. Kyebaek organized 5,000 soldiers into a band, all of whom were determined to die. At Hwangsan (present-day Yŏnsan, South Ch'ungch'ŏng province), he won the battle but could not win the war, as he was killed in the battle. Now the allied forces of Silla and Tang rushed to the Paekche capital, Sabi. Soon the capital fell. With the surrender of King Ŭija, who had taken refuge at Ungjin, the kingdom of Paekche, which had produced a brilliant civilization and transmitted its high culture to Japan, finally perished in 660. The king and crown prince and more than 12,000 others were taken prisoner and sent to Tang.

Tang established five occupied regions in the former Paekche territory and began to administer it directly. Meanwhile, the remaining Paekche forces gathered volunteers at Churyu-sŏng (present-day Hansan, South Ch'ungch'ŏng province) and Imjon-sŏng (present-day Taehŭng, South Ch'ungch'ŏng province). Their leaders Poksin, a member of the royal family, and Toch'im, a Buddhist monk, invited Prince Puyŏ P'ung, who was visiting Japan, to become their king while they sought military aid from Japan. The Wae Japanese, who had maintained close ties with Paekche, tried their best to save the Korean kingdom by dispatching an army, some 30,000 strong, but at the estuary of the Paekch'ŏn (present-day Kŭm River), their naval forces were defeated by the joint Silla-Tang navy.

The effort to restore Paekche continued for four years. Paekche forces at one point laid siege to Sabi and Ungjin, and occupied other strongholds. They also harassed the Tang garrisons, and on a number of occasions defeated the Tang and Silla armies dispatched against them. But the restoration movement collapsed as a result of internal schism. Poksin, who distinguished himself on the field of battle and became increasingly arrogant, killed Toch'im, and was in turn killed by Puyŏ P'ung, who escaped to Koguryŏ. Seizing upon this opportunity, the allied forces of Silla and Tang attacked and captured the main restorationist stronghold of Churyu-sŏng in 663. Two years later, in 665, the final redoubt of the restoration forces, Imjon-sŏng, fell, putting an end to the struggle to restore Paekche.

The Downfall of Koguryŏ

Having destroyed Paekche in 660, the victorious allies of Tang and Silla continued their assault on Koguryŏ for the next eight years. In 661 Tang armies, with the aid of Silla troops, encircled the Koguryŏ capital of Pyongyang for several months. But they were defeated by Yŏn Kae-somun and had to withdraw in 662. Although Koguryŏ survived this attack, its power to resist had been seriously weakened. The exhaustion caused by long years of continuous warfare with China together with the disaffection engendered by Yŏn Kae-somun's dictatorial rule prompted Kogyryŏ's ultimate downfall.

After the death of strongman Yŏn Kae-somun in 666, a power struggle erupted among his three sons and younger brother. The eldest son, Nam-saeng, who succeeded his father as mangriji, was driven out by his two younger brothers, Nam-gŏn and Nam-san. He fled to the old capital of Kungnae-sŏng and voluntarily surrendered to Tang. Yŏn Kae-somun's younger brother, Yŏn Chŏng-t'o, surrendered to Silla, and was joined by the people of 12 castles in the southern region. Taking advantage of this opportunity, Tang mounted a fresh invasion of Koguryŏ in 667 that was coordinated with a Silla offensive. This time the Tang army, commanded by Li Ji, captured most of the fortresses in Manchuria and encircled Pyongyang. After holding out for another year, the weary kingdom of Koguryŏ met its final destruction in 668. King Pojang and more than 200,000 Koguryŏ people were forced to settle in Tang.[6]

After Koguryŏ's collapse, many of its people rebelled against Tang by starting a movement to restore the state. Among them, Kŏmmojam, a former middle-ranking official, elevated Ansŭng, King Pojang's illegitimate son, to the throne and, in 670, carried on a resistance movement at Hansŏng (present-day Cheryŏng, Hwanghae province). But the restoration movement ended in failure, mainly because of internal dissension. Kŏmmojam was assassinated by Ansŭng, who then fled to Silla for protection and was given the title of "King of Koguryŏ," which Silla later changed to "King Podŏk." To drive Tang from the Korean peninsula, Silla gave its full support to the Koguryŏ people's restoration efforts.

Silla's Expulsion of Tang

Although Tang succeeded in destroying two of the Korean kingdoms with Silla's help, it did not share the fruits of the conquest with Silla but instead directly administered the former Paekche and Koguryŏ territories. The Chinese expected to incorporate their Korean conquests into their empire, as had Han China. Tang broke its promise to give the territory south of the Taedong River to Silla and made no attempt to disguise its ambition to dominate the entire Korean peninsula. In 663 Tang created the Great Commandery of Kyerim as the means through which it would rule the Silla territory and appointed the Silla king Munmu (661–681) as its governor-general. In 664, to weaken the Paekche people's resistance to its domination, Tang named Puyŏ Yung, a son of King Ŭija, governor of the Ungjin Commandery in the former Paekche territory. The next year Tang forced Puyŏ Yung and King Munmu to meet at Mount Ch'wiri (present-day Mount Ch'wimi) on the north bank of the Kŭm River and to en-

ter into a pact of friendship. Tang's action aimed not only at winning over the
Paekche people but at thwarting Silla's designs on the former Paekche territory.
Immediately after the fall of Koguryŏ in 668, Tang established nine additional
occupational regions to govern the ruined kingdom's former domains. At the
same time it created the Andong Duhufu, or Protectorate-General to Pacify the
East, at Pyongyang and gave it jurisdiction not only over the former Koguryŏ
territory but also over Paekche and Silla. Indeed, Silla feared for its survival, as
it received the same treatment from the Chinese empire as did the conquered
Koguryŏ and Paekche domains.

Of course, Silla was unwilling to accept Tang's intentions on the Korean peninsula, but it needed foreign help to destroy its rival kingdoms. Soon yesterday's
allies became today's foes. Fortunately for Silla, at that time the Tibetans rapidly
increased their military strength to the extent that they cut Tang off from its
territorial possessions farther west. Tang had to cope with the new situation
and therefore could not concentrate its energies on the Korean peninsula. Almost from the moment of Koguryŏ's destruction, then, Silla launched military
campaigns against Tang and lent assistance to Koguryŏ's restoration movement led by Kŏmmojam. It invested Ansŭng as "King of Koguryŏ" in 670, and
later, in 674, it made Ansŭng "King of Podŏk." Silla forces also began to invade
the former territories of Paekche and Koguryŏ on its own. Inevitably Silla and
Tang forces clashed in many places, and Silla defeated Tang in numerous battles. In 671 Silla captured Sabi-sŏng and created the province of Soburi at the
old Paekche capital, thus seizing control over all the old Paekche territory. In
embarrassment, Tang declared Kim In-mun, King Munmu's younger brother
and longtime resident of China, as the king of Silla, without his consent, in
order to sow dissension between the brothers, and also launched an offensive
against its former Korean ally. But the Silla army defeated Tang forces in a series
of battles, including at Maeso-sŏng (present-day Yangju, Kyŏnggi province) in
675 and Kibŏlp'o at the estuary of the Kŭm River in 676, and finally succeeded
in driving out the Andong Duhufu from Pyongyang to the Liaodong fortress
in Manchuria. Now Tang was forced to accept Silla as an autonomous state and
recognize its claim to hegemony on the Korean peninsula. Silla could not occupy the entire Koguryŏ territory, but it could now control the area south of a
line extending roughly from the Taedong River in the west to the Wŏnsan Bay
in the east. Thus Silla finally unified the two other Korean kingdoms, preserving the independence of the Korean peninsula from foreign domination and
averting a second possible period of Chinese colonialism. This date of 676, for

many Korean historians, marks the beginning of a unified Korea. Korea's political, cultural, and linguistic unity dates back to this unification of the Three Kingdoms, making the country one of the oldest unified nations in the world.

POLITICAL AND SOCIAL STRUCTURE
OF THE THREE KINGDOMS

Establishment of a Centralized Aristocracy

The Three Kingdoms boasted an aristocratic social structure and centralized institutions of government. From the Three Kingdoms period on, the monarch always governed his domains directly, without granting autonomous powers to local administrators. The effectiveness of the central government varied from dynasty to dynasty, and from period to period, but the principle of centralization involving a system of provinces, districts, towns, and villages was never modified. Another feature inherited from this period that endured for centuries was the existence of a stratified social system characterized by a clear distinction between the rulers and the ruled. In particular, Silla society was rigidly organized into the hereditary caste system of kolp'um.

Beginning as tribal walled-town states, the Three Kingdoms first developed into confederated kingdoms and then centralized kingdoms. In the course of consolidating royal authority, tribal chieftains who were scattered throughout the country became part of the central aristocracy, and their aristocratic status depended on their relationship with the king and on their power and wealth. Koguryŏ was the first to be transformed in this way, followed, respectively, by Paekche and Silla. By the sixth century, however, all three states achieved the same aristocratic level in the centralized state.

The emergence of a centralized aristocratic state centered on monarchical power led to the concept that all the nation's land belonged to the king and all the people were his subjects. This does not mean, however, that private ownership of land disappeared or that all people in the nation came under the king's direct domination. Aristocratic families could still own land and wield control over others, a privilege they had continued to enjoy ever since the period of walled-town states. Members of the aristocracy privately enslaved hundreds or thousands of prisoners of war, and the state often granted them large tracts of land in the form of *sikŭp*, or tax villages, in which the recipients held hereditary rights to levy grain and tribute taxes on the farm households and to exact corvee labor from the farming populations under their authority. Therefore the private land and slave holdings of the aristocracy continued to increase. Based on their economic wealth, aristocrats enjoyed various political privileges, and the ruling aristocracy resided mainly in the kingdom's capital. Because the power and wealth of each of the Three Kingdoms were concentrated in its capital, the fall of the capital inevitably led to the destruction of the state itself. Aristocratic status was inherited from generation to generation. As the centralized kingdom was established, the aristocracy was gradually transformed into the monarch's officialdom, without being deprived of its status and privileges. In the period of the Three Kingdoms, then, a limited number of aristocratic lineages enjoyed a dominant status and position.

In Koguryŏ the most honorable title of esteem in the nation, *koch'uga,* was bestowed on members of the royal Ko house of the Kyeru-bu lineage, the former royal house of the Sono-bu lineage, and the Myŏngnim house of the Chŏllo-bu (Yŏnna-bu) lineage that furnished the royal consorts. Only a small minority of the uppermost layer of the aristocracy could be promoted to *taedaero,* the highest office rank of the kingdom's 14 ranks. Beneath this distinct stratum of the aristocracy were several other social strata termed *taega* and *soga,* whose members could not advance to the highest office rank.

In Paekche eight renowned clans (Sa, Yŏn, Hyŏp, Hae, Chin, Kuk, Mok, and Paek) constituted the powerful aristocracy. The royal Puyŏ house and the Chin and Hae families, both the queen houses, not only monopolized the principal government offices but occupied the predominant position in Paekche society. Only a minority of aristocratic households could attend the *chŏngsaam* council, which, it is believed, elected a chief minister to head the officialdom.

Silla's kolp'um system illustrates most clearly the rigid stratification of aristocratic society in the period of the Three Kingdoms. Governance, social status, and official advancement were all dictated by a person's bone rank, or hereditary bloodline. This strict lineage-based institution also dictated clothing, house size, and the choice of a marriage partner. There were two levels of bone rank: *sŏnggol,* or sacred-bone; and *chingol,* or true-bone. There were also six grades of *tup'um,* or head rank: head rank 6 through 1. The sacred-bone status was held by those in the royal house of Kim who had the qualifications to attain the kingship, though this higher bone rank ceased to exist just prior to Silla's unification. Queen Sŏndŏk (632–647) and Queen Chindŏk (647–654) were able to become queens, because at the time there were no men of sacred-bone status available to take the throne. When each ascended her throne, however, the two queens faced stiff opposition from some male true-bone aristocrats, also members of the Kim royal house. Although they originally lacked eligibility for the kingship, when the sacred-bone rank ceased to exist with the death of Queen Chindŏk, those of true-bone rank became eligible to take the throne. The first king of true-bone status was King Muyŏl (654–661). The true-bone rank also included the Pak lineage, which had earlier been the royal house from which royal consorts later came, as well as the "new Kim lineage" descended from the royal house of the Kŭmgwan Kaya kingdom. The change in the royal house from sŏnggol to chin'gol suggests that a wider range of aristocratic strata attained the qualifications to become king. The reason for the distinction between those of sŏnggol and chin'gol within the royal house of Kim is not entirely clear, but apparently distinctions were made based on maternal lineage. In other words, scions whose parents were all from the royal house had the status of sŏnggol, whereas the chin'gol status was held by those whose mothers were not from the royal house.

Head ranks 6, 5, and 4 comprised the general aristocracy. Head rank 6, called *tŭngnan*, or obtained with difficulty, was right below the true-bone status. Head ranks 3, 2, and 1 were originally the lower-ranking aristocracy but later ceased to exist and were called *p'yŏngin*, or common people, or simply *paeksŏng*, or people. Because members of these lower head ranks also had their own family names, they were still distinguishable from the general populace.

The bone-rank institution was closely associated with the allocation of office rank and government position. Holders of true-bone rank could advance to the highest-ranking office of *ibŏlch'an* (or *kakkan*) in Silla's 17 office ranks, but holders of head rank 6 were restricted to no higher than the 6th office rank of *ach'an*; holders of head rank 5, to the 10th office rank of *taenama*; and holders of head rank 4, to the 12th office rank of *taesa*. These strict limitations were also reflected in appointments to official positions. The post of *yŏng*, or minister, could be filled by those of the true-bone rank alone. The post of *kyŏng*, or vice minister, could be occupied by holders of either head rank 6 or 5. Lower posts in the ministries, *taesa, saji,* and *sa*, could be held by men of head rank 4 as well as by those of the higher head ranks and bone ranks. On the military side, holders of office ranks ranging from 1 (ibŏlch'an) through 9 (*kŭppŏlch'an*) could be appointed as general officers who exercised the highest command in the army, but only those of the true-bone rank customarily received such vital appointments. In Silla's hierarchic society, therefore, only those of the highest hereditary social status could wield dominant power and enjoy special privileges. The honorific title of *kalmun wang*, equivalent to Koguryŏ's koch'uga, was given only to members of the royal and consort families.[7]

In the Three Kingdoms the central government controlled the villages in the countryside through village chiefs or headmen who were usually natives of their local areas. Although they, too, possessed a considerable amount of land and a large number of slaves, these village chiefs received office ranks only at local government grades and were denied access to any central government office.

Below these village chiefs were self-supporting peasants with the social status of freemen who cultivated their own plots of land. These independent farmers comprised the numerically predominant class in each society of the Three Kingdoms and were the main providers of food for the society. Their lives and livelihood were subject to the direct control of the state, and they were required to pay grain and tribute taxes, the latter in the form of local products. The state also commandeered their labor services, mobilizing peasant farmers as conscripts or as corvee laborers for a prescribed time. One example is that of a youth named Kasil, who, during the reign of the Silla king Chinp'yŏng (579–632), saw much military service as a guard in a remote region in place of a girl's old father and returned home in six years looking worn down and defeated. Forced mobilization, specifically military service, was a hard obligation for the general populace.

Even lower than this general population on the social strata were outcast groups who led a caste-like existence in separate and ostracized villages. In Silla prisoners of war and criminals were forcibly resettled in villages known as *pugok,* communities of low-caste people. These low-caste laborers groaned under much heavier burdens than were suffered by the general peasants.

In each society of the Three Kingdoms, slaves, who were mainly prisoners of war, murderers, and debtors, constituted the lowest class. Owned by aristocratic families, these individuals led slavish lives, cultivating their masters' land or attending to household duties. It is apparent that aristocratic families owned a large number of slaves. In Silla, for example, a young hwarang warrior named Sadaham, who rendered meritorious services in the conquest of Tae Kaya in 562, was granted 300 slaves by the state. Further, the Silla general Kim Yu-sin, a hero of Silla's unification, is said to have held some 6,000 slaves. In brief, the Three Kingdoms comprised a rigidly stratified society based on an aristocratic social structure.

Administrative Structure

As territories expanded and populations increased, each of the Three Kingdoms established a bureaucratic structure centered on the kingship. As royal authority was increasingly strengthened, a hereditary-based monarchy became firmly established. In Koguryŏ the officialdom was classified into 14 grades, the topmost of which was the taedaero, or chief minister. Noteworthy in Koguryŏ's administrative structure was the existence of several *hyŏng*, or elders, ranks, such as *t'aedaehyŏng* (2nd rank), *choŭidudaehyŏng* (5th rank), *taehyŏng* (7th rank), *sohyŏng* (10th rank), and *chehyŏng* (11th rank), as well as *sa*, or stewards, ranks, including *t'aedaesaja* (4th rank), *taesaja* (6th rank), *suwisaja* (8th rank), and *sangwisaja* or *sosaja* (9th rank). As the nation grew into a centralized kingdom, former tribal or clan chieftains were given the hyŏng rank appropriate to their earlier positions, whereas previous retainers of the royal or powerful aristocratic houses received the saja rank suitable to their earlier standings. In these ways former tribal or clan leaders and their retainers were integrated into the new aristocratic-bureaucratic structure, and Koguryŏ became a centralized aristocratic state with a monolithic ranking system for officials.

Rare records exist describing Koguryŏ's government organization. Some documents reveal that at first the *kuksang,* and then the taedaero or mangriji, functioned as prime minister. In its later period the kingdom created the posts of *taemodal* and *malgaek,* which administered military affairs; *palgoch'uga, sain, t'ongsa,* and *chŏn'gaek,* which were responsible for diplomacy; and *kukcha paksa* and *t'aehak paksa,* who served as scholars.

Paekche, unlike Koguryŏ, from its earliest times created a central government structure with a three-tier office ranking system, distinguished by the color of official attire worn by those in each tier. At the top were chwap'yŏng and several *sol* ranks represented by purple robes. In the middle stratum were the various *tŏk* ranks symbolized by scarlet robes. The bottom layer included the *mun-dŏk* and *mudŏk,* as well as three lower ranks signified by blue robes. Like Koguryŏ, Paekche also instituted a unitary office ranking structure in the process of creating a centralized aristocratic kingdom.

Compared to Koguryŏ and Silla, Paekche had a highly refined government organization, with six chwap'yŏng ministers forming a cabinet: *naesin* chwap'yŏng for performing royal secretariat duties, *naedu* chwap'yŏng for fiscal administration, *naebŏp* chwap'yŏng for conducting rites and ceremonies, *wisa* chwap'yŏng for palace and capital security, *chojŏng* chwap'yŏng for penal and justice administration, and *pyŏnggwan* chwap'yŏng for overseeing provincial military forces. After moving its capital from Ungjin to Sabi in 538, Paekche created 22 new departments to administer the palace and government affairs, demonstrating that it had an elaborate government structure.

Silla's 17 office ranks consisted mainly of *ch'an, ma,* and *chi.* These terms, all meaning tribal or clan chieftains, suggest that the earlier tribal elements were integrated into the nation's centralized government structure. Holders of the 17 office ranks were distinguished by the color of their official attire, such as purple for the 5th rank (*taeach'an*) and above, scarlet for the 9th rank (*küppŏlch'an*) and above, blue for the 11th rank (*nama*) and above, and yellow for the 12th rank (*taesa[ji]*) and below. Several central government departments were established over a period and assigned responsibilities for military affairs (Pyŏng-bu), surveillance of official conduct (Sajŏng-bu), royal secretariat duties (Wihwa-bu), fiscal administration (Cho-bu), and the conduct of rites (Ye-bu).

The most peculiar feature of the political process in each of the Three Kingdoms was the councils for political decision making, which demonstrates that each of the Three Kingdoms was a union of the aristocracy. In Koguryŏ, in the reign of King Sindae (165–179), the post of kuksang (prime minister) was established. Unlimited in tenure, kuksang headed Koguryŏ's council of the high aristocracy. Later kuksang was replaced by the position of taedaero with a three-year term of office. In the sixth and seventh centuries, when the aristocracy regained strength, taedaero was elected by the high aristocracy, but sometimes the most powerful aristocrat took it by force. When the aristocracy could not reach an agreement on the right person for the position, the contestants would resort to arms. The king, unable to control them, would be forced to close his palace gates to protect himself from the struggle. Also, the high aristocracy of the 5th rank and above assembled in council to discuss and decide important affairs of state.

In Paekche high aristocratic officials met and elected the chief minister on a large rock called chŏngsaam. In Silla a council of the high aristocracy, termed the Hwabaek, consisted of aristocrats called *taedŭng.* Headed by a top aristocrat called *sangdaedŭng,* the Hwabaek council decided the most important state affairs, such as succession to the throne and declarations of war. Both taedŭng and sangdaedŭng were members of true-bone lineage. The principle of unanimity governed Hwabaek decisions, and council meetings were convened at one of the four sacred sites—Mt. Ch'ŏngsong to the east of the capital, P'ijŏn field to the west, Mt. Uji to the south, or Mt. Kŭmgang to the north. This council institution of the Three Kingdoms implies that political decision making at the time took the form of an "aristocratic democracy." The Ŭijŏngbu, or State Council, system of the later Chosŏn dynasty seems to have followed the tradition of these earlier council institutions.

The central government gradually extended its authority over the country-side and established a system of local administration. Small "states" formerly ruled by independent tribal chieftains were now reorganized into castle towns and villages in accordance with their size and importance. Castle towns were more populous, covered larger areas than villages, and were surrounded by ramparts. These towns were made the centers of local administration, and later the local administrative units were designated by the Chinese term *kun,* or districts. The central government dispatched its officials to these districts. In Koguryŏ the magistrate of such a district held the title of *ch'ŏryŏgŭnji* (or *tosa*), in Paekche *kunjang,* and in Silla *kunt'aesu,* but the general term *sŏngju,* or castle lord, was applied to all the district magistrates. The central government did not dispatch its officials to villages but allowed village headmen to govern themselves. A number of districts later combined to form larger, provincial-type administrative units, consisting five pu in Koguryŏ, five pang in Paekche, and six *chu* in Silla. The governors of these were called *yoksal,* a transliteration of a native word meaning "clan elder," in Koguryŏ; *pangnyŏng,* or provincial governor, in Paekche; and *kunju,* or military commandant, in Silla. Special administrative units were created in the capitals of the Three Kingdoms, for example, five pu, or districts, in both Koguryŏ and Paekche, and six pu in Silla. Each of the Three Kingdoms, in other words, established an elaborate system of central and local administration in its own way to effectively rule the whole country.

Military Organization

The Three Kingdoms were implacable enemies and frequently battled with one another for some 300 years. As the three states developed into centralized kingdoms, military units were organized on a national level and placed under the monarch's authority. As the commander-in-chief of their state's military forces, the kings of the Three Kingdoms often led their troops and fought alongside them in battle, as exemplified by the Koguryŏ king Kwanggaet'o. This phenom-enon was quite unlike that of the later Koryŏ and Chosŏn dynasties, where the king did not accompany his generals and soldiers to the battlefields.

Little is known about the military structure of the Three Kingdoms. Few re-cords remain regarding Koguryŏ's military system. Every man in the kingdom appears to have been required to serve in the military. There were five "divi-sions" in the capital, one in each of its five pu, and these units largely consisted of cavalrymen, numbering approximately 12,500, personally commanded by the king. Detachments, ranging from 21,000 to 36,000 troops, were stationed in the five provinces and led by provincial governors.

Early on, the Silla army was built around a small number of royal guards assigned to protect the king and in wartime to serve as the primary military force. After frequent conflicts with Paekche and Koguryŏ, and also the Japanese, Silla increased its army to six divisions, called chŏng, or garrisons, one in each of the chu provincial administrations. Garrison troops were responsible for local defense and also served as a police force. They were commanded by generals of the true-bone rank and were recruited from among men of elite lineages. These soldiers looked upon their military service as an honor and privilege, not as a burdensome duty. Additional military units termed sŏdang, or oath banners, pledged their individual service and loyalty to their commanders. In the Three Kingdoms military service was not only a duty but also an important means of pursuing a successful career.

Each of the Three Kingdoms seems to have organized its military forces based on conscripts drawn from the general population on the local level. Local administrative units functioned as the basic units of the local military organization. As implied by Silla's term for its governor, kunju, castle lords and provincial governors served as the commanders of the military contingents garrisoned in their own administrations.

Instituted to reinforce existing military units, companies of young men, usually in their mid-teens, were organized to cultivate moral values and practice military arts. In Koguryŏ they were called sŏnbi (or sŏnbae), meaning virtuous men; susa, meaning ascetics, in Paekche; and hwarang, meaning flowering youth, in Silla. The hwarang bands of aristocratic lineage had a special character, however, dating back to Silla's formative period. Having originated in the communal assemblies of youth in the earlier clan-centered society, the elite youth corps emphasized moral and physical training, military skill, and comradeship. Hwarang warriors honored the so-called sesok ogye, or five secular injunctions, laid down in the early seventh century by the Buddhist monk Wŏn'gwang, who stressed Buddhist and Confucian virtues in the education of Silla youth. They were to serve the king with loyalty, serve one's parents with filial piety, practice fidelity in friendship, never retreat in battle, and refrain from wanton killing. Hwarang youth bands made pilgrimages to well-known mountains and large rivers throughout the nation, and prayed for the tranquility and prosperity of their country by performing ceremonial singing and dancing, which demonstrates that their activities had a religious, specifically Taoist, character. In times of peace these young warriors cultivated military arts in preparation for war. In wartime they comprised the core of the Silla army, fighting in the front lines. All were prepared to sacrifice themselves for their nation. In the course of unifying the Korean peninsula Silla produced such well-known hwarang heroes as Sadaham, Kim Yu-sin, and Kwanch'ang.

Each of the Three Kingdoms not only defended its own domain and conquered other territories but ruled its own population with an iron hand. The general populace of the three states was subjected to severe coercion and government oversight, as opposed to the relatively gentle civil rule of the later Chosŏn dynasty.

CULTURE OF THE THREE KINGDOMS

The Koreanization of Chinese Writing

Originally Koreans may have had their own ancient writing system, probably a hieroglyph, but no one knows for certain. In China the complex pictogram writing on oracle bones and turtle shells of the Shang (Yin) dynasty evolved into Chinese characters. The East Asian peoples who engaged in cultural exchanges with China all adopted the Chinese writing system. A writing system with Chinese characters was first introduced to Korea in early times along with iron culture. After Han China established four commanderies in Manchuria and northern Korea in the later part of the second century BC, Chinese characters and documentation in Chinese writing became the standard usage. The Chinese writing system was adopted more broadly during the period of the Three Kingdoms, when widespread use of the Chinese system contributed greatly to the advancement of learning in the three states.

Because the Korean language differed entirely from Chinese in its lexicon, phonology, and grammar, however, the use of Chinese writing caused a great deal of inconvenience. Thus Koreans devised two modified systems for writing Korean with Chinese characters (*idu* and *hyangch'al*) and one system for reading Chinese texts (*kugyŏl*). The *idu* system used Chinese characters along with special symbols to indicate Korean verb endings and other grammatical markers where Korean differed from Chinese. Characters were selected for idu based on their Chinese sound and their adopted Korean sound or Korean meaning, and some were given a completely new sound and meaning. This process led Koreans to borrow numerous Chinese words, which made the idu system so difficult to learn that only a small minority of the aristocracy gained literacy. To transcribe the Korean language into Chinese characters under the hyangch'al system, characters were given a Korean reading based on the syllable associated with the character. This system is often classified as a subgroup of idu and was used mainly to write poetry. Today 25 *hyangga*, old Silla songs, are extant and show that vernacular poetry followed Korean word order and each syllable was transcribed with a single character.

Some Korean writings followed the Chinese literary style. One such example is the inscription on the memorial stele of the Koguryŏ king Kwanggaet'o of 414, written in Chinese characters. But novices in Chinese writing had difficulty understanding it. Therefore a method of reading Chinese texts was developed, where additional markers, called kugyŏl or *t'o*, written in Chinese characters, were appropriately inserted between phrases of the text. The kugyŏl system sought to render Chinese texts into Korean with minimal distortion. The Silla scholar Sŏl Ch'ong is said to have used this kugyŏl system when he read Chinese classics. Koreans finally dropped these modified writing and reading systems, including idu, hyangch'al, and kugyŏl, when, in the mid-fifteenth century, they invented a true scientific phonetic alphabet, han'gŭl.

Historiography

Each of the Three Kingdoms compiled its own history around the time it laid the groundwork for national development. The compilation of national history, therefore, was almost synchronized with the promulgation of a code of laws, the establishment of national institutions, and the striving for territorial expansion. In this light, the compilation of history represented an expression of desires to demonstrate the nation's legitimacy and authority abroad, and to win the allegiance of people at home by stressing national pride.

Koguryŏ was the first to compile its national history. It is said, early on, the kingdom produced a 100-volume *Yugi*, or Extant Records, and that this voluminous historic work was rewritten into a five-volume *Sinjip*, or New Compilation, in 600 by Yi Mun-jin. Precisely when *Yugi* was written is unknown, but it is surmised that it was written in the reign of King T'aejo who secured the right to the throne by the Ko house of the Kyeru-bu lineage and vigorously expanded the state's territory. *Sinjip* seems to have added post-*Yugi* Koguryŏ history to the original work.

In Paekche the scholar Kohŭng compiled a history called *Sŏgi*, or Documentary Records, in 375 in the reign of King Kŭnch'ogo. Japan's *Nihon shogi*, produced in 720, was modeled after Paekche's *Sŏgi*. The Silla scholar-general

Kŏch'ilbu also compiled his kingdom's history in a work titled *Kuksa,* or National History, in 545 during King Chinhŭng's reign.

None of these histories has survived, but *Samguk sa,* or History of the Three Kingdoms, compiled in the early Koryŏ dynasty, may have included many references to these works. Their contents also seem to have been largely incorporated by Kim Pu-sik in his twelfth-century *Samguk sagi.* But because Kim Pu-sik, a Silla offspring, compiled his work centering on Silla, *Samguk sagi* seems to have deleted much of the content that was disadvantageous to Silla from the written histories of Koguryŏ and Paekche.

Acceptance of Confucianism and Taoism

Using Chinese characters and writing, Koreans were able to read Chinese scriptures on Confucianism, Taoism, and Buddhism, and thus significantly raised the level of their spiritual culture. Confucianism comprised the teachings and lessons of famous Chinese scholars, particularly those of Confucius and Mencius, and its central idea was that the government should treat its people humanely and that people should do the same with one another. People should conduct themselves according to five principles: loyalty to the king, filial piety to parents, trust between friends, respect for elders among siblings, and love and peace between husband and wife. Confucian philosophy was a moral code for governing a country as well as for familial relations. The emperors of Han China adopted Confucianism as the official philosophy, because it inspired loyalty to the monarch among his subjects. When the Han commanderies were established on the Korean peninsula in 108 BC, Confucianism, the Han empire's code of conduct, was introduced into Korea, and thereafter it became deeply embedded in the fabric of Korean society.

The Three Kingdoms attempted to inculcate the Confucian ethos as a means of maintaining their hierarchic social orders. Koguryŏ established a national academy, called T'aehak, in 372, modeled after one where the Chinese taught Chinese philosophy, literature, and literary writing, as well as military arts. At T'aehak, the institution of five *paksa,* or scholars, equivalent to today's Ph.D.s, was established to teach the Five Classics of Confucianism, including *Shijing,* or Book of Poetry; *Shujing,* or Book of History; *Yijing,* or Book of Divination; *Chunqiu,* or Spring and Autumn Annals; and *Liji,* or Book of Rites. Later unmarried youth were assembled at kyŏngdang, or the local academy, in each area for instruction in reading Chinese texts and for practicing archery. It is recorded that the Koguryŏ scholars read the Five Classics, as well as Sima Qian's *Shiji;*

Ban Gu's *Hanshu,* or History of the Han Dynasty; *Yupian,* a Chinese character dictionary; and *Wenxuan,* or Literary Selections, an anthology of Chinese literature. Thus it was not accidental that the people of Koguryŏ compiled their history and had a fluent command of Chinese writing, as evinced in the inscription on the stone monument of King Kwanggaet'o.

Paekche also actively accepted Confucianism, which helped shape the nation's administrative system, culture, and art. Confucian educational institutes must have flourished to teach Chinese philosophy, art, literature, poetry, and other subjects. Educated Paekche scholars such as Wang In, Agikki, Tanyangi, Ko An-mu, and Wang Yu-gui later introduced Confucian classics to Japan and taught the Japanese royalty.

Silla was the last of the Three Kingdoms to accept the Confucian way of life, but Confucian moral values were already widely disseminated among the people in the kingdom. This is demonstrated by the monk Wŏn'gwang's five secular injunctions and by the Oath Inscription of 732, a text incised on a stone tablet where two Silla youth swore to strictly observe the code of loyalty and complete the reading of three Confucian classics—the Book of Poetry, the Book of History, and the Book of Rites—within three years. After unification, Silla established a national university called Kukhak, or the National Confucian Academy, in 682.

In China, however, Confucianism declined as the Han dynasty declined and fell. During the Tang period, Taoism gained popularity among Chinese scholars. The Tang rulers, whose family name was Li, traced their ancestors back to the founder of Taoism, Laozi, who also had been named Li. In earlier times Tang ranked Laozi above Confucius or Buddha. As Koreans increasingly felt the strength of the Tang dynasty, they, too, adopted Taoism.

Taoism was first introduced to Koguryŏ in 643 as a result of Koguryŏ's active cultural exchange with China. Later it was also introduced to Paekche and Silla. Taoism was vehemently taken up by Silla's young hwarang bands, as Taoist philosophy supported the ideal of promoting the self-development of body and soul.

In accepting both Confucianism and Taoism, Koreans in the Three Kingdoms enjoyed an enriched spiritual life. Whereas Confucianism served as a moral principle of human behavior for social order, Taoism became a form of religion in which people sought spiritual strength. People believed that, through Taoism, they could attain earthly perpetual life.

Acceptance of Buddhism

Each of the Three Kingdoms also accepted Buddhism in the course of establishing a centralized kingdom. Before the introduction of this foreign religion, the king ruled his country by virtue of the authority that his progenitor had been the son of heaven, or a demigod. This was based upon the myth of how the state had been born. As time went on, however, the general populace no longer believed that the king was the son of a heavenly god. Needing something new to legitimize or authorize his rule, the king turned to the Buddhist teaching that the king was the Buddha. Although he was not a god but a human being, Buddha attained spiritual awakening, and, accordingly, by identifying with Buddha, the king became endowed with new authority over his people. Furthermore, the Buddhist teaching of an endless cycle of reincarnation, a rebirth based on *karma*, retribution for the deeds of a former life, justified strict social stratification. Buddhism was a doctrine that justified the privileged position of the establishment and, for this reason, it was adamantly welcomed by the king, the royal house, and the aristocracy.

Buddhism was first introduced to Koguryŏ in 372, when the Chinese monk Shundao (Sundo in Korean) came to the Korean kingdom from the Chinese Earlier Qin state, then in control of northern China, and brought with him images of Buddha and Buddhist sutras. Twelve years later, in 384, another monk, Marananta (Maluonantuo in Chinese), brought Buddhism to Paekche from Chinese East Jin. Since Koguryŏ and Paekche had already actively accepted Chinese culture, Buddhism was conveyed from states in China with friendly ties to the recipients as part of an officially sanctioned cultural exchange. The new religious doctrine was well received by the ruling class without causing significant discord.

In Silla Buddhism was first disseminated in the fifth century by the monk Mukhoja, also known as Ado, who entered the kingdom from Koguryŏ.[8] Although this missionary effort was based on an individual initiative and attracted the common people to Buddhism, there was considerable resistance to the alien religion among the central aristocracy which adhered to traditional shamanist beliefs. Buddhism was brought to the royal house a century later, with the arrival of the monk envoy Wŏnp'yo from the southern Chinese state of Liang. For a considerable period, however, it was not accepted because of stiff opposition by the ruling aristocracy. Buddhism was officially recognized only after the storied martyrdom of the high court aristocrat Ich'adon in the reign of King

Pŏphŭng in 527.[9] The next king Chinhŭng encouraged the growth of Buddhism, and eventually it was recognized as the national religion of Silla.

In the Three Kingdoms the king took the initiative in accepting Buddhism. This is particularly remarkable in the case of Silla, where, only after the alien religion had been transmitted to the king and royal house, was the way opened for official recognition. Buddhism was strongly supported and promoted by the Silla king and royal house, because it was regarded as a spiritual prop to consolidate kingly authority. Four Silla kings and two queens—King Pŏphŭng (514–540), King Chinhŭng (540–576), King Chinji (576–579), King Chinp'yŏng (579–632), Queen Sŏndŏk (632–647), and Queen Chindŏk (647–654)—adopted Buddhist names and portrayed themselves as Buddha-kings, based on the belief that the king was the Buddha. Further, all of the nation's land ruled by the king was identified with the Buddha land, and thereafter Buddhist temples were built throughout the country.

In each of the three states, Buddhism was welcomed as a vehicle offering the rich promise of worldly rewards to the individual, for instance, through prayers for recovering from illness or for having children. More important, it functioned as a doctrine or faith assuring protection of the state. In Silla, the sutra *Inwang-gyŏng*, or Sutra of the Benevolent Kings, which contained the doctrines of state protection, was held in particular esteem. The numerous Buddhist temples in the Three Kingdoms dedicated to disseminating the doctrine of the state's well-being included Paekche's Wanghŭng-sa, or Temple of the King Ascendant, and Mirŭk-sa, or Temple of Maitreya, and Silla's Hwangyong-sa, or Temple of the Illustrious Dragon. In particular, the nine-story wooden pagoda, built in 645 at Hwangyong-sa and perhaps, at 70 meters in height, East Asia's tallest manmade structure of the period, was said to symbolize the nine nations, including China and Japan, that were destined to submit to Silla rule. The young hwarang warriors had strong connections to the worship of the Maitreya Buddha and were regarded as the avatar of the future Buddha who would bring enlightenment and abundance to mankind.

The Buddhist sect that flourished most during the Three Kingdoms period was the Vinaya, or *Kyeyul*, sect, which was mainly concerned with the study and implementation of moral discipline. The Paekche monk Kyŏmik and the Silla monk Chajang were major figures in this sect. Chajang, in particular, is credited with having been a major force in adopting Buddhism as the state religion. Because of the close nexus that existed between Buddhism and the state, Silla established a hierarchy of abbot administrators at the district, province, and national levels who applied the disciplines of the Vinaya order to control the temples and monks throughout the state. Chajang occupied the position of chief abbot of the state and supervised the entire Buddhist establishment in the kingdom. In later years, in Koguryŏ and Paekche, the Nirvana, or *Yŏrban*, sect, most notably espoused by the Koguryŏ monk Podŏk, increasingly gained popularity among the general populace.

Buddhist monks in this time of the Three Kingdoms were pioneers in bringing new elements of Chinese culture, at the time known as "Western study," into Korea. Monks also served as spiritual leaders for the people, as illustrated by the Silla monk Wŏn'gwang's formulation of the five secular injunctions for the hwarang bands. Because Buddhism received extensive support and protection from the state, monks frequently acted as political advisers, as shown by the high-level appointment of monk Chajang as chief abbot of the state; it was he who proposed the construction of the nine-story pagoda at Hwangyong-sa, noted above. In short, the Three Kingdoms each embraced Buddhism as a highly disciplined philosophical religion to make the alien religion a spiritual prop that would bring national unity and solidarity to the states. The rulers also sought to consolidate regal power with the Buddha serving as a venerated symbol of authority.

Literature and Music

As Koreans in the Three Kingdoms became accustomed to Chinese writing, they composed Chinese poetry, as seen in the Koguryŏ general Ŭlchi Mun-dŏk's poem, which scoffed at the commanding generals of the invading Chinese Sui forces in 612. Although Chinese poetry was composed by a small minority of the educated elite, in vogue among the masses were the *sin'ga*, literally meaning "divine songs," closely related to shamanism. Among a few remaining sin'ga is the well-known *kujiga*, or turtle song, believed to have been sung by nine village headmen who climbed up the Kuji-bong (hill) to find nine "golden eggs" at Kimhae in A D 42.

The sin'ga, thought to have been composed by shamans, evolved into the hy-angga, or native songs, through the influence of Buddhist monks and hwarang warriors. The hyangga also took on the religious character of shamanism and often functioned as vehicles for entreating divine intervention in human affairs. The Silla monk Yungch'ŏn, for instance, composed *Hyesŏngga*, or Song of the Comet, which, when sung, is said to have successfully eliminated a comet, regarded as an ill omen, and also to have caused Japanese pirates to retreat.

It is one of 25 hyangga still extant. Singing these hyangga, the hwarang warriors might make a pilgrimage to sacred mountains and rivers throughout the kingdom.

Musical instruments also emerged in this period. Master Paekkyŏl of Silla is believed to have composed the pestle-pounding refrain called *taeak*, which had the miraculous power of onomatopoetic sound. In the sixth century Urŭk, from the Kaya area, created the 12-stringed zither called the *kayakŭm*. The 12 strings symbolized a year. He brought the instrument to Silla and taught many disciples the art of playing it. When the Silla king Chinhŭng attacked the upper Han River region in the mid-sixth century, at Nang-sŏng (present-day Ch'ungju, North Ch'ungch'ŏng province), he summoned Urŭk to perform music for him. In Koguryŏ, in the mid-sixth century, Wang San-ak created the *kŏmun'go* (*hyŏnhakkŭm* [black crane zither]) by modifying the seven-stringed zither that was popular in the Chinese state of Jin. He is said to have composed more than 100 melodies for his instrument. Later the kŏmun'go came to Silla, where it was played by distinguished performers such as Okpogo. Besides these string instruments, there were also scores of percussion and wind instruments introduced from Central Asia. A repertoire of 185 melodies may have existed for the kayagŭm and some 860 melodies for the *pip'a*, a Korean mandolin. Korean music, including instruments, instrument makers, and master performers, found its way into Japan, greatly contributing to the development of Japanese music.

Architecture and Fine Arts

The Three Kingdoms each created many works of architecture, as well as paintings, sculptures, and handicrafts of extraordinary beauty. Above all, each kingdom appears to have constructed magnificent palace buildings, but none of these still exists. Judging only from the excavated site of the Anhak-kung palace, constructed by the Koguryŏ king Changsu, in Pyongyang, in 427, one guesses it was majestic in size, some 622 meters long between the eastern and western edges, and 620 meters long between the southern and northern edges. Now one can see only where huge Buddhist temples once stood, particularly Hwanyong-sa at Kyŏngju and Mirŭk-sa at Iksan. As noted above, the famed nine-story wooden pagoda at the Hwangyong-sa temple was built at the suggestion of the Silla monk Chajang, under the supervision of the Paekche master craftsman Abiji, in the mid-seventh century. Regrettably the masterpiece was destroyed by fire during the thirteenth-century Mongol invasions. Near

Hwangyong-sa, however, the Punhwang-sa temple, constructed in 614, still stands along with a majestic stone-brick pagoda at the site. The Mirŭk-sa temple, built by the Paekche king Mu in the early seventh century, is said to have been the largest Buddhist temple in East Asia, but a refined stone pagoda at the site represents the only surviving evidence of that giant temple. Another stone pagoda also remains at the site of the Chŏngnim-sa temple at Puyŏ.

The Ch'ŏmsŏngdae, or Star-Gazing Platform, represents the quintessence of Three Kingdoms architecture. In Silla astronomy comprised an important part of the study of science. Star charts were made by observing the night skies. To observe the stars, Silla built an observatory at its capital in 647. The observatory was built with 364 carved stones which, including the sky in the count, represented the number of days in a calendar year. This milk-bottle-shaped observatory, some nine meters in height, likely served Silla scientists well.[10]

Tombs from the Three Kingdoms period remain abundant. Used as burial sites for kings, queens, and other members of the royal family, as well as for high-level aristocrats, the tombs themselves reflect Koreans' ingenious engineering skills. At first, the people of Koguryŏ built tombs by placing slabs of stone one atop the other. An outstanding example of these earlier tombs is the pyramid-shaped Changgun-ch'ong, or Tomb of the General, which is more than 12 meters in height to symbolize the unyielding power of the figure interred. Later the stone tombs were supplanted by huge earthen tombs, which were mounds of earth piled atop a burial chamber formed from stone slabs. A typical example of these later tombs is Ssangyŏng-ch'ong, or Tomb of the Twin Pillars, which has octagonal twin columns at the entrance of the burial chamber.[11]

Influenced by the structures in Koguryŏ, the people of Paekche also built pyramid-shaped tombs of stone. Later, however, under the influence of China's Southern dynasties, they made brickwork tombs and stone-chambered earthen tombs. Silla tombs, on the other hand, were made of wood, sealed with clay, and covered with mounds of stone and earth.

The tombs of Koguryŏ and Paekche, constructed with a horizontal entranceway leading to the burial chamber beneath the earthen mound, were vulnerable to grave robbing, and so virtually no tomb artifacts have been found. But because Silla tombs had no entranceway beneath the stone mound, they were relatively impenetrable and so many dazzling burial objects have been unearthed.

The Korean custom at the time was to bury the deceased's belongings in chambers within the tombs, as people believed in the immortality of the soul.

Unlike tombs in those of Koguryŏ and Paekche, as noted above, Silla tombs have preserved hoards of precious burial goods. Chief among the treasures are accessories of pure gold—crowns, caps, belts, earrings, necklaces, finger rings, bracelets, and shoes. Numerous ornaments have been recovered, fashioned from silver, gilt bronze, crystal, glass, beads, and jade. The objects were designed not for actual wear but as burial goods. Gold crowns have also been excavated from a number of Silla royal tombs, including Kŭmgwan-ch'ong, or Tomb of the Golden Crown; Sŏbong-ch'ong, or Tomb of the Lucky Phoenix; Kŭmnyŏng-ch'ong, or Tomb of the Golden Bell; and Ch'ŏnma-ch'ong, or Tomb of the Heavenly Horse. Unearthed in 1973, Ch'ŏnma-ch'ong reveals more than 10,000 artifacts that were buried with the deceased person, who is believed to have been a king. Among the more important objects are a beautiful gold crown and a painting of a heavenly horse, for which the tomb was named. The burial objects unearthed from Silla tombs attest to the exquisite sophistication of those ancient craftsmen.[12]

The best paintings from the Three Kingdoms period are the murals of Koguryŏ tombs. Up to the present, it is known that more than 80 Koguryŏ and Paekche tombs contain mural paintings. The various themes painted on the four walls and ceilings of the burial chamber of earthen tombs offer unique insight into the way of life and thinking of the Koguryŏ people. The paintings are colorful representations of mythical birds and animals, as well as human figures displaying marvelous vitality and animation. These Koguryŏ tombs are customarily named after the theme of the mural paintings, such as Kakchŏ-ch'ong, or Tomb of the Wrestlers; Muyong-ch'ong, or Tomb of the Dancers; and Suryŏp-ch'ong, or Tomb of the Hunters. Perhaps the most famous of the Koguryŏ murals is the painting of the four spirits—the azure dragon of the East, the white tiger of the West, the vermilion phoenix of the South, and the tortoise and snake of the North.[13] These four mythical animals were believed to guard the deceased from the four directions. An excellent painting of the four spirits is found in a great tomb known as the Kangsŏ Taemyo, or Great Tomb of Kangsŏ, at Uhyŏn-ni near Pyongyang.

Mural paintings are also found in Paekche tombs, perhaps the result of Koguryŏ influence. The best known are those in the brickwork tomb at Songsan-ni, Kongju, and in the stone-chambered tomb at Nŭngsan-ni, Puyŏ. Whereas Koguryŏ murals are full of gumption and enterprise, the Paekche murals convey tranquility and refinement. No wall painting is found in Silla tombs, as they have no burial chamber.

Buddhism was the dominant artistic influence during the later years of the Three Kingdoms and the unified Silla and Koryŏ kingdoms. Themes and motifs originating in India passed to Korea through Central Asia and China. Sculpture of the Three Kingdoms is almost entirely of images of Buddha and the Bodhisattvas. The images were not mere copies of Indian or northern Chinese models but have a distinctively Korean spirit representing an indifference to sophistication and artificiality, and a predisposition toward nature.

Each of the Three Kingdoms boasts of outstanding Buddha images, particularly those of the gilt-bronze, half-seated, meditating Maitreya Bodhisattva. The production of large numbers of statutes of Maitreya Bodhisattva suggests that at the time the Maitreya faith pervaded the three nations. In addition, Paekche produced stone Buddha images like the stone Buddha carved in the face of a cliff at Sŏsan, South Ch'ungch'ŏng province. The Paekche Buddha statues demonstrate the quintessence of the kingdom's artistry—elegant facial contours and benign smiles. The smile of the Sŏsan stone Buddha is well known as the "smile of Paekche."

A splendid gilt-bronze incense burner found at a temple site located at Nŭngsan-ni, Puyŏ, in 1993, exhibits exquisite metal-arts workmanship in the Three Kingdoms period. This Paekche piece has a base, body, and lid, and 12 holes through which the smoke of burning incense wafted upward. It appears to have been used in rites of the royal house and reflects the thinking and values of the Paekche people who vehemently embraced Buddhism and Taoism.

Before Buddhism was introduced to the Three Kingdoms, Korean artistic creations were characterized by unsophisticated beauty. Later Buddhism greatly encouraged an aesthetic sense in Koreans, driving them to produce more refined artistic works in large quantities.

THE THREE KINGDOMS AND JAPAN

Korean Settlers in Japan

Many archeological findings in Japan as well as Japanese historical records suggest that Korean culture was imported to Japan from the prehistoric age and that, until the end of the eighth century, the Japanese ancient state and culture were greatly influenced by the Korean people. The Paekche people especially were greatly responsible for the development of the Japanese state and culture.

Archeological evidence reveals that a series of different cultures existed in early Japan. The first major culture was Jomon, named after the shape of its

cord-patterned pottery, which spread over the islands in about the third millennium BC. The Jomon people were essentially Stone Age cave dwellers who
subsisted by hunting and gathering roots, nuts, and shellfish. Beginning about
the third or second century BC, an entirely new culture began to develop in the
northern part of Kyushu Island and the southern tip of Honshu Island, clearly
under influences from the continent, and spread rapidly to the Kanto plain, replacing the old Jomon culture. This more developed Yayoi culture, named after
a type of site in the city of Kyoto and characterized by rice cultivation, appears
to have been imported to the Japanese islands by people who came across the
sea from the Korean peninsula.

From the mid-third century AD, Japan entered the era of the "Tomb Culture"
typified by large, round tombs modeled after the Korean tombs. Japan's modern
imperial line undoubtedly dates back to the "Tomb Culture" rulers. At that time
Japan comprised many semi-autonomous units called *uji* (clan). In the Kyushu
region, Yamato rulers, simply the chieftains of the Yamato *uji,* established their
strength. Later they moved to the Nara region of Honshu Island. By the sixth
century the Yamato state had been firmly established and was actively inter-
acting with the southern part of the Korean peninsula. The Yamato government moved its capital from Nara to Heian (present-day Kyoto) in 794, and the
"Heian-jo (dynasty) period" began. From this time on, the Japanese began to
develop their own culture independently of Korean influences.

From early on, continuous waves of Korean settlers established the economic,
political, and military foundations of the new state in Japan. At first, the small
Kaya kingdoms provided Japan with people and a new civilization. Silla's annexation of Tae Kaya, or Imna, in 562 caused more people and materials to flow
into Japan. During the period when the Kaya kingdoms frequently contacted Japan, Paekche also had close ties with the Japanese. After Tae Kaya fell, Paekche
emerged as Japan's main source of new people, scholarship, technology, and
arts, and introduced Confucian classics and Buddhism to the Japanese people.
The Japanese welcomed and encouraged the newcomers from Paekche, granting them high-level posts in the government, social standing, and opportunities to amass wealth. Such encouragement and special treatment resulted in a
flood of immigrants from Paekche to Japan. Many Paekche scholars, artists, and
craftsmen migrated to Japan, seeking safety from the never-ending warfare on
the Korean peninsula and responding to the Japanese government's welcome.
Some of the immigrants were members of the royalty and the aristocracy. Overall these people of Paekche became powerful forces in Japanese society.[14]

The Aya, Hata, and Soga households, all immigrants from Paekche, wielded great influence in Japanese politics between the fourth and seventh centuries. The Hata household lent financial support to the Japanese "Emperor" Kammu (or Kanmu [781–806]) when he transferred Japan's capital from Nara to Heian in 794. The Soga household practically dominated Japan for 100 years, from the sixth through the seventh century. A member of the family, Soga Noumako, built Asuka-ji (temple), the oldest Japanese temple, in the late sixth century.

From the fourth century on, the Paekche royal household forged a marriage alliance with the Japanese royal household. Paekche crown princes often went to Japan to get married to Japanese princesses. And Paekche princesses, who went to Japan, gave birth to Japanese crown princes. Accordingly, the two royal households had a shared blood inheritance. Three Paekche kings, King Chŏnji (405–420), King Tongsŏng (479–501), and King Muryŏng (501–523), were born in Japan or returned home after a long stay there. The Paekche prince Ajwa painted the portrait of the Japanese crown prince Shotoku in 597, and the mother of the Japanese "Emperor" Kammu is known to have been a Paekche princess.[15] As the two states were on intimate terms, it was quite natural that Japan aided Paekche militarily at crucial moments.

Among the many Paekche people who contributed to the development of Japanese culture, the most noteworthy were the scholars Ajikki and Wang In, who introduced, in Japan, the Confucian classic *Lunyu* and *Ch'ŏnjamun,* or Thousand-Character Text. They tutored Crown Prince Shotoku, who established a new government structure modeled on the government of Paekche and promulgated a code of laws. Other contributions include the introduction of Buddhism by the Paekche monk Norisach'igye in 538 and the construction of magnificent temples such as Horyu-ji by the Paekche people. Sculptures produced by Koreans and preserved in these Buddhist temples are the finest art creations in Japan of any age. Paekche so influenced Japan that Japanese culture of the sixth and seventh centuries might be considered an extension of Paekche culture. The great influence Paekche had on Japan led the early Japanese people to call the Korean kingdom *Kudara,* meaning "bear," which was an alteration of the Korean word *Ku-nara* or *K'ŭn-nara,* meaning "home country" or "great country."[16]

Koguryŏ and Silla also transmitted their advanced culture to Japan. The Koguryŏ monk Tamjing, for instance, painted the murals at the Horyu-ji temple in 610, and monk Hyeja became Crown Prince Shotoku's mentor. Although Silla was on bad terms with Japan, it transmitted the arts of fortification, shipbuilding, and medicine to Japan, as well as Buddhist statues and music.

The three Korean kingdoms each provided Japan with their people and civilization in different ways. These developments were recorded in the oldest Japanese history books, the *Nihon shogi*, compiled in 720, and the *Kojigi*, or Record of Ancient Matters, which appeared in 712. In a word, Koreans of the Three Kingdoms played a beneficial role in ancient Japan's development.

The "Mimana Nihon (Japan)-fu" Story

Some Japanese historians have falsely argued that from the late fourth to the mid-seventh century, the Yamato government extended its control to Paekche, Silla, and Kaya, and established the "Nihon-fu" in Imna (Kaya). The mention of the "Nihon-fu" was quoted in the history book *Nihon shogi*, which recorded that, in 369, Japanese forces occupied seven states and four towns on the Korean peninsula, creating the "Nihon-fu" at Mimana (Imna). The book also noted that Imna fell to Silla in 562. According to *Nihon shogi*, Japan ruled the southern part of the Korean peninsula for some 200 years, from 369 to 562, and the "Nihon-fu" was established as a mechanism for Japan's colonial rule in Korea.

But *Nihon shogi* essentially lacks historical reliability. Records in the history book before the fifth century are usually regarded as mythic legend. During the eighth century, when *Nihon Shogi* was written, Japan was in an inferior position in East Asia. To enhance Japan's national image, Japanese historians at the time inserted fictitious tales, including the story of the Japanese conquest of the southern part of the Korean peninsula and the establishment of the "Nihon-fu." First of all, the term "Nihon-fu" is invalid, as the name "Nihon" (Japan) first appeared in the seventh century. Furthermore, *Nihon shogi* did not describe its function, nor did it indicate that it was a governing body. Also, extensive Korean history texts, such as *Samguk sagi* and *Samguk yusa*, make no mention of a Japanese governing body anywhere on the Korean peninsula. If there were an important Japanese government office and military forces ruling Paekche, Silla, and Kaya, there should have been lengthy descriptions of it in these Korean historical works.[17]

To demonstrate an ancient Japanese conquest of Korea, Japan's nationalist historians have interpreted the inscription on the stone monument of the Koguryŏ king Kwanggaet'o as describing a Japanese invasion in the southern portion of the Korean peninsula. The inscription was partially destroyed and was incomplete, and thus these historians have interpreted it to say that the Wae Japanese came over by sea, conquered "something" (which cannot be read but was assumed to be Paekche and Silla), and made them subjects of "something" (which also cannot be read but was assumed to be Japan). The contents relating to Japan in the inscription are generally regarded as fiction or exaggeration. In fact, Koguryŏ appears to have fabricated a Japanese invasion to justify its conquest of Paekche.

In reality, there was no Japanese conquest of Korea at that time. When the Japanese Yamato state was just beginning to consolidate its new territory in the Kinki region of Japan, the Three Kingdoms of Korea were already fully developed, centralized powers. Even Kaya (Imna) had far more advanced culture and technology than the Japanese state. It is highly unlikely that a developing state, such as Yamato, had sufficient military power to conquer Kaya or any other part of Korea. There is absolutely no evidence to support the Japanese historians' contention. Historical evidence shows that the Japanese forces who came to the Korean peninsula were mercenaries employed by Kaya. The people of Kaya strengthened their national defense by reinforcing their insufficient military force with Japanese soldiers whom Kaya obtained in return for its export of iron to Japan. It is true that many Kaya people migrated to Japan for a new life, and they could have maintained an official diplomatic mission or a trade center in Imna. But if Japan had a strong enough military force to have conquered Paekche and Silla, Imna would not have been so easily annexed into Silla in 562. Moreover, the "Nihon-fu" story was written for the first time in 720, nearly 200 years after Imna was annexed by Silla, and therefore it has no historical value. Even many Japanese historians dismiss the "Nihon-fu" theory as false, and in March 2010 historians from both South Korea and Japan agreed that it was false.[18]

A "HISTORY WAR" WITH CHINA

China's Attempt to Distort Koguryŏ History

The long-simmering and recent controversy over whether the ethnically Korean kingdom of Koguryŏ was historically Korean or historically part of China has angered Koreans who have considered Koguryŏ a source of national pride. Because the ancient kingdom has always remained a proud legacy of Korean history, Koreans have accused China of "hijacking" their history.

In 2004 the Chinese declared that the Koguryŏ kingdom actually belonged to the Chinese Middle Kingdom. This claim emerged from China's "Northeastern Project," a state-funded program conducted by the Center for Chinese Borderland History and Geography, which was based on the belief that the histories of all ethnic groups that live or once lived within the present national border are part of China's legacy. This dispute between South Korea and China dates back to 2002, when China launched the five-year Northeastern Project to review the history of its northeastern region of Manchuria. Two years later, in 2004, the wrangling between the two countries was the worst it had ever been since they had normalized diplomatic ties in 1992. The flare-up arose when China registered certain Koguryŏ relics with the World Heritage website, claiming they had been found in Chinese territory. Moreover, the name Koguryŏ was found to have been deleted from the Korean history section on the Chinese Foreign Ministry's Internet homepage. After the South Korean government, academia, and political groups strongly protested the Chinese move, the two nations verbally agreed, in August 2004, not to allow the row to damage their ties. But the dispute over history between South Korea and China resurfaced in September 2006 with the revelation that China had posted a blueprint of its controversial geo-historical project that allegedly rewrote Korea's history. China has continued its history project and still refuses to recognize that the Koguryŏ kingdom is part of Korea's heritage. Koguryŏ seems destined to join Taiwan, Tibet, and Mongolia on a long list of disputes involving territories on China's periphery.

The Chinese unreasonably see Koguryŏ as a Chinese state, more precisely as a Chinese provincial government rather than a sovereign Korean kingdom. To make the Koguryŏ kingdom historically part of China, or to "own" the historical heritage of Koguryŏ, Chinese historians argue that the people of Koguryŏ were actually Chinese, thus denying Koreans any link whatsoever with Koguryŏ. But Koreans, with considerable historical justification, claim that Koguryŏ was a predecessor state of modern Korea with no ethnic links or political subordination to China. The people who established Koguryŏ were the Yemaek people, who were quite different from the Chinese. These people originally lived in Manchuria and the northern part of the Korean peninsula far from China proper.

Chinese historians also maintain that Koguryŏ was a Chinese state because it developed from the Han Chinese commandery of Hyŏndo (Xuantu in Chinese) and because Koguryŏ kings accepted investiture from Chinese emperors. In their eyes, Koguryŏ at first emerged as a tribal state in the Hyŏndo Commandery and later was raised to the status of a provincial regime belonging to the Chinese commandery. Historically Chinese dynasties diplomatically invested rulers of neighboring states with the kingship. Chinese historians emphasize that Koguryŏ kings paid tribute to Chinese emperors and were invested with the kingship. In other words, investiture of Koguryŏ kings implies that they ruled the people in the Koguryŏ region on behalf of Chinese dynasties. But the Chinese misinterpret the system of tribute and investiture as simply the internal political structure between the central government and provincial officials. The institution was only one of the diplomatic forms existing between Koguryŏ and China. Historical records demonstrate that Koguryŏ ruled itself independent of Chinese influence. If the Chinese view is justified, then Paekche, Silla, and Japan, as well as Koguryŏ, must all be part of China, as all those nations had a relationship of tribute and investiture with China.

Finally, Chinese historians argue that the history of Koguryŏ should be part of Chinese history because, after Koguryŏ's downfall, many of its people went over to Tang China and were assimilated by the Chinese. Actually, at the time, many Koguryŏ people were sent to Tang against their will, but many more other displaced people migrated to Silla, merging into the mainstream of Korean history. Later, another Korean kingdom, that of Parhae, received most of the Koguryŏ population.

Today, many Koguryŏ customs remain in some form in Korean culture. Indeed, the name "Korea" has its roots in the word "Koryŏ" which in turn is derived from "Koguryŏ." Koryŏ is actually the more correct term for Koguryŏ, as Koguryŏ is mainly referred to as Koryŏ in most Chinese and Japanese historical texts. The very founding of Koryŏ was based on the fact that it was the descendant state of Koguryŏ, which is why it adopted the name Koryŏ. The view that Koguryŏ was Chinese contradicts the Chinese historical records of the past Chinese dynasties. In short, Chinese arguments that Koguryŏ was one of the minorities of ancient China and was merely a dependent regional authority of China are all groundless, full of distortions of historical facts.

China's remapping of its ethnic frontiers, specifically the inclusion of Koguryŏ in the annals of Chinese history, is not an isolated attempt by zealous Chinese researchers to make history conform to their beliefs about China's centrality and omnipotence in the greater region. In the minds of Chinese historians and politicians, China's borders know no limits. The Chinese Communist Party (CCP) has continuously changed its views of China's territorial borders. In the first two decades of its existence (1921–1942), the CCP identified Taiwan as separate from China. In 1942 it suddenly changed its view without explanation or international challenge. Thereafter China declared Taiwan an integral part of its territory. In this light, China's decision to include the Koguryŏ kingdom in the annals of Chinese history might not bode well for the long-term independence of the northern half of the Korean peninsula.

China's Distortions of the Histories of Old Chosŏn, Puyŏ, and Parhae

Koreans proudly declare that their country's history dates back 5,000 years, as its first kingdom, Old Chosŏn, was established in 2333 BC. That ancient kingdom is considered the root of the Korean nation, and many elementary schools in South Korea have statues of Tan'gun, Korea's legendary founding father. Young Korean students learn that Old Chosŏn was founded in an area covering the northeastern part of present-day China and the Taedong River valley now in North Korea. Korean historians are uncertain, however, about when the first Korean kingdom was established, as little evidence exists to support their arguments.

Recently Koreans dispute China's contentions arguing that Old Chosŏn was part of Chinese history, and they reject the conclusion of the Northeastern Project that all ancient Korean kingdoms had been under Chinese dominion. Under this project, Chinese historians claim that not only Koguryŏ but also Old Chosŏn, Puyŏ, and Parhae are part of China's history. The Chinese argue that Korea began in the southern part of the Korean peninsula, below the Han River, with the Silla kingdom. They maintain that Silla later gave way to the Koryŏ and Chosŏn kingdoms, which then invaded China to expand their territories and "stole the history of China."

The Chinese argue that the roots of Old Chosŏn stem from the ethnic Chinese. In September 2006 the Chinese Academy of Social Sciences, which is under the direct jurisdiction of the Chinese government, maintained that the history of Old Chosŏn, Puyŏ, and Parhae all belonged to Chinese history, as did their territories. That month the Academy's Center for Chinese Borderland History and Geography that had taken the lead in distorting Koguryŏ history through the Northeastern Project since 2002 published 18 abstracts of research papers. One of them argued that descendants of China's Shang (Yin) dynasty founded Kija Chosŏn on the Korean peninsula. A Chinese local government, Kija Chosŏn was, so to speak, an overseas tributary of the Chinese Zhou and Qin dynasties. Kija Chosŏn, which Korean historians regard as a myth, gave rise to the history of Koguryŏ and Parhae, and was where the history of northeast China began. The Chinese seem to claim preemptive rights to North Korea by arguing that ancient China's territory extended to the Han River valley in the central part of the Korean peninsula.

The Chinese also maintain that Parhae was not an independent state but a local government under the Tang dynasty and is inseparable from Chinese history. In 1980, when it tried to co-opt annexed Tibet and the Uyghur region into its history, China also claimed that these regions were "inseparable" from China. Chinese historians argue that at the time of its establishment Parhae was a nation of the Chinese Magya (or Mohe; Malgal in Korean) tribe. The Chinese say that South and North Korea claim Parhae as part of their own history to serve their own political purpose of claiming territorial rights. They argue that China never invaded nations on the Korean peninsula, whereas the Korean kingdoms of Silla, Paekche, Koryŏ, and Chosŏn expanded their borders to the north and gradually eroded Chinese territory. The research organization posted three papers on Parhae alone. The Chinese also contend that even Puyŏ, the ethnic foundation of Koguryŏ and Paekche, was founded by a minority Chinese tribe in the northeastern region of China.[19]

China's recent attempts to distort ancient Korean history is potentially disturbing. These efforts constitute an open challenge to Koreans. Chinese distortions of ancient Korean history are designed mainly to deal with territorial issues, rather than history. The most likely explanation for China's claims is that China has been preparing a case for a preemptive territorial claim questioning the current border in the case of a North Korean collapse. Preparations for the collapse of North Korea have been deemed necessary, and an advance into North Korea would require both psychological and cultural justification, at least within China. Presenting what is now North Korea as an ancient and integral part of China might create the political and psychological environment for supporting this plan.

The international community, however, would never allow China to assert sovereignty over any part of the Korean peninsula. It is not because the world does not want to see a strong and dangerous China. More simply, it is because such a claim must be regarded as nonsense. Most Japanese, for example, accept Koguryŏ as part of Korean history and find South Korea's strong rebuttal of China's claims entirely understandable.

The historically flawed Chinese distortions of the Korean past are closely related to China's territorial concerns elsewhere. China, with its more than 100 different ethnic groups, needs to suppress restive minorities such as the Tibetans and their histories, or else its ethnic minorities will try to form their own independent states if China's rule is loosened. There may be some concerns among some Chinese scholars and officials that a North Korean collapse might result in a change in the borders, but to China's disadvantage. The Chinese do not have any particular fear that ethnic Koreans in China's Northeast might want to break away. More important, they fear that any admission that Koreans might have a valid historical claim to some Chinese territories might incite unrest among other border groups, particularly in the Southwest and Northwest.

China's distortions of ancient Korean history are also related to rising nationalism among the Chinese. China intends to include the histories of all the ethnic minorities in its present territory into Chinese history to confirm China's greatness. Historically the Chinese have wanted to place their country at the center of the world. They have been taught that their culture radiated far and wide over the centuries, embracing great historical events, ranging from Genghis Khan's empire to the invention of spaghetti and meatballs. In the background of the recent distortions of ancient Korean history lies a "great power" consciousness. According to Chinese history, not only the ancient Korean kingdoms of Old Chosŏn, Puyŏ, Koguryŏ, and Parhae began as ethnic minority states in the Chinese fold, but neighboring Japanese civilization began when 1,000 Chinese boys and girls sailed over in 219 BC to colonize the islands in the hope of finding pills that would ensure immortality. China's recently rising power gives its historians the opportunity to again rethink their history and try to restore past greatness by absorbing the histories of neighboring countries. Over the last 150 years, as China suffered from foreign occupation, civil war, and extremist ideology, modern advances largely passed the country by. Only in recent years has China begun to regain its role in the world. For most Chinese, the idea that their culture is a source of past greatness and future strength has never faded. But China has failed to realize that it has nothing to gain by promoting its greatness without supporting evidence, especially when dealing with ancient times.

The Three Kingdoms period is traditionally dated from 57 BC to AD 676, but it actually covered no more than three to four centuries in terms of the actions, reactions, and interactions of Koguryŏ, Paekche, and Silla. Along with the three major kingdoms, Kaya was another important actor in this era. With all four states sharing a similar language and culture, this age could in fact be called the "Four Kingdoms period." The era of the Three Kingdoms came to an end with Silla's unification of its rival kingdoms. Silla thus accomplished the unification of Korea for the first time in Korean history and laid the foundation for the development of a Korean national culture.

In becoming centralized states, the Three Kingdoms established a principle of centralization for subsequent Korean dynasties that was not modified until recent years. They also created an aristocratic, stratified social order that was inherited by the following Korean kingdoms and survived for centuries. In all these ways the Three Kingdoms served as a model for the political culture of future Korean states.

3

PARHAE, UNIFIED SILLA, AND THE LATER THREE KINGDOMS
(676–936)

THE RISE AND GROWTH OF PARHAE

The Period of the Northern and Southern States

AFTER SILLA PUSHED TANG CHINA off the Korean peninsula in 676, it asserted authority over the Korean peninsula south of the Taedong River-Wŏnsan Bay line and thus unified Korea south of the peninsula's narrow waist. The old domain of Koguryŏ above that line on the Korean peninsula and in Manchuria then came under the rule of Tang, which, to govern that vast territory, established the "Protectorate-General to Pacify the East." But Tang's rule met with stiff resistance from those displaced from Koguryŏ. To placate them Tang invested Pojang, the last king of Koguryŏ, with a fiefdom, giving him the title "King of Chaoxian (Chosŏn)," and in 677 it appointed him governor of Liaodong. His descendants succeeded him in that position and gradually secured virtual autonomy for the region they governed. This "state," which remained in existence until the early ninth century, was often referred to by historians as "Lesser Koguryŏ." In 698 Tang was forced to abolish the Protectorate-General to Pacify the East.

Meanwhile, in that same year in the vast plains of eastern Manchuria, the new state of Parhae was established by a former Koguryŏ general, Tae Cho-yŏng.

Tang China, which had exerted great power when the dynasty first started to rule, began to wane by this time. Empress Wu (685–705), the one-time consort of Tang emperor Gaozong, was unable to pay much attention to the affairs of Northeast Asia, as she was busy consolidating her own power through bloody struggles in which, on two occasions, she even removed her own sons from the imperial throne. Seizing upon this opportunity, Tae Cho-yŏng led a band of followers, from both Koguryŏ and Malgal, eastward to Dongmushan (near present-day Dunhua in Jilin province, China), where he proclaimed himself king of "Chin" (literally, "eastern land," "dawn," or "morning," and interpreted as "state of sunrise"). He took the name King Ko (698–719). The name "Parhae," from the name of the sea surrounding the Liaodong and Shandong peninsulas, dates from 713 and was bestowed by Tang China, when the state of Parhae paid tribute to Tang as a formality. Parhae soon gained control of most of the former Koguryŏ territory.

Chinese historians have claimed that the Parhae kingdom was historically part of China, arguing that Parhae was a state of the Malgal people rather than a successor kingdom of Koguryŏ. They have also maintained that, Parhae, like Koguryŏ, was one of China's provincial governments for several reasons. First, the territory was named "Parhae" by Tang. Second, its kings continued to pay tribute to Tang and remained invested in the kingship of the Chinese dynasty. Third, Parhae embraced Chinese culture, including the use of Chinese characters and Chinese writing.

But old Chinese historical records clearly indicate that Tae Cho-yŏng was from Koguryŏ. That Parhae maintained a system of tribute and investiture with the Tang dynasty was merely for diplomatic purposes. Further, Parhae's use of Chinese characters and Chinese writing only reflects its willingness to accept more advanced Chinese culture. Parhae's kings called themselves "emperor" or "great king" and declared the names of their own era. Finally, Parhae was a sovereign state independent of Chinese suzerainty or influence and styled itself as Koguryŏ's successor state. The text of an official communication conveyed by a Parhae envoy to Japan in 727 emphasized that Parhae "has recovered the lost land of Koguryŏ and inherited the old traditions of Puyŏ." In its return message Japan referred to Parhae as the "state of Ko[gu]ryŏ." Thus it is evident that Parhae was indeed a revival of Koguryŏ. The state, in fact, was inhabited by people displaced from Koguryŏ. With the establishment of Parhae, Korea entered the era of the Northern (Parhae) and Southern (Silla) States.[1]

The Flourishing and Fall of Parhae

Parhae's rule extended not only over Koguryŏ's ethnic inhabitants but also included the large Malgal population, then living mainly in eastern Manchuria. Although the king and aristocracy were descendants of the Koguryŏ people, the people of Malgal formed the general populace. A semi-nomadic Tungusic people, the Malgal were organized into tribes scattered over a wide expanse of Manchuria, southern Siberia, and the northeastern Korean peninsula.

In the reign of King Mu (719–737), Parhae greatly extended its territory to encompass the whole of northeastern Manchuria. Wary of Parhae's territorial expansion, Silla constructed a defensive wall along its northern frontier in 721. After Parhae was established, its rulers and people, unable to forgive Silla for siding with Tang to destroy Koguryŏ, viewed Silla with distrust. Because of the inhumane treatment of the people of Koguryŏ by the Tang Chinese after Koguryŏ's fall, Parhae also bore a deep resentment toward Tang for some decades.

Parhae's hostility culminated in a direct military attack on the Chinese dynasty. In 732 King Mu sent a force led by the commander Chang Mun-hyu by sea to attack the port of Dengzhou on the Shandong peninsula. This military action was carried out partly to recover residents of Koguryŏ who had been kidnapped by Tang forces when Koguryŏ fell; as many as 200,000 had been taken prisoner and traded as slaves, with the Shandong peninsula serving a slave trade center. Parhae forces succeeded in returning many of these people home to Parhae. At this time Parhae established close ties not only with the neighboring peoples of Tujue and Qidan but also with Japan in order to cope with a pincer attack by Tang and Silla.

In the ensuing reign of King Mun (737–793), Parhae took advantage of the An Lushan and Shih Siming rebellions (755–761) in China and extended its territory as far as the Liao River. King Mun also subjugated many Malgal people in the northeastern region. In 755 he moved the capital northward to Sang-gyŏng. By the latter part of the eighth century Parhae harbored little anger toward Tang and Silla, and therefore established peaceful diplomatic relations with the Chinese dynasty. King Mun began to exchange diplomatic representatives with Tang, eventually dispatching envoys to Tang as many as 98 times. To greet Parhae envoys, Tang set up a reception center at the port town of Dengzhou. Parhae enthusiastically accepted Tang institutions and culture, and conducted trade with Tang within the framework of China's tribute system. It exported raw materials such as horses, and imported a large number of books and art works. With the importation of Chinese civilization, Parhae culture blossomed. Silla sent its envoys to Parhae to promote a better relationship in 790. Parhae maintained close contact with Japan, and diplomatic, trade, and cultural exchanges between the two states continued for several centuries. In the reign of kings Mu and Mun, Parhae sent its envoys to Japan as many as 12 times.

In terms of both territorial expansion and cultural achievement Parhae civilization reached its zenith in the time of King Sŏn (818–830), when its territory had expanded beyond Koguryŏ. Under King Sŏn, almost all the Malgal people were forced into submission, and the Liaodong peninsula also came under Parhae's dominion. Parhae was then in control of the northernmost areas of the Korean peninsula and much of Manchuria, and further expanded its territory into the present-day Maritime Province of Russia. Parhae's level of civilization was so elevated at this time that the Chinese designated Parhae as the "Flourishing State East of the Sea."

Since the end of the ninth century the Parhae kingdom rapidly declined. After enjoying a long peace, its military preparedness relaxed. Finally, in 926, it was invaded and destroyed by Qidans. A people of Mongoloid ethnic stock, the Qidan people became increasingly strong under the able military leadership of Yelu Abaoji (Yehlu Apochi) and conquered neighboring tribes in Mongolia by 916, when he proclaimed himself emperor of the state of Liao which had been established in 907. Once this was accomplished, Yelu Abaoji turned his forces toward the east and crushed Parhae. Because its population was comprised of two disparate elements, the ruling elite of Koguryŏ descent and a subjected class of people from Malgal, Parhae's social fabric was inherently weak and it easily succumbed to the Qidans attack. In fact, Qidans officially recorded that it was able to destroy the kingdom without warfare because of the restlessness that prevailed among the people of Parhae. One recent theory suggests that Parhae's fatal weakness was the result of the catastrophic volcanic eruption in the tenth century at Paektu-san (mountain) at the center of the Parhae territory. This massive explosion completely devastated the kingdom's capital, Sang-gyŏng, located not far from the volcanic mountain, and damaged the agricultural and even societal integrity of the state. Qidans took advantage of this natural disaster, and the Parhae kingdom, which lasted 228 years, finally came to an end.

After the fall of the kingdom, the displaced people of Parhae began the restoration movement, establishing "Later Parhae." Taking the place of the royal Tae family, the Yŏl house later controlled the nation and changed its name to the

State of Chŏngan. The Parhae aristocracy, which numbered more than 50,000 including the royal family of Tae, sought refuge in the nascent Koryŏ kingdom on the Korean peninsula, contributing to that state's reunification of the Korean people. Parhae was the last state in Korean history to hold any significant territory in Manchuria. Later Korean dynasties continued to regard themselves as successors of Koguryŏ and Parhae, and pursued their northward expansion.

Parhae's Political and Social Structure

The people of Parhae called their king *kadokpu,* from a native word meaning "great king," and often added the honorific title of *hwangsang* (emperor) or *taewang* (great king). From the start, the succession to the throne in Parhae was from father to son, and its kings instituted the names of their own eras independently of China. After resuming relations with Tang and exchanging diplomatic representatives with the Chinese dynasty, Parhae accepted many of the Tang institutions, including its system of government. Parhae's administrative system was indeed modeled after that of Tang. The basic organs of the central government consisted of three chancelleries and six ministries. Among the three chancelleries, the Chŏngdang-sŏng, equivalent to Tang's Shangshusheng, was responsible for the actual administration of state affairs. The Sŏnjo-sŏng, the counterpart of Tang's Webxiasheng, functioned as the royal secretariat, promulgating royal edicts and reviewing government policies. Equivalent to Tang's Zhongshusheng, the Chungdae-sŏng initiated royal edicts and government policies. Under the Chŏngdang-sŏng, there were six ministries—the Ch'ung-bu for personnel administration, the In-bu for taxation, the Ŭi-bu for rites, the Chi-bu for military affairs, the Ye-bu for judiciary affairs, and the Sin-bu for construction.

Parhae's central administrative structure did not entirely conform to that of Tang. In China the Zhongshusheng, the Imperial Secretariat, was the chief originator of government policies and imperial orders. The Webxiasheng, the Imperial Chancellery, had the right to review these orders and was the stronghold of bureaucratic power. The Shangshusheng, the Secretariat of State Affairs, had the duty of executing the orders that had been agreed upon by the two other bodies. Thus the three chancelleries had almost equal power. In Parhae, however, the chief minister of the Chŏngdang-sŏng, whose title was *taenaesang,* or "great minister of the court," occupied a superior position to that of the "chief minister of the left" or "chief minister of the right" who headed the other two chancelleries. This form of administrative structure was inherited from the tradition of the Three Kingdoms in which a prime minister exercised much stronger power than his colleagues in the officialdom and was succeeded by the later Koryŏ and Chosŏn kingdoms. Parhae also was distinctive in its use of Confucian terminology for the names of its ministries—*ch'ung, in, ŭi, chi, ye,* and *sin.* They were all major virtues of Confucianism, meaning, respectively, loyalty to the king, good heartedness or benevolence, uprightness, wisdom, politeness, and faithfulness.

In addition to these three chancelleries and six ministries, Parhae had several other offices or agencies. The Chungjŏngdae served as the inspection-general, and the Chŏnjung-si functioned as the court secretariat. The Chongsok-si was responsible for the business transactions of royalty. The Munjŏkwŏn was the national library, and the Chujagam the national academy. The T'aewang-si took charge of ancestral rites, and the Sabin-si was in charge of receiving foreign envoys. The Taenong-si was empowered to administer nationally owned warehouses, and the Sasŏn-si administered food provisions furnished to the royal court. Finally, the Sasang-si managed national finance, and the Hangbaekkuk was the agency of eunuchs.

Parhae had a well-established structure for provincial and local administration. Modeled on the Tang's five-capital system and succeeding the five-pu institution of Koguryŏ, the kingdom established five capitals. Its capital, Sang-gyŏng, or the High Capital, was located at present-day Dongjingcheng in Heilongjiang province, Manchuria, and there were four secondary capitals: Chung-gyŏng, or the Central Capital, at present-day Hualong in Jilin province, Manchuria; Tong-gyŏng, or the Eastern Capital, at Hunchun in Jilin province, Manchuria; Nam-gyŏng, or the Southern Capital, at present-day Pukch'ŏng, in South Hamgyŏng province, North Korea; and Sŏ-gyŏng, or the Western Capital, at Linjiang in Jilin province, Manchuria. Fifteen other major towns, called *pu,* were created throughout the country. Parhae also established 62 provinces for local administration. In the kingdom ten divisions called *wi,* or defenders, were formed as the central army, and, comprising this nucleus army were local military forces conscripted from the local population.

Parhae was founded by the people of Koguryŏ ethnic stock, and they monopolized political power in the kingdom. Even most of the village heads, called *suryŏng,* or chief, were men of Koguryŏ descent. Parhae's ruling class was composed of such aristocratic families as Ko, Chang, O, Yang, Tu, and Yi, including the royal house of Tae, all of Koguryŏ lineage. The majority of the general populace ruled by this elite class were the people of Malgal. Only a small minority of them succeeded in moving upward into the ruling elite; one such individual was Kŏlsabiu, who helped Tae Cho-yŏng in founding Parhae. These Malgal men held the title of *suryŏng* and were on the periphery of Paehae's elite stratum. Some of the Malgal were reduced to becoming laborers or slaves. Parhae's social structure was so sharply divided along ethnic lines that it accounted for the kingdom's inherent fragility.

Because Parhae was situated in the vast plains of Manchuria, cold weather prevented the cultivation of rice. Instead, dry-field farming thrived, and the people raised millet, beans, barley, and Chinese millet. They also hunted and raised livestock. Parhae produced horses, hemp cloth, silk, fur, young antlers, musk, ginseng, and pottery, exporting them to Tang China and Japan.

Parhae's Culture

Like the preceding Koguryŏ culture, Parhae culture vigorously embraced Tang culture. In fact, the kingdom developed a more advanced culture than that of its predecessor, and its cultural level equaled the standard of its southern neighbor, unified Silla. The kingdom established the Chujagam as a national academy to teach Confucian ethics and Chinese classical literature. Students at the national academy were children of the aristocracy. Parhae also created the Munjŏkwŏn, which functioned as a national library. A large number of students were sent to Tang to study, and many of them passed the Tang civil service examinations reserved for foreigners. Parhae students competed with those from Silla to achieve the highest standing in the examinations. The level of Parhae's Confucian culture was so high that the names of its six ministries, as noted above, all include the major Confucian virtues: ch'ung, in, ŭi, chi, ye, and sin. Parhae's high level of Chinese classical literature is well demonstrated in the memorial inscriptions on tombs of princesses Chŏnghye and Chŏnghyo, the daughters of King Mun, which contain passages from five Confucian classics, *Shijing, Shujing, Yijing, Chunqiu,* and *Liji,* and from Chinese historical works such as *Shiji* and *Hanshu.* Parhae also met high standards in the fields of astronomy, mathematics, and medicine.

The remains uncovered in Parhae's capital, Sang-gyŏng, demonstrate the kingdom's advanced cultural level. The capital city was organized in a manner similar to that of the Tang capital Changan. Residential sectors were laid out on either side of the palace surrounded by a rectangular wall. Nine sites of Buddhist temples found in the remains of the capital show that Parhae was also a Buddhist state where the belief in Buddhism was encouraged by the king.

Many elements of Koguryŏ culture are found in Parhae culture. The most typical example is the ondol installation, Korea's traditional heating system, which was uncovered in the inner citadel of the palace and many others adjacent to it. Parhae tombs, modeled on those of Koguryŏ, had the stone burial chamber structure with a horizontal entranceway, seen in the tomb of Princess Chŏnghye unearthed at Dunhua, in Jilin province, Manchuria, in 1949.

Parhae produced fine pottery, which was light in weight, lustrous, and varied in size and shape. The kingdom exported its pottery to Tang. Parhae's pottery seems to have influenced the well-known Koryŏ porcelain. In short, by actively accepting advanced Chinese culture, Parhae developed its own superior indigenous culture.

THE GOVERNMENT AND SOCIETY OF UNIFIED SILLA

Consolidation of Royal Authority

Integrating Paekche and Koguryŏ into its domain, Silla greatly increased its territory and population. Silla's unification inevitably led to profound changes in its politics, economics, society, and culture. The people of Silla themselves described these changes as "ilt'ong samhan," or unification of the three Hans (Mahan, Chinhan, and Pyŏnhan, or Koguryŏ, Paekche, and Silla). The most important political changes accompanying Silla's unification included the weakening of the bone-rank system and the consolidation of the centralized bureaucracy.

In the Three Kingdoms period the kingship had been monopolized by those of sacred-bone lineage, but the highest bone-rank lineage came to an end with the death of the two queens, Sŏndŏk and Chindŏk. The next monarch was King Muyŏl (654–661), a man from true-bone lineage. King Muyŏl (Kim Ch'un-ch'u) ascended the throne after he suppressed the rebellion of Pidam, then a sangdaedŭng, or one who represented the interests of the aristocracy. King Muyŏl was also victorious in a keen competition for the kingship with Arch'ŏn, another sangdaedŭng. Both men were of prominent aristocratic lineage and were Kim Ch'un-ch'u's archrivals for the kingship. To consolidate his royal authority, King Muyŏl abolished the honorific title kalmun wang, and, instead of the hitherto used Buddhist title, he adopted the posthumous title King T'aejong, as in the Chinese system. He also chose the younger sister of Kim Yu-sin, Mun-hŭi, as his queen consort, breaking away from the tradition that the king's queen come from the former royal house of Pak. Kim Yu-sin's Kaya

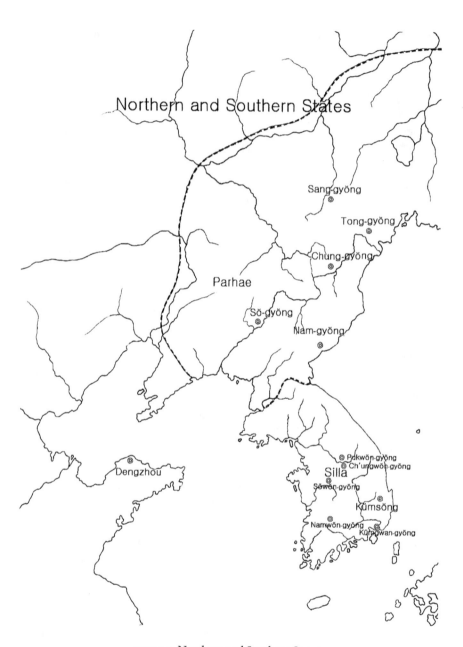

Northern and Southern States

Sang-gyŏng

Tong-gyŏng

Chung-gyŏng

Parhae

Sŏ-gyŏng

Nam-gyŏng

Dengzhou

Pukwŏn-gyŏng
Ch'ungwŏn-gyŏng
Silla
Sŏwŏn-gyŏng
Kŭmsŏng
Namwŏn-gyŏng
Kŭmgwan-gyŏng

MAP 3.1. Northern and Southern States

royal lineage was called the "new house of Kim." Finally, King Muyŏl strengthened royal authority by establishing a system whereby successors to the throne had to be his direct lineal descendants.

At the suggestion of the Buddhist monk Ŭisang that the nation's tranquility be achieved by constructing a "castle of popular confidence," King Munmu (661–681) pursued a civil administration, adding the word *mun,* or learning, to his posthumous title. His successor, King Sinmun (681–692), carried out a determined, large-scale purge of the high aristocracy and firmly established royal authority. Taking advantage of an abortive coup in 681 led by Kim Hŭm-dol, the father of his first queen, he searched out all implicated aristocrats and had them slaughtered. The king restructured administrative and military institutions so as to better serve the throne. Finally, in the reign of King Sŏngdŏk (702–737), the power of the monarch was firmly secured, and Silla was able to enjoy unprecedented domestic tranquility.

As royal authority was further consolidated, some important changes occurred in the balance of power between the two highest central government organs. The position of sangdaedŭng, which had been established in 531, remained intact as before. But the creation of the Chipsabu, or Chancellery Office, in 651, inevitably reduced the powers of the sangdaedŭng. The Chipsabu, now the highest administrative apparatus, executed the dictates of the throne. The head of the Chipsabu, *sijung* (at first *chungsi*), served in effect as a prime minister. Based on the strengthened regal power, the highest executive official became politically more important than the sangdaedŭng.

Although royal authority was considerably consolidated, the traditional bone-rank system itself was not shaken. Those of true-bone lineage continued to form the dominant power center and monopolized high-level government posts. As the monarch's power became increasingly strong, however, the power of the true-bone aristocracy inevitably weakened. Instead, those of head rank 6 lineage began to come to the fore in politics. As this politically less important aristocracy was still barred from serving in the topmost positions, members of head rank 6 background naturally allied with the monarch to check the power of the true-bone aristocracy. Because of the deeper learning and insight of these discontented men of head rank 6 status, the king sought their advice on governmental affairs. Thus such persons of head rank 6 lineage as Kangsu, Sŏl Ch'ong, Yi Sun, and Kim Chi-sŏng played an important political role. Immediately after unification, in other words, royal authority grew strong, and the power and influence of the high aristocracy of true-bone lineage became increasingly weakened.

Local Administrative Structure

To effectively administer its enlarged domain, unified Silla created an expanded system of provincial and local government. Local administration was restructured along Chinese lines, specifically the system of 9 provinces and 5 secondary capitals. Thus, in 685 King Sinmun established nine provinces called *chu* (*-ju*) and five "secondary capitals" called *so-gyŏng*. In addition to the three provinces in the old Silla-Kaya territory (Sangju, Yangju, and Kangju), Silla created three provinces for the old Paekche territory (Ungju, Chŏnju, and Muju) and three in the old Koguryŏ territory (Hanju, Sakchu, and Myŏngju). During the Three Kingdoms period governors of these provinces were called *kunju*, or military commandant. After unification they were renamed *ch'ŏnggwan*, or general commandant, and their functions changed from being more military in nature to more administrative. This tendency was further strengthened in the ninth century, when the title was changed again to *todok*, or governor, modeled on that of the Chinese Tang dynasty. These 9 provinces were divided into 117 prefectures (*kun*), headed by *t'aesu*, or prefects, and these prefectures in turn were subdivided into 293 counties (*hyŏn*), headed by *yŏng*, or magistrates. Each county consisted of villages (*ch'on*) headed by *ch'onju*, or village headmen, as well as special settlements known as *hyang*, *so*, and *pugok*.

Unified Silla also designated five strategically important towns as the secondary capitals—Namwŏn-gyŏng (present-day Namwŏn, North Chŏlla province), Kŭmgwan-gyŏng (present-day Kimhae, South Kyŏngsang province), Sŏwŏn-gyŏng (present-day Ch'ŏngju, North Ch'ungch'ŏng province), Chungwŏn-gyŏng (present-day Ch'ungju, North Ch'ungch'ŏng province), and Pukwŏn-gyŏng (present-day Wŏnju, Kangwŏn province). The capital city of Kyŏngju, then called Kŭmsŏng or Sŏrabŏl, was located in the southeastern corner of the peninsula. In 689 King Sinmun considered moving its capital westward to Talgubŏl (present-day Taegu). Because of stiff opposition by the true-bone aristocracy that had established its power base in the capital, however, he failed to do so. As a result, the secondary capital system functioned as a counterbalance to the capital's unfavorable geographical location. Since some members of the capital and local aristocracy were forced to resettle in the secondary capitals, these "little capitals" became political and cultural centers second to Kyŏngju. Members of the central aristocracy were appointed to head these local administrative units of the provinces, prefectures, counties, and secondary capitals. Inspectors, called *oesajŏng*, were periodically dispatched to supervise their conduct.

As the lowest local administrative unit, villages consisted of scattered hamlets and were administered by village headmen who were from influential local households. To prevent these local elites who were allowed to govern themselves from growing too strong, the central government instituted the system of *sangsuri*, in which representatives of these powerful local households, their eldest sons in particular, were required to undertake low-level military or court duties in the capital on a rotational basis.

The people formerly of Peckche and Koguryŏ were absorbed into this newly created administrative structure. Some were given a bone-rank status and office rank in accordance with their previous social status in their own societies. Prisoners of war were enslaved, and the inhabitants of rebellious districts were reduced to un-free status and forcibly transported to the special settlements of hyang, so, and pugok. These new systems of local administration, ranging from the institution of provinces, prefectures, counties, and secondary capitals to the institution of sangsuri, allowed the central government to effectively control the countryside and thus consolidate regal authority.

Reorganization of the Military System

Before unification, Silla possessed six chŏng as the nucleus of its army. After unification, they ceased to exist. Instead, in the reign of King Sinmun, a new pattern of military organization was instituted, with nine sŏdang divisions as the central army and ten garrison units, again called chŏng, as the local army.

The system of nine sŏdang was completed in 687. Stationed in the capital, the sŏdang military units were differentiated by their tunics. Each unit had collars of a distinctive color—green, purple, white, scarlet, yellow, black, cobalt, red, and blue. The sŏdang army drew its recruits not only from the natives of Silla but also from the people from the former Paekche and Koguryŏ states, and even from the Malgal tribesmen. The sŏdang forces seem to have been placed under the direct command of the monarch, to whom each unit took an oath of loyalty. Thus the establishment of the nine sŏdang army represented the monarch's deliberate effort to consolidate royal authority.

The ten chŏng garrisons were stationed outside the capital. The creation of the ten chŏng divisions was closely related to the establishment of the nine chu provinces. Two chŏng were deployed in Hanju province, the largest province and strategically important for the defense of the state, and the remaining eight chŏng were positioned in each of the other eight provinces—Namch'ŏn-jŏng at present-day Ich'ŏn, Kyŏnggi province; Kolnaegŭn-jŏng at present-day Yŏju, Kyŏnggi province; Ŭmrihwa-jŏng at present-day Sangju, North Kyŏngsang province; Koryangburi-jŏng at present-day Ch'ŏngyang, South Ch'ungch'ŏng province; Kŏsamul-jŏng at present-day Namwŏn, North Chŏlla province; Samyanghwa-jŏng at present-day Talsŏng, Taegu; Sosam-jŏng at present-day Haman, South Kyŏngsang province; Midaburi-jŏng at present-day Naju, South Chŏlla province; Pŏlyŏkch'ŏn-jŏng at present-day Hongch'ŏn, Kangwŏn province; and Ihwahye-jŏng at present-day Ch'ŏngsong, North Kyŏngsang province. In other words, these chŏng units were stationed throughout the nation, including in old Paekche and Koguryŏ. Unified Silla reorganized its military system so as to promote efficiency in national defense and internal security, which conformed with the monarch's efforts to consolidate kingly authority.

The Life of the Aristocracy

The aristocracy in the unified Silla period possessed enormous wealth and a large number of slaves, which formed the foundation of its economic and military strength. Originally the aristocracy had received various economic privileges from the state. In particular, those who distinguished themselves in battle were awarded the sikŭp. For example, Kim Yu-sin was rewarded hereditary rights to a tax village of 500 households. He was also granted 500 kyŏl of farmland and six horse farms.[2] Kim In-mun also received a tax village of 300 households. In addition to the right to levy taxes and tributes, these men could also command the labor services of the peasants who toiled their land. Government officials were also paid for their services to the state by allocations of nokŭp, or stipend villages. Like the recipients of sikŭp, those who received nokŭp also could levy a grain tax as well as exact corvee labor from the peasants.

To consolidate his power, however, the monarch had to impose restrictions on the aristocracy's economic strength. After unification in 687, in the reign of King Sinmun, officials were allocated chikchŏn, or office land, from which they could receive only the grain tax. Subsequently, in 689, the institution of nokŭp was abolished. These changes represented the monarch's attempt to limit the aristocracy's direct control over the peasant population. In 722, in the reign of King Sŏngdŏk, peasants generally were allocated the so-called chŏngjŏn, or able-bodied land, which was designed to free them from the control of the aristocracy. In 757, in the reign of King Kyŏngdŏk (742–765), however, the nokŭp system was revived and the chikchŏn institution was abolished. These changes demonstrate that the aristocracy reasserted itself by relaxing the restrictions that the monarch had placed on the power elite.

As the aristocracy regained strength, the capital city of Kyŏngju, the power base of the ruling class, became increasingly a city of luxury and enjoyment. In the "city of gold," the pleasure-seeking aristocracy led a gay life. It is said that in the ninth century Kyŏngju had 178,936 households divided among 1,360 residential quarters in 55 wards. The enormous number of households, equivalent to a population of some 900,000, may have included the households of neighboring areas as well as those of Kyŏngju. If not, the number probably indicated the population of the capital city rather than the total number of households. As a comparison, for example, in the early and late Chosŏn periods, the population of Seoul was, respectively, about 100,000 and about 200,000. In the capital, it was said, there was not a single thatched-roof house but, instead, unbroken lines of tiled-roof and tiled-wall houses, and the sounds of music and song filled the streets day and night. It was also reported that emoluments flowed unceasingly into the houses of the highest officials, each of whom possessed 3,000 slaves, with corresponding quantities of armor, weapons, cattle, horses, and pigs. There were 35 mansions owned by the immensely wealthy, who had separate residences for each of the four seasons.[3] These records show the extravagant lives and pleasures of the Silla aristocracy living in the capital city. Moreover, in the last years of unified Silla, the monarch also was addicted to extravagance and enjoyment.

The Life of the People

The local farming population usually lived in villages or hamlets called ch'on, the lowest and smallest local administrative unit. A village was normally composed of ten or more blood-related households. These villages were under the control of the central government, and groups of villages, usually three or four, were administered by village headmen.

In 1933 a portion of one Silla census register, believed to date from the unified Silla period, was discovered in the Shosoin imperial repository of the Todai-ji temple in Nara, Japan. As for the date when it was drawn up, several years have appeared—755, 815, and 875. The most persuasive view is that the census register was made out in 815. It contains detailed census figures for covering the secondary capital of Sŏwŏn-gyŏng, present-day Ch'ŏngju, and its neighboring four villages. The contents of this document demonstrate that the central government took very thorough censuses of its local population and society, and that

Silla census registers were compiled anew every three years. This document recorded the numbers of households, population, cattle and horses, mulberry trees, big cone pines, and walnut trees as well as the area of different types of farmland, including paddy fields and dry fields. It also put on record changes from the previous census in both human and livestock populations. The state seems to have levied taxes on the local population in accordance with these census statistics.

This census document indicates that at the time the local population was registered in six categories based on age—able-bodied adult men and women, adolescents, pre-adolescents, small children, the aging, and the aged, all arranged as the basis for exacting labor services from the population. Households were classified into nine categories by the number of able-bodied adults under the obligation of corvee labor.

The people of Silla believed that all their nation's land belonged to the monarch and that they were all his subjects. Unlike the principle of state ownership, this concept made possible private ownership of land given to them by the monarch. The state allotted separate farmlands to village headmen and villagers. Allotments for village headmen, called *ch'onju widap,* are thought to have been a kind of chikchŏn, and those for villagers, called *yŏnsuyu chŏndap,* are believed to have been the so-called chŏngjŏn. These farmlands were originally in the possession of self-supporting village farmers, and the state simply authorized their ownership of the land. Although these villagers cultivated their own plot of farmland, the government took a certain amount of their crops as tax. The above census document recorded several categories of paddy and dry fields, as well as hemp fields, outside yŏnsuyu chŏndap. These were cultivated by village people, and the yield of these agricultural lands went to the state.

In addition to farming villages, there were other special units called hyang, so, and pugok. Contrary to the free commoner population of the villages, un-free humble people inhabited these special settlements. Either conquered people or those who were found guilty of crimes against the state were forcibly transported to these special administrative units to labor at such tasks as farming, livestock raising, fishery, or other manual work.[4]

The lowest class in unified Silla society consisted of slaves. Slavery was prevalent, particularly in the capital. Large numbers of artisans and laborers with slave status were attached to various palace and government agencies, temples, as well as private houses of the aristocracy, and they supplied the needs of the royal and aristocratic households and temples. They also cultivated farmland for their masters. Considering that the households of the highest officials in the capital possessed a large number of slaves, up to some 3,000 each, it may be surmised that the number of slaves owned by the aristocracy comprised a substantial portion of the total Silla population.

In unified Silla, the general population was occupied mainly with agriculture. The farming population paid grain and tribute taxes to the state. Peasant farmers were also mobilized for corvee labor exacted by the state. Unified Silla drew this threefold tax system from the Chinese Tang model.

The Maritime Empire of Silla

Because Silla did not suffer any foreign invasion for 200 years after unification, it was able to achieve remarkable development in agriculture and handicraft manufacturing. This industrial development in turn led to the rapid growth of domestic commerce and international trade. The reservoir at Pyŏkkol county (present-day Kimje, North Chŏlla province), which had existed since the three Han period, underwent a large-scale extension in the late eighth century to irrigate paddy fields in seven neighboring counties. The term *pyŏkkol* literally means a "rice-producing county." Improvement of not only the Pyŏkkol-je reservoir but other irrigation facilities and reclamation of wasteland brought about high productivity in agriculture.

The central government established the Kongjangbu, or Office of Artisans, as an agency to take charge of the nationwide manual industry. Silla handicraftsmen manufactured silk products, ornaments for royal and aristocratic households, arms for the state, images of Buddha and temple bells for Buddhist temples, and various kinds of pottery. The gathering of agricultural and handicraft products in the capital from every corner of the country resulted in the opening of various markets, the *sŏ-si*, or western market, and the *nam-si*, or southern market, along with the existing *tong-si*, or eastern market, as well as the creation of an office to administer these markets. Silla also opened markets in the five secondary capitals and in the nine provincial capitals where the products of different localities were traded on the barter system.

Silla traded with Tang China, Japan, Parhae, and even the Arab world. Silla and Tang conducted two types of trade with each other, one official and the other private. Official commercial exchange was carried on in the form of a tribute to Tang. In reality, it was just another form of foreign trade and took place on a large scale. Private trading activities also flourished between the two countries. Silla exported gold, silver, ginseng, silk and hemp products, gold and silver artifacts, horses, and seal skins to Tang, and Tang returned tea, books, silk clothes, and luxurious articles. Two routes linked Tang China to Silla, one from the present-day Inch'ŏn area of central Korea to the Shandong peninsula of China and the other from the coast of Chŏlla province to the Shanghai area.

Extensive and flourishing trade between Silla and Tang led to the appearance of special Silla settlements in areas of the Shandong peninsula and the lower Yangtze River basin. These were called the Silla-bang, or Silla Quarters. In these settlements, Silla-so, or Silla Offices, were established and had jurisdiction over the affairs of Silla residents. As self-governing bodies for Silla residents, these agencies were administered by the people of Silla themselves who resided in Tang and established their own Buddhist temples, where they prayed for the safe journey of their sailors and ships. These temples were called Silla-wŏn, or Silla Temples, and the best known among them was the Pŏphwa-wŏn temple built at Chishan village in Wendeng prefecture, Shandong province, by Chang Po-go. It is said that as many as 250 Silla people assembled at one time in Pŏphwa-won to listen to a sermon on Buddhist scripts.

Silla's trade flourished not only with Tang but also with Japan. Because of frequent trading activities with Silla, the Japanese even posted additional Silla language interpreters on Tsushima Island. Silla even had contact with Arab merchants, who frequently visited present-day Ulsan, just southeast of Kyŏngju. These Arab merchants brought carpets, glass vessels, spices, and jewelry to be consumed by the royal and aristocratic households as luxury articles.

Flourishing trade with Tang China and Japan led Silla to establish the Ch'ŏnghae-jin garrison, a naval and trade base, in 828, on present-day Wan-do Island off the southwest coast of South Chŏlla province. Ch'ŏnghae-jin was located on the sea route between China and Japan, a site of great commercial importance. As the threat of Chinese piracy to Silla's maritime trade intensified, the kingdom stationed more than 10,000 military forces and hundreds of sea-going vessels at Ch'ŏnghae-jin.

Chang Po-go (or Kung-bok) was the man who established the Ch'ŏnghae-jin garrison. When he was young, Chang had journeyed to Tang and pursued a successful military career in the service of Tang. Indignant at the frequent incidents of Chinese pirates capturing his countrymen and selling them into slavery, Chang Po-go returned to Silla and appealed to King Hŭngdŏk (826–836) to formally establish a garrison on Wan-do, where he had already built a strong military base. He asked the king for an army of 10,000 men and ships, which was granted. In 828 King Hŭngdŏk appointed him to command the Ch'ŏnghae-jin garrison as its "commissioner." Chang Po-go patrolled the Yellow Sea and the South Sea, and eliminated Chinese pirates who had raided Silla's coastal areas to capture slaves. At the same time he built a great commercial fleet, monopolizing international trade in East Asia. As the master of the Yellow Sea and the South Sea, Chang established a maritime empire and gained great power and wealth. At the time the Japanese called him a "sea god."

Finally, Chang Po-go intruded into the fierce political struggle in the capital, providing military support to Kim U-jing, who later ascended the throne as King Sinmu (839–839). With Chang's help, Kim, who had lost out in an earlier struggle for the throne, rushed to the capital and took the throne for himself in 839. Chang Po-go's sudden attainment of power aroused the jealousy and fear of the central aristocracy in Kyŏngju. A few years later the aristocracy in the capital prevented King Munsŏng (839–857, King Sinmu's son) from taking Chang Po-go's daughter as his second queen. The enraged Chang revolted against the central government, but his rebellion ended with his assassination in 846. After his death, the Ch'ŏnghae-jin garrison itself was abolished in 851. The 10,000 troops under Chang's command were removed to Pyŏkkol county, where they were made peasants. From the time of unified Silla, for many centuries Korea maintained advanced shipbuilding technology, maritime leadership, and strong naval power in East Asia.

UNIFIED SILLA'S FLOURISHING CULTURE

Thriving Buddhism

Before unification Silla had already adopted Buddhism as its national religion. All the people of unified Silla, from the king on high to the general populace below, including peasants and slaves, were enthusiastic about Buddhism. As the dominant system of thought, then, Buddhism played a vital role in Silla society. As pointed out in chapter 2, before unification Buddhism in Silla functioned as a political ideology purporting that the king was the Buddha. After unification, however, the religion evolved increasingly into a system of philosophy, an abstruse creed that was developed by the many great monks who journeyed to Tang or even to far away Central Asia and India to study the way of the Buddha. Their pilgrimage brought back to Silla the views held by different sects then popular in China. Although Buddhism's different philosophical leanings had given rise to various sects, these sects did not develop into mutually exclusive schools, as occurred with the Christian sects.

Five major Buddhist sects became firmly established in Silla: the Nirvana (Yŏrban in Korean), the Vinaya (Kyeyul), the Buddha-Nature (Pŏpsŏng), the Avatamsaka (Hwaŏm), and the Dharmalaksana (Pŏpsang) schools. Among these, Avatamsaka emerged as the premier school, especially among the aristocracy. The Hwaŏm doctrine was implanted by Ŭisang, who had been a leading disciple of the Chinese monk Zhiyan, the founder of the Avatamsaka sect. After returning to Silla in 670, Ŭisang established the Pusŏk-sa temple at present-day Yŏngju, North Kyŏngsang province, making it the center for the new sect. The doctrines of Korean Buddhism were greatly influenced by the work of Hwaŏm. As the founder of Hwaŏm in Silla, Ŭisang advised King Munmu politically, on the king's request, and preached his Hwaŏm doctrine of wŏnyung, or all encompassing harmony, that the one was the very multitude and yet the multitude was the very one and that all creations were not mutually separable. In other words, wŏnyung was a concept that all things in nature were not mutually conflicting beings but had harmonizing and encompassing relationships with one another. The wŏnyung doctrine contributed, immediately after unification, to regions and classes being able to spiritually overcome conflicts and feuds and inspired a spirit of unity in the hearts of the people. Because it established a centralized power structure, the Hwaŏm teaching was particularly well received by the monarch. To disseminate the Hwaŏm doctrine, the Silla government established ten great temples throughout the country.

The well-known monk Wŏnhyo did not go to China to study Buddhism.[5] While principally espousing the doctrine of the Pŏpsŏng sect he attempted to Koreanize the different Buddhist doctrines. As a result, he established his own doctrine, which synthesized the teachings of the different sects and is memorialized in his treatise Simmun hwajaeng non, or Treatise on the Harmonization of Disputes among the Ten Schools, which was even translated into Sanskrit. Later, in the reign of King Sukchong (1095–1105) of Koryŏ, he was given the posthumous title of Hwajŏng kuksa, or the National Preceptor of Harmonious Quiescence. Because of his profound Buddhist learning, he gained respect even in China.

The Silla monk Wŏnch'ŭk did not return home but contributed to the development of Buddhism in Tang China through the sutra translations and other writings. Another Silla monk, Hyech'o, went to Tang China in 719 and then made a pilgrimage to Buddhist holy places in Central Asia and India. After returning to China in 727, he wrote the well-known, three-volume account of his travels titled Wang och'ŏnch'ukguk chŏn, or Record of a Journey to the Five

Indian Kingdoms. The original text, now housed in a Paris library, is regarded as an important historical record on eighth-century India.

In unified Silla, the *Chŏngt'o,* or Pure Land, faith was widely prevalent particularly among the common people. This Buddhist creed had its strongest appeal to the masses and, numerically, became the greatest force. It was a faith that the ignorant and poor could easily profess. It did not involve understanding the abstruse doctrines of the Buddhist sutras but stressed the simple act of faith, of calling the name of Amitabha, the Buddha of Infinite Light, by continuously chanting "Nammu amit'a pul." If one only reiterated this extremely simple devotion, then one could be reborn in the "Pure Land," or the Western Paradise, where Amitabha resided, without being reincarnated to earthly existence, which was a "sea of torment." The Pure Land faith became the Buddhism for the masses, as it encouraged hope in those whose daily life was full of suffering. It was Wŏnhyo who contributed most to the widespread dissemination of Pure Land Buddhism. He was admired by the people because of his great attainments in Buddhist learning, as well as his preaching as an itinerant monk. He fell in love with Princess Yosŏk, the daughter of King Muyŏl, and fathered a son, the famous scholar Sŏl Ch'ong. Traveling to villages throughout the country in penance for his transgression of the Buddhist commandments, Wŏnhyo preached the Pure Land creed that if all the people called Amitabha millions of times, they might be reborn in true paradise. Thanks to his efforts, Buddhism was brought to the masses as a popular religion, for it is said that his efforts led eight or nine of every ten Silla people to embrace Buddhism.

Since the mid-eighth century, in areas far from the capital, the Maitreya faith of the Pŏpsang sect spread quickly. This Buddhist doctrine proclaimed that some time in the future the Maitreya Buddha would come down to earth to bring about an earthly paradise. The widespread popularity of Maitreya Buddhism was owing mainly to the efforts of the monk Chinp'yo, who preached this doctrine at the Kŭmsan-sa temple, located in present-day Kimje, North Chŏlla province. As a displaced person of the old Paekche kingdom, he seems to have spiritually pursued the revival of the fallen state through the proliferation of Maitreya Buddhism, which was welcomed particularly by the displaced people of the old Paekche and Koguryŏ kingdoms.

In the late Silla period, *Sŏn* Buddhism became popular. The Sŏn, or Meditation, school was close to primitive Buddhism in its stress on meditation and intuitive insight, or "enlightenment." This anti-scholastic, anti-textual sect was in striking contrast to the *Kyo,* or Textual, school, which included different sects based on the particular sutra each relied upon. The Sŏn sect rejected control by any outside forces, including scriptures, and advocated reliance on one's own power for salvation of the soul. According to the Sŏn doctrine, it is possible to comprehend the Buddha nature that inherently exists in the human mind through sŏn, or meditation. In Sŏn Buddhism, therefore, concentration, contemplation, and absolute silence were of primary importance. To achieve these goals, Sŏn Buddhists in Silla built their temples in remote mountains, away from mundane human society and town life. Because of this, the Sŏn sects were known as *san*, or mountains.

Started in China and called "Chan," Sŏn Buddhism was first introduced to Silla in the seventh century during the reign of Queen Sŏndŏk, but at the time it had little appeal for the people. When introduced to Japan, it was called "Zen." When the monk Toŭi returned from China in 821 and founded the Kaji-san sect at the Porim-sa temple, the Sŏn faith spread widely and ultimately led to the establishment of the so-called Nine Mountain Sects of Sŏn.

Because the Sŏn creed contained strong elements of individualism, it was warmly received by the newly rising *hojok*, or local gentry, who acted independently of the central government's influence in the late Silla period. Most of the nine sects of the Sŏn school had close ties with the local gentry. For instance, the Sumi-san sect at Kaesŏng had close relations with Wang Kŏn, who later established the Koryŏ dynasty. Thus Sŏn Buddhism evolved into the religion of the local gentry and became an ideological foundation for their assertion of local independence. It was also prevalent particularly in the old Paekche and Koguryŏ territories.

In unified Silla, at any rate, Buddhism ceased to function as a political ideology and instead developed into a system of spiritual thought for the masses. It became firmly established as a state religion and contributed greatly to the kingdom's flourishing culture.

The Growth of Confucianism

Although Buddhism was the predominant religion or philosophy in unified Silla, it did not serve the monarch's intention to establish a centralized bureaucratic kingdom. The king needed a political ideology to justify the consolidation of royal authority, and he turned to Confucianism to pursue his goal.

To teach Confucian ethics and literature, a national university called the Kukhak was established in 682. Admission to the national Confucian academy was granted only to members of the aristocracy who held the 12th office rank of taesa or below. This meant that only those of head rank 6 lineage could enter the Kukhak. In 717 portraits of Confucius and his disciples—the *sipch'ŏl*, or ten philosophers, and the 72 Confucian worthies—were brought from Tang China and installed in the Kukhak. In 759 the Kukhak was renamed the T'aehakkam, or Great Academic Institute, and two faculty ranks were created to teach students. The curriculum was divided into required subjects (*Analects* and *Classic of Filial Piety*) and optional subjects (*Book of Poetry, Book of History, Book of Divination, Zuozhuan*, or Tradition of *Zuo* interpretation of the *Spring and Autumn Annals, Book of Rites*, and *Literary Selections*). In accordance with the subjects taught in each course, there were three courses, or majors: *Book of Rites* and *Book of Divination, Zuozhuan* and *Book of Poetry*, and *Book of History* and *Literary Selections*. The division of courses was intended to train specialists in the subdivisions of the Confucian doctrine.

As the foundation of a national educational institution was laid, the *toksŏ samp'um kwa*, or examination in the reading of texts in three gradations, a state examination, began in 788. In this state examination to select government officials, the candidates were graded on three levels of proficiency in reading Confucian texts and then given appointments to office. The examination was based on the texts studied at the national university, with particular emphasis on *Analects* and *Classic of Filial Piety*. Because of the deep-rooted bone-rank institution, however, the state examination system failed to open the offices to talent on a broad basis.

The promotion of education in Confucianism did produce several distinguished scholars who achieved great expertise in Confucianism and Chinese literature. In particular, Confucian philosophy was championed by those of head rank 6 lineage, who were frustrated by the traditional bone-rank order. Among them Kangsu, based on his profound learning in Chinese literature, placed himself at the service of his country by authoring Silla's diplomatic correspondence with Tang China. He criticized Buddhism for its "otherworldly" teachings and stressed that Confucian morals be firmly established in Silla. Obviously he leveled his criticism at the insurmountable bone-rank system. Another blow was dealt to Buddhism when Sŏl Ch'ong, the son of the prominent Buddhist monk Wŏnhyo and best known for developing the *kugyŏl* system of explicating and reading Chinese texts, became a great Confucian scholar, symbolizing the alienation of those of head rank 6 lineage from the values of the bone-rank order and the Buddhist doctrine that buttressed the rigid class system.

Unified Silla actively engaged in cultural exchanges with Tang China, and thus large numbers of students, officials, and monks traveled to China for study and observation. In the late Silla period, many Silla students went to China to study Confucianism firsthand. After becoming famous in China, these students returned home. Ch'oe Ch'i-wŏn was an outstanding representative of this group. He was particularly renowned in Tang China for his literary ability, including passing the Tang civil service examination. He is remembered for a number of literary works, including the 20-volume collection of essays known as *Kyewŏn p'ilgyŏng*, or Anthology of Silla. After his return to Silla in 884, Ch'oe Ch'i-wŏn, a man of head rank 6 background, served as a low-ranking government official for a while. When the government rejected his policy proposals, however, he became disillusioned with the stubborn bone-rank order. He gave up his position and spent the rest of his life in self-imposed exile in a remote region.

Kim Tae-mun, who served as governor of the Hansan (formerly Hanju) province in 704, was the author of a number of writings on Silla history and geography, such as *Kyerim chapchŏn*, or Tales of Silla; *Kosŭng chŏn*, or Biographies of Eminent Monks; *Hwarang segi*, or Chronicles of the Hwarang; *Ak pon*, or Book of Music; and *Hansan gi*, or Records of the Hansan Province. Although he studied in Tang China, Kim Tae-mun, a man of true-bone lineage, attempted to preserve traditional Silla culture rather than devote himself to the study of Chinese Confucianism. None of his works has survived, but his works contributed greatly to the writing of the later historical texts, such as Kim Pu-sik's *Samguk sagi* and Iryŏn's *Samguk yusa*. In unified Silla, then, Confucianism developed to the extent that it laid the groundwork for its future growth in the later Koryŏ and Chosŏn dynasties.

Geomantic Theories

In the late Silla period members of the hojok, who warmly welcomed Sŏn Buddhism, also were interested in geomantic (*p'ungsu* in Korean, *fengsui* in Chinese) theories, that is, theories involving wind-and-water magic. The Buddhist monk Tosŏn greatly enhanced the appeal of geomancy and, thanks to his efforts, the Chinese concept of geomancy became intertwined with Buddhism. Tosŏn traveled throughout the nation, grasping its human geographical character from personal experience and laying the foundation of Korean geomantic studies. According to geomantic theories, the life force was generated by the interplay of *yin* (dark) and *yang* (light) and the five elements or powers (tree, fire, earth, metal, and water). Places where large quantities of the life force converged were considered auspicious sites, and so individuals or nations would enjoy good fortune if they selected propitious sites for constructing villages, graves, and the like. An inauspicious site, on the other hand, would lead to misfortune. Tosŏn divined the auspiciousness and inauspiciousness of the topographical features of the Korean peninsula, and he predicted that Kyŏngju would have bad luck and, instead, Kaesŏng, Pyongyang, and Seoul would become the future centers of the nation. He also saw his nation in the shape of a ship and stressed that, just as a ship maintained its safety by keeping its balance, the regions of the country needed to maintain balance.

The geomantic theory influenced the rulers of the Koryŏ and Chosŏn dynasties but not those of the Silla kingdom. Wang Kŏn, the founder of the Koryŏ dynasty, was a devotee of geomantic theories and, in his testament known as the *Hunyo sipcho*, or Ten Injunctions, he commanded his successors to follow the advice of the p'ungsu theories.

Geomantic theories influenced the Koryŏ kingdom to such an extent that it chose Kaesŏng as its capital, and made Pyongyang and Hanyang (Seoul) its *Sŏgyŏng*, or Western Capital, and *Nam-gyŏng*, or Southern Capital, respectively. Geomancy has continued to influence Korean thinking until recent years. The p'ungsu theory appears to have been suited for those areas of the Korean peninsula where mountains and rivers conform to the theory. Throughout Korean history, therefore, geomantic considerations have played an important role in deciding such significant affairs of state as the selection of a national capital. But it has sometimes been used for political purposes, which has exacerbated certain regional conflicts. It is said, for example, that Wang Kŏn, in his Ten Injunctions, labeled the area of Later Paekche, which had resisted him to the end, as a "perverse and rebellious land," admonishing his successors not to allow the people from that area to enter government service.

Science and Technology

Silla's science and technology was at a high level. Astronomy, which is closely tied to astrology, was an important element of science in Silla, and the *Samguk sagi* is full of reportedly accurate records of solar eclipses, lunar eclipses, earthquakes, appearance of comets, and abnormal weathers. The Silla people made serious astronomical observations, as astronomy was closely related to agriculture and there was a belief that natural calamities reflected popular unrest.

In unified Silla, mathematical knowledge greatly advanced and was put into practice in a variety of areas. The application of precise mathematical concepts include the plan for the Sŏkkuram grotto and the balanced proportions of the Tabo-t'ap, or Pagoda of Many Treasures, and the Sŏkka-t'ap, or Pagoda of Shakyamuni, at Kyŏngju's Pulguk-sa, or Buddha Land Temple.[6]

In Silla, the art of woodblock printing developed so greatly that it was used to disseminate Buddhist sutras and Confucian classics. A scroll of Dharani sutra, discovered within the Sŏkka-t'ap in 1966, may have dated from before the erection of the pagoda in 751, making it the oldest printed material ever found in the world. Silla also displayed its skill in the manufacture of paper, and its science of printing and papermaking were inherited by the Koryŏ kingdom, laying the foundation for its invention of metal printing and enabling the Koryŏ kingdom to manufacture the best-quality paper in East Asia.

Architecture, Sculpture, and Craft

Korean arts flourished during Silla's unified period, when its artistic creations were largely the products of Buddhism, including Buddhist temples, pagodas, temple bells, images of the Buddha, and stone lanterns. But these Buddhist objets d'art had a distinctive Korean style and made use of materials that differed from those used in other countries, particularly China.

As Buddhism became a veritable national faith, its influence on the arts and crafts in unified Silla was profound. The most typical representatives of unified Silla's Buddhist arts are the Pulguk-sa temple at Kyŏngju and its nearby Sŏkkuram grotto, a World Heritage site. Both are said to have been built in 751 by Kim Tae-sŏng, then the chungsi, or prime minister. But, in fact, they were erected and created with the king's patronage. The Silla kings expended great sums to build Buddhist temples around the capital and throughout the country, and several government offices were established to maintain and repair these monasteries. At the time unified Silla's strength, wealth, and artistic achievement reached its maximum, as demonstrated by the construction of the Pulguk-sa and Sŏkkuram. The huge Pulguk-sa temple, which the Silla people regarded as an earthly embodiment of the "Buddha land," is considered a masterpiece of architecture in its symmetry and beauty. Two magnificent stairways, a lower flight named the Paekun-gyo, or Bridge of White Clouds, and an upper flight known as the Ch'ŏngun-gyo, or Bridge of Azure Clouds—both of which symbolized the overpass rising to the Buddha land—lead to the entrance gate called the Chaha-mun, or Mauve Mist Gate. Passing over the entrance, one finds a pair of stone pagodas, the Tabo-t'ap and Sŏkka-t'ap, standing opposite each other at the front yard of the taeungjŏn, the hall of Shakyamuni, the temple proper. The two pagodas are suggestive of Indian rather than Chinese proto-types. All these structures display a mature, harmonious beauty.

The two pagodas, together with the three-storied Four-Lion Pagoda at the Hwaŏm-sa temple, located at present-day Kurye, South Chŏlla province, and the three-storied pagoda at the ruins of the Kamŭn-sa temple near Kyŏngju, are regarded as the finest examples of stone pagodas in unified Silla.

The Dharani sutra, printed between 706 and 751, and, as noted, the oldest woodblock printing found in the world, was brought to light during the restoration of the Sŏkka-t'ap in 1966. Compared to those in China and Japan, Korea's pagodas were made of unique construction materials. Whereas the emphasis in China was on brick and in Japan on wooden construction, Korea's pagodas were constructed from granite.

The Sŏkkuram grotto was modeled after the stone cave temples at Yunggang and Longmen in China. In China these Buddhist temples were cut into the face of natural rock cliffs, but the Sŏkkuram is an entirely man-made stone grotto that enshrines the principal statue of the Buddha. The grotto has a rectangular antechamber, symbolizing the earth, and a circular interior chamber with a doomed ceiling, representing the sky. The Sŏkkuram grotto was erected on the top of the T'oham-san (mountain) toward the east, thus commanding a glorious view of the East Sea. It is assumed that the people of Silla, with the aid of Buddha, were defending their nation from Japanese pirates, then on a rampage.

The Sŏkkuram is widely admired for its unique sculpture, which may be described as a symphony of beauty in its entirety. The grotto houses the historic great stone statue of Shakyamuni Buddha in its inner sanctum, with the figure situated so that the rising sun over the East Sea strikes it in the middle of the forehead. The Sŏkkuram also contains the 11-headed Goddess of Mercy (Avalokitesvara), the Bodhisattva of Wisdom and Intellect, the Bodhisattva of Compassion, the Brahma-Dava, and the ten Arhats, disciples of the Buddha, carved in relief in a semicircle on the surrounding wall of the interior chamber. The two *Inwang*, or Benevolent Kings, are carved on the walls of the antechamber, and the grotesque-looking Four Devas standing guard against sundry evil spirits along the passageway leading from the antechamber to the interior chamber.

Architecturally and artistically the Sŏkkuram is taken to be a worldwide masterpiece. The width of its chambers, the height of its domed ceiling, and the size of its sculptures are all in perfect balance, attesting to the Silla people's great technical skill as well as their sophisticated knowledge of mathematics.

Other famous sculptures include the stone statues of the Amitabha Buddha and the Maitreya Boddhisattva at the Kamsan-sa temple in Kyŏngju, which indicate the increasing popularity among the populace of their beliefs in the Amitabha and the Maitreya. In the later period the construction of images of the Vairocana Buddha, a celestial Buddha interpreted as the Bliss Body of the Shakyamuni Buddha, won great popularity. Unlike those of the earlier period, many of these images were cast in iron.

In fashion in the later period of unified Silla were memorial stupas, mound-like structures preserving cremated remains of noted monks. Because Sŏn Buddhism was popular among the local gentry at the time, memorial stupas to honor *sŏnsa,* or Sŏn masters, were made in considerable numbers. The oldest known stupa for Monk Yŏmgŏ was constructed in 790, but the best known stupa is Master Ch'ŏlgam's memorial for Toyun, the founder of the *Saja-san* sect, one of the Nine Mountain Sects of Sŏn, at the Ssangbong-sa temple, located in present-day Hwasun, South Chŏlla province. Accompanying the memorial stupa is a monument stone recording the Sŏn master's lifetime achievements. The inscriptions on these monuments are important as materials for the study of calligraphic styles of that age and as historical sources for the development of Sŏn Buddhism.[7]

Another form of Silla's Buddhist arts is the castings of *pŏmjong,* or bronze bells. The oldest extant bell at the Sangwŏn-sa temple on Odae-san (mountain) dates back to 725, but the best known is the so-called Emille Bell, or the Pongdŏk-sa Bell, cast in 771 to posthumously honor King Sŏngdŏk. The bell, decorated with beautiful figures in low relief, is an outstanding relic of Silla Buddhism. It measures 7 feet, 6 inches (227 centimeters) in diameter and 11 feet (333 centimeters) in height, and weighs 18.9 tons, making it the largest surviving Korean bell. The Emille Bell is distinguished by the shape of the exquisitely wrought bell itself and the beauty of the flying angel-Buddha and lotus flowers carved in relief on its surface. The bell is particularly famous for its mysterious tone. The flying angel-Buddha and the sound of the bell symbolize the Silla people's dearest wish to go to the Buddha land. The bell at the Hwangnyong-sa temple was said to have been enormous, weighing 500,000 *kŭn,* or 300 tons, but it did not survive. The Silla bell has a unique shape, with a wind tube beside the hanger on the top that gives the bell its unique sound.

Tomb mounds also demonstrate the unique artistry of unified Silla. Before unification, the construction of tombs had been based on a vertical shaft for interment beneath an earth-covered mound of stones. After unification, influenced by Koguryŏ and Paekche tombs, the prevalent style of tomb architecture was characterized by a horizontal entrance shaft leading to a stone burial chamber. In some cases, the lower part of the much smaller earthen mound covering the burial chamber was posted by upright supporting slabs of stone, on which the 12 animal deities of the Zodiac were carved (rat, bull, tiger, rabbit, dragon, snake, horse, sheep, monkey, chicken, dog, and pig). In other cases, the stone statues of the animal deities encircled the tomb. The former is represented by Kwaerŭng, or the Hanging Tomb, thought to be the tomb of King Wŏnsŏng, and the latter is exemplified by the tomb of King Sŏngdŏk. At the time the people of Silla believed that these animal figures, all bearing weapons, would guard the soul of the deceased. The idea of a Zodiac of 12 animals was borrowed from China, but Silla used the animals uniquely in tomb architecture. Kwaerŭng has additional stone statues of a civil official and a military official, both appearing to be Arabians, and of two lions. These uncommon stone images of Arabians suggest that at the time Silla and the Arab world were engaging in active human and material exchanges.

Literature, Calligraphy, and Painting

Literature in unified Silla, especially the hyangga, was closely related to Buddhism. The hyangga was a poetic genre that had already appeared before unification. As Buddhism flourished and monks mainly constituted the intellectual class after unification, many hyangga poems were composed by these Buddhist monks. In 888 Queen Chinsŏng commanded the high courtier Wihong and the monk Taegu to compile an anthology of hyangga, titled *Samdaemok*, or Collection from the Three Periods of Silla History, but it has not survived. Fortunately *Samguk yusa* contains 14 hyangga poems on subjects that mainly include extolling the virtue of the Buddha, longing for a deceased loved one, praying for an easy passage into eternity, and entreating heaven to bring tranquility to the state. Although the hyangga was literature for the intellectual class, narrative literature appealed to the common people. *Samguk yusa* recorded a number of these Silla tales on subjects such as loyalty to the king and the state, and filial piety to parents.

As the study of Chinese classics became prevalent, unified Silla produced noted calligraphers. The most renowned Silla calligrapher was Kim Saeng, but no actual specimen of his calligraphy still exists. Kim In-mun, the son of King Muyŏl, was another well-known Silla calligrapher, and several specimens of his calligraphy have survived. *Samguk sagi* recorded the names of master painters, including Sŏlgŏ, who was said to have drawn a mural painting on the wall of the Hwangnyong-sa temple, but none of their works remains today.

Unified Silla, in sum, developed a flourishing indigenous civilization, one of the most advanced in the world, and its high level of cultural achievements was well known to Tang China. Indeed, the Chinese called Silla the "country of courteous people in the East" and accorded the highest respect to the Silla envoy among the foreign representatives dispatched to the state.

THE LATER THREE KINGDOMS

Great Split of the True-Bone Aristocracy

Until the mid-eighth century, unified Silla enjoyed prosperity and a high level of civilization, but thereafter the kingdom experienced fierce struggles for power within the true-born aristocracy in the central government, the ensuing rise of the local gentry in the countryside that seized control over certain regions, and, later, "invasions" by Paekche and Koguryŏ restorationists that finally led to the establishment of the Later Three Kingdoms in the early tenth century. Finally, the exhausted Silla kingdom faced its end by abdicating the throne in favor of Koryŏ's Wang Kŏn in 935.

By the period of King Kyŏngdŏk, Silla's civilization had reached its climax both politically and in its artistic creativity. Kingly authority in Silla was so firmly established that it could easily control aristocratic defiance against the power of the throne. Beneath the surface, however, a movement to weaken regal power had already started among members of the true-bone aristocracy. Finally, in the period of King Hyegong (765–780), a rebellion against the king erupted.

The turning point in Silla's fortunes began in 768, when Kim Tae-gong led a plot against the monarch. Heralding the beginning of the "late period" of Silla, this incident soon grew into a fierce power struggle involving 96 aristocrats who held the highest office rank of kakkan.[8] The power struggle among the true-born aristocracy continued for several years, in which a series of plots could be interpreted as an attempt to restore royal authority. Finally, in 780, in the course of suppressing the revolt of Kim Chi-jŏng, Kim Yang-sang, a highborn aristocrat, and his partisans killed King Hyegong. With his death, the direct line of royal descent from King Muyŏl came to an end. Now Kim Yang-sang, who claimed to be a 10th-generation descendant of the late fourth-century king Naemul, himself took the throne as King Sŏndŏk (780–785). He was succeeded

by Kim Kyŏng-sin (King Wŏnsŏng, 785–798), said to have been a 12th-genera-
tion descendant of King Naemul. Kim Kyŏng-sin, in a contest for the throne,
then defeated his rival Kim Chu-wŏn, who was a direct descendant of King
Muyŏl. Subsequent kings all came from King Wŏnsŏng's line of descent.

Now kingly authority virtually disappeared, and politics in the capital was
characterized by the decisive role played by ephemeral coalitions of aristocratic forces. While the traditional aristocracy retained its prestige, the bone-
rank system split into contending family groups, each struggling to maintain
its own interests at the expense of the others. The kings were selected from
among a large number of royal aspirants from collateral lines. During the remaining 155 years of its existence (780–935), Silla had 20 kings, many of whom
met violent deaths in the vortex of the competition for the throne. Revolts
and coups followed in rapid succession, as one group after another among the
true-born aristocracy placed its candidate on the throne and massacred its
rival candidates.

Political turbulence in the capital occasionally spilled over into the provinces.
For instance, in 822, Kim Hŏn-ch'ang rose up in rebellion at Ungju (present-day
Kongju). Kim Hŏn-ch'ang was the son of Kim Chu-wŏn whose rightful claim
to the throne upon the death of King Sŏndŏk in 785 had been forcibly usurped
by King Wŏnsŏng. Driven by this old grudge, Kim Hŏn-ch'ang rebelled against
the central government and proclaimed a new state, called Changan, or Long
Peace. For a time, a wide area in present-day Ch'ungch'ŏng, Chŏlla, Kyŏngsang,
and Kangwŏn provinces rallied to his cause, but government forces defeated
him. Three years later, in 825, his son, Kim Pŏm-mun, again revolted and set
up the capital at Hansan near present-day Seoul, but he, too, failed. Kim Hŏn-
ch'ang committed suicide, and Kim Pŏm-mun was captured and executed by
government forces.

After the suppression of the rebellion led by Kim Hŏn-ch'ang and Kim Pŏm-
mun, the political situation was stabilized for a period. But the succession struggle among the true-bone aristocracy again erupted upon the death of King
Hŭngdŏk (826–836) in 836. At first King Hŭngdŏk's cousin, Kim Kyun-jŏng,
was set up as king, but he was killed by a nephew, Kim Che-ryung, who ascended
the throne as King Hŭigang (836–838). Two years later, in 838, however, King
Hŭigang himself was killed and succeeded by a second cousin, King Minae
(838–839). At this point Kim U-jing, the son of Kim Kyun-jŏng, garnered the
support of Chang Po-go, who controlled the Ch'ŏnghae-jin garrison on Wan-
do. With Chang's forces, he attacked King Minae, killed him, and ascended the

throne as King Sinmu in 839. Since the period of King Munsŏng (839–857) these fierce struggles for power among the warring factions of the central aristocracy considerably abated, as a spirit of reconciliation was forced upon them by the increasing threats to their hegemony posed by regional power centers.

The Rise of the Local Gentry

The power struggle within the true-bone aristocracy in the capital and ensuing political turmoil gave men of head rank 6 background and indigenous local elites, who had been greatly dissatisfied with the rigid bone-rank system, an opportunity to extend their power and influence. Members of head rank 6 lineage had long been discriminated against by true-born aristocrats in holding real power. Many of them studied in Tang China, acquired new knowledge, and returned home to emerge as the dominant intellectual class in Silla. They severely criticized unfair discrimination under the bone-rank institution. Some of them turned their backs on their nation, as exemplified by Ch'oe Sŭng-u, who served as Kyŏnhwŏn's political adviser, and Ch'oe Ŏn-wi, who acted as Wang Kŏn's brain trust.

Relaxed government control over the countryside caused the growth of powerful local elites, called the hojok, because they possessed wealth and armed might. Members of this local gentry grew from commanders of powerful military garrisons at strategic locations, individuals who engaged in maritime trade, and local landlords. As they emerged as power elites in the countryside, authority rapidly shifted away from the capital toward key regional centers.

Among members of the local gentry, leaders of military garrisons and seaborne commerce were more powerful than inland landlords, as they were in a better position to amass wealth and military force. To defend the country's land frontiers, unified Silla originally established several military garrisons at strategically important locations, such as the Puk-chin, or Northern Garrison, located in present-day Samch'ŏk, Kangwŏn province, and the P'aegang-jin garrison in present-day P'yŏngsan, Hwanghae province, created in 658 and 782, respectively. As the threat of piracy to Silla's thriving maritime trade intensified, several garrisons were established at important coastal points, such as the Ch'ŏnghae-jin garrison on Wan-do, the Tangsŏng-jin garrison in present-day Namyang, Kyŏnggi province, and the Hyŏlgu-jin garrison on Kanghwa-do in the Yellow Sea, created in 828, 829, and 844, respectively. The most important of these was Chang Po-go's Ch'ŏnghae-jin. These garrisons also were sources of military strength for the ambitious local power elites.

Chang Po-go apparently descended from a powerful local family that had already solidified its footing on the island of Wan-do. Thus, he could base his maritime operations on the island, organize other members of his lineage into his personal armed force, and finally become a virtual merchant prince who secured command of the Yellow Sea and the South Sea. Chang Po-go was the most prominent of these figures because of the scale of his maritime activity, but others also acted as seaborne power elites including Wang Pong-gyu, operating out of Kangju (present-day Chinju, South Kyŏngsang province), and the man known as Chakchegŏn, the grandfather of Wang Kŏn, who was active in the Songak (present-day Kaesŏng) area.

Meanwhile, powerful local families for several generations had exercised de facto control over particular regions in the countryside. Most of these local forces were indigenous local elites who had served as village headmen generation after generation. These local officials originally administered the rural population assigned to them on behalf of the central government, but as stronger village headmen brought weaker headmen in neighboring areas under their control, they increasingly expanded their power base in the countryside. These landlord elites usurped administrative power of officials dispatched from the central government and secured virtual independence in certain localities. They built fortifications around their power centers and therefore were known as sŏngju. They commanded their own private forces recruited from the local populace who were under their control, or from the roaming landless peasantry, and thus became known as *changgun,* or generals.

The Establishment of the Later Three Kingdoms

By the late ninth century unified Silla had plunged into utter, uncontrollable confusion and this gave rise to the tumultuous Later Three Kingdoms period. The central government's power dissipated when members of the influential local gentry splintered central government authority and a succession of peasant rebellions shook the state's foundations. In particular, the growing strength of the local gentry weakened the sway of the central government over the countryside to such an extent that the government could not collect taxes from the local population. Confounding matters, King Hŏn'gang (875–886) and Queen Chinsŏng (887–897) indulged in luxury and pleasure which exhausted the government's financial resources. In a desperate attempt to overcome its financial crisis, the central government, in 889, used force to collect taxes from the peasant population. Now suffering the burden of heavy taxation levied by both the central government and the local gentry, many peasants abandoned their land and roamed the countryside. Some of these landless wanderers barely subsisted, and others entrusted themselves to the protection of powerful local gentry households. Still others joined together in bands and lived by plundering. These so-called *ch'ojŏk* gangs, or grass brigands, comprised of impoverished peasants, became active throughout the country, and as they experienced a succession of alliances and ruptures, they grew into larger groups. Some attempted to rebel against the state and seize power.

The first peasant rebellion erupted in the present-day Sangju area in 889. This uprising was led by two men, Wŏnjong and Aeno. Soon one revolt followed on the heels of another throughout the country. Yanggil, in present-day Wŏnju, Kihwŏn in present-day Chuksan, and Kyŏnhwŏn in present-day Chŏnju were among the most prominent rebel leaders. In 896 a large force of brigands calling itself the *Chŏkkojŏk*, or Red Trousers Banditti, rebelled in the southwest coastal region and mounted a drive on the suburbs of the capital. Now, rebel strongholds were firmly established and the authority of the central government was limited to a small area around the capital.

Lacking statecraft, most of these early rebel leaders were no more than men who controlled a particular locale. Soon, however, two rebel leaders emerged to establish new state entities in the areas they controlled. They were Kyŏnhwŏn and Kungye, who encouraged restorationists of the former Paekche and Koguryŏ kingdoms to bring Silla to an end. As they challenged Silla's legitimacy by claiming that their states were restorations of the two former kingdoms, a three-way contest for mastery of the Korean peninsula developed. Thus Korean history entered the period of the Later Three Kingdoms which spanned nearly half a century.

Kyŏnhwŏn, a man of peasant stock in the Sangju area, started his career as an ordinary soldier and was promoted repeatedly as a reward for valor in defending Silla's southwest coastal region. As peasant uprisings flared throughout the country, Kyŏnhwŏn rebelled at Wansanju (present-day Chŏnju) and proclaimed himself king at Mujinju (present-day Kwangju) in 892. To put the anti-Silla feelings of the former Paekche people to good use, he vowed vengeance on the last Paekche king Ŭija. He marched north and occupied Wansanju, where he founded the state of Later Paekche in 900.

Later Paekche extended its power and influence to the north, recovering most of the old Paekche territory, thanks to the active support of the local gentry in the region. In 927 Kyŏnhwŏn pillaged the capital and captured the Silla king

Kyŏngae, who had been hosting a feast at the pleasure resort of P'osŏkjŏng. He forced the king to commit suicide, raped the queen, and abducted the king's younger brother, the highest officials, as well as skilled craftsmen, and seized large quantities of treasure and arms. He enthroned Kim Pu, a member of the Silla royalty, as King Kyŏngsun (927–935) and then withdrew from the capital. Only the existence of Wang Kŏn could prevent Kyŏnhwŏn from destroying Silla. His ruthless action, which demonstrated his bitter enmity toward Silla, also stirred up anti-Kyŏnhwŏn feelings among the Silla people and ultimately led them to surrender voluntarily to Wang Kŏn's Koryŏ.

Originally a scion of Silla's royal family, Kungye was driven out of the palace as a victim of the political power struggle. At first he became a monk, but as Silla fell into confusion he entrusted himself to Kihwŏn at Chuksan and later became a lieutenant of Yanggil at Wŏnju. At first Kungye commanded a contingent of Yanggil's forces, but soon he assembled a large army under his personal control. Eventually he drove out Yanggil and, in 901, established the state of Later Koguryŏ at Songak (Songdo). In 904 he renamed his kingdom Majin and, in 905, transferred its capital to Ch'ŏrwŏn in central Korea. Once more, in 911, he gave his state a new name, T'aebong. At first he adopted the era name Mut'ae for his kingdom in 904, and then he changed it to Sŏngch'aek in 905, to Sudŏkmanse in 911, and finally to Chŏnggae in 914. This frequent renaming of his country and his era demonstrates his heightened emotional state and instability.

Kungye's T'aebong expanded its territory to the Taedong River to the north and to present-day Kongju and Sangju to the south, where it was bordered by Later Paekche and Silla. The government he created replicated that of Silla. It included a chancellery, termed Kwangp'yŏngsŏng, several ministries, and other offices such as the Pyŏng-bu; the Taeryong-bu, or Ministry of Finance; and the Such'un-bu, or Ministry of Rites, as well as an office ranking system in 9 grades. Kungye's success was the result of several factors. First, he garnered support from members of the local gentry in the former Koguryŏ territory by arousing anti-Silla feelings among them. Second, he won his subordinates' favor by distributing the spoils of war among them. Third, he won the confidence of the people who had strong faith in the Maitreya Buddha by claiming that he himself was the Maitreya Buddha incarnate and by designating his eldest and second sons both Bodhisattvas.

But Kungye's reign was short-lived. Lacking royal virtues, he ruled his kingdom ruthlessly, as did Later Paekche's Kyŏnhwŏn. From the beginning, he had a burning personal hatred of Silla and required his subjects to refer to his homeland of Silla as the "nation of the damned." Moreover, he was inordinately suspicious of the motives of those around him, including his own family members. He claimed that he possessed supernatural powers and could read the minds of others, which led him to kill many who served him. When Wang Kŏn was victorious in a series of battles with Later Paekche and gained public confidence, Kungye showed impatience and became even more cruel. Obsessed with the conviction that he would be killed by his subordinates, he mercilessly executed many of them over the slightest matters. He even killed his wife and two sons in 915. As he turned into a crazed tyrant, Kungye was eventually driven from his throne by his own generals, including Hong Yu, Pae Hyŏn-gyŏng, Sin Sung-gyŏm, and Pok Chi-gyŏm, and was killed by his people as he fled in 918.

Koryŏ's Unification

Immediately before Kungye's death, one of his generals, Wang Kŏn, succeeded him as king of T'aebong. Viewing his kingdom as the legitimate successor to Koguryŏ, Wang Kŏn renamed his state Koryŏ, from which the name "Korea" derives. He adopted the era name Ch'ŏnsu, or Heaven's Mandate, for his kingdom in 918 and the next year moved the capital to Kaesŏng (Songak), his home area.

Wang Kŏn had emerged from a local gentry family in the Kaesŏng area. He was a descendant of a trade merchant household that had amassed enormous wealth through trade with China. To firmly secure his military and political base, he moved his capital from Ch'ŏrwŏn to Kaesŏng, which demonstrates his standing as a local gentry figure in the area. As a member of this powerful elite class, unlike Kyŏnhwŏn and Kungye, he was able to establish a strong local power base among the local gentry. As demonstrated later, he forged strong ties with other local gentry families, primarily through marriage. He also had close connections with maritime activities centered around the Hyŏlgu-jin garrison on Kanghwa-do. Thanks to his long familiarity with maritime activities, he succeeded in seaborne operations against the southwest coastal region of Later Paekche. For much of its existence, Later Paekche was greatly troubled by his naval raids along its coast. Wang Kŏn occupied Kŭmsŏng (present-day Naju, South Chŏlla province), Chin-do, and other coastal points, which worked to disrupt Later Paekche's trade and diplomatic ties with China and Japan. His military skill at the battle of Kŭmsŏng led Kungye to appoint him sijung of the Kwangp'yŏngsŏng. He was then set up by Kungye's generals as king.

After he established a new kingdom of Koryŏ, Wang Kŏn pursued a policy of friendship with Silla both to secure his position as the successor to Silla's traditions and authority, and to isolate Later Paekche from the people of Silla. Upon hearing that Later Paekche's Kyŏnhwŏn had raided the Silla capital of Kyŏngju and forced King Kyŏngae to commit suicide, Wang Kŏn personally led his forces into battle against Kyŏnhwŏn. This policy of friendship led the last Silla king, Kyŏngsun, to voluntarily surrender to Koryŏ in 935.

On the other hand, Wang Kŏn had fought ceaselessly with Later Paekche for many years. Responding to Silla's call for help after King Kyŏngae's death, Wang Kŏn went into battle against Kyŏnhwŏn but suffered a crushing defeat at Kongsan near Taegu in 927. He barely escaped the battlefield and saved his life through the daring self-sacrifice of his generals, Sin Sung-gyŏm and Kim Nak. After the battle, Later Paekche dominated Koryŏ militarily. At the time the battlefield between Koryŏ and Later Paekche was concentrated in Silla's outer perimeter just west of the Naktong River, from Koch'ang (present-day Andong, North Kyŏngsang province), past Sangju, to Kangju. In 930 Koryŏ scored a decisive victory over Later Paekche at the battle of Koch'ang. Thereafter, as the tide of battle turned in favor of Koryŏ, Later Paekche was pushed back into its own heartland. There it suffered a further crippling defeat at the battle of Unju (present-day Hongsŏng, South Ch'ungch'ŏng province) in 934.

Kyŏnhwŏn took many wives and is said to have fathered ten sons. This laid the groundwork for the familial strife that ended the kingdom. After his long rule, in 935 the aged Kyŏnhwŏn designated his fourth son, Kŭmgang, to succeed him. The eldest son, Sin'gŏm, became outraged at that and, after conspiring with his brothers, staged a coup against his father. He killed his half-brother, Kŭmgang, confined Kwŏnhwŏn to the Kŭmsan-sa temple, located at Pyŏkkol, and took the throne for himself. Kyŏnhwŏn managed to escape to Koryŏ, and, to avenge his eldest son, he entrusted himself to his old rival Wang Kŏn. Meanwhile Silla's last king, Kyŏngsun, formally surrendered to Koryŏ along with his kingdom whose territory was now confined to the narrow Kyŏngju region. Wang Kŏn warmly treated the ruling elites of the fallen Silla kingdom, including King Kyŏngsun. In fact, he paid Kyŏngsun every possible respect, even seeming reluctant to accept his surrender. He gave his eldest daughter in marriage to the former Silla king and reestablished him in a supervisory capacity in the old capital district of Kyŏngju. The remains of the Silla administration were peacefully incorporated into the new kingdom of Koryŏ. In the following year, in 936, Koryŏ forces attacked Later Paekche, bringing the state to its final collapse. Kyŏnhwŏn is said to have led an army of 100,000 against his former kingdom. After his defeat in a battle at Illich'ŏn (present-day Kumi [Sŏnsan], North Kyŏngsang province), Sin'gŏm surrendered to Wang Kŏn. Thus ended the period of the Later Three Kingdoms, and in this way Wang Kŏn again unified the Korean peninsula.

When Parhae fell to Qidan Liao in 926, much of its ruling class of Koguryŏ descent, amounting to more than 50,000, fled to Koryŏ. Wang Kŏn welcomed them and generously gave them government posts, farmlands, and houses. He bestowed the name Wang Kye on the Parhae crown prince, Tae Kwanghyŏn, and entered his name in the royal household register. Wang Kŏn also allowed him to perform rituals in honor of his progenitor, Tae Cho-yŏng. Koryŏ achieved a true national unification that embraced all Koreans from the "Northern and Southern States." At the time of its unification, Koryŏ extended its territory to the north as far as the line starting from the Ch'ŏngch'ŏn River on the west and reaching the Hamhŭng plain to the east. The Koryŏ kingdom survived for 474 years, until 1392, and in its heyday ranked among the most advanced civilizations in the world.

Recently Chinese scholars have argued that no successive relationship existed between Koguryŏ and Koryŏ. They claim that the two kingdoms were established by different people, Koguryŏ by people of Chinese stock and Koryŏ by Koreans. In other words, Koryŏ, the Chinese contend, was a state founded by the ancestors of present-day Koreans, whereas Koguryŏ was founded by the forefathers of today's Chinese. They assert that although people have called each of the two kingdoms Koryŏ from ancient times, it is a misnomer that causes confusion.

Koryŏ, however, was indeed the successor kingdom of Koguryŏ. Historical records written during the Chinese Song and Yuan dynasties classified Koryŏ as well as Koguryŏ into a category of foreign nations and admitted that Koryŏ was the successor to Koguryŏ. The official historic work on the Song dynasty began with a chapter on Koryŏ and stated that "Koryŏ originally was Koguryŏ"; it also portrayed its founding. In fact, the name "Koryŏ" is one of the most distinctive factors to testify that the kingdom was the successor to Koguryŏ. Wang Kŏn designated the name of his state as Koryŏ to signify that his new kingdom succeeded Koguryŏ. The Koryŏ founder also forged a "northward policy" to recover the old territory of Koguryŏ and established Pyongyang, the old capital of Koguryŏ, as another capital of his kingdom. The capital was called "Sŏ-gyŏng." All his efforts should be understood as formal moves to declare his kingdom's succession to Koguryŏ. Some Chinese scholars have argued that Wang Kŏn was of Silla descent, but a range of historical records such as *Koryŏ segye*, or Lineage of the Koryŏ Royal Family, written during the Koryŏ period, demonstrate that his ancestors came from the north, either from Koguryŏ or the Parhae kingdom. The people of Koryŏ also claimed to have descended from the people of Koguryŏ.

The period of the "Northern and Southern States," which includes Parhae and unified Silla, occupies a unique place in Korean history. Both kingdoms competitively introduced advanced culture and institutions from China and achieved highly developed civilizations, which were inherited intact by the Koryŏ kingdom. By ending the period of the Three Kingdoms and accepting the survivors of Koguryŏ descent from the Parhae kingdom, Koryŏ accomplished the second national unification of Koreans. By integrating all the people and culture of Korea into a single homogeneous nation, Koryŏ was able to achieve a flourishing indigenous civilization.

4

THE FIRST HALF OF THE KORYŎ PERIOD
(918–1170)

King T'aejo and the Local Gentry

AFTER UNIFYING THE LATER THREE KINGDOMS, King T'aejo (Wang Kŏn's posthumous, official title, meaning "Great Progenitor") sought to achieve national integration by forging alliances with members of the local gentry, who were scattered throughout the country, and by recovering the former territories of Koguryŏ and Parhae. He regarded his state as the successor to Koguryŏ and pursued a policy of northern expansion. He extended Koryŏ's borders to the Ch'ŏngch'ŏn River, some 45 miles north of Pyongyang.[1] Meanwhile, in domestic affairs, T'aejo faced difficulties dealing with the recalcitrant local gentry. Despite unification, members of the local gentry, within their regional strongholds, still maintained quasi-independent status. As a result, the central government could not dispatch its officials to administer the local areas. Needing consent and cooperation from local gentry figures to rule effectively, T'aejo forged marriage ties with 29 local gentry families throughout the country, including the Chŏngju Yu clan, the Naju O clan, the Ch'ungju Yu clan, the Hwangju Hwangbo clan, and the Kyŏngju Kim clan. He fathered 25 sons and 9 daughters. In some cases he strengthened the alliance by bestowing the royal surname, Wang, or other family names on powerful local elites and creating fictive family ties with them. To curry favor with the local gentry, to whom he owed his throne, T'aejo adopted men of local gentry lineage as merit subjects, bestowing upon them land and high office ranks.

Despite these policies, powerful political forces among the local gentry continued to pose a grave threat to royal power. Thus T'aejo made every effort to restrict the privileges of the local gentry to prevent them from dominating the populace. He wrote and promulgated *Chŏnggye*, or Political Precautions, and *Kye paengnyo sŏ*, or Book of Bureaucratic Precepts, setting forth norms to govern the conduct of the king's subjects. Up to his death in 943, however, T'aejo was never able to establish stable royal power. For his heirs, he left behind the testament known as *Hunyo sipcho*, precepts to be observed and honored by his successors in the realm of government. In his *Hunyo sipcho*, T'aejo instructed later kings to protect Buddhism and monasteries, to rule their state based on Confucian virtues, to promote the peasants' livelihood, to follow geomantic theories, to preserve Korea's cultural traditions, to attach great importance to Sŏ-gyŏng (Pyongyang), and not to draft men into government service from the region south of the Ch'aryŏng mountain range and the Kŭm River, in other words, men from the former territory of Later Paekche.

The Reforms of Kings Kwangjong and Sŏngjong

In 943 T'aejo was succeeded by King Hyejong (943–945), the son of his second queen, but after only two years Hyejong died of illness and was succeeded by his half-brother, King Chŏngjong (945–949), the son of T'aejo's third queen. Chŏngjong also died of illness in 949 and was succeeded by his younger brother, King Kwangjong (949–975).

In the course of these successions, in which the throne was passed between princes born of different queens, a serious power struggle ensued. This was the inevitable result of T'aejo having fathered a number of princes, all potential candidates for the kingship, from 6 queens and 23 royal concubines. Each prince's bid for power was based on the power of his maternal in-laws or on his own connections with powerful forces in the local gentry. Thus the same policies that helped T'aejo win over men of local gentry in order to take the throne ultimately threatened his successors' throne.

In 945 Wang Kyu, a royal in-law, plotted to kill King Hyejong. He had given T'aejo two of his daughters as his 15th and 16th concubines—the latter of whom bore a son, the Prince of Kwangju—and sent another daughter into the palace as a secondary queen for Hyejong. He then resorted to every strategy to bring the Prince of Kwangju to the throne, ultimately even attempting to assassinate King Hyejong. With his position in dire threat, Hyejong survived uneasily for a time, protected day and night by an armed bodyguard. Before long, under heavy stress, he died. Immediately before Hyejong's death, Wang Sing-nyŏm, the commander of the Sŏ-gyŏng garrison, killed Wang Kyu, crushing his treason plot and demonstrating the frailty and instability of royal authority at the time.

Having defeated Wang Kyu's treason plot with the help of Wang Sing-nyŏm, King Chŏngjong tried to strengthen royal authority by transferring the capital to Sŏ-gyŏng. In this design, geomantic theories played a role. But Chŏngjong had a strong desire to escape the hands of those influential men who, as merit subjects at the founding of the Koryŏ kingdom, wielded enormous power in the capital. But after a brief reign of just four years, Chŏngjong died of illness.

Two kings, Kwangjong (949–975) and Sŏngjong (981–997), enacted reforms that greatly strengthened royal authority in Koryŏ. To weaken the power of influential men, Kwangjong enacted the *Nobi an'gŏm pŏp,* or Slave Review Act, in 956. During the chaotic period of the Later Three Kingdoms, warlords of local gentry lineage had illegally forced prisoners of war and refugees, mainly commoners by birth, into slavery. This increase in slaves in turn increased their masters' economic and military strength. The Slave Review Act determined those who originally had been commoners and restored their free status, thus undermining the local gentry's power and influence. In addition, by increasing the number of commoners who were liable for taxation, the law increased state revenues while remaining popular among the people who had been unjustly forced into slavery. Despite stiff opposition to the law from powerful warlords in the local gentry, Kwangjong held his ground.

In 958 Kwangjong adopted the proposal of the naturalized Chinese scholar Shuangji and established a system using a civil service examination as the principal means of selecting government officials. The results of the state examination gave a presumptive measure of one's loyalty to the king, and candidates were selected as government officials on the basis of learning, not bloodline. The institution of this civil service examination constituted a fundamental effort to create a new bureaucracy that would strengthen regal power. Thereafter the institution of yangban, consisting of civil and military officials, emerged.

A firm hierarchy was necessary to establish a new bureaucracy. A number of aesthetic or symbolic steps were also undertaken by Kwangjong as part of his effort to consolidate royal authority and enhance national prestige. In

960 he designated purple, red, scarlet, or green as the colors for official attire. New rules specified the proper terminology to be used in the courts, adopting the title system of an empire rather than that of a kingdom. For example, the capital, Kaesŏng, was called *Hwang-do,* or Imperial Capital, and the palace was referred to as *Hwang-sŏng,* or Imperial Palace. Other terms, such as "your majesty" and "imperial ordinance," also suggest that Koryŏ adopted the title system of an empire. He also reinstituted independent era names for his rule, which had been temporarily suspended in the reign of kings Hyejong and Chŏngjong.

Kwangjong answered the continuing resistance to his reforms from powerful men at court with a series of merciless purges. In 960 he executed two high-level officials, Chunhong and Wang Tong, on charges of treason. Finally, Kwangjong was able to assert royal authority over at least the aristocracy in the capital. In 976, following his political reform, the next king, Kyŏngjong (975–981), enacted a stipend land law, the *Chŏnsikwa,* meaning farmland and forest land institution, designed to guarantee the livelihood of the newly created bureaucracy.

It was King Sŏngjong who firmly established centralized government in Koryŏ. He filled government posts vacated by high-level officials of local gentry origin and replaced radically reformative officials appointed by King Kwangjong with new bureaucrats who had passed the civil service examination. He also ruled his country in a more refined way based on Confucian virtues. He relied on Confucian scholars of Silla's head rank 6 lineage, such as Ch'oe Sŭng-no. Ch'oe, unlike members of the local gentry, had no power base in the countryside and so preferred a centralized government structure. In 981, when Sŏngjong ascended the throne, Ch'oe presented a 28-point policy memorial to the king, suggesting that Confucianism become the country's governing philosophy and that Buddhism become the religion by which individuals cultivate a moral culture. Based on his proposal, Koryŏ established its version of the principle of separation of government and religion. He also recommended the creation of a new political structure modeled on Chinese education, ethics, and political institutions but adapted to Koryŏ's cultural climate, with its own unique customs which were quite different from those of China.

Under Sŏngjong, a foundation was laid for a centralized political order in Koryŏ. In 983 Sŏngjong, for the first time, dispatched central officials to head provincial administrative units, called *mok.* He reformed the local government structure in a way that weakened the power and influence of the local gentry throughout the country, and in 992 he established the Kukchagam, or

National University. These accomplishments earned him his posthumous title "Sŏngjong." Koryŏ followed the Chinese style which, unlike in Silla, named kings using the posthumous titles of *cho,* or progenitor, and *chong,* or ancestor.[2] In East Asia the posthumous title "*Sŏngjong*" (Chengzong in China) was usually given to a king who completed the establishment of the ruling structure of his kingdom or empire.

RULING STRUCTURE

Administrative Structure

Koryŏ's centralized government drew on the Chinese model in organizing its political institutions. Based on the institutions of the Tang and Song dynasties, Koryŏ's new political structure began to take shape in 983 under King Sŏngjong and was completed in 1076 under King Munjong (1046–1083). The administrative structure was centered around three chancelleries. Unlike Tang China, Koryŏ merged the first two of the three chancelleries (Chungsŏ-sŏng, Munha-sŏng, and Sangsŏ-sŏng) into a single organ called the Chungsŏmunha-sŏng, or Chancellery for State Affairs. It was also called the Chae-bu, or Directorate of Chancellors, and was headed by *munha sijung* who, as prime minister, oversaw various aspects of governmental affairs. The officials of the Chae-bu consisted of *chaesin,* or directors, who made policy decisions and held an office rank of 2 or above in the 18 office-rank system, and *nangsa,* or deputy directors, of office rank 3 or below, who were responsible for proposing and criticizing policy. The third chancellery, the Sangsŏ-sŏng, or Secretariat for State Affairs, was empowered to carry out policy through six subordinate ministries: the Yi-bu, the Pyŏng-bu, the Ho-bu, the Hyŏng-bu, the Ye-bu, and the Kong-bu. The Yi-bu was responsible for personnel matters for civil offices, including the ennoblement of merit subjects; the Pyŏng-bu managed personnel matters for military offices, other military affairs, and postal stations using horses; the Ho-bu handled the census of the population, households, and farmlands, and was also responsible for tax collections; the Hyŏng-bu administered statute law, litigation, and the management of slaves; the Ye-bu dealt with the conduct of ceremonies, foreign relations, government schools, and state examinations; and the Kong-bu was empowered to administer the state's woodlands and fishing ponds, the output of artisans at government workshops, and general construction activities. Unlike those in the subsequent Chosŏn dynasty, the highest officials in the Chancellery for State Affairs headed the six ministries directly in accordance with office rank, and thus the ministries were seen as unable to properly manage matters under their purview.

Another major organ of the central government, equally important as the three chancelleries, was the Chungch'uwŏn, later called the Ch'umirwŏn, or Royal Secretariat. Sometimes termed the Ch'u-bu, or Directorate of Advisers, the Chungch'uwŏn was responsible for transmitting royal commands and managing urgent military affairs. In other words, it functioned as the royal secretariat as well as the military intelligence agency. The Directorate of Chancellors and the Directorate of Advisers together were known as either the Yang-bu, or Two Directorates, or the Chaech'u, or Privy Council, and the joint sessions attended by their highest officials decided important matters of state by unanimous consent. This joint session was called the *Todang,* or Convening of the Privy Council, and the decision making was termed *ŭihap,* or consensus. This Koryŏ system in which overall state policy was discussed in a high council followed the tradition of the Three Kingdoms where council institutions acted as political decision-making organs.

In addition to the powerful Two Directorates, another important organ called the Ŏsadae (later called the Sahŏnbu), or Censorate, was empowered to evaluate any official's administrative performance and censure any wrongdoings. Significant restrictions were placed on the exercise of royal power by the Censorate and the deputy directors in the Directorate of Chancellors (together known as the Taesŏng or Taegan, or Surveillance Chancellery), through their mandate to scrutinize the royal appointments of officials, propose changes in state statutes, and return royal commands to the monarch without enforcement. The Koryŏ government structure, unlike that of the Chinese Tang on which it was modeled, had firmly established the power to admonish the monarch and censure royal decisions made by officials. In short, Koryŏ was an aristocratic state in which the aristocratic officialdom had considerable power to restrain the crown.

Other offices or agencies in the central government included the Singmok togam, or Directorate for Legislation, which enacted detailed regulations of the kingdom's statutes; the Samsa, or Agency for Financial Affairs, which handled the nation's finances; the Hallimwŏn, or Academy of Letters, which was responsible for preparing royal edicts and diplomatic correspondence; the Ch'unch'ugwan, or Office of Records, which compiled national history; the Pomungak, or Royal Library, which maintained the books and records at the palace; and the Sach'ŏndae, or Astronomical Observatory, which, as the name makes clear, functioned as the nation's astronomical observatory.[3] In sum, the central administrative structure of Koryŏ was more specialized and more refined than that of unified Silla.

In 983 the central government established 12 mok and dispatched its officials for local administration. Later the number of mok decreased to 8. In 1018, after years of alterations, the structure of local government was finally completed. The whole country was divided into a capital region (kyŏnggi), five large circuits (to), and two border regions (kye), within which were established three capitals (kyŏng), five regional military commands (tohobu), and eight provinces (mok), which were further subdivided into districts (kun), counties (hyŏn), and garrisons (chin). The capital region of kyŏnggi was equivalent to the present-day metropolitan area. The number of circuits fluctuated over time but was finally set at five (Yanggwang-do, Kyŏngsang-do, Chŏlla-do, Kyoju-do, and Sŏhae-do). Because these circuits had no permanent administrative organs, the superintendents, called anch'alsa, were dispatched to make rounds as inspectors. Together with these circuits, two border regions, the Puk-kye (Sŏ-gye), or Northern (Western) Border Region, and the Tong-gye, or Eastern Border Region, were created along the state's northern frontier and the northeast littoral. As special military zones, these border regions were administered by military commanders, called pyŏngmasa, and were subdivided into military garrisons, whereas large circuits were divided into districts and counties.

At first, the three capitals were situated at Kaesŏng (Kae-gyŏng; the Main Capital), at Pyongyang (Sŏ-gyŏng; the Western Capital), and at Kyŏngju (Tong-gyŏng; the Eastern Capital). Since the period of King Munjong, Nam-gyŏng (the Southern Capital) at Seoul (Hanyang) replaced Tong-gyŏng as one of the three capitals. The emergence of Seoul as a secondary capital was closely related to geomantic theories. The creation of these secondary capitals was designed to rebuild the old capitals of the Three Kingdoms and to implement balanced development of the nation. The five regional military commands entrusted with the defense of the realm were strategically located at Andong (present-day Andong, Kyŏngsang-do), Annam (present-day Chŏnju, Chŏlla-do), Ansŏ (present-day Haeju, Sŏhae-do), Anbuk (present-day Anju, Puk-kye), and Anbyŏn (present-day Anbyŏn, Tong-gye). Later, as military tensions were eased in the south, two military commands, Andong and Annam, were abolished. The eight provinces were located at Sangju and Chinju (Kyŏngsang-do), Naju and Chŏnju (Chŏlla-do), Kwangju, Ch'ŏngju, and Ch'ungju (Yanggwang-do), and Hwangju (Sŏhae-do).

The central government dispatched its officials to head the provincial and local administrative units. But central government officials were not sent to all districts, counties, and garrisons. They were selectively dispatched to some important local units called *chu-gun,* or major districts, and *chu-hyŏn,* or major counties. Many more districts and counties—*sok-kun,* or minor districts, and *sok-hyŏn,* or minor counties—were administered by the major districts and counties, and were thus under the indirect control of the central government. With a far greater number of minor districts and counties than major districts and counties, the central government's control over the countryside was curtailed. Fearing the growth of local power centers, rather than appointing officials to administer their own home districts, the central government dispatched officials from the capital and assigned them fixed term limits. These dispatched officials were responsible for levying taxes and tributes, and mobilizing corvee labor, but because local functionaries were better acquainted with the conditions of their home areas than the centrally appointed officials, in practice the local functionaries ended up performing the important administrative tasks. Unlike their counterparts of the later Chosŏn dynasty, these Koryŏ functionaries, called *hojang,* were originally of local gentry descent and therefore formed an elite stratum of local society. Recognizing their status as local headmen, the central government made efforts to check their power and influence by sending officials from particular localities as *sasimgwan,* or inspectors-general, to their home districts to investigate and supervise the local elites. The last Silla king, Kyŏngsun, was appointed to be the sasimgwan of Kyŏngju. Also the *kiin,* or hostage, institution forcibly assigned young male members of local influential families to minor duties in the capital.[4]

The district, county, and garrison administrative units all consisted of ch'on. A ch'on was an administrative unit comprised of several hamlets. These villages were headed by village chiefs who mediated between local officials, their functionaries, and the people of the village. The influence of these Koryŏ village chiefs was much weaker than that of their Silla counterparts. Special settlements, called hyang, so, and pugok, were administered by the major districts or counties. The local administration of Koryŏ, in sum, had a well-organized political structure.

Military Organization

In its early years Koryŏ's pursuit of a policy of northward expansion forced the state to confront Qidan Liao. It therefore needed to maintain a strong military

Koryŏ

Puk-gye

Anbuk

Sŏgyŏng

Anbyŏn

Kyoju-do

Hwangju

Sŏhae-do Kaegyŏng

Asŏ Namgyŏng

Tong-gye

Kwangju

Ch'ungju

Andong

Kangwang-do

Ch'ŏngju Sangju

Tonggyŏng

Ch'ŏnju

Kyŏngsang-do

Annam Chinju

Chŏlla-do

Naju

Legends

◎ Capitals
○ Tohobu
● Mok

MAP 4.1. Koryŏ

130

force and to devote considerable attention to national defense and military organization. Koryŏ adopted the *pubyŏng* (*fubing* in Chinese), or militia, system, in which the military trained able-bodied peasants between the ages of 16 and 60, organized them into regular forces, and allotted them tracts of land. Those who did not comply with their military duty or did not complete their training were called *paekchŏng*, meaning "white men," and did not receive land allotments.

T'aejo (Wang Kŏn), of a warlord background, commanded his own, war-experienced army to destroy Later Paekche. These central forces—called the *kyŏng-gun*, or capital army—were organized into the Two Guards and Six Divisions. The Two Guards units, which formed the royal guards and ranked above the Six Divisions, were comprised of the Ŭngyang-gun, or Soaring Falcon Guards, and the Yongho-gun, or Dragon and Tiger Guards. The other pillar of Koryŏ forces, the Six Divisions, consisted of the Chwaui-wi, or Left and Right Division; the Sinho-wi, or Divine Tiger Division; the Hŭngwi-wi, or Rising Authority Division; the Kŭmo-wi, or Internal Security Division; the Ch'ŏnu-wi, or Thousand Bull Division; and the Kammun-wi, or Capital Guards Division. The first three divisions (the Chwaui-wi, Sinho-wi, and Hŭngwi-wi)—the core of the kingdom's combat forces—were responsible for defending the capital and guarding the frontiers. The Kŭmo-wi functioned as the police force in the capital, the Ch'ŏnu-wi was organized for state ceremonies, and the Kammun-wi guarded the palace and castle gates in the capital.

The Two Guards and Six Divisions had a total strength of some 45,000 soldiers, a majority of whom were conscripted peasants. Each conscripted soldier was assigned two supporting households, responsible for supplying the soldier's provisions and equipment, and cultivating his land during the term of his military service. These conscripted soldiers were supplemented by professional soldiers from military households, who were recorded as such in a military census roster. Their social status and military service passed from generation to generation. In return for the military service of these professional soldiers, the state allocated each military household "soldier's land" and assigned two supporting households to cultivate it.

In addition to the Two Guards and Six Divisions, local forces were permanently stationed in the two border regions, where they cultivated "garrison farms." They were organized into three units—the *ch'o-gun*, or assault force; the *chwa-gun*, or left force; and the *u-gun*, or right force. Local forces stationed in Koryŏ's districts and counties functioned as reservists.

The central army of the Two Guards and Six Divisions and the local army were composed of *yŏng,* or regiments, of 1,000 soldiers each. The commanding officer of a regiment was called *changgun,* or commander. Each of the Two Guards and Six Divisions was commanded by a *sangjanggun,* general, and a *taejanggun,* lieutenant general. These commanding officers of the Two Guards and Six Divisions and *yŏng* had their own joint deliberative organs—the Chungbang, or Council of Generals, for generals and lieutenant generals, and the Changgunbang, or Council of Commanders, for regiment commanders.

Educational Institutions and Civil Service Examination

In Koryŏ the political elites were trained through education and selected by the civil service examination. T'aejo had already taken scholars of Silla's head rank 6 lineage into government service and established schools in Kaesŏng and Pyongyang. But it was King Sŏngjong who laid the foundation for Koryŏ's educational system. He established the Kukchagam as a national university in 992 and founded national libraries and archives. The king's libraries, the Pisŏsŏng, meaning Secretariat, in Kaesŏng, and the Susŏwŏn, or Academy of Books and Records, in Pyongyang, housed tens of thousands of books. The national university had a book publishing department called the Sŏjŏkp'o, meaning Book Concern. It also established the Ch'il che, or Seven-Course Academy, where lectures were given on seven specialized areas of Confucianism, and a scholarship fund was set up for needy students. Later the Kukchagam created the Kyŏngsa yuk hak, or Six Colleges of the Capital, including Kukcha-hak, or University College; T'ae-hak, or High College; Samun-hak, or Four Portals College; Yul-hak, or Law College; Sŏ-hak, or Calligraphy College; and San-hak, or Accounting College. Admission to these six colleges reflected Koryŏ's aristocratic society, marked by precisely defined rankings based on bloodline. Kukcha-hak, T'ae-hak, and Samun-hak were all established to teach the *Five Classics* of Confucianism, the *Classic of Filial Piety,* and the *Analects.* The three colleges differed only in their entrance requirements: Kukcha-hak admitted the sons of civil or military officials of the 3rd rank or higher; T'ae-hak, the sons of 4th and 5th rank officials; and Samun-hak, the sons of 6th and 7th ranks officials. The sons of 8th and 9th rank officials, and of commoners, were admitted to Yul-hak, Sŏhak, and San-hak to study one of the miscellaneous technical specialties called *chap-hak,* or miscellaneous subjects, which were held in contempt.

Although education was also encouraged in the countryside, local educational facilities had still not been established by the reign of King Sŏngjong. At first the king brought local youth to the capital, where they were educated to become future government officials. After this program failed, in 987 the king sent two scholars, one of Chinese classics and the other of medicine, to each of the 12 mok to educate the youth. By 1127, under King Injong (1122–1146), local educational institutions, called *hyanghak,* or local schools, were established in those areas.

To promote education, Koryŏ published many books and imported a number of books from Song China. Soon publication in Koryŏ was so prolific that, during the reign of King Sŏnjong (1083–1094), the Chinese dynasty began importing or transcribing rare books not found in Song and, in fact, is said to have transcribed thousands of books found only in Koryŏ.

The *kwagŏ,* or civil service examination, established in 958, was the mechanism through which candidates for the officialdom were selected throughout the entire Koryŏ period. Three different types of civil exams were offered, and were tailored for candidates from different backgrounds and seeking different posts: the *chesul-ŏp,* or composition examination; the *myŏnggyŏng-ŏp,* or classics examination; and the *chap-ŏp,* or miscellaneous examination. The chesul-ŏp tested candidates' literary ability to compose *si* (*shi;* poetry), *pu* (*fu;* rhyme prose), *song* (*song;* sacrificial ode), and *ch'aek* (*ce;* an essay discussing a problem) in Chinese; and the myŏnggyŏng-ŏp examined candidates' knowledge of Confucian works such as the *Book of History, Book of Divination, Book of Poetry, Book of Rites,* and *Spring and Autumn Annals.* The subjects covered in these two exams were almost identical to those taught at Kukchagam, the national university, and so both exams were conducted to select qualified officials from Kukchagam. Because Koryŏ society held literary accomplishment in greater esteem than knowledge of the Confucian classics, the chesul-ŏp was regarded as the more important exam. During the Koryŏ period, more than 6,000 men passed the composition examination, whereas only 450 passed the classics examination. This was also partly because of the demand in Koryŏ for qualified officials with outstanding literary abilities, far greater than the demand for officials who were experts on the Chinese classics. The chap-ŏp was used to select specialists to serve in posts calling for technical knowledge, principally in statute law (*myŏngpŏp-ŏp*), accounting (*myŏngsan-ŏp*), medicine (*ŭi-ŏp*), divination (*pok-ŏp*), and geomancy (*chiri-ŏp*). Within Koryŏ's aristocracy, the chap-ŏp had far lower standing than the chesul-ŏp and the myŏnggyŏng-ŏp. An independent state examination for the selection of military officials did not exist until the reign of King Kongyang (1389–1392). By the time of the last king, the civil examinations selected military officials as well as civil officials, although military candidates constituted a very small portion of all those selected. Then, by the end of the dynasty, Koryŏ created an independent examination for the selection of military officials.

In theory, the people of *yangin,* or commoner, origin or higher were all qualified to sit for the state examination, whereas *ch'ŏnmin,* or the lowborn, and the children of monks were ineligible. In reality, however, the commoners' lack of time for continued Chinese classical studies, their exclusion from many government schools, and other petty restrictions inspired by class prejudice prevented them from taking advantage of this theoretical opportunity. Therefore the successful candidates of the composition and classics examinations were mostly the sons of incumbent officials. Indeed, the examination was so difficult that only those who studied at the national university could pass it. Commoners usually sat for the chap-ŏp.

The civil service examination was not the only mechanism used to select government officials. The *ŭmsŏ (munŭm),* or protected appointment, institution enabled one son (or grandson, son-in-law, younger brother, or nephew) of an official of the 5th rank or higher to receive an official appointment, without passing the difficult state examination. Thus this system preserved the permanence and heritability of special aristocratic privilege. Although it was a more closed society than that of the subsequent Chosŏn dynasty, whose leaders came from a broader social base, Koryŏ, compared to Silla, was relatively open. Because Silla society was based on the bone-rank system, in which the only criterion for appointment to office was hereditary social status, Silla had no need for an examination to select officials. In Koryŏ, on the other hand, the civil service examination enabled large numbers of men, including local functionaries, to become government officials. In other words, the Koryŏ aristocracy was a broader constituency, far more inclusive than Silla's true-bone aristocracy.

ECONOMIC AND SOCIAL STRUCTURE

The Land System and the Life of the Peasants

In Koryŏ's predominantly agricultural society, peasant farmers were the main providers for society and the aristocracy acted like parasites. In the late Silla period, both the central government and the local gentry excessively burdened and exploited the peasant population, causing large-scale rebellions. Fully aware of this situation, T'aejo and his successors in the early Koryŏ period lightened the people's burdens in an effort to stabilize their livelihood. At the time the peasants, who comprised the large majority of the population, cultivated their own privately owned land, commonly known as the "people's land." Although the state authorized their ownership of this land, the king, based on the idea that he actually owned all the land in the country, considered the people's land to be "public land" and levied a tax in kind.

In 940, to guarantee the livelihood of merit subjects and government officials, the state allotted them *yŏkpun-jŏn,* or land grants as rewards, in varying quantities. Of course the state did not endow these men with the right of ownership but instead granted the right to levy taxes on these farmlands. By 976 the yŏkpun-jŏn system had evolved into the *Chŏnsikwa,* a stipend land system, which, after undergoing several changes, was finally completed in 1076, under King Munjong. Under this system, the state allocated land in 18 stipend grades based on the office rank structure. The allocation of land included both farmland (*chŏn*) and forestland (*si*)—hence the term "Chŏnsikwa"—and the state gave the right of taxation on the people's land as well as public land. At first, however, officials were strictly banned from collecting land taxes directly; instead, the state collected the taxes on their behalf. Because the land granted an official was considered his salary, in principle, upon the official's death, the allocated land was to be returned to the state. In time, however, the aristocracy and officialdom gained increasingly greater control over their landholdings, thus weakening the authority of the monarch and the central government.

To provide economic benefits to a few privileged aristocrats, the state gave officials of the 5th rank or higher so-called *kongŭm-jŏn,* or privileged merit land, in graded amounts. Since kongŭm-jŏn could be bequeathed to the recipient's descendants, it was also called *yŏngŏp-chŏn,* or land held in perpetuity. The grantee of kongŭm-jŏn could freely dispose of it and collect taxes on his authority from the tenant farmers who cultivated it. The land was thus, in effect, privately owned. Together with the ŭmsŏ (protected appointment) institution, discussed above, kongŭm-jŏn further perpetuated the privileges of the high aristocracy.

Land, or more precisely the right to levy taxes on land, was also allocated to local government functionaries and professional soldiers. The former received *oeyŏk-chŏn,* or local service land, and the latter *kunin-jŏn,* or soldier's land. Local service land served as the salaries of local functionaries. And since their positions were inherited, this oeyŏk-chŏn land was also a type of yŏngŏp-chŏn (land held in perpetuity). Furthermore, it was effectively private land, as taxes were directly collected by the local functionaries. Soldier's land was granted to professional soldiers in compensation for military service. Because soldiers inherited their military service obligations, soldier's lands were held in perpetuity, passed down through generations of military households.

There were other land allotments: *naejang-jŏn*, or royal estate land, was given to the royal household; *konghae-jŏn*, or public agency land, was allocated to government offices; *kungwŏn-jŏn*, or palace estate land, was given to the palace; and *sawŏn-jŏn*, or temple land, was given to Buddhist temples. The allocation of these lands allowed these organs to meet their expenses via their right to impose rents.

Immediately after its final establishment in 1076, the Chŏnsikwa began to collapse. As the power of the aristocracy and officialdom grew, stipend land, like privileged merit land, was also inherited and finally turned into private land, allowing the recipients of the land to collect rents directly. As the Chŏnsikwa remained in name only, the aristocracy and bureaucracy increased their landholdings by reclaiming wasteland, receiving special grants from the monarch, and forcefully seizing land owned by others. Gradually these private landholdings grew into large, well-organized estates, bestowing their surplus produce directly to their aristocratic owners rather than to the state.

The self-supporting peasants cultivated their farmland and usually paid one-fourth of the harvest as a state tax. The peasants, who had little or no land, tilled the private farmlands of aristocrats and officials, and paid one-half the yield as rent. The peasantry also had to pay a tribute tax, usually in cloth, to the state. Tributary payments had to be made in the form of specialized products from a particular area, such as fur, fruit, paper, and hemp cloth. Furthermore, adult males between the ages of 16 to 60, in addition to their required military service, were liable for corvee labor duty and were mobilized without pay for all sorts of construction projects.

Koryŏ had at least some minimal relief programs for the people's welfare. To secure funds for a variety of purposes, the state established a number of *po* (-*bo*), or endowments, which profited from the interest on grain loans: *Hak-po* provided support for students at the national university; *Kwanghak-po* provided funds for Buddhist monks; *Chewi-bo* provided relief for the poor; and *P'algwan-bo* covered expenses for the Buddhist *p'algwan-hoe* festivals. The Buddhist temples and the aristocracy built granaries, called *changsaenggo*, to store their share of the harvest, and then profited by lending grain at a high interest rate. The state developed a social welfare system to address the economic hardship of the peasantry. In addition to Chewi-bo, the state operated several relief organizations for the people. The Tongsŏdaebiwŏn, or East and West Infirmaries, functioned as a national hospital that cared for the sick and needy. The Hyemin'guk, or Dispensary for the People's Benefit, was a public dispensary of free medicine. The *ŭich'ang*, or righteous granaries, a network of state storehouses, stored grain during normal times for relief in years of poor harvests. The *sangp'yŏngch'ang*, or ever normal storehouses, held grain in storage for use in smoothing out price fluctuations.

Handicraft and Commerce

Handicraft manufacturing in the Koryŏ kingdom was mainly performed under the government's aegis, but it was also undertaken on private initiatives. Craftsmen and artisans throughout the country were enrolled by the state in separate rosters and manufactured weaponry, pottery, furniture, gold and silver wares, clothes, and silk. In some cases the state allocated farmland to craftsmen and artisans where they could maintain their livelihood. As tribute payments to the state, the inhabitants of special settlements of so mined gold, silver, copper, and iron or made yarn, cloth, paper, India ink, and tea. In Buddhist temples monks and their slaves produced various kinds of goods, both for sale and self-consumption, as did peasant farmers during the off-season, putting out hemp cloth, silk, ramie cloth, farming appliances, vessels, and straw mats.

In the early period, domestic commerce formed the nucleus of commercial activity. From early times on, markets were established in the larger cities of Kaesŏng, Pyongyang, and Kyŏngju, where there were also shops specializing in books, tea, medicines, and so forth. Peddlers in the countryside engaged in itinerant trades in small-scale markets.

Later, Koryŏ actively engaged in international commerce with neighboring Song China, Qidan Liao, Japan, and even the Saracens. Pyŏngnando, at the estuary of the Yesŏng River, flourished both as the port for Kaesŏng and for international trade. It was with Song China that Koryŏ carried on its most active trade. Through the visits of official envoys and the travels of private merchants, Koryŏ exported such items as paper, India ink, ginseng, and straw mats and, in return, imported products such as silk, books, porcelain, and medicines. Arab merchants entered Pyŏngnando, bringing goods like mercury, spices, ivory, and medicines. These Arabians introduced Koryŏ to the West as "Korea."

The development of commerce led to a need for currency. At first, both grain and cloth were used in commercial activity. Koryŏ developed the necessary metallurgy skills and scientific technology to mint coins displaying names on their faces. The first metal coins, *Kŏnwŏn chungbo*, or Heavy Treasure of Kŏnwŏn (era name), were minted in 996 and were made of iron. Then, in 1102, copper coins, called *Haedong t'ongbo,* or Circulating Treasure East of the Sea, were produced. At about the same time silver coins, called *hwalgu* (*ŭnbyŏng*), or silver jar money, were made in the shape of the Korean peninsula. These silver coins—each weighing 1 *kŭn,* or 600 grams, were widely used among the aristocracy for large-scale transactions. Both grain and cloth, however, were still the currency used by the general population. Despite a remarkable growth in handicraft manufacturing and commerce, a monetary economy was never activated in Koryŏ.

Class Structure

Koryŏ's class system was not as strict as Silla's bone-rank institution, which conferred a variety of special privileges exclusively on the true-born aristocracy who lived in the capital of Kyŏngju and monopolized the state's economic wealth and political power. In Koryŏ, however, schools and government jobs were open to the yangin class, which included everyone except slaves and inhabitants of the special settlements of hyang, so, and pugok. Intermarriage between commoners and slaves was prohibited. Although commoners were all legally freeborn, even they were never on an equal standing but were divided into several classes. By the beginning of the twelfth century the Koryŏ's class division was well established, with roughly four classes—upper, middle, lower, and humble.

The upper class comprised the ruling aristocracy. The governing elite in the earlier Koryŏ period largely consisted of Silla's head rank 6 aristocrats, those of the local gentry from the area around the capital of Kaesŏng, and Wang Kŏn's merit subjects and their heirs. Those of head rank 6 lineage greatly contributed to the reordering of Koryŏ's political and social structure, in which they consolidated their position as the new ruling aristocracy. The members of the local gentry in the districts around Kaesŏng, along with the merit subjects of T'aejo, ultimately emerged as central government officials in the new state. These new ruling elites from many different clans comprised the Koryŏ aristocracy.

Koryŏ society attached great importance to lineage and, indeed, the extended family system in the kingdom was even stronger than in China. Aristocratic clans adopted the areas from which their ancestors had originated as their *pon'gwan,* or clan seat, and therefore the pon'gwan represented aristocratic power and privilege. The state, as discussed above, sometimes bestowed family names on the merit subjects. It also allowed some families to use surnames that had long been in use and then to adopt the places where they had long lived as their pon'gwan. Other families adopted Chinese surnames as their own. Thus most of contemporary Korean family names date back to the Koryŏ period.

Because social status was inherited, few people could exceed their inherited social position. The state adopted a number of measures to ensure the inheritance of social status, establishing, for example, the ŭmsŏ and kongŭm-jŏn institutions, discussed above. Local functionaries and professional soldiers also passed on their occupations to their descendants. This inheritance of social status led to the emergence of several clans of famous lineage.

Aristocratic families consolidated their privileges and political power through marriage. The most prominent aristocrats, in particular, strove to win places for their daughters as the kings' consorts. Successful unions with the royal house enabled them, as royal in-laws, to monopolize the highest government posts and obtain more land. Such clans as the Ansan Kim and the Inju (Inch'ŏn) Yi families are prime examples. The Ansan Kim clan monopolized power under four kings, for more than 50 years, from the time Kim Ŭn-bu presented his three daughters as queens to Hyŏnjong (1009–1031) down to Munjong's reign (1046–1083), when the Inju Yi clan took over the monopoly of political power by marrying Yi Cha-yŏn's three daughters to King Munjong. The Inju Yi family continued its domination for more than 80 years, until the reign of Injong (1122–1146). Its power was so strong that Yi Cha-gyŏm, a grandson of Yi Cha-yŏn, even dreamed of the Inju Yi clan founding a new dynasty. Other famous lineages of this time, which came into repute not by becoming the monarch's in-laws but by scholarly attainments, included Ch'oe Ch'ung's Haeju Ch'oe clan, Yun Kwan's P'ap'yŏng Yun clan, and Kim Pu-sik's Kyŏngju Kim clan.

In Koryŏ, the aristocratic elite monopolized political power and economic wealth and made class position hereditary. Aristocrats, especially from famous lineages, were mostly concentrated in the capital in central government positions. Higher-level officials took posts in local administration only rarely and with reluctance. Returning to their former places of origin in the countryside was regarded as a bitter experience. They were forced to do so only if they were found guilty of official misconduct. Banishment from the court was considered one of the severest punishments for an aristocrat in the capital. Later the term *kwihyang*, or return to the rural life, evolved into *kwiyang*, or banishment to remote regions as a penalty for criminal activity.

The hereditary aristocracy was divided into the *mun-ban,* or civil official order, and the *mu-ban,* or military official order. Both were known as yangban, with the former filling civil offices and the latter filling military offices. Although they contributed to the security of the kingdom, military officers were left far behind in social standing within the ruling class.

Below the upper class, the middle class was primarily lower-government officials and their descendants. Called the *nam-ban,* or southern order, those in the court functionary sector filled various court service offices, and those in the *kun-ban,* or soldiering order, filled the military units. Specialists selected by the chap-ŏp examinations filled offices demanding technical knowledge. The functionary force in the countryside, called *hyangni,* meaning local officials, also belonged to this middle class.

The lower class, the foundation of Koryŏ society, was the most numerous and consisted of common people such as peasants, merchants, and artisans. The peasantry formed the majority of the population. Anyone without a fixed role in the service of the state, including military service, was commonly called paekchŏng. Thus its meaning in Koryŏ was quite different from that in Chosŏn, where it referred to butchers and wicker workers. Because they had no fixed role, they were ineligible to receive a land allotment from the state. The social standing of merchants and artisans was generally lower than that of peasants.

Below the common people were those living in special administrative districts such as hyang, so, pugok, *chang, ch'ŏ, chin, yŏk,* and *kwan.* Among them, inhabitants of the hyang, pugok, chang, and ch'ŏ settlements were assigned to farm labor, whereas the so residents engaged in handicraft manufacturing or mining. At important overland and sea routes throughout the country Koryŏ established many yŏk, or post stations; chin, or ferries; and kwan, or hostelries. Anyone working in these transportation establishments was regarded with contempt. Another lowly despised status included the *ŏ-gan,* or fishermen; the *yŏm-gan,* or salt makers; the *mokcha-gan,* or shepherds; the *ch'ŏl-gan,* or miners; and the *ponghwa-gan,* or men of signal fire. At the time the term *nom,* or bastards, was synonymous with *gan* and *ch'ŏk.*

The *nobi,* or slaves, constituted the absolutely lowest stratum of Koryŏ society. The term *no* meant male slaves, and the term *pi (bi)* meant female slaves. Slaves inherited their status and could be bought or sold. There were government slaves who belonged to the state and private slaves owned by individuals. Temple slaves were owned by Buddhist monasteries. Government slaves performed miscellaneous duties in the palace and government offices. Otherwise, they did farm work and paid their harvest as rent to the government. Government slaves were freed from all duties when they reached the age of 60. Private slaves were owned by members of the royal household and the aristocracy, and mainly worked at household chores. Private slaves included nonresident slaves who cultivated their masters' farmland and paid rent, but some owned their own property. There were also outcast groups such as *hwach'ŏk*, or butchers; *chein*, or clowns; *yangsuch'ŏk*, or wicker workers; and *kisaeng*, or female entertainers, many of whom were of Qidan and Nuzhen stock. Because their occupations were deemed contemptible, they were treated socially as slaves.

All these class positions were inherited, although some significant changes, such as upward mobility to a higher status, often occurred. Although this class structure provided stability to Koryŏ society, its underlying unfairness, where, except in rare cases, personal talents were totally ignored, frustrated people and made them dissatisfied with their society.

FOREIGN RELATIONS IN THE EARLY KORYŏ PERIOD

The First War with Liao

Qidans of Mongolian stock established their country, Liao, in the upper reaches of the Liao River in 907 and later moved eastward to destroy Parhae in 926. Qidans even invaded northern China, occupying the so-called Yanyun Districts, including present-day Beijing, in 936, and calling their country Liao in 946. In 960 the Song empire was established in China proper, bringing an end, in 979, to the turbulent period of Five Dynasties and Ten Kingdoms. Qidan Liao and Song China competed keenly for supremacy over northern China.

After Qidans destroyed Parhae and now shared a common border with Koryŏ, they attempted to make peace with Koryŏ. Confronted by Song China, Qidans tried to prevent Koryŏ from harassing the rear. In 942 they sent more than 30 envoys and 50 camels to Koryŏ. T'aejo, however, refused the gift, as he regarded Qidans as an immoral people who renounced an alliance with Parhae and ruined it "overnight." In his *Hunyo sipcho*, T'aejo described Qidan Liao as a "state of brutes." He banished the envoys to an island and starved the camels to death under the Manbu-gyo bridge in Kaesŏng. At the same time he welcomed refugees from Parhae and sought to recover the former territory of the Koguryŏ kingdom. Thus, in his time, Koryŏ's northern boundary expanded to the Ch'ŏngch'ŏn River. Koryŏ also pursued a pro-Song policy after the Chinese empire was founded. T'aejo's successors continued his anti-Qidan policy. To

prepare for an eventual conflict with Qidans, King Chŏngjong organized and
trained some 300,000 troops, called the *Kwang-gun,* or Resplendent Army, as
a reserve force in 947. To defend against Qidans, Kwangjong built fortresses
along the northwestern frontiers.

As expected, Qidan Liao sought to counter regional isolation by invading
Koryŏ in 993. At the time the kingdom of Chŏngan (Dingan in Chinese) was
founded by some Parhae refugees along the middle reaches of the Yalu River
and, using Nuzhen (Jurchen) envoys, communicated with Song to launch a
pincer attack on Liao. Feeling insecure, Liao destroyed the Chŏngan kingdom
in 980 and built a fort at Naewŏn-sŏng (fortress) in the lower reaches of the
Yalu River, severing communications between Song and Nuzhens. Then, in
993, to prevent Koryŏ from forging a military alliance with Song, Liao sent a
large-scale invasion force, said to have been some 800,000-strong, across the
Yalu River under the command of Xiao Xunning. Koryŏ checked the advance
of the Liao forces at the Ch'ŏngch'ŏn River and resolved the crisis through the
diplomatic maneuvers of Sŏ Hŭi. Sŏ Hŭi not only managed to persuade Liao
forces to voluntarily withdraw but, with Liao's approval, incorporated the area
up to the Yalu River into Koryŏ territory. In his negotiations with Qidans, Sŏ
Hŭi stressed that Koryŏ was the successor to Koguryŏ, which had occupied
the Manchurian territories. He promised that Koryŏ would enter into friendly
relations with Liao once the Nuzhen lands south of the Yalu had come into
Koryŏ's possession, opening a land link between Koryŏ and Liao. Koryŏ also
agreed to end its ties with Song China. Because at the time Liao was entrenched
in an armed struggle with Song China, it was forced to be satisfied with Koryŏ's
promise. Thus, without a single battle, Koryŏ triumphed over Liao by taking
advantage of the contemporary international situation.

The Second and Third Wars with Liao

After the Qidan army withdrew, Koryŏ continued to communicate with Song
and strengthened its position by building fortresses in the area southeast of the
Yalu against any future Liao raids. The newly constructed fortresses were known
as *Kangdong yuk chu,* or Six Garrison Settlements East of the River, which referred to garrison forts at Hŭnghwajin (present-day Ŭiju), Yongju (present-day
Yongch'ŏn), T'ongju (present-day Sŏnch'ŏn), Ch'ŏlchu (present-day Ch'ŏlsan),
Kwiju (present-day Kwisŏng), and Kwakchu (present-day Kwaksan). All these
places are now located in North Korea's North P'yongan province. Meanwhile,
Liao enlarged its territory and became a mighty empire in control of northern

China north of the Yellow River, most of Mongolia, and almost all of Manchuria. Liao was dissatisfied, however, that Koryŏ controlled the region between the Ch'ŏngch'ŏn and Yalu rivers and demanded that Koryŏ turn over the Six Garrison Settlements. Koryŏ flatly rejected Liao's demand.

At this perilous moment, political turbulence in the Koryŏ court gave Liao the pretext for its second invasion. In 1009, under King Mokchong (997–1009), one of the king's in-laws, Kim Ch'i-ryang, staged a coup to enthrone his own son. But Kang Cho, the commander of the northwestern frontier region, deposed and killed Mokchong, purged the Kim Ch'i-ryang faction from the court, and enthroned Hyŏnjong (1009–1031). Under the pretext of accusing the subject Kang Cho of killing King Mokchong, the Liao emperor Shengzong personally led 400,000 troops across the Yalu and invaded the Koryŏ territory in 1010. Hyŏnjong gave a 300,000-strong army to Kang Cho to defend the country, but Kang Cho underestimated the enemy's strength and was defeated in battle and captured. To the end he refused to vow allegiance to the Liao emperor and died a heroic death. Liao troops occupied Kaesŏng and burned it to the ground in 1011. Hyŏnjong was forced to flee south all the way to Naju. Koryŏ suffered initial losses but won other battles. Unable to establish a foothold and fearing a counterattack, Liao forces withdrew without gaining any particular advantage but did stipulate that the Koryŏ king should pay homage in person at the Liao court. This was not a commitment that Koryŏ would honor, and thus Hyŏnjong did not personally appear at the Liao court.

In 1018 Liao invaded Koryŏ for the third time. This was a major invasion that followed several small-scale attacks to press demands for Hyŏnjong's presence at its court and the surrender of the Six Garrison Settlements region. Led by Xiao Paiya, this time the Liao army of 100,000, while marching into the Koryŏ capital, was defeated by Koryŏ forces at Hŭnghwajin and Chaju. The retreating Liao forces, having failed to take the capital, were routed at Yŏnju and Wiju in the Ch'ŏngch'ŏn river basin by massive Koryŏ attacks led by Kang Kamch'an. Finally, the Koryŏ forces almost annihilated the Liao army at Kwiju. Only a few thousand escaped alive. After this crushing defeat, Liao never again violated Koryŏ territory. It also withdrew its demand that the Koryŏ king personally appear at the Liao court and that Koryŏ surrender the Six Garrison Settlements.

In addition to Koryŏ resolutely resisting Liao's three massive invasions and driving back the invaders, Koryŏ also succeeded in recovering part of old Koguryŏ territory. After its defeat in the war against Koryŏ, Liao also failed to conquer the Song. Thus, in East Asia, the balance of power remained with Koryŏ, Liao, and Song. In the course of the Liao invasions, tens of thousands of Qidans were taken prisoner or surrendered to Koryŏ. Constituting the majority of Koryŏ's chein and kisaeng, they formed their own villages and made a livelihood by various means.

Relations with Song China

Koryŏ's resounding victory over the powerfully militant Liao was a great boost to its national prestige among neighboring countries. For about 100 years or so, between the early eleventh and early twelfth centuries, Koryŏ enjoyed a golden age marked by thriving commercial, intellectual, and artistic activities. At the time Song China, which had lost its territory north of the Yellow River to Liao, wanted to forge close ties with Koryŏ. The Song dynasty looked upon Koryŏ as a potential ally against neighboring tribal invaders. On the other hand, Koryŏ sought to gratify its material and cultural desires by maintaining friendly relations with Song. Thus the two countries promoted cultural and economic exchanges. Song did not regard Koryŏ as its tributary state, but it treated the Korean kingdom as an equal partner and extended extraordinarily cordial treatment to Koryŏ's envoys in Song.

Koryŏ's trade relationship with Song was carried on through traveling merchants as well as visiting envoys. Buddhist monks played an important role in cultural exchanges between the two countries, and many Koryŏ monks went to Song to study or preach Buddhism. Overall, Koryŏ's economic and cultural exchanges with Song benefited its own culture. For instance, Song woodblock editions contributed to the development of Koryŏ's woodblock printing, and Song porcelain enhanced the development of Koryŏ's celadon ware.

The main traffic route to Song was the sea lane between Koryŏ's Pyŏngnando at the estuary of the Yesŏng River and China's Hangzhou at the estuary of the Yangtze River. The Shandong peninsula had been occupied by Liao and was no longer an important traffic center.

Koryŏ also carried on small-scale economic exchanges with Qidans, Nuzhens, and the Japanese. Qidans and Nuzhens brought silver, furs, and horses to Koryŏ and in return received grain, stationery, and iron agricultural implements and weapons. The Japanese, a majority of whom came from Tsushima, sent tangerines, pearl, mercury, swords, and horses in return for grain, books, and stationery. Koryŏ had never imported grain, whereas Nuzhens and the Japanese had always suffered food shortages.

Relations with Nuzhen Jin

Koryŏ's military victory over Liao gave the Nuzhen, formerly Malgal, people a chance to regroup and strengthen their power. Thus, for defense against both Qidans and Nuzhens, Koryŏ, from 1033 to 1044, built a wall stretching from the mouth of the Yalu a thousand *li* (about 300 miles) eastward to the East Sea at Toryŏnp'o (present-day Yŏnp'o, South Hamgyŏng province).The Malgal people had been under Koguryŏ and Parhae rule. After Parhae fell to Qidans they called themselves Jins, but the Chinese called them Nuzhens. Koryŏ adopted the Chinese name Nuzhen and called them *Yŏjin*. Nuzhens were scattered into many tribes throughout eastern Manchuria and the northern Korean peninsula. The tribes that inhabited the reaches of the Tumen River looked upon Koryŏ as their "parent country" and as the source of a highly advanced civilization. Koryŏ was the main supplier of their necessities of life, especially grain. The Nuzhen chieftains visited Koryŏ regularly and made annual tributes. Many Nuzhens migrated into the Koryŏ territory. By the early twelfth century more than 4,700 households of Nuzhens had been naturalized in Koryŏ. Koryŏ gave land and dwellings to these naturalized Nuzhens so that they could maintain a livelihood.

In the first half of the twelfth century, however, this harmonious situation rapidly changed when Koryŏ grew troubled by Nuzhens. At the time the Nuzhen people were well organized under the leadership of Wuyashu, the chieftain of the Wanyan tribe in northern Manchuria, and they began to invade Liao territory to the west. As the power of the Wanyan tribe extended to the south, the relationship between Koryŏ and Nuzhens became increasingly strained. Several military clashes resulted in Koryŏ's defeats. Koryŏ's Six Divisions were mostly infantry, who fought against heavy odds in battling the mounted Nuzhens. Under these circumstances, on Yun Kwan's advice, King Sukchong (1095–1105) created a new military force, the Pyŏlmuban, or Extraordinary Military Corps, in 1104. This new force was established in addition to the existing Six Divisions to contend against Nuzhens who were getting stronger by the day. It was organized into a cavalry corps, the Sin'gi-gun, or Divine Cavalry Corps; an infantry, the Sinbo-gun, or Divine Infantry Corps; and the Hangma-gun, or Corps to Subdue Demons. Commanding officers in the Sin'gi-gun and the Sinbo-gun were members of aristocratic families, the rank and file were made up of peasants, and the Hangma-gun corps was composed of Buddhist monks.

In 1107, in the reign of King Yejong (1105–1122), Yun Kwan's Pyŏlmuban army launched a massive attack against Nuzhens. Crossing the thousand-*li* wall at present-day Chŏngp'yŏng, Koryŏ forces occupied the Hamhŭng plain and further advanced to the Tumen River basin. In the occupied area Yun Kwan built the so-called Nine Forts and garrisoned them for defense against Nuzhens. In 1109, however, Koryŏ returned the region of the Nine Forts to Nuzhens, as a result of Nuzhens' unceasing attacks, coupled with Nuzhens' fervent appeals to reclaim their residential areas, and because of jealousy in the Koryŏ court over Yun Kwan's success.

Later Nuzhens produced a great military leader, Aguda, who changed the entire political structure of the East Asian mainland. Aguda, Wuyashu's younger brother, integrated all the Nuzhen tribes under his rule and founded a powerful state. By 1115 he had occupied most of Manchuria and declared his nation Jin. In 1125 Jin destroyed the Qidan Liao dynasty. Jin also captured the Song capital of Kaifeng in 1126 and, in 1127, took the Song emperor and his father prisoners. In that same year the Song empire finally fell. Aguda settled in Zhongdu (present-day Beijing) and made it the capital city of the Jin empire, which now included all of northern China, Mongolia, and Manchuria.

In 1126 Aguda sent an emissary to the Koryŏ court, demanding that Koryŏ enter into a suzerain-subject relationship. Angered Koryŏ officials called it an insolent demand, but they could not stand up to the mighty empire in the north. With hurt pride Koryŏ accepted the new relationship and the high state of tension between the two countries was relieved peacefully. Thereafter Jin never invaded Koryŏ by force.

DEVELOPMENT OF ARISTOCRATIC CULTURE

Confucianism

Confucian scholars of Silla's head rank 6 background, such as Ch'oe Ŏn-wi and Ch'oe Ung, assisted Wang Kŏn in founding his Koryŏ dynasty, and thus Confucianism exercised greater influence in Koryŏ than in Silla. Because Confucian political ideology espoused a centralized kingdom under a powerful monarch, Koryŏ kings greatly encouraged the activities of Confucian scholars and Confucianism gained new adherents among the country's aristocracy and scholars.

Koryŏ enjoyed peace for some 100 years from the early eleventh to the early twelfth centuries, and Confucianism, which championed civil administration, greatly flourished. This period witnessed the emergence of private academies as the principal agencies for the education of aristocratic youth. In Munjong's reign, the great Confucian scholar Ch'oe Ch'ung, known as the *Haedong kongja*, or Confucius East of the Sea (Korea), established a school, Kujae haktang, or Nine-Course Academy, where lectures were given on nine Confucian scriptures and three works of Chinese history. Known as Master Ch'oe's Assembly, it heralded the beginning of the private academies. Soon, 11 other private academies sprang up, and these, together with Ch'oe Ch'ung's Assembly, were known as the Sibi to, or Twelve Assemblies. The sons of aristocratic families deemed it a great honor to attend one of these 12 private academies and attached greater importance to them than to the national academy of Kukchagam.

As private academies flourished, the state schools inevitably declined. Thus several kings attempted to revive the state school system. King Sukchong, who was dedicated to furthering education, created the Sŏjŏkp'o at the Kukchagam to publish a variety of books. In imitation of Ch'oe Ch'ung's Nine-Course Academy, King Yejong set up, at the national academy, lectures in seven specialized fields—the *Book of History,* the *Book of Poetry,* the *Book of Divination,* the *Book of Rites,* the *Spring and Autumn Annals,* the *Rituals of Zhou,* and a new field of military studies. In each area he appointed an outstanding scholar as the lecturer. He also established a scholarship foundation, called the *Yanghyŏn'go,* or Fund for Nurturing Worthies, as well as the Ch'ŏngyŏn-gak (pavilion), Pomun-gak, Ch'ŏnjang-gak, and Imch'ŏn-gak, not only as academic institutes but as libraries at the palace through which he recruited scholars and collected tens of thousands of books. King Injong completed the reconstruction of the government school system by instituting the "six colleges" at the national academy and establishing more local schools.[5] A number of eminent scholars emerged from these revived national institutions including Kim Pu-sik, Kim In-jon, Yun Ŏn-i, Yi In-sil, Yi Chi-jŏ, Pak Sŭng-jung, Chŏng Kŭk-yŏng, Chŏng Hang, and Chŏng Chi-sang. Injong frequently held the *kyŏngyŏn,* or royal teaching, where he discussed Confucian ethics, politics, and history with these Confucian scholars. As Koryŏ improved its school system, both state and private, Confucianism greatly developed in the kingdom.

The development of Confucianism in this period was notably represented by the compilation of the 50-volume *Samguk sagi* by Kim Pu-sik in 1145. The oldest extant Korean history, *Samguk sagi* was an orthodox Confucian work, compiled in the form of annals, chronological tables, treatises, and biographies. The Chinese Song envoy Xu Jing, who came to Koryŏ in 1123, marveled at the high level of Koryŏ education and scholarship. In his 40-volume *Gaoli tujing* (*Koryŏ togyŏng* in Korean), or *The Illustrated Script on Koryŏ*, which appeared in 1124, he recorded his observations of the Korean kingdom and included illustrations.

Buddhism Flourishes

Whereas Confucianism was established as a political philosophy for statecraft, Buddhism developed as a religious doctrine to achieve spiritual tranquility and otherworldly salvation. Buddhism greatly influenced daily life and, in Korea, achieved the height of its influence in the Koryŏ dynasty. The kingdom built many temples and monasteries, and dutifully observed the various, expensive Buddhist ceremonies. Many of the temples were richly endowed with lands, and in some cases built up their own military power to protect their large holdings. Koryŏ also produced woodblock editions of the Tripitaka, the Buddhist canon. As it gained enormous popularity from all social classes, Buddhism became, in effect, the state religion.

T'aejo, in his *Hunyo sipcho*, stressed that the success of his dynasty depended on the Buddha's protection. He and his successors ardently patronized Buddhism, emphasizing the Buddha's protective powers, and he built many temples including Pŏpwang-sa, Wangnyun-sa, and Hŭngguk-sa. The Hŭngwang-sa temple was extraordinarily large. Established near Kaesŏng in the reign of King Munjong, it had more than 2,800 *kan*, or floor space, and was completed after 12 years of construction, in 1067. It was the most well-known temple where the Koryŏ people prayed for the well-being of the state. In this period there were 70 temples in Kaesŏng alone.

A variety of state Buddhist festivals were dutifully observed in Koryŏ. The most important were the *yŏndŭng-hoe*, held on the 15th day of the first lunar month, and the p'algwan-hoe, held on the 15th day of the 11th lunar month. The yŏndŭng-hoe was performed as a purely Buddhist event, but the p'algwan-hoe combined Buddhist rites with Korea's indigenous practices. Whereas the former was held throughout the country, the latter was observed only in Kaesŏng and Pyongyang. In both festivals the king and officialdom lit up the night with candlelight and presented performances of music, dance, and other entertainments in order to entreat the many Buddhas, the spirits of heaven and earth, and national heroes who sacrificed themselves for the kingdom to bring tranquility to the nation and to the royal house. T'aejo had greatly emphasized these two festivals in his *Hunyo sipcho*. In addition to these two large festivals, there were many other annual Buddhist ceremonies, and the Koryŏ kingdom incurred enormous expenses for these Buddhist festivals that later were criticized by Neo-Confucian scholars.

To improve the quality of monks and select the best persons as monks, Koryŏ established the *sŭng-kwa*, or monk examination, modeled on the civil service examination. Divided into two sections, one was for monks of the *Kyojong*, or Textual School, and the other for Sŏn, or Meditation, monks. Those who passed the examination received graded cleric ranks. The highest rank for a Textual School monk was *sŭngt'ong*, or patriarch monk, and for a Sŏn monk, it was *taesŏnsa*, or great Sŏn mentor. Higher than these were the titles of *wangsa*, or royal preceptor, and *kuksa*, or national preceptor. Holders of these titles were advisers to the king and the royal household.

In return for their service, temples and monks received various favors from the state. Temples received land allocations, called sawŏn-jŏn, and monks were exempt from taxes, tributes, and corvee labor duties, which resulted in increased numbers of monks. Temples expanded their landholdings by different means, especially through donations from the royal household and the aristocracy. They conducted money-lending businesses, lending grain at high interest, and produced much wealth for themselves. By actively engaging in commerce and handicraft manufacturing, they exerted significant influence on the national economy. Temples essentially acted as the corporate conglomerates of the day.

To protect their growing wealth, temples organized monks into private armies. When the nation was in crisis, armed monks fought for their country, and when the Pyŏlmuban army was established for a massive attack on Nuzhens in 1104, the Hangman-gun corps was comprised of monk soldiers. These monk forces also engaged in power struggles within the aristocracy.

Koryŏ Buddhism systematized the Tripitaka by publishing the Chinese translations as mammoth wooden-block print editions. Koryŏ undertook major projects to publish Buddhist scriptures so as to elicit Buddha's help in the national crisis. Begun in 1011, the first set, originally undertaken as a prayer to repel the Qidan invasions, was completed in 1087. The printing of the Tripitaka was also intended to display the superiority of Koryŏ culture by systematizing the doctrines of the Buddhist canon. The 6,000-volume woodblocks were stored at the Puin-sa temple in Taegu, but were destroyed during the Mongol invasion in 1232. The second set of 81,137 woodblocks, completed in 1251, is preserved today at the Haein-sa temple, located at Hapch'ŏn. A UNESCO Memory of the World, it has been praised for its accuracy, containing not one misspelled word or missing letter, and for the perfection of its contents. One of the oldest extant woodblock editions of the Tripitaka originating in East Asia, it describes the contents of the woodblocks produced in Song China or Qidan Liao that no longer exist. Meanwhile, feeling the need to supplement the first Tripitaka, the monk Ŭich'ŏn, the fourth son of King Munjong, established the Kyojang togam, or Directorate for Buddhist Scriptures, at the Hŭngwang-sa temple in 1086. The same year he collected treatises and commentaries found in Song, Liao, and Japan, as well as in Koryŏ, and began to publish the *Sok changkyŏng,* or Supplement to the Tripitaka. The *Sok changgyŏng* was completed in 1096 and stored, together with the first woodblock edition, at the Puin-sa temple. It also perished in the 1232 Mongol invasion. The *Sok changgyŏng,* a set of 4,760-odd woodblocks, became the parent of the extant 81,137 woodblock edition, preserved at the Haein-sa temple. Ŭich'ŏn also compiled the voluminous Buddhist works as the three-volume *Sinp'yŏn chejong kyojang ch'ongnok,* or New Catalogue of Buddhist Sectarian Writings, in 1090. Although he compiled the *Sok changgyŏng* as a complete collection of Buddhist scriptures, it did not include Sŏn-related works but systematized the doctrines of the Kyo school.

As members of the local gentry came into power in Koryŏ, their Buddhism, the Sŏn school, exercised power. The monarchs, on the other hand, seeking a powerful, centralized government, preferred the established Kyo school. Thus, in Koryŏ, both the Sŏn and Kyo schools prospered but at the same time stood in conflict with each other. Attempting to unify the two schools, Ŭich'ŏn studied the *Ch'ŏntae* (Tiantai in Chinese) doctrine in China, and, upon returning to Koryŏ in 1086, established the Ch'ŏnt'ae sect as an independent denomination that embraced both the Sŏn and Kyo schools. Because his new denomination favored the Kyo sect, however, he ultimately failed to unify the two schools. Instead, his efforts led the Sŏn sect to become more cohesive, and this allowed it to later evolve into the *Chogye* sect. This new Buddhist sect then proceeded to absorb the Kyo school.

Buddhism not only controlled the spiritual life of the Koryŏ people but had absolute power over their mundane lives. With unreserved support from the royal household and the aristocracy, Koryŏ Buddhism inspired the flowering of Buddhist arts and architecture, including the Tripitaka Koreana. But the great power and influence of Buddhism was attended by many evils, including corruption.

Literature and Fine Arts

When the civil service examination, particularly the chesul-ŏp, appeared in 958, literature written in Chinese flourished. In the reign of King Sŏngjong, the so-called *Munsin wŏlgwa pŏp*, or Monthly Composition Exercise for Civil Officials, required civil officials to compose poems monthly on themes set by the king. Also, under the practice of the *Kakch'okbusi*, or Notched Candle Poetics, Confucian students in schools competed in writing poetry. Thus learning Chinese literature, poetry in particular, became essential to the education of aristocratic youth. As a result, Koryŏ produced a number of distinguished poets including Pak In-nyang, Kim Hwang-wŏn, Chŏng Sŭm-myŏng, Chŏng Chi-sang, and Kim Pu-sik. Koryŏ, as a whole, was influenced by Tang poetry and Song prose.

In the early Koryŏ period the Silla hyangga tradition remained vital. But only the works of the tenth-century monk Kyunyŏ, the 11 poems of *Pohyŏn sipwŏn ka*, or Ten Vows of Samantabhadra, still exist today. Thereafter, although hyangga poems were steadily composed for a time, the traditional Korean literary genre was gradually replaced by Chinese poems and ultimately disappeared.

Koryŏ's fine arts were represented by craftworks that mainly ended up in the royal house and Buddhist temples in Silla, but they were widely used as utensils in the homes of the aristocracy in Koryŏ. Celadon ware best exemplifies Koryŏ's highly superior crafts. Inheriting the tradition of unified Silla and Parhae pottery, Koryŏ artisans produced an imposing array of ceramic pieces known as Koryŏ porcelain. Although Koryŏ porcelain developed under the influence of Song celadon, by the eleventh century it had attained full maturity in the diversity of its shapes, its skillful decorations, and its elegant colors. Even the Song people praised it as the world's finest ceramic art.

Koryŏ's porcelain was used not only as daily utensils in aristocratic homes but also in Buddhist temple ceremonies. The porcelain appeared in widely varied shapes including jars, flasks, teapots, plates, cups, wine pitchers, water droppers (to mix India ink), brush holders, incense burners, and flower vases. These were usually fashioned after the shapes of plants or animals including chrysanthemums, lotus flowers, pomegranates, bamboo shoots, melons, parrots, mandarin ducks, the phoenix, rabbits, monkeys, turtles, dragons, lions, and fish. The plants represented fecundity, richness, and fidelity, and the animals symbolized longevity, majesty, and love between husband and wife. Another outstanding feature of Koryŏ celadon ware was the beautiful decorations on their surfaces. Initially the designs were either incised or carved in relief, but beginning in the twelfth century the technique of *sanggam,* or inlay, appeared. The sanggam method, in which intricate designs were carved into the surface of the celadon ware and other materials added to the forms, was a distinctive technique found only in Koryŏ porcelain. The design motifs employed combinations of animals and plants symbolizing longevity, richness, and nobility including cranes with clouds, waterfowls with willows, peonies, chrysanthemums, melons, pomegranates, gourds, grapes, lotus flowers, and arabesque scrolls. The excellence of Koryŏ porcelain is also seen in its beautiful colors. Many were done in jade green and are known as *ch'ŏngja,* or jade green ceramic. Other beautiful pieces are in yellow-green, yellow-brown, white, or black. Koryŏ celadon ware was a poetic embodiment of the refined aristocratic culture of the day and the longing of the Koryŏ aristocracy for the ideal world of Taoism and Buddhism. The best-known places of production of Koryŏ porcelain included present-day Kangjin in South Chŏlla province and present-day Puan in North Chŏlla province.

In addition to porcelain, many items fashioned of bronze, most notably Buddhist bells, incense burners with silver inlay, ritual ewers, candelabra, and mirrors, are also among Koryŏ's beautiful craftworks. Regrettably, most of these have flowed from Korea to foreign countries, particularly to Japan, and only a few remain in Korea. The stone memorial stupas also demonstrate the elaborate and delicate workmanship of Koryŏ artisans. Representative specimens include the Silsang-t'ap, erected in 1017 for the National Preceptor Hongpŏp at the Chŏngt'o-sa temple located in present-day Ch'ungju; the Hyejin-t'ap, built in 975 for the National Preceptor Wŏnjong at the Kodal-sa temple located in present-day Yŏju, Kyŏnggi province; and the Hyŏnmyo-t'ap, constructed in 1085 for the National Preceptor Chigwang at the Pŏpch'ŏn-sa temple located in present-day Wŏnju, Kangwŏn province.

As Koryŏ's structures and sculptures became larger, their workmanship became clumsy. The pagodas of the early Koryŏ period, for example, followed the unified Silla style, but they generally deteriorated in terms of their beauty and balance. Later, influenced by Song China, Koryŏ's pagodas became distinctive by taking on a soft look, with round, hexagonal, or octagonal shapes rather than the sharp, straight lines of the unified Silla pagodas. Some of the Buddhist statuary were masterpieces, but Koryŏ sculptures had generally inferior beauty and balance compared to those of unified Silla.

As Buddhist structures and sculptures degenerated rapidly, more secular arts took their place. Landscape painting flourished under Chinese Song and Yuan influences, but few authentic works remain from this period. Yi Nyŏng was a renowned master painter who drew *Yesŏng-gang to*, or the Yesŏng River Scene, and *Ch'ŏnsu-sa nammun to*, or Painting of the Southern Gate of the Ch'ŏnsu-sa Temple. He was invited by the Song emperor Huitzong to visit China. Yi Kwang-p'il, Yi Nyŏng's son, was also a famous painter. But no works of these two artists have survived. As Chinese literature developed in Koryŏ, the quality of calligraphy was greatly improved. Yu Sin, the monk T'anyŏn, and Ch'oe U were the best known calligraphers, and, along with Silla's Kim Saeng, they have been called *Sinp'um sa hyŏn*, or the Four Worthies of Divine Calligraphy. In sum, at this time Koryŏ's highly advanced culture was represented by masterly ceramic art, which even the Chinese admired.

Historiography

In its early period Koryŏ compiled *Samguk sa*, or History of the Three Kingdoms, which is said to have seen Korean history as originating in Old Chosŏn, succeeded by Koguryŏ and then by Koryŏ. In the reign of King Hyŏnjong (1009–1031), the kingdom compiled the *sillok*, or official annals, for the first seven kings of the dynasty. Today, however, none of these survives.

Samguk sagi, the oldest extant history, was compiled by the politician-historian Kim Pu-sik at the command of King Injong in 1145. Modeled on Sima Qian's *Shiji*, it consists of annals containing records of events in the reigns of the main lines of the Three Kingdoms' rulers; tables outlining the chronology of the period; treatises on subjects of interest to the government such as rituals, geography, government offices, astronomy, music, law, and economic matters; and biographies of prominent individuals such as generals, government officials, patriotic martyrs, scholars, artists, rebels, and national traitors. An official history of the Three Kingdoms, *Samguk sagi* was compiled on the basis of native sources as well as Chinese histories. It described Silla as the first state of the Three Kingdoms to be founded and saw its people as the most patriotic and moralistic. Thus it stressed that Koryŏ should become the successor to Silla which had had a long history and time-honored traditions. *Samguk sagi* criticized Koguryŏ for having been warlike and Paekche for having been devious, and deleted the history of Old Chosŏn and the three Han (Mahan, Chinhan, and Pyŏnhan) federations as they were considered to be closely related to Koguryŏ and Paekche. Upholding governance based on Confucian moral virtues, *Samguk sagi* negatively depicted the Buddhist culture and primitive religions of the Three Kingdoms period and thus laid the foundation for the Confucian view of history. *Samguk sagi* reflected the political intentions of the contemporary ruling elite who sought to preserve a government led by civil officials that had peaked in the mid-Koryŏ period by fostering Confucian morality and to maintain the status quo in international relations by promoting the idea that Koryŏ succeeded Silla and thus sternly opposed the policy of northward expansion.

From start to finish, Koryŏ was an aristocratic state. Domestically, by inheriting and integrating the advanced cultures of the preceding dynasties of unified Silla and Parhae, Koryŏ developed a brilliant aristocratic culture. Externally, the Koryŏ kingdom won the war with Qidan Liao and thereby preserved its national identity as one of the most highly developed and powerful nations in all of Korea's history.

5

THE SECOND HALF OF THE KORYŎ PERIOD

(1170–1392)

DISTURBANCES IN KORYŎ SOCIETY

The Revolts of Yi Cha-gyŏm and Myoch'ŏng

IN THE TWELFTH CENTURY, some 200 years after Koryŏ's founding, conditions in the kingdom began rapidly to deteriorate, an apparent outcome of the dynastic cycle. The cycle was an inevitable result of the periodic weakening of royal authority, the corruption of officials, rivalry between court factions, the growth of tax-exempt aristocratic landholdings, and indifference to the problems of the masses. Beginning in the mid-twelfth century several rebellions erupted, and Koryŏ society entered a period of rebellions that spanned more than 150 years.

As a small minority of renowned aristocratic lineages in the capital monopolized wealth and power, Koryŏ's officialdom began to split and develop internal power struggles, starting with the reign of King Injong (1122–1146). The long period of domestic tranquility was first broken by the treason of Yi Cha-gyŏm. In the period of Injong, the Inju Yi clan emerged as the most powerful aristocratic family. Meanwhile, the Koryŏ kings frequently married their own close relatives to consolidate the ruling family. At the time they increased the number of intermarriages with the Inju Yi clan, increasing the number of in-law connections to gain power. Yi Cha-yŏn had already married off his three daughters to King Munjong (1046–1083). Then Yi Cha-gyŏm, a grandson of Yi Cha-yŏn, elevated his Inju Yi family to the pinnacle of its power. He had given a daughter as queen to King Yejong (1105–1122), and the son of that union ascended the throne as King Injong in 1122. He gave two daughters to Injong as his consorts and, through this duplicated in-law connection, monopolized power completely. At 14 years of age Injong acceded to the throne, and thus, as both the king's father-in-law and grandfather-in-law, Yi Cha-gyŏm held real political power. Supported by the military officer Ch'ŏk Chun-gyŏng, Yi also assumed military power and wielded more authority than the king himself. It is said that he trafficked in government positions, and that meat, amounting to tens of thousands of pounds, which was offered as bribes, grew rotten at his house. Yi and his faction enlarged their personal landholdings and property by seizing real estate from others, thereby also achieving a dominant economic position.

As the kingdom was by now exhausted, a popular prophecy among the populace was that a man of the *sipp'al cha,* or eighteen child, an anagram on the character for the surname Yi, would become king and the transfer of the capital to Namgyŏng (Seoul) would lead to the nation's prosperity. Because his family name was Yi and the place of his family origin was Inch'ŏn, close to Seoul, Yi Cha-gyŏm believed that the prophecy was accurate, and he hoped to usurp the throne. Scenting Yi's plot, Injong laid plans with officials close to him, such as Kim Ch'an and An Po-rin, to oust Yi from power. The king's scheme was foiled, however, by the prompt military response of Yi's henchman, Ch'ŏk Chun-gyŏng. In 1126 Yi Cha-gyŏm burned down the palace, scorching tens of thousands of books in the royal library and the national academy, and confined Injong at his house while those close to the king were all put to death. Yi then attempted to poison the monarch, but at this point he himself was driven out by the opportunistic Ch'ŏk Chun-gyŏng, who now sided with the king, and was banished to what is present-day Yŏnggwang, South Chŏlla province. To remove Yi Cha-gyŏm from power, Injong won support from officials of Pyong-yang origin, such as Chŏng Chi-sang. The power of the Inju Yi clan that had spanned more than 80 years fell apart. Later Yi Cha-gyŏm was put to death, and Ch'ŏk Chun-gyŏng, who was accused of a misdemeanor by Chŏng Chi-sang, was purged. Landholdings and property that Yi Cha-gyŏm and his faction had seized from others were restored to their former owners.

Yi Cha-gyŏm's treason revealed the weakness of royal authority and the power potential of the high aristocracy. Thus, in 1127, after the grave crisis had been overcome, Injong initiated political reform that would restore kingly authority by issuing a 15-point decree. This was also a time of tribulation in foreign relations. In 1126 the Nuzhen Jin empire sent an envoy, demanding that Koryŏ acknowledge Jin's suzerainty. At this point, some officials of Pyongyang origin, including Paek Su-han, Chŏng Chi-sang, and the monk Myoch'ŏng, tried to take advantage of the troubled situation to seize the reins of power.

Not satisfied with Injong's political reform, the "Pyongyang faction," Myoch'ŏng in particular, urged the king to move the capital to Pyongyang. At the time Myoch'ŏng had become extremely popular among the masses as an expert on geomancy. To achieve his goal, Myoch'ŏng used geomantic theories, claiming that Kaesŏng's topography was depleted of virtue whereas Pyongyang's was filled with vigor, and that moving the capital to Pyongyang would reinvigorate Koryŏ; the result would be that 36 states, including Jin, would pay homage to Koryŏ. Myoch'ŏng and his supporters further proposed that Injong declare himself emperor, secure an equal standing with the Song and Jin empires by instituting his own era name, and launch an attack on the arrogant Jin. Injong aligned himself with Myoch'ŏng for a time and constructed a palace, called *Taehwagung*, or Great Flowering Palace, in Pyongyang, which was completed in 1129.

Because moving the capital to Pyongyang meant that the Pyongyang faction would seize power, the "Kaesŏng faction," represented by Kim Pu-sik, now holding the reins of government, stubbornly opposed the transfer, denouncing it as an unrealistic, superstitious act. When Myoch'ŏng was unable to sway the king to his side in the face of mounting opposition from the "Kaesŏng faction," he and his supporters, including Cho Kwang, rose up in rebellion in 1135. Myoch'ŏng went so far as to name his short-lived state *Taewi*, meaning Great Accomplishment. At first the rebels, led by Myoch'ŏng and his "Pyongyang faction", were in high spirits, having gained enthusiastic support from people in the northwest region. Soon, however, Myoch'ŏng was assassinated by his own army, and in early 1136 Pyongyang fell to government forces commanded by Kim Pu-sik. Myoch'ŏng's revolt had finally come to an end. Kim Pu-sik's *Samguk sagi,* compiled in 1145, reflected the political intentions of the ruling aristocracy in the capital to establish a stable aristocratic-bureaucratic government and prevent another Myoch'ŏng from mounting a new nationalist push.

The Revolt of the Military Officers

Thirty-five years after Myoch'ŏng's rebellion, in 1170, Koryŏ was thrust into the vortex of another rebellion. This time military officers staged a coup d'état to seize power. Koryŏ ended the period of the Later Three Kingdoms by military force. In the course of consolidating royal authority, however, the dynasty proceeded to establish the principle of civil supremacy, which resulted in lowering the positions of military officials in government and society. The military had been less favored than the civil officials politically as well as economically, and had been systematically subordinated to their civil counterparts. Even the highest military command posts were given to civil officials. Sŏ Hŭi and Kang Kam-ch'an, the two war heroes who defended Koryŏ from Qidan invasions, were civil officials, and the same was true of Yun Kwan, who subjugated Nuzhens, and of Kim Pu-sik, who suppressed the rebellion of Myoch'ŏng. Military officials could only move up to government positions less than the second rank. Allocations of soldier's land, stipulated by the Chŏnsikwa, did not usually benefit professional soldiers, and the land that had been allocated to these soldiers was often taken from them and reassigned to pay official stipends. A long peace further reduced the status of military officers in Koryŏ society. For some 150 years, from the end of war with Liao in 1019 to the revolt of military officers in 1170, Koryŏ had not experienced any major war disturbances.

In the reign of King Ŭijong (1146–1170), the mistreatment of military officials reached a climax. Ŭijong, a monarch who enjoyed a carefree life, built a number of royal villas, pavilions, and temples in and around the capital, and indulged in a hedonistic lifestyle, exhausting the nation's financial resources. Although civil officials who followed the king shared in his pleasures, life was wretched for most military officials, including the highest-ranking officers, the sangjanggun and taejanggun, as they served as mere military escorts to the king and his civil officials. Discontent among the military officials had already reached an explosive point when some of them suffered indignities at the hands of civil officials. In the reign of King Injong, for example, Kim Ton-jung, the son of Kim Pu-sik, incurred the wrath of Chŏng Chung-bu, a high-level military officer, by setting his beard on fire with a candle.

A military revolt finally broke out in 1170. The military officers who escorted King Ŭijong on a royal procession to the Pohyŏn-wŏn temple, outside Kaesŏng, rose up in protest. The proximate spark igniting the riot was the insulting behavior of civil official Han Noe, who slapped Yi So-ŭng, a taejanggun, on the cheek. Under the direction of Chŏng Chung-bu, Yi Ŭi-bang, and Yi Ko, the outraged military officers raised the cry "Death to all who wear the civil official headdress!" and they won an easy victory in their rebellion. The military officers removed Ŭijong and instead enthroned his younger brother, Myŏngjong

(1170–1197). Ŭijong was banished to Kŏje-do off Pusan, and the offending Kim Ton-jung and Han Noe, as well as countless other civil officials, were massacred. Another ruthless purge of civil officials followed in 1173, when Kim Po-dang failed in his attempt to restore Ŭijong to the throne. After Kim Po-dang was captured and executed, Ŭijong was killed by military officer Yi Ŭi-min in 1173. The next year Cho Wi-ch'ong, commander of the Pyongyang garrison, raised an army at the secondary capital to oust military officers in Kaesŏng. When this effort failed, political power was transferred completely from civil officials to military officers. Military rule lasted for 100 years until 1270.

After their successful bid for power, military officials managed state affairs through the Chungbang and monopolized government positions. At the time success in grasping political power depended on the size of each military official's personal military force. Thus military officers made the most of their newly acquired positions and political power to secure financial resources to build their own private military force. As a result, they exploited the country's economic resources more harshly than their civil official predecessors, using their enormous economic wealth to arm family retainers and household slaves. The situation remained unsettled, with power transferred from one military official to another, until Ch'oe Ch'ung-hŏn finally seized power and established a military dictatorship in 1196.

Initially political power was shared by Chŏng Chung-bu, Yi Ŭi-bang, and Yi Ko, the main protagonists in the military revolt, and they made decisions jointly in the Chungbang junta. Soon, however, they developed internal power struggles among themselves. First, Yi Ŭi-bang killed Yi Ko in 1171 and consolidated his power by giving his daughter in marriage to the crown prince, but he in turn was killed by Chŏng Chung-bu's son in 1174. Chŏng remained a dictator until 1179, when he was killed by a young, unsullied officer named Kyŏng Tae-sŭng, who sought to stop the military officers' despotic behavior and thus incurred their hatred. Sensing that his life was in danger, he established a security squad of some 100 handpicked men, calling it the Tobang, or Residence Squad. Before long, however, amid the growing tension, Kyŏng became ill and died at the age of 30 in 1183. After his death Yi Ŭi-min seized power in early 1184. Yi had been in self-exile in his hometown of Kyŏngju, for fear of Kyŏng Tae-sŭng. Originally of ch'ŏnmin status, Yi Ŭi-min's rule was marked by extreme tyranny and corruption, until he was killed by Ch'oe Ch'ung-hŏn in 1196. Ch'oe's ascension marked the end of these decades of disorder and upheaval, and opened a new era of the Ch'oe regime which spanned 62 years (1196–1258).

Dictatorship of the Ch'oe Family

Ch'oe Ch'ung-hŏn, having ruthlessly eliminated his opponents, succeeded in establishing a dictatorship. To consolidate his power, he purged everyone without distinction, including kings, rendering royal authority completely powerless. During his lifetime he deposed two kings, Myŏngjong (1170–1197) and Hŭijong (1204–1211), and enthroned four, Sinjong (1197–1204), Hŭijong (1204–1211), Kangjong (1211–1213), and Kojong (1213–1259). As a result, the monarchy was completely under his control. His power structure was similar to the shogunate system in Japan, and under impotent kings his family held power for four generations and more than 60 years.

To win the people's confidence, Ch'oe Ch'ung-hŏn first crippled the power of Buddhist temples and monasteries. He mobilized armed forces to suppress the armed monks who violently resisted his measures. Against the rampant peasant and slave uprisings he employed a carrot-and-stick policy. While subduing them by military forces, on the one hand, he pacified the lowborn inhabitants of hyang, so, and pugok by freeing many of them and often merging the special administrative units into the regular hyŏn counties. To boost the morale of civil officials who were excluded from political power, he enlisted such men of letters into government service as Yi Kyu-bo and Chin Hwa. In these ways, he firmly established the Ch'oe regime, which was made much stronger by his son, Ch'oe U (also known as Ch'oe I).

The power of the Ch'oe house was based primarily on its own private army. Kyŏng Tae-sŭng's Tobang security squad was the model for Ch'oe Ch'ung-hŏn's similarly named personal armed force, said to have numbered 3,000. In addition to this elite band of warriors on a retainer, Ch'oe U established the Ya-byŏlch'o, or Night Elite Patrols, as a police force. As its numbers grew, the Ya-byŏlch'o was divided into two units and reorganized as the Chwa-byŏlch'o, or Left Elite Patrols, and the U-byŏlch'o, or Right Elite Patrols. Ch'oe U also formed another military unit, Sinŭi-gun, or Divine Righteousness Army, with soldiers who had escaped after being captured in the war with Mongols. Together these three came to be known as the Sam-byŏlch'o, or Three Elite Patrols. Although in form the Sam-byŏlch'o appeared to function as a police and combat force, in reality it was just another private army to provide further military support to the Ch'oe regime.

To rule the nation more effectively, the Ch'oe house established new control mechanisms. Ch'oe Ch'ung-hŏn exercised his dictatorial power through an ad-

ministrative body called the Kyojŏng togam, or Directorate for Decree Enactment. Created in 1209, it functioned as the highest organ of the Ch'oe regime.
After Ch'oe Ch'ung-hŏn first established it, his heirs, U (I), Hang, and Ŭi, in
turn headed it. As directors of this powerful office, Ch'oe Ch'ung-hŏn and his
successors issued orders to collect taxes and investigate official wrongdoing.
In 1225 Ch'oe U created the Chŏngbang, Administrative Authority, in his own
residence to handle official appointments and attached men of letters to this office, calling them *chŏngsaek sŭngsŏn*, or secretaries for personnel administration.
This paved the way for the gradual reappearance of civil officials in positions
of power. In 1227 Ch'oe U also formed the Sŏbang, or Household Secretariat,
comprised of men of letters among his household retainers. It was divided into
three *sukwi*, or watches, that stood duty in turn. For his rule, Ch'oe U relied not
only on a retinue of military men from the Tobang security squad and Sam-
byŏlch'o units but on a civilian staff from the Chŏngbang and the Sŏbang.

To consolidate his family's political power, Ch'oe Ch'ung-hŏn expanded
his personal landholdings. He possessed large-scale agricultural estates in
the Chŏlla and Kyŏngsang regions. In fact, the whole of the fertile Chin'gang
(present-day Chinju) region was bestowed on him by the state as sikŭp, and
all the revenues from this vast private preserve went only to him. To administer the enfeoffed region, he obtained the title of *Chin'gang-hu*, or Marquis
of Chin'gang (Chinju), from King Hŭijong and established the Hŭngnyŏng-bu
(Chin'gang-bu), or Office of Flourishing Tranquility, in his residence in 1206.
The Hŭngnyŏng-bu was a special organ for the Ch'oe house to administer the
Chin'gang region, and the house's vast wealth was the economic foundation
sustaining its private armed force.[1]

Ch'oe Ch'ung-hŏn died in 1219, after a 23-year rule, and was succeeded by his
son, Ch'oe U. The ablest ruler of the Ch'oe house, Ch'oe U was in command
for 30 years, until his death in 1249. His political position and power were succeeded by his illegitimate son Ch'oe Hang. When Ch'oe Hang died in 1258, his
power passed on to his son, Ch'oe Ŭi. This last ruler from the Ch'oe house was
assassinated by the civil official Yu Kyŏng and the military official Kim Chun
in the same year, 1258. The reins of government briefly reverted to King Kojong,
with Kim Chun as another military strongman. In 1268 the military official Im
Yŏn killed Kim Chun and seized power. After Im Yŏn's death, in 1270, another
military official, Im Yu-mu (Im Yŏn's son), exercised dictatorial power for a
short time. His execution in the same year led to the final restoration of royal
rule, thereby ending the long period of military rule in Koryŏ.

Peasant and Slave Uprisings

Since the second half of the eleventh century, Koryŏ achieved remarkable advances in agriculture, commerce, and handicraft manufacturing. But the main beneficiaries of this great economic growth were the aristocracy and Buddhist temples, while the peasant population remained impoverished. In the reign of King Ŭijong, in particular, when royal extravagance and personal pleasures went to extremes, life among the masses further deteriorated following years of bad harvests and excessive government exploitation. The peasants were in serious distress owing to the severe land tax, tribute exactions, and corvee mobilizations, all of which only benefited the aristocracy. In fact, much of the aristocracy was a parasitic class, living in great luxury and addicted to literary and artistic diversions. The peasantry had already been consumed by restlessness, and now people of lower social status, including the peasants, were further agitated by the social upheaval caused by the military revolt, which had created a social climate in which those on the lower stratum challenged those on top. Finally, large-scale popular uprisings erupted in many parts of the country.

The first uprising flared in the Western Border Region, presently P'yŏngan province, in 1172, during military rule. The region's inhabitants were enraged by an oppressive government comprised of local officials of military background. The uprising was immediately suppressed by government forces. When Cho Wi-ch'ong rose in revolt against the military regime in 1174, many peasants in the northwestern region gave him their support. The remnants of Cho's defeated forces, numbering more than 500, entrenched themselves on Myohyang-san (mountain) and continued organized resistance for many years.

Popular uprisings also arose in the southern regions. In 1176 Mangi and Mangsoi led a revolt in the Myŏnghak-so forced labor district attached to Kongju. The rebels occupied Kongju and then advanced northward to Kaesŏng, but after holding out for more than a year in some areas of present-day North Ch'ungch'ŏng and Kyŏnggi provinces, they were finally suppressed in 1177. The previous year, in 1176, the central government in Kaesŏng had organized a large-scale government force to put down this and other ensuing rebellions. A few years later, in 1182, soldiers and government slaves in Chŏnju rebelled and held the town for some 40 days. In the meantime, small-scale outbreaks occurred one after another, particularly in southern parts of the kingdom.

Overall these early uprisings broke out sporadically, as these were the desperate acts of soldiers, peasants, and slaves attempting to shed some of their economic burdens, spontaneously resisting the oppression of local officials and aristocrats. In the 1170s and the 1180s, however, rebels did not attempt to join forces with other lower-class rebel forces in efforts to achieve emancipation.

But a new situation developed after the 1190s, with the uprisings of Kim Sa-mi and Hyosim in 1193, where the two rebel bands united to form a common front. First Kim Sa-mi rose up in revolt at Unmun (present-day Ch'ŏngdo, North Kyŏngsang province), and then Hyosim began a separate riot at nearby Ch'ojŏn, thought to be present-day Ulsan; later the two merged into a single force of tens of thousands. When the rebels were defeated in a battle at Milsŏng (present-day Miryang, South Kyŏngsang province) in 1194, more than 7,000 were killed. This united revolt was finally subdued in the same year as Kim Sa-mi surrendered to the government forces and Hyosim was captured.

The peasant rebels who revolted at Myŏngju (present-day Kangnŭng, Kangwŏn province) in 1199 occupied Samch'ŏk and Ulchin to the south on their way to join forces with a rebel band at Kyŏngju. This uprising was suppressed in 1200. That same year slaves of Chinju increased their strength by forming a common front with lowborn inhabitants in revolt at Hapchu (present-day Hapch'ŏn, South Kyŏngsang province). In 1202 soldiers, monks, and peasants at Kyŏngju, Ch'ŏngdo, Ulchin, and Ulsan also revolted with the battle cry of reviving old Silla, engaging in fierce battles with government forces for some two years. Uprisings erupted not only in the countryside but also in the capital. An insurrection was plotted by Manjŏk, one of Ch'oe Ch'unghŏn's privately owned slaves, in 1198, just two years after he came into power, with the aim of emancipating the entire slave population and seizing power. The plot was uncovered before the uprising even got under way, and Manjŏk and his supporters faced a river burial. By this time the goal of the popular rebellions was to restructure the existing social order and, beyond that, to seize power.

Finally, although all these popular uprisings were subdued by the central government, they did not end in total failure. The military regime abolished the special forced labor districts of pugok and so, raising the status of their inhabitants to that of commoners, and emancipated many slaves. Clearly the uprisings during military rule changed Koryŏ's social order to a great extent. These popular rebellions, in other words, provided a major momentum for the reshuffling of the social status system in the late Koryŏ period.

Culture in the Age of Military Rule

As military officials seized control and civil officials fell from power, Confucianism was in a steep decline, and men of letters who were frustrated with the situation abandoned thoughts of government careers. Some of them lived in rural retirement, passing their days enjoying poetry and wine. Figures such as Yi In-no, Im Ch'un, O Se-jae, Cho T'ong, Hwangbo Hang, Ham Sun, and Yi Tam-ji compared them to third-century China's "Seven Sages of the Bamboo Grove" and called them *Haejwa ch'il hyŏn*, or Seven Sages of the Left of the Sea. They spent their days writing poems and tales, including, for example, Im Ch'un's *Kongbang chŏn*, or Tale of the Fortunes of Master Coin, in which the main character, Master Coin, personified money, and Yi In-no's *P'ahan chip*, or Collection to Dispel Leisure.

After Ch'oe Ch'ung-hŏn established a military dictatorship in 1196, some men of letters sought to enter government service as retainers of the Ch'oe house. Yi Kyu-bo and Ch'oe Cha were two outstanding figures of this sort. Enjoying the confidence of the Ch'oe regime, Yi Kyu-bo enhanced his reputation when he wrote his national epic *Tongmyŏng wang p'yŏn*, or Saga of King Tongmyŏng (Chumong), the semi-legendary founder of Koguryŏ. In this work, composed of verses with five words to each line, Yi suggested that the people of Koryŏ, the successor to the great Koguryŏ kingdom, take pride in being a cultured people possessed of a long history and tradition. Yi also wrote *Kuk sŏnsaeng chŏn*, or Tale of Mr. John Barleycorn, in which the main character personified wine.

Yi In-no's *P'ahan chip*, Yi Kyu-bo's *Paekun sosŏl*, or Novel of White Clouds, a collection of poems and trifles ranging from the period of the Three Kingdoms to his day, and Ch'oe Cha's *Pohan chip*, or Supplement to *P'ahan Chip*, were all collections of anecdotes, poems, stories, and casual commentaries designed to entertain. Starting with Pak In-nyang's *Sui chŏn*, or Tale of the Bizarre, writings of this genre were enormously popular in the period of military rule and later influenced such works as Yi Chae-hyŏn's *Yŏkong p'aesŏl*, or Scribbling of Old Man Oak.

After military rule was established, a new development appeared in Koryŏ Buddhism. While the Kyo school, which had had close ties with civil officials, was declining, the Sŏn school distinguished itself under the aegis of the military rulers and finally gained the upper hand over the Kyo sect. Also, at this time the Chogye sect was established within the Sŏn school. During the period of military rule, in 1200, the Koryŏ Chogye sect was founded by the monk Chinul, also known as the National Preceptor Pojo. The Nine Mountain Sects of Sŏn took the name of the Chogye School, which accepted the Hwaŏm doctrines of the Kyo sect and would greatly flourish.

In 1200 Chinul moved to the Songgwang-sa temple, located in present-day Sunch'ŏn, South Chŏlla province, and converted it into a base for the propagation of his new Chogye sect. He thoroughly analyzed and reformulated the methodologies of Sŏn study and practice. After Chinul, the Chogye sect continued to develop by the efforts of such outstanding successors as Hyesim, known as the National Preceptor Chin'gak, and Ch'ungji, known as the National Preceptor Wŏn'gam. The Chogye sect gained substantial support from military rulers, and beyond uniting the Sŏn and Kyo schools, the monk Hyesim even attempted the unification of Buddhism and Confucianism. The Chogye Order would, in fact, develop as the mainstream of Korean Buddhism.

The age of military rule, which spanned 100 years, witnessed the collapse of Confucianism-oriented government as well as great confusion in the existing administration and social order. On the other hand, this was a transitional period when general disorder led to improvements in the social status of the lower classes and the gradual decline of the aristocratic order.

KORYŎ AND THE MONGOLS

War with the Mongols

While Koryŏ was undergoing internal upheavals by the establishment of military rule, an unprecedented situation developed in north-central Asia. A man named Temujin in Mongolia succeeded in conquering and integrating the neighboring tribes of Mongolia, and in 1206 he proclaimed himself Genghis Kahn, or Almighty Emperor. Until he died of battle wounds suffered when he invaded Xixia (West Xia in Tibet) in 1227, he had already conquered a vast territory on the Eurasian continent. His third son, Ogodei, succeeded him and continued his campaign of conquest.

The Nuzhen Jin empire, which had acted as a shield for Koryŏ against Mongols, fell in 1234, placing Mongols at Koryŏ's doorstep. Now Mongols had a reason to make Koryŏ an object of their conquest, for their ultimate aim was to use Koryŏ as a base for conquering Southern Song and Japan.

The first contact between Koryŏ and Mongols resulted from their joint military operation to destroy remnants of Qidans who had fled from Manchuria

across the Yalu into Koryŏ to escape Mongols. Sustained Mongol attacks on Jin
had afforded Qidans an opportunity to reassert their independence. Following
the fall of the Jin capital in 1215, however, Mongol pressure drove Qidans into
Koryŏ territory to find shelter. From 1216 to 1218 Qidans created considerable
turmoil in Koryŏ. They even raided the town of Chech'ŏn in the central Korean peninsula, and in 1218 they entrenched themselves in the Kangdong-sŏng
fortress, east of Pyongyang. The next year the combined Koryŏ-Mongol forces
took the fortress, causing Qidans to surrender. Thereafter Mongols considered
themselves Koryŏ's benefactors and, in this capacity, demanded heavy tribute
annually, although on several occasions Koryŏ flatly rejected the Mongol demands. Amid rising tensions between the two states, the Mongol envoy Zhu-
guyu, who had acted disrespectfully while in Koryŏ, was killed as he traveled
back to his country in 1225. Mongols used this incident as an excuse to invade
Koryŏ.

In 1231 Mongols launched their first invasion of Koryŏ. Mongol forces, under the command of Salledei (Salietai), crossed the Yalu and took the towns
of Ŭiju and Anju in the northwestern region, but they were met with stubborn
resistance from Koryŏ general Pak Sŏ at the Kwiju-sŏng fortress. Frustrated
by siege warfare, Mongol forces used their superior mobility to bypass the
Koryŏ army and pressed hard against the capital, Kaesŏng. When Koryŏ sued
for peace, Mongols withdrew in early 1232, leaving 72 *daruhachi*, administrative officials, in the northwestern region to ensure that Koryŏ kept to its
peace terms, including heavy tribute. Immediately after dodging the brunt
of the Mongol attack, however, the military regime of Ch'oe U resolved to
renew the resistance against Mongols. Thus, against the pleas of King Kojong
and many civil officials, he moved the capital to the island of Kanghwa-do
for the purpose of mounting a more effective defense against the enemy. In
doing so, he exploited Mongols' primary weakness, which was fear of the sea,
as Kanghwa-do was separated from the mainland by several hundred yards
of waterway. Ch'oe U proceeded to move the ruling class to Kanghwa-do and
build significant defense structures in preparation for the Mongol threat. With
the construction of small forts and a double wall on Kanghwa-do, the island
was transformed into a mighty defense fortress. The general population was
ordered to take shelter in the mountain fortresses or on offshore islands. But
members of the ruling class were still able to maintain their extravagant lifestyle on Kanghwa-do, as the Ch'oe U regime built luxurious facilities there

for their comfort, sustained by grain tax revenues that were sent by ship along safe coastal routes.

Mongols regarded the transfer of Koryŏ's capital to Kanghwa-do as an act of defiance and immediately resumed their invasion of Koryŏ. For more than 20 years, until 1259 when Koryŏ finally surrendered, the invaders continued their attacks. In 1232 Ogodei again sent Salledei's Mongol forces to invade Koryŏ, where he succeeded in capturing the empty capital but could not touch the new capital on Kanghwa-do. His forces crossed the Han River and continued the invasion of the southern Korean peninsula. Throughout the struggle Koryŏ's resistance to Mongol forces was carried out mainly by the peasants and lowborn classes. In the battle at the Ch'ŏin-sŏng fortress (present-day Yongin, Kyŏnggi province) in 1232, Salledei was shot to death by the monk Kim Yun-hu, and the Mongol army became disorganized and again withdrew. At the time of the first invasion in 1231, the brigand bands on Kwanak-san (mountain) in present-day Seoul fought the invaders fiercely, and at Ch'ungju, in the central Korean peninsula, the Mongol advance was halted by a slave army led by Chi Kwang-su who fought bravely to his death, even though the aristocratic officials had all fled. The resistance of these lowborn people resulted in their emancipation from their lower-class status.

As the battle continued, Mongols repeatedly overran and despoiled Koryŏ. The villages were devastated and the people suffered heavy losses. Faced with strong resistance from the people of Koryŏ, Mongols burned towns and villages everywhere they went and destroyed buildings and temples, leaving nothing but ashes. Many innocent people, including women and children, were cruelly slaughtered. Many irreplaceable cultural treasures were lost, outstanding among them the nine-story wooden pagoda at the Hwangyong-sa temple in Kyŏngju and the woodblocks for the Tripitaka stored at the Puin-sa temple in Taegu.[2] Thus, at the court on Kanghwa-do, sentiment for peace with Mongols arose among the king and moderate officials. In 1258 moderate military official Kim Chun and civil official Yu Kyŏng assassinated Ch'oe Ŭi, the last ruler of the Ch'oe house. Authority reverted to King Kojong and a decision was reached to make peace with Mongols. The next year the crown prince, later King Wŏnjong (1259–1274), conveyed to Mongols Koryŏ's desire for peace. To clearly demonstrate Koryŏ's intent to cease resistance, the walled fortifications on Kanghwa-do were torn down. The peace terms between Koryŏ and Mongols allowed Koryŏ to maintain its sovereign power and traditional culture, implying that Mongols had abandoned their aim of conquering and directly dominating Koryŏ.

But struggles within the court continued over peace with Mongols until 1270. The hard-line military official Im Yŏn killed Kim Chun and seized power in 1258. In 1269 Im Yŏn deposed King Wŏnjong, who ascended the throne in 1259, in opposition to the king's pro-Mongol policy. Because Koryŏ had already been under strong Mongol influence, however, five months later Mongol interference restored Wŏnjong to the throne. In 1270 Im Yŏn died, and his role as a powerful military official was taken over by his son, Im Yu-mu. Three months later, when Im Yu-mu was executed by royal command, the long military rule finally ended. Koryŏ returned the capital to Kaesŏng and surrendered completely to Mongols.

The collapse of military rule in 1270 did not completely end Koryŏ's resistance to Mongols. The toppling of the military regime and peace with Mongols infuriated the Sam-byŏlch'o army, the Ch'oe house's core military force which was the vanguard in the struggle against Mongols. Immediately after the government returned to Kaesŏng, the Sam-byŏlch'o forces revolted under the leadership of Pae Chung-son. They placed Wang On, the Marquis of Sŭnghwa, a member of the royalty, on the throne and established an anti-Mongol regime in opposition to the pro-Mongol government in Kaesŏng. In order to secure a permanent base of military operations out of reach of the central government in Kaesŏng, the rebel forces went south to the island of Chin-do, off the southwestern tip of the Korean peninsula. They placed the nearby islands and the adjacent coastal region under their control, once more establishing a maritime kingdom.

When Chin-do fell to a combined Koryŏ-Mongol force commanded by the Koryŏ general Kim Pang-gyŏng in 1271, the major figures in the revolt, including Pae Chung-son, lost their lives. Led by Kim T'ong-jŏng, the survivors fled to Cheju-do, then called T'amna, to continue their resistance. Cheju-do also fell to Kim Pang-gyŏng's forces in 1273, terminating the Sam-byŏlch'o rebellion that had spanned almost four years. The Sam-byŏlch'o forces' stubborn resistance led Mongols to stand in awe of Koryŏ. Finally, after a quarter-century of fierce armed struggle, the Korean kingdom fell under Mongol domination.

Koryŏ as Yuan's "Son-in-Law Nation"

With their titles and privileges greatly reduced, Koryŏ's kings were married to Mongol princesses, and the sons born to these Mongol queens ascended the throne. Mongol officials closely watched over the Koryŏ administration, and the Mongol culture strongly influenced Koryŏ, particularly its ruling class.

Mongols proclaimed their state the Yuan empire in 1271, and their domain reached Central Asia, Persia, Mesopotamia, Russia, and China proper. Kublai Khan, who ascended the throne in 1260, finally destroyed Southern Song in 1279. Koryŏ's dogged resistance against Mongols led this mighty empire to recognize the small kingdom's independence. But the northern part of Koryŏ territory, along with Cheju-do, was placed under direct Mongol domination. Yuan established the Ssangsŏng ch'onggwan-bu, or Two Castle Commandery, at present-day Yŏnghŭng, South Hamgyŏng province, in 1258, to administer the territory north of the Ch'ŏl-lyŏng pass, which is the present-day Hamgyŏng region; the Tongnyŏng-bu, or Eastern Tranquility Administration, at Pyong-yang, in 1270, to govern the area north of the Chabi-ryŏng pass, which is today's P'yŏngan region; and the T'amna ch'onggwan-bu, or Cheju Commandery, on Cheju-do, in 1273, to direct the Mongols' livestock-raising operation on the island. Upon persistent requests from Koryŏ, however, the territories under the administration of the Tongnyŏng-bu and the T'amna ch'onggwan-bu were returned to Koryŏ in 1290 and 1294, respectively. The Ssangsŏng ch'onggwan-bu continued to exist until King Kongmin (1351–1374) recovered its territory by military force in 1356.

The Koryŏ royal house was linked to that of the Mongol empire through marriage and blood ties. To boost royal authority and prestige among Mongol officials in Koryŏ, King Wŏnjong sought to marry his son, the later King Ch'ungnyŏl (1274–1308), to a Yuan (Mongolian) princess. The Yuan emperor Kublai acceded to this request, and the Koryŏ crown prince was given one of Kublai's daughters as his consort. From Kublai's view, it was a political marriage to assist his ambition to conquer Japan. Thereafter it became standard procedure for Koryŏ kings to marry princesses of the Yuan imperial house. Koryŏ became Yuan's "son-in-law nation," and the royal house of Koryŏ became nothing more than a branch of the Mongol ruling family. The Mongol consorts of the Koryŏ kings exercised great power. Koryŏ crown princes had generally resided at the Yuan court in present-day Beijing as hostages before they were called up to the kingship. Even after they took the throne, they were required to visit the Yuan capital frequently and stay in the imperial capital rather than their Korean capital. The customs of the ruling class, particularly those of the king, became strongly Mongolized, and despite its external independence, Koryo was reduced to a dependency of the Yuan empire.

Koryŏ as Yuan's Tributary State

In 1280 Mongols established the Chŏngdong haengsŏng, or Eastern Expedition Field Headquarters, in Koryŏ to carry out the second military campaign against Japan. Even after they gave up any thought of conquering Japan, Mongols continued to operate the field headquarters for a while, and transformed it into a means for interfering in Koryŏ's domestic affairs. The Koryŏ king was automatically appointed to head this organization, with the title of chwasŭngsang, or state minister of the left. Two years later, in 1282, after the disastrous failure of the second invasion of Japan, Mongols abolished this colonial agency.

Once the Koryŏ king became a son-in-law of the Yuan emperor he was no longer the independent ruler of his kingdom, and Koryŏ became a tributary state of the Yuan empire. The king was forced to endure degrading royal titles and privileges. In 1276 Yuan compelled Koryŏ to downgrade all the terms relating to the king and his actions. The Koryŏ kings were no longer given the posthumous titles of cho or chong that suggested equality with the Yuan emperors. Instead, the character wang was used as a suffix, with the character ch'ung, or loyal, added as a prefix to express the Koryŏ kings' spirit of loyalty to Yuan.[3] Other terms were similarly degraded, for example, the royal first-person pronoun was downgraded from chim to ko, the mode of addressing the king from p'yeha to chŏnha, the term designating the crown prince from t'aeja to seja, and the name for a royal decree from sŏnji to wangji. These changes indicate that the status of the Koryo king was demoted from imperial ruler of a kingdom to ruler of the vassal state of an empire. Government organs also experienced the downgrading of their names. The three chancelleries were merged to form the Ch'ŏmŭibu, or Council of State, and the Ch'umirwŏn (formerly the Chungch'uwŏn), the Ŏsadae, and the Hallimwŏn were renamed, respectively, the Milchik-sa, the Kamch'al-sa, and the Munhansŏ, respectively. These nominal changes suggest that the importance of these offices was also diminished. Moreover, Koryŏ was forced to abolish the Kong-bu and combine the Yi-bu and the Ye-bu to establish a new agency, the Chŏnri-sa, or Office of Proprieties. Further, the Pyŏng-bu was renamed the Kunbu-sa, or Office of Military Rosters; the Ho-bu became the P'ando-sa, or Office of Census Registration; and the Hyŏng-bu was now called the Chŏnpŏp-sa, or Office of Legal Administration. On the other hand, Koryŏ voluntarily reorganized the Tobyŏngmasa, or Supreme Council of Military Affairs, into the Top'yŏngŭisasa, or Supreme Council. In the early period the Tobyŏngmasa had been a nonpermanent government organ that had commanded the Koryŏ army in wartime. In this period, however, the Top'yŏngŭisasa became the government's permanent, highest decision-making organ. The deprecating rechristening and restructuring of government organs was forcibly carried out by Mongols and paralleled the downgrading of terminology related to the monarch. In sum, although Koryŏ maintained political independence, its relationship with Yuan was that of sovereign and subject.

Koryŏ-Yuan Expeditions against Japan

As time went on, Kublai's ambition to conquer Japan continued to inflict great pain on Koryŏ. Although Mongol forces excelled in land warfare, they had little experience in naval war and lacked the technology for building seagoing vessels large enough to carry a great armed force, and so they ultimately turned to Koryŏ to make up for these deficiencies. Initially Kublai sent envoys to Japan several times in an effort to subjugate the island country by diplomatic means, but these attempts failed. Having already suffered from extensive warfare with Mongols and wanting to avoid another war with Japan, Koryŏ tried to mediate the two parties. Kublai was adamant, however, and ordered Koryŏ to provide vast quantities of provisions and hundreds of ships for a large-scale military campaign against Japan.

In 1274 a 40,000-man army left the Koryŏ port of Happ'o (present-day Masan) for Japan. Koryŏ provided most of the warships and 8,000 men, and the rest was comprised of Mongol forces. After first taking the islands of Tsushima and Iki, this allied force landed on Hakata beach in northern Kyushu. Although the Kamakura shogunate offered stout resistance, initially the Koryŏ-Yuan forces easily defeated the numerically superior Japanese. But then a typhoon struck and wrecked some of the invaders' ships, and the subsequent arrival of Japanese reinforcements sent Mongols sailing back to Koryŏ.

Having failed in this first invasion of Japan, Kublai became even more aggressive and demanded that Koryŏ make greater preparations for another expedition. The Koryŏ king Ch'ungnyŏl dispatched a mission to Yuan, explaining that his country could not afford another invasion of Japan. Kublai was not moved, however, and sent two missions to Japan with threatening letters in 1275 and 1279, but the Japanese refused to accept Mongol suzerainty and killed his envoys. The enraged Kublai demanded that Koryŏ speed up preparations for a second invasion of Japan. He assembled a far larger expeditionary force, numbering 170,000, composed of Mongols, the Chinese, Koreans, and the Vietnamese, with 4,500 warships. Koryŏ contributed 10,000 men and 900 vessels.

In 1281 the invasion force sailed toward Japan. As in their invasion of 1274, these combined forces again captured Tsushima and Iki as staging areas and then struck Hakata beach. This time the Japanese were better prepared and put up a fierce resistance. At first it appeared that Mongols and their allies could not be stopped, but in August a violent typhoon struck once again and wrecked most of the Mongol ships. Only some 200 ships and 20 percent of the invaders survived the storm or the Japanese soldiers waiting for them as they swam ashore. Cut off from their supplies, Mongols and their allies were easily defeated, and the Japanese reportedly enslaved some 12,000 invaders. The Japanese named the storms that saved them from the Mongol fleets *Kamikaze*, or divine wind.

Undeterred by this disaster, the indefatigable Kublai planned another invasion of Japan, but Koryŏ could no longer support Kublai's unreasonable demands for its participation. Partly because of Koryŏ's stubborn refusal and mainly because of unrest in China, Kublai finally gave up his ambition to subjugate Japan. The two invasions of Japan, in any case, imposed some of the heaviest burdens on the Koryŏ peasantry.

Yuan's Exploitation of Koryŏ

After the abortive invasions of Japan, Yuan demanded, under the cloak of tributes, that Koryŏ provide gold, silver, cloth, grain, ginseng, and even falcons, more precisely duck falcons (*haedongch'ŏng*), for hunting. The demand for falcons resulted in many abuses including corruption and high-handedness of Koryŏ officials. In 1275 Yuan established *ŭngbang*, or falconries, to catch falcons in numerous places, and Koryŏ officials in these falconries who were backed by Mongol power enjoyed a variety of special privileges, incurring the people's grievances. Mongols' excessive impositions of tributes, along with the luxury and extravagance of the Koryŏ kings, exacerbated the economic hardships among the people.

Mongols even demanded that young women and eunuchs work at the imperial palaces. To meet their requirements, in 1274 Koryŏ established the Kyŏrhon togam, or Directorate for Marriage, to seek out young women and, in 1275, placed a ban on marriage throughout the country. Many Koryŏ families were forced to dress young women in men's clothing to hide them. Once Mongols took Koryŏ's young women in, however, they gave them respectable positions. The Koryŏ women who went to Yuan, either willingly or unwillingly, were usually married to Mongol aristocrats, high-level officials, or rich men, even members of the royal family, and ended up in the higher echelon of Mongol society. The later empress Ki, for example, became the consort of the Mongol emperor Shundi and bore him a son, Zhaozong, who became the next emperor of the Yuan dynasty.

Under Yuan domination, Koryŏ kings detested the presence of the so-called King of Shenyang, who had jurisdiction over the Koryŏ people living in Manchuria. When King Ch'ungnyŏl was in the Yuan capital as crown prince, he was invested as King of Shenyang, and later, when King Ch'ungsŏn (1298, 1308–1313) was forced to abdicate the throne in 1298 and reside in the Yuan capital, he, too, was given that title. Appointing Koryŏ royalty as kings of Shenyang was a maneuver on the part of Mongols to further consolidate their control over Koryŏ by pitting members of Koryŏ's royalty against each other. The result was a constant confrontation between the Koryŏ king and the King of Shenyang. For instance, a bitter struggle for the succession to the Koryŏ throne erupted between Wang Ko, King Ch'ungsŏn's nephew and his successor as King of Shenyang, and King Ch'ungsuk (1313–1330, 1332–1339). As a result of this struggle, King Ch'ungsuk, in 1330, was forced to abdicate the throne in favor of his young son, King Ch'unghye (1330–1332, 1339–1344), only to take the throne again two years later. Yuan also held sway over royal succession by frequently deposing a king and raising another to the throne.

The Rise of Powerful Families

Under Yuan aegis, new forces among powerful families emerged in Koryŏ society. Some of these families had remained powerful from the early period, whereas others became prominent during military rule. On the other hand, new families distinguished themselves by their relations with Mongols. Some of them became powerful as Mongolian language interpreters or officials of the falconries, and others assumed prominence by taking public office in the Yuan government or forging marital relations with Mongolian royal and aristocratic families.

Members of these powerful families served as high-ranking civil and military officials in the government. They participated in the deliberations of the Top'yŏngŭisasa, the highest decision-making organization. Participants in this body had originally numbered just 10 or so, but now the number had reached 70 or 80. They also possessed vast estates and hundreds of slaves. Their unrestricted personal landholdings gave rise to the so-called *nongjang*, or agricultural estates, which were enormous tracts of farmland. It is said that at the end

of the Koryŏ dynasty, the landholdings of powerful families were so vast that
mountains and rivers formed their boundaries or they extended across entire
counties. The royal house also possessed many nongjang estates, indeed more
than 360. These nongjang were cultivated by the owners' retainers and slaves.
Powerful families secured special privileges such as tax and corvee exemptions
on their lands and retainers. As a result, the increase in private estates seriously
cut into state revenues. The increased population of privately owned slaves
also reduced the number of peasants that the state could mobilize for corvee
labor. In fact, to escape heavy taxation and corvee labor, many peasants entered
nongjang estates to be reclassified as slaves or serfs, either at their own or the
owners' wish. The situation had now reached the point where the state had to
carry out reforms from top to bottom.

THE DOWNFALL OF KORYŎ

The Reforms of King Kongmin

The Yuan empire, which had once had dominion over most of the Eurasian
continent, rapidly faded, as the fires of its conquest were extinguished. After
Kublai's death in 1294, all Mongol rulers degenerated quickly. The descendants
of erstwhile conquerors were no longer formidable and instead became weak
and corrupt. Within half a century after Kublai, all of China was embroiled
in serious rebellions. Zhu Yuanzhang, who revolted against Yuan in southern
China, expelled Mongols from China proper and founded the new Ming dynasty in 1368. The ousted Mongols renamed their state Northern Yuan.

Upon learning that Mongols began to recede from China proper, King Kongmin (1351–1374) initiated his reform movement, which basically pursued two
goals: eliminating Yuan's control and influence over Koryŏ and suppressing
the nation's own powerful families. In 1352 he prohibited his officials and the
people of Koryŏ from wearing their hair in the pigtail style of Mongols and
from wearing Mongol dress. In 1356 he purged the pro-Yuan faction led by Ki
Ch'ŏl, the elder brother of Empress Ki of Shundi, discontinued the use of Yuan
era names, restored the old government structure, abolished the Imunso, or
Office of Interrogation and Punishment, which was subordinate to the former
Chŏngdong haengsŏng, and recovered Koryŏ's territory that the Ssangsŏng
ch'onggwan-bu had taken by military force. In 1369 he sent troops across the
Yalu into Manchuria to recapture Koguryŏ's lost territory. The Koryŏ general
Yi Sŏng-gye, later the founder of the Chosŏn dynasty, took the Liaoyang for-

tress, the major stronghold of the remaining Yuan forces in Manchuria. The occupation did not last long, however. Fearing a counterattack from the Yuan army, Yi withdrew, having first received a pledge of loyalty to Koryŏ from the tribes in the area. King Kongmin's aggressive defiance toward Yuan provoked a strong reaction from both Yuan and its supporters within Koryŏ. Kim Yong, a major pro-Yuan figure at the Koryŏ court, attempted to assassinate the king at the Hŭngwang-sa temple in 1363. King Kongmin barely escaped the assassination attempt. Although Yuan proclaimed that the king had been dethroned, he stood firm and resolutely proceeded with his anti-Yuan policy. When the Ming dynasty was founded in 1368, he took measures to open relations with the new Chinese empire.

Internally King Kongmin made every effort to undermine the dominant position of powerful families. In 1352 he abolished the Chŏngbang, which had functioned as an instrument of the Ch'oe house's autocratic rule and placed restraints on the exercise of royal authority over personnel matters. In 1365, when his Mongol queen died during a difficult childbirth, however, he lost interest in political affairs and instead devoted himself entirely to Buddhism, believing it would soothe his wife's soul. That same year he took into government service a humble Buddhist monk named Sin Ton, formerly called P'yŏnjo, establishing for him a new high-level government post the Samjung taegwang yŏngdo ch'ŏmŭi, or Prime Minister Plenipotentiary, in which capacity he carried out sweeping reforms. Sin Ton first expelled from the court several influential officials from powerful families such as Yi Kong-su and Kyŏng Ch'ŏn-hŭng. Then, with the consent of the king, in 1366 he created the Chŏnmin pyŏnjŏng togam, or Directorate for the Reclassification of Farmland and the Farming Population, and set about returning land and slaves seized by powerful families to their original owners; in many cases he actually set slaves free. Sin Ton's actions were well received by the general population, and he was even hailed as a "saint." At the same time he provoked the antipathy of powerful families and grew so arrogant that he became involved in wrongdoings including abuses of power under the pretext of royal command. After losing the confidence of King Kongmin, he plotted treason against the king. Finally, he was banished to Suwŏn, just south of Seoul, and executed in 1371.

In his later years King Kongmin increasingly indulged in artistic activities and was killed by a eunuch in 1374. Although he succeeded in freeing Koryŏ from Mongol domination, King Kongmin failed to free its society from the grip of powerful families.

The Emergence of the Literati

Following the period of military rule, a new educated bureaucratic class, called the *sadaebu,* or literati, emerged. The literati were literally scholar-officials, but in the late Koryŏ period the term defined educated and knowledgeable men, particularly Neo-Confucian scholars. Members of the literati generally sought political advancement through the civil service examinations, based purely on scholarly achievement. Some of them passed the Yuan civil service examinations and entered government service in Koryŏ. Others distinguished themselves on the battlefield and became military officers, called *hallyang.*

Many members of the literati emerged from among local functionaries in local administrations. The literati of this hyangni background were generally small- and mid-level landowners or self-supporting farmers who had built up their meager landholdings by reclaiming wasteland, improving agricultural techniques, or by purchasing them. These literati despised powerful families who acquired their huge estates by illegal means, including using their political clout to extort land from others, and thus they were quite reform-minded.

The emergence of the literati profoundly changed Koryŏ's political scene. During military rule, they did not play a major role in government or society, as they functioned only as the retainers of the Ch'oe house. During the period of Yuan domination, however, they were completely overwhelmed by Koryŏ's powerful families and accepted Neo-Confucianism brought from Yuan as their political ideology. After the reign of King Kongmin, they enjoyed relatively favorable circumstances and began to perform important political roles. As abuses of powerful families reached a climax in the reign of King U (1374–1388), the literati joined forces in an all-out effort to reform Koryŏ society. But, in the end, the literati split into moderates and radicals, and whereas the former tried to reform the Koryŏ dynasty, the latter wanted to establish a new dynasty in its place.

Culture in the Late Koryŏ Period

The Introduction and Spread of Neo-Confucianism

Neo-Confucianism was first established by Zhu Xi, the great Chinese philosopher of the Southern Song period. This "new Confucianism" was an abstruse philosophy that explicated the origins of man and the universe in metaphysical terms. It espoused a political ethic that stressed joint rule by monarchs and their subjects, thus strengthening the power of the latter. The new literati class in the late Koryŏ period, satisfied neither with Buddhism nor with earlier belletristic, speculative Confucianism, accepted Neo-Confucianism as their spiritual doctrine. The first to profess Neo-Confucianism was An Hyang (An Yu), who, after returning from Yuan in 1290, disseminated the new doctrine in Koryŏ. In the reign of King Ch'ungnyŏl, the efforts of An Hyang and others greatly encouraged the study of Neo-Confucianism. For instance, in 1304, a *munmyo*, or Confucian shrine, was built, and an endowment for the support of students was established at the Kukhak (formerly the Kukchagam but renamed in 1275). King Ch'ungsŏn, after his throne had been returned to his father, King Ch'ungnyŏl, in 1298, went to the Yuan capital with the Koryŏ scholar Paek I-jŏng and forged close relations with eminent Yuan scholars. Ten years later he returned to Koryŏ to succeed to the throne. After he was dethroned again in 1313, however, he built the Man'gwŏndang, or Hall of Ten Thousand Volumes, in the Yuan capital in 1314. Paek I-jŏng studied Neo-Confucianism in Yuan, and his studies were furthered by his disciple Yi Che-hyŏn. The study of Neo-Confucianism greatly advanced in the reign of King Kongmin, when many famed Neo-Confucian scholars appeared in succession. Well-known Neo-Confucian scholars at the end of Koryŏ included Yi Saek, Chŏng Mong-ju, Chŏng To-jŏn, Kim Ku-yong, Pak Sang-ch'ung, Yi Sung-in, Kil Chae, and Kwŏn Kŭn.

As Neo-Confucianism spread, Buddhism was increasingly repudiated. During most of the Koryŏ period, Buddhism and Confucianism coexisted with little conflict. But now Neo-Confucian scholars did not agree with the idea that one should renounce one's family ties to become a monk, as the very basis of Confucian philosophy was founded on strong family and social relationships. More important, the wealth and power of the Buddhist temples and the enormous expense incurred by the state for Buddhist festivals became a major target of criticism. At first, rather than denouncing Buddhism itself, moderate Neo-Confucian scholars, such as Yi Che-hyŏn and Yi Saek, were content to attack the abuses of the temples and the misconduct of the monks. Later, however, radical Neo-Confucian scholars, such as Chŏng To-jŏn and Kwŏn Kŭn, completely rejected Buddhism as destructive of mores and ruinous to the state. Because these hard-liners assisted Yi Sŏng-gye in founding the later Chosŏn dynasty, the influence of Buddhism would inevitably diminish in the new kingdom.

The Writing of Histories

Unlike the earlier kingdoms, Koryŏ produced many historical writings. In 1215 the monk Kakkhun, by royal command, wrote *Haedong kosŭng chŏn*, or Lives of Eminent Korean Monks, which contained biographies of Korea's most distinguished Buddhist monks since the period of the Three Kingdoms. A portion of this work still exists. In the early reign of King Ch'ungnyŏl, Chŏng Ka-sin wrote a Koryŏ history titled *Ch'ŏnch'u kŭmgyŏng nok*, or Records from the Mirror of This Age. In 1284 Wŏn Pu and Hŏ Kong, on the king's command, compiled a history of Koryŏ's founding in *Kogŭm nok*, or Chronicle of Past and Present. In 1319 Min Chi wrote of Koryŏ's history chronologically from King Munjong to King Kojong in his *Ponjo p'yŏnnyŏn kangmok*, or Annotated Events of the Present Dynasty in Chronology. In 1357 Yi Che-hyŏn summarized the achievements of Koryŏ kings from King T'aejo to King Sukchong in his *Saryak*, or Concise History. None of these works has survived, and only Yi Che-hyŏn's personal judgments on history, contained in his *Saryak*, remain. Following the tradition of *Samguk sagi*, these government-sponsored histories were compiled from the perspective of Confucian morality which viewed history didactically as a mirror for good government.

Quite different in character from the above works were *Samguk yusa*, written by the monk Iryŏn in 1285, and *Chewang un'gi*, or Songs of Emperors and Kings, compiled by Yi Sŭng-hyu in 1287. Unique about these works is that both saw Korean history as beginning with Tan'gun. Thus both sought to recover Koreans' national identity and national pride, which had disappeared in the period of Mongol domination, by strengthening their sense of identity as a distinct race with a common ancestor, Tan'gun. Because they emphasized traditions and the legacy of history, these writings used many historical materials neglected by Kim Pu-sik's *Samguk sagi*. Iryŏn's *Samguk yusa* is particularly valuable, as it contains the history of Old Chosŏn and the three Han federations which were ignored in Kim Pu-sik's *Samguk sagi*. Yi Sŭng-hyu's *Chewang un'gi* more closely resembles a work of literature than a work of history, as it is in the form of an epic. Fortunately both are still with us today.

Literature and Fine Arts

The emergence and growth of the Neo-Confucian literati class brought a change to literature. Members of the literati expressed themselves in the literary form of the so-called *kyŏnggi*-style poem. Although it succeeded the tradition of Silla's hyangga, this newly developed poetic form was influenced by the literature and music of the Chinese Song dynasty and was written in Chinese. This new literary genre mainly depicted either the exultant and proud life of the emerging literati class or Korea's beautiful scenery. The former is exemplified by

Hallim pyŏlgok, or Song of the Academicians, composed by the young Confucian scholars of the Hallimwŏn, and the latter by An Ch'uk's *Kwandong pyŏlgok,* or Song of Kwandong Region, and *Chukkye pyŏlgok,* or Song of Chukkye Valley.

Although kyŏnggi-style poems were mainly composed by scholar-officials, the literary form of the common people was the *changga,* or long poem, written in the style of a folk song. Examples of the changga, whose authors are generally unknown, include *Ch'ŏngsan pyŏlgok,* or Song of Green Mountain, which sings of life conversing with nature; *Sŏgyŏng pyŏlgok,* or Song of the Western Capital, which describes love between a man and a woman; *Kasiri,* or Would You Now Leave Me? depicts the sorrow of parting; *Chŏngŭp sa,* or Song of Chŏngŭp County, delineates a wife's fervent prayer for her husband, who is away on business, to return; *Tongdong,* or Tongdong Refrain, describes the moon's 12-month cycle; and *Ssanghwajŏm,* or the Turkish Bakery, which sings of decadent love between a man and a woman. These changga poems all frankly express the feelings and realities of life among the common people.

Regarding Koryŏ's architecture, the oldest surviving wooden building is the Kŭngnakchŏn, or Hall of Paradise, at the Pongjŏng-sa temple, in present-day Andong, thought to date from 1363. The best example of Koryŏ's wooden architecture, however, is the Muryangsujŏn, or Hall of Eternal Life, at the Pusŏk-sa temple, in present-day Yŏngju, which seems to have been built in 1376. Other well-known structures from the late Koryŏ period include the Chosadang, or Hall of the Founder, at Pusŏk-sa, and the taeungjŏn at the Sudŏk-sa temple, in present-day Yesan, South Ch'ungch'ŏng province.

Representative of the late Koryŏ stone pagodas is the one at the Kyŏngch'ŏn-sa temple at Kaep'ung, North Korea (now housed in the National Museum of Korea in Seoul), built in the mid-fourteenth century. This ten-story pagoda, constructed in marble rather than granite, exhibits a Yuan and Lamaist influence and became the model for the Wŏngak-sa pagoda, built in 1467 at the time of the Chosŏn dynasty, located in Seoul.

Paintings of this age were mainly done by the literati. One example is the *sakunja,* or the four gracious plants (also known as the four gentlemen), referring to the orchid, bamboo, chrysanthemum, and plum blossom, intended to portray the elegant lifestyle of the newly emerging literati class. A few paintings from this period have survived, and the most noteworthy is *Ch'ŏnsan taeryŏp to,* or Painting of the Great Hunt on Heavenly Mountain, thought to have been done by King Kongmin in 1352. Some Buddhist paintings still exist, and those known as the *Yangnyu kwanŭm to,* or Portrait of the Willow Goddess of Mercy, rank as masterpieces of refinement and splendor. A few of these paintings, done by the court painter Kim U-mun, the monk Hyehŏ, and another artist named Sŏ Ku-bang, are now preserved in Japan.

In calligraphy, the laconic style of Ouyang Xun of the Chinese Song period, widely practiced in the earlier period, was replaced by the elegant style of *songxue* (*songsŏl* in Korean), after a penname of the famed scholar-calligrapher Zhao Mengfu of the Yuan period. A representative calligrapher of this school in Koryŏ was Yi Am. This songxue style would become the predominant mode of calligraphy in the later Chosŏn dynasty.

Science and Technology

Gunpowder was manufactured in this late Koryŏ period for the first time in Korean history. It had already been produced and used in the Song and Yuan eras, but the Chinese kept the method of its manufacture a closely guarded secret, never revealing it to Koryŏ. When Japanese pirates raided Koryŏ, Ch'oe Mu-sŏn, a minor official, realized he needed more powerful weapons and succeeded in learning the secret of manufacturing gunpowder from a Yuan Chinese named Li Yuan. This allowed Koryŏ to produce formidable weapons using gunpowder and cannons. In 1377 Ch'oe persuaded the government to establish the Hwat'ong togam, or Directorate for Gunpowder Weapons, under his supervision. In 1380 he equipped the Koryŏ navy with cannons and gunpowder, and inflicted a crushing defeat on the Japanese pirates at the estuary of the Kŭm River.

Another major development occurred in the materials used for clothing. Until the late Koryŏ period, hemp had been the principal material for commoners' clothing, and ramie and silk were used for the clothing of the aristocracy and the wealthy. In this period the introduction of cotton seeds and the successful manufacturing of cotton cloth revolutionized Korean clothing, and cotton emerged as a major material for clothing. Cotton seeds were secretly brought to Koryŏ from Yuan in 1364 by Mun Ik-jŏm, who had gone there as secretary to a Koryŏ envoy. He gave the seeds to his father-in-law, Chŏng Ch'ŏn-ik, who not only succeeded in growing cotton but learned to devise a cotton gin and build a spinning wheel from a Chinese monk. Subsequently cotton cloth was mass-produced as the principal material for clothing and would even be used as currency in the later Chosŏn kingdom.

The spread of disease brought on by the many wars of this period encouraged the development of an indigenous medical science. The oldest extant medical work, *Hyangyak kugŭp pang,* or Emergency Remedies of Folk Medicine, published in 1236, was based on Korea's traditional folk remedies. Later, similar works appeared including the thirteenth-century work *Samhwaja hyangyak pang,* or Folk Medicine Remedies of Samhwaja, which served as a diagnostic guide. These medical works laid the groundwork for *Hyangyak chipsŏng pang,* or Compilation of Native Korean Prescriptions, published in the Chosŏn dynasty in 1433.

An especially noteworthy cultural achievement in Koryŏ in this period was the invention of movable metal type, its first appearance in world history. Printing flourished in Koryŏ, and a wide variety of books, including the Tripitaka, was published. Initially most of the printing was done using the woodblock technique. Woodblock printing was convenient to meet the widespread demand for a specific work. When many different works were printed in limited numbers, however, printing by movable type was more efficient and reduced publishing costs. With the emergence of the literati in the late Koryŏ period, the demand for various kinds of books clearly increased.

Printing by movable type is said to have been invented in the eleventh century by Bi Sheng in the Northern Song dynasty, but the material he used for the type was clay. The inconvenience of using clay soon put that material out of use. According to a contemporary record, Koryŏ printers used cast metal type in 1234 for publishing *Sangjŏng kogŭm yemun,* or Prescribed Ritual Texts of the Past and Present. Clearly the type used to print this work was movable metal type. This is hard to confirm, however, as the book has not survived. The oldest extant work printed by movable metal type, now housed in a Paris museum, appeared in 1377; titled *Chikchi simch'e yojŏl,* or An Abstract on Looking Straight at the Mind and Perceiving Buddha's Mind, it is an anthology of the Sŏn teachings of great Buddhist priests. Thus the world's first printed material with metal type was produced in Koryŏ 216 years before Johannes Gutenberg, or at least 73 years before. Koryŏ also produced paper with wooden fiber of the best quality in Asia. In sum, in this late period, Koryŏ achieved great scientific and technological development.

The Founding of the Chosŏn Dynasty

In the reign of King Kongmin, Koryŏ was invaded by the so-called *Honggŏnjŏk,* or Red Turbans, a powerful Chinese peasant force who rebelled against Yuan twice, in 1359 and 1360, and suffered enormous human and material losses. In their first invasion, in late 1359, these Chinese bandits, numbering more than

40,000, occupied Pyongyang. They were repulsed by Koryŏ forces in early 1360; only some 300 escaped alive across the Yalu. These Chinese brigands, amounting to 200,000, invaded Koryŏ again in late 1360 and occupied the capital of Kaesŏng. The king was forced to flee as far south as present-day Andong. They were finally repelled in early 1362, when more than 100,000 of them were killed by the Koryŏ defenders. Koryŏ took advantage of these Chinese invasions to regain control of its northern territory from Yuan. On the other hand, Koryŏ suffered an irreparable blow, which in part caused the kingdom's ultimate downfall.

As already pointed out, another external trouble that shook the Koryŏ dynasty to its core was the Japanese piratical raids that were later stopped by the use of Koryŏ's new gunpowder weaponry. Unlike short-lived Chinese incursions, the raids of *waegu*, or Japanese pirates, extended over a lengthy period and greatly affected the entire country. Piracy of the seaborne Japanese marauders had already begun as early as 1223 and continued until the mid-Chosŏn period. The impoverished Japanese in Tsushima, northern Kyushu, southern Honshu, and along the Sedo-naikai seacoast frequently raided Koryŏ's coastal areas. By 1353 Japanese piracy had become an annual occurrence. The Japanese pirates despoiled the coastal districts and villages on a large scale. Piracy became so severe, in fact, that people had to vacate the seacoast areas for many miles inland, turning the entire coastal region into a no-man's land. At first the Japanese pirates raided the Korean coast, later extending their raids to the Chinese coast. These bands of seagoing bandits gradually increased in number, constituting a small army. They became ever bolder, even raiding towns and villages located 30 to 40 miles inland.[4] Damage from these raids was so severe that the very nation was endangered. The Japanese pirates prevented the vital transportation of grain taxes by sea, and because local taxes could not be brought to the capital, the central government at Kaesŏng faced virtual economic collapse.

Koryŏ's initial attempts to end these waegu attacks by diplomatic means failed, as the Japanese authorities were powerless to suppress these pirates; meanwhile, the impetus for piracy and the poverty of the Japanese continued. But then Koryŏ resorted to military campaigns and, under the command of Ch'oe Yŏng and Yi Sŏng-gye, succeeded in repulsing the Japanese raiders. With his fearful gunpowder weapons, Ch'oe Mu-sŏn also had remarkable success in repelling the Japanese pirates. In 1389 Pak Wi led a direct assault on these pirates' den on Tsushima, destroying more than 300 Japanese ships. Japanese piracy gradually diminished, and thanks to their victorious battles against the Japanese, the influence of Ch'oe Yŏng, and particularly Yi Sŏng-gye, greatly increased.

After Japanese piracy was essentially brought under control, sharp disagreement arose between Ch'oe Yŏng and Yi Sŏng-gye over Koryŏ's policy toward the continent. After expelling Mongols from China proper, the Ming dynasty gradually extended its strength into southern Manchuria, and then shared the border with Koryŏ across the Yalu. In 1388 Ming formally notified Koryŏ of the establishment of the Tianling-wei, or Ch'ŏllyŏng Commandery, to administer the vast area from the Liaodong region of Manchuria to Koryŏ's northeastern territory north of the Ch'ŏl-lyŏng pass, or present-day Hamgyŏng province. Ming demanded the "return" of the Koryŏ territory on the grounds that it had been occupied and administered by Yuan's Ssangsŏng commandery. Upon receiving this demand, the outraged Ch'oe Yŏng, who held power in the government, determined to invade the Liaodong region with a force of 40,000. That same year the expedition was launched, with Ch'oe Yŏng as commander-in-chief and Cho Min-su and Yi Sŏng-gye as deputy commanders.

Yi Sŏng-gye, however, had opposed the expedition from the start. Thus he did not cross the Yalu but marched his troops back from Wihwa-do at the mouth of the river. In a nearly bloodless coup Yi Sŏng-gye ousted King U and Ch'oe Yŏng from power, seizing the reins of government himself. He deposed King U under the pretext that he was not the true heir but the son of the monk Sin Ton. The king, said to have been born to King Kongmin and a slave woman of Sin Ton, was succeeded by King Ch'ang (1388–1389), nine year old. Yi Sŏng-gye removed or exiled many old-line members of powerful family lineage from the court and consolidated his power. As a result of Yi's march back from Wihwa-do, Koryŏ did not conquer the Liaodong region, but, in the end, Ming was unable to take possession of the land belonging to the Tianling-wei, and so Koryŏ did not lose its territory.

Yi and his Neo-Confucian literati supporters such as Chŏng To-jŏn and Cho Chun also deposed King Ch'ang on the grounds that he was a grandson of Sin Ton, and in his place raised King Kongyang (1389–1392) to the throne. Then they carried out a sweeping land reform that had long been advocated by the literati class and dreamed of by the populace for many years. These radical elements were opposed by a moderate group led by Yi Saek, but these moderates were swiftly purged from the government. Because opponents of land reform offered stubborn resistance, Yi Sŏng-gye had to keep them in submission by the power of the sword. Land reform represented the destruction of the old economic order that had been maintained and enjoyed by Koryŏ's powerful families and its replacement by a new order that would benefit the rising literati class.

In 1390 Yi Sŏng-gye and his supporters, in a dramatic move, burned the land registers, which were in flames for days, and confiscated all public and private lands. In 1391 an ordinance stipulating a new land system, called the *Kwajŏnpŏp*, or Rank Land Law, was promulgated. Its terms provided for the allocation of land stipends, taken only from the Kyŏnggi region around the capital, to incumbent and former government officials for life in accordance with the rank they had achieved. The land allocated would vary from 10 kyŏl to 150 kyŏl and would be cultivated to support the central bureaucracy. The Yi Sŏng-gye faction was the greatest beneficiary of the land reform. Those who disobeyed Yi received land allotments of just 5 to 10 kyŏl. Recipients were given the right to collect rent, and peasants were given the right to cultivate. The level of taxation to be imposed on farmlands was set at 30 tu, or some 160 kilograms, per kyŏl.

The peasants' livelihood would be stabilized, as they were guaranteed land tenure in terms of cultivation rights and their lands were not subject to confiscation. Further, the accumulation of land by the recipients, namely, office holders, was strictly controlled by the stipulation that land would be granted only in the Kyŏnggi areas, where land accumulation was placed under government supervision and surveillance. The land in the rest of the country was all subsumed under the category of state land, which meant that the agricultural estates of the former powerful families were confiscated, thus completely destroying their economic foundation and causing their ultimate demise. At the same time the land reform represented the eventual downfall of the Koryŏ dynasty and heralded the coming of the new Chosŏn dynasty. The increase in state land resulted in a corresponding increase in government revenues, which secured the economic foundation of the new kingdom.

After completely ousting moderate literati such as Chŏng Mong-ju, who opposed the establishment of a new dynasty and was killed, Yi Sŏng-gye finally ascended the throne in 1392. His crowning was legitimized by the confirmation of the Top'yŏngŭisasa. Yi Sŏng-gye became the founder of Korea's longest-ruling dynasty, Chosŏn, more accurately "Modern Chosŏn," which would survive into the early twentieth century. To make a clean break with the previous dynasty, Yi Sŏng-gye was determined to move the capital to Hanyang (present-day Seoul), which he did in 1394, and the next year Hanyang was renamed Hansŏng. From this time on, Seoul would become the political, economic, social, and cultural center of Korea. Finally Korean history had entered a new era.

From the mid-twelfth century on, the Koryŏ kingdom was afflicted with several rebellions and gradually declined. The turn of the dynastic cycle manifested itself by rebellions and uprisings. After the deadly Mongol invasions, Koryŏ barely preserved its political independence and actually fell under Yuan domination. After freeing itself from Yuan control, Koryŏ failed to recover its previous strength and finally gave way to the new Chosŏn kingdom. Compared to its successor state of Chosŏn, Koryŏ was distinguished by its independence and autonomy. Thus North Korea, a self-proclaimed "state of self-reliance," contends that Koryŏ was superior to any other Korean kingdom in Korean history. North Koreans have even suggested that the name of the unified Korean state be the "Koryŏ Democratic Confederate Republic." An open society, Koryŏ actively accepted foreign cultures from many parts of the civilized world and produced brilliant cultural achievements characterized by cosmopolitanism and diversity.

6

THE FIRST HALF OF THE CHOSŎN PERIOD
(1392–1650)

THE ESTABLISHMENT OF A NEW ORDER

The Beginning of a New Dynasty

THE FIRST CENTURY OF THE CHOSŎN DYNASTY, which ranged from King T'aejo (1392–1398) to King Sŏngjong (1469–1494), saw a new ruling order established and witnessed the dynasty's greatest strength, prosperity, cultural brilliance, and unprecedented vitality. Inheriting the brilliant Koryŏ civilization, the Chosŏn kingdom created its own developed civilization.

Chosŏn was sinicized far more than any previous Korean kingdom in terms of its institutions and culture. Within the first two centuries of its reign, Chosŏn became recognized as even more sinicized than China itself. It was often called *So chunghwa*, or "Little China," meaning that Chosŏn was the perfect embodiment of Chinese ("Middle Kingdom") civilization.

It was also in this period of the new dynasty when the influence of Buddhism greatly diminished. The Chosŏn kingdom launched a sweeping attack on Buddhism and its institutions, with profound and enduring effects on the character of subsequent civilization in Korea. In place of Buddhism, Confucianism, particularly Neo-Confucianism, was instituted as a state philosophy. The Neo-Confucian literati managed to inculcate Confucianism throughout Chosŏn society, which had a profound effect on the position of women. As time went on, women were increasingly relegated to the category of the so-called *naeja,* or "inside people," who devoted themselves to the domestic chores of child rearing and housekeeping.

Confucianism is based on an ideal model of relations between family members that called for special bonds between sovereign and subject, father and son, and husband and wife, as well as five moral disciplines. Confucianism generalized the family model and relationships of subjects to the state and to an international system. In political terms, these principles meant that a village followed the leadership of venerated elders, and citizens revered a king who was thought of as the father of the state. Generalized to international relations, the Chinese emperor was the big brother of the Chosŏn king. A conservative philosophy, Confucianism stressed tradition, strict social hierarchies, obedience to superiors, and identification of the father with the monarch. It adopted the proper rite as one of its major virtues and therefore paid careful attention to the performance of ritual. In the international context, it envisioned a China-centered world order.

Yi Sŏng-gye, known by the posthumous title T'aejo, promptly sought confirmation of his status by the Chinese Ming emperor and eventually received it. In 1393 he renamed the new dynasty Chosŏn, with the Ming emperor's approval. Two names, Chosŏn and Hwaryŏng, had been presented to the Chinese, and although Hwaryŏng was Yi Sŏng-gye's birthplace, Chosŏn was presented to the Ming emperor based on the idea that the new dynasty would succeed Korea's ancient state of "Old Chosŏn." Thus the Chinese recommended Chosŏn as the name of their neighboring state.

In 1394 the new dynasty moved its capital to Hanyang (Seoul), located almost in the center of the Korean peninsula. To the south of Hanyang was the Han River, which enabled the new capital to secure good facilities for water transport, and it was surrounded by high mountains, creating a heaven-sent fortified zone. Already in the earlier Koryŏ dynasty Hanyang had been regarded as a propitious locale. King Munjong (1046–1083) elevated the city to the status of Nam-gyŏng. King Sukchong (1095–1105) constructed a palace in the town, frequently touring and staying there for several months annually. Several Koryŏ kings attempted to move the capital to this southern town, but this was blocked based on the geomantic belief that not the Wang house but the Yi house would become the master of the city. Yi Sŏng-gye finally succeeded in relocating the capital, and built royal shrines, palaces, and a fortified wall surrounding it, making it the center of political power.

After six years on the throne Yi Sŏng-gye wearied of the power struggles within his family and, in 1398, abdicated the throne in favor of his second son, King Chŏngjong (1398–1400). The transition of power from the Koryŏ kingdom to the Chosŏn kingdom was relatively peaceful, with little damage to property or life. But there was a power struggle within the royal Yi family, in which Yi Pang-wŏn, the fifth son of Yi Sŏng-gye, was behind most of the plots and undertakings that had made his father the founder of the Chosŏn kingdom. He used extraordinary measures, including the assassination of political foes such as Chŏng Mong-ju, a moderate Neo-Confucian scholar-official loyal to Koryŏ, whom he killed in 1392. His father never approved his son's aggression and cruel behavior.

As soon as Yi Sŏng-gye ascended the throne, he named the youngest of his eight sons, Pang-sŏk, the crown prince, bypassing Pang-wŏn. Confounding matters, each son had a private army of his own. In 1398 in the "First Strife of Princes," Pang-wŏn attacked and killed two of the king's youngest sons, including the crown prince (his half-brother). He also slaughtered his father's two eminent merit subjects, Chŏng To-jŏn and Nam Ŭn, who then patronized the crown prince. Yi Sŏng-gye, aghast that his sons were willing to kill each other for the throne, abdicated, and the second son, Pang-gwa, was made king. But he was a puppet of Pang-wŏn, who watched his every move. Pang-gwa was named King Chŏngjong but was not much of a king, as Pang-wŏn controlled every affair of the nation. Then Yi Sŏng-gye's fourth son, Pang-gan, emerged as Pang-wŏn's political rival. In 1400 in the "Second Strife of Princes," Pang-gan attacked his younger brother with his own army but was defeated. Pang-wŏn exiled his older brother and killed his brother's subordinates.

Thoroughly intimidated, King Chŏngjong abdicated the throne in favor of his younger brother, Pang-wŏn. In 1400 Pang-wŏn became the third king of the Chosŏn kingdom, King T'aejong (1400–1418). Yi Sŏng-gye was so disheartened that he returned to his birthplace, now called Hamhŭng. Once he ascended the throne, King T'aejong became an effective ruler who did much to consolidate royal authority. Before actually taking the throne, T'aejong had already seized political power and made drastic reforms. In 1400 he abolished private armies, thereby instituting centralized military control and increasing the number of men employed in the national military. At the same time he changed the Top'yŏngŭisasa into the Ŭijŏngbu, with greatly diminished power and authority. All decisions passed by the Ŭijŏngbu could only come into effect with the king's approval. He entrusted the overall conduct of government business to six ministries, each authorized to receive royal commands directly. In these ways the monarch could participate directly in the administration, bringing royal power to new heights. He confiscated a great deal of Buddhist property, thus completing the land reform. In 1413 he initiated the first population survey and ordered the documentation of family names and clans, as well as places and dates of birth and death for all males. He required males over the legal age of 16, whatever their class in society, to carry wooden tablets, called *hop'ae*, or identification tags, engraved with their name, date of birth, birthplace, and other information, in effect preventing peasants from abandoning the land they tilled or evading the mandatory military draft service. Although he was an effective monarch, his brutal method for ascending the throne had set a precedent of bloody purges among royalty and the bureaucracy that continued throughout the Chosŏn dynasty and greatly contributed to the weakening of the kingdom.

King Sejong the Great

In its heyday, the Chosŏn dynasty produced its greatest king in Korea's long history and through its many different dynasties. Given the reign name Sejong (1418–1450), King Sejong was not only a wise, benevolent ruler but a noted scholar, scientist, and inventor, who organized the best talent of the country and achieved unprecedented advances for his country and people. He established the Chipp'yŏnjŏn, or Hall of Worthies, assigned outstanding scholars to it, and had them study the ancient statutes and institutions of Korea and China and provide him with advice and suggestions. He sent Yi Chong-mu to attack Tsushima, the lair of the Japanese pirates, in 1419, and ordered Kim Chong-sŏ to establish the *yuk chin*, or six garrison forts, in the northeastern part of the peninsula in 1437. He delegated Ch'oe Yun-dŏk and Yi Ch'ŏn to create the *sa gun*, or four outposts, along the upper Yalu in 1433, thus extending Korea's northern frontier to the Yalu and Tumen rivers.

King Sejong's greatest achievement was the scientific systematization of the Korean written alphabet, han'gŭl. Promulgated to the public in 1446, han'gŭl, a UNESCO Memory of the World, is one of the world's premier phonetic alphabets for accurately representing the sounds of words. Perhaps the most scientific system of writing in general use in any country, the Korean alphabet, which now consists of 10 vowels and 14 consonants, possesses geometric beauty, simplicity, and scientific accuracy, and, as such, can be learned by an uneducated man in a matter of hours.

King Sejong pursued the realization of Confucian humanism through his numerous accomplishments, including the invention of han'gŭl and the reduction in the land tax rate from one-tenth of the harvest to one-twentieth, all of which contributed to improving people's lives.[1] He also engendered a modern national consciousness in the minds of the people. After his death in 1450, the people venerated King Sejong as *Haedong yosun,* or Yao-Shun East of the Sea (Korea), named after China's two legendary sage kings.

Kings Sejo and Sŏngjong

After the reign of King Sejong, a rift developed between the king and Confucian scholar-officials. The first son of Sejong succeeded him to become King Munjong (1450–1452), but he was ill and died after two years. His son, Tanjong (1452–1455), was only 12 years old when he became king in 1452, and state affairs were left to state councilors, as monarchical power declined. At this very point the king's uncle, Prince Suyang, seized control of the government. He removed the opposition by killing his own younger brother, Prince Anp'yŏng, as well as many able government officials including the elder politicians Hwangbo In and Kim Chong-sŏ. When Prince Suyang finally seized the throne as Sejo (1455–1468) three years later, in 1455, many Confucian officials disapproved of Suyang's usurpation of the throne as a violation of Confucian ethics. In 1456 some of these officials, including Sŏng Sam-mun, Pak P'aeng-nyŏn, Ha Wi-ji, Yi Kae, Yu Ŭng-bu, and Yu Sŏng-wŏn, who came to be known in later days as the *sa ryuksin,* or six martyred subjects, gathered secretly and plotted to depose Sejo. Unfortunately for them, the plan came to light before they were ready to take action. Many were ruthlessly slaughtered, and others went into hiding. Sejo sent his young nephew into exile but then killed him in 1457. Although immoral in terms of Confucian ethics, Sejo's accession to the throne not only consolidated kingly authority but also led to national prosperity.

In 1468 Sejo was succeeded by his second son, Yejong (1468–1469), and following Yejong's death in 1469, his nephew succeeded him as King Sŏngjong (1469–1494). As his posthumous title implies, the administrative structure of the Chosŏn dynasty was set in place under his reign. Sŏngjong set about compiling a statutory code that would define the structure and functioning of the Chosŏn government, and, in 1470, he produce the *Kyŏngguk taejŏn,* which became the cornerstone of the dynastic administration and provided a sort of constitutional law in written form. Sŏngjong's reign also saw the compilation of poetry and prose from the past ages in a volume titled *Tongmun sŏn*, or Anthology of Korean Literature (1478); a geographical work on Korea titled *Tongguk yŏji sŭngnam*, or Augmented Survey of the Geography of the Eastern Kingdom (1481); and a general Korean history titled *Tongguk t'onggam*, or Comprehensive Mirror of the Eastern Kingdom (1484). Thus, 100 years after the establishment of the Chosŏn dynasty, a new ruling order and culture finally were completed.

Yangban Society

From the beginning Chosŏn was an utterly hierarchical society. At the apex stood the yangban whose members served in the bureaucracy as civil or military officials. Along with the royal family, they were the social aristocracy of the state, virtually monopolizing the state's education, official positions, and farmland. Although Chosŏn's yangban class was far more broadly based than the ruling classes of Koryŏ or earlier ages, it was still a privileged minority group, comprising less than 10 percent of the entire population. A sharp social cleavage existed between the yangban and other lower classes, as members of the yangban class became government officials almost entirely through the kwagŏ, or state examination. The examination system was virtually the only road to attaining a high-level official position throughout the Chosŏn period. Confucian academic training was an indispensable condition for appointments to office through the examination system, and a number of educational institutions were established to provide this training to those in the yangban class. Many yangban members were not in government office, mainly because there were no vacancies. Those without government positions lived as scholars, many of them teachers or agrarian landlords who hoped to take or resume office based on their own merit or through factional patronage.

The yangban were exempt from nearly all the exactions placed upon commoners, whether land and tribute taxes, corvee labor, or military conscription. As Confucianism disdained working with one's hands, the yangban avoided manual labor even to the point of starvation. They only gave themselves up to study, cultivating themselves to become sŏnbi, or men of virtue. The yangban, in short, were a parasitic, privileged class. Because Confucianism emphasized proper form in social activity, rites and ceremonies were as important for the yangban as the substance of government. In Korea, as in China, one of the six government ministries, Ye-bu in Koryŏ and Ye-jo in Chosŏn, specialized in rites which, in the Confucian view, included relations with foreign states.

The yangban closed the door to other social classes aspiring to attain their status and special privileges. In fact, virtually no movement occurred into or out of the yangban class. Yangban members married only persons within their own class, securing them hereditary yangban status. They did not even reside in the same villages as those who were not yangban, preferring to live in the capital although they also resided in countryside estates. In any cases, separate villages were formed as yangban residences. But even within the yangban class, strict social distinctions were drawn. First, the military order was less well treated than the civil order, as the Chosŏn kingdom had become dominated by Confucian scholars who generally despised the military. In the beginning of the dynasty, the princes and other men of military-officer background had commanded their private armies and used them to gain personal power. As a result, a deep-seated distrust of the military developed, and military officials were rarely appointed to ministerial or higher posts. Those of illegitimate birth were also excluded from important government office. Sons of the yangban by secondary wives and their descendants were not regarded as yangban and were barred from sitting for the state examinations. In Chosŏn's strict Confucian society, where women's fidelity was highly prized, sons and grandsons of yangban widows who remarried could not serve in government office. There was regional discrimination as well; residents of the northern provinces of P'yŏngan and Hamgyŏng would find it almost impossible to obtain an appointment to higher office. All these restrictions were designed to maintain the yangban's position as a privileged minority, for yangban members feared that an increase in their numbers would deprive them of their special social position.

Although the yangban all aspired to public office, they seldom served in the lower-ranking technical posts. The so-called *chungin,* or middle people, occupied these technical specialties on a hereditary basis, serving as scribes, medical officers, translators and interpreters, technicians in science-related fields, government artists, and local functionaries called hyangni or *ajŏn.*

Although Chosŏn was a hierarchical society from the start, initially it was not so closed as to make upward mobility completely impossible. As time went on, however, yangban society was firmly established, with yangban members constituting a select ruling elite and enjoying all sorts of special privileges. Even the most talented in the kingdom could find little opportunity to exercise their faculties if they were from the lower classes.

REORGANIZATION OF THE RULING STRUCTURE

Administrative Framework

Although in theory the king held autocratic power, in reality he could exercise his exclusive authority only regarding personnel appointments and acts of treason. Under Confucian precepts, he was required to govern his country wisely and thus had to heed the advice of the Confucian scholar-officials who, in effect, could curb the excessive exercise of regal power. Every day the king deliberated and decided state affairs with key government officials, a process termed *sangch'am*, or constant attendance. Along with the monarch, a bureaucracy of scholar-officials, acting as the agent of the king's will, controlled central government functions and extended its control into the countryside, from the provincial to the county level.

The Chosŏn kingdom's basic administrative structure was established during its first quarter-century of rule, but important additions were made in the next half-century. This structure was not much different from that of Koryŏ's government. The highest government organ was the Ŭijŏngbu, which had evolved from Koryŏ's Top'yŏngŭisasa, or Supreme Council. In 1400 the Top'yŏngŭisasa was replaced by the Ŭijŏngbu as a deliberative organ. Joint decisions of the Ŭijŏngbu were made by three high-level state councilors, called *chŏngsŭng*. These three top-ranking officials included the *yŏngŭijŏng*, or chief state councilor, *chwaŭijŏng*, or left state councilor, and *uŭijŏng*, or right state councilor, who preliminarily discussed important matters of state, agreed upon decisions, and, after receiving the king's approval, transmitted them to appropriate government agencies. At the same time they were in charge of several other organs, such as the Ch'unch'ugwan. In addition, they were responsible for *kyŏngyŏn*, or royal teaching, and *sŏyŏn*, or teaching the crown prince. Both were usually conducted three times a day for delivering lectures on Confucian classics to the king and the crown prince. Compared to Koryŏ's Top'yŏngŭisasa, Chosŏn's Ŭijŏngbu had far fewer officials and far less power, consisting of only seven members, including three high-level state councilors. Also, as many important government matters were referred for disposition directly to the six ministries, political power of the Ŭijŏngbu was relatively weak. The Ŭijŏngbu primarily served an advisory role to the throne.

The yuk-cho, composed of the Yi-jo, Pyŏng-jo, Ho-jo, Hyŏng-jo, Ye-jo, and Kong-jo, in order of importance, functioned as the chief executive organs. The six ministries received royal commands directly on matters under their purview and then execute the king's decisions. Although the respective areas of juris-diction of Chosŏn's yuk-cho were almost the same as those of Koryŏ's yuk-pu, the political importance of the former was much greater. High-level officials of these six ministries not only executed the king's decisions but also sat in company with the king and with high-level state councilors of the Ŭijŏngbu to deliberate important matters of government.

There were two censoring organs—the Sahŏnbu, or Office of the Inspector-General, and the Saganwŏn, or Office of the Censor-General. The former was created to scrutinize and criticize government policy and the actions of offi-cials, whereas the latter censured the conduct of the king. These two oversight bodies were joined by the Hongmun'gwan, or Office of Propagation and Lit-erature, to form the so-called sam-sa, or three offices. Whereas the Sahŏnbu was responsible for criticizing daily political issues and ferreting out officials' dishonesty and maladministration, the Saganwŏn complained to the sovereign in the event of wrongful or improper action or policy, and thus imposed con-siderable restraint on arbitrary actions of the monarch. The Hongmun'gwan, which succeeded the Chipp'yŏnjŏn that Sejo had abolished in 1456, oversaw the royal library and served as an advisory body to the king as well as a research institute for the study of Confucian classics. It also authored major state docu-ments. Overall, this was a delicate system of checks and balances that prevented concentration of political power in any one branch of government. Officials who served in the three offices were generally younger and of lower rank but they gained strong academic reputations, and these three offices offered the fastest route to the highest posts.

Other important offices included the Sŭngjŏngwŏn, or Royal Secretariat; the Ch'unch'ugwan; the Ŭigŭmbu, or Royal Investigation Bureau; and the Hansŏngbu, or Capital Office. The Sŭngjŏngwŏn's primary role was to transmit royal decrees to the appropriate offices and present the king with petitions from officialdom and the populace. Court historians of the Ch'unch'ugwan recorded daily occurrences in the court, made verbatim records of royal conversations, and were empowered to criticize the king and keep him under close observa-tion. The Ŭigŭmbu dealt with treason and other serious cases that concerned the monarch, and the Hansŏngbu was responsible for running the capital.

Peculiar to the Chosŏn's political system was the institution of *sangso*, or memorials to the throne. Every Chosŏn official was able to send a memorial to the king, and the general population could memorialize the government on its policies or unjust treatment. Local government transmitted these memorials from the people to the central government, and in turn the central government reviewed these individually to understand the people's will regarding its policy.

In 1413 Koryŏ's former division of the country was reorganized into eight provinces: Kyŏnggi, Ch'ungch'ŏng, Kyŏngsang, Chŏlla, Hwanghae, Kangwŏn, P'yŏngan, and Hamgil (Hamgyŏng). These were divided into more than 350 counties of several types, specifically pu, mok, kun, and hyŏn. Chosŏn elevated Koryŏ's special administrative units—the hyang, so, and pugok—to the higher status of counties. Chosŏn regarded the figure "eight" as sacred and preferred it, as it represented a "tree" and symbolized the kingdom. According to the Naturalists of the yin-yang school in China, the "tree" was one of "five elements" or "five powers" (along with fire, earth, metal, and water), varying combinations of which constituted all of nature.[2] The counties numbered 350 to represent the days of the year.

In the Koryŏ period central government officials were not sent to all the local administrative units, but Chosŏn's central government dispatched its officials to every county to maintain central control over the local inhabitants. A governor, called *kwanch'alsa*, or *kamsa*, as well as *pangbaek*, was appointed to each province, which, as noted, was subdivided into counties of various types: pu, headed by the *puyun* or *pusa*, administrative offices in charge of major cities; mok, administered by *moksa*, administrative offices that governed the large counties; and kun and hyŏn, headed by the *kunsu* and *hyŏllyŏng* or *hyŏn'gam*, respectively, administrative offices that were responsible for the smaller counties. Often called the "people's shepherd," the county magistrate governed the local populace on behalf of the central government; his duties, known as the *suryŏng ch'il-sa*, or seven affairs of a county magistrate, included promoting agriculture, increasing the population by encouraging childbirth, advancing education and military preparedness, collecting land and tribute taxes, mobilizing corvee labor, ensuring fair justice, and maintaining public peace and order. His principal duty, however, was to collect taxes and mobilize corvee labor for the central government.

Empowered with broad administrative and judicial duties, the provincial and county officials were appointed for fixed terms limited to one year for provincial governors and five years for county magistrates in order to prevent corruption. Also, central government officials were never assigned to posts in their home districts. In local provincial and county administrations, duties were allocated among the *yuk-pang*, or six chambers, which included personnel, military affairs, taxation, punishment, rites, and engineering, modeled on

MAP 6.1. Chosŏn

the six ministries in the capital. Provincial governors and county magistrates were reassigned frequently, providing an essential connection and continuity between the central government and the local population to *yuk-pang* functionaries, called hyangni or ajŏn. Not included in the civil service structure, these men often inherited their posts and served for life. Native to the area where they served, they played an important liaison role with the agricultural villages where the bulk of the population lived. Hyangni had also existed in Koryŏ, and at the time they were a powerful local elite. In Chosŏn, however, members of the hyangni class only acted as aides to the provincial governor or county magistrate and were barred from rising to yangban status.

A self-governing organ existed for local populations. The central government organized the *Yuhyangso,* later renamed the Hyangch'ŏng, or Local Agency, in each county, which was comprised of its leading residents whose opinions wielded considerable influence on the local government. This office was directed by an overseer, called the *chwasu,* and his assistants, called *pyŏlgam.* It assisted the magistrate, edified local inhabitants, and reported functionaries to the magistrate for misconduct. In short, the Yuhyangso or Hyangch'ŏng functioned as a local assembly. In Seoul, meanwhile, each county was represented by another office, called the Kyŏngjaeso, or Capital Liaison Office. Headed by an influential person dispatched from his county, it served as a link between the central government and the Yuhyangso.

This refined system of government worked well in the early period and contributed to the realization of Chosŏn's golden age. Power centers in the central government, however, were increasingly transformed into battlegrounds for high-level government officials. Political infighting and factional struggles within the central government bureaucracy led to continual vicious bloodlettings.

Military Organization

The early Chosŏn period witnessed the reinforcement of its national defense force. Immediately after the founding of the new dynasty, members of the royal household, merit subjects, and others still retained their own personal armed forces. In 1400 T'aejong, who held real power under his older brother Chŏngjong, abolished these private armies, transforming them into national defense forces. From the beginning the Chosŏn kingdom implemented the universal conscription system recruiting soldiers from among commoners. Incumbent government officials and Confucian students were exempt from military service but, otherwise, every able-bodied man from 16 to 60 years of age was required to serve as a soldier or as a sustainer who would provide economic support to conscript soldiers on active duty. The latter generally paid the nation a bolt of cotton cloth a year. Regular army soldiers served for two or three months annually. These peasant-soldiers were called up to active duty in Seoul or at the garrisons or navy garrisons in the provinces and then returned to their farms on a rotational basis. There were also professional military men who usually guarded the royal palace and defended the capital, or became low-ranking commanding officers in the local army commands. They were selected through tests of their military skills.

In 1457 King Sejo divided the country into five military districts—the center, east, west, south, and north—and integrated the various army units scattered throughout the country into five *wi*, or commands. In 1466 the king placed the five commands under the newly established Owi toch'ongbu, or Five Military Commands Headquarters, which was given authority over Chosŏn's central forces commanded by a civil official.

Ever since the reign of King Sejo, each province had its own army command, called *pyŏngyŏng*, and navy command, called *suyŏng*, each placed under a commanding officer. Under these pyŏngyŏng and suyŏng were a number of garrisons, called *chin*, and navy garrisons, called *p'ochin*. Hamgyŏng and Kyŏngsang provinces, which were exposed to Nuzhen (*Yain*) and Japanese incursions, had two army commands and two navy commands, and Chŏlla province had two navy commands because of its long coastline. Chosŏn also constructed citadels in more than 100 strategically important towns, strengthening its defense in the countryside.

The strong national defense system established in the fifteenth century gradually weakened since the sixteenth century. Thus, in 1583, before the massive Japanese invasion of Chosŏn, the well-known Neo-Confucian scholar-official Yi I proposed that the government build military forces numbering up to 100,000.

Education and Examinations

Because of Confucian reverence for education, the Chosŏn kingdom stressed education, which started very early as students had to learn the extraordinarily difficult classical Chinese language by rote. In their childhood, yangban youth attended the *sŏdang*, or village schools, where they learned the basic Chinese characters with *Ch'ŏnjamun* as the primer, practiced writing them, and studied the basic Chinese classics. They then advanced to one of the four *puhak*, or section schools, in Seoul: the *tong-hak*, or eastern school; the *sŏ-hak*, or western school; the *nam-hak*, or southern school; and the *chung-hak*, or central school. Alternatively, they went on to the *hyanggyo*, or county school, established in each county. They studied Confucian classics, specifically the Four Books and Five Classics of China. After several years of study, the Confucian students in these schools were qualified to sit for the *saengjin-kwa* (*so-kwa*), or licentiate examinations. Those who passed, depending on which examination they took, were called *saengwŏn*, or classics licentiates, or *chinsa*, or literary licentiates. These licentiates could enter the Sŏnggyun'gwan, or National Confucian Academy, in Seoul, which had a capacity to accept 200 students, or sit directly for *mun-kwa*, or the civil examination. Students attending the Sŏnggyun'gwan were the privileged elite whose objective was to prepare for the kwagŏ examination.

The Koryŏ kingdom had already adopted the kwagŏ examination system as a means of selecting competent officials, and the Chosŏn dynasty placed even greater importance on it. Chosŏn strictly restricted privileged appointments to the sons of merit subjects and officials of the 2nd rank and higher, and usually assigned the beneficiaries of the institution to the lower-ranking posts. Therefore, unless one passed through the national examinations, particularly the civil examinations, the path to higher office was virtually closed. The subject matter of the kwagŏ consisted almost entirely of the Chinese classics, history, and belles-lettres. In theory, anyone of commoner status was qualified to sit for the examination; in reality, however, members of the yangban class monopolized the examination, because the educational opportunities needed to pass the examination were available almost exclusively to them. In fact, the commoner population generally lacked the time for studying the difficult Chinese classics.

Qualifying examinations for appointments to civil office were carried out at two levels—saengjin-kwa (so-kwa) and mun-kwa (*tae-kwa*). The saengjin-kwa examinations were of two kinds. Whereas the *saengwŏn-kwa*, or the classics licentiate examination, tested candidates on China's Four Books and Five Classics, the *chinsa-kwa*, or literary licentiate examination, examined skills in composing such Chinese literary forms as poetry, rhymed prose, documentary prose, and essay writing to discuss a specific topic. Each of the two examinations selected 100 successful candidates every three years. Those who passed one of the two examinations were called sangwŏn, or chinsa, and could sit for the higher mun-kwa examination. To become successful candidates in mun-kwa, typically 33 in number, they had to survive both the *ch'o-si*, or preliminary examination, and the *pok-si*, or second-stage examination. The former selected 240 successful candidates, and the latter picked 33. Finally, those who passed the *chŏn-si*, or palace examination, held in the king's presence, were individually ranked and assigned to various office ranks between the 6th junior (12th rank) and the 9th senior (17th rank), and to the corresponding government posts in accordance with their examination grades. When an incumbent official passed the examination, his rank was raised one to four ranks.

The civil examinations were held regularly every three years, and thus the examination was called the *singnyŏn-si*, or triennial examination. In time, the examination was held more frequently than every third year. These irregular examinations included the *chŭnggwang-si*, or augmented examination, conducted to celebrate a national festivity such as the ascension of a new monarch; the *pyŏl-si*, or special examination, held to commemorate other auspicious occasions, including the birth of the future crown prince; and the *alsŏng-si*, or royal visitation examination, held for students of the Sŏnggyun'gwan when the king visited there to perform sacrificial rites at the Confucian shrine in the national academy.

The *mu-kwa*, or military examination, was also held every three years and selected 28 men. Skills in military arts were tested, especially archery, as well as one's knowledge of military science. Like the civil examination, the military exam was held in three stages. During the Korean-Japanese War of 1592–1598, every Chosŏn male of commoner status or higher could sit for the military examination, thus allowing many sons of the yangban by second wives, who were of the lower chungin class, to undertake successful careers as military officers.

To select technical specialists, the Chosŏn dynasty established four *chap-kwa*, or miscellaneous examinations: the *yŏk-kwa*, or translation-interpretation exam; the *ŭi-kwa*, or medical exam; the *ŭmyang-kwa*, or astronomy exam; and the *yul-kwa*, or law exam. These chap-kwa examinations were also carried out every three years and selected a total of 46 men—19 for the yŏk-kwa and 9 each for the ŭi-kwa, the ŭmyang-kwa, and the yul-kwa. The yangban always derided these specialized technical studies and examinations, and generally it was the youth of the chungin class who devoted themselves to these studies and sat for examinations on a hereditary basis.[3]

The kwagŏ system produced a bureaucracy based on personal merit rather than bloodline, placing men of intellectual inclination and philosophical training in charge of government machinery. But this also put government service exclusively in the hands of the upper class, namely, the yangban. Also, because it stressed scholarly, literary, antiquarian, and historical interests, it produced an impractical bureaucracy.

SOCIAL STRUCTURE AND ECONOMIC LIFE

Class Structure

In the early Chosŏn period, the population is estimated to have numbered some five million. The people of Chosŏn were largely divided into four social classes—the yangban, chungin, *sangmin*, or commoners, and ch'ŏnmin. Whereas in the Koryŏ period the yangban had included both civil and military officials, in the Chosŏn dynasty the term referred to social status, specifically the ruling elite class. Members of the yangban class were largely descendants of the newly emerged literati class of the late Koryŏ period. The chungin was comprised of hyangni of the countryside, technical specialists who passed the chap-kwa examinations, and the like.

The vast bulk of society was comprised of people in the sangmin class, mainly peasant farmers, craftsmen, and merchants. These people carried the main burden of producing life's daily necessities and paying taxes. Confucianism, which sought to maintain the social and political status quo and disdained material goods, commerce, and reconstructing society through industrial and commercial development, stressed the importance of farmers as the producers of rice and other foodstuff while minimizing the value of industry and commerce. As a result farmers or peasants, who made up the overwhelming majority of the sangmin people, had a higher status than craftsmen and merchants.

Slaves comprised the most significant component, some 95 percent, of the ch'ŏnmin class, which in the early period amounted to one-third of the total population. In the late Koryŏ period many commoners had fallen into slavery as a result of hardships. Since the reign of King T'aejong, the government emancipated these commoners-turned-slaves, and, moreover, some 100,000 slaves owned by Buddhist temples became commoners or public slaves. In these ways the number of slaves greatly decreased.

Slave status was strictly hereditary, and the Chosŏn law accorded a child the status of his or her mother. As their owners' possessions, slaves were bought and sold, turned over to others, and inherited by heirs, but owners were forbidden to punish slaves to the point of death. Although slaves were called the "hands and feet of the sŏnbi (yangban)" and moved at their beck and call, commoners

—even slaves—could own slaves. In some cases, a master's goodwill could result in the emancipation of a slave.

Slaves were either public slaves possessed by the government or private slaves owned by individuals. Public slaves included those who supported themselves and paid a kind of head tax, particularly in cotton cloth, and those who were mostly artisans and manufactured industrial products at the behest of government offices for a certain portion of the year. Government slaves had better living conditions than private slaves, and were allowed opportunities to earn unlimited wealth. Privately owned slaves included *solgŏ nobi,* or household slaves, and *oegŏ nobi,* or nonresidential slaves. Whereas the former performed every kind of labor in their master's house, the latter kept house for themselves but cultivated their master's land and paid a fixed fee to their owners.

Besides slaves, social and economic outcasts also constituted a small group in the ch'ŏnmin class. These lowborn people engaged in such occupations as butchering, tanning, wickerwork, and entertainment on a hereditary basis, and lived together in separate hamlets. To assimilate them into the general farming population, King Sejong, in 1423, gave them farmland and called them paekchŏng, the term originally used to designate general peasant farmers. Thus outcasts of lowborn status were treated in same manner as commoners, but they did not become peasant farmers. They pursued their hereditary occupations uninterrupted and were treated as ch'ŏnmin. Thereafter the term paekchŏng designated lower-class people in humble occupations.

Chosŏn's class structure was not as rigid and closed as that of Koryŏ. In this early period upward mobility, although a singular phenomenon, was not impossible. Nevertheless, Chosŏn was certainly a hierarchical society.

Patterns of Landholding and Taxation

Like the earlier kingdoms, the Chosŏn dynasty was based on the concept that the monarch formally owned all of the nation's land. What is meant by "formally" is that the state and government recognized private ownership rights to land but levied taxes on the land. With regard to public land, including land confiscated from Buddhist temples, the state directly collected rent, usually 10 percent of the harvest. With private land, allotted to those of high rank or office holders, the government granted the recipients only the right to collect rent, but the original landowners still held ownership rights.

The Kwajŏnpŏp, promulgated in 1391, stipulated that both incumbent and former government officials were to receive land allotments as a substitute for salary in accordance with their rank in the 18 office-rank structure. Only the land in Kyŏnggi province around the capital was allocated to prevent extending the economic strength of the new ruling elite into the countryside. In principle, the land was allocated to recipients for life only. But an official's widow, if she did not remarry, was allowed to retain a portion of her husband's land, and, similarly, if both parents were deceased, part of their land could be held for fostering the children. The former was called *susin-jŏn,* or fidelity land, and the latter *hyuryang-jŏn,* or fostering land. In these ways, land allocated to officials could be held hereditarily.

With the increased number of persons newly eligible to receive land allocations, available land under this program ran short. Within a few years of its promulgation, controversies arose over how this problem would be solved. In 1466 King Sejo replaced the Kwajŏnpŏp with the *Chikchŏnpŏp,* or Office Land Law, in which land was to be allotted only to incumbent officeholders. But this new system also could not sustain itself for long, and in the mid-sixteenth century it was abolished. At this point officials received only a stipend in kind.

Besides lands allocated to officials under both the Kwajŏnpŏp and the Chikchŏnpŏp, several other land allotment programs exacerbated the problems of land allocation. Above all, grants of *kongsin-jŏn,* or merit subject land, increased. The founding of the new dynasty and the ensuing succession struggles added to the number of merit subjects to such an extent that a great deal of land was granted to them as kongsin-jŏn. In 1392, for example, King T'aejo allocated kongsin-jŏn to 43 merit subjects according to their merits. Thereafter his successors followed suit, and vast areas of land were granted to merit subjects whenever political changes occurred. From the beginning it was recognized that lands allotted to merit subjects were hereditary property and might be confiscated later only as punishment for very serious crimes. Increasing kongsin-jŏn led to a shortage of land that could be allocated to prospective officials, a situation aggravated by the fact that *kun-jŏn,* or military land, was assigned to junior military officers who were required to serve as professional military men. Additional allotments included *naesusa-jŏn,* or royal household land, given to the royal family to finance itself; and *konghae-jŏn,* or public agency land, allocated to central government offices to defray their expenses, although this allocation soon came to an end and was replaced by receipts for land and tribute taxes. To meet their expenses, the local government, local schools, Buddhist temples, and provincial and local military garrisons were all granted land allotments. These allocations of land to individuals and organs were the result of the poorly developed monetary economy in this early Chosŏn period.

As time went on, certain aspects of the landholding pattern of the Koryŏ period reappeared. Between generous grants to merit subjects and the enterprise of some leading families, large estates reappeared, owned by yangban bureaucrats in the capital.

In return for cultivation rights, peasant farmers were required to pay a land tax, which the Kwajŏnpŏp set at one-tenth of the harvest. To lighten the peasants' burden King Sejong, in 1444, displaying his great concern for the livelihood of the peasantry, lowered the tax rate to one-twentieth. The land tax was levied differentially in accordance with six grades of fertility and weather conditions, which were judged by nine criteria. Thus, for example, the tax burden on peasant farmers was relatively light when lands were barren and was reduced in less productive years.

The unit measuring the area of farmland was still the kyŏl. At the time when the Kwajŏnpŏp was promulgated in 1391, the total amount of farmland throughout the country was no more than 600,000 to 800,000 kyŏl. Thereafter, land surveys indicated that farmland increased to 1.20 million kyŏl and 1.72 million kyŏl in the reign of T'aejong and Sejong, respectively, as a result of confiscation of Buddhist land, acquisition of territory in the northern region, and reclamation of tideland. Some 90 percent of farmland was public land on which, as noted, the government directly collected rent. Although Sejong reduced the tax rate from one-tenth to one-twentieth, national revenues did not decrease because there was an increase in the total kyŏl of farmland.

Government officials were permitted only to collect rent from land allocated to them by the state, but they gradually gained possession of the allocated land. In fact, private ownership of land was widespread from the start. Extensive land areas were cultivated either by the landowners' slaves or by tenant farmers, who usually hired out their labor and had to pay 50 percent of the harvest as rent. Landholders in turn paid only 10 percent of the harvest to the state as rent and therefore could secure the remaining 40 percent of their share. In this way the big land grantees could accumulate more holdings. The government levied the land tax on peasants but also imposed a business tax on craftsmen and merchants. The tax in kind was collected by the local government and transported to Seoul by riverine and coastal shipping. For example, the grain tax collected in Kyŏngsang province was shipped to Seoul by water traffic through the Naktong and South Han rivers, whereas P'yŏngan and Hamgyŏng provinces in the north consumed the tax paid in kind for their own military expenditure instead of transporting it to Seoul.

In addition to the land tax, peasants were required to pay the tribute tax in kind. Because it was levied on local specialties to meet a wide range of government needs, the tax was known as *t'ogong*, or local tribute. This tax was much more burdensome to the peasantry than the land tax, particularly because the process of paying it always overtaxed the peasants' income.

In addition to conscription for military service for two or three months each year, able-bodied commoner males between 16 and 60 years old were under government obligation to perform corvee labor for six days each year. The government often mustered corvee drafts whenever it saw fit, and so the obligation was an onerous burden for peasant farmers. As before, Chosŏn's commoner population, especially peasant farmers, groaned under heavy obligations.

The Development of Agriculture

In the early Chosŏn period, remarkable growth occurred in agricultural production as a result of territorial expansion in the north, the aggrandizement of agricultural land mainly resulting from the reclamation of coastal areas, population growth, the government's policy to encourage farming, and Confucian literati's study of agricultural management. Improvements in fertilization, including the use of human manure and ashes as fertilizer, contributed to growing multiple crops in dry fields. The development of intensive agriculture made double-cropping possible, specifically beans and barley in dry fields and rice and barley in paddy fields.

Originally the size of Korea's dry fields was more than twice that of paddy fields because of its half-dry climate. Embarking on improving irrigation facilities, the Chosŏn government repaired existing reservoirs and constructed many new dammed pools for irrigation. As a result, by the mid-fifteenth century, Chosŏn had more than 3,000 reservoirs throughout the country. As the use of water wheels improved irrigation efficiency, the total area of paddy fields greatly increased.

Koreans, because of arid spring weather, first sowed rice seeds in dry paddies and then, after the rice plants began to grow, irrigated the paddies. Beginning with the early Chosŏn period, they developed hydroponics, in which they sowed rice seeds directly in the irrigated paddy fields. Also, the technique of rice transplantation developed, in which rice seeds were first planted in a small seedbed, and then, when they reached a suitable stage of growth, were transplanted to the paddies. In the early Chosŏn period, however, the government banned farmers from practicing rice transplantation because of the lack of irrigation facilities.

Still, improved agricultural techniques in the early Chosŏn period greatly increased Korea's rice crop. The 1444 rice crop, for example, was four times higher than the crop in 1391, when the Kwajŏnpŏp was promulgated. This means that the size of kyŏl for rice farming quadrupled after a lapse of some 50 years.

Besides rice, Koreans cultivated millet, beans, barley, Chinese millet, barnyard millet, and Indian millet. In addition, to provide material for clothing, fiber crops such as cotton, hemp, and ramie were raised in large quantities; sericulture also rapidly developed. The government maintained ranches to breed cattle, horses, and sheep. Fifty-eight nationally operated ranches throughout the country raised cattle for use as draft animals and for meat, horses for the military and for tribute gifts to China, and sheep to use in various sacrificial rites.

Handicraft and Commerce

Like their predecessors in the Koryŏ dynasty, craftsmen and artisans in the early Chosŏn period performed their handiwork mainly under government aegis, not private initiatives. The government enrolled all skilled workers on *kongjangan,* or artisan rosters, attached them to various agencies in the capital or to provincial and local governments, and had them manufacture goods to meet the government's needs. In the capital these workers were mainly assigned to agencies such as the Kun'gisi, or Government Arsenal, to produce weapons; the Sangŭiwŏn, or Bureau of Royal Attire, to make court robes; the Saongwŏn, or Bureau of the Palace Kitchen, to manufacture utensils for the royal table; the Kyosŏgwan, or Government Publisher, to print books; and the Chojiso, or Paper Manufactory, to manufacture paper. Altogether some 2,800 skilled workers were employed in the 30 government agencies, undertaking 129 manufacturing assignments. In the provinces, of the more than 3,500 artisans engaged in 29 assignments, most were paper manufacturers, metal workers, mat manufacturers, bow and arrow makers, tanners, and lacquerers.

These skilled workers were required to serve the government for a certain period of time each year and were on the government's payroll. But they did not devote themselves exclusively to supplying the government's requirements. After performing their duties, they worked for themselves on orders from private clients, paying the government a tax for the privilege to do so.

Peasant farmers also engaged in household industry, producing cotton cloth, ramie cloth, hemp, and silk, as well as brassware, farm implements, and paper. Most of the products were used for paying the tribute tax, and surpluses were sold in the markets. The production of cotton cloth was particularly important; as cotton growing rapidly increased, the manufacturing of cotton cloth became widespread. Cotton cloth was not only used by peasants for their own clothing but was also important to the government for military dress and as a major item in the nation's foreign trade. Cotton cloth, as noted previously, was also used as currency.

The development of agriculture and handicrafts led to brisk commercial activities. Commerce mainly developed in populous cities and towns. Seoul in particular, with a population of some 100,000 in the early Choson period, was the commercial center. Already in the reign of King T'aejong, the government established a chain of shops, amounting to 2,600 kan, centered along the main thoroughfare of Chongno, and leased them to merchants. These government-licensed merchants were required to deal in designated articles. In return for their monopolistic commercial rights, these merchants paid a tax in kind and purveyed items required by the government. Since the sixteenth century the so-called *yukŭijŏn*, or six licensed stores, appeared, dealing in drapery, cotton cloth, silk, paper, ramie cloth and hemp, as well as marine products. There were also small stores in Seoul and similar markets in large cities including Kaesŏng, Pyongyang, and Chŏnju.

In the countryside itinerant vendors, called *pobusang*, or pack and back peddlers, engaged in commercial activity. Pack peddlers usually dealt in luxury goods of fine craftsmanship, whereas back peddlers mainly sold the coarse necessities of life such as farm and sea products, and, most important, salt. These peddlers organized themselves into a guild that was sanctioned by the government. Starting in the late fifteenth century peasants in Chŏlla province began to establish irregular markets, called *changsi*, or market, or *changmun*, or market gate, and these soon spread throughout the country. The government suppressed these markets, fearing that the peasants would flee their land and engage in commercial activity. The government's efforts failed, however, and markets began to spring up periodically. Usually open every five days, these markets attracted peasants, artisans, and peddlers, trafficking in such items as agricultural products, handcrafted articles, marine produce, and medical supplies. Because these commercial activities were conducted on the barter system, a monetary economy could not develop. During the sixteenth century the medium of exchange continued to be cotton cloth, called *p'ohwa*, or cloth currency.

TERRITORIAL EXPANSION AND FOREIGN RELATIONS

Relations with Ming China

The relationship Chosŏn established with Ming China was termed *sadae*, or "serving the great." In the sovereign-subject relations between the two countries, a new king ascending the throne in Chosŏn sought the Ming emperor's formal confirmation of his status. By doing so, Chosŏn became Ming's "little brother" and a tributary state. Absolutely convinced of its own superiority, China indulged in a policy that might be called benign neglect, thereby allowing Chosŏn substantive autonomy as a nation. The relationship between Chosŏn and Ming was, indeed, amicable, and when the Japanese invaded Chosŏn in 1592, Ming helped Chosŏn at that critical time by dispatching an army called the *ch'ŏnbyŏng*, or heavenly army. In the seventeenth century, when Ming was attacked by the Manchu people, Chosŏn reciprocated, sending an army to help its Chinese ally.

In the course of paying homage to Ming, Chosŏn sent its envoys to the Chinese empire at any opportunity available. For instance, each year a Chosŏn envoy was sent to Ming to offer felicitations on the New Year. Envoys were also dispatched on the occasions of a Ming ruler's death or a successor's accession to the throne, and Ming acted similarly. Although all these diplomatic missions were meant to strengthen ties with Ming, they were also opportunities for economic exchange. The articles Chosŏn exported to Ming included paper, writing brushes, straw mats with floral designs, gold, silver, ginseng, furs, ramie cloth, and horses, and in return Chosŏn imported books, silk fabrics, medicines, and stationary. In particular, Chosŏn's paper was so durable and smooth that the Chinese nicknamed it the "paper of mirror surface." Because Chosŏn was praised as the "country of courteous people in the East," Chosŏn's envoys were given special, favorable treatment at the Chinese court.

Acquisition of the Northern Regions and Relations with Nuzhens

The early Chosŏn kings actively sought to incorporate the regions south of the Yalu and Tumen rivers into their kingdom's domain. In the reign of King Sejong the two rivers made up Korea's northern frontier, whose native inhabitants were Nuzhens, who at the time Koreans called *Yain*, or barbarians. In 1433 King Sejong sent an expeditionary force against the Yain people in the upper Yalu region, with Ch'oe Yun-dŏk and Yi Ch'ŏn in command, which led to the establishment of four outposts along the river, at Yŏyŏn, Uye, Chasŏng, and Much'ang. The region long held by the Nuzhen people was incorporated into the territory of Chosŏn. In 1437 another army, commanded by Kim Chong-sŏ, was sent to exercise Chosŏn's sovereign power over the territory south of the Tumen River and also drive the Yain people beyond the river. Kim Chong-sŏ created six garrisons in the northeastern part of the Korean peninsula, at Chongsŏng, Onsŏng, Hoeryŏng, Kyŏngwŏn, Kyŏnghŭng, and Puryŏng. As a result, the domain that Korea now occupies was finally fashioned, and inhabitants of the three southern provinces of Kyŏngsang, Chŏlla, and Ch'ungch'ŏng were encouraged to migrate to this newly acquired northern region.

Originally the Yain people led a half-agricultural, half-hunting life, and from Chosŏn they obtained grain, clothing, and other basic needs. To acquire these daily necessities, they sometimes invaded Chosŏn territory. To pacify them, Chosŏn opened markets at Kyŏngsŏng and Kyŏngwŏn, where the Yain people bartered their horses and furs for grain, cloth, and farm implements. Chosŏn also welcomed their formal submission and immigration, granting titular rank, food and clothing, and houses to those who pledged their loyalty. Nevertheless, because of the basic shortage of daily necessities, the Yain continued their pillaging.

Relations with the Japanese

The Chosŏn policy toward Japan was known as *kyorin*, or neighborly relations, and was one of equality. Although Japanese piracy had almost subsided by the end of the Koryŏ dynasty, it had not been completely eliminated but continued to occur from time to time in the early Chosŏn period. The impoverished Japanese, particularly those on Tsushima, frequently raided the costal areas of Chosŏn. In 1419 King Sejong sent a punitive expedition of 227 ships and some 17,000 naval forces, under the command of Yi Chong-mu, to Tsushima. For 15 days Chosŏn forces killed 114 Japanese pirates, burned 2,000 houses to the ground, and captured 129 Japanese ships, which finally led the lord of Tsushima to surrender. Thereafter, to pacify the Japanese, Chosŏn granted them limited trading privileges. In 1426 three ports were opened to the Japanese along the southeast coast, at Pusanp'o (Tongnae, today part of Pusan), Naeip'o (Ungch'ŏn; present-day Ch'angwŏn, South Kyŏngsang province), and Yŏmp'o (present-day Ulsan). For the Japanese to conduct business with Chosŏn, trading and living quarters called the *waegwan*, or Japanese quarters, were established in each of the three open ports. Later the Japanese imported large quantities of rice and cotton cloth from Chosŏn. In 1443 Chosŏn worked out a treaty, in which the number of Japanese ships that might trade with Chosŏn was set at 50 each year, and the ships were permitted in port only upon presenting credentials issued by the lord of Tsushima.

Items exported to Japan included life's necessities such as rice and beans, cotton cloth, hemp and ramie cloth, handcrafted articles such as porcelain ware, and books. In return, the Japanese sent minerals including copper, sulfur, and tin, as well as dyestuffs, medicines, and spices. In 1411 the Japanese presented an elephant to King T'aejong, causing widespread excitement in the country.

Chosŏn also engaged in economic and cultural exchanges with the Ryukyu Islands, Siam, and Java. Ryukyu, in particular, actively sent envoys to Koryŏ and Chosŏn, paying homage to these Korean kingdoms with its indigenous products in return for the Buddhist Tripitaka, temple bells, and Buddhist images. The streets in front of the Kyŏngbok-kung palace were said to have thronged with foreign envoys, and with merchants from Japan and Southeast Asian countries. As time went on, however, Chosŏn increasingly pursued an isolationist policy, closing its door to foreigners, and such lively scenes no longer occurred.

CULTURE IN EARLY CHOSŎN

The Creation of Han'gŭl

From early times Koreans wrote their literary works in classical Chinese and accepted Chinese culture. They always wanted an indigenous alphabet, however, because of the discordance between their language and Chinese writing, as well as the difficulty in studying the latter. Thus Koreans created several primitive alphabets, but they were all inadequate to express their spoken language and still difficult to learn.

As the need for a writing system designed to express the everyday spoken language increased, King Sejong, in 1446, created han'gŭl, which was initially called the *Hunmin chŏngŭm*, or Correct Sounds to Instruct the People. The people readily learned and used this new system of writing, and indeed it promoted literacy among the common people.

Although han'gŭl was a simple and almost perfect system for writing the native Korean language, this masterful creation functioned only as an auxiliary to Chinese writing. The official written language continued to be Chinese, although han'gŭl contributed to pronouncing the Chinese characters in a way that conformed to the Korean language. There had been many phrases with Chinese characters in Korean vocabularies, and so the Korean language could not be understood without them. Furthermore, as Chinese had already taken root as the common writing system, Koreans could not help using it. Han'gŭl, therefore, was not well received by the ruling yangban class of the day, as they wanted to retain their monopoly on access to learning through the use of the difficult Chinese writing system. In the Confucian state of Chosŏn, literacy was power itself.

After it was created, however, han'gŭl was put to practical use in several ways. First, a number of major works written in Chinese were translated into the Korean alphabet and could be more widely read among the general population. In the reign of kings Sejong and Sejo, several important opuses were translated into han'gŭl, including *Yongbi ŏch'ŏn ka,* or Songs of Flying Dragons, which was a eulogy of the virtues of the royal ancestors; and two hymns titled *Wŏrin ch'ŏn'gang chi kok,* or Songs of the Moon's Reflection on a Thousand Rivers, and *Sŏkpo sangjŏl,* or Episodes from the Life of the Buddha, which together were titled *Wŏrin sŏkpo.* These han'gŭl translations were known as a special genre, *ŏnhae,* or vulgate elucidations. In the sixteenth century Confucian texts such as the Five Classics, agricultural manuals, and military texts were also translated into the Korean alphabet. Thus han'gŭl was known as *ŏnmun,* or vulgate writing. Government clerks who engaged in routine administrative affairs used han'gŭl to enable common people to easily understand national policies. Ladies of the palace and wives and daughters of yangban families used han'gŭl extensively in exchanging letters and writing literary works, and even scholar-officials, with a profound knowledge of the Chinese writing system, composed poems and prose in han'gŭl. *Tongguk chŏngun,* or Correct Pronunciations of the Eastern Kingdom, compiled in 1447, was a text for studying how to conform pronunciation of Chinese characters to the native Korean language. Although initially rebuffed by the yangban literati, han'gŭl's increasingly extended use ultimately made it the national script for Koreans.

Compilation of Histories, Geographies, and Rites

In the reigns of King Sejong through King Sŏngjong, a variety of scholarly works on history, geography, and rite were compiled and produced under government aegis. These were mainly written from a Confucian perspective and so were closely related to the realities of the Confucian Chosŏn dynasty. Past history was regarded as an exemplar for the king and government, which heightened interest in the compilation of historical works. The work to compile a history of each reign already began in 1392, immediately after the founding of the dynasty, and *T'aejo sillok*, or Annals of King T'aejo, was completed in 1413. Thereafter the process of compiling *sillok* lasted until the end of the dynasty, producing the basic record known collectively as *Chosŏn wangjo sillok*, or Annals of the Chosŏn Dynasty, a UNESCO Memory of the World. *Sillok* records were drafted by *sagwan*, or history officials, at the Ch'unch'ugwan, and, to safeguard them, copies were placed in four widely separated depositories called *sago*, or history archives, in Seoul (Ch'unch'ugwan), Chŏnju, Sŏngju, and Ch'ungju.

When special events such as royal marriages, royal funerals, palace festivals, and royal visits occurred, the government kept detailed records of the activities, participants, and expenses of the events, with illustrations, in specially complied works called the *Ŭigue*, or Royal Protocols. Throughout the Chosŏn dynasty, a total of 3,895 volumes of the *Ŭigue*, a UNESCO Memory of the World, were compiled. Only the Chosŏn kingdom created such special works in East Asia. The Chosŏn government also compiled *Kukcho pogam*, or A Precious Mirror for Succeeding Reigns, which drew examples from *sillok* of the good governing practices of earlier monarchs for the edification of their successors. The *Kukcho pogam* first appeared in 1458 and continued throughout the dynasty until 1909, immediately before the downfall of the dynasty, totaling 90 volumes when completed.

The Chosŏn kingdom rewrote the Koryŏ kingdom's official history from a Neo-Confucian perspective. In East Asia, the current dynasty traditionally established the official account of its preceding dynasty. Thus, just as Koryŏ had written *Samguk sagi*, the Chosŏn dynasty compiled works on Koryŏ history. After a prolonged effort that began in the reign of King T'aejo, the much revised final version of *Koryŏ sa*, or History of Koryŏ, was completed in 139 volumes by Chŏng In-ji in 1451.[4] It was compiled in the format of annals, chronological tables, treatises, and biographies modeled on Kim Pu-sik's *Samguk sagi*. At almost the same time, in 1452, the 35-volume *Koryŏ sa chŏryo*, or Essentials of Koryŏ History, was written in strictly chronological form by Kim Chong-sŏ. Both *Koryŏ sa* and *Koryŏ sa chŏryo* were written from a Neo-Confucian perspective. Whereas the former emphasized the role of the monarch, the latter stressed the function of bureaucrat-officials. Chŏng To-jŏn and Kim Chong-sŏ each wrote a history of Koryŏ that made the role of bureaucrat-officials more prominent than that of the monarch; as a result, they incurred the hatred of Kings T'aejong and Sejo, respectively, and were put to death. Naturally the monarchs attempted to disseminate *Koryŏ sa* rather than *Koryŏ sa chŏryo*.

After a series of revisions, Korea's first overall history, *Tongguk t'onggam*, or A Comprehensive Mirror of the Eastern Kingdom, was completed in 1485 in 56 volumes, offering, chronologically, the entire Korean history from Tan'gun through the end of Koryŏ. At the time Tan'gun was honored as the progenitor of the Korean race, and a comprehensive history naturally began with an account of the Tan'gun era.

In order to rule the local population effectively, the Chosŏn government conducted a geographical survey of the entire kingdom and compiled works on the cultural and physical geographies of the country. The first was *Sinch'an p'alto chiriji*, or Newly Compiled Geographical Descriptions of the Eight Provinces, which appeared in 1432. It was incorporated as an eight-volume treatise into *Sejong sillok*, or the Annals of King Sejong, in 1454, and thus was titled *Sejong sillok chiriji*. It included more than 60 items of information deemed necessary for the governing of the country, including each county's administrative history, historical figures, historical remains, surnames, population, land area, topographical features, control checkpoints, fortifications, native products, roads and post stations, garrisons, troop levies, and beacon communication sites. An even more detailed work, the 50-volume *Tongguk yŏji sŭngnam*, or Augmented Survey of the Geography of the Eastern Kingdom, compiled in 1481, treated all aspects of the country's cultural geography mainly to reflect the interests and values of the literati class. The existing version is a revised edition, in 55 volumes, called *Sinjŭng tongguk yŏji sŭngnam*, or Newly Enlarged Survey of the Geography of the Eastern Kingdom, completed in 1530. The Chosŏn dynasty also set about creating maps of the country, and an atlas titled *Tongguk chido*, or Map of the Eastern Kingdom, appeared in 1463.

Rites and ceremonies were especially important in a Confucian state, and so, in 1474, the Chosŏn dynasty compiled *Kukcho orye ŭi*, or Five Rites of State, an eight-volume work prescribing the mode of conduct of the state's major ceremonies. The five major rites included royal succession and various sacrifices, marriage and other sanctified occasions, welcoming ceremonies for foreign envoys, military reviews, and funerals. In 1432 an earlier three-volume work, *Samgang haengsil to*, or Drawings of the Conduct of the Three Bonds, had been compiled by Sŏl Sun and others at Sejong's command; this book of moral virtues for the general populace employed drawings and accompanying texts of more than 300 Korean and Chinese loyal retainers, filial sons, and faithful women to portray models of the three bonds of loyalty, filial piety, and fidelity. It was designed to promote Confucianism's three ethical values and five moral disciplines that were most important for the general population. As this work of ethics was compiled in Chinese, Sejong strongly believed that a Korean alphabet was needed, and so he accelerated the creation of han'gul. In short, to rule more effectively and realize a more perfect Confucian state, the Chosŏn kingdom compiled many different works on its history, geography, and ritual ceremonies.

Science and Technology

In the fifteenth century Chosŏn attained its apogee in science and technology, as a number of inventions and publications were produced. As agricultural techniques developed, several agricultural manuals were compiled. The first work, *Nongsa chiksŏl,* or Straight Talk on Farming, compiled by Chŏng Ch'o, appeared in 1429 under the reign of Sejong and was replete with information collected from experienced elder peasants throughout the country. Although it referred to agricultural techniques used in northern China, because the climate and soil of Korea differed from those of northern China, the manual was designed to meet the needs of Korean agriculture. It had become the classic work on Korean farming until a later agricultural work appeared in 1655, *Nongga chipsŏng,* or Compilation for Farmers, which was compiled by Sin Sok and introduced the more advanced agricultural techniques used in southern China. Later, in the reign of King Sŏngjong, the scholar-official Kang Hŭi-maeng wrote *Kŭmyang chamnok,* or Miscellaneous Notes on Farming in Kŭmch'ŏn County, where he described the cultivation methods for 81 kinds of grain based on his own experience and what was taught in his home town of Kŭmch'ŏn, present-day Sihŭng, which is part of Seoul. In 1492 the contents of this work were appended to a new edition of *Nongsa chiksŏl.*

Astronomy and meteorology, which were highly advanced particularly in the period of Sejong, were closely related to agriculture. In addition, especially because of the widespread belief that government decisions, good or bad, affected astronomical phenomena, astronomy was of great importance. In 1441 Chosŏn scientists, notably Yi Ch'ŏn and Chang Yŏng-sil, invented a rain gauge, the pluviometer, which preceded by almost 200 years Gastelli's invention of a similar instrument in Europe in 1639. Sejong distributed copies of the pluviometer to Seoul and the rest of the country to record precipitation. Famed scientist and astronomer Chang Yŏng-sil specialized in sundials and water clocks, and other scientists refined the Chinese and Arabic sciences of the calendar. Important progress in astronomy led to the development, in 1444, of Korea's indigenous calendar, the *Ch'ilchŏngsan,* or Calculations of the Motions of the Seven Celestial Determinants, based on new calculations defining the geographical location of Korea, which differed in longitude from that of China. *Chosŏn wangjo sillok* detailed abnormal natural occurrences, including solar and lunar eclipses, earthquakes, halos of the sun and moon, and the observation of comets, reflecting the Chosŏn people's interest in astronomy and atmospheric phenomena.

In medical science, No Chung-nye and others, in 1433, compiled the 85-volume *Hyangyak chipsŏng pang,* which included 959 entries on disease diagnoses, 10,706 prescriptions, and 1,477 items on acupuncture therapy. Inheriting a tradition that began in the Koryŏ period, this work firmly established an independent Korean medical science based on the Korean experience. In 1445 a medical encyclopedia titled *Ŭibang yuchw'i,* or Classified Collection of Medical Prescriptions, was published by No Chung-nye and others in 365 volumes. No comparable medical work existed anywhere in the world at the time.

In the fifteenth century a variety of books on military science appeared, and new types of artillery were produced by military technicians. In 1450 a two-volume work on the military history of Korea and China, titled *Tongguk pyŏnggam,* or Military Exemplar of the Eastern Kingdom, was published. The next year another book on tactics, *Chinpŏp,* or Battle Formation, was published to explain how to drill troops and take assault positions. This was later revised in 1492 to become *Pyŏngjang tosŏl,* or Descriptions of Officers and Men. Techniques for casting and using cannons were described in a publication entitled *Ch'ongt'ong tŭngnok,* or Records on Gunpowder Weaponry, that appeared in 1448. In 1451 a new weapon, the *hwach'a,* or launching vehicle, was invented that used gunpowder ignited by fuse wicks to fire 200 arrows at one time. As a rocket launcher, it had a range of 1,000 meters.

Accompanying all the scholarly works produced in this period was a tremendous amount of activity in the field of printing, including the development of improved movable metal type. Most printing was previously done with metal type invented in the thirteenth century in the preceding Koryŏ dynasty, but the new movable metal type, in the Chosŏn kingdom, was cast in great quantities and widely used in the publication of state-sponsored books including Confucian classics and historical works. In 1403 a type-casting foundry was established and copper printing type, called *kyemi* type (after the designation for the cyclical year of 1403), was cast.[5] Typography was developed and improved by the repeated casting of new fonts. At first beeswax was used to fasten the type on a plate; Sejong improved this inconvenient method by assembling the type into squares on a plate. This new system doubled the efficiency of printing. After 1437 copper was replaced by lead for metal type. Sejong ordered the casting of two new types of *kyŏngja* and *kabin* in 1420 and 1434, respectively. The *kabin* type has been rated as the best type, as it consisted of exquisitely wrought Chinese characters and was cast in large quantities (more than 200,000 types) to make printing more efficient. Chosŏn's advanced art of printing greatly influenced neighboring countries, including China and Japan. Clearly the early Chosŏn period was a golden age in terms of scientific and technological developments.

Literature and the Arts

Buddhism was no longer a source of literary and artistic inspiration in the Chosŏn dynasty, and although Chinese models influenced the literature, art, and music of the period, all three exhibited a distinct Korean style. In its preface the compilers of *Tongmun sŏn*, or An Anthology of Korean Literature, stressed that the Chinese literature of Koreans was strictly Korean and was not the literature of the Song, Yuan, Han, or Tang. Korean scholar-officials cultivated and developed their skills in the arts of Confucian culture—poetry, painting, and calligraphy. Poetry was considered the most important of these arts, and men who lacked poetic ability could not pass the civil service examinations.

In 1478 the high-ranking scholar-officials Sŏ Kŏ-jŏng and No Sa-sin, at the king's command, compiled the 133-volume *Tongmun sŏn*, a collection of poetry and prose written by Koreans in Chinese in the period from the Three Kingdoms to the early Chosŏn dynasty. In 1517 the 23-volume *Sok tongmun sŏn*, or the Succeeding Anthology of Korean Literature, appeared, containing the writings from the post-*Tongmun sŏn* period. At the same time the so-called *p'aesŏl munhak*, or literature of tales and anecdotes, was popular among the yangban literati. Works of this genre include Sŏ Kŏ-jŏng's *P'irwŏn chapki*, or An Author's Miscellany; Sŏng Hyŏn's *Yongjae ch'onghwa*, or Assorted Writings of Yongjae; and O Suk-kwŏn's *P'aegwan chapki*, or The Storyteller's Miscellany. This genre developed into "novels," or fictional tales; an example is Kim Si-sŭp's *Kŭmo sinhwa*, or New Stories of the Golden Turtle.

Portrait and landscape paintings were done mainly by government artists, who painted them at the request of members of royalty and the yangban literati. Landscapes of the period portrayed idealized settings not found in the natural world. This style of painting was influenced by China and later changed to the new mode of portraying real scenery as seen by the painters themselves. The most highly praised early Chosŏn painter was An Kyŏn whose famous landscape *Mong yu towŏn to,* or Painting of a Dream of Strolling in a Peach Garden, painted in 1447, has been recognized as a supreme masterpiece. It is said to have been an artistic representation of a dream of Prince Anp'yŏng, the third son of King Sejong. Another renowned painter of that period, Ch'oe Kyŏng, was particularly skilled in painting portraits. In the sixteenth century Yi Sang-jwa, who had been born a slave, was selected as a government artist because of his outstanding talent. The yangban literati took an interest in painting for their pleasure; this genre, known as *muninhwa,* or literati paintings, was characterized by India ink and brush drawings. A master of these paintings was Kang Hŭi-an in the reign of King Sejong.

Unlike painting, training in calligraphy was an essential adjunct of education for the yangban, and a number of calligraphic masters emerged among the yangban literati. The ornamental writing of Chinese characters in calligraphy was considered an art in itself. Since the late Koryŏ period, the songxue style of Chinese Zhao Mengfu continued to be popular, and its acknowledged master was Prince Anp'yŏng; excluded from succession to the throne, he took pleasure in artistic pursuits and produced graceful calligraphic works. Yang Sa-ŏn and Han Ho were also famous calligraphers of the sixteenth century.

In the early Chosŏn period the royal family and the yangban literati led a relatively simple life. As the royal court used ceramic instead of gold and silver vessels, pieces called *punch'ŏng,* or powder blue-green, were produced in great quantities. The period of Koryŏ celadon came to an end with the disappearance of the Koryŏ government's kilns which had produced these articles. Beginning in the late Koryŏ period, as jade green color disappearared, Koryŏ celadon was gradually transformed into punch'ŏng porcelain. These punch'ŏng pieces lacked the refined beauty of the Koryŏ celadon but were attractive and calming, with designs that were usually of flowers and fish. These punch'ŏng porcelains were a transitional stage that led to the famous *paekcha,* or white porcelains. This Chosŏn ceramic ware, made by painting a clear glaze over ceramic made of white clay, first emerged during the Koryŏ era along with ch'ŏngja, but it came into its own only during the Chosŏn period. Paekcha most often was pure white in color, but sometimes green or a milky color was added to the clay to lend it a pale hue. If the Koryŏ ch'ŏngja could be seen as the embodiment of the era's aristocratic culture and luxuries, then paekcha was a fitting expression of the tastes of Chosŏn's yangban literati. This less refined porcelain of the Chosŏn dynasty greatly influenced the development of Japanese artistic appreciation since the late sixteenth century and is still far more artistic than the porcelains found anywhere else in East Asia.

In a Confucian state that stressed ritual, music was naturally a vital component of statecraft. Music always accompanied various national ceremonies, and the Chosŏn dynasty established the *Changakwŏn*, or Office of Music, which took charge of music at the court. In the reign of King Sejong, additional musical instruments were introduced into the realm and musical texts were arranged. The man who contributed most to these efforts was Pak Yŏn. Sejong also composed several pieces of music. In 1493 a nine-volume publication on musicology, titled *Akhak kwoebŏm,* or Canon of Music, was compiled by Sŏng Hyŏn and Yu Cha-gwang. This work classified music into three categories: *aak,* or ceremonial music; *tangak,* or Chinese music; and *hyangak,* or native music. With the enhanced musical standard, dance also developed, which was characterized by dignity and elegance.

THE GROWTH OF THE NEO-CONFUCIAN LITERATI

Rule by the Hun'gu Elite and the Peasants' Heavy Burdens

By the early sixteenth century, serious problems began to surface throughout Chosŏ society. A keen desire for reform spread and, particularly in circles of political power, challenged the dominance of the "*hun'gu,* or meritorious elite, a political faction composed of merit subjects and their descendants. This elite faction held the reins of power, occupying high government posts and possessing abundant farmlands and slaves. Their dominant position was largely the result of special meritorious awards bestowed for services under kings Sejo and Sŏngjong. Taking advantage of their position and power, many members of this faction expanded their landholdings, thereby reducing government tax receipts and impoverishing peasant farmers. The deepening misery of the peasantry led to rampant brigandage throughout the country. The best-known brigand leader was Im Kkŏk-chŏng; a righteous outlaw, he rose up against greedy officials, seized government granaries, and provided relief to the hungry in Kyŏnggi and Hwanghae provinces for three years, from 1559 to 1562. Although he was caught and executed in 1562, his cavalry and revolutionary ideas captured the admiration of the populace and inspired the writing of the popular novel *Hong Kil-tong chŏn,* or Tale of Hong Kil-tong.

The rule of the meritorious elite was challenged by the so-called *sarim,* or Neo-Confucian literati, a group of newly rising yangban scholars based in the countryside. The hun'gu faction brought the sarim faction under control by a series of *sahwa,* or literati purges. Ultimately, however, the sarim survived and were victorious as a result of its continual manpower supply.

As the Chikchŏnpŏp was abolished in the mid-sixteenth century and yangban bureaucrats were paid only in salaries, they expanded their personal landholdings and secured them through purchases, seizures, and reclamation. Finally, many of them, especially the meritorious elite who had already been awarded a great deal of merit-subject land, came to possess large agricultural estates.

The expansion of landholdings by yangban bureaucrats even further impoverished the peasantry. Many tenant farmers had to pay not only a tenancy rent to landowners but a land tax to the state. In the sixteenth century the tribute tax was mostly responsible for depressing the income of peasant farmers. Beginning with the reign of Yŏnsan'gun (1494–1506), not only was the tribute tax a heavy burden, but the process by which it was paid was still more onerous. The peasants also had to deliver tribute goods that were not produced in their native districts or else pay one or two years' tributes in a lump sum in advance. Moreover, the *pangnap,* or indirect payment system, developed, in which *sŏri,* or petty clerks, of government offices, in collusion with merchants, delivered tribute items to the state and then collected an overly high cost for them, further adding to the peasants' plight. As increasing numbers of peasants could not meet their tax obligations and abandoned their land, tax collection was enforced on their kinsmen or neighbors. Finally, the heavy burden of the tribute tax was lifted by the enforcement of the *Taedongpŏp,* or Uniform Land Tax Law, which allowed tax to be paid in rice. Carried out first in 1608 and finally enforced throughout the country in 1709, the Taedongpŏp virtually abolished the institution of the tribute tax.

Another source of suffering for peasant farmers was military service. Initially the principle that military service was imposed upon the individual and corvee labor was assigned to a household had been strictly kept. As military rosters increased with the reign of Sejo, however, it was impossible to fill the quotas for corvee labor and thus soldiers were frequently mobilized for this duty. The increase in military rosters was a result of the adoption of the *popŏp,* or paired provisioner system, which required peasant farmers to serve alternately as conscript soldiers or as sustainers who would provide economic support for conscripts called to active duty. The nature of military service was increasingly transformed into the corvee labor obligation. To escape this double burden, the men in the military rosters either hired slaves of yangban or landless wanderers to perform corvee labor in their place; the *choyŏkka*, or support in kind, which these substitutes received from their *poin*, or provisioners, was usually 17–18 bolts of cotton cloth (for men registered as land soldiers) or 20 bolts (for men registered as naval soldiers) for 20 months. Soon payment for corvee service was required to be made directly to the office in charge of corvee labor mobilization in a particular locality. As this was a very high payment, a great number of conscript soldiers and provisioners fled to escape this burden.[6] As a result, reportedly nine out of ten houses were abandoned in many rural villages. The escapees moved to other regions to become merchants or slaves, or only to hide.

As compulsory military service proved an increasingly onerous duty to the peasantry, the government doubted the effectiveness of the conscription system manned by the peasants. In 1537 it levied two bolts of cotton cloth, called *kunp'o*, or military cloth, yearly on every prospective conscript and recruited professional soldiers with the payments. Thus the military organization shifted from a system of compulsory conscription to one of career soldiers in the late sixteenth century. This was immediately before the Korean-Japanese war (1592–1598), when the strength of Chosŏn's active duty army numbered no more than 1,000.

Since the sixteenth century the grain loan system drove the peasantry further to the wall. In the fifteenth century the government had operated the ŭich'ang program, giving loans of grain to needy peasants in the lean spring season. Only the principal sum of grain loans was repaid from the harvest in the fall. Since the late fifteenth century the responsibility for this aid program was transferred to the sangp'yŏngch'ang, established to control violent fluctuations in grain prices that occurred because the ŭich'ang program lacked adequate supplies. Under this new relief system, the peasants paid interest when paying back their grain loans. Although the government set the interest rate at 10 percent, the peasants usually borrowed grain at a far higher interest, thus incurring yet another heavy burden.

The Rise of the Neo-Confucian Literati

By the early sixteenth century Chosŏn officialdom was divided into two distinct factions, the hun'gu and sarim forces, that were enmeshed in fierce power struggles. Whereas members of the hun'gu faction lived in districts clustered around the capital, those in the sarim faction mainly led a rural life initially devoted to the education of their youth. Struggles between the two factions, culminating in a series of sahwa, or literati purges, along with subsequent *tangjaeng*, or factional strife, among the literati themselves, were bitter and bloody, splintering the government and sapping the Korean nation of its former vitality.

In the reign of King Sŏngjong, the locally based Neo-Confucian literati entered the central bureaucracy for the first time. In an effort to check the further expansion of power by the meritorious elite, Sŏngjong took Kim Chong-jik and his disciples into government service, appointing them to positions in the samsa of the Sahŏnbu, Saganwŏn, and Hongmun'gwan, where they took charge of criticisms of the government and the preparation of important state documents. Sŏngjong proved to be unusually tolerant of official criticism, perhaps because he had acceded to the throne as a child and had been subjected to heavy indoctrination regarding a ruler's Confucian duty to heed his advisers.

Kim Chong-jik was a member of the Neo-Confucian literati from Kyŏngsang province and a son of Kim Suk-cha, the leading disciple of Kil Chae, a man who had remained faithful to Koryŏ by refusing to accept office in the Chosŏn dynasty. Following the teachings of Kil Chae, Kim Chong-jik and his disciples were more thoroughly indoctrinated in Confucian principles than were the meritorious elite, and they were characterized by idealism, were less experienced in administration, and tended to be idealistic moralists. Under the aegis of King Sŏngjong, the influence of these Neo-Confucian literati-officials rapidly grew into a major force challenging the preponderant power of the meritorious elite. Thus conflict inevitably developed between the two forces and led to bloody political convulsions of sahwa.

Sŏngjong managed to balance power between the two factions, and so no direct collision occurred under his reign. This changed dramatically, however, after Yŏnsan'gun, who subsequently was denied the usual posthumous title, ascended the throne in 1494. Yŏnsan'gun sought to strengthen royal authority by bringing both the meritorious elite and the Neo-Confucian literati under his control. A man whose outlook differed from his father's, he gradually sided with the meritorious elite faction, as he hated the literati force that attempted to restrain royal authority through unlimited criticisms. Divining Yŏnsan'gun's thoughts, members of the meritorious elite such as Yi Kŭk-ton and Yu Cha-gwang incited the king to purge the court of the Neo-Confucian literati. In doing so, they brought to the fore Kim Il-son's draft of the annals of King Sŏngjong's reign, discussed earlier.While serving as a state historian,

Kim Il-son, a disciple of Kim Chong-jik, had incorporated into his draft for the *Sŏngjong sillok,* or Annals of King Sŏngjong, his teacher's *Cho ŭije mun,* or Lament for Emperor Yidi. In his writing Kim Chong-jik had mourned the killing of the young Chinese emperor Yidi by his general Xiang Yu. He criticized, metaphorically, King Sejo's usurpation of the throne and the subsequent murder of his young nephew, King Tanjong. When Kim Il-son's draft was discovered by Yi Kŭk-ton, who was in charge of compiling the *sillok,* the meritorious elite incited the king to execute Kim Il-son and those closely linked to him. Scores of the Neo-Confucian literati were executed or banished, including Kim Il-son, Chŏng Yŏ-ch'ang, Pyo Yŏn-mal, and Ch'oe Pu. Kim Chong-jik's corpse was dug up and beheaded. The power of the Neo-Confucian literati was greatly weakened. This event has been called the *Muo sahwa,* or Purge of 1498, after the designation for the cyclical year of 1498, or the *Sahwa,* History Purge.

After purging the Neo-Confucian literati from the government, Yŏnsan'gun sought to eliminate all opponents of his kingly authority, including the meritorious elite. He finally found an opportunity in 1504; a group of courtiers connected to the king by marriage, including Im Sa-hong, exposed the fact that key members of the meritorious elite were involved in an incident that occurred in the reign of Sŏngjong, in which Yŏnsan'gun's mother, the Lady Yun, was deposed as the king's consort and poisoned to death. The enraged Yŏnsan'gun executed or banished not only many members of the meritorious elite, such as Yun P'il-sang, but also some Neo-Confucian literati who had survived the 1498 purge, such as Kim Koeng-p'il, and then appropriated the property of the ousted meritorious elite. This massive second purge has been known as the *Kapcha sahwa,* or Purge of 1504. Essentially the motive was not Yŏnsan'gun's revenge for his mother's tragic death but rather his intentions to consolidate royal authority.

After eliminating nearly all his critics in the two purges, Yŏnsan'gun was said to indulge in spending sprees and lewd activities, leading to massive squandering of the state's fiscal resources. Setting out to undo what his predecessors had done, he banned the Korean alphabet, han'gŭl, for males, simply because a wall poster criticizing his misconduct was written in that alphabet. For two years he carried on a reign of terror, executing or banishing hundreds of hapless officials. Finally, in 1506, he was forcefully dethroned by the meritorious elite, including Pak Wŏn-jong, Sŏng Hŭi-an, and Yu Sun-jŏng, and was replaced by his half-brother, King Chungjong (1506–1544). He was dishonored after his death and called "Yŏnsan'gun," or Prince of Yŏnsan. The prime players in the coup included opportunists who had even abetted his purges. Yŏnsan'gun's folly was that instead of ousting the Neo-Confucian literati along with the meritorious elite, he should have made the former his allies by having them fill the posts left vacant by the latter and distributing the forfeited property to the populace. The meritorious elite, after all, had expelled him from the throne by force, whereas the Neo-Confucian literati had simply justified the coup by pen. Perhaps, had he acted more wisely, he might not have been dethroned.

Increasingly tired of the abuse of power by the meritorious elite who had brought him to the throne, King Chungjong took the young Neo-Confucian scholar Cho Kwang-jo into government service in 1515, appointing him to a succession of influential government positions, including that of inspector-general. Securing the confidence of Chungjong, Cho Kwang-jo carried out a series of reforms to create the hypothetical, ideal Confucian state. In an effort to correct the behavior of the king in the aftermath of Yŏnsan'gun's tyranny, he tightened up kyŏngyŏn. To inculcate Confucian ideals in the general populace, he implemented the *hyangyak,* or village code, a rule for local self-government. To stabilize peasants' livelihood, he attempted to redress the abuses of expanded agricultural estates and indirect payment of the tribute tax. Cho proposed in 1518, and secured in 1519, enactment of the *hyŏllyangkwa,* or examination for the learned and virtuous; this required that individuals holding responsible central and local government posts recommend men of talent and integrity to take a simplified examination, held in the presence of the king, for recruitment into officialdom. In 1519, 28 successful candidates were selected from 120 who had been recommended to take the exam. Most of them, like Cho Kwang-jo, were dedicated Neo-Confucian literati, who furiously attacked existing institutions and high-level officials. In the process they incurred the enmity of the meritorious elite and even alarmed Chungjong by their obvious threat to the exercise of strong regal power.

In 1519 Cho Kwang-jo launched a campaign to rescind the awards, including the titles of merit subjects, farmland, and slaves, that had been bestowed on many as a reward for setting King Chungjong on the throne. He succeeded in persuading the king to delete 76 names from the 100 on the merit roster. The enraged merit subjects, particularly Sim Chŏng and Nam Kon, incited Chungjong's fear that his own position might be in jeopardy, as they unjustly accused Cho Kwang-jo of committing high treason by planning to enthrone himself. Having tired of Cho's excessive pressure on him, Chungjong executed Cho and his leading supporters in an event that is known as the *Kimyo sahwa,* or Purge of 1519, which again dealt a severe blow to the power of the Neo-Confucian literati.

The fourth purge, known as the *Ŭlsa sahwa*, or Purge of 1545, resulted from the successive enthronement of two sons of King Chungjong by different consorts. Even before Chungjong's death, government officials had formed factions around brothers of the two queens. The accession of King Injong (1544–1545), Chungjong's eldest son, led his maternal uncle, Yun Im, and his faction, the *Taeyun*, or Senior Yun, to seize power. The Taeyun faction consisted mainly of locally based young Neo-Confucian scholars identified with Cho Kwang-jo. Injong's untimely death, however, brought his younger brother, King Myŏngjong (1545–1567), to the throne. This time Myŏngjong's maternal uncle, Yun Wŏn-hyŏng, and his faction, the *Soyun*, or Junior Yun, came into power. The Soyun faction was made up largely by Seoul-based established men. The Yun Wŏn-hyŏng faction charged the Yun Im faction with attempting to kill Myŏngjong, with the intent of purging the latter force from the government. Once again, many promising Neo-Confucian scholar-officials were killed or banished.

The main theme of all four literati purges was the struggle for power between the meritorious elite and the Neo-Confucian literati. In the course of the bloody purges, the Neo-Confucian literati suffered blow after blow, but despite their repeated setbacks, they slowly and steadily took back the political initiative from the meritorious elite. Their continual supply of manpower made this possible. After these purges, factional rivalries became a major motif of Chosŏn politics, taking precedence over the general welfare of the populace.

Factional Strife

After its brilliant first century the Chosŏn dynasty gradually declined in administrative efficiency and effective unity. The turn of the dynastic cycle manifested itself in disruptive factional struggles within central officialdom. Chosŏn had already experienced sahwa between the hun'gu and sarim factions in the first half of the sixteenth century, and then, in the second half of the century, as the Neo-Confucian literati grew in strength, tangjaeng began in earnest. The number of literati eligible to serve in the bureaucracy markedly increased, while the number of government positions remained essentially fixed. Thus, when those aspiring to government office all competed to occupy the limited number of posts, conflict between the aspirants inevitably developed. Furthermore, because actual appointments to office and subsequent promotions frequently depended on the patronage of high officials, competing factions formed in the bureaucratic hierarchy based on shared scholarship and political inclinations, and centering on well-known scholar-officials. Because Neo-Confucian teachings originally encouraged sŏnbi to organize in cliques, it was quite natural that factions formed in the Neo-Confucian state of Chosŏn.

According to conventional wisdom, factional strife appeared in the early reign of King Sŏnjo (1567–1608). In 1575 a conflict developed between two segments of the bureaucracy coalescing, respectively, around Sim Ŭi-gyŏm and Kim Hyo-wŏn. Those who sided with Sim Ŭi-gyŏm were called the *Sŏin,* or Westerners, because Sim lived in the western part of Seoul, and those who supported Kim Hyo-wŏn were called the *Tongin,* or Easterners, because Kim lived in the eastern part of Seoul. At first the Westerners were mainly the established literati from Seoul, Kyŏnggi, Ch'ungch'ŏng, and Chŏlla, and the Easterners were largely the newly rising literati from Kyŏngsang.

The immediate cause of the conflict between Sim Ŭi-gyŏm and Kim Hyo-wŏn was a personal quarrel over appointments to coveted positions in the Yi-jo, known collectively as the *chŏllang.* Although these posts were mid-level (5th or 6th rank), their holders were authorized to recommend and appoint candidates to some lower offices in the ministry. Because the chŏllang were important positions, they were usually filled by officials of high academic repute from the Office of Propagation and Literature. The posts also functioned as a shortcut to promotion to the highest offices. Incumbents customarily recommended their successors; for example, Kim Hyo-wŏn, as a younger reputable official, was recommended for a chŏllang position by his predecessor O Kŏn in 1574. But Sim Ŭi-gyŏm accused him of being a sycophant and opposed his appointment. Although Kim Hyŏ-won had once been supported by Yun Wŏn-hyŏng, who was hated by the Neo-Confucian literati, Kim nevertheless secured the post. When Kim left office in 1575, Sim Ŭi-gyŏm's younger brother, Sim Ch'ung-gyŏm, was suggested as a potential successor, and this time it was Kim Hyo-wŏn who objected. Sim Ch'ung-gyŏm failed to obtain the appointment to the post. Soon officialdom began to take sides between the two protagonists and to regard their opponents with contempt.

Immediately after a factional split between the Easterners, who were mainly disciples of Yi Hwang and Cho Sik, and the Westerners, who largely followed Yi I and Sŏng Hon, a balance of power was achieved between the factions. Then, in 1589, the Westerners, led by Chŏng Ch'ŏl, charged Chŏng Yŏ-rip, a member of the Easterners, with high treason, which resulted in the execution of many

Easterners, including Chŏng Yŏ-rip himself. This incident exacerbated the conflict between the two factions, and two years later, in 1591, Chŏng Ch'ŏl and his Westerners proposed to designate an heir to Sonjo's throne. This incurred Sonjo's wrath, and they were driven from power. At this point the Easterners split into two sub-factions over the issue of how Chŏng Ch'ŏl and the Westerners should be punished. The sub-faction known as the *Pukin,* or Northerners, urged a harsh punishment, as it was the scholar-officials of Northerner background who suffered a severe blow in the Chŏng Yŏ-rip incident. The opposing *Namin,* or Southerners, on the other hand, was took a more moderate stance. In terms of philosophy and scholasticism, the two sub-factions represented the division between the disciples of Cho Sik and those of Yi Hwang. Initially the Southerners were in the ascendancy, and then the Northerners took the lead. The victorious Northerners then differed internally over the appointment of Hong Yŏ-sun as inspector-general and split into two sub-factions, the *Taebuk,* or Senior Northerners, and the *Sobuk,* or Junior Northerners. Consolidating their power in the years during and following the war with Japan, the Senior Northerners helped Kwanghaegun, or the Prince of Kwanghae, ascend to the throne, and, accordingly, they dominated the political scene during the king's reign (1608–1623).

Factional strife was a life-and-death struggle between political cliques. Whereas successful factions constantly split into sub-factions, defeated factions retired and recouped their strength in rural villages, where their leaders surrounded themselves with large numbers of relatives and disciples for support. Members of a particular faction bequeathed their factional affiliation to their descendants as an inheritance, and thus, rather than remaining ephemeral groupings, the factions were essentially foreordained and permanent. Factionalism was seriously disruptive, as no mechanism existed for reconciling policy differences if the throne failed to settle them through strong leadership. Because of the Confucian emphasis on ethics as the basis of good government, opposing policies were frequently regarded as signs of the opponents' depravity and even tantamount to treason. The factional struggles were so ferocious and enduring that even wars with foreign countries could not resolve them.

The Sŏwŏn and the Hyangyak

Despite successive harsh purges, the Neo-Confucian literati increasingly consolidated their strength and ultimately dominated the political scene thanks to the *sŏwŏn,* or private academies, and the hyangyak. Along with agricultural landholdings, these provided the literati with a solid power base in the rural community. In their early years the sŏwŏn contributed to greatly reinvigorating Neo-Confucian scholarship. Soon, however, by dividing education along family and factional lines, they accentuated the growing factionalism in officialdom involving the highest scholar-officials to the lowest student candidates in controversies dividing the government.

In the late Koryŏ period, Confucian scholars built *sŏjae*, or private academies, where they devoted themselves purely to education. In the sixteenth century, for the first time in Korean history, the sŏwŏn, which added Confucian shrines dedicated to worthies of the earlier period to the existing sŏjae, appeared.

The first sŏwŏn, the Paekundong, was established in 1543 by Chu Se-bung, then magistrate of P'unggi county in Kyŏngsang province. In his sŏwŏn, Chu honored An Hyang (Yu), the famed Koryŏ Neo-Confucian scholar. In 1550, when Yi Hwang became magistrate of P'unggi, he presented a memorial to King Myŏngjong, in which he persuaded the king to bestow on the Paekundong sŏwŏn a wooden hanging board inscribed, in the king's own hand, with four Chinese characters, the *sosu sŏwŏn*, meaning "academy of received learning," as well as books, farmlands, and slaves. Now known as the Sosu sŏwŏn, the Paekundong was the first of the sŏwŏn to receive a royal charter. The sŏwŏn was also granted the right of exemption from taxation and corvee labor. The king's gift of a hanging board represented the state's official approval of the sŏwŏn.

Subsequently sŏwŏn sprang up throughout the country, and by the end of King Sŏnjo's reign, in 1608, they numbered more than 100, distributed mostly in Kyŏngsang province. At the same time the number of royally chartered sŏwŏn greatly increased, amounting to one-third of the total. Following the precedent of the Sosu sŏwŏn, the state bestowed grants of books, farmland, and slaves on the sŏwŏn. At first the sŏwŏn competed with the hyanggyo for leadership in education, but soon they not only outnumbered the hyanggyo but had greater authority than the local schools. The sŏwŏn now occupied a position that had been enjoyed by the Buddhist temples in the Koryŏ period. Since the late sixteenth century the sŏwŏn were the major foundation, or stage, of the internal power struggles plaguing the Neo-Confucian literati and functioned, in particular, as a political base where the defeated literati regained their strength.

The hyangyak was another mechanism through which the Neo-Confucian literati strengthened their position in the rural community. The hyangyak basically sought four objectives that originated in Song China: encouragement of moral integrity, regulation of misconduct, observance of decorum, and provision of aid in the event of disasters. Cho Kwang-jo had initially implemented the hyangyak in 1519, but his downfall brought its enforcement temporarily to a halt. When the Neo-Confucian literati finally gained strength in King Sŏnjo's reign, the hyangyak became widely instituted throughout the country. Because powerful figures among the local Neo-Confucian literati usually administered the hyangyak, it actually had great authority over the peasantry in the rural villages.

Through the widespread operation of the hyangyak, self-government took root in the countryside, and the yangban literati held real power in the rural community. This was accompanied by the reinforcement of the landowner-tenant system in rural villages. Scholar-officials were employed by the government service in the capital and at the same time were sustained by their agricultural landholdings in the countryside. Meanwhile, the defeated faction patiently waited for a ripe opportunity to return to power in the rural villages.

Neo-Confucianism Flourishes

As already pointed out, Neo-Confucianism had two overall aims: to cultivate an individual's own virtue and to establish an ethical basis for a virtuous, enlightened political order. As the literati increasingly emphasized cultivation of the mind following successive literati purges since the early sixteenth century, Neo-Confucianism increasingly became a metaphysical philosophy that sought to find the essence of the human psyche and the seminal components of the universe. Following the same path as their Chinese peers, Korean Neo-Confucians divided all existence in the universe into two interdependent, inseparable components, i and ki (li and qi in Chinese), and they pursued the essence of human nature more deeply compared to their Chinese counterparts.

According to the Neo-Confucian doctrine, i was a patterning or formative element, and ki a concretizing and energizing element understood as matter or "ether." Fundamental principles of form could not exist concretely without ki, which, without i, would only be directionless energy. Thus, for example, i could provide the plan of a boat or house but actual boats and houses are made of ki. Elaborate theories specified the relationships between i and ki, and to explain the essence of the universe and human nature, two distinct schools of Neo-Confucian thought emerged in Chosŏn: the Yŏngnam school, which primarily emphasized i, and the Kiho school, which stressed the primacy of ki.

Yi Ŏn-jŏk pioneered the theory of the primacy of i, but Yi Hwang (T'oegye) developed a full philosophy based on this view and is known to posterity as "Korea's Zhu Xi," after the Chinese founder of the Neo-Confucian school. In fact, a street in downtown Seoul is named T'oegye, his pseudonym, in his honor. In centering on the role of the metaphysical element i, Yi Hwang saw the universe as essentially spiritual, and because human nature was pure and good, all of us could perceive moral principles, norms, duties, and inner experience. This school of thought was carried on by such figures as Yu Sŏng-nyong, Kim Sŏng-il, Chŏng Ku, and Chang Hyŏn-gwang; it became known as the Yŏngnam (Kyŏngsang province) school and exerted great influence on Confucian scholarship in Japan.

The formulation of the material ki doctrine was completed by Yi I (Yulgok), following the thinking of such scholars as Sŏ Kyŏng-dŏk and Ki Tae-sŭng. Contrary to Yi Hwang's concepts, Yi I thought that human nature, i, could be manifested only through its ki, or physical aspects. Along with his followers he sought to grasp the laws governing the material world, and thus emphasized external experience and observation of nature, as well as breadth of learning. A famed philosopher almost equal to Yi Hwang, Yi I thus advanced many proposals for reforming government, economics, and national defense. The ki school of thought was carried on by scholars including Sŏng Hon, Song Ik-p'il, Kim Chang-saeng, and Chŏng Yŏp, and became known as the Kiho (Kyŏnggi and Ch'ungch'ŏng provinces) school.

THE STRUGGLE WITH THE JAPANESE AND MANCHUS

The First Japanese Invasion (1592)

As factional struggles grew increasingly intense in the late sixteenth century, disaster struck Chosŏn in the form of a massive Japanese invasion. Already in 1510, as a result of Chosŏn's tightening grip on Japanese trade, Japanese residents in the three open ports had rebelled. At the time Chosŏn felt threatened by the Japanese demand to expand trade and by the growing number of Japanese residents in the three ports. After this rebellion was suppressed, Chosŏn cut in half the number of Japanese ships permitted in the ports and limited the volume of rice and beans to be given or traded with the Japanese. The result was occasional large-scale attacks by Japanese pirates on the Chosŏn coast. In 1555 the Japanese plundered Chosŏn's southwest coastal regions but were repelled by Chosŏn forces. Suffering sporadic Japanese attacks on its coasts, in 1517 Chosŏn established the Pibyŏnsa, or Border Defense Council, jointly staffed by civil and military officials, which was responsible for all matters relating to national defense. By the end of the sixteenth century, however, Chosŏn society as a whole was accustomed to centuries of peace and sank into complacency.

At this very point, a new political development in Japan brought the return of centralized control. In 1590 Toyotomi Hideyoshi emerged as the power behind the throne, establishing mastery over the entire Japanese nation. He then decided to invade China, indirectly, through Chosŏn. Apart from his desire to make Japan the dominant power in East Asia, he also wished to distract his warlords, restless from inactivity, from domestic affairs. Thus he demanded that Chosŏn give him free passage to China.

To determine Toyotomi's intentions, in 1590 Chosŏn sent two emissaries, one each from the Easterners and Westerners, to meet with him in Japan. When they returned in 1591, their opinions were divided. Hwang Yun-gil of the Westerners reported that war was imminent, whereas Kim Sŏng-il of the Easterners claimed that Toyotomi was merely bluffing, thus leaving the Chosŏn court uncertain about a possible Japanese attack. The returning emissaries carried back a letter from Toyotomi demanding that his forces be allowed to pass through Chosŏn in order to attack Ming China. Chosŏn refused this demand, which would have meant the Japanese occupation of Chosŏn.

After two centuries of peace, Chosŏn forces were disorganized, ill-trained, and ill-equipped, and were scattered across the country. Koreans were totally unprepared for warfare. The only preparations at the time were by Admiral Yi Sun-sin, the commander of the left naval command of Chŏlla province, guarding the southwestern coastline. Yi Sun-sin was an inventor and one of history's most effective naval commanders. Appointed to the post in 1591, he strengthened his naval forces and set about building warships and training their crews. Specifically, on the model of vessels already in use in the mid-fifteenth century, he built his well-known *kŏbuksŏn,* or turtle ships, the world's first ironclad warships, which would play a leading role in the forthcoming war.

In May 1592, a Japanese force of 158,000 launched a surprise attack on Chosŏn, first landing at Pusan. Taking advantage of a unified command and superior weaponry, particularly matchlock guns that were unfamiliar to the Chosŏn military, the invaders soon overwhelmed the numerically inferior and ill-equipped defenders. Chŏng Pal, commander of the Pusan garrison, and Song Sang-hyŏn, magistrate of neighboring Tongnae, tenaciously defended the two beachheads, but to no avail. The Japanese then launched a three-pronged attack northward to Seoul. The Japanese met with little effective resistance, as the Chosŏn leadership was disorganized and had failed to prepare for the invasion. The stunned Chosŏn court pinned its hopes on General Sin Nip, but he suffered utter defeat at Ch'ungju in late May. Two days after the defeat, King Sŏnjo escaped to

Pyongyang and then to the northern border town of Ŭiju. The Japanese occupied the capital in June, but by then parts of Seoul had already been looted and burned (particularly the registry that maintained the slave rosters), and the entire capital had been abandoned by its inhabitants.

After occupying Seoul, Japanese forces divided and took two opposite directions: Konishi Yukinaga's forces took Pyongyang, and Kato Kiyomasa's troops advanced on the east coast toward the Tumen River. At the border area in the northeastern part of the Korean peninsula, Kato captured two Chosŏn princes who had been dispatched to raise troops in Hamgyŏng and Kangwŏn provinces. The situation went from bad to worse, as Koreans were massacred by Japanese forces everywhere. The invaders collected enough ears and noses (cutting parts off enemy bodies for making casualty counts was accepted practice) to build a large mound, which the Japanese termed *Mimizuka*, or the Mound of Ears, in their country.

The overall Japanese strategy was to invade and occupy Chosŏn's southeast and central regions with ground forces while its navy attacked and occupied the rice-rich areas of Chŏlla and Ch'ungch'ŏng provinces, ensuring a food supply for their land forces. This general plan failed, however, as the Japanese suffered defeats at sea.

Chosŏn dominance at sea was credited to the brilliance of Admiral Yi Sun-sin, who gained decisive victories in a series of naval battles, intercepting and scattering a large Japanese reinforcement convoy. His first triumph was at Okp'o, followed by victories at Sach'ŏn, Tangp'o, Tanghangp'o, Angolp'o, Hansan-do, and Pusan, from June to October 1592. The battle in the seas off Hansan-do in July is particularly well known as one of the three great victories of the war against the Japanese. There Yi's navy sank 63 large Japanese ships. Beginning in October Yi's navy seized complete control of the sea, cutting off Japanese forces in Chosŏn from their homeland. No more reinforcements or supplies could be shipped from Japan.

On land, as well, the Japanese positions increasingly weakened. The general populace at first was infuriated at the government's incompetence and irresponsibility, and some even collaborated with the enemy. But now the same people began to volunteer for the militia called the *ŭibyŏng*, or righteous army, mostly because they were enraged by Japanese atrocities against Korean civilians. The yangban literati, peasants, and even slaves in a single district coalesced around a ŭibyŏng leader and constantly harassed the Japanese. The ŭibyŏng leaders were generally Neo-Confucian literati of high repute in their locales and included such outstanding figures as Kwak Chae-u, Kim Myŏn, Chŏng In-hong, and Kwŏn Ŭng-su of Kyŏngsang province; Cho Hŏn of Ch'ungch'ŏng province; Ko Kyŏng-myŏng of Chŏlla province; Kim Ch'ŏn-il, Sim Tae, and Hong Kye-nam of Kyŏnggi province; Yi Chŏng-am of Hwanghae province; Cho Ho-ik and Yang Tŏk-nok of P'yŏngan province; and Chŏng Mun-bu of Hamgyŏng province. Bands of Buddhist monks, led by honored figures such as Hyujŏng and Yujŏng, often struck severe blows to Japanese military operations.

In January 1593, with its own security threatened, Ming China dispatched a 40,000-strong relief army commanded by Li Rusonh to Chosŏn. In early February the combined Ming and Chosŏn troops recaptured Pyongyang and pushed the Japanese southward. After suffering a heavy loss in a battle at Pyŏkchegwan just north of Seoul, however, the Chinese withdrew to Pyongyang. Meanwhile, a Chosŏn force of a few thousand under Kwŏn Yul, which had been garrisoned in the mountain redoubt at Haengju on the north bank of the Han River, attempted to launch a combined operation with Chinese forces to retake Seoul. But when the Ming army pulled back to Pyongyang, the Korean defenders, including women, were left isolated. Bolstered by the victory at Pyŏkchegwan, 43,000 Japanese troops repeatedly launched large-scale assaults against the mountain fortress at Haengju. After nine massive assaults and enormous casualties, the Japanese retreated in March 1593. The battle at Haengju was an important victory for the Korean army, as it greatly raised its morale. The battle has been celebrated as one of the three great Chosŏn victories in the struggle against the Japanese invaders.

Under multiple pressures, particularly the interruption of supplies from Japan, the Japanese experienced many setbacks in Chosŏn. The top Japanese generals, including Konishi Yukinaga, sued for peace and began negotiations for a truce with Ming forces that desired to return home. While negotiations for peace were under way, Japanese forces retreated from Seoul to an enclave around Pusan. They were determined to occupy the Chosŏn stronghold of Chinju, situated in the Japanese-held areas, which was blocking the coordination of Japanese forces as well as defending the rice-rich Chŏlla province. Already in November 1592 a 3,000-man Chosŏn force commanded by Kim Si-min had soundly defeated a major Japanese force, which lost more than 30,000 men. This decisive Japanese defeat is considered one of the three great Chosŏn victories of the war. In July 1593 some 79,000 Japanese troops attacked the town once again, and despite a heroic defense led by Kim Ch'ŏn-il, Chinju fell and the Japanese slaughtered many of its inhabitants.

From April 1593 on, truce negotiations continued between Ming and Japan but with no agreement. Meanwhile, Japan withdrew almost all its forces from Chosŏn, and Ming also pulled most of its troops out. The Japanese now believed that they won the war, but the Chinese insisted that Japan become a vassal state to Ming. The truce talks dragged on for three years and eventually ended with each side far apart in their demands. The Chinese tried to enfeoff Toyotomi as the king of Japan, but Toyotomi, for his part, demanded that Chosŏn first cede four southern provinces to Japan, that Ming send a daughter of the emperor to Japan as a consort of the Japanese "emperor," and that Chosŏn send a prince and several high officials to Japan as hostages. Because of the huge gap in the bargaining positions, there was no hope for a settlement. In the end peace negotiations dissolved, and the war entered its second phase when Toyotomi sent another force to invade Chosŏn.

The Second Japanese Invasion (1597)

In February 1597 141,000 Japanese troops again sailed to Chosŏn. This time, however, the Japanese met much stronger opposition, as the Chosŏn forces were better equipped and prepared to fight. Landing near Pusan, the Japanese drove north, devastating much of Chosŏn and causing Ming China to step in again and send forces. Throughout the second invasion, however, the Japanese were confined mainly to Kyŏngsang province. At sea, however, the Chosŏn navy suffered a crushing defeat in July 1597. This came about when Yi Sun-sin learned that the Japanese were attempting to lure him into a trap and so he refused a royal order to attack. Thereupon Yi Sun-sin was dismissed as commander-in-chief of the Chosŏn naval forces and was replaced by Wŏn Kyun. But Wŏn proved incompetent, leading the Chosŏn fleet to destruction off Pusan in the battle at Ch'ilch'ŏnnyang. He was killed in action, and 157 of 169 Chosŏn ships were lost.

Dismayed by the debacle at Ch'ilch'ŏnnyang, the Chosŏn government reinstated Admiral Yi Sun-sin, who reorganized the navy, now reduced to only 12 ships and 200 men. With these few ships, Yi Sun-sin engaged a Japanese fleet of 300 ships in the Myŏngnyang strait, near present-day Mokp'o, South Chŏlla province, and, using his wide experience and knowledge of tides and currents, he achieved a smashing victory in October 1597 and regained control of the sea.

While the war was turning to Japan's disadvantage, in August 1598 Toyotomi, the prime player behind the invasion, suddenly died. Under the pretext of his death, the Japanese determined to withdraw from Chosŏn. In December 1598

Japanese forces were in full-scale retreat, but attacking the retreating Japanese to the end, Yi Sun-sin was struck by a stray Japanese bullet and killed in the sea off Noryang point. The battle at Noryang point ended with a Chosŏn victory and the Japanese loss of nearly 250 of the original 500 ships. Finally, the Korean-Japanese war of 1592–1598 came to a conclusion but with grave consequences for Chosŏn, Japan, and Ming China.

The Aftermath of the War

For Chosŏn, the war of 1592–1598 was a tragedy, more devastating than any other event in Korean history (even the Korean War of 1950–1953). Japanese forces had ravaged and despoiled the entire nation, and today's anti-Japanese sentiment can be traced back to this unprovoked Japanese invasion. The Chinese armies that came to Chosŏn's aid were not much better. For the duration of the war, the administration and the economy were entirely disrupted. The Chosŏn dynasty never fully recovered from these blows.

Of all the devastation and suffering the Japanese invaders caused, the worst occurred in Kyŏngsang province, the main theater of war. For example, 90 percent of the farmlands there had turned into wasteland. The Japanese slaughtering of the people markedly decreased the entire population of the nation. The Chinese were no better than the Japanese in the destruction they caused and the crimes they committed. Famine and disease ensued, which led to the compilation, in 1610, of a great medical treatise, *Tongŭi pogam,* or Precious Exemplar of Korean Medicine, by Hŏ Chun. Because land and census registers had been destroyed, the government had great difficulty collecting taxes and enforcing corvee levies. In efforts to overcome its financial difficulties, particularly the shortage of food grains, the government sold office titles and ranks in exchange for *napsok,* or grain contributions, in set amounts. The cultural treasures lost in fires set by Japanese troops included the Kyŏngbok-kung palace and Pulguk-sa temple. The irreplaceable cultural materials rooted out of Chosŏn and taken to Japan included royal and government records, historical documents, art objects, paintings, Koryŏ porcelains, tens of thousands of books, and hundreds of thousands of handmade cast-movable metal type made over two centuries. The loss of artisans and technicians caused a decline in the quality of handiwork as well as in manufactured goods such as pottery and book printing. Neo-Confucian norms and values were gradually shaken. The dynastic cycle leading to the decline of the kingdom was initiated by the factional struggle within officialdom and was accelerated by this war.

On the other hand, the Japanese greatly benefited from their contact with Korea's higher civilization. That civilization was transmitted mostly through Japanese plunder and looting. But Japan also gained from the captives who were taken to Japan, including scholars and craftsmen who brought with them cultural and technological gains. The famous Japanese pottery of Satsuma, Karatsu, Hagi, and Raku were all made by kidnapped Korean potters. The numerous books seized and the many scholars captured by the Japanese also contributed to the development of learning in Japan, especially the study of Neo-Confucianism. Among the tens of thousands of Koreans shipped to Japan as prisoners of war, many were sold to European traders, mainly the Portuguese, as slaves at Nagasaki. The Portuguese merchants then resold them in Southeast Asia.

The war with Chosŏn caused political upheavals in Japan. After Hideyoshi's death, his son Hideyori, then only five years old, became head of the Toyotomi clan. But the clan's power and prestige greatly weakened. Tokugawa Ieyasu, who did not dispatch his troops to Chosŏn and thus kept his military strength intact, won the decisive battle of Sekigahara, defeating the Toyotomi forces, in October 1600, and then established himself as shogun in 1603. The Tokugawa shogunate lasted until the Meiji Restoration of 1868.

After the war Chosŏn severed diplomatic relations with Japan. But in its efforts to repatriate Korean prisoners of war and at Japan's earnest request, Chosŏn entered into friendly relations with Japan in 1607. Soon after the Chosŏn envoy Monk Yujŏng brought back more than 7,000 Korean captives, both countries exchanged delegates. Between 1607 and 1811 Chosŏn dispatched its envoys to Japan 12 times, and Japan sent its emissaries to Chosŏn more than 60 times. Whenever Chosŏn envoys arrived in Japan, the Tokugawa shogunate sent welcoming parties and treated them with courtesy equal to that given to the highest-ranking daimyos, powerful feudal lords.

The war also shook the balance of power on the Asian continent. By ridding Manchuria of Ming garrisons, the war paved the way for the Nuzhen Manchus to rapidly grow in strength in Manchuria, conquer Ming, and become the masters of China proper.

Kwanghaegun's Postwar Reconstruction and Neutral Diplomacy

In 1608 Kwanghaegun ascended the Chosŏn throne, succeeding his father, King Sŏnjo. The intelligent Kwanghaegun displayed uncommon capacities in directing both domestic and foreign affairs. In his reign (1608–1623), the Taebuk faction assumed the reins of government. To reconstruct his state, which had been in a completely debilitated condition, Kwanghaegun, with the help of the Taebuk faction, executed a new land survey and reinstituted census registers. To alleviate some of the burdens on the peasantry, who had to pay the heavy tribute tax, in 1608 he enforced the Taedongpŏp, a measure for paying taxes in rice, in Kyŏnggi province. He also rebuilt the *sago,* or history archives, and printed many books, such as duplicate sets of *Chosŏn wangjo sillok.*

Among Kwanghaegun's other accomplishments, the most noteworthy was his adroit foreign policy, which kept Chosŏn from being drawn into the acutely developing conflict on the Asian continent. The rise of the Nuzhen Manchus in Manchuria had already posed a grave threat to Chosŏn. At the time the Manchus produced a great leader, Nurhachi. By 1592, when the Korean-Japanese war began, Nurhachi was in command of a considerable force. An outstanding organizer of military as well as political institutions, he organized his army under eight banners of different colors and raised his troops as a formidable force. Nurhachi formally rebelled against Ming in 1616 and named his new nation Later Jin. Ming sent a large force to put down the revolt and asked Chosŏn for assistance.

Kwanghaegun was the only person in the Chosŏn court who viewed Ming not in terms of Neo-Confucianism but realistically. He thought Ming was no longer a match for Later Jin, but bowing to pressure from his subjects, he reluctantly sent a token force of 13,000 men commanded by Kang Hong-nip. After Kang's relief army arrived in Manchuria in 1619, Later Jin persuaded the Chosŏn forces to surrender repeatedly. On the verge of annihilation, Kang had no alternative but to surrender for survival. When the Westerners deposed Kwanghaegun in 1623, they denounced the king for not wholeheartedly helping Ming, which the Westerners perceived as the "parent country," and made this a major pretext for their coup against him.

Before he was overthrown, Kwanghaegun had actually pursued a neutral or balanced policy toward Later Jin and Ming. For instance, he never offended Later Jin, and at the same time permitted the Ming general Mao Wenlong, who planned to recapture the Liaodong peninsula, to encamp on the Chosŏn island of Ka-do near the estuary of the Yalu River. Also, he did not neglect, but enhanced, his country's state of military preparedness against any possible Manchu invasion.

At this perilous point, in 1623, the dethroned Kwanghaegun was succeeded by King Injo (1623–1649), and the factional strife, which had temporarily subsided in the face of the Japanese invasion, returned with renewed intensity. The Westerners deposed Kwanghaegun on the grounds that, besides betraying Ming China, in 1613 he had deposed his stepmother, Queen Dowager Kim, and slaughtered her son, his half-brother, Prince Yŏngch'ang, who was patronized by the Sobuk faction. After the coup, Kwanghaegun was banished to Kang-hwa-do and leading members of the Taebuk faction were all executed. Like Yŏnsan'gun a century ago, Kwanghaegun was no longer called king but was named "Kwanghaegun," or the Prince of Kwanghae.

The Manchu Invasions

King Injo, heavily influenced by the Westerners, including Kim Yu, Yi Kwi, and Yi Kwal, who had put him on the throne, abandoned his predecessor's posture of watchful waiting in favor of avowedly pro-Ming and anti–Later Jin policy. This change in Chosŏn policy was taken by Manchus as a serious affront. Manchus felt it necessary to secure their flank before proceeding with their campaign to conquer China proper. At this point, in February 1624, Yi Kwal led a rebellion against the government and occupied Seoul, believing he had been inadequately rewarded for his services in bringing Injo to the throne. When he was defeated and killed by government forces in March, remnants of his troops fled to Manchuria, where they seem to have urged Manchus to invade Chosŏn to redress the immorality of Kwanghaegun's dethronement.

Nurhachi died of battle wounds in 1626, and his son, Abahai, succeeded him. Under the pretext of righting the wrong of Kwanghaegun's deposal, Abahai dispatched 30,000 men to Chosŏn in February 1627. Still not recovered from the war with Japan, the Chosŏn army was ill-prepared to defend against these Manchu forces, which quickly moved as far south as P'yŏngsan, Hwanghae province. While advancing, Manchus sent envoys to the Chosŏn government demanding a negotiated settlement. Stubborn resistance of the ŭibyŏng militia slowed the invaders' advance and forced them to make peace with Chosŏn. The Chosŏn government had also desired a peaceful settlement, and so they reached an agreement in April. In exchange for the withdrawal of the Manchu forces, Chosŏn agreed on terms with Later Jin and the two established a brotherly relationship, with the Later Jin as the older brother and Chosŏn as the younger.

In May 1636 Abahai, Emperor Taizong, renamed his state of Later Jin to Qing. After the invasion of 1627 Chosŏn continued to defy Manchus, and so the relationship between the two countries remained bleak. Chosŏn's Neo-Confucian scholar-officials believed that it would be treachery to abandon Ming China after its assistance during the war with Japan, and they also resented the Manchu invasion of 1627. This resentment grew deeper when Qing sent a diplomatic representative to Chosŏn demanding that the country acknowledge the sovereign-subject relationship between the two states. The Chosŏn government rejected this demand, and King Injo even refused to receive the Qing envoys and the documents they carried. In January 1637 the angry Qing emperor personally led 100,000 troops in an assault against Chosŏn, knowing that Chosŏn maintained close relations with Ming and that he could not afford to face two enemies from the west and south. The southern front had to be secured before he could invade China proper.

Qing troops were mostly cavalry who moved quickly, and they reached Seoul in a few days. King Injo sent his queen, his sons, and their wives to seek refuge on Kanghwa-do, but Manchu forces prevented Injo himself from fleeing to the island, as Korean kings traditionally did. He hurriedly escaped, with barely 14,000 soldiers, to the Namhansan-sŏng fortress just south of Seoul. In the fortress the Chosŏn army was suffering from a scarcity of food and other supplies, as well as cold weather. Immediately upon Injo's arrival, the fortress was besieged by Manchus. Confounding matters, Kanghwa-do fell to Manchus, its royal refugees were taken prisoner, and several attempts by Chosŏn forces from various provincial and local garrisons to break the siege were foiled. Heeding the pleas of Ch'oe Myŏng-gil and other moderate officials who advocated peace, Injo surrendered, and in February 1637, at Samjŏndo (present-day Songp'a in Seoul), he capitulated to the Manchu emperor in a ceremony known as kowtow (*ketou*), the act of supplication (in which one kneels three times and prostrates oneself nine times). By the terms of the surrender, Chosŏn vowed to sever its ties with Ming, acknowledge the suzerainty of Qing, and delivered Injo's two eldest sons as hostages. Subsequently Crown Prince Sohyŏn and his younger brother, Prince Pongnim, along with some hard-line Chosŏn officials, accompanied the withdrawing Manchu forces as hostages. Reportedly 100,000 women were also sent to Qing as its spoils of war. Among the hard-liners, scholar-officials Hong Ik-han, Yun Chip, and O Tal-che refused to surrender to the end and were executed in the Qing capital of Shenyang. Another high-level official, Kim Sang-hŏn, was held in harsh confinement in a Manchu prison for three long years.

The two Manchu invasions deeply injured Korean pride and earned their hatred. Although their country officially yielded in obeisance, Koreans remained defiant toward the Qing empire, although privately. They considered Manchus uncivilized *orangk'e,* or barbarians. King Hyojong (1649–1659), who lived as a hostage for seven years in Shenyang and succeeded Injo, planned an unrealistic expedition to Qing during his ten-year reign. His death on the eve of the northern expedition ended the plan. On the other hand, because Chosŏn was forced to be a vassal state of the Qing empire, loyalty to Ming remained strong in Korean hearts for many years. Qing conquered Ming in 1644, and Manchus reigned as the masters of China until 1911. Content with degrading Chosŏn to a tributary state, the Qing empire respected the Korean kingdom's political independence and territorial integrity.

The Chosŏn kingdom may be summed up as replacing the aristocratic Koryŏ dynasty and, in its stead, establishing a strictly bureaucratic order led by the yangban. Based on Neo-Confucian institutions and culture, it achieved an advanced civilization in its first century. Subsequently, however, the bloody literati purges and fierce factional struggles greatly sapped its earlier vitality and strength. Finally, the decisive turn of the dynastic cycle came with the massive Japanese invasion of Chosŏn in the late sixteenth century, which virtually sealed the fate of the kingdom. Another important aspect should be mentioned concerning the Chosŏn kingdom. Its Neo-Confucian scholars spontaneously confined the scope of Korean history to the Korean peninsula, denying the close ties it had forged earlier with many states and civilizations on the Asian continent.

FIGURE 1. Comb Pattern Pottery (Neolithic Age).

신22891(2).

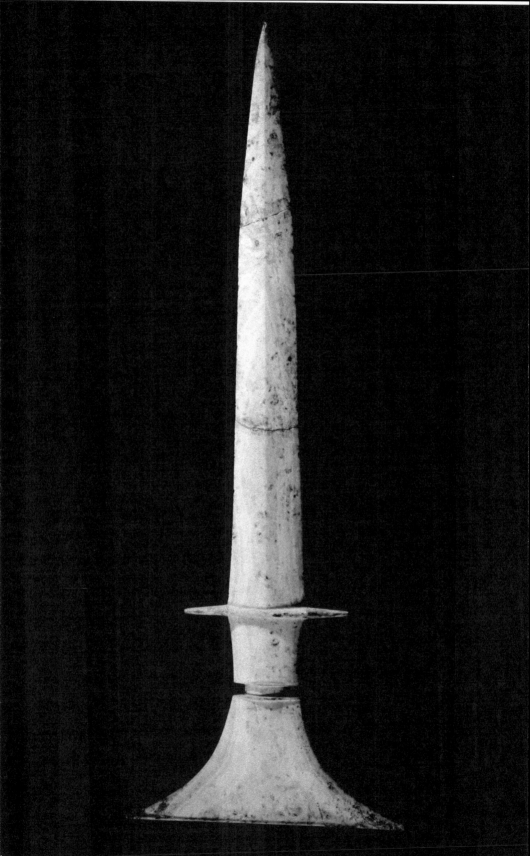

FIGURE 2. Facing. Polished Stone Sword (Bronze Age).
FIGURE 3. Above. Gold Crown (Silla, fifth century).

FIGURE 4. Facing. Gilt-Bronze Half-Seated Meditating Maitreya Bodhisattva (Three Kingdoms Period, seventh century).

FIGURE 5. Above. Gilt-Bronze Incense Burner (Paekche, seventh century).

FIGURE 6. Facing. Koryŏ Ch'ŏngja (Koryŏ, twelfth century).
FIGURE 7. Above. Chosŏn Paekcha (Chosŏn, fifteenth–sixteenth century).

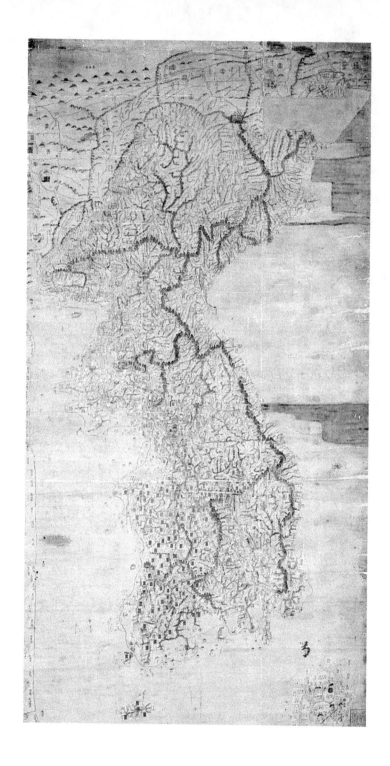

248

FIGURE 8. Facing. Map of the Eastern Kingdom by Chŏng Sang-gi (Chosŏn, 1728).

FIGURE 9. Above. A Dancing Boy in Kim Hong-do's *Genre Album* (Chosŏn, eighteenth century).

7

THE SECOND HALF OF THE
CHOSŎN PERIOD
(1650–1910)

THE REVIVAL OF THE DYNASTY

Factional Struggles

IN THE LATER CHOSŎN PERIOD fierce factional struggles developed, in which scholar-officials quarreled even over minor points of Confucian ritual and etiquette, especially the proper mourning period following the death of a royal personage. Neo-Confucian doctrine rewarded tedious scholasticism and inflexible orthodoxy, and encouraged the Neo-Confucian literati to avoid "forged factions" and join "authentic factions." The Neo-Confucian literati also argued that their own faction was orthodox and denounced their rivals as heterodox. This bitter strife deteriorated further as the number of aspiring officials grew while the number of available positions became scarce.

After the two wars with the Japanese and the Manchus, the power struggle among the yangban scholar-officials intensified. Bloody purges took many talented lives every time power changed hands. The winners threatened the losers' persons, property, and families, even their graves. Each faction sought to desecrate the power and influence of its rivals, always in the name of a higher morality, but every time a faction took power, the group splintered into smaller units. Meanwhile, with officials engaged in a life-and-death struggle, they had no time to attend either to national matters or the needs of the populace.

After Kwanghaegun was charged with misrule and deposed in 1623, eventually the Westerners dominated the political scene. For example, King Hyojong (1649–1659) brought members of the *sallim*, or rustic literati, from the Westerners into government service, such as Song Si-yŏl, the king's former mentor, Song Chun-gil, Kim Chip, Kwŏn Si, and Yi Yu-t'ae. Of course, the Westerners frequently faced challenges to their power. In 1674, following a dispute concerning how King Hyojong's stepmother, the Queen Dowager Cho, was to mourn the death of one of Hyojong's consorts, the Southerners drove the Westerners from power and took their place. Later, in 1680, the Westerners struck back, accusing the Southerners of plotting high treason against King Sukchong (1674–1720) and succeeded in purging them from the court. The Southerners' two top leaders, Hŏ Chŏk and Yun Hyu, were executed. Then, in 1683, the Westerners themselves split into two factions: the *Noron*, or Old Doctrine, faction, led by Song Si-yŏl, and the *Soron*, or Young Doctrine, faction that coalesced around Yun Chŭng. The Old Doctrine faction wanted the Southerners to be purged and harshly punished, whereas the Young Doctrine faction remained relatively moderate on the issue of retribution against its political rivals. After the division, it was principally the Noron faction that seized power. The downfall of the Westerners, however, came after the group discordantly opposed the king's intention to make a child of Southerner lineage the crown prince. When Sukchong, long without an heir, proposed this investment of the newborn son of his favorite concubine, the Lady Chang of Southerner lineage, in 1689, the Westerners' opposition enraged the king, who was driven to kill Song Si-yŏl by poisoning him. Then, in 1694, only a few years after the Southerners assumed the reins of government, Sukchong lethally poisoned the Lady Chang and ousted the Southerners from power. For quite a long period following these bloody political intrigues, the Westerners, particularly the Old Doctrine faction, enjoyed political supremacy, and there was no chance of the Southerners ever returning to power again. After the Old Doctrine faction won a lasting victory over its chief rival, the Southerners, and Kings Yŏngjo and Chŏngjo made strong efforts toward reconciliation, factionalism subsided considerably.

Kings Yŏngjo and Chŏngjo

After the short reign of the sickly Kyŏngjong (1720–1724), the son of the Lady Chang, King Yŏngjo (1724–1776) ascended the throne in 1724. He was on the throne for 52 years and was succeeded by his grandson, King Chŏngjo (1776–

1800), in 1776. During the reign of the two kings, the Chosŏn dynasty enjoyed a period of revival. They tried their best to remedy the adverse situation caused by factional fights, without much success, but the two kings were able, like the Roman emperors Diocletian and Constantine, to slow the dynasty's rapid decline.

Yŏngjo and Chŏngjo weakened factional struggles by advancing a policy of impartiality, called *t'angp'yŏngch'aek*, in which no faction was favored over another for official appointments among men of the so-called *sasaek*, or four colors, the four major factions at the time: the Old Doctrine, the Young Doctrine, the Southerners, and the Northerners. But the policy of distributing posts equally failed to completely root out chronic factional strife. In 1762 Yŏngjo, on the instigation of the Old Doctrine faction, ordered his officials to execute his own son, Crown Prince Sado (Changhŏn), who was friendly to the Young Doctrine faction. Out of this tragedy a new conflict arose within the bureaucracy between the *Sip'a*, or Party of Expediency, and the *Pyŏkp'a*, or Party of Principle. Whereas the Party of Expediency deplored the crown prince's tragic fate, the Party of Principle justified the king's action. Although the confrontation between the two new groups partially cut across the earlier factional lines, essentially the *Pyŏkp'a* party consisted of the Old Doctrine faction and the *Sip'a* party was composed of the Southerners.

Because of their enhanced royal authority, Yŏngjo and Chŏngjo reformed the tax system, increased government revenues, improved military preparedness, and oversaw the revival of learning during their reign. The two kings revived printing by using newly cast movable metal type and published numerous well-known works. Specifically, the scholarly Chŏngjo employed young scholars from various factions in the *Kyujanggak*, or Inner Royal Library, established in 1776, to partake in these projects.

Changes in the Tax Collection System

The Advent of the Taedongpŏp

In the aftermath of the Japanese invasion, the Chosŏn government had urgent matters to resolve; it needed to revive the ruined economy, provide job stability, and increase national revenues. Farmlands had been completely devastated in the war, and the total area under cultivation had greatly decreased. Many land registers had been destroyed, which resulted in illegal transfers of taxpaying lands into the hands of powerful tax-free landlords. The nation's total taxable land fell from 1.70 million kyŏl before the war to only 0.54 million kyŏl in the reign of Kwanghaegun. The amount the nation could collect in land taxes decreased proportionally.

In the postwar years improvement and reclamation of agricultural land and increased land registers led to the steady growth of taxable farmlands from 0.54 million kyŏl in the Kwanghaegun period to 1.20 million kyŏl in the Injo period, 1.40 million kyŏl in the Sukchong period, and 1.45 kyŏl in the Yŏngjo and Chŏngjo periods. At the same time the total amount of land taxes the state could collect also increased, which contributed to the nation's economic stability.

The government sought to improve the tax collection system at a time when the tribute tax accounted for some 60 percent of Chosŏn's national revenue. Further, gross overcharging of taxes (a practice called *pangnap*) and the exploitation of peasant farmers by tax collectors were among many of the problems causing a disproportionate burden to the peasantry. After the war, the government finally initiated the Taedongpŏp, a rice payment law that allowed tribute taxes to be paid in rice, which had already been suggested before the war as a means of alleviating the suffering of those who paid the tribute tax. In 1608, urged on by Chief State Councilor Yi Wŏn-ik, the Taedongpŏp was first carried out in Kyŏnggi province, and by 1709 it was enforced throughout the country.

The terms of the Taedongpŏp set a rate of 12 tu (64 kilograms) of rice, about 1 percent of the harvest, for each kyŏl of farmland, in addition to the standard land taxes. To administer the Taedongpŏp, the government established the Sŏnhyech'ŏng, or Agency to Bestow Blessings. Implementation of the new tax law, and the abolition of the tribute tax system, improved state revenues and lightened the economic burden of the peasantry by some 80 percent.

Changes in the Military Cloth Tax

By the time of the Japanese invasion, the Five Commands system was not operational and existed in name only. By 1594, during the course of the war, a special agency for military training, called the Hullyŏn togam, or Military Training Command, was established. It drilled a new fighting force known as the *samsubyŏng*, or three combat forces, consisting of *p'osu*, or musketeers; *sasu*, or archers; and *salsu*, or lancers and swordsmen. Later, four new army garrisons were created around the capital, forming a total of five army garrisons, with the Hullyŏn togam as the core element; the four included the Ch'ongyungch'ŏng, or Command of the Northern Approaches, in 1624; the Ŏyŏngch'ŏng, or Command of the Royal Guards, in 1624; the Suŏch'ŏng, or Command of the Southern Approaches, in 1616; and the Kŭmwiyŏng, or Capital Garrison, in 1682.

Soldiers under the command of the five army garrisons were paid their wages by the government. Instead of being called up for military duty themselves, all able-bodied men, specifically peasant farmers, were required to pay a military cloth tax, or kunp'o, of 2 bolts, or 40 feet, of cotton cloth per year, which was used to pay the expenses for the maintenance of professional soldiers. Because powerful landlords were able to shelter their tenant-farmers from this military cloth tax, the entire tax burden again fell to the peasants. And because the price of a bolt of cotton cloth was equivalent to that of 32 kilograms of rice at the time, the peasants' burden was all the more crushing. Moreover, as targets for extortion, many peasants were forced to flee their land to escape unlawful practices including *hwanggu ch'ŏmjŏng,* or fledgling legerdemain, registering boys as adults on whom the military cloth tax could be levied; and *paekkol chingp'o,* or skeleton levies, keeping dead men's names on tax rosters in order to continue collecting from their surviving relatives. Even as many peasants fled their land to escape these unreasonable charges, their unpaid taxes were forcibly collected from their neighbors (called *injŏng,* or neighbor levies) or from their kinsmen (termed *chokching,* or kinsmen levies).

The malfeasance involved in the collection of the military cloth tax reached a climax in the late seventeenth and early eighteenth centuries, and the governemt began to recognize an urgent need for military tax reform. In 1750 a government decree reduced the military cloth tax from two bolts to one. The government compensated for the lost revenue by taxing fish traps, salt production, and private fishing and trading vessels, and by instituting a grain surtax, called *kyŏlchak (kyŏlmi),* or kyŏl rice, charging landowners 2 tu, or 11 kilograms, of rice per harvest. The new measure, appropriately called the *Kyunyŏkpŏp,* or Equalized Tax Law, along with the implementation of the Taedongpŏp, succeeded in alleviating much of the suffering endured by the peasantry.

Economic Growth

Changes in Farming

Historically rice has been the staple food of the Koreans. In Chosŏn rice also was used as currency. Following the wars against the Japanese and the Manchus, the government strove to increase rice yields, which depended on the availability of water. Thus the construction of irrigation facilities became a pressing problem. In 1662 the Cheŏnsa, or Office of Embankment Works, was formed, and in 1778 the *Cheŏn chŏrmok,* or Comprehensive Plan for Embankment Works, was promulgated to provide for the maintenance and repair of irrigation facilities throughout the country. In the meantime, many reservoirs for irrigation were developed. By the end of the eighteenth century almost 6,000 reservoirs existed. At the same time reclamation projects were actively undertaken along the west coast, considerably enlarging the farmlands.

As irrigation facilities expanded, the farming of rice fields developed. Dry fields were transformed into paddies on a vast scale, and the technique of transplanting rice seedlings became widespread. Rice transplantation made possible the double-cropping system, in which the paddies, before rice planting, could be used for the ripening winter barley crop, resulting in a marked increase in food grains. The technique of dry-field cultivation was also developed, in which fields were plowed so as to form an alternating pattern of ridges and furrows, with the seed being sown in the furrows at the same time.

As the development of agricultural techniques reduced labor requirements, the practice of *kwangjak,* or enlarged-scale farming, became prevalent, in which one farmer alone worked a good-sized area of land. These farmers emerged as agricultural entrepreneurs, capable of producing not only for their own consumption but also for the market. They also hired farm laborers. Indeed, most of the landless labor force in rural society became the hired hands of their wealthier neighbors or were driven elsewhere for employment. Some became mountain recluses living by slash-and-burn agricultural practices.

Since the early eighteenth century, the growing commercial production of specialized crops, particularly ginseng, tobacco, and cotton, transformed rural life. The cultivation of ginseng was popular in the Kaesŏng area both as a product for the domestic market and for exporting to China and Japan. Tobacco, first introduced in the early seventeenth century from Japan, was also widely grown for domestic consumption as well as for exporting to China. The cultivation of cotton gradually increased for both market and home consumption, and vegetables were widely grown for subsistence in the increasingly populated suburban areas of Seoul.

The experiences of war had led farmers to recognize the need for hardy plants and for better general preparations in case of crop failures. Thus, new crops such as sweet potatoes, potatoes, tomatoes, squash, and red peppers were widely cultivated. Sweet potatoes were brought from Japan by Cho Ŏm, who had been dispatched to Japan as Chosŏn's envoy in 1764, and potatoes were introduced from China in 1824.

As large landholdings became widespread, a majority of peasant farmers were reduced to working the land as tenants, although at the same time a new class of commoner landlords emerged. In this period a tenant farmer who usually paid 50 percent of his harvest as rent could farm the leased land at his own discretion. Later, the tenant system developed to where rent for tenancy could be paid in cash rather than in kind.

Changes in the Handicraft Industry

In this later Chosŏn period a new phase developed in the handicraft industry. Production under government auspices gradually declined, and private industry took its place. The manufacture of weapons, paper, clothes, chinaware, silk, brassware, and mintage still remained government activities for some time, but even commodities in state demand such as these ultimately came under private management. By the end of the eighteenth century artisans and craftsmen of all kinds had become private producers independent of government control. The enactment of the Taedongpŏp was a prelude to the development of private industry. With the abolition of the tribute tax, merchants, called *kongin*, or tribute men, acted as purchasing agents, ordering craftsmen to supply the goods necessary to meet the government's requirements.

In the seventeenth and eighteenth centuries, most craftsmen did not finance their own operations but mostly relied on capital provided by the merchants. Upon receiving an order from a merchant, the craftsman was given raw materials and advance payment for his labor. Called the *mulchu*, or financier, the merchant controlled the craftsman's production. Some craftsmen, however, did produce goods with their own capital, selling them on their own or through the pack and back peddlers. For example, the makers of brassware who were concentrated at Ansŏng, Kyŏnggi province, and Chŏngju, P'yŏngan province, used their own capital to build workshops, procure raw materials, and employ labor, and then sold their output to merchants at markets that were set up.

In the early period the state had a monopoly on mining rights and banned the private development of mines. Beginning in the mid-eighteenth century, however, the government permitted private mining operations, and with the growing demand for silver in the trade with Qing China, the number of silver mines sharply increased. Indeed, by the end of the century, as many as 70 silver mines were operating, particularly at Tanch'ŏn, Hamgyŏng province, and P'aju and Kyoha just north of Seoul.

The majority of these and other mines, however, were operated without the government's knowledge or approval in order to avoid paying the generally excessive mining taxes; such operations were known as *chamch'ae*, or covert diggings, and many of them employed a labor force. The undue tax burden on miners greatly reduced the number of officially sanctioned silver mines, and thus gold mining, conducted at Chasan and Sŏngch'ŏn, P'yŏngan province, and at Suan, Hwanghae province, surpassed silver mining in importance. The government also authorized copper and iron mining to supply the need for coins, brassware, and weapons.[1] But, like the other mining operations, these were also covert diggings.

Changes in Commerce

This period saw the proliferation of monopolistic wholesale commerce, called *togo,* in which government-licensed merchants operated through the yukŭijŏn, or private merchants in Seoul, and the tribute men carried on wholesale commerce, specifically as purchasing agents who supplied government-required goods. These wholesale merchants accumulated vast amounts of capital and in time grew into a specialized class of wealthy merchants, each handling large quantities of one particular type of good and paying a tax for their monopolistic privilege.

Numerous private merchants also engaged in commerce in Seoul as well as throughout the country. Their activity extended along the major transportation routes to markets everywhere. The "river merchants" of Seoul marketed, quite profitably, grain, salt, and fish along the reaches of the Han River in Kyŏnggi and Ch'ungch'ŏng provinces, and their activities resulted in many ferry crossings along the river. This brought many local people into Seoul, who built a number of new villages outside the capital. Merchants of Kaesŏng, Kyŏnggi province, extended their activities over land routes to Hwanghae and P'yŏngan provinces to the north and Ch'ungch'ŏng and Kyŏngsang provinces to the south. They even accompanied official envoys to China in their quest for profits. The Kaesŏng merchants themselves managed the cultivation and sale of ginseng, a major item in their trade.

The escalating activity of private merchants greatly changed the appearance of Seoul's commercial streets. The *Sinhae t'onggong,* or Commercial Equalization of 1791, abolished special privileges granted to licensed merchants, except for the original yukŭijŏn. Three great markets operated by private merchants flourished in Seoul: at Ihyŏn inside East Gate, at Ch'ilp'ae outside South Gate, and at Chongnu in the present-day Chongno area. These three markets dealt not only with local products from the country's eight provinces but also with goods imported from China and Japan. The well-known song "Hanyangga," or "Song of Seoul," much in vogue in the early nineteenth century, expressed the appearance of the capital as a prosperous commercial city.

Markets in the countryside, called *changsi*, first emerged in Chŏlla province in the fifteenth century and, by the eighteenth century, numbered more than 1,000 throughout the country. These markets were generally open every five days, but the larger ones were established on a permanent basis. In the markets *kaekchu*, or inland market brokers, and *yŏgak*, or coastal trade brokers, provided various services to the itinerant pack and back peddlers. These not only carried on a wholesale trade but engaged in commission sales, warehousing, transportation, inn-keeping, and banking activities.

As markets developed in the countryside, new roads were constructed and new sea routes were opened. Also, active water transportation led to the development of a boat-building industry. Well-known markets at the time were located in Kanggyŏng, Ch'ungch'ŏng province; Taegu, Masan, and Andong, Kyŏngsang province; Ŭnp'a, Hwanghae province; Wŏnsan, Hamgyŏng province; and P'yŏngch'ang, Kangwŏn province. Some towns grew into commercial cities.

Alongside the development of internal commerce, foreign trade also grew considerably. The merchants of Ŭiju near the estuary of the Yalu River traded privately with the Chinese, importing silks, hats, medicines, horses, and stationery from Qing China, and exporting silver, furs, paper, and cotton cloth. Since the nineteenth century the chief article for export to China was Kaesŏng ginseng. Merchants of Tongnae, near Pusan, engaged in trade with the Japanese, exporting ginseng, rice, and cotton cloth, and importing copper, sulfur, and pepper. Later, Chosŏn merchants of Kaesŏng, Ŭiju, and Tongnae acted as intermediaries in commissioning trade with China and Japan.

Expanding commercial activity spurred the use and circulation of coin currency, which acted as a bridge linking rural life to the urban economy. After copper coins known as *Sangp'yŏng t'ongbo*, or Ever Constant Circulating Treasure, were minted in 1678, large quantities of coins were continuously issued. By the end of the seventeenth century, coins were in wide circulation throughout the country. Among the general populace, however, coins were an auxiliary currency, trailing behind their extensive use of rice and cotton as money. But as the government increasingly collected tax payments in cash beginning in the late eighteenth century, coins began to serve as the main medium of exchange. This extensive use of coins as currency accelerated the commercialization of production. Marketing transactions and payments of wages and taxes in cash also greatly increased.

Coins were often hoarded for their intrinsic value by many yangban, rich merchants, and landowners, who consequently amassed great wealth and became usurers. Despite the mass mintage of coins, the increase in hoarding led to coin shortages known as *chŏnhwang*, or coin famines. As internal commerce and international trade flourished, commercial capital began to accumulate, along with increasing mercantile wealth, comprised not of land and slaves but of commodities for trade.

Economic Changes and a New Class Structure

Economic growth inevitably led to profound changes in the existing class structure. Although the traditional yangban-centered status system essentially remained in place, the status of many yangban had greatly eroded mainly because of their declining fortunes. Having become increasingly impoverished, the yangban could no longer maintain their dignity and authority, and some actually fell to the level of commoners. The yangban population had steadily grown as well, further marring their prestige and influence. Between the 1690s and 1850s, for example, the number of yangban in Taegu increased from 9.2 percent to 70.2 percent of the total population. Whereas the profound economic changes drove the peasantry further into poverty, rich farmers of commoner background purchased yangban titles at set prices. In fact, throughout the eighteenth century, the purchase and forgery of genealogical tables of yangban families were prevalent.

Another major class shift occurred among former slaves. Many slaves had escaped in the confusion brought on by the wars with the Japanese and the Manchus. Moreover, the government, beset by a shortage of military conscripts and chronic financial difficulties, viewed emancipation of the slaves as advantageous to the state. Therefore slaves who distinguished themselves on the battlefield or donated food grains under the "napsok" system were set free, and gradually the entire slavery system collapsed.

Under these circumstances, in 1801, all the rosters of government slaves were destroyed in an effort to set them free. Almost all slaves in the central government offices were emancipated, but slaves belonging to local government offices remained in bondage, and the system of private slavery was not abolished until the *Kabo kyŏngjang*, or Reform of 1894.

CULTURAL REHABILITATION

The Rise and Development of Sirhak

Beginning in the early seventeenth century Neo-Confucianism strayed from its original intent and degenerated into a mere instrument for the civil service examination. In its place, a new philosophical movement termed *Sirhak,* or Practical Learning, was initiated by scholars in Seoul and became popular among members of the literati, particularly those out of power. This new intellectual movement, which advocated putting human knowledge to practical use, was inspired partly by Chosŏn's deteriorating social conditions and partly by new currents of thought in China, introduced by young members returning from official missions in China. In fact, it was stimulated primarily by the recognition that Chosŏn's well-being as a nation was in need of dramatic improvement.

At the time when the Northerners seized political power in the reign of Kwanghaegun, scholars and literati of the Westerners in Seoul were pursuing a new scholarly approach to literature and the Chinese classics and, in so doing, proposed various social reform programs. Yi Su-gwang (Chibong) is remembered as the first Sirhak scholar, whose fundamental work, *Chibong yusŏl,* or Topical Discourses of Chibong, appeared in 1614. In this 20-volume encyclopedic work, which included 3,435 entries, Yi discussed, among other subjects, astronomy, geography, the kingly virtues, military administration, Chinese classics, botany, animals, and insects, and offered his own views of the society and government of earlier Korean dynasties. *Chibong yusŏl* greatly expanded the available knowledge in Korea about Europe and Southeast Asia, and for the first time explained the nature of Catholicism in Korean history. In his prolific work, Yi stressed the idea that pure knowledge without action had no value. In the early period of King Injo, Yi presented the king with a 12-article memorial containing proposals for government and social reform.

After the Westerners came into power with Injo's accession to the throne in 1623, Neo-Confucianism regained its strength as the main current in scholarship. From the late seventeenth through the early eighteenth century, when the Westerners, particularly the Old Doctrine faction, held the reins of government, Chosŏn scholarship was overwhelmingly influenced by Neo-Confucianism again, and scholars who criticized Zhu Xi Confucianism were considered betrayers of Confucianism. During these times many Sirhak thinkers emerged from the Southerners, whose members had long been excluded from important government positions. These Sirhak scholars pondered the way to achieve an ideal society in their country. Although they were all essentially Neo-Confucians, their inquiry emphasized not the primacy of i or ki but actual worldly manifestations. Their scholarship thus embraced many disciplines, including politics, economics, geography, astronomy, agriculture, natural science, Catholicism, and Confucianism. Seeking to find solutions to the difficult problems facing their country, Sirhak scholars devoted themselves to the study of Korea.

Starting in the late seventeenth century, famed Sirhak scholars including Yu Hyŏng-wŏn (Pan'gye), Yi Ik (Sŏngho), and Chŏng Yak-yong (Tasan) stressed the need for reform of the land system, personnel administration, and military organization. They were particularly concerned about agricultural reform and sought to achieve a sound agricultural economy based on independent, self-supporting farmers.

Yu Hyŏng-wŏn spent his life in self-imposed exile in the isolated farming village of Puan, Chŏlla province, where he devoted himself to studying the local society, based on his personal experience. In his work, Pan'gye surok, or Treatises of Pan'gye, compiled in 1670, he criticized the existing land system, education, official appointments, government structure, and the system of military service. He urged the redistribution of farmlands to the people, including the yangban literati, so they could become self-supporting farmers. He also suggested that soldiers in the armed forces be allocated land by the state and that the kwagŏ institution be replaced by a system of recommendations. Although his proposals found no official acceptance, his reformist school of thought became the mainstream philosophy of Sirhak.

One of Yu Hyŏng-wŏn's relatives, Yi Ik, another scholar of established repute, founded the "Sŏngho school." In his basic work, Sŏngho sasŏl, or Encyclopedia of Sŏngho, Yi Ik criticized the institutions and culture of both Chosŏn and China. The subject matter covered in the book was arranged under five broad headings: the world, all of creation, human affairs, Chinese classical scholarship, and belles-lettres. The section on human affairs specifically treated such important subjects as politics and administration, economics, and the family. Another book, Kwaku rok, or Record of Concern for the Underprivileged, set forth Yi Ik's ideas for reform. He believed that knowledge should not be acquired unless it benefited the daily lives of the general populace. His sharp analysis of the causes of factionalism stemmed from a deep-seated concern for people's welfare. Yi Ik's chief concern was the need to reconstruct impoverished farming communities, and he proposed that each peasant be allotted land to be held in perpetuity. Because factionalism mainly resulted from competition for government office and securing a livelihood, he maintained that those who had chosen to remain out of office should be afforded the opportunity to enter government service upon recommendation, and that the literati should also engage in farming. He wanted to abolish all class distinctions and emancipate the slaves. His ideas for reform greatly influenced Chŏng Yak-yong, one of the most eminent Sirhak scholars, although Chŏng was also influenced by the Pukhak, or Northern Learning, movement.

An early-nineteenth-century scholar, Chŏng Yak-yong, set forth the most comprehensive, progressive reform programs yet suggested. As a result of the *Sinyu saok,* or Catholic Persecution of 1801, Chŏng was banished for 18 years at Kangjin, Chŏlla province, and forced into retirement for 17 more years in his hometown of Yangju, Kyŏnggi province, during which time he wrote more than 500 works. These included *Kyŏngse yup'yo,* or Design for Good Government (1817), *Mongmin simsŏ,* or Admonitions on Governing the People (1818), and *Hŭmhŭm sinsŏ,* or For a New Jurisprudence (1822), in which he sharply analyzed and criticized the institutions and conditions of Chosŏn society. Comparing provincial governors, county magistrates, and local functionaries to robbers or rapacious birds, he wrote *Mongmin simsŏ* as a textbook to instruct these local officials on how to cultivate their moral culture. In *Hŭmhŭm sinsŏ,* Chŏng Yak-yong advanced his ideas on reforming the penal administration, and in *Kyŏngse yup'yo* he proposed reforms in central and local government institutions. He maintained that the monarch should hold the reins of government and rule the people directly, with the assistance of local officials, but at the same time he believed that the people should be allowed to govern themselves as much as possible. He also suggested that wealthy farmers be appointed to government offices based on their contributions to the rural community. He proposed creating an agency to oversee science and technology. Regarding land, he urged that each village be allocated farmland to be run under a system of collective ownership and cultivation, in which individual peasants would receive shares of the harvest based on their labor contribution.

Sirhak emerged as a new intellectual movement starting in the early seventeenth century as an alternative to Neo-Confucianism which had degenerated into dogma. Sirhak scholars, ranging from Yu Hyŏng-wŏn to Chŏng Yak-yong, especially advocated a "physiocracy," in which they envisioned an ideal agricultural society based on independent, self-supporting farmers. They never realized their goal, however, as officialdom rejected their reform proposals.

The Rise of Pukhak

Since the mid-eighteenth century a new school of thought arose among a group of scholars from the Old Doctrine faction, adding a new dimension to the development of Sirhak thought. As the new doctrine actively introduced cultural and institutional reforms borrowed from Qing China, then at its height, it became known as Pukhak, or Northern Learning. Although its proponents did not admire China, they ardently wished to model Chosŏn society after China's, seeking to enrich the nation and secure the people's livelihood by embracing Qing civilization and its commercial and manufacturing achievements.

The pioneer scholar of this Pukhak persuasion, Yu Su-wŏn, advanced a systematic plan for political, economic, social, and cultural reform in his major work *Usŏ*, or Idle Jottings, which appeared in 1737. He proposed that Chosŏn transform its economic structure from one centered on agriculture to one based on commerce and manufacturing. In the new economy he envisioned, the yangban would engage in agriculture, commerce, and manufacturing. Instead of unrealistic land reform, he suggested that agricultural productivity might be improved through commercial management and the introduction of new technology. He also urged that merchants engage in joint ventures to enlarge the scale of commercial management and that they employ craftsmen in order to control production and marketing.

Hong Tae-yong saw in the natural sciences the essence of all spiritual activities, refuting the traditional Confucian conception of science and technology as marginal branches of knowledge. The reason for the earth's rotation, the cause of eclipses, and the nature of rainbows, for example, were included among his valid scientific findings. He wrote an account of his travels to Qing China, titled *Yŏn'gi*, or Beijing Memoir, in 1765. In it, he denied that China was the center of the world, a view previously undisputed by scholars. He believed that Western science and technology surpassed anything that Chinese civilization could provide, and that the acceptance of Western learning would aid in Chosŏn's development. He also thought that introducing new technology, eliminating yangban lineages, and rejecting Neo-Confucianism would enrich his nation.

Pak Chi-wŏn, who lived in retirement at Yŏnam of Kimch'ŏn, Hwanghae province, declared that unique talents were bestowed on all men from heaven. He wrote the *Yŏrha ilgi*, or Rehe Diary, documenting his journey to Beijing, in 1780, in the entourage of a Chosŏn envoy. In that work he introduced Qing civilization and expressed his views on Chosŏn society, culture, and history.

Although he was concerned about the redistribution of farmland, he worried more about raising agricultural productivity by reforming farmland management, encouraging commercial farming, improving farming appliances, and expanding irrigation facilities. He also showed particular interest in the promotion of commerce and manufacturing, stressing the importance of transportaion by wagon and ship and the need for a stable currency. Finally, he strongly assailed the parasitic life of the yangban.

Pak Che-ga described his experiences in Beijing in *Pukhakŭi*, or Discourse on Northern Learning, which, like the work of Pak Chi-wŏn, addressed the need to reform Chosŏn society. It was this treatise, written in 1778, that gave rise to the term "Northern Learning." In his work Pak Che-ga urged the fostering of commerce and manufacturing, transportation by wagon and ship, trade and commerce with Qing China, and the abolition of class distinctions. Clearly Chosŏn's economic growth in the mid-eighteenth century owed much to the Pukhak-oriented scholars leading this new intellectual movement.

New Interest in the Study of Korea

Wars with the Japanese and the Manchus inspired a national consciousness and patriotic spirit among Koreans, which stirred their interest in the nation's history, geography, and culture. In his major work, *Chibong yusŏl*, Yi Su-gwang advised Koreans not to overestimate China and its civilization, and encouraged people to take pride in their history and relish the proclaimed fact of Korea's more highly refined culture relative to that of China. He also claimed that ancient places presumed to have existed in the Korean peninsula were actually in Manchuria, thereby urging Koreans to remember the "lost territory of Manchuria." Prepared at King Yŏngjo's command in 1770, the 250-volume work *Tongguk munhŏn pigo*, or Compilation of Reference Documents on the Eastern Kingdom, was a true encyclopedia of Korean studies offering a chronological overview of Korea's geography, government, economy, and culture.

In the eighteenth century some important historical works based on the thorough study of old records appeared. In his *Tongguk yŏktae ch'ongmok*, or Complete Account of Successive Generations of the Eastern Kingdom, written in 1705, Hong Man-jong claimed that Korean history began with Tan'gun Chosŏn as the first legitimate Korean nation and was succeeded by Kija Chosŏn, Mahan, and unified Silla, and that the period of the Three Kingdoms should not be considered a legitimate part of Korean history. He wrote a history of the dynasties of Koryŏ and Chosŏn from the perspective of royal households. His proclamation that Tan'gun Chosŏn was the first legitimate Korean nation was reinforced by the findings of An Chŏng-bok, who completed his *Tongsa kangmok*, or Annotated Account of Korean History, in 1778. An's work presented a full chronology of Korean history from Tan'gun through the end of the Koryŏ dynasty. His contribution to Korean historiography emphasized the roles of the common people who expelled foreign invaders, and he blamed the ruling classes for having devoted themselves only to the exploitation of the people. His work made a lasting impression on such modern historians as Pak Ŭn-sik and Sin Ch'ae-ho. In 1797 Yi Kŭng-ik wrote *Yŏllyŏsil kisul*, or Narratives of Yŏllyŏsil, which, based on his research of more than 400 unofficial histories, provided descriptions of the major events in each Chosŏn king's reign through King Sukchong.

At the time the consensus among Korean scholars was that Korea's scope of activity extended beyond the Korean peninsula into Manchuria. In his work, *Tongsa*, or History of Korea, which appeared in 1803 after the author's death, Yi Chong-hwi emphasized the role played by the Koguryŏ kingdom in Manchuria. He also claimed that old territories of Puyŏ and Parhae in Manchuria were under the domain of the Korean people. Yu Tŭk-kong's *Parhae ko*, or Study of the Parhae Kingdom, written in 1784, placed Parhae on an equal footing with unified Silla, suggesting for the first time the idea of the period of the "Northern and Southern States." In agreement, Han Ch'i-yun's *Haedong yŏksa*, or History East of the Sea (Korea), compiled in 1823, which covered the kingdoms of Koguryŏ and Parhae in detail, viewed the latter as integral to Korean history.

Studies of historical geography also developed alongside those of historical scholarship. The pioneer work in this field of study was *Tongguk chiri chi*, or Treatise on the Geography of the Eastern Kingdom, written by Han Paek-gyŏm in 1640. Han's work gave impetus to the study of historical geography with its new inquiries into the names of ancient places. Han asserted that Old Chosŏn and the three Han federations had been situated, respectively, north and south of the Han River. He was also the first to provide proof that Koguryŏ was not established in the area of Sŏngch'ŏn, P'yŏngan province, as was generally accepted at the time, but was located in Manchuria, and this greatly influenced later studies of Korean history. His work was succeeded by Sin Kyŏng-jun, who wrote *Kanggye chi*, or Treatise on Domains, in 1756.

A major work on cultural geography was *T'aengni chi*, or Treatise on the Ecology of Korea, also known as *P'aryŏk chi*, or Treatise on the Eight Provinces, written by Yi Chung-hwan in 1751. Based on geomantic theories, it covered the economies, politics, customs, and community values of Chosŏn's eight provinces. Important geographical work included Sin Kyŏng-jun's *Toro ko*, or Study of Routes and Roads, appeared in 1770, and his *Sansu kyŏng*, or Study of Mountains and Rivers, written in the mid-18th century. Also, Chŏng Sang-gi completed *Tongguk chido*, or Map of the Eastern Kingdom, in 1728, and his invention of an ingenious scaling device encouraged the development of Korean cartography. He greatly influenced Kim Chŏng-ho who, in 1861, drew up *Taedong yŏjido*, or A Detailed Map of Korea.

Interest in the study of Korea gave rise to the study of the Korean alphabet, han'gŭl. Sin Kyŏng-jun wrote *Hunmin chŏngŭm unhae*, or Explication of *Han'gŭl*, in 1750, and Yu Hŭi completed his work, *Ŏnmun chi*, or Treatise on *Han'gŭl*, in 1824. These works introduced several views concerning the origins, forms, and phonemes of han'gŭl.

Science and Technology

During this period Chosŏn scholars and scientists accepted Western civilization from China on the basis of their own scientific and technological achievements. This helped spark the development of science and technology in the country, which greatly strengthened the nation and helped spur industrial growth.

Interest in farm management and agricultural technology encouraged many publications on agriculture, such as *Nongga chipsŏng*, or Compilation for Farmers, written by Sin Sok in 1655, introducing advanced technology for rice cultivation. Appearing in 1676, Pak Se-dang's *Saekkyŏng*, or Farming Manual, focused on the cultivation of fruit trees, the raising of livestock, horticulture, irrigation, and weather. Hong Man-sŏn, in 1710, wrote *Sallim kyŏngje*, or Farm Management, a small encyclopedic work considered to be the first Korean text on natural science and technology, dealing with many topics concerning agriculture and the daily lives of farmers. *Haedong nongsŏ*, or Work on Farming East of the Sea (Korea), compiled by Sŏ Ho-su in the late eighteenth century, was the first work to systematize Korea's agricultural science by emphasizing indigenous Korean agriculture and accepting certain agricultural techniques from China.

On the subject of marine life, Chŏng Yak-chŏn wrote *Chasan ŏbo*, or Register of Hŭksan Fish, which appeared in 1815 and is seen as Korea's oldest ichthyological work. The author wrote this while exiled on Hŭksan-do, off the southwest Chŏlla coast. Based on his personal observations and collections, his work recorded the names, distribution, morphology, habits, and uses of 155 varieties of marine life in the waters surrounding the island. His younger brother,

Chŏng Yak-yong, researched numerous Chinese writings on smallpox to compile a medical work, *Magwa hoet'ong*, or Comprehensive Treatise on Smallpox, in 1778, which discussed the symptoms and treatment of this life-threatening disease. Suggesting therapeutic practices based on the physical features of mankind, Yi Che-ma, in the mid-nineteenth century, classified men into four different physical types and developed different medical treatments for each.

In 1603 Yi Kwang-jŏng, the Chosŏn envoy to Ming China, brought a map of the world to Chosŏn, and in 1631 Chŏng Tu-wŏn, another Chosŏn emissary to Ming, returned home with a musket, telescope, alarm clock, and books on astronomy and Western culture that had been written by the Jesuit missionary Matteo Ricci. Crown Prince Sohyŏn, who had been taken hostage by Qing China, became acquainted at the time with another Jesuit missionary, Adam Schall, and, in 1645, he returned to Chosŏn with a number of works on Western science, including astronomy and mathematics, and on Catholicism. After a Dutchmen named Jan Janse Weltevree was shipwrecked on Cheju-do in 1628, he took the Korean name of Pak Yŏn and lived out his life in Chosŏn; he was assigned to the Hullyŏn togam and engaged in casting cannons. In 1653 Hendrick Hamel and his company of 36 Dutch sailors were shipwrecked on Cheju-do. After many attempted escapes, Hamel and seven others managed to escape to Nagasaki, Japan, in 1666. Hamel's account of his years in captivity in Chosŏn gave the West its first direct knowledge of the "hermit kingdom," and the book was highly popular among Europeans.

With the growing interest in Western science and technology, the study of these subjects increased in Chosŏn. Kim Sang-bŏm, with the help of Kim Yuk, studied the newly introduced calendrical science, producing a revised Korean calendar in 1653. Sirhak thinkers Yi Ik and Hong Tae-yong advanced their views on terrestrial movement within a solar system. Chŏng Yak-yong proposed the establishment of the Iyonggam, or Office of Science and Technology, to study Western civilization. He believed that technological progress would greatly enhance human development, and to this end he devised and assembled many machines. Researching Jean Terreng's *Qiqi tushuo*, or Descriptions of Ingenious Devices, contained in the Chinese collection of some 5,000 volumes *Gujin tushu jicheng*, or Collection of Books Old and New, he devised pulley mechanisms that were used to build the fortifications at Hwasŏng (present-day Suwŏn, Kyŏnggi province), and he also designed a pontoon bridge on the Han River.

Scientific and technological development in this period mainly focused on agriculture and medicine, and progress in transportation and communication, manufacturing, and the military were largely ignored. By the early nineteenth century Western science and technology was fairly well accepted, but thereafter the influence of Western civilization stagnated because of the suppression of Catholicism that accompanied the introduction of Western culture and institutions.

New Approaches in Literature and Arts

Literature

In the seventeenth century a new literary trend emerged highlighting the importance of emotion rather than reason. Hŏ Kyun's *Hong Kil-tong chŏn*, written in han'gul in 1607, was the pioneer work in this new genre. This first vernacular novel, severely critical of the inequities of Chosŏn society, particularly its discrimination against illegitimate yangban offspring, was followed in 1689 by another litereay work written in han'gŭl by Kim Man-jung titled *Kuunmong*, or A Nine Cloud Dream.

This new seventeenth-century trend encouraged Sirhak scholars to create works in this new literary form. Pak Chi-wŏn's fictional writings, in which he satirized the parasitic life of the yangban literati, are good examples, including *Hŏ Saeng chŏn*, or Tale of Hŏ Saeng; *Hojil*, or A Tiger's Rebuke; *Yangban chŏn*, or Tale of a Yangban; and *Min ong chŏn*, or Tale of Elder Min. In *Yangban chŏn*, Pak characterized members of the yangban as people who do nothing but read while subsisting on government assistance.

In this period men of chungin status and even commoners produced a variety of literary works, including poetry anthologies. In 1712 Hong Se-t'ae compiled *Haedong yuju*, or Pearls from the Real Korean Poetry, and in 1737 Ko Si-ŏn supplemented this work with his *Sodae p'ungyo*, or Poems of a Peaceful People. The two anthologies contained poems written by the people of the chungin class. *P'ungyo*, or poems of the people, included poetry that represented the lower social classes. Two additional anthologies of p'ungyo, *P'ungyo soksŏn*, or Further Selection of Poems of the People, and *P'ungyo samsŏn*, or Third Selection of Poems of the People, appeared in 1797 and 1857 respectively. Kim Ch'ŏn-t'aek and Kim Su-jang, both petty clerks, compiled, respectively, *Ch'ŏnggu yŏngŏn*, or Enduring Poetry of Korea, in 1728, and *Haedong kayo*, or Songs of Korea, in 1763. These works were anthologies containing Korea's earlier *sijo*, Korean odes composed of three couplets, written by known and unknown authors of various social origins, including the yangban literati.

Since the eighteenth century, novels written in han'gŭl were widely popular among the general populace. Some of these were didactic novels, in which virtue was rewarded and evil punished, such as *Changhwa Hongnyŏn chŏn*, or The Tale of Changhwa and Hongnyŏn; *K'ongjwi P'atchwi chŏn*, or The Tale of K'ongjwi and P'atchwi; *Sim Ch'ŏng chŏn*, or The Tale of Sim Ch'ŏng; and *Hŭngbu chŏn*, or The Tale of Hŭngbu. Other such novels, including *Imjin nok*, or A Record of the War with Japan, and *Im Kyŏng-ŏp chŏn*, or The Tale of General Im Kyŏng-ŏp, dealt with the theme of military exploits. *Ongnumong*, or The Dream of the Jade Chamber, *Sukhyang chŏn*, or The Tale of Sukhyang, and *Ch'unhyang chŏn*, or The Tale of Ch'unhyang, portrayed the theme of love between a man and a woman. The authors of these novels have not been identified. The most widely read novel among them was *Ch'unhyang chŏn*, which involved the subjects of love and class discrimination. This popular satirical novel, which was dramatized as a quasi-opera, exposed the greed and snobbery of government officials. The rise of popular fiction and verse drew people's attention to government abuses and encouraged their participation in social reform.

Art

New trends also appeared in art. First, the so-called *chin'gyŏng sansu hwa*, or realistic landscape painting, became firmly rooted among Chosŏn artists. Rather than portraying idealized scenes modeled on Chinese landscape painting, artists now depicted Korea's own natural scenery as seen firsthand. The painter Chŏng Sŏn pioneered this realistic landscape style. As shown in his *Inwang chesaek to*, or Painting of a Storm Rising over Inwang-san, and *Kŭmgang chŏndo*, or Complete Drawing of Kŭmgang-san, he portrayed the scenic beauty of the Kŭmgang-san mountains and the outskirts of Seoul.

Following Chŏng Sŏn, Kim Hong-do opened new paths in landscape painting and in *p'ungsok*, or genre, painting which portrayed ordinary scenes from everyday life. Kim Hong-do was also from the realism school of painting, but he concentrated on depicting scenery in a natural way, in contrast to Chŏng Sŏn's personal interpretation of the landscape. Kim Hong-do's *Kŭmgang-san ongch'ŏn*, or Ongch'ŏn of Kŭmgang-san, is a typical example of his work. Chŏng Sŏn also produced a version of this painting, and the contrast between the two is readily seen. Kim Hong-do is also rated among the most famous masters of genre painting. As demonstrated by his masterful *P'ungsok hwach'ŏp*, or Genre Album, his principal themes included the typical activities in the working lives of commoners, such as plowing, harvesting, and laboring in a smithy, as well as events including marriage and *ssirŭm*, or Korean wrestling. His most well-known works include *Muak*, or Dancer with Musicians, and *Ssirŭm*. Another painter, Sin Yun-bok, portrayed mainly the mores of the townspeople, with an emphasis on women's activities. The best examples of his work include *Miin to*, or Picture of a Beauty, and *P'ungsok hwach'ŏp*, or Genre Album. The popularity of genre painting represented the resistance of artists to yangban society.

THE DYNASTY IN DISTURBANCE

Government by Royal In-Law Clans

During the reigns of Kings Yŏngjo and Chŏngjo, monarchical authority was strengthened and the political scene generally remained stable. Although Hong Kuk-yŏng won the confidence of Chŏngjo in 1776 by preserving his throne against the Pyŏkp'a party of the Old Doctrine faction, wielding power for some time after, he was driven out in 1779. The era of so-called *sedo chŏngch'i*, or royal in-law government, began after King Sunjo (1800–1834), a ten-year-old boy, ascended the throne in 1800, at which time the royal in-law family, the Andong Kim clan, took complete control of power. Now Sunjo's father-in-law, Kim Cho-sun, from the Sip'a faction that had sided with Chŏngjo, held the reins of government in 1805, and many of his close kinsmen occupied key positions in the court. When Hŏnjong (1834–1849), a boy of just seven years, ascended the throne in 1834, this time the P'ungyang Cho clan held real power in the government. Since the mother of Hŏnjong was the daughter of Cho Man-yŏng, later the queen dowager Cho, his clan seized power in the reign of the king. Power again returned to the Andong Kim family after Ch'ŏlchong (1849–1863), an 18-year-old boy, ascended the throne in 1849. As the king's consort was the daughter of Andong Kim Mun-gŭn, his clansmen wielded predominant power.

During the period of royal in-law government, the power of the throne was purely nominal, as true power was entirely in the hands of the influential Andong Kim clan. The most influential organ of the day was the Pibyŏnsa, an inner circle comprised of a small number of officials who monopolized power. Any challenge to the powerful family was not tolerated; even those in the royal household of Yi who criticized the abuses of the Andong Kim clan were exiled or charged with treason and executed.

Disorder in the "Three Administrations"

The monopolization of power by the sedo regime left the nation in complete administrative upheaval, and the consequent suffering fell on the shoulders of the general populace, especially the impoverished peasantry. The Andong Kim oligarchs exploited the population by trafficking in the prized government positions, particularly the posts of provincial governor and county magistrate. Meanwhile, conditions in the countryside rapidly deteriorated, as the central government paid scarce attention to the people's welfare. Those who obtained official appointments with bribes attempted to redeem their bribe money by levying excessive taxes on the peasantry, leading to the overtaxation of the peasants and the resultant decline in their living standards.

Confounding matters, a succession of natural disasters brought a rage of epidemics and famines to the state, rapidly depleting the population. But, though continuing to collect taxes, the inefficient and corrupt government provided its people with no protection against bad harvests. In these circumstances, the primary sources of government revenue, the "three administrations"—namely, *chŏnjŏng*, or administration of the land tax; *kunjŏng*, or administration of the military cloth tax; and *hwan'gok*, or administration of the state granary loan— fell into total disarray.

According to law, the total land taxes to be paid per cultivated kyŏl was less than 20 tu, or 107 kilograms, of rice, or less than one-tenth of the harvest. In practice, however, total tax collections rose to as much as 100 tu, or 535 kilograms, per kyŏl, an amount equal to roughly half the harvest. The military cloth tax levied on each able-bodied male had been the payment of one bolt of cotton cloth, or the equivalent of six tu, or 32 kilograms, of rice. The peasants were under ever greater duress, as they were subject to various illegal exactions, for example, being charged a military cloth tax on behalf of deceased family members and nursing babies. The military cloth tax, in fact, caused greater pain to the peasantry than the land tax. Rich farmers evaded payment by forging or purchasing yangban titles. Under the national granary system, loans of grain had been made to poor peasants in the lean spring season to be repaid at harvest time at an interest of 10 percent. But now this same system that had been designed to offer a helping hand to the impoverished peasants was transformed into an instrument of exploitation. Officials in charge of the granary loan system forced peasants to borrow more than they needed, fabricated false reports on their transactions for their own profits, and even multiplied the quantities of rice borrowed severalfold by mixing husks in with the grain.Corrupt local officials and hyangni also became rich by pocketing large portions of the taxes collected for the central government, further diminishing government revenues. Such corruption was a primary cause of the significant peasant rebellions that erupted throughout the country.

Peasant Resistance

In this period of rule by royal in-laws, peasant life was grinding poverty itself. In addition to oppressive government measures, draughts and floods, alternately striking the country, caused a succession of bad harvests, which in turn generated a grim cycle of famines. Many starving peasants were forced to become landless wanderers or try to survive in the upland areas as *hwajŏnmin,* or slash-and-burn farmers. Many others migrated across the border into the Jiandao region of Manchuria or the later Russian Maritime Province.

In the mid-eighteenth century discontented and anguished peasants began to form armed brigades. *Hwajŏk,* or fire brigands, who usually set fires to commit burglaries, were often on horseback and armed with muskets. *Sujŏk,* or water brigands, pillaged along the rivers and seashores. Some hwajŏk groups became better organized and developed into more powerful forces such as the Sŏgangdan, or West River Band, and the P'yesagundan, or Northwest Frontier Corps, mainly robbing government storehouses. For now, however, a massive uprising was deferred, and the peasant resistance was limited to brigandage.

Beginning in the early nineteenth century, the angry peasantry became increasingly organized. At first, streamers and wall posters with inflammatory rhetoric appeared throughout the country. In 1804 the *Kwansŏ pigi,* or Secret Account of Conditions in P'yŏngan Province, was affixed to the four main gates of Seoul. Similar incidents also took place at Anak, Hwanghae province, and at Ch'ŏngju, Ch'ungch'ŏng province. At the same time the peasants' opposition to government taxation grew increasingly intense.

The sporadic dissatisfaction among the general populace exploded into massive uprisings nationwide. The first major rebellion broke out in the northwestern region of P'yŏngan province, led by a fallen yangban named Hong Kyŏngnae. Frustrated by continually failing to pass the civil service examinations, he conspired with other malcontents in his area, including U Kun-ch'ik, Kim Sayong, Yi Hŭi-jo, and Kim Ch'ang-si. In January 1812, upon distributing a manifesto throughout the northwestern region complaining of government corruption and centuries-old discrimination against the northerners, Hong organized a rebellion with an army of 1,000 men. Because the people of P'yŏngan province were already in a volatile mood, the rebels made notable military achievements, immediately occupying nine towns north of the Ch'ŏngch'ŏn River. Soon, however, government forces defeated them at Songnim-ni in Pakch'ŏn county, and the routed rebels were only able to hold out at the Chŏngju fortress for four months. In May 1812 Hong was killed in the final battle for the town, and the largest rebellion in the Chosŏn dynasty finally came to an end.

Peasant uprisings again broke out throughout the country in the mid-nineteenth century, specifically in March 1862, when a serious peasant revolt erupted in the town of Chinju, Kyŏngsang province. Ouraged at the rapacious exploitations of Paek Nak-sin, a provincial army commander, the populace took up arms, all wearing white caps as a mark of their unity. Under the leadership of Yu Kye-ch'un, a former yangban fallen to peasant status, the rebels killed local government officials and burned down government buildings. The uprising subsided as the peasants voluntarily dispersed, but it gave rise to a series of similar riots. In April 1862, for instance, a peasant rebellion broke out at Iksan, Chŏlla province, and other popular disturbances rocked 20 counties in Kyŏngsang province, 37 counties in Chŏlla province, and 12 counties in Ch'ungch'ŏng province. The central government dispatched troops to crush the rebellions, but at the same time it punished corrupt local officials and took steps to lighten the peasants' burden. These positive efforts resulted in gradually ending the popular disturbances.

CULTURE IN THE EARLY NINETEENTH CENTURY

Scholarship

Over the course of the nineteenth century, the addition of a wide range of new disciplines further enriched the existing Chosŏn scholarship. Korean scholars, as in previous periods, worked to uncover solutions to the day's pressing problems and to advance reform proposals. In their efforts to "modernize" the country, a new system of thought known as *kaehwa sasang,* or enlightenment thought, emerged.

The most well-known scholar at the start of the century was Chŏng Yak-yong. The author of more than 500 works, he is best known for synthesizing Sirhak scholarship with Pukhak scholarship. In 1810 Yi Kyu-gyŏng compiled *Oju yŏnmun changjŏn san'go,* or Random Expatiations of Oju, a 60-volume encyclopedic work that expounded upon 1,417 disciplines, including history, astronomy, geography, economics, music, medicine, and agriculture. His penname,"Oju," meaning "Five Continents," reflects his vast outlook on scholarship. The work of another scholar, Sŏ Yu-gu—compiled in 1835, comprising 113 volumes, and titled *Imwŏn simnyuk chi*, also known as *Imwŏn kyŏngje chi*, or Sixteen Treatises Written in Retirement—dealt with agriculture and farm life. In these volumes, the author urged the government to raise agricultural productivity and improve the living standard of the peasantry through managerial reform and technological innovation. The scholar Ch'oe Han-gi advanced various reform programs aimed at promoting commerce and industry, suggesting, overall, that the government abandon its isolationist policy and open its doors to the outside world. His book, *Chigu chŏnyo*, or Descriptions of the Nations of the World, written in 1857, was the first Korean work on world geography.

Chŏng Yak-yong's remarkable historiographical work, *Abang kangyŏk ko*, or A Study of Korean Territory, appearing in 1810, uncovered previously unknown facts about ancient Korean kingdoms. For example, he discovered that present-day Seoul had been chosen as the first capital of the Paekche kingdom and that the center of the Parhae kingdom had been located east of Paektu-san. These and other ideas he revealed have since become widely accepted as established truths. In the realm of cartography, Kim Chŏng-ho, who is regarded as the greatest geographer in pre-modern Asia, completed his *Taedong yŏjido* in 1861, based on his lifetime work observing the geographical features of the Korean peninsula. Lastly, in 1852, Kim Chŏng-hŭi, an epigraphist who adopted the approach of the Qing empirical school, wrote *Kŭmsŏk kwaan nok*, or Observations on Examining Two Stone Inscriptions, a study of two stelae erected during the royal tour of Silla king Chinhŭng at Pukhan-san and Hwangch'o-ryŏng.

The Spread of Catholicism

Catholicism was first introduced to Chosŏn between the late sixteenth and early seventeenth centuries as part of the transmission of Western culture rather than as a religion, and was therefore known as *Sŏhak*, or Western Learning. It was the Sirhak scholars who were first interested in studying Catholicism as a new religion. In his work, *Chibong yusŏl*, Yi Su-gwang referred to *Ch'ŏnju sirŭi*, or True Principles of Catholicism, written by Matteo Ricci, a Jesuit missionary in Ming China, clarifying the difference between Catholicism and Buddhism. Later, based purely on intellectual curiosity, Yi Ik and his disciples discussed the Western religion in their writings but showed no disposition toward believing its doctrine.

Catholicism penetrated Chosŏn on a significant scale in the second half of the eighteenth century. Catholic doctrines appealed particularly to scholars from the frustrated Namin faction, who had long been excluded from political power. In 1784 Yi Sŭng-hun, who had accompanied his father on a diplomatic mission, returned to Chosŏn after being baptized in Beijing by a Western priest. Other Namin figures who converted to Catholicism included Yi Pyŏk, Yi Ka-hwan, the brothers Chŏng Yak-chŏn, Chŏng Yak-chong, and Chŏng Yak-yong, and the brothers Kwŏn Ch'ŏl-sin and Kwŏn Il-sin. Members of the chungin class such as Kim Pŏm-u also became members of the Catholic Church.

Unprecedented in world history, Catholicism was widely accepted by the Koreans without any proselytizing efforts on the part of Western missionaries. The Koreans' traditional worship of heaven facilitated the diffusion of the religion among the general populace. Furthermore, as in many other parts of the world, Catholicism served as a solace for physically distressed people. Sirhak scholars attempted to find a solution to the dismal conditions of Chosŏn society by embracing the Western religion.

As the number of Catholic converts grew, othodox Confucianists naturally looked upon Catholicism as subversive and especially as questioning the Confucian system of loyalties and ancestor worship on which the state rested. The Catholics' denial of ancestral ritual was considered especially immoral and lacking in filial piety. Some Neo-Confucian thinkers criticized the religion theoretically and took the anti-Catholic position, which was typified by An Chŏng-bok's Ch'ŏnhak mundap, or Questions and Answers on Heavenly Learning, which appeared in 1795. In 1785 King Chŏngjo designated Catholicism a heresy, and the next year he banned the importation of books of any kind from Beijing. In 1791 Yun Chi-ch'ung, a yangban residing in Chinsan, Chŏlla province, was put to death for failing to prepare an ancestral tablet for his deceased mother, an essential practice in Confucian memorial ritual. But because King Chŏngjo was friendly with the Namin faction and held a relatively benign view of Catholicism, the religion was tacitly tolerated and no further severe persecutions occurred. Meanwhile, the Chinese Catholic priest Zhou Wenmo secretly entered Chosŏn in 1795 and engaged in proselytizing activity.

With Sunjo's ascension to the throne in 1800, the Pyŏkp'a clique of the Noron faction gained power and the cruel suppression of Catholics, known as the Sinyu saok, immediately followed. More than 300 Korean Catholics, including Yi Sŭng-hun, Yi Ka-hwan, Chŏng Yak-chong, and Kwŏn Ch'ŏl-sin, as well as the Chinese priest Zhou Wenmo, were executed, and Chŏng Yak-chŏn and Chŏng Yak-yong were exiled. This persecution of Catholics was accompanied by a ban on importing Western science and technology. A political motive for the persecution was that the ruling Pyŏkp'a clique sought to stage a purge of its rival Sip'a clique, mainly consisting of the Namin faction. A few months later a Korean Catholic convert, Hwang Sa-yŏng, secretly attempted to send the "silk letter" to the Catholic bishop in Beijing, a Frenchman, but the letter was discovered in advance and Hwang was executed. In this letter, written on silk, Hwang had asked the French to dispatch armed troops to force the Chosŏn government to grant religious freedom. But this traitorous action only intensified the government's anti-Catholic policy.

As demonstrated by the Sinyu saok, the government's Catholic policy was closely related to factional strife. Whereas the Pyŏkp'a faction were sternly anti-Catholic, the Sip'a group maintained a moderate stance. Thus once Kim Cho-sun of the Andong Kim clan, who was a member of the Sip'a faction, took power in 1805, Catholicism was no longer suppressed. Thereafter the Catholic faith was widely accepted in Chosŏn; in fact, the Vatican appointed a vicar apostolic for Chosŏn in 1831, and French priests entered the country—Maubant in 1836 and Chastan and Imbert the following year. But when the P'ungyang Cho family, belonging to the Pyŏkp'a faction, held power during the reign of King Hŏnjong, Catholic converts were persecuted once again. During the *Kihae soak,* or Catholic Persecution of 1839, three French Catholic priests and scores of Korean converts were executed. A few years later, in 1845, the first Korean Catholic priest, Kim Tae-gŏn, who had been trained at a seminary in Macau, secretly returned to Chosŏn to proselytize in Ch'ungch'ŏng province. The next year, however, he was apprehended and sacrificed his life to become a martyr. When Ch'ŏlchong ascended the throne in 1849, the Andong Kim family again seized power and once more the government relaxed its anti-Cathloic policy.

The total number of Korean converts, amounting to some 10,000 in the mid-nineteenth century, reached 30,000 by the end of the century. This increase was the result of people of the lower social classes entering the Church. Although at first Catholicism attracted yangban adherents, especially members of the Namin faction, with the turn of the nineteenth century most converts, along with those, were from the lower social classes and were the uneducated rather than the educated, the poor rather than the better off, and women rather than men. Most of the Korean converts were attracted by the alien religion's creed of equality, and so Catholicism became firmly established among urban dwellers in the capital and neighboring areas. While Catholicism failed to attract villagers and peasant farmers, despite its strong appeal to commoners, a new semi-religious doctrine called the *Tonghak,* or Eastern Learning, movement, which had some elements of Catholicism, won wide adherents among the peasantry.

The Rise of the Tonghak Doctrine

Founded by an idealistic, frustrated yangban man, Ch'oe Che-u, at Kyŏngju in 1860, Tonghak was a reaction against the introduction of alien Catholic doctrines. To devise a new faith opposing Sŏhak, Ch'oe not only adopted the best precepts of Confucianism, Buddhism, and Taoism but accepted some elements of Catholicism, such as congregational worship. He also embraced features of Korea's native shamanistic practices, especially the belief in amulets and incantations. The Tonghak doctrine was presented in such writings as *Tonggyŏng taejŏn,* or The Great Scripture of Tonghak, and *Yongdam yusa,* or Hymns from Dragon Pool, both written by Ch'oe Che-u. The former, written in Chinese, was designed to be read by intellectuals, whereas the latter, written in han'gŭl, could easily be understood by peasants. Ch'oe Che-u believed that all human beings were equal, that humankind and God were one and the same, and that serving humankind constituted serving God. In short, he preached humanitarianism and equality for all human beings. A revolutionary idea in a traditional Confucian society, Tonghak was a product of the frustration of the era and gained growing support from the oppressed peasantry.

Tonghak increasingly evolved from a religious movement into a social reform movement, somewhat similar to the Taiping movement in China at roughly the same time. It steered clear of such complicated questions as the nature of humankind and life after death but sought to regenerate existing society by purging it of misrule and corruption. Its leaders not only demanded reform from the corruption-ridden government but also sought to protect Chosŏn against the influx of Western and Catholic influence. As the Tonghak faith won acceptance among the general populace, the panicked government arrested Ch'oe Che-u on charges of deluding the world and deceiving the people, and executed him in 1864. Because adherence to Tonghak was criminalized, its practice was forced underground. Before long, however, the Tonghak faith recovered under Ch'oe Che-u's successor, Ch'oe Si-hyŏng, and its appeal spread rapidly among the peasantry in response to economic and political oppression.

Literature and the Arts in the Mid-Nineteenth Century

Fallen yangban, illegitimate yangban descendants, and chungin produced literary works on a large scale in the mid-nineteenth century. In 1857 Yu Chae-gŏn compiled *P'ungyo samsŏn,* comprised of writings by some 300 authors, including members of non-yangban social classes. Literary men, mainly chungin in Seoul, formed several *sisa,* or fellowships of poets, and their writings in Chinese were almost on a par with those of reputed yangban authors. Well-known chungin writers included Chang Chi-wan, Chŏng Chi-yun (also known as Chŏng Su-dong), Cho Hŭi-ryong, Yi Kyŏng-min, Pak Yun-muk, and Cho Su-sam.

In this period noteworthy literary achievements appeared in different forms including *p'ansori,* or one-man opera, *chapka,* or folk song, and *kamyŏn'gŭk* (also known as *t'alch'um*), or masked dance. Combining music and literary expression in ballad form, the p'ansori genre comprised popular tales sung to outdoor audiences by a professional performer accompanied by a drummer. P'ansori performers used monologues and certain tunes adapted from earlier Korean vernacular novels such as *Ch'unhyang chŏn, Sim Ch'ŏng chŏn,* and *Hŭngbu chŏn.* The man who contributed most to developing the p'ansori texts was Sin Chae-hyo, who is said to have created a repertoire of 12 tales. Chapka songs, full of jest and satire, were the favorites of commoners in towns. T'alch'um also flourished in this period. Although usually translated as "masked dance," this genre, which interspersed song and dance with satirical narrative, was not just a "masked dance" but was designed to reveal the "absurdities" (the literal meaning of *t'al*) of Chosŏn society, especially the striking distinctions between the yangban, who were often mocked in the performance, and other social classes. Storybooks written in han'gŭl were widely read, particularly by women. Songs widely sung by the general populace included *Hanyangga,* or Song of Seoul, which described the beauty and prosperity of the capital, and *Yŏnhaengga,* or Song of a Journey to Beijing, which depicted a diplomatic mission to China.

Paintings reflecting the development of Seoul and the aristocratic tastes of the yangban in the capital had a showy and refined look. Large paintings depicting palaces and prosperity in Seoul appeared, represented, for example, by *Tongguŏl to,* or Painting of Eastern Palaces, a work portraying the entire view of the Ch'angdŏk-kung and Ch'anggyŏng-gung palaces and painted collectively by more than 100 artists in the 1820s.

The most renowned Korean painter of the nineteenth century was Chang Sŭng-ŏp, who is seen as one of the three great masters of the Chosŏn period, along with An Kyŏn and Kim Hong-do. The great scholar of epigraphy Kim Chŏng-hŭi was also a foremost master of calligraphy, who studied the work of famed calligraphers of the past and developed a new mode of brushwork called the Ch'usa style, after his penname.

POLICIES OF THE TAEWŎN'GUN

Reforms of the Taewŏn'gun

In January 1864 Kojong (1864–1907) ascended the throne at the age of 12, and the new king's father, Yi Ha-ŭng, became the *taewŏn'gun*, or lord of the great court, and ruled Chosŏn with an iron fist in his son's name. In 1873, however, he was forced to retire by the king's consort, Queen Min, and her clan. Originally the term *taewŏn'gun* referred to any person who was not actually the king but whose son took the throne. Four men were called the taewŏn'gun in the Chosŏn dynasty, but three of them died even before their sons took the throne, and thus the fouth man, Hŭngsŏn Taewŏn'gun (Yi Ha-ŭng), became the only living taewŏn'gun. Thereafter the use of the term "taewŏn'gun" referred only to this man. The Taewŏn'gun and his primary political rival, Queen Min, held sway over the destinies of Chosŏn for almost the rest of the century.

When the stern and arbitrary Taewŏn'gun secured absolute power of the government as the king's regent shortly after his son took the throne, he set about reshaping the country according to his own governing principles. To that end, he expelled members of the Andong Kim family from their positions in the national bureaucracy, targeted bureaucratic corruption, instituted administrative reforms, and sought to enhance the dignity of the royal house.

He replaced high-level officials from a few powerful lineages or royal in-law families, particularly the Andong Kim clan, as noted, with an equal number of members from the four main factions. He was determined to close down the sŏwŏn academies, the stronghold of the yangban literati; so long as the sŏwŏn academies were permitted to remain intact, the Taewŏn'gun believed it would be impossible to establish a strong monarchy. By this time the sŏwŏn possessed vast farmlands, a number of slaves, and the special privilege of exemption from taxation and corvee labor. Thus they ravaged the economic foundation of the state and remained a formidable force unrestrained by the government. In 1865 he demolished the *Mandongmyo,* or Ten-Thousand East Shrine, the spiritual mainstay of the Noron faction; this edifice was erected to honor the last two emperors of Ming China, who helped Chosŏn during the war with Japan, and was built according to the wishes of Song Si-yŏl. In 1868 the Taewŏn'gun levied taxes on the sŏwŏn, and in 1871 he shut down more than 1,000 academies, leaving only 47 scattered throughout the country. His suppression of the sŏwŏn incurred the wrath of the Confucian literati and ultimately was one of the main factors that later caused his downfall, when Queen Min allied with the angry Confucian scholars to oust him from power.

Before the Taewŏn'gun's forced withdrawal, however, he sought to increase national revenues and equalize tax burdens among the entire populace, including the yangban. Thus he conducted a land survey to locate the "hidden fields" that had been omitted from government registers and made them taxable farmlands. He also converted the military cloth tax levied only on commoners into a household tax imposed on the yangban as well. Further, he reorganized the existing grain loan system, which had been subject to usury, into locally administered village granaries, thus putting an end to the plundering of corrupt local officials and functionaries.

To weaken the power of high officials, the Taewŏn'gun, in 1865, abolished the Pibyŏnsa, the power center of royal in-law government. To enhance the monarch's image, he ordered a lavish reconstruction of the Kyŏngbok-kung palace, which was then a mere ruin since its destruction during the Japanese invasion of the 1590s. Giving no thought to the government's precarious finances, he set about reconstructing the palace, completed the project in 1867, and moved Kojong into the new palace the following year. To meet the huge costs incurred, he levied a special land surtax of 1 tu, or about 5 kilograms, of rice per kyŏl on all landowners and charged a "gate tax" on goods transported in and out of the four gates of Seoul. The Taewŏn'gun also forcibly extracted contributions for the construction work in the name of wŏnnapchŏn, or the voluntary offering of coins. Moreover, he minted a special currency, the tangbaekchŏn, or arbitrary hundred coin, with a value far above its intrinsic worth, causing considerable inflation. He aroused bitter resentment among the laborers who were forced to work on the project.

Despite some economic confusion, overall the internal reforms carried out by the strong-willed Taewŏn'gun contributed considerably to terminating the oligarchical royal in-law government, establishing a strong monarchy, increasing state revenues, and enhancing defense capabilities. His reform measures garnered popular support and built national strength to the extent that he

was able to circumvent the difficult situation brought on by the French and
U.S. invasions.

Clashes with France and the United States

Isolationist Policy

Long before the nineteenth century Chosŏn had maintained diplomatic relations only with its suzerain, China, and with neighboring Japan. Foreign trade
was mainly limited to China, at designated locations along the Korean-Manchurian border. By the mid-nineteenth century Westerners had come to refer
to Chosŏn as the "Hermit Kingdom," suggesting that Chosŏn's diplomacy was
characterized not just as isolationism but, more precisely, as "exclusionism."

The Taewŏn'gun was determined to continue Chosŏn's traditional isolationist policy and to purge the kingdom of any foreign ideas that had filtered into
the nation. The disastrous events occurring in China, including the Opium
War (1840–1842), reinforced his determination to separate his country from
the rest of the world, a path, though perhaps understandable, that ran counter
to the tide of history.

Even since the mid-nineteenth century Western vessels made frequent
appearances in Korean waters, surveying sea routes and seeking trade. The
Chosŏn government, extremely wary, referred to these vessels as "strange-looking ships." In June 1832 a ship from the British India Company, *Lord Amherst*,
appeared off the coast of Hwanghae province seeking trade. In June 1845 an
English warship, *Samarang*, surveyed the coast of Cheju-do and Chŏlla province, and the next month the Chosŏn government filed a protest with British
authorities in Guangzhou through the Chinese government. In June 1846 three
French warships dropped anchor off the coast of Ch'ungch'ŏng province and
conveyed a letter protesting Chosŏn's persecution of Catholicism. In April 1854
two armed Russian vessels sailed along the coast of Hamgyŏng province, in
the East Sea, causing some deaths and injuries among the Koreans they encountered. This prompted the Chosŏn government to issue a ban forbidding
the people of Hamgyŏng from having any contact with foreign vessels. Ships
manned by the German adventurer Ernst J. Oppert appeared off the coast
of Ch'ungch'ŏng province twice, in January and July of 1866, seeking trade.

In August 1866 an American merchant ship, *General Sherman*, appeared
off the coast of P'yŏngan province, ascended the Taedong River to the provincial capital of Pyongyang, and asked permission to trade. Local officials refused
to enter into trade talks and demanded the ship's departure. A Korean official

was then taken hostage aboard the ship, and its crew members fired guns at enraged Korean officials and civilians on the shore. The crew then came ashore, plundered the town, and killed seven Koreans. The governor of P'yŏngan province, Pak Kyu-su, ordered his forces to destroy the ship, and in the event the *General Sherman* ran aground on a sandbar and Korean forces burned the ship and killed the ship's entire crew of 23. Korean officials never admitted that an American ship had been destroyed in Pyongyang; they described it as a French vessel or simply as a "strange-looking ship."

The Western Disturbance of 1866

While this troubling affair was developing in northern Chosŏn, a much greater crisis was coming to a head. At the time, as noted earlier, Koreans increasingly turned to the religious teachings of Catholicism. After experiencing several major persecutions, Catholicism was reinvigorated by the proselytizing activities of 12 French priests, including Siméon-François Berneux and Felix-Claire Ridel, who had secretly entered the country. As the number of domestic converts grew into the tens of thousands, the Taewŏn'gun concluded that Catholicism posed a direct challenge to the state's Neo-Confucian ideology.

Although at first relatively tolerant of Catholicism partly because his wife had converted, the Taewŏn'gun came to believe that French priests and Catholicism were spearheading Western aggression against his country. He took the advice of a Korean Catholic, Nam Chong-sam, and attempted to block Russia's southward advance into Chosŏn territory, assisted by France, a major Catholic state. Negotiations did not go well, and high officials in the court unanimously urged him to expel Catholicism from Chosŏn. He had to heed their advice if he was to maintain his power, and so he launched a massive persecution of the Western religion. In February 1866, in what became known as the *Pyŏngin saok,* or Catholic Persecution of 1866, nine French priests were killed along with large numbers of Korean believers, including Nam Chong-sam. Between 1866 and 1872 approximately 8,000 Korean Catholics were executed and thousands more were imprisoned.

When word of the French deaths leaked out (Father Ridel had escaped to China), French authorities in China concluded that punitive action had to be taken. In September 1866, to make a show of force, Admiral Pierre G. Roze, commander of the French Asiatic Squadron, came to Chosŏn with three ships, steamed up the Han River, and reconnoitered within sight of Seoul. The next month he again appeared in Korean waters, this time with a flotilla of seven warships and about 1,000 troops. The French demanded that the Chosŏn government both severely punish the murderers of the French priests and enter into a trade treaty with France. These demands were ignored by the Taewŏn'gun. A French detachment then landed on Kanghwa-do, seizing the administrative center of the island, pillaging it, and carrying away weapons, gold and silver equivalent to some 200,000 contemporary francs, and more than 300 precious books (now housed in a museum in Paris). Another French force attempting to blockade the mouth of the Han River, the gateway to the capital, was beaten back by Chosŏn troops led by Han Sŏng-gŭn at the Munsu-san fortress, on the mainland just opposite Kanghwa-do. Also, a French landing party sent to attack the Chŏngjok-san fortress on the island was repulsed by Chosŏn units under the command of Yang Hŏn-su. Following these defeats, the French squadron withdrew without accomplishing its mission. These engagements with the French, called the *Pyŏngin yangyo,* or Western Disturbance of 1866, resulted in a "Chosŏn victory" and reinforced not only the Koreans' fear of outsiders but Taewŏn'gun's determination to maintain a foreign policy of seclusion.

The French invasion was followed by another incident that would reinforce the Koreans' negative view of Westerners. In May 1868 Ernst J. Oppert, the German adventurer cited earlier, was determined to forcibly open Chosŏn's doors to foreign trade. To this end he concocted a scheme to break into the tomb of Prince Namyŏn, the Taewŏn'gun's father, at Tŏksan county, Ch'ungch'ŏng province. In this expedition his intention was to steal the body and hold it for ransom; he would return the body to Chosŏn only if it permitted the West to trade with the kingdom. This scheme ended in failure as a result of Chosŏn's quick reaction. When word of his "invasion" became known, the Chosŏn government swiftly dispatched troops to the area. Opert hastily retreated to his ship, and instead of opening Chosŏn's doors to Western trade, Oppert's actions only reinforced the Koreans' suspicion about the West and Western traders. Given the importance of filial piety in Chosŏn society, a more insulting and barbaric action than that perpetrated by Opert could not be found.

The Western Disturbance of 1871

In 1871, five years after the *General Sherman* debacle, the U.S. government dispatched a naval expedition to Chosŏn using the incident as a pretext to force Chosŏn to enter into a commercial treaty opening the kingdom to U.S. trade and providing protection for shipwrecked American sailors. Rear Admiral John Rodgers, commander of the U.S. Asiatic Squadron, was selected to lead the expedition. Frederick F. Low, the U.S. minister to China, would take charge of the diplomatic negotiations. Using the 1853–1854 Perry expedition to Japan as a model, the Americans would make a show of force with five naval ships and more than 1,200 troops.

The U.S. fleet arrived off the west coast of Chosŏn in May 1871 and contacted local officials to inform them of the purpose of the expedition. The Chosŏn officials answered that they could not act upon the U.S. request but would receive government approval for any diplomatic talks. While waiting for an official response from the capital, the Americans decided to conduct preliminary surveys along the Korean coastlines, dispatching a small crew to a narrow channel leading into the mouth of the Han River, where the French had invaded Chosŏn five years earlier. Fearful that this foreign force might pose a grave threat to national security, Chosŏn's coastal artillery fired upon the Americans. Although no Americans were killed or seriously injured, leaders of the U.S. expedition interpreted this incident as an unprovoked attack upon the U.S. flag and demanded an apology. When their demand was ignored, the Americans attacked the Korean fortifications and then landed 759 marines and sailors along the southeastern coast of Kanghwa-do. They quickly advanced upon the Chosŏn forts in the vicinity, and although the Chosŏn defenders fought courageously, the Ch'oji-jin and Kwangsŏng-jin forts fell and more than 240 Chosŏn soldiers, including their commander, Ŏ Chae-yŏn, were killed. The U.S. forces suffered 13 battle casualties, including 3 dead.[2] Because of the Koreans' determined defensive action, the Americans withdrew in June, with both sides claiming victory. This incident, called the *Sinmi yangyo*, or Western Disturbance of 1871, provided another impetus for the Taewŏn'gun to continue his closed-door policy in foreign relations.

Exultant at "victories" over the invading French and American forces, the Taewŏn'gun and his government were filled with even greater anti-foreign spirit than ever before and viewed Westerners as barbarians. The Taewŏn'gun had stone tablets erected on the Chongno main thoroughfare in Seoul and at points throughout the country declaring: "The barbarians from beyond the seas seek to invade our land. If we do not fight them, we must appease them. But to appease them is to betray the nation."

As in previous Korean kingdoms, in the Chosŏn dynasty the king's in-laws enjoyed great power. The Taewŏn'gun, knowing that his sons-in-law might threaten his authority, attempted to block the possible threat by selecting as a new queen an orphaned girl from among his wife's relatives, the Yŏhŭng

Min clan, who lacked powerful political connections. With this woman as his daughter-in-law he felt safe, but he failed to consider the cleverness and intelligence of the woman herself. After Queen Min took her place in the palace, she recruited all her relatives and appointed them to influential positions in the name of the king. She allied with the Taewŏn'gun's political enemies, including the Confucian scholars whom he had so antagonized, and by late 1873 she mobilized enough influence to oust the Taewŏn'gun from power. When the Confucian scholar Ch'oe Ik-hyŏn submitted a memorial urging Kojong to rule in his own right in October 1873, Queen Min seized the opportunity to force her father-in-law's retirement as regent. The Taewŏn'gun's departure led to Chosŏn's abandonment of its rigid isolationist policy.

THE OPEN-DOOR POLICY AND THE REFORM MOVEMENT

The Opening of Chosŏn

When Kojong began to rule in his own right in December 1873, he initiated a more moderate policy toward the outside world. Soon after his father had been forced into retirement, he surrounded himself with a number of young advisers, many of whom concluded that the Taewŏn'gun's foreign policy of seclusion could not be maintained in an age of growing foreign imperialism. The advisers were aware of what had happened to China in the 1840s and 1850s, and also of Japan's more positive response to the Western powers. Thus Kojong sought to open his country to foreign trade based on the idea of *kaehwa*. Originally "kaehwa" was a Confucian term, an abbreviation meaning achievement of a project by inquiring into life's basic principles and establishing public morals through education. Thus, it did not refer to learning about Western culture or achieving modernization but instead referred to carrying out favorable reforms, which at the time inevitably focused on the advanced science and technology of the West and Japan.

Already in the eighteenth century the Pukhak scholars had suggested promoting foreign trade, and their ideas were followed up by nineteenth-century kaehwa thinkers such as Yi Kyu-gyŏng, Ch'oe Han-gi, Pak Kyu-su, O Kyŏng-sŏk, and Yu Tae-ch'i. When the British ship *Lord Amherst* sought trade with Chosŏn in 1832, Yi Kyu-gyŏng urged that Chosŏn comply with the British request. After reading *Haiguo tuzhi*, or Illustrated Treatise on the Sea Kingdoms, written by the Chinese scholar Wei Yuan in 1844, Ch'oe Han-gi authored *Chigu chŏnyo* in 1857 and called for Chosŏn to open itself to foreign trade. Pak Kyu-su, who had commanded his men to destroy the *General Sherman* in 1866, was one of the rare enlightened high-ranking officials in the Chosŏn government; he had visited China several times and had gained considerable information about the outside world. He maintained that Chosŏn should be open to Western ideas and approaches, and stressed, in particular, that his country should attempt to establish trade relations with the United States. A translator-interpreter of the Chinese language, O Kyŏng-sŏk, acquired books such as Wei Yuan's *Haiguo tuzhi* and another Chinese scholar Xu Jiyu's *Yinghuan zhilue*, or Record of the Ocean Circuit, written in 1848, and he encouraged his countrymen to read them. O Kyŏng-sŏk's close friend Yu Tae-ch'i, a medical practitioner, read books on Western civilization obtained from O Kyŏng-sŏk and urged his country to engage in foreign trade and embark on enlightened reform. As the voices in Chosŏn calling for change and reform grew louder with the downfall of the Taewŏn'gun, conditions within the country became more favorable to opening its doors to the outside world.

Japan was the first nation to pressure Chosŏn to reconsider its isolationist policy. Westerners had not yet perceived Chosŏn as an important trading and diplomatic partner, whereas the Japanese saw it as a prime area for domination and expansion. Early in the Meiji period, aggressive factions in the new Japanese government demanded that their country remove Chosŏn from Chinese suzerainty and establish control over the peninsula. Perhaps recalling their own experiences at the hands of Commodore Matthew Perry in 1853–1854, the Japanese government dispatched a naval squadron to Chosŏn to force the country to enter into a new relationship with Japan.

In September 1875, in a deliberate effort to confront Chosŏn, the Japanese warship *Unyo Maru* sailed to Korean waters off Kanghwa-do, under the cloak of surveying Korean coastlines. The ship was promptly fired on by Chosŏn defenders at the Ch'oji-jin fort on the southeastern tip of the island. As planned, the Japanese government strongly protested that Chosŏn had made an unprovoked attack on a Japanese ship engaged in a peaceful mission, when, in fact, the true intent was to create a disturbance. In the ensuing period, the *Unyo Maru* destroyed the Ch'oji-jin fort, and a Japanese detachment occupied the nearby Yŏngjong-jin fort, killing 35 Korean defenders and taking 16 prisoner before withdrawing. In late January 1876, using the *Unyo Maru* incident as a pretext, Japan dispatched a minister plenipotentiary, Kuroda Kiyotaka, along with five warships and some 400 troops, to Chosŏn; Kuroda landed on Kanghwa-do and demanded that Chosŏn enter into treaty negotiations with Japan. Although it could have withstood this pressure (as it had previously with the the French and the Americans in 1866 and 1871, respectively), the Chosŏn government decided to negotiate a modern, Western-style treaty with Japan and sent Sin Hŏn to receive Kuroda and negotiate with him. The result was the Treaty of Kanghwa or the Friendship Treaty of 1876, signed on 26 February 1876. Following a textbook display of gunboat diplomacy, the Japanese succeeded in opening Chosŏn's doors to their country.

Perhaps the most important provision in the Treaty of Kanghwa was Article 1, which stated: "Chosŏn, as an independent state, enjoys the same sovereign rights as Japan does."[3] The Japanese insisted on this article in the treaty because it meant that, as an independent state, Chosŏn was no longer subject to China's traditional suzerainty claims. Thus Japan could begin to exercise economic and political influence over Chosŏn without Chinese interference. The 12-article treaty opened up three Chosŏn ports, including Pusan, to Japanese trade. The designation of two other ports was left to Japan's discretion. The two ports later designated were Wŏnsan on the east coast, in 1880, and Inch'ŏn (then called Chemulp'o) on the west coast, in 1883. The treaty also granted the Japanese the right of extraterritoriality, which Japan wanted to remove from their treaties with the Western powers.

The Treaty of Kanghwa caused considerable concern in China, but in the late 1870s China, because of its own serious problems, could not afford to thwart Japanese designs in Chosŏn. As the Chinese government mulled this dilemma, the United States provided a possible solution. America once again showed an interest in entering into treaty negotiations with Chosŏn and had already dispatched a naval officer, Commodore Robert Shufeldt, to East Asia to achieve this goal. First, Shufeldt visited Japanese officials in 1880 to see if Japan would mediate between U.S. officials and the Koreans, but the Japanese did not respond to his offer. Shufeldt then traveled to China, where he met with Li Hongzhang who was in charge of China's Chosŏn policy. Li concluded that if he encouraged Chosŏn to enter into treaty talks with Shufeldt, China could use the United States to offset Japan's growing influence in Chosŏn. Following up on this strategy, Li represented Chosŏn at the treaty talks with Shufeldt in Tianjin, China, during April and May 1882, and produced a diplomatic agreement between Chosŏn and the United States.

The treaty, titled the "Treaty of Peace, Amity, Commerce, and Navigation between the United States of America and the Kingdom of Corea," was formally signed in Inch'ŏn on 22 May 1882 by Shufeldt and Chosŏn's two senior officials, Sin Hŏn and Kim Hong-jip. The document provided for the protection of shipwrecked American sailors, the securing of coal supplies for U.S. vessels entering Chosŏn, trading rights in selected Chosŏn ports, and the exchange of diplomatic representatives. It also granted the Americans extraterritoriality rights and most-favored-nation status in Chosŏn. In return for these benefits, the United States agreed not to import opium or arms into Chosŏn. The 14-article treaty was a typical nineteenth-century settlement, in which a nation of superior power dictated the terms. Compared to treaties that other East Asian nations concluded with the West, however, the terms were less overbearing.

Two significant issues, one regarding China and the other Chosŏn, were raised by this treaty. The first concerned Chosŏn's status as an independent nation. During the talks with Shufeldt, Li Hongzhang insisted that the treaty contain an article declaring that Chosŏn was a dependency of China. He argued that Chosŏn had long been a tributary state of China, but Shufeldt firmly opposed such language, arguing that a U.S. treaty with Chosŏn should be based on the Treaty of Kanghwa, which stipulated that Chosŏn was an independent state. A compromise was finally reached, with Shufeldt and Li agreeing that the Chosŏn king would notify the U.S. president in a letter that Chosŏn had special status as a tributary state of China.

The other important controversial issue grew out of the second paragraph in Article 1 of that document. The paragraph, in the English-language version, stated: "If other Powers deal unjustly or oppressively with either Government, the other will exert their good offices, on being informed of the case, to bring about an amicable arrangement, thus showing their friendly feelings."[4] The Korean version, written in Chinese, employed far more emphatic language, using, for example, the term *p'ilsu sangjo* (literally, "good offices"), meaning "shall surely render mutual aid," and the Koreans, in desperate need of outside help, took this as a firm commitment by the United States to come to Chosŏn's assistance if its sovereignty and independence were threatened. To Americans, however, this statement in the treaty was nothing more than an expression of friendship between nations. Over the next two decades Kojong earnestly tried to persuade the United States to implement the clause according to the Korean interpretation but without success.

The treaty between Chosŏn and the United States became the model for all treaties between Chosŏn and other Western powers. Chosŏn signed trade and commerce treaties with Great Britain and Germany in 1883, with Italy and Russia in 1884, and with France in 1886. Subsequently commercial treaties were concluded with, among others, Austria, Belgium, and Denmark. Thereafter Chosŏn was plunged into a whirlpool of international rivalries, with imperialist intrusions and ensuing struggles for supremacy among foreign powers that ended in Japan's annexation of Chosŏn in 1910.

Pursuit of the Enlightenment Policy

Immediately after opening Chosŏn to the outside world, Kojong and his reform-minded advisers pursued a policy of enlightenment aimed at achieving national prosperity and military strength through the doctrine of *tongdo sŏgi*, or Eastern ways and Western machines. To modernize their country, they tried selectively to accept and master Western technology while preserving their country's cultural values. Despite some reforms, however, such halfway modernization efforts and policies failed to strengthen and stabilize Chosŏn.

In the wake of welcoming the outside world, the Chosŏn government first launched administrative and military reforms along enlightenment lines. To carry out the enlightenment policy, in January 1881 the government established the T'ongni kimu amun, or Office for Extraordinary State Affairs, modeled on Chinese administrative structures. Under this overarching organ were 12 *sa*, or agencies, dealing with relations with China (Sadae), diplomatic matters involving other foreign nations (Kyorin), military affairs (Kunmu), border administration (Pyŏnjŏng), foreign trade (T'ongsang), military ordnance (Kunmul), machinery production (Kigye), shipbuilding (Sŏnham), coastal surveillance (Kiyŏn), personnel recruitment (Chŏnsŏn), special procurement (Iyong), and foreign-language schooling (Ŏhak).

Following the conclusion and implementation of the Treaty of Kanghwa, Kojong also turned to modernizing his troops and military organization. To this end, in May 1881, the Chosŏn government organized the Pyŏlgigun, or Special Skills Force with 80 recruits, instructed by Horimoto Reizo, a lieutenant in the Japanese army's engineering corps. In January 1882 it reorganized the existing five-army garrison structure into the Muwiyŏng, or Palace Guards Garrison, and the Changŏyŏng, or Capital Guards Garrison.

The reform-minded Chosŏn leadership sent out observation groups to gather the knowledge of foreign nations, and, upon their return, these groups recorded their experiences so they could be used to pursue a policy of enlightenment. In March 1876, immediately after the conclusion of the Treaty of Kanghwa, special envoy Kim Ki-su was sent to Japan. Upon returning home, he presented the king with the journal of his observations abroad, titled *Iltong kiyu*, or Record of a Journey to Japan. In April 1880 another envoy, Kim Hong-jip, went to Japan. Upon returning in September 1880, he presented Kojong with a booklet titled *Chaoxian celue,* or A Policy for Chosŏn, written by Huang Zunxian, a counselor in the Chinese legation in Tokyo. In the treatise Huang advised Chosŏn to accept Western institutions and technology for the sake of its economic development. More important, he proposed that, in view of potential Russian threats, Chosŏn should strengthen itself by maintaining close ties with China and Japan, and allying with the United States. Kojong generally agreed with its policy recommendations, and he even ordered his officials to circulate copies of *Chaoxian celue* among Confucian literati throughout the country. In May 1881 Pak Chŏng-yang, Cho Chun-yŏng, Hong Yŏng-sik, and 60 others were sent to Japan as an inspection team called the *sinsa yuramdan,* or gentlemen's sightseeing group. This was a technical mission to survey a wide range of Japan's modernized facilities, and until their return home in September of the year, they traveled all over Japan inspecting, for example, administrative, military, educational, and industrial facilities. In October 1881 Kim Yun-sik and his 38-man group went to Tianjin to study methods of modern weapons manufacture, and Chinese technicians were invited to manufacture weapons in Seoul. In July 1883 a fact-finding diplomatic mission, led by Min Yŏng-ik, toured the United States, meeting with U.S. government leaders, including President Chester A. Arthur, and observing the startling urban and industrial development of the United States.

Opposition to the Enlightenment Policy

The enlightenment policy of Kojong and his adherents met with stiff opposition from the Confucian literati who believed that Confucianism was the only valid system of belief and that civilizations based on any other ideology should be excluded from their country. They propounded the doctrine of *wijŏng ch'ŏksa,* or the defense of orthodoxy and rejection of heterodoxy. The term *chŏng* (orthodoxy) referred not only to Chosŏn but to the entire country's traditional Confucian values, and *sa* (heterodoxy) referred to all of Western civilization as well as the Western powers and Japan.

The wijŏng ch'ŏksa movement reached an intital climax soon after the French invasion of Kanghwa-do in 1866, when the Confucian scholar Yi Hang-no submitted a memorial to the king arguing that Chosŏn should battle foreign aggression to the end in defending itself and its traditional Confucian culture. He cautioned that advocating peaceful relations would transform Chosŏn into a colony of the Western powers and cause its people to behave like animals. In late January 1876, immediately before the signing of the Treaty of Kanghwa, Ch'oe Ik-hyŏn, a disciple of Yi Hang-no, presented a memorial to the king in which he sternly opposed concluding the treaty. He warned that Japan and the West were one and the same in the grave threat that they posed to Chosŏn.

When *Chaoxian celue* was in wide circulation, on Kojong's orders, in late 1880, the members of the wijŏng ch'ŏksa movement again became agitated. Kojong had the booklet copied and distributed to educate the Confucian literati who opposed his enlightenment policy. Contrary to his expectations, however, the circulation of the booklet triggered a stormy controversy nationwide. The Confucian scholars immediately organized a mass protest movement in the form of memorials to the king. Initiated by the *Yŏngnam manin so*, or Memorial of Ten Thousand Men of Kyŏngsang Province, authored by Yi Man-son, a deluge of memorials soon flooded the government. In these outpourings, the Confucian literati violently denounced the arguments articulated in the *Chaoxian celue* and demanded that Kim Hong-jip be punished for having brought the booklet into the country. Thereafter the government resolutely suppressed memorials to the king regarding the doctrine of wijŏng ch'ŏksa.

Under these unsettling circumstances, in September 1881, a coup d'état was revealed in which Taewŏn'gun's illegitimate eldest son Yi Chae-sŏn would have ascended the throne in Kojong's stead, at the same time eliminating the Min clan and supporting the Taewŏn'gun as regent. Yi Chae-sŏn and his accomplices were executed in November. This incident demonstrated that the antagonism between advocates and opponents of the enlightenment policy was intertwined with the struggle for power between the Taewŏn'gun and Queen Min.

The Soldiers' Revolt of 1882 and Chinese Intervention in Internal Affairs

The government's open-door policy benefited government officials in Seoul and merchants in treaty ports at least for a short time. On the other hand, a steep increase in rice prices followed the export of large quantities of grain, especially rice, and spread misery among the peasantry in the countryside and the lower classes in Seoul. The traditional military units also were financially distressed. Kojong and his enlightenment-oriented government discriminated against the veteran soldiers of the Muwiyŏng and the Changŏyŏng, while favoring the elite Pyŏlgigun. On 19 July 1882, infuriated soldiers revolted after not being paid for

13 months, and when depot officials of the Sŏnhyech'ŏng, which administered grain taxes, embezzled the rice intended for soldiers' salaries. Many inhabitants of the slum sections in Seoul took sides with the mutinous troops. The mutineers killed Min Kyŏm-ho, Queen Min's nephew and superintendent of the Sŏnhyech'ŏng who was responsible for controlling soldiers' pay. They also murdered the Japanese training officer Horimoto Reizo, and burned the Japanese legation building to the ground. The Japanese minister Hanabusa Yoshitada, who had come to Chosŏn in November 1877 as the first Japanese minister to Chosŏn, barely escaped to Japan. Hungry soldiers, believing that Queen Min and her family had stolen their pay, sought vengeance, but the queen managed to escape to the countryside in disguise.

To dodge the difficult situation, on 26 July Kojong reinstated the Taewŏn'gun as regent. In the midst of the soldiers' mutiny, the Taewŏn'gun had been asked to support the mutineers and he agreed, inserting himself into the scene and seizing power once again. In deference to the demands of the veteran soldiers, he dismantled the Palace and Capital Guards garrisons as well as the Special Skills Force, and revived the former five-army garrison structure. He also abolished the newly created T'ongni kimu amun and freed the Confucian literati who had been exiled as a result of the wijŏng ch'ŏksa movement. Thus the Taewŏn'gun's reemergence temporarily suspended the enlightenment policy.

With China's and Japan's intervention in Chosŏn's internal affairs, however, the Taewŏn'gun's triumph was short-lived. On 2 August 1882 the Chosŏn government asked China to send troops to resolve the chaos it faced, thus giving China the opportunity to reclaim suzerainty over Chosŏn which Japan had usurped. On 10 August a Chinese force of 4,500 men and three warships arrived at Inch'on, and soon after Chinese troops entered Seoul and stationed themselves at strategic points in the capital. Sixteen days later, on 26 August, they abducted the Taewŏn'gun as he was making a courtesy call at the Chinese headquarters and sent him under protective custody to Tianjin. Once again the Taewŏn'gun lost power.

Earlier, on 12 August, Japanese minister Hanabusa Yoshitada had returned to Chosŏn with 1,500 troops and four warships, and on 30 August the panicked Chosŏn government concluded the Treaty of Chemulp'o (Inch'ŏn) with Japan. By its terms, the Chosŏn government was forced to punish the leaders of the Korean mutiny within 20 days, pay the families of Japanese victims 50,000 yen and the Japanese government 500,000 yen for damages, and order its troops to guard the Japanese legation in Seoul until they could be replaced by Japanese guards. The treaty further increased the scope of Japan's aggressive activity, centering on the ports of Inch'ŏn, Pusan, and Wŏnsan. Finally, the treaty required Chosŏn to formally apologize to Japan, and, to do so, a delegation headed by special envoy Pak Yŏng-hyo was sent to Japan.[5]

After the solders' revolt, China reasserted its suzerainty over Chosŏn and stationed troops there commanded by Yuan Shikai, as well as two special advisers on foreign affairs, the German Paul Georg von Möllendorf, a close confidant of Li Hongzhang, and the Chinese diplomat Ma Jianzhong. In December 1882 two high-level offices, the Oeamun, or Foreign Office, and the Naeamun, or Home Office, were established. The former dealt with foreign affairs and trade, and the latter was responsible for military matters and internal affairs. The Ch'in'gunyŏng, or Capital Guards Command, was also created comprised of four barracks designated the right, left, front, and rear. The new Chosŏn military was trained along Chinese lines by Yuan Shikai.

Now that Chosŏn was again reduced to a tributary state of China, Kojong could not appoint his diplomats without Yuan's approval. On 4 October 1882 the two countries concluded the *Choch'ŏng sangmin suryuk muyŏk changjŏng,* or Regulations for the Maritime and Overland Trade of Merchants of Chosŏn and Qing China, stipulating that Chosŏn was a dependency of China and granting Chinese merchants the right to conduct overland and maritime business freely within Chosŏn. Under this treaty the number of Chinese merchants and traders greatly increased, striking a severe blow to Chosŏn merchants' business transactions.

The Coup d'état of 1884

After the soldiers' mutiny of 1882 the conservatives, often called the *Sadaedang,* or Servers of the Great Party, including not only the Min Yŏng-ik from the royal in-law Min family but also prominent political figures including Kim Yun-sik and Ŏ Yun-jung, who wanted to maintain power with China's help. Although the conservatives supported the enlightenment policy, they favored gradual changes based on the Chinese model. They were opposed, however, by the *Kaehwadang,* or Enlightenment Party, comprised of younger men such as Kim Ok-kyun, Pak Yŏng-hyo, Sŏ Kwang-bŏm, and Hong Yŏng-sik. These progressives, whose careers had been blocked by the Min family, looked to Japan to learn from the Meiji government's rapid reform program. They were also strongly nationalistic and tried to make their country truly independent by ending China's interference in Chosŏn's internal affairs.

The progressives failed to secure appointments to vital offices and so were unable to advance their reform plans. Prepared to seize power by all means, they found an opportunity to stage a coup d'état in 1884, when hostilities between France and China erupted over Annam (now modern Vietnam) in August 1884 and half the Chinese contingents were withdrawn from Chosŏn. On 4 December 1884, with the help of Japanese minister Takezoe Shinichiro, who promised to mobilize Japanese legation guards to render assistance, the progressives staged their coup under the cover of a banquet hosted by Hong Yŏng-sik, director of the Ujŏng ch'ongguk, or General Postal Administration, to celebrate the opening of the new national post office. The king was expected to be there, along with several foreign diplomats and high-ranking officials, most of them members of the pro-Chinese Sadaedang faction. Kim Ok-kyun and his cohorts approached King Kojong, falsely reported that the Chinese troops had created a disturbance, and escorted him to a small palace, the Kyŏngu-gung, where they placed him in the custody of Japanese legation guards. They then killed and wounded several senior officials of the Sadaedang faction.

After the coup, called *Kapsin chŏngbyŏn*, or the Coup d'état of 1884, the Kaehwadang members formed a new government and formulated a program of reform. A drastic 14-point reform proposal urged that the following conditions be met: an end to Chosŏn's tributary relationship with China; the abolition of ruling-class privilege and the establishment of equal rights for all; the reorganization of the government as virtually a constitutional monarchy; the revision of land tax laws; cancellation of the grain loan system; the unification of all internal fiscal administrations under the jurisdiction of the Ho-jo; the suppression of privileged merchants and the development of free commerce and trade, the creation of a modern police system including police patrols and royal guards; and severe punishment of corrupt officials.

Despite all its good intentions, however, the new government totally failed, lasting no longer than a few days. The Kaehwadang was supported by no more than 140 Japanese troops facing at least 1,500 Chinese forces in Seoul. Even before the reform measures were made public, Chinese troops attacked and defeated the Japanese forces and restored power to the Sadaedang. Hong Yŏng-sik was killed but others escaped to Japan, including Kim Ok-kyun, Pak Yŏng-hyo, Sŏ Kwang-bŏm, and Sŏ Chae-p'il, as well as the Japanese minister Takezoe.

After the abortive coup, Kojong voided the reform measures proposd by the Kaehwadang and sent an envoy to Japan protesting its cooperation in the coup and demanding repatriation of the conspirators. Japan demanded, instead, reparation for damages, and in January 1885, in a show of force, dispatched two battalions and seven warships to Chosŏn. Confronted with Japanese saber rattling, on 9 January 1885 the Chosŏn government concluded the Treaty of Hansŏng (Seoul) with the Japanese envoy, Foreign Minister Inoue Kaoru. By its terms, Chosŏn indemnified the Japanese victims and paid 100,000 yen to Japan for damages to the Japanese legation.

To overcome his country's disadvantageous position in Chosŏn followed by the abortive coup, the Japanese prime minister, Ito Hirobumi, visited China to discuss the matter with his Chinese counterpart, Li Hongzhang, and succeeded in concluding the Convention of Tianjin on 31 May 1885. The two countries pledged to withdraw their troops from Chosŏn within four months, with prior notification to the other party if troops were to be sent to Chosŏn in the future.

China and Japan withdrew their troops from Chosŏn, leaving behind a precarious balance of power in Chosŏn between those two nations. Meanwhile, Yuan Shikai remained in Seoul and continued to interfere with Chosŏn politics. Japan, on the other hand, in a strategic retreat, was prepared to pounce upon any suitable opportunity for future encroachment.

THE TONGHAK PEASANT WAR AND THE KABO REFORM

Spreading the Enlightenment Policy

The Chosŏn government pursued the enlightenment policy in various fields, including the press, education, medical treatment, and science and technology. The Pangmun'guk, or Office of Culture and Information, was created on 17 August 1883, and the office published the *Hansŏng sunbo*, or Tri-Monthly Gazette of Seoul, Korea's first modern newspaper, on 30 October 1883. It stopped publication in October 1884 and, on 25 January 1886, was reissued with a new title, the *Hansŏng chubo*, or Weekly Gazette of Seoul.

The first modern, government-founded school, established in August 1883, was the Tongmun haksa, or Academy of Common Script, where foreign languages were taught,. On 23 September 1886 the government created a special institute, the Yukyŏng kongwŏn, or Public Institute for Education, to educate the sons of high-ranking officials in the new knowledge gleaned from the West. This royal school invited American teachers including George W. Gilmore, Homer B. Hulbert, and Delzell A. Bunker to teach, respectively, English, social sciences, and natural sciences. In 1894, disappointed with the school's failure, Kojong brought in British teachers to start a new government school.

The first modern private school was the Wŏnsan haksa, or Wŏnsan Academy, which taught mainly foreign languages and natural sciences, founded in the port town of Wŏnsan, Tongwŏn county, in September 1883. Established by Chŏng Hyŏn-sŏk, the reform-minded magistrate of Tongwŏn county, the school reflected the residents' strong urging that a modern school was needed. American missionaries founded several schools in Seoul, enabling them to expand their proselytizing efforts and introduce modern, Western-style education to Chosŏn. The American Methodist missionary Henry G. Appenzeller established Paejae haktang (Academy), a boarding school for boys, in August 1885; another American Methodist missionary, Mary F. Scranton, founded Ihwa haktang, a school for girls, in April 1886; the American Presbyterian missionary Horace G. Underwood built Kyŏngsin hakkyo (school) for boys, in May 1886; and another Presbyterian missionary, Annie J. Ellers, established Chŏngsin yŏhakkyo (Girls' school), in June 1887. The names of these missionaries became synonymous with Korea's modern education.

The Chosŏn government introduced modern, Western-style hospitals and initiated modern medical treatment in February 1885, with the Wangnip kwanghyewŏn, or Royal Widespread Relief House, at the suggestion of the American Presbyterian medical missionary Dr. Horace N. Allen. This first modern hospital was soon renamed the Chejungwŏn, or House for People's Relief, in March of that year, and Allen was installed to administer it. Allen, who later joined the diplomatic corps, enjoyed Kojong's confidence and friendship, as he had saved the life of Min Yŏng-ik, Queen Min's nephew, who had been seriously wounded during the failed coup of 1884. As a preventive measure against smallpox, the government founded the Uduguk, or Office of Cowpox, at Kongju, Ch'ungch'ŏng povince, in July 1883, and in May 1885 it assigned Chi Sŏk-yŏng the task of writing a book titled the *Udu sinbang,* or New Methods of Vaccination for Smallpox.

As the government's interest in acquiring new agricultural technology grew, it established agricultural and stock-farming experimental stations. To introduce modern Western farming methods, An Chong-su wrote *Nongjŏng sinp'yŏn,* or New Compilation of Farm Management, in 1881, and Chŏng Pyŏng-ha compiled *Nongjŏng ch'waryo,* or Essentials of Farm Management, in 1886.

Beginning in the 1880s electricity was used in Chosŏn, and the introduction of the telegraph greatly improved the country's communication system. At first the government obtained a loan from China to build telegraph lines between Seoul and Inch'ŏn, and between Seoul and Ŭiju in 1885. Later, to free itself from

Chinese interference, the government asked Germany for a loan and installed telegraph facilities between Seoul and Pusan, and between Seoul and Wŏnsan, in 1888 and in 1891, respectively. In 1887 electric lights were installed for the first time at the Kyŏngbok-kung palace.

In the 1880s the Chosŏn government adopted the doctrine of tongdo sŏgi to pursue the enlightenment policy in many areas. The results fell short of its expectations, and the effort only invited foreign interference in the country.

New Neighbors: United States and Russia

United States

Ever since the coup d'état of 1884 China enjoyed an overwhelmingly dominant position in Chosŏn. Yuan Shihkai controlled Chosŏn's internal affairs and blocked interference by foreign powers in order to maintain China's suzerain-dependency relations with Chosŏn. Also, under his protection, Chinese merchants thronged to every part of the country and established a settlement in Seoul's downtown area which virtually became Seoul's "Chinatown."

After concluding the friendship treaty between Chosŏn and the United States in 1882, Kojong embarked on freeing his kingdom from Chinese domination and using U.S. aid to modernize the country. The king and his adherents regarded the United States as a benevolent power that would guarantee Chosŏn's territorial integrity and political independence, and viewed the bilateral treaty as an instrument to free Chosŏn from Chinese control. They interpreted the "good offices" provision of Article 1, as pointed out above, to mean that the United States would guarantee the integrity and independence of their country by taking sides with Chosŏn in the event of foreign aggression. With his favorable impression of the United States, Kojong was said to have "danced for joy" when Lucius H. Foote arrived in Seoul in May 1883 as the first U.S. minister. The king wanted to employ several American advisers in the Chosŏn government, and encouraged U.S. investment and trade to induce and strengthen U.S. interests in Chosŏn. As a result, the Americans invested in railroads, streetcars, a telegraph system, and the Unsan gold mine.

The United States had concluded, however, that Chosŏn was of less value economically and strategically than it had expected, and so it increasingly distanced itself from the kingdom. Thus, despite Kojong's strong desire for more American involvement, the United States turned him down, although it formally supported Chosŏn's independence.

Russia

U.S. reluctance to help Chosŏn led Kojong to turn to Russia. Unlike the indifference displayed by the United States, Russia took a great interest in making inroads into Chosŏn, particularly to secure an ice-free port. After signing a treaty of friendship and commerce between Chosŏn and Russia in 1884, Karl Woeber was sent to Chosŏn as a Russian minister. An able diplomat, Woeber frequently visited the court to foster a pro-Russian faction in the government. Responding to Russian efforts, a pro-Russian clique emerged among those who resented China's excessive interference in internal affairs. This development was further accelerated by Möllendorf, Kojong's special adviser on foreign affairs. Although he was appointed, on Li Hongzhang's recommendation, as vice minister of the Foreign Office and inspector-general of Chosŏn's customs service, Möllendorf tried to free Chosŏn from Chinese control by allying the kingdom closely with Russia.

Concerned about Chosŏn's leanings toward Russia, the Chinese responded initially by returning the Taewŏn'gun to Chosŏn. But then, in August 1886, Yuan Shihkai considered dethroning Kojong. This move was frustrated by Li Hongzhang's opposition, and, instead, China pressured the Chosŏn government to dismiss Möllendorf. After the latter's dismissal in September 1885, Li Hongzhang divided Möllendorf's responsibilities between the American Owen Nickerson Denny, who became the foreign affairs adviser, and another American, Henry F. Merrill, who was made chief of the customs service. During his tenure between 1886 and 1890, however, Denny, too, advocated close ties with Russia. In August 1888 he concluded an overland-trade agreement with Russia that opened Kyŏnghŭng, on the Russian border, , to the Russians for trade and granted Russia full navigation rights on the Tumen River.

Russian inroads into Chosŏn aroused uneasiness in Great Britain, which at the time was dealing with Russia's southward advance into Asia Minor, among other places. With China's full knowledge, in April 1885 the British illegally occupied Kŏmun-do off the southern coast of Chŏlla province to defend against Russia in case of an Anglo-Russian war. By building troop encampments and gun emplacements there, Great Britain demonstrated that Kŏmun-do would be used as a permanent gateway to the Korea Strait. The British called the island "Fort Hamilton."

The Chosŏn government vigorously protested the British infringement of its sovereignty, while Russia, alarmed by the British incursion, pressured China to intervene with the British or else it, too, would occupy Chosŏn's territory. China interceded, and two years of negotiations finally led to the British evacuation of Kŏmun-do in March 1887. Great Britain withdrew its forces from the island on the condition that no nation would be permitted to seize Chosŏn's territory. As international rivalry over Chosŏn intensified, Chosŏn was urged to become an unaligned nation by such notables as Kim Ok-kyun, Yu Kil-chun, and Möllendorf. These urgings were ignored, and by the early 1890s Chosŏn had become the focus of a three-way power struggle between China, Japan, and Russia. In its effort to preserve its political independence and territorial integrity, the Chosŏn kingdom's only weapon was to play off one powerful nation against another.

The Tonghak Peasant War

By the early 1890s Chosŏn was ripe for a peasant rebellion as a result of the kingdom's deteriorating economic and social conditions. Government officials were so corrupt that much of the tax collected for the central government was sidetracked by local officials. The government's vigorous pursuit of enlightenment policy had worsened already troubled public finances, as the steep cost of huge indemnities to Japan and the introduction of new modern facilities had to be financed mostly by the peasants.

The peasantry was also wounded financially following Japan's economic penetration, for the conclusion of the Treaty of Kanghwa in early 1876 had given Japan almost a monopoly on Chosŏn's foreign trade. Two years later, in 1878, Japan's Daiichi Bank established a branch office in Pusan, encouraging Japanese merchants to find their way into the Chosŏn market. (Indeed, Chosŏn gold was used as a reserve fund for the Bank of Japan.) The Japanese merchants purchased rice, soy beans, cattle hides, and alluvial gold at incredibly low prices, making huge profits at home. On the other hand, Chosŏn was faced with the pressing need of devising some way to protect its national economy against Japan. Although its position in Chosŏn weakened for a short period after the abortive coup of 1884, Japan quickly recovered its former position. By the early 1890s Japanese economic activity had reached a standard that no other nation could rival. Chosŏn's exports, chiefly rice, soybeans, and cowhides, went almost entirely to Japan, and Chosŏn's rice, superior in quality to Japanese rice, was used to feed the Japanese. Japan imported cowhides for military use, and Chosŏn imported cotton goods and other industrial products, mostly sundry goods for daily use, from Japan. These trade practices devastated Chosŏn's village economy, seriously aggravating the food situation.

To resist Japan's economic penetration, especially its huge rice imports, the Chosŏn government prohibited certain provinces from exporting rice. Large-scale bans were imposed in Hwanghae and Hamgyŏng provinces in October 1889. Because of strong Japanese protests, however, the Chosŏn government lifted the embargo on rice and indemnified Japan for damages. The continuously deteriorating village economy aroused deep animosity among the peasantry toward its exploiters, foreign as well as Korean. This discontent of the peasantry combined with the Tonghak movement to provoke the Tonghak peasant war.

As the country opened to foreign trade and the peasants' plight deepened, the popular, nationalistic, and religious Tonghak movement gained wide support in the farmlands. A network of Tonghak churches had been established in the countryside, and its members were organized into p'o, or parishes, creating a hierarchy of church leadership, mainly educated men of considerable fortune. Since the late 1870s, the Tonghak had firmly taken root in the three southern provinces of Ch'ungch'ŏng, Chŏlla, and Kyŏngsang.

As the Tonghak became increasingly influential in Chosŏn society, its members channeled their energies into a movement both to clear the name of its founder, Ch'oe Che-u, of false charges that had led to a death sentence in 1864, and to allow missionaries to carry on their activities freely. To this end, several thousand Tonghak members gathered at Samnye in Chŏlla province in December 1892, demanding that the governors of Ch'ungch'ŏng and Chŏlla provinces posthumously exonerate Ch'oe Che-u and end the suppression of the Tonghak movement. The two governors rejected the first demand, claiming that it was beyond their jurisdiction, but they pledged that Tonghak believers would no longer suffer persecution by local officials.

Not persuaded by this pledge, in March 1893 more than 40 Tonghak members, led by Pak Kwang-ho, held vigil before the palace gate for three days where they petitioned the king directly. The government arrested the leaders of the petitioners and forcibly dispersed the throngs. The next month, some 20,000 infuriated Tonghak members gathered at Poŭn, Ch'ungch'ŏng province, hoisted banners calling for a "crusade to expel the Japanese and Westerners," and confirmed their determination to fight to the death. Soothing the Tonghak crowd at first with promises to punish officials who had harshly persecuted the Tonghak, the government then proceeded to subdue them with a 600-man force commanded by Hong Kye-hun. The exhausted Tonghak members dispersed voluntarily on the condition that the governor of Ch'ungch'ŏng province would be punished.

In 1894 the simmering protest came to a head, as the Tonghak movement evolved into a large-scale peasant revolution focused in the Chŏlla region, historically the granary of Korea. This region had suffered the most severe exploitation by the financially crippled central government and corrupt local officials, and witnessed the shipping of rice to Japan in greater quantities than any other province. Thus the Chŏlla people's hostility toward the central government, local officials, and Japan was exceptionally fierce.

The specific trigger of the rebellion, however, was the excessive exploitation of the peasantry by Cho Pyŏng-gap, the magistrate of Kobu county. A typical corrupt official, Cho had taken every opportunity to illegally extort large amounts of grain from the peasantry, collecting, for instance, more than 1,000 yang, equivalent to some 1,500 contemporary silver dollars, to erect a pavilion to protect his father's tombstone. Most enraging to the peasants was the tax he forcibly levied on irrigation water from the Mansŏk-po reservoir. He had already exacted corvee labor from the peasants to construct the reservoir, and yet charged a large quantity of rice for water use. The angry peasants had repeatedly appealed for redress to the Kobu county and Chŏlla provincial offices but to no avail. Finally, in February 1894, under the leadership of Chŏn Pong-jun, the head of Tonghak parish of Kobu county, more than 1,000 peasants seized the county office, punished corrupt functionaries, returned illegally collected tax rice to the taxpayers, and took weapons from the armory. After occupying the town of Kobu, the peasant forces called upon the government to punish Cho Pyŏng-gap for his abuses and block the inroads of Japanese merchants into the Chosŏn market.

Thoroughly alarmed, the government dispatched a specially empowered inspector, Yi Yong-t'ae, to investigate the incident. Yi, however, wanted to place responsibility for the uprising on the Tonghak movement and was intent on ferreting out and punishing Tonghak members. This was the final blow. Enraged by this betrayal, the peasants rallied around Tonghak leaders Chŏn Pong-jun, Son Hwa-jung, Kim Kae-nam, and O Chi-yŏng and, in April 1894, they rose in rebellion armed with bamboo spears and cudgels, declaring they would drive out Japan, the West, and the privileged few, and provide for the people's welfare. As peasants from the neighboring areas joined forces with the Tonghak rebels, their ranks swelled to some 8,000.

The Tonghak forces moved northward to Paeksan in battle formation and defeated government troops sent from Chŏlla province at Hwangt'ohyŏn hill south of Kobu in May 1894. They then marched southward, successfully seizing Chŏngŭp, Koch'ang, Mujang, and Yŏnggwang, and then further south to occupy Hamp'yŏng, Muan, and Naju. After this successful campaign, they turned northward. To suppress the rebellion, the central government had already dispatched Hong Kye-hun, commanding some 800 men from the elite capital garrison. Hong's forces proved no match for the confident, spirited Tonghak insurgents. Routing these government troops in a clash at Changsŏng in their northern campaign, the Tonghak forces met with virtually no resistance and easily occupied Chŏnju in late May 1894. By early June all of Chŏlla province was under the occupation of the Tonghak forces.

The Chosŏn government panicked and asked the Chinese government for military support. China immediately sent an army of 3,000 men, landing them at Asan Bay, Ch'ungch'ŏng province, in June 1894. Japan responded by quickly sending a counterforce of 7,000 men in July. Now the two powers were pitted against each other, and the confrontation became increasingly tense. In light of this new situation, the Chosŏn government now believed that the Tonghak had to be appeased without depending on a foreign power and proposed that a truce be negotiated. Negotiations between the government and Tonghak forces led to the "Peace of Chŏnju" of 10 June 1894. The agreement specified comprehensive reform programs that would end government misrule. The Tonghak peasant soldiers withdrew from Chŏnju and returned to their homes. But because they were authorized to extend their organized network into new areas, they established the Chipkangso, or Local Directorate, in 53 counties of Chŏlla province and set about redressing local government abuses. A headquarters of these popular organs was established in the provincial capital of Chŏnju, with Chŏn Pong-jun at the helm.

Regardless of efforts by the Koreans themselves to reach an amicable settlement, the explosive situation caused by the presence of both Chinese and Japanese forces in Chosŏn soon resulted in the outbreak of the Sino-Japanese War. The Japanese defeated the Chinese in the war, but the bigger losers were the rebellious peasantry of Chŏlla province. Angered at Japan's having taken virtual control of all internal matters during the war, the Tonghak peasants raised another army in November 1894 and again moved northward, intent on expelling the Japanese from Chosŏn. They were defeated, however, by Chosŏn government troops reinforced by a Japanese army contingent at Kongju, Ch'ungch'ŏng province, in late November. After some 500 survivors retreated to Chŏlla province, Chŏn Pong-jun was captured in Sunch'ang, Chŏlla province, and executed in Seoul. The Tonghak peasant war finally came to an end in January 1895.

The first Tonghak peasant war was not only a revolutionary movement of the peasantry against their autocratic, oppressive government but was also a struggle against Japanese economic aggression. The second Tonghak uprising, in addition to resisting Japanese economic encroachments, was a direct challenge to Japanese intervention in Chosŏn's internal affairs. Although the peasant war ended in failure, the Tonghak lived on in the religious *Ch'ŏndogyo*, or Heavenly Way Teaching movement, which influenced Korean peasants for decades thereafter and ignited the spark of Korean nationalism. On 1 December 1905 the Tonghak was renamed the Ch'ŏndogyo, which remains North Korea's powerful state religion.

The Sino-Japanese War

China responded immediately when Chosŏn requested help to suppress the Tonghak uprising. Within a month 3,000 men had been dispatched to Chosŏn, an action reported to Japan in accordance with the terms of the Convention of Tianjin. Under the pretext of protecting its citizens residing in Chosŏn, Japan sent seven warships and 7,000 troops to the country, occupying Seoul, Inch'ŏn, and the central region. By this time, however, the Tonghak peasant army had already withdrawn from Chŏnju in compliance with the "Peace of Chŏnju." At that point the Chinese and Japanese had no reason to be in Chosŏn. China proposed a joint withdrawal of Chinese and Japanese troops, which was welcomed by the Chosŏn government. Japan, however, was determined to take this opportunity to completely remove Chinese influence from Chosŏn, and so rejected the Chinese proposal. Instead, Japan suggested that the two powers push ahead with Chosŏn's internal reform. By making a proposal that would clearly be unacceptable to China, Japan's aim was to incite hostilities between the two powers. As expected, China rejected the offer, and a clash between China and Japan became inevitable.

The Sino-Japanese War began with a preemptive attack by Japanese warships against a Chinese troop convoy bringing reinforcements to Chosŏn at Asan Bay on 25 July 1894. At the same time fighting also broke out on land. Thereafter the Japanese won victories on land and sea, including a battle at Pyongyang in Sepember, humiliating China. The Japanese penetrated southern Manchuria, occupying Liaodong peninsula. With Japanese forces in a position to advance on the capital of Beijing, China sued for peace in early 1895, and on 17 April of that year, the Japanese-dictated Treaty of Shimonoseki was signed, specifically calling upon China to recognize Chosŏn's complete independence. This meant that Chosŏn would be separated from its centuries-old political relationship with China and placed under Japan's wing. The war and the Treaty of Shimonoseki clearly established Japanese dominance in East Asia and set the stage for the Japanese annexation of Chosŏn in 1910.

The Reform of 1894

The First Kabo Reform

During and after the Sino-Japanese War, Japan's position in Chosŏn was greatly enhanced, as the main obstacle, China, had been removed. On 10 June 1894, the very day when the Peace of Chŏnju was concluded between the Chosŏn government and the Tonghak army, Japanese troops entered Seoul. In July, after occupying the capital, Japan demanded by armed threat that Chosŏn carry out internal reform. But the Chosŏn government refused to accede to the demand and called for the withdrawal of Japanese forces. Japan responded by forcibly expelling the pro-Chinese faction, mostly the Min family, out of the government and restoring the reluctant Taewŏn'gun to power as a figurehead. Then it formed a new government mainly of pro-Japanese elements headed by Kim Hong-jip, which pressed ahead with the radical Kabo Kyŏngjang against the conservative opinions of the people.

On 27 July 1894 the new government established the Kun'guk kimuch'ŏ, or Deliberative Council, to carry out the reform program. Under the direction of Kim Hong-jip, this temporary and extraordinary governmental organ enacted 208 reform bills by December 1894, which has been called the First Kabo Reform. The reform program emphasized administrative and economic reforms. With regal power reduced, the power of the Ŭijŏngbu was strengthened under a prime minister, with two new ministries for foreign affairs and for agriculture and commerce added to the original six. Modeled on the Japanese system, the institution of office rank was modified. The Kungnae-bu, or Department of the Royal Household, was set up to deal only with matters concerning the palace and royal family, and the Kyŏngmuch'ŏng, or Agency of Police Affairs, was responsible for public safety. The traditional examination system, kwagŏ, was abolished and replaced by two styles of civil service examinations for both higher and lower positions. To demonstrate that Chosŏn had eliminated the traditional suzerain-subject relationship with China, the government ceased using the Chinese era name.

Economic reforms included placing all fiscal matters under the jurisdiction of the new T'akchi-bu, or Ministry of Finance. A new currency system was also instituted, based on the new silver standard. Japanese currency was permitted to circulate; embargoes on rice exports were permanently prohibited; and taxes and monthly salaries of government officials were paid in cash, not in kind.

The social reforms of 1894 included, first of all, the termination of the traditional class-status system, thus ending class distinctions between yangban and commoners; the yangban's pipe-smoking status was eliminated as well by banning the inordinately long pipes they smoked, sometimes one to three feet long (the longer the pipe, the greater the status). The system of slavery was abolished, as were the social and ritual distinctions between civil and military officials. Widows were allowed to remarry, and illegitimate sons now had the right to succeed their fathers. People were encouraged to replace traditional Korean attire with more practical clothing.

The Second Kabo Reform

As victory in the Sino-Japanese War became certain in late 1894, Japan appointed Inoue Kaoru, Japan's former foreign minister, as minister to Chosŏn and began to intrude in the kingdom's internal affairs. In November 1894 Inoue compelled the Taewŏn'gun, who bitterly opposed the reform program, to retire from politics. He also forced Kojong to appoint Pak Yŏng-hyo and Sŏ Kwang-bŏm, who were now home following a long exile in Japan, as cabinet members. In December Japanese advisers were employed in each government ministry. The so-called Second Kabo Reform took place from December 1894 to July 1895, during which time 213 reform bills were enacted. On 7 January 1895 Kojong, along with the Taewŏn'gun, the crown prince, and members of the royal family and officialdom, visited the *Chongmyo*, or Royal Ancestral Shrine, in Seoul and there, before the tablets of his ancestors, Kojong proclaimed the 14-article *Hongbŏm*, or Guiding Principles for the Nation, pledging to modernize his country.[6] Generally considered Korea's first constitution, the Hongbŏm was an embodiment of the Kabo Reform.

In this second reform program, the Ŭijŏngbu was renamed the Naegak, or Cabinet, which comprised seven ministries, including foreign affairs, home affairs, finance, justice, education, defense, and agriculture, commerce, and

industry. In June 1895 the former 8 provinces were reorganized into 23 prefectures, which were subdivided into 337 counties in order to better adapt local
administration to local conditions. The 23 prefectures were restructured into 13
provinces in August 1896. In the Ministry of Finance, 220 *chingsesa*, or taxation
agencies, were established nationwide, under the supervision of nine *kwansesa*,
or regional taxation agencies. An independent judiciary was created with district courts, open-port courts, circuit courts, and a Supreme Court. Military
reform was not enacted, however, as the man in charge of the mission, Pak
Yŏng-hyo, was suspected of treason and fled to Japan.

The Kabo Reform appeared to transform Chosŏn into a Western-style, modern nation, but the reform program actually facilitated Japanese penetration
into Chosŏn; the currency reform, in particular, was a major instrument in
furthering Japanese economic encroachments. Moreover, the Kabo Reform
did nothing to ensure the military manpower resources and new weaponry,
essential to the security of a modern state. The reform program also neither
considered the modern parliamentary system, the very basis of a representative
government, nor carried out land reform needed to relieve the peasants' suffering. The Kabo Reform was therefore ignored by the king and encountered bitter
opposition among the Korean people.

THE DOWNFALL OF CHOSŎN

The Murder of Queen Min

Because of Kojong's irresolution, Chosŏn at the time was virtually ruled by
Queen Min on behalf of the king. The Japanese attempted but failed to drive her
out of power, for she and the king turned to Russia for help to counterbalance
Japan's influence. Opportunely the "triple intervention" of Russia, France, and
Germany, in the spring of 1895, forced Japan to give back to China the Liaodong
peninsula, a major trophy Japan had won in the Sino-Japanese War. With this
blow to Japan's strength, Kojong and Queen Min seized a rare opportunity
to finally rid their country of Japanese control. But the pro-Japanese minister
Pak Yŏng-hyo got word of their intentions and plotted to depose Queen Min.
His conspiracy was detected in advance, however, and he and his pro-Japanese
cohorts were tossed out of the government, and once again Pak was exiled to
Japan. In August 1895 men of the pro-Russian faction such as Yi Pŏm-jin and Yi
Wan-yong joined the cabinet and succeeded in transforming the pro-Japanese
government into a government that was pro-Russian. The Japanese, who had

already lost the Liaodong peninsula to Russia, were now in danger of losing Chosŏn altogether.

Uneasy with Russia's increasing influence in Chosŏn, Japan saw the need to restore its control as a matter of life and death. The Japanese plotted to assassinate Queen Min, who led her kingdom's pro-Russian diplomacy, and mapped out a plan of operation code-named "fox hunting." At about the time the pro-Japanese elements were ousted from the government, Miura Goro was sent to Chosŏn as the new Japanese minister with a secret mission to assassinate Queen Min. As soon as he arrived in Seoul, Miura secretly organized a Japanese gangster-like group called *ronin*, and on 8 October 1895 the group launched a surprise attack on Queen Min's residence, the Kyŏngbok-kung palace. After killing the guards stationed at the palace gates, the attackers dashed into the queen's chamber. Although it is commonly believed that she was killed in her bedroom, she was actually dragged to a courtyard and publicly hacked to death with a sword. The queen's body was burned, and the remains were buried to destroy proof of the atrocity.

The Japanese government denied any involvement, but Miura had obviously orchestrated the murder. At the time Queen Min was slaughtered Japan had extraterritorial rights in Chosŏn but, fearing condemnation from abroad, the Japanese government recalled Miura and his 47 accomplices to stand trial in Japan. Even with the testimony of numerous eyewitnesses at trial, the assassins were found not guilty on the grounds of insufficient evidence.

Immediately after Queen Min's murder, a new, pro-Japanese cabinet was formed with Kim Hong-jip again appointed prime minister. The new government advanced far more radical reforms, passing more than 140 bills, labeled the Third Kabo Reform. The solar calendar was adopted, and on 26 October 1895 the government changed the date of 17 November 1895 (by the lunar calendar) to 1 January 1896 (by the solar calendar). A new system for naming eras was instituted, in which a single era name was to be used during each king's reign. From 1 January 1896 the era name *Kŏnyang,* or Lustrous Inauguration, was used for Kojong. Other important reform measures included the prescription of smallpox vaccinations for children; the establishment of an elementary school in Seoul; the initiation of postal service in Ch'ungju, Andong, Taegu, and Tongnae; and a reorganization of the military into assigning capital guards in Seoul and local garrison forces in the provinces. The most controversial reform, however, was the mandatory removal of males' traditional topknot, or *sangt'u.* Koreans traditionally never cut their hair for the duration of their lives out of respect for the Confucian belief that one's body and hair were given by one's parents. Violating this tradition, on 30 December 1895, at Japan's instigation, the government put out the order, enforced under protest, that all males cut off their topknot. In doing this, the Japanese tried to symbolically wipe out Korea's heritage, but the order aroused widespread popular resistance, with cries of "Cut off my head rather than my hair."

Japan's brutal assassination of Queen Min and the order for men to cut off their topknots finally led to a nationwide armed uprising against the Japanese by bands of civilian volunteers known as ŭibyŏng, or "righteous armies," mobilized by Confucian scholars such as Pak Chun-yŏng, Yu In-sŏk, Sŏ Sang-yŏl, Min Yong-ho, Kim Pok-han, Kwak Chong-sŏk, Yi Kang-nyŏn, and Ki U-man.

When the capital guards were deployed through the countryside to put down the ŭibyŏng forces, the pro-Russian faction in the government, led by Yi Pŏm-jin and Yi Wan-yong, secretly arranged with Karl Woeber, the Russian minister, to place Kojong under Russian protection and thus restore their power. First, Woeber brought 150 Russian sailors and a single cannon from Inch'ŏn to Seoul under the pretext of guarding the Russian legation. Then, at dawn on 11 February 1896, Kojong, seized with the fear of being killed by the Japanese, and the crown prince slipped away from the royal palace and made their way to the Russian legation, where the king remained as a guest for approximately a year. Kojong had chosen the lesser of the two evils, Russia over Japan. After an arrest warrant was issued for men of the pro-Japanese faction, Kim Hong-jip, Chŏng Pyŏng-ha, and Ŏ Yun-jung were killed by angry mobs, but Yu Kil-chun and others fled to Japan. A new pro-Russian cabinet was formed with no trace of the pro-Japanese element. Japan believed that it was not yet prepared for a final showdown with Russia to decide Chosŏn's fate.

While Kojong was in the Russian legation for almost a year, the Chosŏn government was under strong Russian influence, with Russian advisers and military instructors having replaced their Japanese counterparts. Economic concessions were first given to Russia and then to other nations. Foreign powers were now intent on the economic exploitation of Korean natural resources.

The Proclamation of the "Taehan Cheguk"

The Korean people as a whole condemned King Kojong's flight to the Russian legation and called upon him to return to his palace. Yielding to this pressure, Kojong moved back to the Kyŏngun-gung palace (today the Tŏksu-gung palace) on 20 February 1897. He chose the Kyŏngun-gung rather than the Kyŏngbok-kung because he thought the new residence neighbored Russian, American, and other Western legations that could better protect him against a Japanese threat.

After returning to his palace, Kojong nullified some reform measures enacted by the former pro-Japanese cabinet, including, on 12 August 1897, the order for males to cut their topknots. Two days later he declared the era name to be *Kwangmu*, or Shining Warrior, making clear his intentions to enhance national prosperity and defense. Then, feeling the need to increase his kingdom's status and reinforce national integrity, on 11 October 1897 Kojong proclaimed to the nation and the world the establishment of the *Taehan cheguk*, or Great Han Empire, whence comes the name *Taehan min'guk* of the present-day Republic of Korea. Taehan refers to the integration of the former three Han federations (Mahan, Chinhan, and Pyŏnhan) or three kingdoms (Koguryŏ, Paekche, and Silla). The next day he ascended the imperial throne and, outwardly, the new Korea assumed the form of an independent, imperial state. But Korean realities had not changed. Russian influence was still dominant, and Western powers were heavily engaged in wringing economic concessions from Chosŏn.

The Activities of the Independence Club

Sensing that Chosŏn was exposed to ruthless aggression by foreign powers, many Koreans were prepared to fight to preserve their country's sovereignty and territorial integrity. A new intellectual class that favored Western liberalism and vowed to secure the nation's independence and people's rights formed a political organization called the Tongnip hyŏphoe, or Independence Club, which was actually founded by Sŏ Chae-p'il (Philip Jaisohn) on 2 July 1896. Sŏ Chae-p'il had participated in the abortive coup of 1884, voluntarily sought exile in Japan and then the United States, and, upon returning to Chosŏn in January 1896, resumed leadership of the nation's modern reform movement. Appointed as a consultant to the Privy Council, he broadened his contacts with prominent government leaders, and on 7 April 1896 he launched the newspaper *Tongnip sinmun*, or *Independence Newspaper*, which was printed entirely in han'gŭl to increase readership among the general populace. The *Tongnip sinmun* called on the nation to devote itself to preserving sovereignty and promoting the public good. It praised Western liberal ideas, including civil rights, and did its utmost to introduce modern science and the perspectives of the Western world. It grew rapidly from an initial circulation of 300 readers to 3,000. Sŏ Chae-p'il demanded that the government preserve national sovereignty by repelling growing foreign influence, and he awakened the people to the urgent needs of the day—eliminating corruption, extending opportunities for education, securing sovereignty, and promoting civil rights. The "independence" advocated by the newspaper was independence from China. After the Independence Club was established in July 1896, the newspaper served to propagate the new organization's cause.

The Independence Club started as a social organization to raise funds to erect the *Tongnimmun*, or Independence Gate, on the recently demolished site of the *Yŏngŭnmun*, or Gate of Welcoming Imperial Grace, where Chinese envoys had been greeted. The funds were also used to renovate the *Mohwagwan*, or Hall of Cherishing China, where Chinese emissaries had been entertained, and which was then renamed the *Tongnipkwan*, or Independence Hall. The campaign was well received by the entire population, including the royal family and high officials. With a large sum of money donated by the crown prince, the ceremony of laying the cornerstone of Independence Gate was held in November 1896 (and construction was completed in November 1897), and Independence Hall, which would be used as the club's office, was completed in May 1897.

By the time the Great Han Empire was inaugurated in October 1897, the Independence Club had been gradually transformed into an enlightenment organization, with the participation of Yun Ch'i-ho and Yi Sang-jae, both of whom were active in the country's diplomatic affairs, as well as Namgung Ŏk, Chŏng Kyo, and Na Su-yŏn, men in middle-level government officialdom, and the ordinary citizens of Seoul. From February 1898 on, as an increasing number of citizens joined its ranks, the nature of the club again became political. By October 1898 the club had some 4,000 members, and its leadership included representatives of the new intellectuals who were inspired by Western thought such as Sŏ Chae-p'il, Yun Ch'i-ho, and Yi Sang-jae. Next in importance were those who, like Namgung Ŏk and Chŏng Kyo, were indoctrinated with the thinking of "tongdo sŏgi."

At its zenith, the Independence Club convened a mass meeting of officials and the people of Seoul at the Chongno intersection on 29 October 1898. With high officials such as Pak Chŏng-yang and a mix of people including intellectuals, students, women, monks, and even paekchŏng outcasts in attendance, the assemblage resolved to present six proposals to the king, essentially calling for a constitutional monarchy and the rule of law. The next day Kojong promised to put the proposals into effect by enacting a law converting the Privy Council into a parliamentary assembly, half of whose 50 councilors would be elected by the Independence Club. But this was only a delaying tactic to save time while the king readied himself for suppressive countermeasures. Soon the government charged that the Independence Club aimed to replace the monarchy with a republic headed by an elected president. Kojong received a false briefing from Cho Pyŏng-sik, a high-ranking official who was critical of the Independence Club, indicating that a republic would be established, with Pak Chŏng-yang as president, Yun Ch'i-ho as vice-president, and members of the Club as cabinet members. The king promptly ordered the Club to be dissolved and its supportive newspaper, the *Tongnip sinmun*, suspended, and at the same time arrested 17 leaders, including the Club's president, Yi Sang-jae. Sŏ Chae-p'il, who was hated by those in power, had already decided to depart for the United States. Independence Club members immediately campaigned vigorously to protest the government's actions, holding continual mass meetings day after day.

At a crucial moment, in late November 1898, the government mobilized 2,000 members of the Hwangguk hyŏphoe, or Imperial Association, a makeshift body organized by thugs from the peddler guild as a government tool to violently suppress the demonstrators. In December 1898 the government called in troops to forcibly break up protest meetings. Finally, the activities of the Independence Club came to an end.

Because the Independence Club had hastily moved to install a constitutional monarchy, its efforts to carry out fundamental reform failed to win public backing from a still conservative citizenry. But the club's efforts did contribute to securing Chosŏn's independence and sovereignty by rejecting Russian influences: Russian military instructors and financial advisers were recalled, the Russo-Chosŏn Bank was forced to close, and Kojong left the Russian legation after a one-year stay and returned to his palace.

The Russo-Japanese War

Once Kojong had returned to his palace in February 1897, Japan quickly resumed its influence in Chosŏn and competed with Russia for domination over the kingdom. At first the two powers sought to reach an accommodation; Russia and Japan secretly negotiated the possible division of Chosŏn between themselves. In May 1896, during the high tide of Russian influence, Japan proposed that Chosŏn be divided along the 38th parallel. Russia rejected this partition, still hoping to gain control of the entire peninsula. In March 1900 Russia leased land at Masan, Kyŏngsang province, with the intention of building an ice-free port. Three years later, in May 1903 a combined force of Russian troops and mounted bandits in Manchuria forcibly occupied Yongamp'o at the estuary of the Yalu River to secure a bridgehead in Chosŏn, causing Japan grave concern. When Japan regained ascendancy, in December 1903, Russia sought an agreement with Japan to create a neutral, arms-free zone in Chosŏn territory north of the 39th parallel while recognizing Japan's special interests south of that line. Japan rejected the plan.

Finally, in early February 1904, the temporary calm that had settled over Chosŏn gave way to a great showdown between Japan and Russia. Neither power would yield to the other, which brought negotiations for compromise to a deadlock. With both powers seeking exclusive economic and military control in Chosŏn and Manchuria, a war between the two was inevitable. Although the major battles took place outside Chosŏn, the Russo-Japanese War had a profound impact on the fate of Chosŏn and its people. Here it is important to examine the series of events that led up to that decisive war between Japan and Russia.

In 1895 Japan had won the Sino-Japanese War decisively, but the triple intervention of Russia, Germany, and France had forced it to give up many of the spoils gained in the Treaty of Shimonoseki. In 1896 Russia signed a treaty with China to extend its trans-Siberian railway across China's Manchurian provinces. In 1900, in response to the Boxer Rebellion in China, the Russians occupied Manchuria and then refused to withdraw. In January 1902, determined to prevent another European revision if it went to war again, Japan signed an alliance with Great Britain. By the terms of the treaty that was aimed at containing the Russian threat, Japan recognized British rights and interests in China in exchange for Great Britain's acknowledgment of Japan's special interests in Chosŏn. If one of them became involved in a war with another power in East Asia, the other would remain neutral. If one of them found itself at war with more than one enemy, however, the other would fight on its behalf. Thus the Anglo-Japanese Alliance meant that when the Russo-Japanese War began, Japan could have greater assurance that France would not intervene on behalf of its Russian ally for fear of Britain coming to the aid of Japan. Emboldened by the Anglo-Japanese Alliance, Japan launched a surprise attack on Russian naval forces at Port Arthur on the tip of the Liaodong peninsula on 10 February 1904, heralding the outbreak of the Russo-Japanese War.

One month earlier, as war between Japan and Russia became imminent, Chosŏn had formally proclaimed its neutrality. Japan ignored this, however, and sent troops into Seoul to occupy a number of government buildings. On 23 February, by threat of force, Japan compelled Chosŏn to sign a protocol seriously infringing on the latter's sovereignty. Under the cloak of a rhetorical provision that Japan would respect Chosŏn's independence and territorial integrity, Japan could interfere in Chosŏn's internal affairs and occupy strategic points throughout the country. On 18 May 1904 Chosŏn was forced to declare that all its agreements with Russia were void. Japan now started construction on the Seoul-Pusan and Seoul-Sinŭiju railroads necessary to wage war with Russia. As the Japanese requisitioned Korean lands and labor, the Korean people violently protested. In June Japan demanded the right to open up all state-owned uncultivated lands, amounting to one-third of Chosŏn's entire territory, to development by Japanese colonists. In the face of the Koreans' stiff opposition, however, Japan dropped its demand.

To further interfere with Chosŏn's internal administration, on 21 August 1904 Japan forced Chosŏn to sign a new agreement stating that foreign advisers should be installed in strategic government ministries. By its terms, Chosŏn agreed to employ a Japanese financial adviser named by Japan and to follow his advice in all matters related to fiscal administration. A foreign affairs adviser recommended by Japan was also to be hired to handle all diplomatic affairs. Megata Tanetaro, a high-ranking official of the Japanese Ministry of Finance, was named as the financial adviser, and an American, Durham W. Stevens, was selected as the foreign affairs adviser. Megata assumed full authority over Chosŏn's financial administration and immediately devalued the Chosŏn currency, absorbing it into the Japanese monetary system. Stevens served as the "hands and feet" of the Japanese government between 1904 and 1907. When he went to the United States to justify and propagate Japanese control of Chosŏn in March 1908, he was assassinated in San Francisco by two Korean expatriates, Chŏn Myŏng-un and Chang In-hwan. Later the Chosŏn government was forced to employ four additional advisers not stipulated in the agreement: an adviser in the Ministry of Defense, a police adviser, an adviser on royal household affairs, and an adviser in the Ministry of Education. In April 1905 Japan took control of postal, telegraph, and telephone services in Chosŏn. Although Japan had created a "government by advisers" in Chosŏn, the actual administrative authority was completely in Japanese hands, and Chosŏn's sovereignty and independence were in name only.

In a series of land and naval engagements, Japan scored startling victories against Russia. The Japanese navy destroyed the Russian Baltic fleet at the Tsushima Strait in May 1905. Great Britain helped Japan by blocking the passage of the Russian fleet at the Suez Canal, which forced the Baltic fleet to circle the African continent, sapping its fighting power. Despite their victories, the financially and militarily overextended Japanese were poorly positioned to carry out a lengthy war. The war nearly bankrupted Japan, while, on the Russian side, popular discontent and revolutionary outbreaks threatened the government's very survival. Eventually, as the war dragged on, the United States stepped in to mediate the conflict. President Theodore Roosevelt, responding to a Japanese request, was eager to see a settlement that would restore peace and the balance of power in East Asia. Offering to be a mediator, he invited Japanese and Russian diplomats to Portsmouth, New Hampshire, for negotiations. Ultimately, a peace was reached, the Treaty of Portsmouth, that signaled victory for Japan and defeat for Russia.

Shortly before the final discussions in Portsmouth were to begin, Roosevelt dispatched his Secretary of War, William Howard Taft, to the Philippines by way of Japan. During his stopover in Tokyo, Taft spoke with Japanese Prime Minister Katsura Taro on 29 July 1905 and reached a secret understanding that would become known as the Taft-Katsura Memorandum: the United States would recognize Japan's paramount interests in Chosŏn in return for Japan's recognition of U.S. special interests in the Philippines. Hence the United States was prepared to sacrifice Chosŏn's independence to strengthen its position in the Philippines. The United States was not alone; on 12 August 1905 Great Britain also agreed to recognize Japan's special interests in Chosŏn. The Treaty of Portsmouth was signed on 5 September 1905, officially ending the Russo-Japanese War. As a result, Japanese rights in Manchuria were extended to include the lease of Port Arthur and Darian and their adjacent territories and the lease of the Changchun–Port Arthur Railroad with all its branches. The southern half of Sakhalin and all the islands adjacent to it (the Kuril Islands) were ceded to Japan. The most important terms in the treaty were Russia's acknowledgment that Japan possessed predominant political, military, and economic interests in Chosŏn, and Russia's pledge not to prevent Japan from taking whatever actions it deemed necessary for the direction, protection, and supervision of Chosŏn. Japan finally succeeded in removing the last threat posed by Russia to its control of Chosŏn. Soon after the Treaty of Portsmouth was signed, Kojong quietly dispatched the American Homer B. Hulbert, a longtime friend of Chosŏn, to the United States to plead the Chosŏn case to President Roosevelt. The plea fell on deaf ears. Now Chosŏn was left to the mercy of Japan.

The Treaty of 1905

Having won firm recognition from Russia, Great Britain, and the United States of its paramount interests in Chosŏn, Japan immediately proceeded to make the kingdom a protectorate, with a semi-colonial government. Aware of the intense anti-Japanese feelings among the Korean people, Japan first employed its front organization in Chosŏn, the Ilchinhoe, or Integration Promotion Society, to justify the need for a protectorate treaty and spread the lie that the Koreans, not the Japanese, demanded a protectorate status. The Ilchinhoe was formed and headed by Song Pyŏng-jun, an interpreter for the Japanese army in Seoul, and Yi Yong-gu, a Tonghak apostate. It was supported financially by the Japanese and directed by Japanese advisers. Japan's attempt to mislead the Korean people through this pro-Japanese body was foiled by the patriotic activities of several anti-Japanese organizations, which condemned the Ilchinhoe's treachery to the nation, and by the Confucian literati who filed protests against Japan's scheme to establish a protectorate. In response, Japan sent its elder politician, Ito Hirobumi, to force the protectorate treaty on Chosŏn. Ito was assisted by Hayashi Gonsuke, the Japanese minister to Chosŏn, and Hasegawa Yoshimichi, commander of Japanese forces in Chosŏn. On 17 November 1905 Ito and Hayashi entered Kojong's palace with Japanese troops and forced the king and his eight ministers into a meeting to accept the treaty that Japan had drawn up. Kojong entrusted each minister with the power to evaluate the fateful treaty. Prime Minister Han Kyu-sŏl violently opposed the treaty and was supported by Minister of Finance Min Yŏng-gi and Minister of Justice Yi Ha-yŏng. Supporters included Minister of Education Yi Wan-yong, Minister of Defense Yi Kŭn-t'aek, Minister of Home Affairs Yi Chi-yong, Minister of Foreign Affairs Pak Che-sun, and Minister of Agriculture, Commerce, and Industry Kwŏn Chung-hyŏn. The supporters have been recorded in history as the "Five National Traitors of 1905." Soon Japanese soldiers went to the Foreign Ministry to deliver the seal of the Minister of Foreign Affairs so that the Japanese themselves could affix it to the treaty. Reportedly Kojong refused to sign the treaty to the end. As the king had the right to enter into a treaty with foreign nations, the protectorate treaty that did not obtain his sanction was legally invalid. The Japanese insisted it was valid, however. Referred to in English as the Protectorate Treaty, the Koreans simply call it the Treaty of 1905. The treaty created the Office of the Resident-General and invested it with full authority over Chosŏn's diplomacy and foreign affairs, eliminating almost all aspects of Chosŏn's sovereignty.[7] Ito

Hirobumi, the chief mastermind of Japanese imperialism in Chosŏn, became the first Resident-General in March 1906. He was shot and killed on 26 October 1909 by a Korean, An Chung-gŭn, at the Harbin railroad station in Manchuria while inspecting Russian troops.The Treaty of 1905 triggered bitter anger and opposition from the Korean people in general. In his 20 November 1905 editorial, "Siirya pangsŏng taegok," or Today We Cry Out in Great Lamentation, in the *Taehan maeil sinbo,* or Great Korea Daily News, Chang Chi-yŏn inflamed the Koreans' resentment of the treaty. Countless memorials, including that of the former prime minister Han Kyu-sŏl, denouncing Japanese aggression were presented to the king. In his indignation and grief, Min Yŏng-hwan, military aide-de-camp to Kojong, left an impassioned testament to the nation and took his own life. Many other outraged officials followed suit including Cho Pyŏng-se, a former left state councilor; Hong Man-sik, a former vice minister; and Song Pyŏng-sŏn, a former inspector-general. At the same time ŭibyŏng militia forces revolted throughout the country against Japan's ruthless aggression. Min Chong-sik and his some 1,000-man army killed more than 100 Japanese troops, seizing Hongsŏng in Ch'ungch'ŏng province. Ch'oe Ik-hyŏn and Im Pyŏng-ch'an raised armed forces at T'aein, Chŏlla province, but they were defeated by the Japanese and sent into banishment on the Japanese island of Tsushima. Sin Tol-sŏk's forces grew into more than 3,000 men and took action in Kyŏngsang and Kangwŏn provinces. But none of these efforts could halt Japan's domination of Chosŏn.

The Japanese Annexation of Chosŏn

In April 1907, as a last-ditch effort to save his country's independence, Kojong dispatched secret envoys to the Second World Peace Conference, to be held in June, in the Hague, the Netherlands. The envoys would plead to the world body that Chosŏn should regain independence, as Japan had forced the Treaty of 1905 on the kingdom. Yi Chun and Yi Sang-sŏl, who were joined by Yi Wi-jong in St. Petersburg, Russia, carried Kojong's sealed letter to the conference. Upon their arrival, however, the Japanese delegates fiercely lobbied to obstruct the envoys' admittance, and the conference rejected Chosŏn's delegates on the grounds that Chosŏn did not have authority over its own foreign affairs. The three Chosŏn envoys then visited the representatives of each country and the press club, asking for their help in the Chosŏn cause. On 8 July Yi Wi-jong spoke before an international meeting of journalists held at the same time in the Hague, assailing Japanese aggression in Chosŏn and seeking international support for the restoration of its sovereignty, but all to no avail. The mission failed. Overwrought with grief, Yi Chun died in the city. Because Chosŏn lacked economic and military strength to preserve its sovereignty, the international effort was ineffective.

Using this incident as a pretext, Japan further strengthened its grip on Chosŏn, forcing the recalcitrant Kojong to abdicate in favor of his son. On 20 July 1907 Sunjong ascended the throne, and his reign was titled *Yunghŭi*, or Abundant Prosperity. The abdication of Kojong further enraged the already stricken people, driving them into a series of daily massive protest demonstrations. The Koreans destroyed the building housing the *Kŭngmin sinbo*, or National News, the official voice of the pro-Japanese Ilchinhoe, and attacked the Japanese everywhere.

Immediately after Sunjong's accession to the throne, on 24 July, the Seven-Article Treaty of 1907 was signed authorizing the Japanese Resident-General to interfere in all matters of internal administration. By its terms, the Chosŏn government was required to receive his prior consent in legislative enactments, major administrative measures, and the appointment and dismissal of high officials. As it was mandatory to appoint Japanese who were recommended by the Resident-General, a number of Japanese officials were named as vice minister of each ministry. Now Japan changed its previous method of governing through advisers to governing by vice ministers, and so the Japanese held the real power. On the same day Japan enacted a law regarding printed news, strictly censoring the anti-Japanese press.

A week later, on 31 July, Japan dissolved the entire remaining Chosŏn army units totaling 8,800 men, reducing Chosŏn to a mere puppet. Courts, prisons, and the police also fell into Japanese hands. The day after the army was disbanded, a battalion commander, Pak Sŭng-hwan, in mortification, took his own life. Soon the ŭibyŏng forces came together to wage an armed struggle against the Japanese. Previously the main component of the volunteer forces had been the peasantry under the leadership of the Confucian literati. This time, however, soldiers from the disbanded Chosŏn army joined the peasant fighters, enhancing the combat effectiveness of these irregular units. Immediately after the Chosŏn army was forced to disband, guard units in Seoul engaged in street fighting with Japanese troops, and when their ammunition and supplies ran out, they retreated into the countryside to join the ŭibyŏng forces. Among the former Chosŏn army units, the provincial garrison troops at Wŏnju, Kangwŏn province, and a detachment force on Kanghwa-do engaged in the fiercest battles to date with the Japanese. The forces at Wŏnju, in particular, under the leader-ship of Min Kŭng-ho and Kim Tŏk-che, enjoyed a series of victories against Japanese troops in central Chosŏn. Along with 600-man ŭibyŏng groups, the former contingents on Kanghwa-do, commanded by Chi Hong-yun and Yu Myŏng-gyu, extended their activities to Kyŏnggi and Hwanghae provinces. Besides these former armed forces, Hŏ Wi led his volunteers in Kyŏnggi and Hwanghae provinces, while Yi In-yŏng fought in Kangwŏn province and Yi Kang-nyŏn operated in the Kangwŏn and northern Kyŏngsang area. Sin Tol-sŏk was still actively fighting in eastern Kyŏngsang region.

At one point these ŭibyŏng groups gathered a united force to drive into Seoul, attack the Japanese residency-general headquarters there, and regain Chosŏn's sovereignty. In the winter of 1907 more than 10,000 ŭibyŏng men, from all over the country, concentrated their forces at Yŏju, near the capital. In January 1908 a 300-man advance unit, commanded by Hŏ Wi, marched on the Japanese positions within eight miles of Seoul's East Gate, but their advance was halted by enemy troops. After the drive on Seoul failed, ŭibyŏng forces dispersed throughout the country to independently wage guerrilla warfare.

Although the volunteer forces were active mainly in Kyŏngsang, Kangwŏn, Kyŏnggi, Hwanghae, and Chŏlla provinces, their operations extended over almost the entire country. The activity of the ŭibyŏng armies peaked in 1908, and then declined. Still, the ŭibyŏng became the main resistance force in all subsequent struggles against the Japanese. After the Japanese annexation of Chosŏn, in August 1910, these irregular volunteers shifted their operations to Manchuria and the Russian Maritime Province, and continued to harass the Japanese, demonstrating the indomitable will of the Koreans to resist Japanese colonialism.

Along with these armed struggles, the Koreans engaged in patriotic enlight-enment activities, where men of property, intellectuals, former officials, and reform-minded Confucian scholars organized educational and reform move-ments to restore their country's sovereignty. They sought to promote public education and develop the nation's industries to enhance Korea's cultural and economic strength. They also established many political and social organiza-tions, and promoted various programs for enlightening the Korean people.

The first such program was the Poanhoe, or Preservation Society, formed by Song Su-man and Sin Sang-jin in 1904. When Japan attempted to seize Chosŏn's uncultivated land, the Society aroused public opposition and succeeded in thwarting the Japanese scheme. As a result, it was dissolved under Japanese pressure. In 1905 Yun Hyo-jŏng, Yi Chun, Yang Han-muk, and others formed the Hŏnjŏngyŏn'guhoe, or Society for the Study of Constitutional Government, hoping to establish a constitutional government, but it, too, was forced to disband in compliance with a Japanese ban on public political assembly after the inauguration of the residency-general. The successor to the constitutional movement was the Taehan chaganghoe, or Great Korea Self-Strengthening Society, formed by Yun Hyo-jŏng, Chang Chi-yŏn, Sim Ŭi-sŏng, and others in April 1906. This organization aroused Korean opposition to Japanese demands for Kojong's abdication, and, consequently, it was forcibly dissolved by the residency-general in July 1907. It reappeared later as the Taehan hyŏphoe, or Great Korea Association.

Harsh Japanese suppression led the Koreans to form a sizable clandestine organization, the Sinminhoe, or New People's Association, in November 1907, created by businessmen, intellectuals, military men, religious men, and journalists, including An Ch'ang-ho, Yang Ki-t'ak, Yi Tong-hwi, Yi Kap, and Yi Sŭng-hun. It sought to develop Korean industry by establishing a ceramic factory in Pyongyang, promote Korean education by establishing schools such as the Taesŏng School in Pyongyang and the Osan School in Chŏngju, P'yŏngan province, and promote Korean public awareness by operating bookstores such as the T'aegŭk bookstore in Taegu. At the same time the organization prepared for armed operations against the Japanese. Soon, however, a sharp conflict over the body's policies developed between moderates such as An Ch'ang-ho, who stressed self-strengthening, and hard-liners such as Yi Tong-hwi, who favored armed struggle. After the Japanese annexation of Chosŏn, An Ch'ang-ho traveled to the United States to continue his cultural and educational enlightenment movement, and Yi Tong-hwi migrated to Manchuria to wage an armed struggle.

In late January 1907 a campaign was launched among the Koreans to repay the huge national debt that the government owed to Japan. The leaders of this campaign worried that this immense debt threatened the nation's independence and sovereignty. Although the movement to redeem the national debt was initiated by men from Taegu, such as Sŏ Sang-don and Kim Kwang-je, it soon spread nationwide. A fund-raising campaign was launched by the nationalistic press, including the *Taehan maeil sinbo*, the *Cheguk sinmun*, or Imperial Newspaper, the *Hwangsŏng sinmun*, or Capital Newspaper, and the *Mansebo*, or Long Live Newspaper. Responding to this nationalistic, patriotic cause, men participated in a no-smoking movement, and women and girls sold their gold ornamental hairpins and rings. The Japanese saw that this campaign threatened their efforts to colonize Chosŏn, and they made every effort to thwart it. After falsely charging Yang Ki-t'ak, editor of the *Taehan maeil sinbo*, with embezzlement of contributions entrusted to the newspaper, the movement to repay the national debt came to an end.

Meanwhile, in May 1910, the Japanese Minister of the Army Terauchi Masatake became the new Resident-General, charged with finalizing Japanese control over Chosŏn by concluding the Treaty of Annexation with the powerless Chosŏn government. Japan disguised its usurpation of Chosŏn's sovereignty as a "duty" to promote the Korean people's welfare and maintain peace in East Asia. The annexation treaty was formally concluded on 22 August 1910. A week later, on 29 August 1910, Sunjong yielded the throne, and Chosŏn became a colony of Japan. The Korean people, except for a small opportunistic minority, deeply resented Japan's domination of their country, and strong Korean resistance to the annexation continued throughout the early years of colonization.

The long rule of the Chosŏn dynasty, spanning 518 years, left a deep impression on the national attitudes and behavior of modern Koreans. Confucian philosophy, ethics, and government became intrinsic to the Korean culture. Indeed, as seen in North Korea's "Kim dynasty," whose ruling ideology is based in part on Chosŏn's Confucianism, the traditional political and social order of the Chosŏn dynasty became the foundation upon which modern Korea has been built.

8

THE PERIOD OF JAPANESE
COLONIAL RULE
(1910–1945)

GOVERNMENT BY THE BAYONET AND
THE MARCH FIRST MOVEMENT

The Nature of Colonial Rule

THE FATEFUL KOREAN-JAPANESE ANNEXATION TREATY not only culminated the process of Japan's domination of Korea but heralded the demise of the Chosŏn dynasty. Despite the people's resentment and bitter opposition, Korea had become a colony of the Japanese empire. Following annexation, the Japanese began a 35-year period of colonial rule that profoundly affected the manner in which modern Korea took shape.

Japanese colonial rule in Korea was unusually harsh and destructive, producing virtually no benefit for the Korean people. It was severely systemic and pervasive, an extension of ingrained feudal attitudes that even today influence the behavior of the Japanese toward one another. Having assigned the Koreans an inferior status, Japanese colonial administrators, with unlimited zeal, naturally applied the hierarchical standards of their own society to the Koreans. Japan built huge bureaucracies in Korea, all of them highly centralized and too big by colonial standards. In the mid-1930s, in India, some 12,000 British governed 340 million Indians (a ratio of 1 to 28,000), whereas in Korea approximately 52,000 Japanese ruled 22 million Koreans (1 to 420). The Koreans could not escape the tight control of a police state, where their political suppression by Japan was thorough and far-reaching. Free speech, free press, suffrage, and representative government were totally absent. Korea escaped the harsh Japanese colonial rule only in August 1945, when Japan yielded to the U.S. and Soviet onslaught that brought an end to World War II.

In the first decade of colonial rule, the Japanese relied on a heavy-handed "military policy," mainly because of the fierce Korean resistance to Japanese control in the period from 1905 to 1910. Even schoolteachers wore uniforms and carried swords to strike terror into Korean hearts, which had been unheard of in colonial history. As a civilian-led government with comparatively liberal political orientations was formed in Japan proper in the early 1920s, these excesses and abuses were curbed somewhat. At this juncture, the Koreans were allowed to publish their own newspapers and organize themselves politically and intellectually. The ensuing intellectual and social ferment of the 1920s marked a seminal period in modern Korean history. Many developments of that time, including the organization of labor unions and other social and economic movements, exerted their influence into the post-liberation period. But when illiberal forces represented by the military reasserted themselves in the mid-1920s, colonial rule became harsh once again. This trend was further strengthened during the 1930s and 1940s.[1] All of Korea was totally mobilized for the Japanese invasion and occupation of China, which expanded into the Pacific, forcing the Koreans to assimilate even more as Japanese within their own country.

The objective of the Japanese colonial administration was always to rule and exploit the colony to serve only Japanese interests. The spearhead of Japanese rule in Korea, and at the apex of a highly authoritarian, centralized government structure, was the Office of the Government-General, formerly the Office of the Resident-General. The governor-general, appointed by the Japanese emperor from among the highest echelons of the Imperial Japanese Army's active list, was independent of the Japanese cabinet.[2] He enjoyed almost complete freedom in the colonial administration. Under his command were five ministries—Secretariat; General Affairs; Internal Affairs; Finance, Agriculture, Commerce, and Industry; and Administration of Justice—which in turn had subordinate agencies including the Interrogation Bureau, the Bureau of the Superintendent-General of Police Affairs, the Railroad Bureau, the Communications Bureau, the Monopoly Bureau, and the Temporary Land Survey Bureau, as well as courts and prisons. The colony was divided into 13 provinces, locally administered, and each was subdivided into *pu* (cities) and counties (made up of townships). The Japanese established a military police system, in which the police exercised vast powers in peacetime as well as in civil administration and judicial affairs. Alarmed at the intense Korean resistance to colonial rule, Japan stationed two army divisions throughout the colony, including in Seoul. Virtually all key positions, both in the government and in major business and financial enterprises, were staffed by the Japanese. Landholding was drastically "reformed," and the Japanese appropriated large agricultural tracts for themselves. Agricultural and industrial production in Korea was directed only to serve the needs of Japan, and enough food was produced for all purposes.

The Koreans, as subjects of the Japanese emperor, could enjoy, in theory, the same status as the Japanese, but in practice Japan treated the Koreans as an inferior and conquered people. The Government-General enacted laws legalizing racial discrimination against the Koreans, making them second-class citizens. Education served as a means of justifying such racism. The Japanese monopolized all supervisory and managerial positions in the government, the police, and the factories, and restricted Koreans to clerical positions. A Korean worker labored much longer hours and received half the wages paid to a Japanese worker.

The average Japanese, whether in Korea or Japan proper, perceived Koreans as inferior and therefore treated them with contempt and cruelty. The Koreans, however, never considered the Japanese to be superior to them; indeed, they viewed themselves as culturally superior to the Japanese. Thus, from start to finish, the Koreans challenged the legitimacy of Japanese colonialism, which resulted in their never-ending resistance to Japanese colonial rule.

Although colonial Korea was generally created to satisfy Japan's political and economic ambitions, at the same time Japan did play a role in Korea's modernization. Before 1900 Korea had a relatively backward agricultural economy. Following the annexation of Korea in 1910, Japan brought modern industrial capitalism to its colony, which industrialized and modernized Korea's once semi-feudalistic agrarian society. Most Koreans have claimed that the benefits of economic growth achieved in the colonial period, if any, went entirely to Japan and that Korea would have developed economically without Japanese help. Some foreign observers argue, however, that remarkable improvements were achieved in colonial Korea, including a state-led economy characterized by strong economic guidance by the administration; the forceful opening of industry and markets, domestic as well as foreign; and the repression of organized labor. They further insist that economic development of the two Koreas in the post-liberation period was modeled on this colonial experience.[3] In particular, South Korean patterns of economic development after the early 1960s under President Park Chung-hee, a former military officer in the Japanese Imperial Army, closely followed the methodology introduced by the Japanese 50 years earlier—industrialization from above using a strong bureaucracy that formulated and implemented economic plans and policies. Simply put, Japan's role in colonial Korea's modernization and development still remains controversial.

Dispossessing the Koreans of Their Farmland

After depriving the Koreans of sovereignty and political independence, Japan systematically integrated Korea's economy into its colonial structure. In the process, the Koreans lost their farmland and other economic resources and accompanying opportunities to improve their economic and social conditions. Further, by introducing "modernization" in economic and social spheres, Japan seriously disrupted traditional economic and social structures.

Already in 1907, before annexation, the Japanese attempted to seize large tracts of Korean land, amounting to one-third of the nation's entire land, under the pretext of reclaiming uncultivated lands. But Japan withdrew its demand following stiff Korean opposition. After annexation, the Japanese Government-General confiscated public land amounting to 25,800 *chŏngbo*, or 66,500 acres, of farmland and 19,400 chŏngbo, or 48,500 acres, of forest land, most of it actually consisting of people's land, which, under nominal state ownership, was designed to escape heavy taxes and usurpation.

After taking over large tracts of public land without compensation, the Japanese Government-General embarked on a land survey for more effective control over Korean farmland. This survey would reestablish ownership based on written proof. To clarify, register, and classify ownership of farmland, the Government-General established the Temporary Land Survey Bureau in 1910. It began the land survey in August 1912 and required landowners to classify their holdings according to ownership, type, and dimensions.

Many Koreans, however, were negligent about registering their land. Because of previous inadequate land surveys, they were accustomed to holding their farmland without legal proof of ownership and unaccustomed to strict registration proceedings. Their antipathy to Japan and purposeful misinformation also interfered with their registering their land. As ownership was denied to those who could not provide written documentation, all those who failed to register by a set date lost their landholdings.

Because of the absence of registrants, land that had formerly been allocated to post stations and military forts in the border regions, amounting to 132,633 chŏngbo, or 331,583 acres, and land that had belonged to clans rather than individuals, became the property of the Government-General. Many Korean farmers who protested the Japanese confiscation were totally ignored. On the other hand, some Koreans, particularly those of the former yangban and bureaucratic classes, were allowed to establish titles to farmland. In this way, the yangban class was transformed into a new landlord class.

The land survey and registration conducted under the cloak of establishing modern ownership of farmland enabled the Japanese to possess large amounts of Korean farmland. By November 1918, when the land survey was completed, the Government-General became Korea's largest landowner. By 1930 the combined total of agricultural and forest land held by the Government-General amounted to 8.88 million chŏngbo, or 22.2 million acres, some 40 percent of Korea's total land area. The Government-General sold this confiscated land at a reduced price or without compensation to Japanese land companies such as the Oriental Development Company, created in 1908 as a semiofficial colonization organ, and to Japanese immigrants. The land, rather than the uncertain annual harvest, became the basis of a land tax system, which was implemented in 1914. As a result, compared to the land tax in 1911, it doubled in 1919. By 1930 the land tax comprised 45 percent of annual government revenues.

Foreign observers argue that most of the land falling into Japanese hands was not formerly held by individual Korean farmers but public land.[4] Because public land confiscated by the Government-General was private land in that heredity guaranteed the cultivation rights of peasant farmers, the Japanese actually dispossessed peasants from their land. In fact, the number of Korean peasants who cultivated the land formerly assigned to the post stations and military forts amounted to 331,748. These peasants who were separated from the land were downgraded to tenants. Simply put, although the Japanese land survey was presumably conducted as a way to consolidate Japan's colonial economic system, in reality it functioned as an instrument for expropriating Korean land.

The Monopoly of Natural Resources, Industry, and Finance

In addition to controlling Korea's farmland, Japan also firmly controlled Korea's forest land, fisheries, mineral resources, industries, and finances. In June 1911 the Government-General enacted a forest ordinance to tighten its control over Korean forest resources. By its terms, the Government-General could classify any forests in the country as "reserved forests," which ordinary citizens were prohibited from exploiting for resources. In May 1918 another law was promulgated to conduct surveys of forest land, by which all forest owners were required to register their forest land with the colonial authorities. As a result, all former state-owned forest land became the property of the Government-General. By seizing Korean forest land in the same way as it had taken over the country's farmland, the Government-General possessed more than 50 percent of Korea's entire forest land. The Government-General sold the forest land to Japanese lumbering companies, and the latter cut down forests particularly in the reaches of the Yalu and Tumen rivers on a large-scale and made huge profits.

In accordance with a fishery ordinance promulgated in February 1912, the vast fishing grounds, held formerly by the Chosŏn royal household and private Koreans, were placed under the administration of the Government-General. The colonial government encouraged Japanese fishermen to immigrate to Korea. Because Japanese fishing techniques were far superior to those of Korean fishermen, the Japanese catch per capita was four times larger than that of the Koreans. Overfishing by Japanese fishermen devastated Korean fishing grounds. The illegal incorporation of Tok-to into Japan proper in February 1905 sought to dispossess Korea of marine resources in its neighboring sea area.

Although the southern part of the Korean peninsula had rich farmland that could feed hungry Japanese who mounted large-scale rice riots in Japan in 1918, the northern part had large deposits of mineral reserves of more than 70 different kinds of minerals, including iron, gold, silver, copper, tungsten, zinc, uranium, and coal. A mining ordinance enacted in December 1915 turned Korea's mineral deposits over to the Japanese mining *zaibatsu* conglomerates, such as Mitsui, for exploitation. In 1920 the Japanese owned more than 80 percent of Korean mines, and the Koreans possessed only 0.3 percent of them.

Virtually all industries were monopolized either by Japanese-based corporations or by Japanese corporations in Korea. To check the growth of native Korean enterprises, the Government-General enacted a company ordinance in December 1910. The law stipulated that the Government-General's approval was required to establish a company. Even the companies that obtained approval were subjected to frequent suspension or dissolution. The underdevelopment of Korean capital resulted in the rapid growth of Japanese investment in fundamental industries. The law was originally designed to stop the advance of foreign capital into Korea, but Korean capital was also hard hit by the Japanese-imposed law. Such vital industries as electricity, railroads, and finance were monopolized by Japanese conglomerates, including Mitsui and Mitsubishi. The Government-General had a monopoly on the sale of ginseng, salt, and opium. Korean entrepreneurs mainly engaged in light industries such as rice polishing, leather, ceramics, spinning, and the processing of agricultural and marine products. In 1919 the Japanese possessed some 91 percent of all capital invested in Korea. The rate of Korean-owned capital continued to fall. In 1942 Korean capital constituted only 1.5 percent of the total capital invested in Korean industries.

The Japanese and some Western observers often cite Japanese construction of an extensive transportation infrastructure of railways, ports, and roads as an important Japanese benefit to Korea. They ignore the fact, however, that the extensive railway and port facilities primarily served Japanese interests and were built to extract and exploit Korea's natural resources, including raw materials, foodstuffs, mineral resources, and industrial products. They were also intended for the strategic purpose of facilitating the transport of large numbers of troops and materials to the Asian mainland.

The first railroad was constructed between Seoul and Inch'ŏn by an American company in 1899, three years after a contract was awarded to the American James R. Morse. A Japanese company built a line between Seoul and Pusan in 1904. As the Russo-Japanese War became imminent, the Japanese hastened the construction of a Seoul-Sinŭiju line, which was completed in 1905, to carry troops and military supplies to Manchuria. The Pusan-Sinŭiju line became the main artery of Japanese troop movement for the invasion of the Asian mainland. Upon the annexation of Korea in 1910, all railway control was transferred to the Japanese Government-General. More precisely, it became a Japanese government monopoly. Railroad lines increased from 674 miles in 1911 to 1,777 miles in 1930. Secondary rail lines linked northeastern seacoast Japanese factories in Wŏnsan, Hamhŭng, and Najin. Other lines were completed in the southwestern region, home to large Japanese-owned farms.

The Chosŏn government had already installed telegraph lines in the 1880s linking Seoul with other important cities such as Inch'ŏn, Ŭiju, Pusan, and Wŏnsan. During and after the Russo-Japanese War, control of these telegraph facilities of course fell into Japanese hands. The postal service conducted by the Chosŏn government since the 1890s was also placed under Japanese control during and after the war.

By 1900 a number of Japanese banks had established branch or agency offices in Chosŏn. In October 1909 the Bank of Korea was created and functioned as a central bank. After annexation, in March 1911, the Bank of Korea was transformed into the Bank of Chosŏn (Chosen in Japanese). There were several Japanese-owned commercial banks whose services were largely limited to the Japanese residents in Korea. After annexation, in other words, the Japanese completely controlled Korea's finances.

In Korea's colonial economic structure, Japan virtually monopolized trade. Some 90 percent of Korean exports, mainly rice and other grains and leaf tobacco, went to Japan, and about 65 percent of its imports, chiefly clothing and other light industrial goods, came from Japan. As Japan's colony, Korea functioned as a source of raw materials as well as a commodity market for Japan.

Japanese Attempts to Annihilate the Korean National Consciousness

After the annexation of Korea, the Japanese were ever sensitive to the education of the Koreans. Even before the annexation, Japan assumed actual power over Korean education, reorganizing the educational system by imperial edict. The Japanese sought to place all schools under government control, reduce the number of schools, adapt the substance of education to their colonial policy, and arrest the development of Korean education by lowering its quality. By a decree enacted in 1908, the Japanese tightened their control over private schools and closed many of them. The Education Act, promulgated in September 1911, was mainly designed to secure manpower for the colonial administration in Korea. On the other hand, to extinguish Korean national consciousness, the Japanese kept the Koreans illiterate, affording them little opportunity to learn.

In a nationwide search conducted in 1910 for works on Korean history and geography, the Japanese confiscated and burned 200,000 to 300,000 works. Included in the vandalism were biographies of Korean national heroes of earlier centuries such as Ŭlchi Mun-dŏk, Kang Kam-ch'an, Ch'oe Yŏng, and Yi Sun-sin; Korean translations of foreign books treating independence, the birth of the nation, and revolution such as biographies of the German Otto von Bismarck and the Russian Peter the Great; and histories of the founding of Switzerland, American independence, and Italian unification. Many ancient Korean texts describing the Japanese as inferior and uncivilized were found and destroyed. The Government-General reinterpreted and distorted Korean history to suit Japanese tastes and, to this nationalistic end, employed many government-patronized historians, both Korean and Japanese. The Japanese specifically tried to limit the scope of Korean history to the Korean peninsula and sever it from the Asian continent, thus seriously distorting Korean history to justify its colonial rule. The "Mimana Nihon-fu" story is a typical example of Japan's desperate efforts to annihilate the Korean national consciousness and national spirit.

The Nationalist Movement in the 1910s

The Koreans had violently resisted Japanese control of their country even before annexation. National consciousness grew increasingly among all classes under Japanese rule, but as overt protests became almost impossible at home, many Korean nationalists fled to safe havens overseas, particularly the Jiandao region in southeastern Manchuria and the Maritime Province of Russia. Beginning in the later Chosŏn period, many Koreans migrated into Jiandao and Russian Siberia across the Tumen River near the Korean border to lead a new life, and after Japanese annexation, Korean migration into the regions continued, this time to escape Japanese oppression. Those who moved to Manchuria developed fertile farmland with new irrigation systems in the vast Manchurian plains. With these financial and population resources, Korean nationalist activists were able to establish military bases there.

One famous base for armed independence operations in Manchuria was the Sinhŭng mugwan hakkyo, or Military School of the New Rising. In 1911 Yi Hoe-yŏng, Yi Si-yŏng, Yi Tong-nyŏng, and Yi Sang-nyong founded the Kyŏnghaksa, or Cultivation and Learning Society, a self-governing body for Koreans in the Jiandao region. The same year they established the Sinhŭng kangsŭpso, or Training School of the New Rising, to train independence fighters, and in 1919 it was renamed the Sinhŭng mugwan hakkyo. In 1914, in the Russian Maritime Province, Yi Sang-sŏl and Yi Tong-hwi established the Taehan kwangbokkun chŏngbu, or Government of the Korean Restoration Army, the first Korean provisional government in Vladivostok, and organized an independence army to wage an armed struggle against Japan.

Another center for the overseas Korean independence movement was established in Shanghai, China. Korean exiles in the area forged covert relations with China, exemplified by Sin Kyu-sik's organization of the Tongjesa, or Mutual Assistance Society, in 1912. In 1919 Korean nationalists formed the Sinhan ch'ŏngnyŏndan, or New Korea Youth Corps, and sent Kim Kyu-sik to the Paris Peace Conference to appeal for self-determination of Korea. Kim left Shanghai in February and arrived in Paris just as the March First Movement began in Korea. Kim submitted two petitions protesting the injustice of Japanese colonialism in Korea and asking for help to achieve independence, but the Allies, including the United States, ignored them, as they feared offending Japan and saw no benefit for themselves in the transaction.

In the United States Syngman Rhee (Yi Sŭng-man) founded the Kungmin-hoe, or Korean National Association, in Hawaii in 1909. When Sŏ Chae-p'il, a reformer and independence activist, established the Independence Club in 1896, Rhee joined it. In 1898 he was charged with government subversion and remained in prison until 1904, during which time he converted to Christianity. Upon his release Rhee went to study in the United States: at George Washington University, where he earned a bachelor of arts degree; at Harvard University, where he received his master's degree in international relations; and at Princeton University, where he was awarded a doctoral degree in political science in 1910. (The topic of his dissertation was "Neutrality as Influenced by the United States.") He stressed that Korea should recover its independence by diplomatic means. When the Korean Provisional Government (KPG) was established in Shanghai in April 1919, he was elected its first president, despite his stay in the United States. He went to Shanghai to take office as president of the KPG in December 1920 and returned to the United States in May 1921. He was impeached by the KPG legislature in March 1925 on various charges, including embezzling funds amassed in the United States, lacking devotion to the KPG, and damaging the prestige of the KPG and the legislature. In the United States, he led the Korean Commission which he established in Washington, D.C., in August 1919 to lobby on behalf of Korean independence. By the time of Korea's liberation in August 1945, he had become Korea's best-known political figure overseas.

In contrast to Rhee, Pak Yong-man advocated armed struggle and established a military school for Korean youth in Hawaii. By 1915 Korean residents in Hawaii split into the pro-Syngman Rhee and pro-Pak Yong-man groups. An Ch'ang-ho, who primarily emphasized education, founded the Hŭngsadan, or Society for the Fostering of Educational Activities, in San Francisco in 1913, to promote Korean education and moral standards.

Within Korea, meanwhile, the Japanese repressed Korean independence activities harshly. In October 1911 the Japanese police arrested more than 600 members of the Sinminhoe, falsely charging them with plotting to assassinate Governor-General Terauchi Masatake when he attended the dedication of the railway bridge over the Yalu River in December of the previous year. These men were imprisoned, without trial, until June 1912, when 123 were indicted before the district court of Seoul. The trial ended in September 1912, with the conviction of 105 men, all of whom had been severely tortured; it has come to be known as the "Case of the One Hundred Five." After this fabricated conspiracy case, the Sinminhoe itself dissolved. Its ideals survived, however, and thereafter a number of secret organizations were established by almost all segments of Korean society, including former ŭibyŏng leaders, religious leaders, teachers, and students.

In 1912 the Tongnip ŭigunbu, or Righteous Army for Korean Independence, was organized by Im Pyŏng-ch'an, who had led a ŭibyŏng unit with Ch'oe Ik-hyŏn in Seoul in 1906. Engaged in armed struggles against Japan in South Chŏlla province, Im was apprehended in 1914 by the Japanese. The year before, in 1913, the Taehan kwangboktan, Corps for the Restoration of Korea's Independence, had been formed in Taegu, but in 1915 it was renamed the Kwangbokhoe, or Society for the Restoration of Independence, with the aim of training independence fighters and punishing pro-Japanese collaborators. In 1915 the Chosŏn kukkwŏn hoeboktan, or Corps for the Restoration of Korean National Sovereignty, was established in Taegu by Sŏ Sang-il, Yun Sang-t'ae, and Yi Si-yŏng. Later it actively participated in the March First Movement in the Kyŏngsang region. In the northwestern area the Chosŏn kungminhoe, or Korean National Society, was organized by Sungsil School students and Christian youth in 1915. It launched a fund-raising campaign for the independence fighters and took part in the March First Movement in the P'yŏngan region. Many clandestine societies also were formed by teachers in Seoul and other cities, advocating the promotion of education and of economic strength for the Korean people. The Korean spirit of resistance, which was strengthened through the nationalist movement at home and abroad in the 1910s, culminated in the March First Movement of 1919.

The March First Movement

On 1 March 1919 Korean nationalism came to the fore in massive demonstrations against Japan's harsh colonial rule. Known collectively as the March First Movement, the seminal event in the growth of modern Korean nationalism was triggered by a number of foreign and domestic factors. Koreans' resentment against the Japanese had only grown stronger with the passage of time, inspired anew by U.S. President Woodrow Wilson's Fourteen Points, and particularly the principle of "self-determination" clarified on 8 January 1918. Wilson may have been thinking primarily of people who had been forcibly placed under the control of the German, Austro-Hungarian, and Ottoman empires, but the term "self-determination" struck a cord with millions of colonial peoples around the world, including Koreans.

As Korean students and intellectuals, especially those abroad, became aware of the principle of self-determination, a national effort to regain independence intensified. To express Koreans' desire to restore independence, leaders of Korean nationalist groups planned to demonstrate against their Japanese colonial rulers.

The massive independence movement was stimulated by Korean students in Japan who had always been sensitive to national consciousness. About 600 Korean students gathered on 8 February 1919 at the hall of the Young Men's Christian Association in Tokyo, where they issued their own declaration of independence. This event ignited nationwide demonstrations for Korean independence.

Although the principle of self-determination renewed hope for Korean independence, the immediate spark for the March First Movement was the death of the former king Kojong on 21 January 1919, when rumors spread that he had been poisoned by a Japanese physician, further inciting the Koreans against Japan. A state funeral was to be held in Seoul on 3 March and large crowds were expected to attend.

Taking advantage of this opportunity, major religious leaders from Ch'ŏndogyo, the successor to the Tonghak movement, and from Christian and Buddhist denominations, secretly gathered and drafted the Declaration of Independence. Thirty-three leading religious figures signed the document as "representatives of all the Korean people," and thousands of copies were distributed throughout the country. Of the 33 original signers, led by Son Pyŏng-hŭi for Ch'ŏndogyo, Yi Sŭng-hun for the Christian groups, and Han Yong-un for the Buddhists, 15 were followers of Ch'ŏndogyo, 15 were Christians, and 3 were Buddhists. They planned to send the declaration, along with a petition, to the Japanese government and the Paris Peace Conference, then under way, two days before the funeral rites for the former king. At the time these religious groups took full responsibility for the actual planning, as under harsh colonial rule only churches were equipped with the necessary infrastructure for communication and mobilization.

At 2:00 on the afternoon of 1 March, 29 of the 33 signers of the Declaration of Independence met at the T'aehwagwan restaurant (also called the Myŏngwŏlgwan) near P'agoda Park where the declaration was scheduled to be read aloud. The signers had not initially planned to provoke nationwide demonstrations with the reading of the proclamation and so had changed the location to a restaurant from the original large outdoor venue, fearing that the latter would incense more radical nationalists to transform a peaceful appeal into a violent uprising. Despite their best-laid plans, however, the reading of the Declaration of Independence, even by these conservative "national representatives," was the catalyst for approximately 1,500 demonstrations that would ultimately involve more than 2 million Koreans nationwide.

Although none of the signers of the Declaration appeared at P'agoda Park after the reading, a crowd of people, mainly students, gathered there and began demonstrating in the streets. As they waved Korean flags, T'aegŭkki, and shouted "Taehan Tongnip Manse!" ("Long Live Korean Independence!"), more and more people joined in the demonstrations, which soon spread across the country, reaching their peak in early April. Similar protests occurred in Manchuria, the Russian Maritime Province, and other overseas areas.

This large-scale independence movement was so well coordinated and planned in such secrecy that the Government-General was caught by surprise. The stunned Japanese reacted to the peaceful demonstrations with harsh repression. By mid-April 1919, throughout the country, more than 7,500 demonstrators were killed, some 16,000 wounded, and more than 46,000 arrested. The Japanese also destroyed or burned 715 houses, 47 churches, and 2 schools. The cruelest and most tragic incident occurred at Cheam-ni near Suwŏn, just south of Seoul, on 15 April. While worshipers were meeting inside the church, the Japanese locked the doors from the outside and torched the building, burning people alive. Twenty-nine people died in this "Cheam-ni massacre." Sadly, after all these sacrifices, Korea had failed to win independence. But the movement inspired Koreans with a spirit of independence and freedom, and served as a major symbol of Korean nationalist aspirations. It also forced Japan to modify and reform its colonial policy as a "Cultural Policy."

The massive Korean struggle against brutal Japanese colonial rule became known to the world primarily through Western missionary channels, inciting strong international criticism. This was not followed, however, by any official response from the international community. Japan's Western allies were reluctant to condemn Japan's cruel actions, mainly because they had their own colonial holdings.

Although the March First Movement failed to win Western powers' support for Korean independence, it awakened an independence-oriented Korean nationalism. The independence movement led, in particular, to the establishment of provisional governments of Koreans. These were organized in Vladivostok on 17 March 1919, in Shanghai on 11 April 1919, and in Seoul on 23 April 1919. Provisional governments were established in three different locations almost simultaneously, because at the time Korean nationalists believed that leadership was essential in the independence struggle. The provisional government in Seoul, the so-called Hansŏng Provisional Government, in which all 13 Korean provinces were represented, proclaimed Korean independence, asking Japan to end its colonial rule and withdraw from Korea, thus posing a direct challenge to the entire Japanese colonial system. After being notified that a provisional government had been formed in Shanghai, known as the Korean Provisional Government, the provisional government in Vladivostok, called the National Council of Korea, attempted to integrate its activities with those of the Shanghai group. When the Hansŏng Provisional Government in Seoul and the National Council of Korea in Vladivostok were integrated into the Korean Provisional Government in Shanghai on 15 September 1919, a united provisional government was finally formed to serve as the representative organization of the Korean people.

To establish the Korean Provisional Government, socialist-inclined nationalists and moderate-conservative nationalists temporarily aligned. The former advocated armed struggle against Japan, whereas the latter preferred peaceful means of resistance, particularly diplomatic approaches effected through Western powers. The Korean nationalists, including Syngman Rhee, Kim Kyu-sik, Yi Tong-hwi, and Yŏ Un-hyŏng, all participated in forming the cabinet, and all of them would play important roles in modern Korean history.

The Korean Provisional Government was created not to restore the old monarchy but as a republic guaranteeing the people an elected government with a president and legislature; freedom of speech, assembly, press, and religion; and separation of state and religion. The Korean Provisional Government was weakened, however, by its difficulty in maintaining contact with the homeland, as well as a lack of significant international support, and, above all, by the ideological left-right split among nationalists fueled by Russia's 1917 Bolshevik Revolution.

On 1 March 1919 the disparate strands of Korean nationalism coalesced in massive demonstrations against Japanese rule. Despite enormous sacrifices, however, independence was still not achieved, though the movement did foster a spirit of independence among the Koreans and brought about the Korean Provisional Government. Despite its many weaknesses, this was a government lawfully striving for Korea's independence. The government of the current Republic of Korea prides itself on successfully attaining the legitimacy of the former Korean Provisional Government.

JAPAN'S SHIFT TO THE "CULTURAL POLICY"
AND KOREAN NATIONALISM

The Nature of the "Cultural Policy"

The March First Movement forced the Japanese to reassess their colonial policy in Korea, and, finally, they modified certain aspects of their colonial policy. Japan's efforts to change its colonial rule in Korea was closely related to new political currents within Japan. Wartime prosperity and its victory in World War I brought a more liberal spirit to Japanese politics. The inauguration of the Hara Kei cabinet, in 1918, opened a new era in Japanese politics, often referred to as "Taisho Democracy," during the first half of the 1920s. A civilian party politician, Hara revealed his distaste for military-oriented colonial rule in Korea.[5] Finally, in August 1919, Japan announced the reshaping of its colonial rule in Korea: the harsh face of military-oriented rule under Governor-Generals Terauch Masatake (1910–1916) and Hasegawa Yoshimichi (1916–1919) was replaced by the softer appearance of Admiral Saito Makoto's rule. Saito proclaimed a number of policy changes known collectively as the "Cultural Policy."

The new policy included five major changes: no longer was it required that the post of governor-general be appointed from active-duty generals or admirals; the gendarmerie police system was replaced by the ordinary police system, and government officials and schoolteachers no longer had to wear uniforms or carry swords; freedom of speech, press, assembly, and association was granted but with limitations; educational opportunities for Koreans were expanded; and Korean cultural self-expression was allowed some free reign.

The new policy proved to be a fraudulent strategy, however. Not one single civil official was appointed as governor-general among six who succeeded Saito Makoto;[6] only generals or admirals in active service were his successors. Further, despite the proclaimed change in the police system, Japan actually reinforced police strength by integrating military policemen into the ordinary police force. Because public order was the first priority among the Japanese, a police force was stationed in every local district in Korea. Saito was also determined to frustrate any anti-Japanese activity, and so, in May 1925, the Government-General promulgated the Peace Preservation Law, which, quite effectively, put an end to anti-Japanese newspapers, assemblies, and associations. Within Korea, even minor pro-independence activity was closely watched and harshly suppressed.

Japan's legal foundation to control publications in Korea began with the Newspaper Law of 1907 and the Publication Law of 1909, enacted by the Japanese during the protectorate period. From 1910 to 1919, a time historians call the "dark period," no Korean newspapers managed by Koreans were permitted. Beginning in 1920, however, Japanese control over newspapers seemed to ease, and the Korean-owned newspapers the *Tonga ilbo*, or East Asia Daily, and the *Chosŏn ilbo*, or Morning Calm Daily, were founded in that year, followed by the *Sidae ilbo*, or Current Daily, in 1924. Still, rigid censorship was exercised on every word and phrase, and the deletion of text, confiscation of papers, levying of fines, and suspension of publication were frequent occurrences. For example, when 28 U.S. Congressmen and their families stopped in Seoul for a brief visit in late 1920 while embarked on a visit to China, the *Chosŏn ilbo* described their visit to Korea as a "law of nature" and subsequently the paper was banned for a week by the Government-General. Clearly the easing of controls on newspapers was for appearances only; the real intention was to mollify international critics and spy on Koreans who held anti-Japanese opinions. Similarly, allowing Koreans the freedom of assembly and association was primarily a way to form pro-Japanese organizations and win over pro-Japanese collaborators.

Another sham was the widely advertised expansion of educational opportunities for Koreans, as, in reality, the previous discriminatory practices continued as before. An education ordinance enacted in 1922 stipulated that Koreans would not be discriminated against in education. In 1924 the Japanese established Kyŏngsŏng Imperial University, present-day Seoul National University, and allocated about one-third of its student quorum to Koreans.[7] Elementary education and industrial education were also expanded, but no more than 18 percent of school-aged children attended elementary schools. Moreover, education was directed only at assimilating Korea's culture and way of life to Japan's. Although, as noted, Japan did allow Koreans some freedom to restore and defend their culture against Japanese encroachment, the new Japanese policy sought to eliminate entirely the Korean spirit of independence. Thus, in 1922, the Japanese established the Korean History Compilation Committee and published a 35-volume *Korean History* in 1937, which seriously distorted Korean history. In so doing, the Japanese aimed to negate the national consciousness and autonomous spirit of the Korean people, as well as their historical traditions. Simply put, Japan's new "Cultural Policy" was a deceitful moderation of its earlier government by bayonet, designed only to blunt international criticism of Japan's harsh, military-oriented colonial rule.

Economic Changes

As a colony of the expanding Japanese empire, Korea was primarily a source of raw materials and food, but it also provided markets for Japan's industrial development. With little interest in the economic development of Korea, Japan continuously exploited Korea's resources at the expense of most Koreans' livelihood.

At the time of annexation, Korea was an overwhelmingly agrarian economy, and so Japan's initial economic policy there was to increase agricultural production to meet Japan's growing need for rice. In the late 1910s, Japan was experiencing a severe crisis in food supply as a result of maladjustments in its rapidly industrializing economy. In 1918 the price of rice skyrocketed, leading to serious social unrest. Finally, rice riots broke out in many parts of Japan in August of that year. As Japanese demand for rice sharply increased, Korea became a rice-based colonial economy tightly controlled in the interests of creating a rice surplus to feed Japan. Beginning in the 1920s huge quantities of Korean rice were shipped to Japan; in the period between 1932 and 1936 the amount of rice exported reached the point where more than half of Korea's total rice production was sent to Japan. As a result, many Koreans had to consume grain substitutes such as barley, sorghum, and millet.

Living conditions for Korea's peasants had seriously deteriorated, with crushing poverty and debt, demanding nothing less than a radical change in the structure of Korea's centuries-old land relations, in which privately owned land was concentrated in the hands of relatively few large landowners. Peasant cultivators were either small holders and tenants or laborers. The Japanese annexation of Korea not only did nothing to alter this structure to improve the peasants' economic status; instead, it encouraged the separation of ownership from actual cultivation of land, which resulted in large-scale absentee landlordism.

As the concentration of landholdings in increasingly fewer hands became the trend, farm tenancy rapidly increased. The rate of Korean farmers owning no farmland rose from 37.7 percent in 1918 to 53.8 percent in 1932. By 1938 less than 20 percent of farmers owned all the land they tilled, about one-fourth owned some land and rented some, and farmers owning no land still amounted to over 50 percent.[8]

Landlessness always makes farmers less self-sufficient. The inequitable distribution of farmland caused great misery to tenants, for as the number of tenants increased and thus sharpened competition for land among tenants, tenancy rents became exorbitant. Generally, in previous years, tenant farmers paid rents amounting to 50 percent of the crop, but during the 1930s these rents in southern Korea ran up to 80 percent of the yield and were among the highest rents in the world. Keen competition among tenants made tenant farming almost a privilege. Many of the lease contracts for land were for a period of just one year, and so tenants faced constant renegotiations of leases, which caused utter insecurity for tenant families. The miserable tenancy conditions depressed Korean agriculture as a whole as well as the tenants themselves. With no promise of tenure on the land beyond a year's lease, tenants made no improvements on the land, nor could they conserve land and resources for increased production.

The destitution of Korean peasants was beyond description. Especially in the period termed "spring suffering," before the summer harvest of barley, they were periodically on the brink of starvation. Already burdened with huge debts, most of them endured food shortages and had to maintain life by searching for edible weeds, roots, and barks on the hillsides, which led the peasants to feel hopeless and see no point in working.[9] Koreans living in urban areas were no better off than those in the countryside. Some 80 percent of urban dwellers were poverty-stricken, and Koreans received wages less than half the amount of their Japanese counterparts.

After the March First Movement major Japanese business interests supported modifications to colonial policy in Korea not out of altruism but out of self-interest. They sought to relax restrictions on business transactions in Korea to expand the market for their surplus capital. Korea offered a more favorable investment climate compared to Japan, as Korean workers were paid less than half of what Japan's competitors were paid, and they worked longer hours (more than ten hours a day). In 1920 the Government-General rescinded an ordinance enacted in 1910, so that now companies only needed to register with the Government-General but no longer needed its approval. Soon large-scale investments of Japanese capital were made in Korea. In 1926 the Japanese established the Chosen Hydroelectric Power Company, which developed a site on the Pujŏn River, a tributary of the Yalu, in South Hamgyŏng province. The following year the Chosen Nitrogenous Fertilizer Company was founded at Hŭngnam in the same province, where it could utilize the new, cheap power supply on the Pujŏn River. This spurred considerable urban growth in Hŭngnam, one of the earliest planned cities in the region. Soon it became the largest industrial center in Korea. The outbreak of the Manchurian Incident in 1931 further accelerated Japanese investment in Korea. Because of the increasing Japanese emphasis on industrialization, the number and distribution of Japanese manufacturing industries grew rapidly.

Koreans benefited little from the developing economy, which was designed to serve the Japanese homeland. Heavy industry was limited mainly to developing raw materials, especially mineral resources, and producing war supplies. The Japanese monopolized all the key positions in the colonial government and business sectors, with few Koreans allowed access to the basic skills essential for the industrialization and modernization of their country.

Cultural Life

Japan's "Cultural Policy," on the other hand, did encourage new developments in Korean cultural life in the 1920s. For example, it brought about the emergence of the "New Literature." Immediately before Japan's annexation of Korea, the "new novel" appeared. Although the new novel retained remnants of the older literary form in that it was still didactic and written entirely in han'gŭl so as to be easily read by everyone, the new novels reflected the values of the contemporary enlightenment movement by advocating Korean independence, educational reform, family ethics based on equality between the sexes, the eradication of superstitious beliefs, and the construction of a rational, enlightened Korean society.

The pioneer among the new novelists, Yi In-jik, authored such representative works as *Hyŏl ŭi nu,* or Tears of Blood; *Ch'iaksan,* or Pheasant Mountain; and *Kwi ŭi sŏng,* or Voice of a Demon. The new novels also included Yi Hae-jo's *Chayu chong,* or Liberty Bell, and *Moran pyŏng,* or the Peony Screen; Ch'oe Ch'an-sik's *Ch'uwŏl saek,* or Color of the Autumn Moon; and An Kuk-sŏn's *Kŭmsu hoeŭi rok,* or Proceedings of the Council of Birds and Beasts. Following Western and Japanese models, the new novel constituted the mainstream of fiction writing in Korea until the end of the 1910s, reaching its peak with the publication of Yi Kwang-su's *Mujŏng,* or the Heartless, in 1917.[10]

Following the March First Movement modern literature, often called the "New Literature," appeared, exemplified by a group of writers active in the 1920s. These new literary men launched the publication of several writers' magazines such as *Ch'angjo,* or Creation (1919); *P'yehŏ,* or Ruins (1920); *Paekcho,* or

White Tide (1922); and *Kŭmsŏng*, or Gold Star (1923). The pioneer of the new literary movement was Kim Tong-in, whose main work, *Kamja*, or Potatoes, introduced the genre of naturalism in its portrayal of the environmental influences on dehumanization. On the other hand, the realistic works of Yŏm Sang-sŏp, such as *Samdae*, or Three Generations, dealt with the dilemma facing Koreans in the transition from a traditional society to a modern society. A literature of sentimentalism, or romanticism, represented by Na To-hyang's *Mullebanga*, or A Waterwheel, also appeared in the early 1920s.

In the mid-1920s two new trends were added to the existing literary corpus: one seeking to promote Korean self-identity during the dark colonial period and the other designed to awaken a social consciousness. Representing the former trend was Han Yong-un, one of the 33 signers of the Declaration of Independence, whose poem, *Nim ŭi ch'immuk*, or The Silence of My Beloved, embodied the spirit of love for one's fellow countrymen. Another poet in this genre was Yi Sang-hwa who, in his *Ppaeatkkin tŭl edo pom ŭn onŭn'ga?*, or Does Spring Come to a Lost Field?, sang of his endless love for his country. The other trend was influenced by the socialist and communist movements, and described the Japanese infiltration of capitalism into Korea and the resultant poverty of the Korean people. The pioneering work of this genre was Ch'oe Sŏhae's *T'alch'ulgi*, or The Account of an Escape, in which the author vividly portrayed the misery of a poor family that migrated to the Jiandao region. Another representative work was Yi Ki-yŏng's novel *Kohyang*, or The Home Country, describing the misery of the villagers and a student's effort to organize them. In his lengthy novel, *Im Kkŏk-chŏng*, Hong Myŏng-hŭi dramatized the activity of Im Kkŏk-chŏng, a bandit leader of the early sixteenth century, Korea's version of Robin Hood, who fought corrupt government officials, and thus he tried to rally the Korean people against their Japanese colonial masters. These works soon evolved into a proletarian, politicized literature, and in August 1925 left-wing writers established the Korea Artista Proleta Federatio, or the Korean Proletarian Artists' Federation (KAPF), which lasted until Japanese authorities dissolved it in May 1935.

Because Koreans were only allowed to organize themselves in limited ways, officially approved organizations sprang up like mushrooms after rain in a variety of areas in the early 1920s. This period also witnessed the emergence of distinctively modern Korean traditions in literature, drama, music, film, and historiography, which profoundly influenced cultural developments of the subsequent era.[11]

A Rising Police State

Japanese colonial policy in Korea remained practically unchanged, despite the fancy appellation of "Cultural Policy," which was, of course, used only to gloss over Japan's harsh colonial strategies after the March First Movement. With Korea already a virtual police state, Japan continued to build up police strength in Korea by rapidly adding to the number of officers. Indeed, the depth of police penetration among the general Korean populace was obvious in that there was one policeman per 722 persons, whereas in Japan there was one policeman per 1,150 persons. Budgetary appropriations for the police force was also greatly increased to the point where the police budget quadrupled in the 1920s, comprising 12 to 13 percent of the Government-General's total budget.

The national police had headquarters in Seoul with main divisions in each province. Within the province, local stations were set up in each municipality, county, or island, with as many substations as needed in towns or townships. The Japanese police possessed broad powers, with a highly centralized system that dominated virtually every phase of Korean life through terror and intimidation. This included maintaining civil order, preventing and detecting crime, and even controlling people's thoughts. The Japanese police were also empowered to make precautionary arrests and imprison individuals without trial, whenever they saw fit. The Korean people were not protected by the writ of habeas corpus or other safeguards against arbitrary police actions. Searches without warrants were commonplace, as was torture. As a result, the police were universally hated and feared, but the people were so intimidated that no one dared complain.

After the March First Movement the general crime rate slowed, but a rapid increase occurred in the arrests of civilians for political offenses, reflecting intensified ideological oppression by the police. To completely crack down on political offenses, along with the appointment of "thought prosecutors" and "thought judges," "special high police" squads were added to each police unit. By targeting communist circles, which had spread rapidly in Korea, the police effectively frustrated communist efforts from 1928 until liberation. Thought control was introduced in December 1936, and the "thought police" were increasingly strengthened.[12]

The Split among Korean Nationalists

The rise of Korean nationalism as a political ideology can be traced to the 1920s, when Koreans mounted a nationalist movement in various forms. They became involved in educational enlightenment activities, patriotic economic activities, tenancy and labor disputes, armed resistance, guerilla warfare, and even terrorism. But this period also saw the beginning of the left-right split in postwar Korea.

In Korea, as in other colonial countries, many disparate forces with different ideological orientations developed nationalist movements, united only in the common cause of resistance to colonial rule but largely divided into moderates and radicals. Moderate nationalists, a loose collection of educated and influential Koreans, were rightists who accepted the reality of Japanese colonial rule and stressed a gradual path to independence through encouraging Koreans' innate abilities. The moderates, specifically Ch'oe Nam-sŏn and Yi Kwang-su, espoused the doctrine of "remodeling the Korean people," urging that Koreans should be reborn as "modern citizens" to sustain an independent, modern nation. The gradualists, or "cultural nationalists," believed that Koreans should devotedly strengthen themselves through education. Emphasizing the need to awaken the ignorant masses, many of these gradualists launched campaigns to educate the masses and eradicate illiteracy. In 1923 Korean educational leaders, led by Han Kyu-sŏl and Yi Sang-jae, began a fund-raising drive to establish a private university, which failed because of Japanese interference and lack of finances. Moderate nationalists also mounted the buy-Korean campaign aimed at supporting Korean-owned businesses. This "Korean Products Promotion Campaign" succeeded a movement launched in 1907 to repay national debts. In July 1920 Cho Man-sik, often called "Mahatma Gandhi of Korea" because of his doctrine of nonviolence, organized the Korean Products Promotion Society in Pyongyang. The organization was enlarged in January 1923, when it moved its headquarters to Seoul. It campaigned to persuade Koreans to refrain from buying Japanese goods and instead purchase their own Korean products, employing the slogan "Let's wear, eat, and use Korean-made products." The campaign began in large cities such as Seoul and Pyongyang, and developed into a nationwide movement in a short time.

As the government in Japan grew illiberal once more under increasing pressure from the military in the mid-1920s, colonial rule in Korea itself became even more repressive. After 1925 most moderate nationalist campaigns rapidly lost momentum. The promulgation of the Peace Preservation Law, in May 1925, marked the beginning of harsher repression. Moderate nationalists were especially vulnerable to Japanese manipulation, and later many of them became Japanese collaborators including Ch'oe Nam-sŏn and Yi Kwang-su. Radical nationalists, in contrast, took an unyielding stand on Japanese colonial rule and advocated direct confrontation with the colonial masters. But most of them had already gone into self-exile abroad. Many were imbued with socialist and communist ideas, and whereas moderate nationalists became less active in the face of severe Japanese pressure after 1925, socialists and communists sought more direct forms of action, including labor and peasant organization, agitation against the Japanese in Korea, and guerrilla and terrorist activities abroad.

Korean nationalists abroad also quarreled among themselves, which seriously weakened the nationalist movement itself. Many prominent nationalist activists participated in the Korean Provisional Government, which had formed in Shanghai in April 1919. But these mutually antagonistic elements worked together only until 1921. During that decade and the next they accomplished little more than simply to exist, as they were weak and did not forge ties with the nationalist movement inside Korea.

The Communist Movement and Tenancy and Labor Disputes

Korea had one of the oldest communist movements in Asia, and after the March First Movement some nationalists sought to forge ties with international socialism. They were helped by the Bolshevik Revolution, by Vladimir Lenin's pledge to fully support independence struggles among the oppressed peoples of the world. Following up on this pledge, in August 1920, Yi Tong-hwi, a veteran independence fighter, and his loyalists secured substantial financing from the Soviet Union to organize the Koryŏ Communist Party in Shanghai.[13] Thereafter Yi devoted himself to the Korean communist movement in Russian Siberia. In February 1921 some 30 Korean nationalists, including Yŏ Un-hyŏng and Kim Kyu-sik, attended the Congress of the Toilers of the Far East in Moscow, where they met Lenin and Leon Trotsky. In April 1925 the Korean Communist Party was established in Seoul but soon dissolved as a result of internal strife. Within Korea, communists directly confronted the Japanese in tenant struggles, labor disputes, and occasional acts of violence.

The growing number of tenant farmers increased tenancy disputes, which further intensified as the farming population became more and more organized. All the farmers' misery, including extreme poverty, widespread debt, and usury, as well as the constant renegotiation of leases to the detriment of the tenant and utter insecurity of the farming family—all this was closely associated with the concentration of land ownership.[14] Tenants comprised a clear majority of the rural population, and, as landlords became the primary beneficiaries of increased agricultural output and higher prices, tenant farmers became more assertive, tenant-landlord antagonism intensified, and the number of tenancy disputes multiplied.

Tenants mainly resisted the landlords' unilateral transfer of their tenancy rights to others and firmly demanded reductions in their tenant rents. Their resistance to the landlords often took the form of organized disputes. The year 1922 saw 124 disputes involving 2,539 tenant farmers, and this number grew to 204 cases with 4,002 participants in 1925 and to 726 incidents involving 13,012 tenants in 1930. Many of the tenancy disputes occurred on the farmlands of the giant Japanese landholding corporations, such as the Oriental Development Company and the Fuji Industrial Promotion Company. The disputes were not only a struggle for economic justice but took the form of a resistance movement against Japan.[15] Following a huge dispute regarding Oriental Development Company land at Chaeryŏng, Hwanghae province, in 1924, area resident Na Sŏk-chu threw a bomb at the company building in Seoul and later, in December 1926, took his own life. With the founding of the Korean General Farmers Union in 1927, tenancy disputes broke out with greater intensity.

As Japanese business interests invested heavily in mining and heavy industry, taking advantage of cheap Korean labor, a small working class emerged in the 1920s and labor unrest grew steadily: 36 labor disputes involving 3,403 workers erupted in 1921, growing to 81 cases involving 5,984 workers in 1926, and then to as many as 205 incidents involving 21,180 participants in 1931. These disputes gathered intensity with the organization of both the Korean Workers Mutual Aid Society in 1920 and the Korean General Workers Alliance in 1927. At first, labor disputes arose mainly over demands for higher wages. Then, as time went by, the workers increasingly demanded an eight-hour workday and better working conditions. The worst labor strife, involving more than 3,000 Korean workers, occurred at Wŏnsan in 1929, and led to a general strike. A Korean worker had been struck by a Japanese foreman in an oil company in the city and, when news of the incident spread, nearly all the workers at Wŏnsan joined in a strike. The strike was resolved by a compromise, but it indicated that labor disputes were an important part of the Korean nationalist movement.

The Japanese saw that tenancy disputes and particularly labor disputes, threatened their colonial rule in Korea, and so the Government-General exhausted every means to thwart them. Thus, although tenancy and labor disputes spread like wildfire in the 1920s, they subsided in the next decade under sustained harsh repression.

The Nationalist Movement at Home

Unchallenged by the disunited nationalist movement, the Japanese remained in firm control of colonial Korea for many years following the March First Movement. On 15 February 1927, however, right- and left-wing nationalists formed a common front to establish the Sin'ganhoe, or New Main Society, as a united nationalist organization. The plan to organize the Society was proposed by right-wing nationalist leaders who keenly felt the need to combine all nationalists, including communists, into a single independence organization. The communist camp, for the purpose of building up its own strength, also sought to form a united front with the right-wing nationalists. The new organization's main platforms called for the political and economic awakening of the Korean people, unity of purpose, and rejection of any compromise with Japan, which remained the ideological mainstay of the body. Still pursuing their heralded "Cultural Policy," the Government-General reluctantly recognized the New Main Society as a legal organization. Soon it grew to encompass more than 140 branches throughout the country, and its membership totaled some 40,000. A parallel women's nationalist organization, the Kŭnuhoe, or Rose of Sharon Fraternity Society, created on 27 May 1927, acted in line with the New Main Society.

Through lecture tours across the country, the united nationalist organization called for dismantling the Japanese colonial apparatus that exploited Koreans, such as the Oriental Development Company; ending Japanese immigration to Korea; disavowing any form of opportunism; establishing an educational system to serve Korean needs; implementing freedom of study and of thought; and abolishing special laws and regulations aimed at repressing the Korean nationalist movement, including communism. The New Main Society also led various tenancy and labor disputes and school strikes among Koreans. When the Kwangju student demonstration arose in November 1929, the Society staged sympathy demonstrations in order to spread the anti-Japanese movement throughout the country. But this move led to the arrest of many of its leading members, making it almost impossible for the Society to continue its activities. Another problem was the conflict between the leftist elements who wanted to continue radical activities and the more conservative nationalists who urged law-abiding tactics. The New Main Society split, and on 15 May 1931 the communists voted to dissolve the nationalist coalition. Without the communists, the right-wing nationalists proved unable to maintain any strong coalition. No other united resistance organization emerged on a comparable scale to replace it.

When the last Chosŏn king, Sunjong, died on 26 April 1926, the Korean people were gripped with sorrow, and their hatred against the Japanese grew even stronger. Left-wing nationalist activists seized this opportunity to hold a massive anti-Japanese demonstration on 10 June, the day of the king's funeral. In an awe-inspiring atmosphere and strictly monitored by the Japanese police, Korean students staged street demonstrations as the funeral cortege passed each location en route to the burial ground. In this "10 June Independence demonstration," more than 200 students were arrested, all shouting "Taehan Tongnip Manse!"—"Long Live Korean Independence!"

Korean students also organized school strikes, and the most dramatic was the Kwangju Student Movement in November 1929. This student movement was sparked when a Japanese male student insulted a Korean female student waiting for a train to take her home after school in late October 1929. By 3 November, a clash between Korean and Japanese students had escalated into open fighting in the streets of Kwangju. As expected, the Japanese police blamed the Korean students for the incident and arrested some 400 of those involved. Angered by this unjust police action, all students in the city participated in anti-Japanese demonstrations and in skirmishes with the Japanese police. These student protests spread beyond Kwangju and by March 1930 were occurring nationwide, involving 194 schools and some 54,000 students. In the end 582 students were expelled from their schools and 2,330 were suspended for an indefinite period.[16]

The Kwangju Student Movement was both a massive school strike and an independence movement strongly demanding freedom of speech, assembly, and publication, as well as the abolition of the colonial educational system and the installment of an educational institution serving Korean needs. These demands were developed with the guidance of the New Main Society. The Kwangju Student Movement represented the only major resistance movement against Japanese colonial rule in Korea between the March First Movement and Korea's liberation at the end of World War II and helped Korean nationalism survive during great adversity.

The Overseas Independence Movement

As armed resistance against Japan became impossible within Korea, many independence fighters who followed the tradition of the former ŭibyŏng militia moved into Manchuria, propitiously located directly across Korea's northern border. Manchuria became a major center for a lasting, tenacious armed fight for Korean independence. Although ill-equipped and outnumbered, the independence fighters in Manchuria were a powerful force of Korean nationalism, sometimes achieving spectacular success.

On numerous occasions these fighters moved in and out of the Korean-Manchurian border area, engaging in guerrilla warfare against Japanese forces. Two of their most spectacular victories occurred in 1920 at Fengwu-dong and Qingshan-li, just across the Korean-Manchurian border in southeastern Manchuria. In the battle at Fengwu-dong, on 4–7 June, the Taehan tongnipkun, or Korean Independence Army, led by Hong Pŏm-do, defeated a Japanese army contingent, killing 160 and wounding more than 300. In the battle at Qingshan-li on 21–26 October, the independence fighters of the Pungno kunjŏngsŏ, or Northern Route Military Command, led by Kim Chwa-jin, routed a Japanese force that far outnumbered and outgunned them, killing more than 1,200 and wounding over 2,000. The victory would remain a landmark in the history of the Korean independence struggle. In retaliation, Japanese forces attacked Korean villages in Manchuria, slaughtering more than 10,000 Koreans and burning down over 2,500 houses and more than 30 schools in what became known as the "Massacre of 1920" or the "Massacre in Jiandao."

To save Korean civilians from Japanese atrocities and elude Japanese follow-up attacks, independence army units scattered into less accessible areas, including Russian territory. In the Russian Maritime Province, in June 1921, Korean nationalist fighters suffered what has come to be known as the "Free City disaster," in which Soviet Korean and Bolshevik forces attacked independence fighters who refused to be disarmed and killed several hundreds at Braweschensk. Despite the adverse conditions facing them, the Korean volunteer fighters regrouped into smaller units, under a single command, to launch more effective operations. As a result, the Ch'amŭibu, or General Staff Headquarters, was formed by Ch'ae Ch'an and Kim Sŭng-hak under the direct command of the Korean Provisional Government in the region of the mid-Yalu River, centered on Jian prefecture, in 1923. The Chŏngŭibu, or Righteous Government, was established in Jilin province by O Tong-jin and Chi Ch'ŏng-ch'ŏn (Yi Ch'ŏng-ch'ŏn) in 1925, functioning in effect as a governing authority for the Korean populace living in southern Manchuria. In northern Manchuria the Sinminbu, or New People's Government, was created by Kim Hyŏk and Kim Chwa-jin in 1925. The independence forces that returned from the Russian

Maritime Province were a core force uniting several independence army units into this Sinminbu. Thus the Korean independence forces scattered throughout Manchuria were organized under three commands. Each functioned not only as a military command to battle the Japanese but also as a means for Koreans to practice self-rule in its sphere of jurisdiction. In 1929 the three commands were integrated into the Kungminbu, or National Government, with a united military headquarters.

In the 1920s, under adverse conditions, Korean independence fighters in Manchuria battled the Japanese and willingly sacrificed themselves. Despite their sustained efforts to work together, however, they failed to resolve the discord among themselves caused by regionalism and disparate ideologies.

JAPAN'S TIGHTENING GRIP ON KOREA AND KOREAN NATIONALISM

Korea as Japan's Military Support Base

In the early 1930s Japan's military-oriented government attempted to find a way out of the economic problem caused by the Great Depression by advancing into the Asian mainland, embarking first on an invasion of Manchuria in 1931 and then on China proper in 1937. These Japanese war efforts transformed Korea as a colony of Japan into a vital military rear-support base, which in turn greatly changed the nature of Japanese colonial rule. The Government-General in Korea mobilized human and material resources more ruthlessly and exhaustively to achieve the Japanese goal of making Korea a military supply base.

In June 1931 Ugaki Kazushige (1927, 1931–1936) replaced Saito Makoto (1919–1927, 1929–1931) as governor-general, heralding a new phase in Japanese colonial rule in which Korea was forced to completely serve the Japanese war effort. The Japanese encouraged military values in every part of Korean society and ruthlessly repressed all opposition. As the Government-General directed its energies to mobilizing all Korean resources for Japanese military campaigns in the Asian continent, Korea was plunged into a wartime economy.

To restore Korea's rural economy, which was severely damaged by the Great Depression, the Japanese launched the so-called Korean Rural Revival Movement in July 1932, declaring a crusade against "spring suffering," that is, the spring shortage of food, and emphasizing self-reliance and the spiritual regeneration of rural villages. In practice, however, it aimed to strengthen Japanese control of the Korean rural community. The Japanese also enacted modest tenancy reform measures, such as the Tenancy Mediation Ordinance and the Farmland Ordinance, promulgated in 1932 and 1934, respectively, to settle tenancy disputes by arbitration and check the growth of absentee landlordism. As the Japanese economy recovered its strength, the Korean rural economy, relying heavily on Japan, repaired itself as well.[17]

As Japan's wars in China and the Pacific rapidly increased the need for military provisions, especially rice, the Japanese sought to boost rice production in Korea. Whereas they shipped tremendous quantities of Korean rice to their country, they brought coarse grain substitutes, such as millet, from Manchuria to stave off starvation in Korea. As time went on, this tendency was intensified. In the 1940s, to exploit more Korean farm products for their war effort, the Japanese employed the method of kongch'ul, or quota delivery, which compelled farmers to grow rice with expensive fertilizers to fulfill their assigned quotas. Because the Japanese usually demanded kongch'ul offerings in excess of the actual year's harvest, Koreans faced mass starvation. Many barely managed to stay alive by eating roots and bark.

As Korea emerged as an important base for Japan's wars on the Asian mainland, Japan sought to stimulate key manufacturing facilities in Korea such as machines, chemicals, and metals to secure sufficient military supplies. Korean industry served only Japanese military needs.

The Japanese war industry needed cheap and plentiful labor, which was met by Korea's immense agricultural labor force. Hundreds of thousands of unskilled Korean workers were pressed into service in industries in northern Korea as well as in Japan and Manchuria. They performed heavy manual labor at wages less than half of those earned by their Japanese counterparts.

To meet Japan's increasing need for military hardware, Koreans, as secondclass citizens, were forcibly mobilized on a large scale; hundreds of thousands of Koreans were requisitioned as laborers. Soon, in March 1943, Koreans were being drafted into the Japanese army, and even college students were being drafter under the Student Volunteer Ordinance of January 1944.

Women were drafted into the Japanese armed forces as sexual slaves in military brothels. Under the "comfort women" practice, tens of thousands of young Korean women, mostly teenagers, were recruited. In the guise of regular employment, they were sent to the front lines of China, Manchuria, the Pacific islands, and Southeast Asia and forced into service for Japanese soldiers. The orders to recruit these so-called comfort women came from the highest echelon of the Japanese government, including the highest military authorities,

and recruiters were the Japanese police and local government officials. The
Japanese military established the brothels not only to boost morale among its
troops but to prevent rapes of local women and the spread of sexually transmitted diseases among Japanese soldiers. Poorly paid, these women were forced to
endure shame and disdain.

By the end of the Pacific war, some 4 million Koreans, almost 16 percent of
the total population, were scattered throughout the Japanese empire. As victims
of the Japanese warmongers, Koreans had been robbed of their rice, exploited
as low-wage earners in factories and mines, and requisitioned as laborers or
soldiers or humiliated as sex slaves.

Japan's Assimilation Policy

From the late 1930s, as Japan consolidated its wartime mobilization, the Japanese organized nearly every aspect of Korean life to serve their war needs. The
National General Mobilization Law, promulgated in April 1938, imposed upon
Koreans mandatory Japanese war conditions. The desires of Koreans were completely ignored, and the Korean people became slaves of the Japanese warlords.
Japan established a policy of *naisen ittai,* meaning "Japan and Korea as one
body," to obtain the Koreans' total loyalty. The Japanese attempted to create
a climate wherein the Koreans and the Japanese would be of one body, one
mind, and one spirit in serving the needs of Japan. The policy of "Japan and
Korea as one body" originated in the Japanese contention of the 1880s that the
Japanese and Koreans had the same ancestors. Koreans were prohibited from
speaking their own language and writing in their own script, and were forced
to assume Japanese names and participate in Shinto worship. Japan organized
numerous "patriotic" and "anticommunist" groups to penetrate Korean society
at every level for the war effort. The Japanese also pressured prominent Koreans
to collaborate with them, holding up the slogan "Japan and Korea as one body,"
Simply put, Japan wanted Korea to cease being a colonial outpost and become
an integral part of the Japanese empire.

The appointment of Minami Jiro (1936–1942) as governor-general in August
1936 marked an intensification of the mobilization and assimilation policies.
After his inauguration, Minami recklessly pushed ahead with the assimilation
plan, contrary to the Koreans' wishes. In 1938, as part of the plan, he ordered
Koreans to recite from memory, in Japanese, the "Oath of Imperial Subjects,"
pledging loyalty to the Japanese emperor while bowing toward the imperial
palace in Tokyo. He also forced the Koreans to worship the Japanese Shinto

spirits of dead Japanese, a practice repellent to them, and closed schools and newspapers that opposed his policy. For instance, he shut down the *Chosŏn chungang ilbo,* or Korean Central Daily, in November 1937, and then the two largest Korean newspapers, the *Tonga ilbo* and the *Chosŏn ilbo,* in August 1940, leaving only the minor pro-Japanese *Maeil sinbo,* or Daily News.

In April 1938 Minami issued an order to extinguish Korean culture altogether by strictly prohibiting the use of the Korean language in all Korean schools, offices, and businesses. All teaching materials written in Korean were forcibly destroyed, and teachers and students who spoke Korean in schools were expelled or severely punished. All government offices or business corporations had to write documents only in Japanese. Novelists, poets, and other creative writers were forced to produce their works only in Japanese. Even mild expressions of cultural and literary nationalism were not tolerated and subject to surveillance and punishment.

In accordance with the Name Order enacted in 1939, Koreans were required to use Japanese names. Family names, for Koreans, represented an essential means through which families and clans forged a spiritual bond. Those who refused to assume Japanese names were discriminated against in every corner of society dominated by the Japanese. They were prohibited from attending schools, from obtaining official documents, and from mail delivery, and were not even allowed to draw provision rations. The law took effect in February 1940, and, to the end, only 14 percent of Koreans refused to adopt Japanese names. In short, the Japanese sought to obliterate Korean national identity which had been maintained for several millennia. Because Japanese efforts to erase Korean identity were so ruthless and tenacious, Koreans might not have preserved their indigenous language, culture, and customs if Japanese colonial rule had not ended in August 1945.

The Preservation of Korean Culture

While Japan stubbornly pursued its assimilation policy in the 1930s and the 1940s, some Korean nationalist scholars made every effort to preserve Korean culture. The Chosŏnŏ yŏn'guhoe, or Korean Language Study Society (currently the Han'gŭl hakhoe, or Han'gŭl Study Society), was founded in 1921 by Yi Chung-hwa, Chang Chi-yŏng, and Ch'oe Hyŏn-bae—disciples of Chu Si-gyŏng, a great scholar in the late Chosŏn period who, in 1910, wrote *Taehan kukŏ munpŏp,* or Korean Language Grammar, and *Kukŏ munpŏp,* or Korean Grammar.[18] This organization of Korean linguists made its greatest contribution in the standardization of both han'gŭl orthography and the transcription system of foreign words. Its monthly journal, *Han'gŭl,* which first appeared in February 1927, broadened and popularized the use of the native Korean alphabet in a country where the educated elite still preferred to write in literary Chinese. At the same time, the linguistic society embarked on the clandestine compilation of a dictionary of the Korean language and commemorated as "Han'gŭl Day" the date in 1446 when the newly created Korean alphabet was first promulgated. Meanwhile, Korean vernacular newspapers launched a campaign to enlighten the masses. In April 1933 these daily newspapers adopted the newly proclaimed spelling system and sponsored a literary campaign enlisting the participation of middle school students. In October 1942, when the clandestine Korean-language dictionary was detected by the Japanese police, leading figures of the society were arrested, charged with conducting anti-Japanese activity. In what became known as the "Incident of the Korean Language Study Society," they were subjected to severe torture, and Yi Yun-jae and Han Ching died in prison.

The Japanese rewrote Korean history from a strongly Japanese viewpoint to denigrate Korean history and culture. To stress the Koreans' cultural inferiority, for instance, the Japanese denied, falsely, that the Paleolithic Age had never existed on the Korean peninsula, but Korean historians, in their quest for independence, refuted and discredited the Japanese historiography. Nationalistic histories of Korea, in the tradition of those published at the end of the Chosŏn dynasty, appeared in the 1910s and the 1920s. In his works *Han'guk t'ongsa,* or The Tragic History of Korea (1915), and *Han'guk tongnip undong chi hyŏlsa,* or The Bloody History of the Korean Independence Movement (1920), Pak Ŭn-sik not only attacked Japan's aggression in Korea but also sought to spiritually support the Korean independence movement, and his works made a lasting impact on the minds of Koreans. Sin Ch'ae-ho devoted himself to the study of early Korean history and wrote his representative work, *Chosŏnsa yŏn'gu ch'o,* or Exploratory Studies of Korean History, in 1929. By gleaning information from the inscription on the stone monument of the Koguryŏ king Kwanggaet'o, Chŏng In-bo was able to correct errors Japanese historians had made concerning early Korean history. Mun Il-p'yŏng understood Korean history as an expression of the country's distinct cultural identity, and he wrote a well-known work titled *Taemi kwangye osimnyŏnsa,* or The Fifty-Year History of Korean-American Relations, which appeared in 1939. Because most of these nationalistic studies were closely related to the struggle for Korean independence, the Japanese suppressed them. Sin Ch'ae-ho died in prison in Lushun (Port Arthur), China, because of his independence activities.

In the 1930s some Korean historians sought to explain Korean history from the perspective of Marxist historical materialism. They tried to awaken class consciousness among peasant farmers and laborers, and, in so doing, conflicted with the nationalist historians who gave priority to the nation over class struggles. Paek Nam-un represented the Marxist historian in his works *Chosŏn sahoegyŏngjesa,* or The Socioeconomic History of Korea, written in 1933, and *Chosŏn ponggŏn sahoe kyŏngjesa,* or The Economic History of Feudal Society of Korea, published in 1937. In 1934 historians who rejected both the nationalistic and materialistic interpretations of history founded the *Chindan hakhoe,* or Eastern Land (Korea) Study Society, which advocated a purely objective study of history, with no rigid theoretical frameworks. The Japanese saw the study of the Korean language and Korean history as dangerous, so they aborted even the activities of Korean historians who belonged to the relatively moderate Chindan hakhoe.

In the 1940s Korean literature faced its darkest hour, its very survival in peril. Most Korean writers yielded to Japanese pressure, publishing their works in Japanese or even allowing their art to serve the Japanese war effort. But the poets Yi Yuk-sa and Yun Tong-ju were exceptions. Speaking out for independence, Yi Yuk-sa composed *Ch'ŏngp'odo,* or Seedless Grape, in 1940; after being arrested many times, he died in prison in Beijing in January 1944. Another poet Yun Tong-ju, famous for his posthumous poem, *Hanŭl gwa param gwa pyŏl gwa si,* or Sky, Wind, Stars, and Poetry, also died in prison in Fukuoka, Japan, in February 1945, just before Korea's liberation. Thus, in the darkest hours of Japanese colonial rule in the 1930s and 1940s, some Koreans did strive and sacrifice themselves to preserve Korean culture by studying the Korean language and history, as well as writing the nation's literary works.

The Nationalist Movement in the 1930s

During the 1930s all Korean nationalists fought bravely against the immense power of the Japanese empire. Within Korea, both active and passive resistance virtually ceased as the police and the military kept close watch on anyone suspected of subversive inclinations and imposed severe punishments. Most Koreans chose to pay lip service to the colonial rulers; others actively collaborated with the Japanese. As a result, the treatment of collaborators became a sensitive and sometimes violent issue during the years following liberation. Even in the twenty-first century, the controversy over these Japanese collaborators still remains a contentious, divisive issue.

As the nationalist movement was completely thwarted at home, Manchuria and later China were the main theaters of émigré nationalist activity, and mainly the communists led the independence struggle. In Manchuria Korean guerrilla forces grew rapidly, and by 1933 they established several liberated districts in mountainous areas near the Korean-Manchurian border. The strength of the guerrilla forces grew to such an extent that they carried the battles into Korea proper. Japanese forces based in the villages of Poch'ŏnbo and Musan were attacked and destroyed in July 1937 and May 1939, respectively, and the guerrilla struggle continued into the early 1940s.

North Korean sources have credited this struggle to Kim Il-sung, the founder of the North Korean regime. It appears, however, that most of Kim's military exploits were either imaginary or greatly inflated and carefully tailored to suit the image of a cult figure. Japanese authorities described Kim as a bandit chieftain in command of about 40 to 50 marauders. The "division" he allegedly commanded in Manchuria consisted of only some 300 men.

Kim was born Kim Sŏng-ju to a peasant family in Man'gyŏngdae near Pyongyang on 15 April 1912, which happens to be the day the *Titanic* sank. His family moved back and forth between Korea and Manchuria while he was growing up, and as a child he was exposed to his parents' deep Christian beliefs; his mother was the devout, churchgoing daughter of a Presbyterian elder, and his father had attended a missionary school, and both reportedly were very active in the religious community. Kim had only eight years of formal education. When he was 17 years old he was expelled from school for revolutionary activities and never returned to the classroom. In the early 1930s, after a brief stint in jail for subversive activities, he joined guerrilla bands fighting the Japanese. Kim was a member of a Korean guerrilla army, organized by and attached to an army led by the Chinese Communist Party (CCP). In 1935 he assumed the name Kim Il-sung, meaning "become the sun," a legendary hero of the Korean independence movement, and under the name became a well-known anti-Japanese guerrilla leader in the 1930s. He also used his assumed name effectively to gain support when he entered northern Korea in 1945. By 1941 Kim's units and other parts of the Chinese guerrilla army were forced to retreat across the Manchurian border to the Soviet army training camps. The existence of Korean guerrilla forces irritated the nerves of the Japanese in Manchuria, and so, in August 1939, the Japanese mobilized six battalions of the Guandong (Kwantung) Army and 20,000 men of the Manzhou State Army and police in a six-month antiguerrilla campaign, mainly targeting Kim Il-sung's guerrilla fighters. In September 1940 the Japanese mounted an even larger counterinsurgency campaign that lasted more than two years and killed thousands of Korean and Chinese guerrillas, but Kim survived.

With Kim hiding in the Soviet Maritime Province for the next four years, the Russians created an international army of 10,000 Koreans and Chinese troops. At Khabarovsk some guerrilla officers were assigned Soviet army officer ranks. At the Voroshilov Camp and Okeanskaya Field School, Kim Il-sung is believed to have been appointed a major and the commander of a Korean detachment in the 88th Special Independent Brigade, an international unit of the Soviet Army's Far East Command. When Kim returned to Pyongyang in September 1945 after Korea's liberation, he wore a Soviet army uniform and had the rank of major. While in the Soviet Union Kim married a fellow partisan, Kim Chŏng-suk, and fathered two sons; the elder, Kim Jong-il, eventually became his political heir and successor. The younger Kim, often called "Yura," was born near Khabarovsk on 16 February 1942.[19]

In northern China some 500 Korean guerrilla forces continued military operations until 1938, when they retreated deeper into China and fought against the Japanese alongside CCP troops. In postwar Korea these pro-CCP forces, including Kim Tu-bong, Kim Mu-jŏng (Mu Chŏng), Pak Hyŏn-sam, Ch'oe Ch'ang-ik, and Han Pin, were known as the Yan'an group and played an important role in the formation of the North Korean state.

While guerrilla forces engaged in armed struggle against the Japanese in Manchuria and northern China, other Korean exiles in China proper adopted terrorist tactics in their fight against Japan. The best known of these organizations were Kim Wŏn-bong's Ŭiyŏltan, or Righteous Brotherhood, and Kim Ku's Aeguktan, or Patriots Corps. Both groups carried out many bombing and assassination plots; the best known included the bomb attack on the Oriental Development Company in Seoul in 1926 by Na Sŏk-chu of the Ŭiyŏltan; the attempt to assassinate the Japanese emperor with a hand grenade in 1932 by Yi Pong-ch'ang of the Aeguktan; and the bombing of Japanese military leaders in China in 1932 by Yun Pong-gil of the Aeguktan. On 29 April 1932 Kim Ku ordered Yun Pong-gil to throw a small-scale bomb at high-ranking Japanese military officials in China who were gathered at Hungkou Park in Shanghai to celebrate Japan's occupation of the city on 28 January. The bomb killed and wounded more than ten military leaders, and Sirakawa Yoshinori, commander of the Japanese armed forces in China, was among the dead.

Three years after the outbreak of the Second Sino-Japanese War in September 1940, the Korean Provisional Government, under Nationalist Chinese sponsorship, formed the Kwangbokkun, or Restoration Army, in Chongqing. On the day after Japan's attack on Pearl Harbor, on 9 December 1941, it declared war against Japan. While conducting a diplomatic campaign to gather support from the Allies, its forces launched military operations against Japan in concert with the Allied armies, particularly the Chinese forces. In June 1943 the Restoration Army concluded a mutual assistance agreement with British forces in India by which its units were sent to the Burma-India war area. Others cooperated with the U.S. Office of Strategic Service, preparing for an advance into Korea proper.

Meanwhile, Japanese pressure was steadily forcing the retreat of the radical Korean National Revolutionary Party, organized under Kim Wŏn-bong in northern China in 1937, and its army, the Korean Volunteer Corps. The Koreans eventually fell back to Chongqing, where they were integrated into the Korean Provisional Government and its Restoration Army.

Altogether, after 1943, more than 5,000 Korean troops joined the Allied forces in military operations against the Japanese throughout the Chinese theater of war. Korean college students and youths drafted into the Japanese army deserted to join the ranks of China's anti-Japanese fight. In the United States a number of Korean immigrants volunteered for the U.S. Army to fight against the Japanese in the Pacific.

Koreans, during this period, were able to have military careers for the first time, based on previous service with either the Japanese or Chinese armies. Some attained officer status, such as Park Chung-hee, who was commissioned a lieutenant in the Japanese Guandong Army in Manchuria and later became president of the Republic of Korea. A few even reached the rank of general, including Kim Hong-il, who became a major general in the Republic of China Army. The officer corps of the later South Korean Army during the Syngman Rhee period (1948–1960) was dominated by Koreans who had gained experience in the Japanese army.

In the 1930s and 1940s disparate elements of Korean nationalists abroad continued their struggle against the Japanese imperial yoke. But these elements of the nationalist movement were so divided and parochial that they never achieved a united front. When Koreans finally freed themselves from harsh Japanese bondage and regained their independence in August 1945, a fundamental question remained: Which ideologies would lead independent Korea?

JAPAN'S REVISIONIST HISTORY OF KOREA

Territorial Claim to Tok-to

Since the early 1950s Japan has claimed sovereignty over the Korea-controlled island of Tok-to and has plotted to make the island a disputed area in the eyes of the international community. So far, Japan has been successful in this currently invisible contest for international recognition, as it has attempted to establish Japanese names for the East Sea ("Sea of Japan") and Tok-to ("Takeshima"). The Japanese laid claim to Tok-to by the unilateral act of a local government in early 1905. On 22 February 1905, in the course of Japan's imperial aggression, the Shimane prefecture, a Japanese local authority, adopted a municipal ordinance to incorporate Tok-to into its jurisdiction without legal foundation or notifying any concerned state.

After Japan's defeat in World War II in August 1945, liberated Korea recovered its territories, including Tok-to. The victorious Allied powers recognized Korea's sovereignty over the island, and the Supreme Commander of the Allied Powers Instruction No. 677, in 1946, excluded Tok-to (referred to as Liancourt Rocks) from Japan's territory with the following edict: "For the purpose of this directive, Japan is defined to include the four main islands of Japan . . . excluding Utsuryo (Ullŭng) Island, the Liancourt Rocks, and Quelpart (Cheju) Island." As a result of Japan's fierce lobbying activity to exclude Tok-to from Korea's sovereignty, however, the 1952 San Francisco Treaty of Peace with Japan stipulated, in Article 2 (a), that "Japan, recognizing the independence of Korea, renounces all right, title and claim to Korea, including the islands of Quelpart, Port Hamilton (Kŏmun-do), and Dagelet."[20] At the time the government of the Republic of Korea (South Korea) under President Syngman Rhee negotiated ineffectively over the ownership of the islands in talks with U.S. authorities but focused, instead, on an unrealistic demand for Korean sovereignty over Japan's Tsushima. Much of Rhee's attention was also on suppressing his domestic political rivals rather than on maintaining his country's territory. Despite Japan's endless attempts to claim sovereignty over Tok-to, since 1954 South Korea has effectively exercised jurisdiction over the islands and has stationed its coast guard on Tok-to as a symbol of Korea's ownership.

Since 1996 South Korea and Japan have had several rounds of talks about the boundary between their exclusive economic zones (EEZs) in the East Sea but with little progress. South Korea proposed a median line between Tok-to and the Japanese archipelago, whereas Japan maintained its position that the line should be drawn between Ullŭng-do and Tok-to. In a tentative step, the parties signed a fisheries agreement in 1998, sharing a joint fishing area in the waters separating the two countries in the East Sea.

Revisionist History Textbooks

Claiming sovereignty over Tok-to, Japanese right-wing nationalists have revised the history of its relations with Korea, raising tensions between the two countries. In the spring of 2001, the Japanese government, which authorizes the use of textbooks every four years, approved, for use in secondary school, a right-wing history textbook titled *New History Textbook*, or Fusosha textbook, named after Fuso Publishing, its publisher, and authored by the Japanese Society for History Textbook Reform, a group comprised of right-wing nationalist scholars and politicians. The textbook first described Japan as aiding in the modernization of Korea: "Since [Chosŏn] opened its doors to the outside world, Japan has supported military reforms of the Korean dynasty as part of its efforts toward the modernization of [Chosŏn]. It was vital to the security of Japan that [Chosŏn] developed into a modern state capable of self-defense without yielding to foreign domination." To justify Japanese colonial rule in Korea, the textbook unreasonably argued that Japan had freed Chosŏn from China's domination and supported the kingdom's modernization, totally ignoring Japan's ruthless aggression to control Korea as a colony.

With regard to the Russo-Japanese War, the textbook explained that "the Korean peninsula protrudes from the continent to Japan like an arm.... If the Korean peninsula came under control of Russia, it could be used as a base for an invasion of Japan.... With its national budget and armed forces ten times greater than those of Japan, Russia reinforced its military presence in Manchuria and established a military base in the northern part of [Chosŏn]. It was evident that Russia's military in the Far East would grow so powerful that Japan could hardly match it. The victory by Japan, a burgeoning modern state and a country of non-white people, over the Caucasian empire of Russia instilled hopes of independence into colonized people." In short, the textbook glorified the war as a defensive measure against threats from a Korean peninsula controlled by Russia and as a purely heroic and patriotic action.

In discussing the annexation of Korea, the textbook stated that "there were some voices within [Chosŏn] accommodating Japan's annexation. The Japanese Government-General in Korea endeavored to modernize Korea." The Japanese annexation of Korea, in other words, was a non-coercive response to the Koreans' wishes and, after annexation, Japan contributed to Korea's modernization.

Concerning the forcible change of Korean names into Japanese names, the textbook pointed out that "on the Chosŏn [Korean] peninsula, the change of Korean surnames into Japanese names was approved [by the Japanese government], and policies were carried out to Japanize the Korean people." This implied that Koreans themselves had wanted the name changes and earned approval for the changes from the Japanese government. The textbook ignored one of the most notorious abuses of human rights perpetrated by the Japanese, the enslavement of tens of thousands of "comfort women" as sex slaves for Japanese soldiers. It did not reveal that many of the comfort women were conscripted from Korea against their will by the Japanese Imperial Army.[21] By doing so, the textbook denied the forcible mobilization of Korean women for prostitution for the Japanese soldiers. Since the 1990s the Japanese government has given only a token apology and has refused to make proper compensation to the victims.

The history textbook prompted criticism from South Koreans for its glorification of Japan's imperialist past. But when the Japanese government approved the controversial history textbook again in 2005, the percentage of secondary schools using the book as their text increased tenfold. In April 2009 the Japanese government approved a history textbook, written by the very same Japanese Society for History Textbook Reform but this time published by Juyu Publishing, and it was used in classrooms in 2010. This second textbook was even worse than the first. As a whole, the textbooks glossed over Japan's invasion of Korea and glorified the invasion by arguing that the Japanese had sped Korea's emancipation.

THE ALLIED POWERS' WARTIME POLICY ON KOREA

The Emergence of the Korean Problem

In the late nineteenth century, Korea was a center of great conflict for its neighboring powers, China, Russia, and Japan. It once again emerged as a focus of international rivalry in the 1940s, almost 30 years after Japan annexed that country in 1910, demonstrating that it was still critical to the peace of Northeast Asia. This time the two archrivals for the strategic peninsula were the United

States and the Soviet Union, and the Korean problem began with the proposition that Korea be placed under the trusteeship of a group of other nations. The trusteeship issue caused a maelstrom in Korea, when it was publicly announced in late 1945. It also influenced to an extent how the United States used the trusteeship arrangement to prevent the sovietization of postwar Korea.

The trusteeship matter surfaced for the first time in 1943, when, on 27 March, in Washington, British Foreign Minister Anthony Eden met with U.S. President Franklin D. Roosevelt, who suggested returning Manchuria and Taiwan to China and establishing trusteeship arrangements for Indochina and Korea. He also recommended that China, the United States, and one or two other countries act as trustees in Korea.[22] Despite opposition from the British, who rejected the trusteeship idea because of their huge colonial holdings, the United States proceeded with Roosevelt's proposals for postwar trusteeships.[23]

Allied military victories in the Pacific during 1943 led the United States to consider more seriously the impact of the Soviets entering the war against Japan. U.S. officials realized that Russia had been deeply involved in Korean affairs ever since the late nineteenth century, and that because the Soviet Union was now in a superior military position on the Asian mainland, it was capable of occupying Korea unilaterally at the end of the Pacific war. The multinational trusteeship was considered a sure way to prevent the Soviet Union from making a unilateral move in Korea, and thus the Soviet agreement to trusteeship assumed greater importance. Although the Roosevelt administration favored trusteeship for certain regions, strategic considerations dominated U.S. thinking with respect to Korea. During the autumn of 1943, the United States concentrated its energies on achieving an accord with the other three major powers—Britain, Russia, and China—for a Korean trusteeship.

The Cairo Conference

An ambiguous commitment to Korean independence was made in a joint communiqué, issued on 1 December 1943, by the three participants in the Cairo Conference held on 22 November 1943, which included President Roosevelt, Prime Minister Winston Churchill, and Generalissimo Jiang Jieshi (Chiang Kai-shek). The part regarding Korea read that "Japan will ... be expelled from all ... territories which she has taken by violence and greed. ... The aforesaid three great powers, mindful of the enslavement of the people of Korea, are determined that in due course Korea shall become free and independent."[24] Although the three powers had officially pledged their support for Korean independence after the war, the phrase "in due course" left some questions as to the nature of the Allied commitment to Korean independence. Thus, although they welcomed the Cairo Declaration, many Koreans worried about the implications of the proviso "in due course," which obviously meant Korean trusteeship. At the time the participants failed to grasp the mood of the Koreans who were impatient for their country's independence. Roosevelt, in particular, linked Korean trusteeship with the Philippine experience. In the Tehran Conference between Roosevelt, Churchill, and the Soviet leader Joseph Stalin, held from 28 November to 1 December 1943, Roosevelt stated that "the Koreans are not yet capable of exercising and maintaining independent government and they should be placed under a 40-year tutelage."[25] When, on 30 November, Stalin said that he approved of the Cairo Declaration, the Allies appeared united behind trusteeship.

The Yalta Conference

From early 1944 U.S. officials, discussing a multilateral trusteeship for Korea, planned for a partial or full military occupation of Korea. In March 1944 they envisioned a U.S. presence in any military occupation of the country. The United States also raised the possibility of a military government for Korea, believing that the Soviet Far East harbored 35,000 Koreans, "thoroughly indoctrinated with Soviet ideology and methods of government." The United States expected Soviet forces to occupy a considerable area of the Korean peninsula, and therefore U.S. forces were to cooperate with Soviet forces in governing Korea prior to the trusteeship. Military occupation was a surer course than trusteeship, in the Americans' view, if the Soviet Union proved uncooperative or if they used their "thoroughly indoctrinated" Koreans.[26] The Americans further believed that total Soviet occupation of Korea might threaten future security in the Pacific, and thus U.S. participation was essential in any occupation of Korea.[27]

In preparing for the pending Yalta Conference, U.S. officials set forth American political objectives in Asia that envisioned a multinational military occupation and trusteeship for Korea. To establish Korean independence, they saw the need for joint action by the Allied powers. Considering that both China and the Soviet Union were contiguous to the Korean peninsula and had historical interests in Korea, military occupation by a single power might cause serious political consequences. Similarly trusteeship should be multilateral, with four powers as trustees, namely, the United States, the Soviet Union, China, and Great Britain.[28]

U.S. officials suggested three steps to achieve Korean independence: first, joint military occupation by the Allied powers; second, establishment of a military government under a single, unified administration; and, third, transfer of the military government's authority to a provisional Korean government under the supervision of the trustees.[29]

On a rising tide of Allied victories, U.S., Soviet, and British leaders met at Yalta from 4 February to 11 February 1945 to discuss a number of pressing issues. First priority was given to European political and military problems, particularly the Polish question, in which the United States and the Soviet Union conflicted sharply over how the postwar Polish government should be formed, and the newly established United Nations Organizations. Another major issue was the Pacific war and the problems that might arise if the Soviets entered the still raging war against Japan. Korea was briefly discussed by Roosevelt and Stalin, and on 8 February, quoting the U.S. experience in the Philippines, Roosevelt proposed that Korea be made a trusteeship for 20 to 30 years. Stalin replied that the shorter the period, the better. He then inquired about stationing foreign troops in Korea during the trusteeship period, and Roosevelt answered in the negative.[30] The conversation between the two leaders produced only a vague understanding, and thus the United States and the Soviet Union failed to reach a firm agreement at Yalta on a postwar trusteeship for Korea. Later official evidence dispelled the misunderstanding that at Yalta the United States and the Soviet Union secretly agreed on the division of the Korean peninsula at the 38th parallel.

The Potsdam Conference

After Yalta, U.S. officials were uneasy about the lack of a detailed, written agreement on the postwar status of Korea, as the Yalta agreements allowed the Soviet Union to play a dominant role in neighboring Manchuria. Thus the issue of the Korean trusteeship urgently needed clarification. When Roosevelt died on 12 April 1945, Harry S. Truman assumed the presidency and dispatched Harry Hopkins, Roosevelt's close aide, to the Soviet Union to resolve differences between the United States and the Soviet Union, and to reaffirm the Yalta agreements. The Truman administration still wanted Russia's agreement on a detailed trusteeship arrangement in postwar Korea through the Hopkins mission. Most of the talks between Stalin and Hopkins, which lasted between 26 May and 6 June 1945, focused on European affairs, but on 28 May Hopkins asked Stalin about his views regarding the Korean trusteeship. Stalin expressed full agreement with the U.S. proposal for a four-power trusteeship for Korea.[31] But, once again, Stalin's apparent support was merely an informal, verbal understanding.

With the Potsdam Conference drawing near, scheduled for 17 July to 2 August 1945, U.S. officials strongly felt that the agenda should include a detailed discussion of a postwar trusteeship for Korea and that the Allied powers should reach an agreement. As before, attempts were made at the conference to organize a multilateral trusteeship to prevent the Soviet Union from dominating the Korean peninsula. On 22 July, however, when Soviet Foreign Minister V. M. Molotov asked for deliberation on the Korean trusteeship, the issue was deflected by a discussion of the Soviets' desire to participate in a trusteeship in the Italian colonies in Africa. Thus the well-laid plans to discuss postwar Korea were foiled, and further discussion about Korea was postponed until a later Council of Foreign Ministers meeting, which did not occur until December 1945.

In the summer of 1945, with the Pacific war still a preoccupation, the United States could not participate strongly in Korean affairs. Thus, having to direct its power utterly against the Japanese home islands, the United States entrusted military operations in Korea, considered more difficult than an invasion of Japan and one that would accrue higher losses, to the Soviet Union. For this, the United States would pay a high price.

At the same time the United States was preparing for the sudden collapse of Japan in the event of a U.S. atomic attack. On 16 July, the day before the Potsdam Conference convened, President Truman had learned of the successful testing of the atomic bomb. At that point, he began to consider "atomic diplomacy," using the atomic bomb to bring an early Japanese surrender as well as derive the great diplomatic and strategic benefits of having a nuclear weapon. Clearly the possible Soviet engagement in postwar Japan would be eliminated. This also meant that the United States could prevent any Soviet military action on the Korean peninsula and establish its own unilateral occupation.

Truman entertained the hope that such a strategy in Korea would be possible, when he heard Stalin's statements at Potsdam. On 18 July Stalin declared that the Soviet Union would not enter the Pacific war before 15 August 1945. He convinced his American counterpart that if the United States could force Japan to surrender during the first two weeks of August, the Soviets would miss the opportunity to participate in the Pacific war and would therefore not acquire the attendant spoils of war. Truman thus concluded that victory over Japan through the use of the atomic bomb would forestall Soviet entry into the Pacific war as well as unilateral Soviet action in Korea.

To end the Pacific war as early as possible, on 26 July the United States and Great Britain issued the Potsdam Declaration, demanding Japan's unconditional surrender. When Japan delayed in answering, the United States forced its early surrender by dropping atomic bombs on Hiroshima and Nagasaki on 6 and 9 August, respectively. On 8 August, still hoping to secure the spoils of war, the Soviet Union declared war on Japan and subscribed to the Potsdam Declaration, which reaffirmed the Allied powers' pledge to strive for the eventual independence of Korea.[32] On 9 August Russian troops went into action in Manchuria and northern Korea, and within five days, by 14 August, they had marched far inside the Soviet-Korean border. Bowing to heavy pressure, particularly from the United States, Japan finally surrendered unconditionally on 14 August 1945, ending the Pacific war.

The 38th Parallel

The decision to divide Korea into two occupation zones at the 38th parallel was entirely the choice of the United States. Soviet entry into the Pacific war had deprived the United States of the opportunity to establish Korea's postwar independence on its own terms. Now U.S. concern was to secure a foothold on the Korean peninsula for political and strategic reasons. The only real decision now was the location of the demarcation line between the occupying forces. Civilians, led by Secretary of State James F. Byrnes, wanted the United States to occupy as much of the region as possible in order to block Soviet expansion. But military leaders realistically pointed out the limited military resources that would be available to deny Soviet expansion into an area that the Soviet Union had the capacity to seize. Here the State-War-Navy Coordinating Committee (SWNCC) took responsibility for dividing Korea. The SWNCC, created by Roosevelt in November 1944, was comprised of assistant secretaries from each department to improve civil-military consultation on major policy questions. At around midnight, on 10 August, John J. McCloy, representing the State Department, allowed 30 minutes for Colonels Charles H. Bonesteel III and Dean Rusk to find a geographical line in Korea that would harmonize the political desire to have U.S. forces receive the surrender as far north as possible, with the obvious limitation of the ability of the United States to reach the area.[33] They were also directed to include in the American zone Korea's capital, Seoul, and two of the three important ports of Pusan, Inch'ŏn, and Wŏnsan. Bonesteel and Rusk studied a National Geographic Society map on the Far East and seized on the 38th parallel as a suitable boundary. The SWNCC promptly incorporated this provision into a preliminary draft titled "General Order Number One." Its final version was dispatched on 15 August to General Douglas MacArthur, the Supreme Commander of the Allied Powers, in Manila, and at the same time communicated to the Soviet Union and Great Britain.

No experts on Korea were involved in the decision to divide the country at the 38th parallel. Dean Rusk later confessed that neither he nor any of the others involved were aware that, at the turn of the twentieth century, the Russians and the Japanese had discussed dividing Korea into spheres of influence at the 38th or 39th parallels. He said, many years later, that "had we known that, we almost surely would have chosen another line of demarcation."[34] The alternative was to divide the occupation zones based on administrative districts, that is, to divide the country between provinces, in order to minimally violate political divisions.

Many U.S. officials doubted whether the Soviets would accept the U.S. proposal, as the 38th parallel clearly did not reflect Russia's superior military position in the region. After the American proposal was communicated to the Soviet Union, a "short period of suspense" ensued in anticipation of the Soviet reply, accompanied by suggestions that U.S. forces move into Pusan if the Soviet Union refused to accept the proposal.[35] To the Americans' surprise, however, the Soviet Union accepted the 38th parallel, permitting joint occupation in an area where the Soviet Union had the power to take full control. When Stalin made no objections, Dean Rusk was "somewhat surprised."[36] While accepting this division of Korea into two spheres, the Soviets were demanding permission to occupy the northern part of Hokkaido in Japan, which the United States refused.

Stalin's decision to accept the U.S. proposal to divide the Korean peninsula at the 38th parallel was, of course, not out of altruism. Most likely, Stalin was content with the 38th parallel, because the United States recognized Russia's "legitimate" rights in Korea north of that line. He may have viewed the 38th parallel as a suitable boundary to divide Korea into two spheres of influence, but he also decided to accept this partition to stave off further Allied discord that had developed mainly over the Polish problem. An attempt to seize all of Korea would alarm the United States and eliminate the possibility of Soviet participation in Japan's reconstruction.[37] After Japan's collapse, therefore, the United States could send its forces into a country that was all but conceded to the Soviet Union at the Potsdam Conference. Later on, in fact, American forces were able to occupy the portion of Korea that included its capital and two-thirds of its population.

The division of the Korean peninsula at the 38th parallel had tremendous consequences for the Korean people who had lived in a unified nation for a millennium. The 38th parallel symbolized a traditional Korean sentiment, *han*, a smoldering bitterness about past wrongs. In fact, the division of Korea along the parallel proved disastrous for Koreans on both sides of the line, as two entirely different political ideologies and societies ultimately emerged on the Korean peninsula and grew increasingly hostile to each other.

No words can easily be found to express the emotional injury that Koreans suffered following the tragic division of their country. Already in the late 1940s they tried to find solace in popular songs such as "P'anmunjŏm ŭi talpam" (A Moonlit Night at P'anmunjŏm) (1946), "Kagŏra samp'alsŏn" (The 38th Parallel Should Be Removed) (1947), and "Hae do hana, tal do hana" (The Sun Is the Same and So Is the Moon in Both Koreas) (1949).

The period of Japanese colonial rule represented the darkest age in the long history of Korea. Japanese colonialism was an exceptionally bitter experience for Koreans who barely managed to keep their national identity. Although the Korean people were freed from Japanese imperialism in August 1945, they had not achieved liberation by their own efforts, and thus they had to endure another hard experience of national division. Liberation on 15 August 1945 was no more than a new beginning of difficulties and suffering caused by the north-south division.

9

LIBERATION, DIVISION, AND WAR
(1945–1953)

FROM OCCUPATION TO A SEPARATE
GOVERNMENT IN SOUTHERN KOREA

Liberation and Division of Korea

THE YEARS FROM 1945 TO 1948 was a difficult and uncertain period in Korean history, only to be followed by the country's division into two Koreas, the North and the South, in August and September of 1948. The three-year U.S. occupation of the area south of the 38th parallel was marked by the absence of a clearly formulated policy for Korea, intense rivalry and confrontation between the United States and the Soviet Union, and the polarization of Korean politics between the Left and Right.[1] Americans, in particular, were ill-prepared for the task of governing Korea and lacked any definite plan of action. Americans were even slow to draw up detailed guidelines for the nation's military occupation. Nevertheless, the United States played a decisive role in the independence and formation of South Korea. Indeed, this momentous three-year period shaped the economy, society, and domestic politics of present-day South Korea.

Although the division of the Korean peninsula into two occupied zones was temporary at first, a means of accepting the surrender of the Japanese forces, the deepening of the Cold War and the growing antagonism between the United States and the Soviet Union on the Korean peninsula made the division permanent. Moreover, the American and Soviet approaches to administering their respective zones were different entirely. In the northern zone, Soviet authorities used the indigenous people's committees and enforced a policy of communization. In the southern zone, on the other hand, the 24th U.S. Army Corps, commanded by Lieutenant General John R. Hodge, established the U.S. Army Military Government in Korea (USAMGIK).The lion's share of responsibility for the division of the Korean peninsula at the 38th parallel was borne by the United States. U.S. officials had consulted no Koreans in making this decision, but the Korean people were still blamed for the political chaos that ensued. In particular, Korean political leaders, sharply divided along ideological lines, engaged in bitter confrontations, and were never able to reconcile their different visions of a future Korea. In the absence of mature leadership, the Korean people failed to unite in presenting a strong alternative course to the occupying powers.

The Korean People's Republic

With their surrender only days away, the Japanese in Korea had good reason to fear Korean reprisals after the end of colonial rule. Hoping to get assurances for the safety of Japanese lives and property until Allied forces arrived, Japanese Governor-General Abe Nobuyuki, on 10 August 1945, took immediate steps to form an interim administration controlled by Koreans. Not surprisingly, there were few Koreans he could approach to run the administration who were moderate, commanded respect, and wielded informal power. Endo Ryusaku, Abe's secretary-general for political affairs, sought to contact Song Chin-u, a rightist, but Song refused even to meet with Endo, fearing that leftists would label him a collaborator. The Japanese then approached left-leaning nationalist Yŏ Un-hyŏng, a well-known moderate figure with great prestige among Koreans based on his long anti-Japanese record. Before accepting responsibility for an interim administration, Yŏ demanded the release of all political prisoners and no Japanese interference in the maintenance of peace or with Korean efforts to gain independence. The Japanese accepted and designated him to head an organization to maintain public order. Yŏ organized the Committee for the Preparation of Korean Independence (CPKI) on 15 August, and his authority was accepted by most Koreans, including landlords, intellectuals, students, and professionals. With CPKI's encouragement, local notables organized 145 people's committees throughout the country, with associated volunteer police forces. The local people's committees effectively maintained law and order despite the lack of coordination with the central authority.[2] The arrangement between Yŏ and the Japanese maintained order, with no serious violence against the Japanese, and by the end of August Yo was the unchallenged de facto leader of Korea.

Until late August it appeared that Soviet forces might accept Japanese surrender throughout Korea, but in the last week news came that the United States would occupy Korea below the 38th parallel. Obviously this development would profoundly affect the political situation in southern Korea, and so Yŏ's CPKI and his followers called a national convention in Seoul on 6 September to provide his regime with the stamp of legitimacy by hastening the creation of a new government before the Americans arrived. At the convention, Yŏ proclaimed the Korean People's Republic (KPR) as a de facto government, with a cabinet that included distinguished nationalists of all political persuasions, both rightist and leftist. Despite efforts to represent all sides, the cabinet was influenced mostly by the Left, but because of his reputation among Koreans, Syngman Rhee was elected president without his knowledge or consent. Rhee refused the offer and remained an ardent anticommunist leader and a pillar of the Right. Although the Korean Communist Party was revitalized as a coalition of several communist factions on 11 September and was quickly building a substantial following among workers, peasants, and students, rightist organizations were also getting stronger as the United States was expected to come to southern Korea. On 16 September several rightist groups united to form the Korean Democratic Party (KDP). As a magnet for rightists in the first few months after liberation, the KDP remained the strongest single right-leaning party throughout the period of U.S. military occupation. The KDP described itself as a party of patriots, notables, and various circles of Korea's intellectual stratum, but leftists and moderates viewed it as a party of landlords, businessmen, and collaborators. In the initial U.S. occupation period, a fierce power struggle would arise between the leftist coalition around the KPR and the rightist coalition around Syngman Rhee and the KDP.

The Establishment of the U.S. Army Military Government in Korea

On 7 September 1945 General Douglas MacArthur, Supreme Commander of the Allied Powers, formally established American control in Korea south of the 38th parallel. The next day Lieutenant General John R. Hodge and his 72,000-strong 24th Army Corps landed in Korea. At the time, the U.S. government had no detailed guidelines for the occupation, and the 24th Army Corps, including the 6th, 7th, and 40th infantry divisions, drew heavy duty in Korea, simply because it was stationed on relatively nearby Okinawa, not because it had any specific qualifications for administering Korean affairs.

On 9 September Lieutenant General Hodge accepted Japan's formal surrender at the capital building in Seoul, but ignorant of conditions in Korea and with no plan of action, Hodge at first directed the Japanese Government-General to continue governing the country until other arrangements could be made. Hodge urged Koreans to be patient, but the Korean outcry forced the Americans to hastily withdraw the Japanese administration and replace it with a U.S. military government. On 12 September, Major General Archibald Arnold, commander of the 7th Infantry Division, was sworn in as governor-general, and two days later all Japanese officials were removed from office. The title of the administration was changed from Government-General to "Military Government," as the former denoted a "colonial status." English became the official language of the occupation, and, naturally, Americans then turned for information and advice to Koreans who spoke English. The U.S. Military Government soon earned the derisive nickname "government by interpreter" and repeatedly made mistakes and misjudgments in administering Korea, ultimately alienating itself from the Korean population.

Forging a New Order

Soon after U.S. forces arrived in southern Korea to oversee the Japanese surrender and established the Military Government, an atmosphere of anarchy enveloped the U.S. occupation zone. To foster stability, Americans asked the best-educated and wealthiest members of Korean society for advice and support, leading to a close relationship between the Military Government and the conservative KDP from the outset of the occupation. In effect, the KDP became the Military Government's ruling party. On 5 October 1945 the Military Government created an 11-member Korean Advisory Council to assist the military governor. Yŏ Un-hyŏng, the only representative chosen from the Left, refused to participate. Most Koreans felt that the Advisory Council did not represent them. Preoccupied with the perceived worldwide threat of communism, Americans believed that Yŏ's Korean People's Republic was under Soviet domination, and was therefore subversive, and refused to cooperate with it. General Hodge dismissed Yŏ's claim to legitimacy and outlawed the people's committees throughout the country. Because the KPR was not recognized by the Americans, Yŏ organized the Korean People's Party on 12 November 1945, thus implicitly consenting to the American demand that the KPR drop its claims to being a government and label itself only a political party.

The Americans brought in Syngman Rhee from the United States and the leaders of the Korean Provisional Government from China. Rhee arrived in Seoul on 16 October 1945, and the KPG officials, including Kim Ku and Kim Kyu-sik, returned to Seoul in late November and early December 1945. Syngman Rhee promptly set about building a political base. He was introduced to the Korean people for the first time at the welcoming ceremony for U.S. forces in Korea, held in Seoul on 20 October 1945, where he stood with the conservatives, particularly the Korean Democratic Party. Indeed, the party and Rhee needed each other. Despite U.S. favoritism toward the KDP, most Koreans considered the party unrepresentative, and so KDP leaders realized that they needed someone who would give their party legitimacy as a party of patriots. Syngman Rhee was considered the most qualified person to do so. Despite his personal prestige, Rhee had lost contact and command over the organized forces of internal political life at home because of his 40 years of exile. Needing a strong, grass-roots political machine, he allied with the KDP because of its newly won power within the Military Government. The alliance between the KDP and Rhee was a marriage of convenience.[3] The KPG exiles, on the other hand, frowned on the KDP and its allies who had seized so many important positions within the Military Government bureaucracy.

The chief concern of the United States in southern Korea was to maintain law and order amid the chaotic situation. To achieve this goal the U.S. Military Government quickly created the necessary police and military forces, and soon thereafter reorganized the police. The first plan was to initially use the Japanese police while training Koreans to take their place, but this proved impossible because the Koreans objected to the continued presence and authority of the hated Japanese police. The alternative plan was to replace all volunteer police and advertise for trained Korean policemen to join the new police force. The result was a wholesale reemployment of Koreans from the former colonial police force. On 21 October 1945 the Korean National Police was formally created and granted significant power, authority, and material and moral support.

In October 1945 the Military Government decided to form a Korean military force, and in early December it began selecting and training Korean military officers. On 15 January 1946, the South Korean Constabulary, the precursor to the South Korean Army, was formally established. Americans called for those who had prior military experience to join as officer candidates. To solve the language problem in training officers, Americans established the Military English Language School on 5 December 1945. With graduates of the Military English Language School as the nucleus, an extensive recruitment of enlisted men began in the spring of 1946. On 1 May 1946, as a replacement for the Military English Language School, the Korean Constabulary Officer Candidate School was established to produce an officer corps for the expanding army. Graduates of the schools later played important roles in the South Korean Army.

Officers with Japanese military experience dominated the South Korean Constabulary and the succeeding South Korean Army. On 5 December 1948 the government of the Republic of Korea created the Ministry of National Defense, the Army, and the Navy. Simultaneously all Constabulary brigades were reclassified as army divisions.

From the start the United States, particularly the officers of the Military Government, acted with Cold War logic. They sought to maintain the social status quo, building a political bulwark against communism, fostering rightist allies, and organizing the police and military to preserve order and stability. The Military Government preferred the police to the fledgling military force, which they viewed as heavily infiltrated by leftists.

The Trusteeship Issue and the U.S.-Soviet Joint Commission

To clarify many problems that arose between Allies after the war, the foreign ministers of the United States, Great Britain, and the Soviet Union met in Moscow from 16 to 26 December 1945. On 27 December the Foreign Ministers' Conference reaffirmed a U.S. proposal for a five-year trusteeship of Korea administered by the three states plus China. The United States and the Soviet Union were to establish a joint commission that would consult with the Koreans to create a provisional Korean government.

News of the Moscow agreement reached Korea on the morning of 29 December 1945. Trusteeship was a major affront to Korean national aspirations for immediate independence. The Koreans saw in the trusteeship proposal a renewal of foreign interference, for the Japanese had used the term to justify their rule. The proposal pulled a psychological trigger in the minds of the Koreans, and in southern Korea the initially warm welcome to U.S. forces as liberators cooled. Strikes and demonstrations occurred throughout Korea but were immediately suppressed in the Soviet zone. Following the line of their northern counterparts, from early January 1946 communist and sympathetic leftist groups in southern Korea began to support the Moscow agreement and trusteeship. As wave after wave of resentment swept the country, dangerous tension was building in Seoul. Specifically Kim Ku mobilized mass demonstrations against trusteeship and finally attempted a coup on New Year's Eve in 1945, issuing a series of proclamations that amounted to a direct attempt to seize the government. But the coup attempt failed, and his stubborn opposition to a trusteeship cost Kim Ku U.S. support in his struggle to attain power in postwar Korea.

Preliminary talks between the American and Soviet commands began in Seoul in January 1946. Each side was deeply suspicious of the other, and apart from agreeing on supplies of electricity from the North to the South, only minor matters were settled such as the exchange of mail.

The U.S.-Soviet Joint Commission held its first meeting in Seoul on 20 March 1946, with five members each from the U.S. and Soviet commands. Major General Archibald V. Arnold and Colonel General Terenti F. Shtikov headed the U.S. and Soviet delegations, respectively. After six weeks of detailed discussion, the two sides were unable to reach any significant understanding concerning which group of Koreans should be consulted to pursue the Moscow agreement to form a provisional Korean government. After 24 fruitless sessions the Joint Commission adjourned in deadlock on 8 May 1946. It reconvened on 21 May 1947 but reached another impasse in July. No agreement could be reached as to which Korean political parties and social organizations were qualified to participate in the Commission's activities. The Russians demanded that only those accepting the Moscow agreement and trusteeship (which the U.S. side interpreted as "leftists") were eligible to participate with the Joint Commission in forming a provisional government; the Americans insisted that all credible groups, including anti-trusteeship groups (which the Soviet side interpreted as "rightists"), should be consulted on the basis of the principle of "free speech." The Joint Commission continued its meetings but progress ceased, and in August 1947 the Commission adjourned for the last time.

In retrospect, the Joint Commission had little chance of success. It could have succeeded only through close U.S.-Soviet cooperation. Unfortunately for Korea, the cooperative spirit among the Allies during World War II had rapidly disappeared, and by early 1947 the United States and the Soviet Union were locked into the Cold War. The newly developed ideological and military stalemate between the two powers adversely affected Korea. The actions of U.S. officials and Koreans in southern Korea made the exact execution of the Moscow agreement impossible, and to guarantee the participation of rightists in the Joint Commission activities, the United States never adhered to the strict application of the accord. Without the participation of the American-supported rightists, it was crystal clear that the future provisional Korean government would be dominated by leftists or communists, as had happened in Poland. The Soviet Union also opposed any compromises that might possibly cause it to lose its predominant role in northern Korea or the opportunity to gain control over the entire Korean peninsula. The failure of the Joint Commission was a foregone conclusion.

Toward a Separate Government in Southern Korea

Efforts of the U.S. Military Government to strengthen southern Korea against communist domination led it to establish a separate southern government. Unlike U.S. officials in Washington, Americans on the scene in southern Korea were actually confronted with the leftist revolutionary thrust and thus earnestly pursued both responsible and anticommunist leadership there from the start of the occupation. At first this policy failed to meet positive approval from the U.S. government. Because negotiations with Russians over Korea had bogged down, however, the policy to create a separate southern government increasingly garnered support from top officials in Washington. At the time, fundamental U.S. policy in Korea was to set up a free, unified government for the entire Korean peninsula through a political settlement with the Soviet Union, or at least to keep southern Korea noncommunist with American support against communized northern Korea.

U.S. occupation officials in southern Korea believed that unless they acted swiftly to bolster conservative elements, the Left, particularly communists, would dominate the American zone. By late January 1946 the Military Government had sought to unify Kim Ku's Korean Provisional Government, the Korean Democratic Party, and other non-leftist political groups under the leadership of Syngman Rhee. With that aim, on 14 February 1946 the South Korean Representative Democratic Council was established as a broad rightist political coalition, with 28 rightist political leaders and with Rhee as chairman.

During early 1946 the Right experienced a steady rise in popularity as a result of American sponsorship as well as popular opposition to trusteeship. In the event of a breakdown at the U.S.-Soviet Joint Commission, the U.S. government could implement a program of "Koreanization" in the southern zone alone. Meanwhile, in July 1946, in order to forestall a unilateral Soviet action to create a friendly regime in the northern zone, the U.S. government instructed the Military Government to forsake its exclusive attachment to the Right in favor of a broad coalition embracing moderates. The Military Government reluctantly attempted to build a moderate coalition around the leadership of Kim Kyu-sik, a leader of moderate rightists. Although the chances of success seemed slim, Kim managed to join forces with Yŏ Un-hyŏng. Initially Yŏ refused to participate in the coalition movement, and he was under intense pressure from extreme leftists to quit the coalition effort. He was even kidnapped, beaten, and warned not to participate, but he finally agreed to take part in it. On 7 October 1946 the Left-Right Coalition Committee was formed, with Kim and Yŏ as cochairmen.[4] Kim emerged as the Military Government's choice for political leadership, but he lacked dynamism and broad support among the Korean masses.

In the meantime, on 1 July 1946, Military Governor Major General Archer L. Lerch announced that the Military Government soon would sponsor the formation of the South Korean Interim Legislative Assembly (SKILA). Rightists began immediately to mobilize in an effort to control the forthcoming SKILA elections. The Korean Communist Party, under the leadership of Pak Hŏn-yŏng, on the other hand, denounced the U.S. policy as premature and in violation of the Moscow agreement.

The SKILA was established as an advisory legislative body, with half the 90-member assembly elected and the other half appointed by General Hodge. Because followers of Syngman Rhee controlled the administrative apparatus, the rightists scored a sweeping victory. From its opening session on 12 December 1946, Rhee's rightists dominated the legislature on almost every major issue.

While preparing for the selection of delegates to the interim legislature, U.S. officials also took steps to provide certain Koreans with experience in government and administration. As the Military Government appointed local leaders to work with its bureaus as a prelude to the creation of the South Korean Interim Government, a growing body of rightist Koreans controlled the central bureaucracy of the interim government.

Cooperation between the United States and the Coalition Committee was short-lived. U.S. officials on the scene were preoccupied with limiting leftist political power and increasingly undermined the Coalition Committee, and the moderate alternative in Korean politics failed to realize the anticipated results. The failure of the U.S.-Soviet Joint Commission in the summer of 1947 had an immediate effect on politics in southern Korea. The moderate coalition that the United States had put together to support its position finally collapsed when Yŏ Un-hyŏng was assassinated in Seoul on 19 July 1947. Syngman Rhee, who had already mounted a campaign to establish a separate government in southern Korea, was confident that the United States would now work with him.[5] In short, the political situation was heading increasingly toward the creation of a separate government in the U.S. occupation zone.

Opposition to the Left

When the Korean People's Republic collapsed under American opposition, the Left created another coalition called the Democratic People's Front (DPF), a group that included all leftists. The opening session of the DPF was held in Seoul on 15–16 February 1946. The DPF platform and programs were similar to those of the Korean People's Republic, for it was, after all, the direct successor of the KPR.

Americans mistakenly viewed the DPF as directed by Soviet-trained Korean communists; none of the key DPF leaders, however, had been trained or directed by the Russians. The organization was actually a response to the inauguration in northern Korea, on 8 February 1946, of the North Korean Interim People's Committee led by Kim Il-sung. It was also a response to the formation of the South Korean Representative Democratic Council by southern rightists on 14 February 1946. The DPF was simply an organization for southern leftists and, like the KPR and the people's committees in the South, was a creation of indigenous southern leftists.

The DPF was doomed to suppression by the U.S. Military Government. From the opening of the Joint Commission in March 1946, the suppression of the Left went hand-in-hand with U.S. policies aimed at creating rightist Korean leadership. As the Joint Commission deadlocked in early May 1946, the Military Government and Korean rightists were determined to root out leftist opposition in southern Korea.

On 15 May 1946 the rightist-controlled Korean National Police announced that it smashed a counterfeiting ring allegedly involving top Korean Communist Party officials and members. The police charged top party leaders with issuing some 12 million *wŏn* in counterfeit bills from October 1945 to February 1946 in the Chŏngp'ansa building housing the KCP headquarters and the party's newspaper, *Haebang ilbo*, or Liberation Daily. The party allegedly used the counterfeit notes as its secret fund. The KCP charged that the entire affair was a frame-up by the police and asked, in vain, for the evidence upon which the charges were made.[6] Despite the party's denial of all charges, a judge associated with the Korean Democratic Party found the accused persons guilty.

Using the opportunity provided by the "Chŏngp'ansa Incident," the Military Government accelerated the suppression of leftists throughout the summer of 1946. In early September 1946 the Military Government issued warrants for the arrest of three top officials in the Korean Communist Party—Pak Hŏn-yŏng, Yi Kang-guk, and Yi Chu-ha. The three went underground to evade arrest. At the same time the Americans ordered the closing of three leftist newspapers—*Chosŏn inminbo*, or Korean People's Newspaper; *Hyŏndae ilbo*, or Modern Daily; and *Chungang sinmun*, or Central Newspaper. By September 1946 most communist leaders in southern Korea were in jail or being hunted down.

Resistance to the U.S. occupation policy spontaneously burst into violence in the fall of 1946, when the "October People's Resistance" was precipitated by a railroad strike in Pusan on 24 September. The strike quickly spread to Taegu and Seoul, and combined with protests against forced grain collections and police brutality to completely engulf the southeastern provinces. The unprompted popular uprising lasted into December 1946. Shocked by the magnitude of the violence, General Hodge suspected that communists in northern Korea or the Soviet Union had ordered the riots and were preparing a military attack from the North. He promptly ordered wholesale suppression of the leftists. Other U.S. observers, within and outside the Military Government, recognized that the uprisings were not a well organized, communist-led revolution but were spontaneous, indigenous peasant rebellions.

During the uprisings many people were killed and injured. The wave of wrath was mainly directed at the police, who lost more than 400 of their members in brutal executions.[7] Property damage was extensive. The total number of arrests is unknown, but it may have approached 30,000 or more in the three-month period of violence.

The people's uprisings represented the failure of U.S. military occupation policies, particularly in the economic realm, specifically mounting inflation and forced grain collection. The successful suppression of the October People's Resistance, however, marked a turning point in the balance of power between the Left and the Right that favored the Right and weakened leftist forces irreparably. After the people's resistance, the remnants of the KCP united with other leftist elements to form the South Korean Workers Party on 23 November 1946.

Throughout 1947 the U.S. Military Government and the Korean police continued their harsh suppression of leftists. In February 1947 police raided the

National Council of the Korean Labor Union, a leftist organization, and the Democratic People's Front headquarters in Seoul and arrested their leaders. On 22 March the leftist labor union called for a general strike of workers throughout southern Korea. The strike began in Pusan and spread rapidly to Seoul, Taegu, Inch'ŏn, and other cities. In Seoul and Inch'ŏn students went on strike in sympathy, but by 24 March severe police suppression swiftly broke the strikers' resolve.

The suppression peaked in August 1947. On 27 July thousands of people carrying banners of the Democratic People's Front gathered in Seoul to celebrate the reconvening of the U.S.-Soviet Joint Commission. This was destined to be the last authorized political assembly of leftists. The participants paid a high price. Workers who attended the meeting were fired on and arrested when they protested. The Military Government and the Korean police initiated the large-scale arrests of leftists throughout southern Korea on 12 August and completed their operation on 23 August, with about 2,000 arrests. Leaders of the Democratic People's Front and other leftist organizations were arrested, and their headquarters searched and finally closed. Many liberal teachers, writers, artists, newspaper reporters, and lawyers were also rounded up.

The widespread crackdown was closely related to a new U.S. policy on Korea. At the time the reconvened Joint Commission had reached another complete deadlock, and the United States was seeking a way out of the impasse. The only alternative under these hopelessly stalemated conditions was to establish a separate southern government. Thus the large-scale suppression of leftists was the direct result of the American plan to create a separate rightist regime in southern Korea.

Following the suppression, major leftist organizations went almost completely underground throughout the country. Leftists maintained offices in only a handful of large cities, and these, too, seemed on the verge of a shutdown. Finally, by the end of 1947, the way had been cleared to establish a separate rightist government in southern Korea.

U.S. Policy in the United Nations

In early 1947 the United States reconsidered its policy toward Korea, but it came at a particularly difficult moment. The crisis in Greece and Turkey had already forced the United States to reassess its overall strategy in the Cold War. As the Joint Commission meetings remained at a standstill throughout the summer of 1947, the United States decided to refer the Korean problem to the United Nations. It even acknowledged that the creation of a separate government would be unavoidable.

On 17 September 1947, over the Soviet Union's objection, the United States placed the Korean issue before the second regular session of the U.N. General Assembly. Although the Soviets argued that the United Nations had no jurisdiction over the Korean problem, the United States at the time had overwhelming support in the international forum. On 14 November 1947 the U.N. General Assembly unanimously adopted a U.S. resolution to hold elections throughout Korea in order to send representatives to a new body, the Korean National Assembly, which would in turn establish a National Government of Korea. The election would be based on a system of proportional representation from the population, and thus southern Korea would be assured roughly two-thirds of the total number of representatives. A Temporary Commission on Korea was to supervise the election, which would occur no later than 31 March 1948. The newly formed National Government would arrange with the occupying powers the complete withdrawal of their armed forces as soon as practical and, if possible, within 90 days. Then the Temporary Commission would report its conclusions to the General Assembly and consult with the Interim Committee.[8]

U.S. policy in the United Nations appeared to be a great victory for the nation itself. But the transfer of the Korean problem to the international body was unfortunate for Korea, for, without Soviet cooperation, a unified Korea would be impossible. Actually, as the Soviet Union refused to help implement the American resolution, U.S. policy to submit the Korean problem to the United Nations only accelerated the creation of two separate Korean regimes and thereby perpetuated the divided Korean nation.

The Role of the UNTCOK and Unification Efforts by Korean Leaders

Because the Soviet Union denied the United Nations Temporary Commission on Korea (UNTCOK) access to northern Korea, the Commission was confined to southern Korea. It had little hope, therefore, of carrying out observations of an election in the northern zone. On 6 February 1948 the Temporary Commission finally decided to consult with the Interim Committee of the General Assembly, now in session in New York.

Meanwhile, the Korean domestic situation seriously worsened. The events in southern Korea had turned extremely violent after the Temporary Commission announced that it intended to consult the Interim Committee. A wave of sabotage and strikes swept southern Korea. Organized by leftists, the sabotage, mass demonstrations, and attacks on the police posed a serious challenge to the authority of the U.S. Military Government. In scores of carefully planned attacks on the police and rightists, more than 40 persons were killed and thousands were arrested. Incidents continued for three months, right up to the 10 May election day.

In New York the Interim Committee considered the Korean problem, and on 26 February 1948 adopted the U.S. resolution by a vote of 31 to 2, with 11 abstentions. The main point of the resolution proposed that the UNTCOK observe elections for representatives to a national assembly in those areas of Korea accessible to the Commission, namely, southern Korea.[9]

Immediately, extreme rightists jubilantly greeted the Interim Committee's decision, whereas moderates and leftists expressed deep disappointment. The moderates and leftists, as well as Kim Ku's rightist group, would not participate in separate election in southern Korea, which meant that the extreme rightist elements would coalesce around the Syngman Rhee–Korean Democratic Party coalition and control practically 100 percent of the vote in the forthcoming election.

News of the Interim Committee resolution reached the Temporary Commission by cable. Members of the Commission held an informal meeting on 28 February, where they agreed to implement the resolution of the Interim Committee and issued a statement that the Commission would observe elections in accessible parts of Korea no later than 10 May 1948.[10]

Two days later General Hodge announced that the election would be held on 9 May, under the supervision of the UNTCOK. South Korean religious groups requested a one-day postponement of the elections, as 9 May was a Sunday, but the Americans refused. Ultimately, however, the date was changed to 10 May on the recommendation of the Chinese representative. A solar eclipse was expected on 9 May, which Koreans would construe as a bad omen.

After several heated discussions, the Temporary Commission formally decided on 12 March, by a small majority, to implement the resolution of the Interim Committee. Everything was now ready for an election in accordance with the wishes of the United States.

Korean political leaders who opposed the separate southern election sought to hold the North-South political leaders' conference as an alternative. On 12 March 1948 certain prominent leaders, including Kim Ku, Kim Kyu-sik, Cho So-ang, and Hong Myŏng-hŭi, issued a joint statement pledging to work for a unified Korea and vowing not to participate in a separate election held in southern Korea alone. In a letter to Kim Il-sung, chairman of the North Korean People's Committee, and Kim Tu-bong, chairman of the North Korean Workers Party, they proposed that measures to establish a unified Korean government be discussed through a conference of political leaders of northern and southern Korea. On 25 March the North Koreans invited all South Korean parties and groups opposing a separate southern election to meet on 14 April in Pyongyang with representatives of the North Korean political parties and social organizations to discuss the unification of Korea. Within a week, the South Korean political leaders accepted the invitation.

Under these circumstances, 7,837,504 voters actually registered during the period of registration from 5 to 10 April. The UNTCOK reported that the estimated population in southern Korea on 1 April 1948 was 19,947,000. The possible total number of registrants, based on the percentage of 49.3 as derived from the 1947 National Registration, was 9,834,000. On this basis, the number of actual registrants was some 79.7 percent of the potential electorate.[11] But the high percentage of registration did not necessarily accurately reflect the popular will. The very high registration number could be partly explained by police threats to withdraw individual rice ration cards from those who failed to register.

The Soviet Union did not sit still. To offset America's success in southern Korea, the Soviet Union attempted to force the United States to recognize the legitimacy of the northern regime. On 17 March 1948 G. P. Korotkov, commander of the Soviet forces in northern Korea, delivered an ultimatum to General Hodge from Kim Il-sung threatening to cut off the flow of electricity to the U.S. zone on 15 April.

The North-South Korean political leaders' conference in Pyongyang opened on 19 April but was delayed because Kim Ku and Kim Kyu-sik, the two leading South Korean delegates, had not yet arrived. Then, after a private meeting on the morning of 30 April between Kim Ku, Kim Kyu-sik, Kim Il-sung, and Kim Tu-bong, the conference was finally held that afternoon and attended by one representative from each of the political parties and social groups. The plenary meeting unanimously adopted a statement attacking the United States, the United Nations, and Syngman Rhee's extreme rightists who were seeking a southern election, and appealing to the Korean people to oppose that election. A resolution also called for the withdrawal of foreign troops.

When they returned to Seoul on 5 May, Kim Ku and Kim Kyu-sik declared that their North Korean counterparts had agreed to hold a nationwide election after foreign troops left Korea and that the North Koreans had promised not to cut off electric power to southern Korea. Because a separate southern election appeared to be inevitable, however, the two Kims gradually retreated from their earlier hard-line positions.

In a move obviously intended to punish and humiliate Kim Ku and Kim Kyu-sik for not taking strong action against the separate election, on 7 May North Koreans renewed their intimidation to cut electric power to their southern neighbors. The unilateral North Korean breach of their earlier promise hit the two leaders hard. The North Korean threat was also designed to force the southern electorate to boycott the voting and to distract their attention from the separate election by arousing fears of suspension of electricity.[12] Finally, North Koreans did stop supplying electric power to southern Korea on 14 May, immediately after the separate election in the U.S. zone.

The Korean leaders' efforts to unify Korea ended in complete failure. Without the close cooperation of the occupying powers, their efforts were fated to fail; from the start, the Korean problem could be solved only by negotiations between the United States and the Soviet Union. Actually, Koreans never had any say in their own destiny.

Immediately following the conference, communists in southern Korea intensified their program of violence and subversion. They used threats of violence and assassination to convince the UNTCOK that it should not supervise the separate election. Even if this strategy failed, the chaos caused by their activity at least would discourage voter turnout. The local police retaliated with accelerated anti-leftist repression. During the first four months of 1948, the police and political extremists killed more than 250 people. Another 200 fell victim to indiscriminate violence in April, including 8 election officials and 2 candidates. Domestic instability peaked during the week just prior to the 10 May election, when more than 300 people died. Threats, beatings, robbery, and imprisonment were the order of the day.

The Birth of the Republic of Korea

Because leftists and moderates opposed and boycotted the separate election in southern Korea, the major concern was not whether a predominantly rightist victory would be possible but whether a successful election could be held at all. The main concern was the activities of the police and rightist youth organizations, as they were closely aligned with the Rhee-KDP coalition that was determined to force the separate election at any cost.

To uphold law and order during the election period, the U.S. Military Government authorized the police to mobilize some one million members of the Community Protection Corps, which was formed on 21 April 1948. Membership was necessarily drawn from among rightists and, in many instances, right-wing terrorist youth organizations. The Military Government also engaged in a large-scale propaganda campaign to persuade people to participate in the election despite the opposition of leftists and moderates.

On election day the voting went smoothly in most areas. Of the 7,837,504 registrants, 7,036,750, or 95.2 percent of registrants, actually took part in the voting.[13] The Americans described the election as a great victory for democracy and a repudiation of communism. Although its members discovered evidence of oppression and intimidation wherever they observed the voting, the UNTCOK reported that the high percentage of voting might be explained by the Koreans' patriotism.

The results of the election were ambiguous nevertheless. Rhee's National Association for the Rapid Realization of Korean Independence elected 55 candidates, the Korean Democratic Party 29, and the rightist Taedong Youth Corps 12; 6 others were elected from another rightist group, the Taehan Youth Corps, which had been supported by the U.S. Military Government. Overall, these rightist parties and social organizations won 102 seats out of 198. Although independents obtained nearly 40 percent of the seats and thus formed the largest single group of successful candidates, they were never a cohesive political force but featured many disparate political elements. Many of them were KDP candidates only disguised as independents to hide their party membership.[14] So, although no party had a clear-cut majority, effectively the National Assembly was predominantly rightist.

After the election the creation of a southern government was just a matter of procedure. The U.S. Military Government and the rightist political parties that participated in the election busily hammered out the final shape of a new government. Politics in southern Korea during that summer centered on a power struggle within the once solid rightist alliance for control of the new government.

A dispute flared between Rhee and the Korean Democratic Party when the National Assembly convened on 31 May 1948, but ultimately the Assembly elected Rhee as chairman. Almost certain to become the first president of South Korea, Rhee was growing increasingly aloof. Concerned about its participation in the new government, the KDP pushed hard for the adoption of a constitutional draft that would establish a parliamentary system. Angry over what he saw as a challenge to his transcendent authority, Rhee threatened to resign his Assembly seat and actively oppose the new government. Yielding to Rhee's intimidation, the National Assembly adopted a constitution incorporating some superficial concessions to the KDP but basically creating a strong presidential system with a four-year term for the presidency. The first constitution was adopted by the National Assembly on 12 July and was promulgated five days later. On 20 July the National Assembly elected Syngman Rhee president of South Korea.

The Republic of Korea was formally inaugurated on 15 August at a ceremony in Seoul attended by General Douglas MacArthur. General Hodge officially proclaimed that the USAMGIK would be terminated at midnight on that date. Unable to eliminate the economic damage done by Japanese colonial rule, the new government was faced with the pressing task of reconstructing the bankrupt economy left by the chaos of the three-year post-liberation period. These, along with various other problems, were too demanding a task for a new and inexperienced government.

The course of events in southern Korea brought a prompt response from northern Korea. On 9 September the North Korean government led by Kim Il-sung was officially established as the Democratic People's Republic of Korea. The two mutually hostile regimes refused to cooperate with each other, even though at least a working relationship between the two governments was necessary to develop a viable economy in either state. Each state saw itself as the only lawful government of all Korea. Nevertheless, the permanent division of Korea was now an accomplished fact.

ECONOMIC AND SOCIAL PROBLEMS IN SOUTHERN KOREA

Economic Difficulties and Social Chaos

The division of the Korean peninsula into the U.S. and Soviet occupation zones in August 1945 further aggravated already serious economic problems. Even if the Americans had arrived with a carefully considered economic plan, the situation would have been difficult, as the Japanese had developed Korea's economy only as part of their empire, with little for Korea's economic welfare. When liberation came in August 1945, therefore, many inherent problems stood in the way of building a self-sufficient economy in southern Korea. Most of the natural resources, particularly mineral resources, heavy industry including fertilizer production, and electric power generation were concentrated in northern Korea. Southern Korea, in contrast, was the food basket and center of the textile and other light industries.

Although trade between the two zones was essential for a viable economy in each area, it was already severely reduced even before the Korean War of 1950. Along with the lack of electricity, the problems were further complicated by the near absence of managerial and technical skills and capital resources. The main source of electricity for both zones was the Sup'ung Electric Plant on the Yalu River, but on 14 May 1948 northern Korea cut off the power supply to its southern neighbor, depriving it of more than half its already inadequate electric power. As the Americans repatriated Japanese holdovers to their homeland in the months following their military occupation, almost all the factories and mines vested in the Military Government as enemy properties were left without managers, technicians, and capital. The inevitable result was high levels of unemployment and severe shortages.

The U.S. Military Government, aided only by complete faith in free private enterprise, removed all wartime economic controls. Hoarding, speculation, food shortages, and massive inflation followed. As the Military Government rescinded Japanese controls on rice, the attempt to establish a free market resulted in disaster. At the time Korea was not yet in an economic stage of development capable of successfully adopting a free market system. The immediate effect of the free market policy was a steep rise in the price of rice, resulting in hoarding and speculation. Moreover, despite a bumper harvest in 1945, maldistribution of food led to food shortages and hunger in the cities. The rice-based South Korean economy began to suffer from severe inflation, and a black market grew and prospered to the point where, lured by high prices, rice disappeared almost entirely from the free market and flowed into the black market. Through its free market policy, the Military Government lost the main strong point of the South Korean economy—its ability to extract large surpluses of grain—and caused, instead, spiraling inflation in early 1946 and a general economic breakdown.

The disastrous shortage of rice in southern Korea caused U.S.-Soviet relations to deteriorate. From 16 January to 5 February 1946, the Americans and Russians held a joint conference in Seoul to consider administrative and economic matters of mutual concern to American and Soviet military authorities in Korea. Whereas the Americans favored complete administrative and economic integration, the Russians sought only an exchange of goods, with one fixed goal in mind—to secure southern Korean rice for the hungry population of northern Korea. Clearly the Russians believed they were being deceived when the Americans professed at the conference that southern Korea was experiencing a severe rice shortage, for only a short time earlier the Americans had announced that there was a surplus of rice. The Russians concluded that the Americans were intentionally undermining the Soviet administration in northern Korea by preventing the use of surplus South Korean rice to alleviate the critical food shortage in northern Korea. All that northern Korea wanted was rice, and the Americans did not have it. It was over this essential issue that the conference stalled and ended in failure.

The U.S. Military Government was flooded with complaints and petitions from Koreans demanding that price controls and rationing be resumed and that it act promptly to stop the rice hoarding. As a result, by February 1946, the Military Government had not only rescinded the free market but had also ordered rice rationing. Indeed, the rice shortage was evident throughout the country, and people everywhere thought, spoke, and wrote of only one thing—food, which meant rice to Koreans. People were generally confused, frightened, and uncertain. The food situation was so serious that in the summer of 1946 the Military Government began to worry about the possible appearance of the "rice communists," who might agitate a revolt among the hungry population. During March 1946 demonstrations were staged in several cities in protest to slim rations. Massive starvation was averted only by U.S. emergency relief under the Government Aid and Relief in Occupied Areas (GARIOA) program, intended to avert disease and unrest that might threaten U.S. forces. The receipt of U.S. grains made it possible to gradually increase rations; from 1945 to 1948, $400 million in aid was given to southern Korea, 90 percent of it in food, clothing, fuel, other consumer commodities, and fertilizer.

The deteriorating food situation forced the Americans to revive the old Japanese rice collection system. Because black-market rice was 7.6 times higher than the price of collected rice, farmers wanted their rice sold on the black market rather than collected by the Military Government. The farmers' reluctance to comply with rice collection led the Military Government to enforce it by all means necessary.

The collection of grain, particularly rice, was carried out throughout the period of U.S. military occupation, and collection results improved as the years passed. The non-farming population was put on rations; non-farmers received individual ration cards, drew their rations at a ration station, and made payments according to the price of rice set by the Military Government. The number of ration recipients was roughly 6.9 million in 1946, 8.5 million in 1947, and 9.6 million, or some 48 percent of the total population, in 1948. The average daily ration per person was 1.2 *hop*, or 630 calories, in 1946; 2.3 hop, or 1,228 calories, in 1947; and 2.4 hop, or 1,236 calories, in 1948. Because the actual ration fell short of the minimum ration (2.5 hop) promised by the Military Government, Korean consumers had to make up the difference through the black market. The price of rice on the black market was usually 5.25 times higher than that of rationed rice, and therefore Korean rice consumers had to struggle against hard times. At the time, expenses for the staple food amounted to 30 percent of the total living expenses for a household.

The socioeconomic situation was complicated by the repatriation of the Japanese, along with their managerial and technical skills, and a huge inflow of Koreans from former Japanese territories and from northern Korea. The U.S. Military Government sped the evacuation of the Japanese from Korea. At the time of liberation there were some 2 million Japanese on the Korean peninsula with about 700,000 in southern Korea. About the same number of Japanese refugees had fled south from northern Korea to avoid persecution by Soviet troops. Roughly 400,000 Japanese troops in Korea were disarmed by American and Russian forces, and many Japanese soldiers who remained in the Soviet occupation zone were sent to forced labor camps in Siberia. All the Japanese in the U.S. zone were repatriated to Japan in an orderly manner.

At about the same time, of the more than 2 million Koreans in Japan, about 1.5 million were repatriated and some 600,000 chose to remain in Japan. At the end of World War II, 1.4 million Koreans were still in Manchuria, 600,000 in Siberia, and 130,000 in China proper. Of these Koreans, some 500,000 returned to their homeland, making the total repatriated from overseas over 2 million. Most of the repatriated went to southern Korea. Along with these overseas Koreans, by the end of 1947 more than 800,000, most of them Christians, came south over the 38th parallel, producing a sudden increase in the population of more than 2.8 million and creating huge problems, including massive unemployment.[15]

As industries became paralyzed, their production was no more than 10 to 15 percent of the pre-liberation potential by the end of 1948. Moreover, southern Korea was exposed to severe inflation when the Japanese recklessly printed money before their surrender. As defeat in the Pacific war was impending, the Japanese, in an atmosphere of hysteria, flooded their colony with paper money. This excessive issue of paper currency was also designed to buy protection. In June 1943 a billion Bank of Chosen yen notes had circulated in Korea; on 6

August 1945, 4 billion notes were in circulation throughout Korea. By October 1945 7 billion or more circulated in the U.S. occupation zone alone. Currency in circulation continued to rise steadily to 18.3 billion in January 1947 and 33.4 billion in December 1947. The newly established Republic of Korea government also issued too many Bank of Chosŏn notes, amounting to 38 billion wŏn (formerly called yen) at the end of 1948. Thus, while retail prices rose 10 times higher between August 1945 and December 1946, wholesale prices soared 28 times higher. The average monthly cost of food per person rose from 8 yen before the war to 800 wŏn (yen) by September 1946, a rise aggravated by the Military Government's release of controls over grain prices in October 1945. Strikes, demonstrations, and demands for more food were the order of the day.[16]

Serious economic distress led to a rapid increase in crime rates, as many city dwellers, especially refugees and repatriates pouring into southern Korea, stole, operated in the black market, or pimped in the alleys and marketplaces of Seoul and other major cities. Also, new refugees went into the business of illegally seizing "enemy properties" of the Japanese. Moreover, corruption pervaded all classes of society.[17] Black markets prospered to the extent that some 15 percent of the 1946 rice yields and 24 percent of the 1947 rice yields were channeled to this underground economy. In short, as suggested by the proverb "Hunger makes any man a criminal," destitution prevented many people from suffering qualms of conscience.

As social chaos added to economic sufferings, southern Korea under the U.S. Military Government was in a difficult situation. South Koreans had led hard lives, troubled by shortages of food, jobs, and all the other commodities needed in daily life.

The Major Accomplishments of the U.S. Military Government

Despite its mistakes and conservative bias, the Military Government generally acted with diligence and fairness in seeking to accomplish land reform, social and educational changes to promote equal opportunity for women and their full equality with men, and the development of a bill of rights. When Korea was liberated in August 1945, it was still an overwhelmingly agrarian nation. In southern Korea some 74 percent of the total population engaged directly or indirectly in agricultural production. Thus, when the Americans arrived in southern Korea in September 1945, they found a nearly universal clamor for land reform. In early October 1945 the Military Government placed a maximum allowable tenancy rent at one-third of the crop, which proved very popular. Unfortunately, however, the rent-reduction measure had no effective enforcement mechanism and Korean officials under the Military Government made few attempts to enforce the regulation. Korean landlords widely violated the measure, which was only effective on former Japanese-held lands vested in the Military Government. On 6 December 1945 the Military Government took ownership of all former Japanese properties, including farmlands, as of 25 September 1945. Late in 1945 the Americans set up the New Korea Company which was charged with managing the former Japanese farmlands.

To keep southern Korea noncommunist, the Americans had to improve the existing land tenure system to deflect peasant farmers from the appeal of communal ownership of farms. From early 1946 the Americans directed their attention to the redistribution of farmland, and in February 1946 they drafted a proposal to sell formerly Japanese-owned farmlands to tenants. Unfortunately the execution of the program was postponed indefinitely, as the Military Government decided that, on the basis of several opinion polls, the Koreans preferred to wait for the establishment of a Korean provisional government before proceeding with farmland reform.

As the U.S.-Soviet Joint Commission reached its final impasse in the summer of 1947, the United States decided to establish a separate rightist government in southern Korea. The creation of a southern regime needed firm support from its people, and because more than 70 percent of South Koreans were farmers, the Americans could find no more effective means than land reform to gain the people's support. Again, in late March 1948, the Military Government announced a program to sell formerly Japanese-held farmland to tenant farmers and to allow tenants, whose holdings did not exceed 2 chŏngbo (approximately 5 acres) to buy their farms. A buyer's total holdings could not exceed 2 chŏngbo through the land sale. Each piece of land was to be sold for three times its historical average yearly production, and the purchase price was to be paid in the principal crop over a period of 15 years, without interest. Therefore a farmer could pay 20 percent of a normal yield each year and eventually own his land, with title and deed. By September 1948, 245,554 chŏngbo, or 613,885 acres, amounting to 91.4 percent of the total farmland vested in the New Korea Company, had been sold. Unsold farmland was transferred to the newly established Republic of Korea government.

The land sale began on the eve of the general elections to establish the National Assembly, which were held on 10 May 1948, and triggered land sales by Korean landlords who feared that the land reform would ultimately be expanded to include their own land. As a result of both the Military Government's sale of previously Japanese-held farmlands and Korean landlords' sales, the land tenure structure in southern Korea underwent significant changes. At the end of 1947, 18.7 percent of the total farmer households were landlord and owner households; 38.8 percent were part-owner/part-tenant households; and 42.5 percent were full-tenant households. By June 1949 the number of landlord and owner households increased to 37.0 percent of the total and that of part-owner/part-tenant households rose to 42.0 percent. On the other hand, the number of full-tenant households decreased to 21.0 percent of the total.[18] It is undeniable that the Military Government's farmland policy produced a beneficial result for the Koreans—an unequivocal, substantial improvement of the age-old tenancy system in Korea.

Another major contribution that the Military Government made to the future growth of South Korea was the development of Korean education. Americans opened educational opportunities to everyone, with the new educational system modeled after the U.S. school system, including six years of elementary school, six years of secondary school (three years of middle school and three years of high school), four years of higher education, and additional years for graduate studies. In January 1948 attendance up to the sixth grade became compulsory. In mid-June 1946 the Military Government announced a plan to establish a Seoul National University, in which the former Kyŏngsŏng Imperial University would be transformed into a Korean national university. The plan caused intense conflict between leftists and rightists, with both vying for the leadership of the university. In September of that year Seoul National University was finally established. In three years of military occupation, the elementary education population doubled, and the number of students in secondary education tripled. The popular educational system that the Americans established in the country ultimately produced the well-educated workforce that was primarily responsible for South Korea's subsequent economic and industrial growth.[19]

During their military occupation, the Americans also introduced important social reforms. As already pointed out, every South Korean was made legally and socially equal, thus laying the very foundation for democracy. The Military Government guaranteed freedom of speech, press, assembly, association, and religion to every Korean, and these basic rights were written into the new constitution of the Republic of Korea in July 1948.

Overall, the U.S. Military Government produced some important achievements in economic and social areas. Exemplified by their efforts to prevent widespread starvation, Americans' goodwill as a whole outweighed the administrative mistakes and individual sins of this foreign occupation force.

NORTHERN KOREA AFTER LIBERATION

The Soviet Occupation

After the Soviet Union declared war against Japan on 8 August 1945, units of the Soviet 25th Army, commanded by Colonel General Ivan Chistiakov, attacked the northernmost Korean towns of Unggi (present-day Sŏnbong) and Najin. After running into light Japanese resistance, Soviet forces entered Korea by 10–11 August. After landing at the port city of Ch'ŏngjin on the East Sea on 12 August, they rapidly occupied most of the country north of the 38th parallel, and on 22 August the Red Army marched into Pyongyang.

The Soviet Union was much better prepared than the United States to deal with the problem of Korean occupation. When Soviet forces entered northern Korea, they encountered the people's committees in all the regions, immediately recognizing these self-governing organs and establishing close working relationships with them. By using these people's committees, the Soviet Union administered northern Korea without establishing a military government. Together with local Koreans willing to cooperate with the occupation forces, the Soviet army was accompanied by many other Koreans who were naturalized Russian citizens or members of the Red Army. The Soviet Union was able to use all these Koreans in fashioning a provisional government in North Korea.

Still, however, the Soviet occupation forces were unpopular among the overall populace, generally because of their crude behavior, specifically raping and looting. Reportedly, after they entered Korea, every night two or three Russians were killed by Koreans who had no weapons other than rocks.[20] In late November 1945, at Sinŭiju on the Yalu River, youth and student groups, mostly Christians, revolted against the Soviet occupation. The Soviet forces cruelly suppressed the anticommunist revolt, killing 23, wounding more than 700, and arresting more than 800. Thereafter freedom of political activity no longer existed in the Soviet occupation zone.

Although it wanted to establish a pro-Soviet power base in North Korea, the Soviet Union initially did not try to create a communist regime directly. It sought to set up a united front of political forces dominated by the communists. Russians were afforded an opportunity to do that when, after liberation, provincial branches of the Committee for the Preparation of Korean Independence (CPKI) were organized in northern Korea. On 17 August 1945 Cho Man-sik, a moderate nationalist, established the South P'yŏngan province branch of the CPKI. At about the same time, other provincial branches were also organized throughout North Korea. On 22 August the Russians arranged a merger of the South P'yŏngan and the Pyongyang branches to form the People's Political Committee. Cho Man-sik was so important that the Russians appointed him chairman of the indigenous interim administration. Although it aimed ultimately at securing communist hegemony, as it had in Eastern Europe, the Soviet Union used Cho as a figurehead leader of the coalition government comprised of communists and nationalists.

By the end of August 1945, people's committees had been in existence throughout northern Korea, and on 6 September they sent their delegates to the national convention in Seoul to establish the Korean People's Republic under the leadership of Yŏ Un-hyŏng. The people's committees in the North recognized the KPR as the sovereign body that would administer the Korean peninsula. Cho Man-sik's People's Political Committee also recognized the KPR and was placed under its authority.

When the Americans in southern Korea refused to recognize the KPR, the northerners created the North Korean Five Provinces Administrative Bureau on 28 October 1945. Again, Cho Man-sik was elected chairman of this body that only coordinated local people's committees and entrusted them with full administrative powers.[21] This form of government did not last long, however, ending in early February 1946 with the establishment of the North Korean Interim People's Committee.

Unlike the Americans who were not equipped with detailed or long-range administrative plans and political guidelines to cope with the problems of Korea, the Russians had arrived with a background of considerable knowledge of Korean affairs and well-prepared plans for administering northern Korea with the cooperation of many friendly Koreans. Obviously their goal was to integrate northern Korea into the Soviet orbit politically as well as economically.

Kim Il-sung's Rise to Power

Six months after liberation North Korean politics entered a new phase, with Kim Il-sung's rise to power. The Russians appear to have chosen Kim as North Korea's leader, as they thought he was cooperative and would be sufficiently pro-Russian.[22]

Kim Il-sung's emergence to power and the rise of the "Kimist" system dated from early 1946. His prime assets were his record of anti-Japanese resistance, organizational skills, and ideology. Kim was fortunate to survive the 40-year independence struggle against the Japanese that had killed off many leaders of the older generation. North Korea claimed that Kim was *the* leader of all Korean independence fighters, but the fact is he was only one among many leaders of the independence struggle. Kim did, however, win the support and firm loyalty of several guerrilla fighters, including Kim Ch'aek, Ch'oe Hyŏn, Ch'oe Yong-gŏn, and others, who were all young and tough, and as nationalistic as Kim Il'sung. The prime test of legitimacy for leadership in postwar Korea was one's record under the hated Japanese rule, but Kim was further helped when his allies assumed military power. This military background functioned as a formidable weapon against rivals with no military experience.

Although he was supported by the Red Army, at first Kim was not North Korea's undisputed leader. To consolidate his power in the later Korean Workers Party, Kim tried to reorganize the party. He probably had gained his organizational skills from his experience in the Chinese Communist Party in the 1930s. Unlike intellectual or theoretical communists such as Pak Hŏn-yŏng, he broke from Soviet orthodoxy and aimed to make the KWP a "mass" party rather than an "elite" or vanguard party by recruiting masses of poor peasants and laborers. In December 1945, when Kim Il-sung replaced Kim Yong-bŏm as head of the North Korean Branch Bureau of the Korean Communist Party, party members numbered no more than 4,500, but its membership soared to 366,000 in August 1946, when the Kim Il-sung group and Kim Tu-bong's Korean New People's Party merged to form the North Korean Workers Party (NKWP). In August 1948, immediately before the establishment of the North Korean regime, its membership rose again to 752,000. Most of the new party members were poor peasants and laborers. Following in the steps of Chinese communist leaders, Kim pursued a style of leading the masses by getting close to the people; for example, he often visited farms or factories for "on-the-spot guidance" and instructed his subordinates to do the same. The unflinching loyalty of newly accepted party members enabled Kim to emerge as the top leader of the North Korean regime.

Kim Il'sung's rise to power, though it fit into the Soviet Union's strategy for Korea, owed mainly to his long history of nationalism rather than any deep communist beliefs. From the 1940s Kim's ideology had already been revolutionary and nationalist rather than communist. Indeed, the prevailing governing ideology in North Korea under the rule of Kim and his son and successor, Kim Jong-il, has been termed the so-called *juche* doctrine. Although the term *juche,* meaning "autonomous subject," is usually translated into "self-reliance," it originated in 1946 but was not officially used until Kim Il-Sung's speech delivered on 28 December 1955. The juche doctrine, in its stress on self-reliance and political independence, was appealing to the Korean people at first.

On 25 September 1945 Kim Il-sung, with a number of other Soviet-trained Koreans, landed at Wŏnsan. Then, on 14 October, the Soviet occupation forces held a ceremony to celebrate Kim's return to Korea. Still in his mid-thirties, Kim represented a new generation in Korean leadership.

When Soviet forces arrived in northern Korea, four major communist groups were available to them for manipulation—Kim Il-sung's followers, known as the "Kapsan [or partisan] faction," who were the smallest; a group returned from Yan'an, China, led by (Kim) Mu Chŏng and Kim Tu-bong, known as the "Yan'an faction"; the Soviet Koreans; and a domestic Korean communist group. Hŏ Ka-i's "Soviet faction" was mostly of second-generation Soviet Koreans who returned to Korea with the Soviet occupation forces, and the less cohesive "domestic faction" comprised northern party leaders who had worked underground during the colonial period and tended to support Pak Hŏn-yŏng, then in Seoul. The strongest and most popular political group in the North, however, was the "nationalists" under Cho Man-sik, who had no ties to the communists. The power struggle among these groups continued for at least a decade, but Kim Il-sung held the upper hand with the support of the Soviet Union. The Russians did not trust the Koreans who lived in Korea and thus helped Kim's accession to power as the surest way to maintain Soviet influence in North Korea.

As part of making Pyongyang the center of Korean communism, Kim Il-sung and his followers, aided by Soviet occupation forces, established the North Korean Branch Bureau of the Korean Communist Party in October 1945, which was renamed the North Korean Communist Party in April 1946. On 17 December 1945 Kim he took office as the party's First Secretary, replacing Kim Yong-bŏm. But Cho Man-sik, as chairman of the North Korean Five Provinces Administrative Bureau, remained the top leader. Until the end of 1945, under the authorization of Soviet forces, a coalition regime of communists and rightist nationalists controlled the political arena in northern Korea. As part of a national united front movement between the communists and nationalists, however, the Russians and Kim Il-sung urged Cho Man-sik's nationalists to form a noncommunist political party. Finally, on 3 November 1945, the Chosŏn

Democratic Party was founded. Later on, as has been demonstrated, the united front proved unstable.

This transitional pattern of politics finally ended in early 1946, as a dispute over the trusteeship issue led to the collapse of the united front movement between the communists and nationalists and the emergence of a separate northern regime. On 31 December 1945 Soviet occupation forces urged Cho Man-sik to declare his support for the Moscow agreement and trusteeship. Shortly after his firm refusal, on 6 January 1946 Cho was confined to a hotel in Pyongyang for months and indeed was never seen in public again.[23] On 8 February 1946 the North Korean Interim People's Committee (NKIPC) became the new governing body under the Soviet occupation. Kim Il-sung was named chairman of the NKIPC, his first major administrative post in the North.

The new governing body soon initiated sweeping economic and social reforms. In March 1946 all lands were expropriated without compensation and redistributed to the peasants. In June major industries owned mostly by the Japanese were nationalized. By August 1946 as much as 70 percent of all industry was under state control; by 1949 the percentage rose to 90 percent. A new law guaranteed equal rights for men and women. The economic and social reforms were brought about peacefully, as former landlords, capitalists, and Japanese collaborators were allowed to flee south. Beginning in 1947 the North Koreans began a two-year economic program based on the Soviet model of central planning, with priority on heavy industry. Thereafter the North Korean economy expanded rapidly under a centrally controlled system.

Kim Il-sung's consolidation of power with the help of the Russians was challenged, however. The Korean New People's Party was formed by returnees from Yan'an, China, under Kim Tu-bong, on 30 March 1946 and demanded a share of power in the new North Korean leadership. As a result, on 28 August 1946, the Kim Il-sung and Kim Tu-bong groups merged and established a new party, the North Korean Workers Party. The chairmanship fell to Kim Tu-bong, not to Kim Il-sung, who settled for the first vice-chairmanship. Nevertheless, firm Soviet support for Kim Il-sung relegated the Yan'an faction to a secondary position in the new party.

On 3 November 1946 elections were held to select local delegates who were to legitimize the reforms that had already taken place. As expected, one candidate ran for each seat. At the election, 99.6 percent of eligible voters cast their ballots and 97.0 percent endorsed the official slates. On 17–20 February 1947, these local representatives elected the Supreme People's Assembly and the Presidium.

On 22 February the Supreme People's Assembly approved the creation of the North Korean People's Committee as the highest executive organization under Kim Il-sung.

By early 1948 Kim Il-sung and his Kapsan faction virtually dominated the political arena in northern Korea. The balance of power among the competing communist factions decisively swung in favor of Kim's faction. Kim's main political power base was the Korean People's Army (KPA), which Kim had organized in mid-1946. When the KPA was formally founded on 8 February 1948, its first commander was Ch'oe Yong-gŏn, one of Kim's confidants. At the formation of the Democratic People's Republic of Korea (DPRK) on 9 September 1948, Kim's power was firmly established.

The Birth of the DPRK

Much like the United States did in southern Korea, the Soviet Union fashioned a separate, friendly regime in the area north of the 38th parallel. Moreover, from 1946 to 1948 the Russians already forged a quasi-colonial relationship with the regime, in which Korean raw materials were exchanged for Soviet manufactured goods, an effort to prevent China from influencing northern Korea.

On 18 November 1947, four days after the U.N. General Assembly passed a U.S. resolution on Korea, the Supreme People's Assembly delegated a special committee to draft a provisional Korean constitution providing for a national government with its capital in Seoul. The constitution was adopted in April 1948 but was not ratified officially until 3 September, following the establishment of the Republic of Korea (ROK) in the South. On 10 June Kim Il-sung announced that the North Korean People's Committee would sponsor elections, on 25 August, for representatives to a Supreme People's Assembly for Korea (212 from northern Korea and 360 from southern Korea). Elections were held under the façade of universal suffrage, with an underground election conducted in the South. The Supreme People's Assembly convened on 2 September, and the next day it ratified the April draft of the constitution. The Democratic People's Republic of Korea (DPRK) was formally declared on 9 September as the legitimate government of Korea. Kim Il-sung was elected premier, and Pak Hŏn-yŏng shared the vice-premiership with Kim Ch'aek and Hong Myŏng-hŭi, and also became minister of foreign affairs. On 12 October the Soviet Union recognized the North Korean government. Because the leaders of both the North Korean Workers Party and the South Korean Workers Party participated in the DPRK regime, the two parties united to form a single communist party, the Korean

Workers Party (KWP), on 30 June 1949. Kim Il-sung was elected chairman of this united party and thus emerged as the undisputed leader of the entire Korean communist movement. On the other hand, Pak Hŏn-yŏng shared the vice-chairmanship of the party with Hŏ Ka-i, a Soviet-Korean, and so had to be satisfied with becoming the number-two man in the North Korean leadership.

The formation of the ROK on 15 August 1948 and of the DPRK on 9 September 1948 formalized the de facto division of the Korean peninsula at the 38th parallel. Each state claimed legitimacy for the entire nation and strove to unify Korea on its own terms and at any cost.

THE TWO KOREAS BEFORE THE KOREAN WAR

The Cheju-do Uprising

On 3 April 1948 a rebellion led by the South Korean communists broke out on the island of Cheju-do. That day guerrilla forces descended from their bases on Halla-san to simultaneously assault 11 of the 24 police stands on the island. The rightist organizations, including the Northwest Youth Corps, were also raided.

Without external interference, the uprising grew out of a campaign launched by the South Korean Workers Party against a separate election scheduled to be held on 10 May 1948. The communists on the island were able to rebel mainly because their strength had been preserved intact since liberation. During the October People's Resistance of 1946, the U.S. Military Government and the Korean police concentrated their suppression of leftists on the mainland, leaving the communists on the remote island more or less alone.

When the uprising erupted, the U.S. Military Government promptly dispatched 1,700 mainland police and 800 constabulary troops to Cheju-do to support the island's meager force of one constabulary regiment (the 9th Regiment), 450 police, and several hundred members of a rightist youth corps. With sporadic fighting continuing, Major General William F. Dean, U.S. military governor, flew to Cheju-do on 29 April to reorganize the Military Government's campaign and order the uprising to be suppressed with minimal force. The Military Government assumed that the newly active Korean police and constabulary forces would eliminate the communist guerrillas. But the situation on the island fell short of its expectations.

Guerrilla activity resumed after the establishment of the Republic of Korea in August 1948. As the insurgency gradually reestablished itself, fighting intensified in early October. As the situation on the island did not turn in its favor, the

Syngman Rhee government sent reinforcements and, in early November 1948, launched a major offensive against the insurgents. The government contained the guerrillas but failed to force them off the island.

By the spring of 1949 the continued guerrilla resistance on Cheju-do had become a major source of anxiety to the Rhee government, and in early March the government sent a special combat command to the island. When the suppression campaign formally ended in mid-April 1949, the Cheju-do rebellion claimed some 30,000 victims, or 10 percent of the island's population, most of them innocent civilians massacred by government forces that also destroyed half the villages on the island.[24]

The Cheju-do rebellion demonstrated the frailty of Rhee's Republic of Korea government. Arguably the rebellion may have caused the spread of guerrilla activity to the mainland and thus may have been the true beginning of the Korean War that would ensue. The Cheju-do uprising has been interpreted quite differently, however, by conservatives and progressives in South Korean society. For instance, the ROK Ministry of National Defense under Lee Myung-bak's conservative administration (2008–2013) insisted that the rebellion was a mutiny by armed communists and thus the "Cheju-do uprising" should be renamed the "Cheju-do riots." On the other hand, Roh Moo-hyun's progressive administration (2003–2008) glorified the tens of thousands of islanders who had died as martyrs while struggling against the U.S. Military and Syngman Rhee governments.

The Yŏsu-Sunch'ŏn Rebellion

With the Cheju-do uprising still under way, another rebellion broke out on the mainland and absorbed much more attention. On 19 October 1948 some 2,000 troops of the 14th Regiment of the South Korean Constabulary rebelled against the government at the port city of Yŏsu, South Chŏlla province, as they were about to embark for Cheju-do to suppress the uprising on the island. For a time the rebellion of South Korea's own security forces seemed to threaten the very foundation of the fledgling Republic of Korea.

The Yŏsu rebellion was sparked by the refusal of elements of the 14th Regiment to leave for Cheju-do to help quell the uprising, but the root cause was the frustrated leftist struggle in southern Korea dating back to the country's liberation. At the time, the police were exclusively occupied by rightists, whereas the constabulary was heavily infiltrated by communists. The uprising, however, was neither centrally planned nor initiated by the South Korean Workers Party, not to mention North Koreans. As on Cheju-do, local circumstances prematurely triggered the revolt.The rebellion erupted on the evening of 19 October at the headquarters of the regiment just outside Yŏsu. Shortly after they rose up, the rebels moved into Yŏsu and were joined by local supporters of the South Korean Workers Party to seize control of the port city and the nearby city of Sunch'ŏn by 20 October. In the occupied areas they killed policemen, executed rightist activists, and reinstated the people's committees, transforming the occupied cities into a "liberated district."

The panicked Syngman Rhee government was not sufficiently prepared to handle the crisis. Threatened with political collapse and in total confusion, the ROK government committed tactical errors in its suppression campaign. Subsequently most of the rebels were able to escape into nearby mountains, particularly Chiri-san, and conduct their guerrilla warfare against the government. By 27 October government forces managed to regain control of the two cities, ending the rebellion. The armed revolt had claimed many lives, including policemen, loyalist soldiers, rebels, and civilians. Many people were arrested and charged with taking part in the riot and, if found guilty, were imprisoned or executed.

As soon as it overcame the immediate crisis, the Syngman Rhee government moved quickly to suppress all forms of dissidence in South Korean society and to strengthen its security forces. A purge of more than 4,700 officers and soldiers that had been staged by July 1949 prevented further military revolts in the South Korean army. Taking advantage of the tense atmosphere, Rhee, on 20 November 1948, secured passage of the draconian National Security Law outlawing communism. At the same time the government began a major buildup of its security forces, introducing compulsory military training in the schools, consolidating rightist youth groups into a nationwide paramilitary organization, creating a centralized military intelligence system, and doubling the size of the army to 100,000 men. Within a few months after the rebellion, South Korea became a police state.

After 27 October 1948 the remnants of the rebels and their civilian supporters who had escaped to Chiri-san controlled an area that was, in effect, two states: the Republic of Korea by day, the People's Republic by night. Not until the winter of 1949–1950 did the government launch a major offensive that finally crushed the guerrillas in the Chiri-san area.[25]

Although the Yŏsu-Sunch'ŏn rebellion was a spontaneous uprising by indigenous communists, without the South Korean Workers Party or the North

Koreans, and although it paved the way for organized guerrilla activity within South Korea, in the end it resulted in transforming South Korea into a "national security state" under Rhee's dictatorship. Meanwhile, North Korea continued to hope that the ongoing guerrilla warfare in the South would lead to the unification of the Korean peninsula.

The Withdrawal of U.S. Forces

The U.S. military occupation of southern Korea officially ended on 15 August 1948 with the formal creation of the Republic of Korea. On 9 September North Koreans proclaimed the Democratic People's Republic of Korea, and the new government there formally requested the withdrawal of occupation troops from the Korean peninsula. In compliance with the DPRK's request, Stalin announced that the Soviet Union would withdraw its forces from North Korea before the end of 1948 and urged the United States to follow suit.

An important development occurred, however, in the fall of 1948. On 13 October a quarter of the members of the ROK National Assembly introduced a resolution calling on the United States to withdraw its troops from their country. But then, as a result of the Yŏsu-Sunch'on rebellion, the public mood shifted to anxiety about national security, causing many lawmakers who had sponsored the U.S. withdrawal resolution now clamoring to halt the pullout.[26]

Stalin's intention to withdraw his forces, however, placed the United States in an embarrassing and dangerous position. Whereas the Soviets could withdraw without hesitation, as North Korea unquestionably was stronger than South Korea militarily, economically, and politically, American withdrawal would imperil South Korea's very existence. The Americans thought that withdrawing their forces would certainly invite a civil war between the two Koreas and that South Korea would have little chance of surviving such a struggle. Despite the compelling reasons for withdrawing, the United States feared that the inevitable collapse of the ROK government would seriously damage America's credibility and prestige.

American resolve to withdraw was strengthened, however, when, on 12 December 1948, the U.N. General Assembly recognized the Republic of Korea as the only legitimate government on the Korean peninsula. The United States concluded that it now could take positive steps in the direction of disengagement. On 27 December 1948 the Soviet Union announced that it had completed withdrawal of its forces from North Korea and demanded that the United States do the same.

Finally, in March 1949, the United States decided to complete the withdrawal of its forces from South Korea by 30 June of the year. To placate Syngman Rhee and bolster South Korean morale, the formation of the Korean Military Advisory Group (KMAG) was announced on 2 May 1949 and it was officially established on 1 July. By the end of May the United States had transferred its remaining arms, ammunition, communications equipment, vehicles, and spare parts to the South Korean army, then numbering approximately 114,000.

Throughout June the ROK government sponsored mass demonstrations in which South Koreans protested the U.S. decision to withdraw its forces. The South Korean government stressed that the United States had an obligation to guarantee the survival of the ROK as a crucial bastion of democracy in Asia. Despite these desperate appeals, the United States refused to alter its plans. On 29 June 1949 the United States withdrew the last of its combat forces from South Korea, ending almost four years of military occupation. U.S. officials were confident that South Korea could survive without American military protection, but it did not take long for them to find out that they were wrong.

Border Fighting and Guerrilla Warfare

The period between the spring of 1949 and the winter of 1949–1950 witnessed the outbreak of large-scale border clashes along the 38th parallel and major guerrilla fighting within South Korea. These incidents took thousands of lives and ultimately led to North Korea's all-out invasion of South Korea in June 1950.

The border fighting, probably initiated by South Korean forces, reflected a new assertiveness by the Syngman Rhee government toward North Korea. Indeed, the ardent anticommunist Rhee government called for a "March North," and some South Korean officials boasted that if war broke out, they would eat breakfast in Seoul, lunch in Pyongyang, and supper in Sinŭiju on the Yalu River at the Korean-Manchurian border.

Rhee and his military commanders appear to have started the border fighting along the 38th parallel in the spring of 1949. Beginning in early May these border clashes often escalated into major battles in the Ongjin peninsula, at Kaesŏng, and at Ch'unch'ŏn, involving battalion-sized units on each side. There were also numerous patrol skirmishes. North Korea, however, was also responsible for the border clashes, and Soviet advisers to the Korean People's Army were often involved in the conflicts. Since late September 1949 no major fighting along the 38th parallel occurred until the outbreak of the Korean War. The fighting that did erupt was confined to minor patrol skirmishes. Both Koreas now devoted themselves to guerrilla warfare in the interior of South Korea. The fighting was costly for the Rhee government, as the United States became deeply suspicious of Rhee's motives and made a fatal decision to limit its military aid to South Korea to "defensive weapons."

Meanwhile, communist policy had changed. On 22 February 1949 a northern delegation, headed by Kim Il-sung and Pak Hŏn-yŏng, left for the Soviet Union. About three weeks later, on 17 March, North Korea and the Soviet Union formally concluded cultural and economic treaties. They also entered into a secret military assistance agreement, with the Soviet Union promising a large-scale buildup of North Korea's military strength. As a result, North Korea accelerated the expansion of its armed forces over the winter of 1949–1950. Although the North Korean delegation succeeded in obtaining Soviet military aid, it failed to secure Stalin's approval for an attack on South Korea.

While accelerating its military preparedness, North Korea deployed its reunification strategy effort, organizing a united front with opponents of Syngman Rhee and reviving the insurgency in South Korea. On 26 June 1949 North Korea formed the Democratic Front for the Unification of the Fatherland (DFUF) to create a political crisis for Rhee. The same day Kim Ku, Rhee's chief political rival, was assassinated by a ROK army officer. The timing of the assassination and the conduct of the assassin's trial aroused suspicion of government complicity at the highest political level. Indeed, Kim Ku's assassin, though sentenced to life in prison, was soon released, reinstated, and promoted.

North Korea also began a large-scale guerrilla offensive. Aided by the infiltration of guerrilla units from North Korea, the South Korean Workers Party established new base areas on the east coast and stepped up its attacks on South Korean security forces. Although guerrilla activity peaked in mid-September 1949 with a succession of attacks on major towns in the countryside, the communist offensive soon collapsed.

After a brief pause, guerrilla warfare was renewed in October 1949. Responding to North Korea's call for another large-scale offensive, the guerrillas mounted a second wave of attacks on towns in early October, but the South Korean government carried out a successful campaign to root out the guerrillas during the winter months. North Korea tried to revive the guerrilla movement early in 1950 but failed, and experienced another major setback on 27 March 1950 with the arrest of two top leaders of the South Korean Workers Party remaining in South Korea, Kim Sam-nyong and Yi Chu-ha.[27] Now North Korea realized that the time for united front tactics had completely passed. The remaining option for the communist country to achieve reunification was a full-scale conventional invasion of South Korea.

Mounting Problems for South Korea

Although it had struck a fatal blow at communist guerrilla activity by the first months of 1950, the South Korean government paid a high price for its border fighting with its northern neighbor and its subsequent military campaign against communist guerrillas in the interior of the country. Because of heavy defense expenditures, it was in severe financial trouble, which was further aggravated by the government's fiscal mismanagement as well as a declining economy, including vicious inflation.

Rhee's maladministration greatly increased political opposition to him in the National Assembly. After the formal establishment of the Republic of Korea on 15 August 1948, the Korean Democratic Party, Rhee's close ally during the U.S. military occupation period, was excluded from participating in the newborn Rhee government. Considering themselves betrayed by Rhee, beginning in late 1948 KDP members established South Korea's first opposition party. On 7 September 1948 the disgruntled National Assembly passed the National Traitors Law to punish pro-Japanese collaborators, and although many members of the party were also vulnerable to such charges, the KDP did not oppose the law to remove the members of Rhee's cabinet that it disliked. In any case, the law had no effect, as Rhee had lined up with many pro-Japanese collaborators. On 10 February 1949 the KDP convinced several Rhee-aligned politicians, including Speaker of the National Assembly Sin Ik-hŭi, to break ranks with the Rhee government and join the KDP. Thereupon it was renamed the Democratic National Party (DNP) and became the first political group whose chief purpose was that of an opposition party.

Unhappy with Rhee's authoritarian style, abuses of power, and fiscal irresponsibility, the opposition party sought power by means of amending the constitution to create a parliamentary system. By the spring of 1950, South Korea was engrossed in a struggle between Rhee and the DNP-led National Assembly over a constitutional amendment and the establishment of a date for general elections. The DNP introduced a constitutional amendment to institute a parliamentary system and extend the term of the Assembly for an additional year, but the proposal was defeated on 14 March 1950, having failed to obtain the necessary two-thirds majority in the Assembly. The vote was 76 in favor of the amendment and 33 opposed, with 66 abstentions. Despite this slim margin of victory, Rhee immediately announced his intention to introduce his own constitutional amendment to increase the power of the chief executive by providing for the direct election of the president. Rhee sought to postpone the general elections several times, but following intense U.S. pressure, the date was finally set for 30 May 1950.[28]

South Korea's relations with the United States increasingly became strained. Doubts about the U.S. security commitment were raised by Secretary of State Dean G. Acheson's National Press Club speech on 12 January 1950, which seemingly left South Korea out of the U.S. defense perimeter in East Asia, and by the difficulty in securing passage of a Korea aid bill. Acheson's speech, some believe, in effect invited the North Korean invasion of the ROK in June 1950. In his speech Acheson stated that only the Aleutians, Japan, Okinawa, and the Philippines fell within a perimeter that would be militarily defended by the United States, thus giving the impression that the United States would not defend South Korea under any circumstances. Whereas the speech shocked the Rhee government, it greatly delighted Kim Il-sung. In fact, Acheson's speech was ambiguous in some ways that could be interpreted differently depending on one's political orientation. Whatever its interpretation, the speech had no impact on the communists' decision to invade South Korea.[29]

One week after Acheson's speech, on 19 January 1950, the U.S. House of Representatives defeated by a single vote (192 to 191) the revised Korea Assistance Bill of 1949 providing South Korea with economic aid for the remainder of fiscal year 1950. This resulted mainly from the rejection of the bill by supporters of Jiang Jieshi's Guomindang (Nationalist) government of Taiwan who assailed the readiness of the Truman administration to aid South Korea while denying economic aid to Taiwan. Rejection of the Korean aid bill further shocked the South Korean government. The Truman administration expressed concern and dismay over the rejection of the Korean aid bill and urged a quick reconsideration. To satisfy the Republican China lobby, the bill included economic aid for Taiwan. Thus, on 9 February 1950, the House passed the revised bill, now titled the Far Eastern Assistance Act, and the next day the Senate approved it. The bill provided $60 million to South Korea and $103 million to Nationalist China. On 31 March the Truman administration obtained congressional consent to another Korea aid bill that appropriated $100 million for fiscal year 1951.

By this time the military balance on the Korean peninsula was clearly tilted in favor of North Korea as a result of increased Soviet military aid and the return of thousands of Korean veterans of the Chinese People's Liberation Army.

Moreover, the Soviet explosion of an atomic bomb and the earlier communist victory in the Chinese civil war had placed South Korea at a political disadvantage in that region of Northeast Asia. In the winter of 1949–1950, therefore, South Korea was in serious crisis both politically and militarily.

The Final Stage for the Outbreak of War

Beginning in early 1949 North Korea was on a war footing. Later Kim Il-sung's 1950 New Year's speech was bellicose, excoriating South Korea as a puppet of the United States. By early 1950 the North Korean army had become a formidable fighting machine, which, by the spring of 1950, clearly held military superiority over its southern neighbor. Under these already perilous circumstances, South Korea was also embroiled in a struggle for power between Rhee and his opponents in the National Assembly.

As scheduled, the National Assembly election was held on 30 May 1950. In the elections Rhee barely clung to power, losing 20 percent of his support, but the Democratic National Party suffered a real defeat. Rhee's seemingly weakened position led North Korea to propose several last-minute unification proposals in the hope of destabilizing South Korea. Although most incumbents were replaced by new figures, the new National Assembly appeared to be dominated by independents who took 126 of 210 seats, while the pro-Rhee parties captured 55 seats and the Democratic National Party elected only 24 assemblymen. The remaining seats were taken by moderate and leftist candidates. Although its own formal ranks thinned in the elections, the DNP still had an excellent chance to increase its power by recruiting the many newly elected opposition independents. Rhee therefore faced a renewed challenge from the DNP when the new assembly convened, and until 1952 the DNP remained a strong, cohesive, and stable political force opposing Rhee.

Immediately after the elections, on 7 June 1950, the Central Committee of the Democratic Front for the Unification of the Fatherland proposed all-Korea elections in early August to elect a unified assembly. To prepare for these elections, the DFUF called for a joint conference of political leaders from both Koreas, scheduled to be held at either Haeju (North Korea) or Kaesŏng (South Korea) in mid-June. It also demanded that Syngman Rhee, along with other rightist politicians and parties, be excluded from the meeting. On 19 June, the day when the new South Korean National Assembly opened, the North Korean Supreme People's Assembly proposed to its counterpart in South Korea that the two legislative bodies merge. North Korea also offered to release Cho Man-sik in exchange for Kim Sam-nyong and Yi Chu-ha, the two South Korean Workers Party leaders who had been arrested on 27 March. These offers were designed only to throw the ROK government into confusion, and the Rhee government flatly rejected them. The atmosphere on the Korean peninsula was ripe for the outbreak of war, and the moment was fast approaching when a Korean People's Army soldier would fire on his enemies in the South.

The North Korean Decision to Attack South Korea

After exhausting other options to reunify Korea under communism, the North Koreans finally decided to conduct an all-out, conventional attack on South Korea. Already in February–March 1949 Kim Il-sung had begun lobbying for a Soviet-backed invasion of the ROK. He had proposed it and struggled for it, and now, with a Soviet army battle plan, he executed it. The invasion of South Korea that began on 25 June 1950 was pre-planned, blessed, and directly aided by Stalin and his generals, and reluctantly backed, at Stalin's insistence, by Communist Party chairman Mao Zedong of the People's Republic of China (PRC).[30]

Between 30 March and 25 April 1950, Kim Il-sung had visited the Soviet Union and secured approval from Stalin for his planned invasion of South Korea. During a secret summit, Kim envisioned realizing his goal in three stages—first, the concentration of the Korean People's Army troops near the 38th parallel; second, issuing an appeal to South Korea for peaceful unification; and, third, initiating military activity after the South Korean rejection of the proposal for peaceful unification. Then, at Stalin's insistence, Kim visited the PRC between 13 and 16 May 1950 and succeeded in securing Mao Zedong's approval for the planned offensive.

At Stalin's order, North Korea's requests for the delivery of weapons and equipment for the formation of additional units of the Korean People's Army were quickly met. Kim Il-sung patiently waited until he secured substantial Soviet military support. In addition to the delivery of arms and ammunition, Stalin sent military advisers experienced in large-scale campaigns to draft a battle plan for the invasion of South Korea. In April 1950 Mao Zedong sent North Korea 12,000 Koreans who had served with the Chinese People's Liberation Army, bringing the strength of these combat-experienced veterans who had been absorbed into the North Korean forces to 30,000, or some one-third of the total forces.

By the end of May 1950 the general staff of the Korean People's Army, aided by Soviet military advisers, announced the readiness of the North Korean army to begin amassing at the 38th parallel. At the insistence of Kim Il-sung, the invasion was scheduled for 25 June 1950. The North Korean armed forces had significant superiority over the ROK forces: in the number of troops, the ratio was 2 to 1; guns, 2 to 1; machine guns, 7 to 1; submachine guns, 13 to 1; tanks, 150 to 0; and planes, 6 to 1. The KPA operational plan envisioned that its troops would advance 15 to 20 kilometers per day and complete the main military activity within 22 to 27 days.[31]

Months earlier, in March 1950, North Korean leaders held a secret Politburo meeting in Pyongyang, where Kim Il-sung discussed with them the possibility of military action against South Korea. Pak Hŏn-yŏng spoke strongly in favor of invasion, predicting that 200,000 underground South Korean Workers Party members would emerge to join the invading northern forces. The consensus at the conference was that U.S. intervention was unlikely or, even if it did occur, would come too late to make any difference.[32]

Revisionist scholarship has argued that the Korean War originated in 1945, with the division of the Korean peninsula along the 38th parallel, but the fact is that the war began with a North Korean invasion of South Korea on 25 June 1950, as a continuation of the developing conflict between the two Koreas prior to 1950. To commemorate the conflict, the successive South Korean governments have set 25 June 1950 as the day the Korean War began.

THE KOREAN WAR

The Outbreak of the War

Early on Sunday morning (4:00 AM), 25 June 1950 (Korea time), the 89,000-strong North Korean forces, supported by tanks, heavy artillery, and aircraft, crossed the 38th parallel. North Korea claimed that it was merely responding to a South Korean invasion of its own territory, a patent lie. The attack struck at four points along the 38th parallel. Comprising the main invasion force were the troops sent across the border near Seoul, their mission to hasten the fall of South Korea by taking its capital city. In Seoul, panicky citizens clamored for information on the acute situation, and for a time South Korean forces appeared to have contained the invasion. It soon became evident, however, that after a brave initial resistance, South Koreans were completely overwhelmed.

U.S. President Harry S. Truman, who had gone home to Independence, Missouri, for the weekend, hurried back to Washington. After meeting with his national security advisers, he believed that the North Korean invasion was an

obvious move to broaden the communist hold in Asia by crushing the South
Korean government, and that the Soviet Union was behind the attack. One
official commented that the relationship between the Soviet Union and North
Korea was the same as "between Walter Disney and Donald Duck." Truman
instructed Warren Austin, U.S. ambassador to the United Nations, to recommend to the Security Council that "members of the United Nations furnish
such assistance to the ROK as may be necessary to repel the armed attack and
to restore international peace and security in the area."[33] At the time Yakov
A. Malik, the Soviet representative to the United Nations, was boycotting the
Security Council to protest that Communist China had not been given a seat in
the international body. With Malik absenting himself from the meeting, where
he could have exercised a veto, the motion was carried on 27 June. The Soviet
Union might have abstained from voting intentionally so that the United States
could quickly get Security Council approval to send American troops into Korea. Stalin, according to this view, wanted to draw the United States and the
PRC into the war in Korea to divert U.S. attention from Europe.

By Wednesday, 28 June, Seoul had fallen to the North Koreans. Early that
morning the main bridges over the Han River had been blown up by ROK
army engineers with no warning to the military personnel and civilian refugees crowding the bridges. By destroying the bridges prematurely, the South
Korean army not only killed hundreds but also trapped 44,000 of its own men
north of the river.

With the North Korean attack on the Republic of Korea, the U.S. attitude was
suddenly transformed. Truman announced military assistance for South Korea
and ordered General MacArthur to support South Korean forces with U.S. air
and sea forces. Air strikes, however, initially were restricted south of the 38th
parallel. He also instructed MacArthur to watch the fighting closely and report
on how South Korea was faring. The general flew to Korea for a firsthand look at
the battlefront on 29 June and reported to the president that U.S. ground troops
would have to come to the ROK's aid to prevent the loss of the entire country.
On 30 June Truman approved the dispatch of U.S. ground forces to Korea,
broadened the range of U.S. air and naval operations to include North Korea,
and authorized a U.S. naval operation to blockade North Korea's ports. At the
time, however, Truman thought that the United States was not undertaking a
war but a "police action," a limited effort meant to push North Korean forces
back into their country. But it was obvious that the United States was at war in
Korea, triggered by unprovoked North Korean aggression.

South to the Naktong

When he was told to commit American ground troops to the Korean fighting, General MacArthur had the 8th Army on occupation duty in Japan. It consisted mainly of four undermanned infantry divisions. The 24th Infantry Division became the first one to send men to Korea when MacArthur ordered one of its battalions to speed to the battlefront.

The 540-man "Task Force Smith," named after its commander Lieutenant Colonel Charles Brad Smith, was dispatched to Korea to buy time for MacArthur to bring enough men and arms into Korea from Japan. On 5 July Task Force Smith stubbornly fought off the North Korean assault at a point three miles above the town of Osan, and the first U.S. battle in the Korean War ended in tragic failure. Of 540 men who faced North Korean forces that July day, Smith lost 150 listed as killed, wounded, or missing. The battle had been a terrible but valiant one. Task Force Smith held up the North Korean advance for seven hours before withdrawing.[34]

Following a Security Council resolution of 7 July, the United Nations Command (UNC) was established, with General MacArthur as its commander. MacArthur would lead all U.S. Army, Navy, Air Force, and Marine personnel in Korea, as well as ROK forces, and the troops, ships, planes, and medical aid sent by 15 U.N. nations that joined the UNC. Lieutenant General Walton H. Walker, commander of the 8th U.S. Army, took command of the UNC ground troops on 12 July. The fifteen nations that committed themselves to the Korean fighting, with some immediately joining the UNC and others coming later, included Australia, Belgium, Canada, Colombia, Ethiopia, France, Great Britain, Greece, Luxembourg, the Netherlands, New Zealand, the Philippines, Thailand, Turkey, and South Africa. On 14 July ROK President Syngman Rhee handed over authority of the entire ROK armed forces to MacArthur. The peak strength of the UNC was 932,964 on 27 July 1953, the day when the Armistice Agreement was finally signed.

Beginning with the battle at Osan, Walker's 8th Army suffered a succession of defeats. From Ch'ŏnan (6–8 July) to Ch'ŏngju (10 July), Choch'iwŏn (11–12 July), the Kŭm River (15–16 July), and finally Taejŏn (19–20), North Korean forces continuously pushed the undermanned and poorly trained 24th Infantry Division, commanded by Major General William F. Dean, southward down the peninsula. At Taejŏn, U.S. and South Korean defenders tried to stave off the North Korean advance without success. Dean became separated and was later captured by North Koreans. He would spend the next three years as a North Korean prisoner. Despite heavy casualties, the battle at Taejŏn enabled the 25th Infantry and the 1st Cavalry Divisions of the U.S. Army to further position themselves to slow the North Korean advance. In the course of continuing retreats, the infamous "Nogŭn-ni railroad bridge incident" occurred, in which up to 300 South Korean civilians were killed by U.S. soldiers of H Company of the 2nd Battalion, 7th Cavalry Regiment of the 1st Cavalry Division.[35] The "Nogŭn-ni incident" would hold the potential for further worsening ROK–U.S. relations, including the "Kwangju incident" of 1980.

By mid-July 1950 the North Korean invaders were spread across the width of South Korea. Having overcome American forces and their South Korean allies on the main axis of advance leading to Pusan, they headed for Korea's southwestern corner. Then they turned to the east and occupied Chinju, a strategically important town located west of Pusan. As North Koreans came closer to Pusan, a battle was raged in the vicinity of the strategic town of Masan. In the central sector North Korean forces were heading for Taegu, an important defensive stronghold for U.N. forces.

General Walker's mission was to trade space for time, delaying and withdrawing until sufficient forces could be built up in Japan for General MacArthur to effect a significant turnabout by landing forces at Inch'ŏn on South Korea's west coast. By the end of July, however, Walker had largely run out of space. He ordered his forces to withdraw behind the line of the Naktong River, making it the last bastion to guard the ROK. By 4 August he established what became known as the Pusan Perimeter, a defensive line with a rectangular shape approximately 100 miles by 50 miles around the port of Pusan, in the southeastern corner of the Korean peninsula.[36] The North Korean forces, under Kim Il-sung's direction, tried but failed to destroy this line as the U.N. forces raced to build up their strength. Pusan was at last safe from North Korean capture.

By mid-September, as the North Korean offensive stalled, the tide had turned in favor of U.N. forces. While the North Korean forces were overextended and out of supplies, the U.N. forces became stronger and seized the opportunity to counterattack.

The Inch'ŏn Landing

On 15 September 1950 U.N. forces conducted a landing operation at Inch'ŏn that constituted a turning point in the Korean war. By mid-July 1950, when

American and South Korean forces fought with their backs to the wall to defend the vital port city of Pusan, MacArthur was preparing to present North Koreans with a two-front war. Confident that the 8th Army could hold the Pusan Perimeter, he diverted his resources to a "second front," landing several divisions of troops at the port city of Inch'ŏn, Korea's second largest port and only 15 miles from Seoul. The area was the most important road and railway hub in Korea and a vital link in the main North Korean People's Army supply line extending to the south. Cutting it off would cause North Korean forces facing the 8th Army to suffer scanty supplies of food and munitions. Furthermore, the capture of Seoul would be a serious psychological blow for North Korea.

Planning for the landing, code-named Operation CHROMITE, began on 12 August. On 28 August MacArthur received formal approval from President Truman for the invasion. He had assembled 70,000 troops and more than 230 ships and transports for the landing. Assigned to the campaign were the 1st Marine Division, the 7th Infantry Division, and the 5th Marine Brigade of the U.S. Army, as well as a contingent of South Korean forces. The force was named the X Corps and placed under the command of Major General Edward Almond, MacArthur's chief of staff in Japan.

At dawn on 15 September the X Corps landed at three points on Inch'ŏn, designated as "Beaches"—Green, Red, and Blue. By midnight of D-day, the Inch'ŏn landing was a definite success. Casualties had been surprisingly light, and the invasion force now turned to the task of recapturing Seoul.

MacArthur was determined to capture Seoul on 25 September, three months to the day after the North Korean invasion. But the capital city was not completely taken by the U.N. forces until 28 September. The next day MacArthur and Syngman Rhee entered Seoul.

MacArthur's plan was for the X Corps, now heading south, to act as an anvil on which North Korean forces would be smashed by Walker's 8th Army and South Korean forces moving up from the south. After a crushing defeat, only one-fourth to one-third of the North Korean forces would eventually escape back across the 38th parallel.

With South Korea almost entirely under U.N. control by the end of September 1950, political leaders had to decide on the next step—whether to cross the 38th parallel. The Korean fighting had always been intended as a "police action," meant only to repel the North Korean invaders and restore peace and security to the South. To carry the fighting into North Korea would go beyond the boundaries of a "police action."

North to the Yalu

Bent on reunifying Korea, on 1 October units of the ROK 3rd Infantry Division crossed the 38th parallel and started to drive North Korean forces up the east coast toward Wŏnsan.[37] That same day MacArthur demanded that Kim Il-sung surrender his country; the demand was ignored. On 2 October, the PRC issued the ominous warning that if U.S. forces crossed the 38th parallel, it would send aid to North Korea. The PRC would not intervene, however, if South Korean troops alone crossed the border. On 7 October the U.N. General Assembly sanctioned the advance of U.N. forces into North Korea to establish a unified and democratic Korea.

To conquer North Korea, MacArthur launched a two-pronged attack northward to the Yalu River. Walker's 8th Army would strike North Korea across the 38th parallel in the west, while Almond's X Corps would conduct an amphibious landing at Wŏnsan on the East Sea with a subsequent attack to link up with the 8th Army. The two forces would then drive North Korean forces back to the Yalu River. When there was no room left for North Koreans in the North, the war would end. The decision to entirely separate the X Corps from the 8th Army would have unfortunate repercussions. Although the Chinese warning triggered uneasiness, both the United States and the United Nations were inclined to accept MacArthur's assessment that Chinese intervention was unlikely and that, in any case, MacArthur's forces could deal with a Chinese attack.

On 9 October the 8th Army, led by its 1st Cavalry Division, crossed the 38th parallel and launched an attack north toward Pyongyang. On the east coast, South Korean army units moved steadily toward Wŏnsan. All went well initially. Wŏnsan fell to South Korean forces on 10 October, and Pyongyang was captured by U.N. forces on 19 October. On 21 October Kim Il-sung established a new capital at Sinŭiju on the Yalu River.

The U.N. advances were swift and smooth, but to ease his mind about the possibility of Chinese intervention, Truman met with MacArthur on Wake Island, in the Pacific, on 15 October. During the conversation, Truman asked about the possibility of Chinese intervention, and MacArthur assured the president that there was little chance of Chinese or Soviet intervention. He claimed that if the occasion arose, his forces could manage it. Truman later complained that MacArthur had misled him.

The participants in the Wake Island Conference were unaware that on 4 October PRC leader Mao Zedong had already decided to intervene militarily in the Korean fighting. Actually, the day after the Wake Island meeting, troops of Lin Biao's 4th Field Army began crossing the Yalu River into North Korea. By 20 October four Chinese field armies of 30,000 men each crossed the Yalu; three positioned themselves opposite 8th Army units on the western front and one opposite the X Corps on the eastern front. By the end of October two additional field armies were positioned in North Korea.

All the while U.N. forces remained unaware of the growing presence of Chinese Communist Forces (CCF), calling themselves the Chinese People's Volunteer Army, a fig leaf enabling the PRC to go to war with the United States without a formal declaration. Obviously they were the regular armed forces of the PRC. Unaware of the Chinese armies amassed deep in North Korea, MacArthur's troops continued pressing north. After taking Pyongyang, Walker's 8th Army quickly advanced to the Ch'ŏngch'ŏn River, some 45 miles north of Pyongyang. For their push toward the Yalu and final victory, on 26 October 8th Army troops crossed the river. That same day a reconnaissance platoon of the ROK 6th Division reached the Yalu at Ch'osan. On the eastern front, the 1st Marine Division of the X Corps climbed to the vast 4,000-foot plateau where they came to the Changjin Reservoir. From there they were to link up with the 8th Army in the west for the final thrust to the Yalu River.

At the time the North Korean forces were, for all practical purposes, dissolved. On 25 October, however, massive numbers of PRC troops attacked U.N. forces on both the western and eastern fronts. The attacks continued into early November. Then, on 6 November, just as suddenly as they began, the Chinese halted operations and broke off contact. The initial Chinese intervention raised questions that no one could answer. MacArthur believed the two-week-long Chinese intervention was only an attempt to save what remained of the shattered North Korean forces and perhaps hold part of the country. But the disappearance of the Chinese troops was to conceal their strength, deceive the enemy, and prepare for future hard blows against MacArthur's army.

Blinded by his own optimism and relying on inadequate intelligence, MacArthur was slow to grasp the measure and gravity of the PRC intervention. Intelligence estimates of Chinese strength were far off the mark. By mid-November some 300,000 Chinese troops were in North Korea. After a three-week lull in the fighting, on 24 November U.N. forces renewed their offensive toward the Yalu River. Within 24 hours, however, the situation changed dramatically. On the night of 25–26 November the Chinese launched a massive assault on U.N. forces, particularly the 8th Army on the western front. With its advance halted, the 8th Army's survival was in jeopardy. The 2nd Infantry Division was charged with the mission of preventing a total catastrophe for the 8th Army. At Kunu-ri it purchased sufficient time for other 8th Army units to cross over the Ch'ŏngch'ŏn River and reach safety south of the river. While fulfilling its mission, however, the 2nd Division suffered appalling losses. With the 8th Army in full retreat, its rear guard under heavy PRC pressure, Walker brought his forces just below the 38th parallel to protect Seoul. There, at the end of the year, the 8th Army awaited a new Chinese offensive. Soon the 8th Army had a new commander, as General Walker was killed in a jeep accident on 23 December. Lieutenant General Matthew B. Ridgway was named to succeed Walker and arrived in Korea on 26 December.

The X Corps at the Changjin Reservoir also opened an offensive on 24 November. Like the U.N. forces in the west, it faced a momentous enemy force that engulfed the reservoir and the entire road back to Hŭngnam, the X Corps' supply base. To escape annihilation, the X Corps would have to battle its way back to the coast, 78 miles away—and they did just that, rumbling past CCF units and entering Hŭngnam on 11 December. The campaign in northeastern Korea had tied down 12 Chinese divisions that could otherwise have been utilized against the 8th Army on the western front.

U.N. forces evacuated northeastern Korea through a U.S. Navy's masterful and massive evacuation plan. With substantial naval air cover and 193 ships, the evacuation at Hŭngnam began on 11 December and cleared out some 105,000 troops, their 17,500 vehicles, and 350,000 tons of equipment, along with some 98,000 Korean civilian refugees who did not want to remain in the North. When it was completed on Christmas Eve, engineers blew up the Hŭngnam waterfront with explosives, again leaving North Korea to the communists.

The "New War"

The Korean fighting would continue for more than two years, but it was to be a totally different kind of war. On New Year's Eve the PRC launched the third phase of their offensive, again crossing the 38th parallel, striking the 8th Army's line in the Seoul area and recapturing the capital on 4 January 1951. They continued advancing southward until the 8th Army stopped them 75 miles below Seoul. On 1 February 1951 the U.N. General Assembly voted to condemn the Chinese "aggression" in Korea. Then, U.N. forces were pressing north against the overextended Chinese, finally liberating Seoul once again on 14 March. It was the fourth (and final) time that the capital changed hands. By the end of March 1951 U.N. forces were once more at the 38th parallel, and in April they crossed it.

In the United States, meanwhile, the Truman administration had now recognized that complete victory was impossible. A way had to be found to end the Korean conflict through talks with the communists. As a result combat activities slowed, and the battle line stabilized along the 38th parallel where the war originally began.

Truman planned to announce that, on behalf of the United Nations, his representatives were willing to meet with PRC and North Korean officials to negotiate an end to the war. He was prevented from doing this, however, when, unexpectedly and without Truman's authorization, MacArthur issued a demand to the North Koreans that they surrender immediately. Behind MacArthur's dramatic move was his long disagreement with Truman's policy of limited war. The general wanted nothing less than complete victory over the communists, no matter the cost. Seeking revenge for his humiliation when the PRC armies invaded across the Yalu, he wanted to bomb their bases in Manchuria to destroy China's industrial capacity to wage war, blockade the coast of the Chinese mainland, and enlist the forces of Jiang Jieshi on Taiwan to fight in Korea. The general was even prepared to use the atomic bomb against the People's Republic of China. Truman, on the other hand, did not want to expand the war beyond the borders of Korea for fear that it would bring in the Soviet Union and possibly initiate a general war and the use of nuclear weapons. Moreover, Truman's advisers feared getting tied down in a war with China when they considered the real danger to be a Soviet incursion into Western Europe or Japan. According to General Omar Bradley, chairman of the Joint Chiefs of Staff, a larger war in East Asia would be "the wrong war, at the wrong place, at the wrong time, and with the wrong enemy."[38]

Increasingly disturbed by the stalemate in Korea and his government's restrictions, on 24 March MacArthur issued his demand for China to surrender, directly violating Truman's directive. Five days later the PRC rejected MacArthur's ultimatum and called for renewed fighting. Truman was convinced that the general had to be discharged, and as if to seal his own dismissal, MacArthur sent an inflammatory letter to U.S. Republican Party House Minority Leader Joseph W. Martin, again calling for victory in the Korean War. With the rift between Truman and MacArthur making world headlines, Truman finally charged MacArthur with insubordination and relieved him of his command on 11 April 1951. Lieutenant General Ridgway succeeded MacArthur as commander of the U.N. forces and faithfully followed the administration's guide-lines, and Lieutenant General James A. Van Fleet took command of the 8th Army.Now the United States decided to end its attempts to "liberate" North Korea and instead concentrated on pushing back the communist forces beyond the 38th parallel. After this goal was achieved in May 1951, the United States proposed negotiations to end the fighting and restore the prewar status quo.

The Static War

With the war now at a stalemate and the U.S. government signaling that it was prepared to accept a truce line in the vicinity of the 38th parallel, on 23 June 1951 Yakov A. Malik recommended talks to bring about a cease-fire and reestablish the status quo ante bellum in Korea. On 30 June, on instructions from Truman, General Ridgway offered to meet communist commanders in the field to dis-cuss a cease-fire and terms for an armistice. The following day, on 1 July, Kim Il-sung and Peng Duhuai, commander of the Chinese forces in Korea, agreed to armistice talks at Kaesŏng.

The truce talks began at Kaesŏng on 10 July 1951 and continued with two long recesses and the relocation of the conference site until the armistice was signed on 27 July 1953. As scheduled, a U.N. team headed by Vice Admiral C. Turner Joy met with North Korean and PRC delegates at Kaesŏng on 10 July. The chief communist delegate at the table was North Korean general Nam Il. Whereas the U.N. delegates were authorized only to discuss military matters, the communists used the talks as a propaganda vehicle, presenting the U.N. side as defeated and suing for peace. Two weeks were needed to hammer out the agenda for armistice talks, and on 26 July the negotiators completed the agenda leading to an armistice. Its major points included the establishment of a military demar-cation line and a demilitarized zone between the opposing armies; the exchange of prisoners of war; and supervision to ensure that the terms of armistice were carried out. The agenda itself raised one problem after another, however, and many obstacles dragged the armistice talks out for two years.

The very first problem was an argument over the conference site. Kaesŏng was in communist-controlled territory. The U.N. side had been dissatisfied with the Kaesŏng site from the beginning and sought to relocate the talks to a more neutral location. The communists suspended the talks, claiming that U.N. planes had strafed its troops at the Kaesŏng site on 23 August, but the two sides resumed the talks on 25 August and agreed to change the site to the nearby village of P'anmunjŏm.

With the truce talks in progress, fighting continued at relatively low intensity. Each side had constructed deep defensive lines that would be very difficult to pierce. After Ridgway ordered an end to UNC offensive operations and the start of an active defense strategy on 12 November 1951, the fighting evolved into a series of raids, limited local attacks, combat patrols, and artillery fire in the valleys and on the ridge spanning the width of the peninsula. With the ground fighting diminished, the air campaign intensified. The U.S. Navy and Air Force conducted the largest air attacks of the war against the North Korean capital of Pyongyang and destroyed hydroelectric dams on the Yalu River. By this time the communists had hundreds of new MIG jet fighters, but U.N. fliers maintained air superiority throughout the war.

On 12 May 1952 Lieutenant General Mark W. Clark replaced Ridgway as head of the Far East Command in Japan and as commander-in-chief of the U.N. forces in Korea. He inherited a frustrating mission, waging a war of limited objectives with no clear end in sight. Then, on 10 February 1953, Lieutenant General James A. Van Fleet retired and was succeeded by Lieutenant General Maxwell D. Taylor as commander of the 8th Army.

A major debate during the truce talks was over the location of the North-South boundary and the demilitarized zone. The communists wanted the 38th parallel as the boundary, but the U.N. side, whose forces had pushed north of the 38th parallel except for an area near Kaesŏng in the west, insisted that the boundary be based on the armies' battlefield positions at the time the armistice was signed. Finally, in March 1953 the communists agreed to a line of ground contact. It was also agreed that the opposing armies would drop back to form a demilitarized zone 4 kilometers (2.5 miles) wide between the opposing forces. But the truce talks still deadlocked on the repatriation of prisoners of war.

At the time many North Korean and Chinese prisoners refused repatriation. The U.N. side proposed voluntary repatriation of prisoners, which the communists opposed. In April 1952, U.N. forces screened more than 170,000 prisoners and reported that only 70,000, including 5,100 Chinese, desired repatriation. The communist side refused to negotiate on the basis of this low figure. Thereupon the U.N. side declared an indefinite recess of the truce talks in October 1952. With the talks still deadlocked, the communists launched an intense propaganda campaign, accusing the United States of conducting germ warfare. This was vigorously denied by the United States, and international observers offered to go to North Korea to investigate the communist charge. Finally, the falseness of the charge became evident, but bloody uprisings in the

U.N.-controlled POW camps provided fuel for the communists to continue their propaganda crusade. Embarrassingly, Chinese and North Korean prisoners at Kŏje-do prison camp actually controlled the camp for a considerable period in May and June 1952.

Following the death of Soviet leader Josef Stalin on 5 March 1953, his successors were clearly predisposed to a settlement in Korea and encouraged the Chinese and North Koreans to conclude an armistice. Thus, on 28 March, the communists finally agreed to the principle of voluntary repatriation.

The following month, in April 1953, sick and wounded POWs were exchanged in Operation Little Switch at P'anmunjŏm. In the exchange the communists released 471 South Koreans, 149 Americans, and 64 other sick and wounded U.N. Command troops, and the U.N. side returned 1,030 Chinese and 5,194 North Koreans, together with 446 civilian internees.

ROK President Syngman Rhee, who had always opposed an armistice that would leave Korea divided, made a final effort to derail the agreement. Threatening to fight on alone, on 18 June 1953 he unilaterally released some 27,000 North Korean POWs, which almost disrupted the armistice talks. The sudden release of the North Korean prisoners was intended to stop the peace process. Responding to Rhee's action, and perhaps seeking to improve the communist line and end the war with a military victory, Chinese forces launched a major offensive in June–July 1953, directed mainly against South Korean positions. U.S. reinforcements pushed back the Chinese who suffered perhaps as many as 72,000 casualties, with 25,000 killed. As a result of the huge South Korean casualties in the fighting, as well as the U.S. promise of a mutual security treaty and a major aid package, Rhee no longer interfered with the armistice talks.

The talks resumed on 10 July, and an armistice agreement was signed on 27 July 1953. Finally, the military demarcation line (MDL)—248 kilometers (155 miles) in length—was drawn at the center of the Korean peninsula, cutting the demilitarized zone (DMZ) in half and establishing the border between the two Koreas. The Korean Armistice Agreement established the Neutral Nations Supervisory Commission (NNSC) to supervise the armistice. The NNSC consisted of four senior officers from "neutral nations," two of whom were nominated by the U.N. Command and two by the communists. The UNC chose Sweden and Switzerland, and the communists designated Poland and Czechoslovakia. The Military Armistice Commission (MAC), comprising representatives of the two opposing sides, would supervise the implementation of the armistice terms.

From 5 August to 6 September 1953, the main and final exchange of prisoners, Operation Big Switch, took place at P'anmunjŏm. The number of POWs returned included 75,823 communists (70,183 North Koreans and 5,640 Chinese) and 12,773 U.N. forces (7,862 South Koreans, 3,597 Americans, and 946 British). More than 22,600 communist soldiers declined repatriation. More shocking was that 23 Americans, 1 Briton, and 333 South Korean soldiers also declined repatriation.

On 30 August 1953 General Mark W. Clark set the Northern Limitation Line (NLL), a disputed maritime demarcation line in the Yellow Sea between North and South Korean waters, as the U.N. and communist sides failed to reach an agreement on a maritime border The U.N. side wanted the border set at 3 nautical miles, whereas North Korea wanted a 12 nautical-mile border. The NLL was based on a 3 nautical-mile limit, recognized in the 1950s, extending from the Han River estuary and cutting between North Korea's mainland and five offshore islands, which now remain under South Korean administrative control. The NLL was not a de jure border, as the U.N. side drew it unilaterally and then notified North Korea. But it has served ever since as a de facto maritime border between the two Koreas. After fierce fighting spanning more than three years, with the establishment of the Korean Armistice, the sound of gunfire was finally silenced.

The Unfinished War

Although the Korean Armistice Agreement ended the fighting in Korea, it did not drastically alter the prewar status quo. Korea remained divided, with the north-south boundary still extending roughly along the 38th parallel. Nor did the agreement require the withdrawal of foreign troops from the Korean peninsula.

The most tragic consequence of the Korean War was the staggering loss of life. South Korea listed its casualties during the war at 901,656 (184,573 killed or missing and 717,083 wounded). U.S. losses amounted to 140,200 (33,667 killed or missing, 3,249 dead from other causes, and 103,284 wounded). Other UNC losses came to 15,488 (3,960 killed and 11,528 wounded), and North Korean casualties were estimated at 520,000, while China's exceeded more than 1 million dead. Perhaps 3 million Korean civilians died as a direct result of the war. More than 80,000 South Koreans were forcibly taken to North Korea.

Both Koreas also suffered an irreparable loss of property. The Korean peninsula was in total ruin, with its cities, towns, and villages ravaged by the battle.

The economic cost for the United States alone was more than $15 billion, making the Korean War one of the most expensive conflicts in U.S. history.

The Korean conflict has long been known as "the war that nobody won," because no outright victor emerged from the conflict. But the United States and the United Nations deserve certain laurels. In coming boldly to South Korea's defense, the United States proved itself an undisputable leader of the free world, prepared to act decisively against communist aggression. It emerged from the war as a superpower with the world's most powerful military, and this situation has continued to the present day. Before the war the United Nations had been widely criticized for its inability in promoting international peace and was in danger of being disbanded. In coming to South Korea's aid, however, it changed its image on the world scene. Its action on behalf of the Republic of Korea enhanced its reputation. The PRC, by entering the war and standing up to the United States, also gained in international stature, and it stood as a major power in Asia. A large number of Chinese forces remained stationed in North Korea until October 1958, and China began to play an increasingly important role in Korean affairs. As time passed, this trend increased. The war also spurred Japan's industrial recovery and the U.S. decision to rearm Japan as a bulwark against communism in Asia.

In the United States, immediately after the fighting ceased, the Korean War was soon forgotten. That it has been called the "forgotten war" may be attributed to the fact that the United States neither won nor lost. Because it was unpopular among the general population, book publishers and movie makers, unlike their response to World War II or the Vietnam War, were reluctant to exploit the Korean War either for educating or entertaining the public. From the early 1980s, however, historians, especially revisionists, began to rediscover and write about the Korean War.

For Koreans, the war hardened the division between the North and South, adding to the enmity between the two Koreas. Particularly in the Republic of Korea, it gave rise to extreme anticommunism and a sense of permanent antagonism that ended up infringing on the basic rights of South Koreans. On the other hand, in some sense the war paved the way for South Koreans to abandon narrow regionalism and their traditional sense of social hierarchy. Also, as a U.S. ally, South Korea was accepted into the circle of "maritime civilizations" as a free market economy.

"The war that has never ended" is an accurate description of the Korean War. The armistice of 1953 was only the first, temporary step along the way to a peace treaty that would formally end the conflict. But because no such pact has ever been arranged, technically the two Koreas are still at war. To this day the border between North and South Korea remains one of the most dangerous flash points in the world, pitting about 1.1 million North Korean troops against some 600,000 South Korean troops and their 28,500 American allies. Korea remains the only divided nation in the world.

The period between 1945 and 1953 is characterized as an era of terrible upheavals in Korean history. As soon as the Koreans were liberated from harsh Japanese colonial rule, they were drawn into the maelstrom of the Cold War and experienced the pain of national division. Their suffering increased with the fratricidal Korean War, a consequence of the tragic division of the country. This period of cataclysm was to have profound impacts on subsequent developments in Korea, including many instances of incurable, continuing rivalry and hostility between the two Koreas. A stark reminder that the Korean War remains unfinished was the unprovoked North Korean artillery attack on South Korean territory (Yŏnp'yŏng-do) near the Northern Limitation Line on 23 November 2010.

10

THE PERIOD OF POSTWAR RECONSTRUCTION

(1953–1971)

THE ESTABLISHMENT OF AUTHORITARIAN RULE IN SOUTH KOREA

The First Republic

SOUTH KOREAN POLITICS DURING the Rhee regime (1948–1960) revolved around his struggle to remain in power indefinitely against the opposition's efforts to unseat him. Since the inauguration of the ROK, on 15 August 1948, Rhee disingenuously portrayed himself as a transcendent leader who stood out above the partisan and factional struggles of daily politics, and at first this proved to be an indispensable political asset for his public image, as well as a key source of his popular support. As time went by, however, this strategy grew increasingly ineffectual in the face of the more stubborn opposition, which forced him to increasingly pursue authoritarian measures to retain power.[1]

The 1948 constitution provided for a popularly elected National Assembly, the members of which elected the president for a four-year term. The president could be elected for a second term. Although he lacked grass-roots support in his homeland, Syngman Rhee was handily elected to the presidency by the National Assembly on 20 July 1948 as a reward for his lifetime struggle against Japanese rule. He garnered 180 votes out of 198, and his rival, Kim Ku, obtained just 13 votes. But Rhee escalated the institutional tension between the president and the legislature by seeking more terms and refusing to share power with the National Assembly.

The outbreak of the Korean War on 25 June 1950 proved fortuitous for the Rhee regime. As the leader of a nation in turmoil, he could rally various domestic political forces behind his leadership, particularly during the first year of the fighting. As the war progressed, however, the battle line was held and the tense atmosphere caused by the war gradually dissipated. Nevertheless, Rhee continued his arbitrary rule, which rapidly deteriorated his relationship with the opposition. At the time his political power base was a loose collection of rightist minor political parties, rightist social organizations, and a majority of independent assemblymen who relied on his patronage. This disparate crew, needing money for political activities and survival, were proving ineffective in the changing political environment. Thus Rhee felt impelled to create a strong ruling party backed by his government apparatus. The police acted to perpetuate his power within an easily maneuverable electoral system. Already in 1949 Rhee had ordered that all rightist youth groups be merged into the Taehan Youth Corps and that all unions join the Federation of Korean Trade Unions. These steps were probably motivated by his desire to strengthen his control over his supporters. In late December 1951 Rhee's supporters in the National Assembly and five pro-Rhee social organizations—the Taehan Youth Corps, the Federation of Korean Trade Unions, the Federation of Korean Farmers Unions, the Korean National Association, and the Korean Women's Association—combined to form the Liberal Party. The new party proved instrumental for gathering and distributing the political funds and patronage that made it a firm political base for Rhee to seek future terms as president. By 1952 Rhee had lost much of his support in the National Assembly and his reelection was in doubt. In an attempt to retain power and weaken the National Assembly, Rhee proposed constitutional amendments providing for direct popular election of the president and a bicameral legislature. On 18 January 1952 the National Assembly, led by the opposition Democratic National Party, overwhelmingly rejected the proposed amendments by a vote of 143 to 19. Rhee then instituted a campaign of political harassment and demonstrations against his opponents. When the opposition legislators held firm, Rhee declared martial law in and around Pusan, the temporary ROK capital, effective 25 May 1952. He also ordered the imprisonment of more than 50 opposition politicians. Most were soon released, but 7 were charged with participating in a communist conspiracy and several others then went into hiding.

Rhee's actions concerned South Korea's wartime allies, as his reckless tactics shattered the image of the ROK as a country moving toward democracy and thus jeopardized international support for the U.S.-led war effort. The United States attempted to persuade Rhee to end martial law and release the jailed politicians but to no avail. It then considered stronger action, including support of an anti-Rhee coup by ROK military officers and even direct military intervention. Ultimately it reverted to its admonitions and encouragement of a political compromise. The crisis ended in early July, not through political compromise but only when Rhee's police rounded up all the legislators and confined them to the National Assembly building until they passed his constitutional amendment. His legislation obtained 163 of 166 votes.

The presidential election was set for 5 August 1952 in the thick of the Korean War, providing the opposition with little time for campaigning. Rhee easily won another presidential term, obtaining 74.6 percent of the popular vote, and an uneasy peace returned to the South Korean political scene. Assisted by the powerful police and local administrations, he manipulated the politically unsophisticated populace, seized with insecurity over the war, into backing him.[2] Although civil war and political chaos were averted, the National Assembly was powerless and excluded from any effective policy-making role. Rhee's political power had become greatly strengthened at the expense of the international as well as domestic legitimacy of his government.

Immediately after the Korean War, Rhee was faced with mounting pressure from DNP-led opponents in the National Assembly, but the malleable general population raised little objection to his continuing rule. Mainly people were more preoccupied with daily survival than with politics, but they also liked Rhee personally and had a sense of national unity based on their antipathy toward communism.[3] Moreover, in the 1950s, South Koreans as a whole were still swayed by the traditional Confucian ideas, which translated into the perception of the president as a monarch who should not be easily replaced.

As people's political intelligence grew, however, Rhee's popular support began to dwindle. Thus, to ensure victory, he inevitably resorted to repression of the opposition and election fraud. Rhee's Liberal Party and the Democratic National Party were pitted against each other in the National Assembly elections, held on 20 May 1954. Using police harassment and restrictive electoral laws aimed at disadvantaging DNP candidates, the Liberal Party became the first party in Korean history to receive an absolute majority in the National Assembly, 114 of 203 seats. The DNP, reduced to just 15, was almost eliminated as a serious political contender. The independents captured 68 seats. Collectively the independents might have maintained a balance of power between the ruling party and opposition forces, but divisions among the members prevented them from wielding such collective power. Desperate to maintain their local constituencies, many independents succumbed to bribery and cajolery by the Liberal Party, so that the Liberals almost acquired the two-thirds majority necessary for another constitutional amendment that would permit Rhee a third term as president in 1956.

At this point, Rhee lacked the statutory two-thirds majority by a mere fraction of one vote. At first the constitutional amendment to abolish the two-term limitation on the presidency was declared to be defeated on 28 November 1954, when 135 of 203 members voted for it and carrying the bill lacked just 0.3 vote (actually 1 vote). But the next day it was announced by the Liberal Party that the amendment had indeed passed, on the grounds that the number of affirmative votes required for passage, 135.3, could be rounded down to the next whole number (135.0). This questionable and unconstitutional move angered and unified all of Rhee's opposition. The Democratic National Party and anti-Rhee independent legislators, with more than 60 assemblymen, united to form the Association for the Preservation of the Constitution, the organization that eventually, on 18 September 1955, fathered the Democratic Party. Rhee's existence in power was all that united the fragmented anti-Rhee forces. In the years to come, the Democratic Party would seek Rhee's removal from power, and once it was achieved, the party would disintegrate.

With Rhee still in power, opportunities for education during the postwar recovery rapidly expanded and a new urban culture based on Western democratic values took hold. This ultimately eroded the foundations of Rhee's dictatorship, particularly in Seoul and other major cities. South Koreans, especially the urban masses, became more politically aware. Higher education provided the youth with greater political understanding, especially given the strong emphasis on democratic values and the views of teachers and intellectuals. For the first time Korean youth were provided with unrestricted access to Western democratic ideas at school and through the mass media. While these Western ideas functioned as the norm against which to judge the government in power, the press frequently exposed government ineptitude and corruption and attacked Rhee's authoritarian rule. The opposition Democratic Party capitalized on these opportunities.

The presidential election on 15 May 1956 provided the first strong indication of a rapidly changing political mind-set. Rhee was reelected, gaining 70 percent of the popular vote. Although Rhee dominated the electoral process and his main opponent, Sin Ik-hŭi of the Democratic Party, died of a heart attack during the campaign, his real electoral support fell far short of his expectations. Moreover, in the separate vice presidential election, the Democratic Party's candidate, Chang Myŏn (John M. Chang), defeated Yi Ki-bung, Rhee's former personal secretary, protégé, and anointed successor. Chang won 41.7 percent of the vote, and Yi won 39.6 percent.[4] Chang was supported mostly by the urban population discontent with economic hardship, particularly the spiraling inflation, and the Rhee government's maladministration and corruption. His victory demonstrated a steep decline in Rhee's popularity and that of his Liberal Party, especially in urban areas. The possibility that the opposition vice president would succeed the aging Rhee made the ruling party very uneasy.

Faced with the new threat to its power, the Rhee government again resorted to severe repression. The first victim was Cho Pong-am, Rhee's first minister of agriculture and forestry and now leader of the Progressive Party, with a "social democratic" platform that included peaceful reunification with North Korea. Representing the moderate Left in South Korean politics, Cho ran for the presidency in 1952 and 1956, obtaining an impressive 30 percent of the popular vote in 1956, thus posing a significant threat to Rhee. In the "Progressive Party Incident" in February 1958, the Rhee administration banned Cho's party, indicted him on charges of spying and violating the National Security Law, and executed him on 31 July 1959. Cho's guilty verdict had been based on false charges of collusion with North Korean agents. In truth, he had never engaged in espionage but was the victim of a president who would remove his political foes by any means necessary.

The National Assembly elections on 2 May 1958 clearly demonstrated the continuously declining support for the Rhee government. The Liberal Party obtained only 38.7 percent of the vote despite extensive electoral fraud, and the Democratic Party, though at a severe disadvantage, won 29.5 percent. Under the single-member constituency system, the ruling party won 126 of 233 seats, the main opposition party took 79 seats, and the independents 27 seats. The two-party system began to take shape, and the major cities emerged as bastions of the opposition party. As the election resulted in the formation of a stronger opposition coalition to Rhee in the National Assembly, Rhee responded with further repression, culminating, on 24 December 1958, with the passage of a new National Security Law that made South Korea a virtual police state. In the course passing the law, the dignity and sanctity of the National Assembly were once again compromised. Outnumbered in the legislature, the opposition staged a sit-down strike in the National Assembly building to block passage of the legislation. In response, the Rhee government mobilized the police force to clear the hall of the opposition. The Liberal Party then rushed through 22 bills, including the new draconian National Security Law. Immediately after the passage of this measure, Rhee organized the Anticommunist Youth Corps, in January 1959 to forcibly and effectively frustrate the opposition's resistance against him.

Under the terms of the new security law, anyone who criticized the president or the Speaker of the National Assembly or the Chief Justice of the Supreme Court was subject to a charge of libel. The law also provided for the extended detention of individuals suspected of crimes and for the arrest of civilians by agents of the armed forces intelligence agencies.[5] Simply put, the law aimed to muzzle any and all anti-Rhee news media and suppress antigovernment activities and rhetoric. A striking example of this was the government's closing of the *Kyŏnghyang sinmun*, or Capital and Country Newspaper, a Seoul-based daily that openly supported Vice President Chang Myŏn, in April 1959.

Because the Rhee regime had lost much of its popular support by the time of the presidential election in March 1960, the only means for Rhee and his party to achieve victory was electoral fraud on a massive scale. Rhee was left unopposed on the ballot when, as occurred in 1956 with Sin Ik-hŭi of the Democratic Party, his chief opponent, Cho Pyŏng-ok of the Democratic Party, died, in this case of cancer while undergoing treatment at Walter Reed Hospital in Washington, D.C., in February 1960. Therefore, had the Rhee regime been content with another term for the presidency, it would have retained power. Foolishly, however, it failed to recognize the public sentiment of the time and chose to heavily rig the elections to ensure Vice President Chang Myŏn's defeat. Because of Rhee's advanced age (then 85 years old), the vice presidential contest became very important. In the election on 15 March 1960 Rhee was declared elected with "100 percent" of the vote, and Yi Ki-bung defeated Chang Myŏn for the vice presidency. The Liberal Party had actually lowered the percentage of votes Yi obtained from 100 percent to 79 percent. As heavy vote rigging was brought to light, waves of violent protest followed. Thousands of university students protested in the streets. The turning point came when police, defending the presidential mansion in Seoul, fired into a crowd of students on 19 April, killing more than 100. Soon the protest escalated into an insurrection in the capital city. Other major cities were also in the throes of a popular revolution that took the lives of an estimated 400 students. The April Student Revolution put an end to the Rhee regime.

After the incident on 19 April, Rhee belatedly declared martial law but without success, as army troops refused to fire on people in the streets. The United States persuaded Rhee not to act against the people's wishes. Finally Rhee resigned on 26 April and three days later left South Korea for exile in Hawaii, where he died in 1965 at the age of 90. On 28 April a caretaker government was formed, and Yi Ki-bung and his family committed suicide. As Rhee's dictatorial rule came to an end, the First Republic and the Liberal Party collapsed swiftly and silently.

Syngman Rhee's legacy has been in considerable dispute. In South Korea the conservatives have generally considered Rhee the "founding father of the Republic of Korea" and believed that he saved the ROK from the "evil power of communism," whereas the progressives have criticized him as the "mastermind of the national division" and a "dictator." In retrospect, Rhee and his rightist allies established a separate southern government in August 1948 and made it a bulwark against communism in South Korea. Rhee was a self-righteous man convinced of his indispensability to his county and thus hated his opponents and considered their criticisms high treason to the nation. In the First Republic he established an unpopular and unrepresentative dictatorship. As time passed, his rule became increasingly personalized, with his government characterized as "personal authoritarianism." Under his charismatic authority, the number-two man (Yi Ki-bung) wielded enormous power, and the Liberal Party established an oligarchy. This system malfunctioned and resulted in the demise of his regime.

The Second Republic

When Syngman Rhee was driven from power, South Koreans seized the opportunity to establish true democracy in their country, but there was no administration to fill its place. Hŏ Chŏng, who was appointed foreign minister one day before Rhee resigned, was given the task of forming an interim government. He had not been implicated in the abuses of Liberal Party rule and thus was acceptable to the opposition. As prime minister and acting president, he organized a caretaker government comprising eminent persons reputed for impartiality. From April to July 1960 his government revised the constitution and organized a new election.

On 15 June 1960 the constitution was amended for the third time since 1948. The newly revised constitution designated the Second Republic to have the form of a parliamentary cabinet system where the president was merely a figurehead. This was the first and only instance that South Korea turned to a system in which the cabinet held responsibility instead of a president. Executive emergency powers were considerably weakened; a central election committee was created to ensure fair elections; a special constitutional court was charged with judicial review; and various legal restraints on civil rights were eliminated. In the National Assembly elections held on 29 July 1960, the Democratic Party, which was still intact as a loose coalition, won an overwhelming victory, gaining 175 of 233 seats in the lower House of Representatives. The second largest group, the independents, won 49 seats. The Liberal Party elected only 2 seats. In the upper House of Councilors, the Democratic Party obtained 31 of 58 seats.

Soon the Democratic Party set about forming a government. The party could not function as the ruling party, however, because electoral success exposed its inherent weakness as an unstable coalition of political leaders drawn together only by their opposition to Rhee. Once their common enemy—Rhee and his Liberal Party—had been removed from the scene and they seized power, these factional leaders began to struggle against one another to obtain the spoils for themselves. The Democratic Party split into two major groups, the "Old Faction" under titular President Yun Po-sŏn and the "New Faction" under Prime Minister Chang Myŏn. During weeks of post-election maneuvering over the choice of prime minister, the two factions were pitted against each other. After Chang successfully secured the premiership and formed his cabinet on 23 August, 86 members of the "Old Faction" left the Democratic Party and organized a new party, the New Democratic Party, on 18 October 1960. Thus Chang Myŏn was left with a weakened cabinet. In time continued factional wrangling caused the public to turn away from the new government.

Although it was a democratic government, the Second Republic was a politically unstable period. The new regime, plagued by inexperience and political infighting, faced massive challenges. Specifically, the Second Republic witnessed the proliferation of political activity that had been repressed under the Rhee regime's First Republic. In the absence of firm central control, and in an atmosphere of unprecedented freedom among a people accustomed to strong leadership, politics approached anarchy. The new government could not secure stability, contain corruption, or provide quick solutions to the economic problems inherited from the Rhee regime, all of which furthered popular discontent. To its credit, the Democratic government introduced the concept of long-range economic planning for the first time; Syngman Rhee had neglected such planning altogether. In economics, as well as in other areas, had the new government been given more time, it might have succeeded.

Continued student activity further exacerbated confusion and disruption following the sudden emergence of freedom. After the success of the April revolution, the students were highly motivated and filled with a sense of mission, regularly taking to the streets and making numerous and wide-ranging demands for political and economic reforms. They insisted that the "criminals" of the Rhee regime be punished, and on 11 October 1960 student mobs invaded the National Assembly chamber and forced the Assembly to enact laws to retroactively punish elements of the Rhee regime. The next day the discouraged National Assembly passed a special law to punish government officials and police officers who had been involved in anti-democratic activities or corruption in the First Republic. Some 40,000 people were investigated, resulting in the dismissal of more than 2,200 government officials and about 4,000 police officers. The students accomplished their objective in this instance, but in the process they made the government appear helpless and discredited the dignity of the legislature itself. Although student activity declined sharply after November 1960, law and order could not be maintained because the police, long an instrument of the Rhee regime, were demoralized and utterly distrusted by the public.

The economic slump that had begun in the late 1950s created unemployment for 2.4 million workers and stopped the operation of some 80 percent of factories in the Seoul-Inch'ŏn area in late 1960. About 2 million people suffered serious food shortages, a period called the "spring suffering." The country was appallingly poor. Per-capita income was $80, putting South Koreans on a par with the people of Sudan and Haiti. People actually cared little about democracy and the finer points of civil rights; they wanted jobs, price controls, and affordable loans.

Under these circumstances, North Korea attempted to take advantage of the internal disorder and stepped up its subversive activity against South Korea. North Koreans proposed unification discussions, to which some South Koreans responded positively. For instance, many students mounted a unification campaign under the slogans "Come to the South! Let's Go to the North! Let's

Meet at P'anmunjŏm!" and "Settlement of the Korean Problem by the Korean People Themselves!" This move produced fears of subversion among a large segment of the population.

Middle ranks of the army's officer corps were most displeased about the developments of 1960–1961. Having experienced the Korean War, the South Korean military emerged as a significant political force. By 1960 the military planned a coup to topple the Rhee government, but it was never implemented because of the student uprising in April 1960. As time went by, however, and the Chang Myŏn government failed to provide effective leadership to cope with the difficulties it faced, a small group of ambitious army officers concluded that the opportunity for a coup had finally arrived. In a carefully designed bloodless coup, staged in the predawn hours of 16 May 1961, some 250 officers, mainly junior generals and colonels, and only 3,500 soldiers out of a 500,000-man army quickly achieved success. The coup leader, Major General Park Chung-hee, dissolved the National Assembly, prohibited all political activity indefinitely, instituted martial law and a curfew, and announced the establishment of a military junta of 32 colonels and brigadier generals. Although Prime Minister Chang Myŏn stubbornly resisted the coup, President Yun Po-sŏn sided with the military junta and persuaded U.S. forces in South Korea and the commanders of various Korean army units not to interfere with the new rulers. Until his resignation on 23 March 1962, he stayed on as president for ten months after the junta took power, legitimizing the coup. The takeover of the government was accepted by a populace that was exhausted by political chaos and economic instability. The experiment in democracy in the Second Republic had lasted only a year.

The leadership of the Second Republic was too weak constitutionally and personally to fill the gap created by the sudden collapse of Rhee's authoritarian regime. Unable to cope with the difficult situation he faced, Chang Myŏn stressed that order based on rifles and swords was undesirable and that order based on freedom was the very foundation of true democracy. Surely Chang Myŏn was a man ahead of his time. But the order based on freedom that he championed was not achieved in the short-lived Second Republic. Although freedom thrived, order disappeared. Excessive freedom stirred up chaos, and a state of anarchy continued. The populace became ever more skeptical about the value of freedom in the face of hunger and was increasingly alienated from the government. Now, at this very moment, a group of politically oriented army officers led by Park Chung-hee conspired to revolt and seize power. Without Park's coup, the Second Republic ultimately might have mustered the united support of the population to cope with the pressing problems of the day. The Second Republic, after all, had produced such major achievements as the experiment in democracy and the formulation of long-range economic planning.[6] Given enough time, the Second Republic might have succeeded in realizing the anticipated benefits in many areas, particularly in economic growth. In fact, after having experienced severe chaos in 1960, the Second Republic had increasingly consolidated its leadership and stabilized the state of affairs from early 1961.

The Military Regime

The coup leaders, including Major General Park Chung-hee and Lieutenant Colonel Kim Jong-pil, staged the coup because they firmly believed that their move would not be seriously challenged by any major forces in South Korean society. In fact, the Second Republic was left with no supporters. President Yun Po-sŏn, who was always at loggerheads with Prime Minister Chang Myŏn, remained in office, shielding the new leaders from being denounced for having destroyed a legitimate government. Many other opinion leaders were passive in defending the Second Republic or even supported the coup. The general population as a whole accepted the coup as inevitable, and the United States did not intervene.

When the coup leaders came into power, they justified their action as a move to save the nation from misrule characterized as aimlessness, inefficiency, and weakness. Despite this justification, their seizure of power by a military coup smothered the growth of democracy in the country. After a short experimental period in parliamentary democracy, South Korean politics returned to the normalcy of strong executive control.

Park Chung-hee, the coup leader, was born at Kumi near Taegu in North Kyŏngsang province on 14 November 1917. He graduated from the Taegu Teachers College and entered the Military Officer Training Academy of the Manchurian Imperial Army in Changchun, China, in April 1940. Thereafter he attended the Japanese Military Academy during 1942–1944, was commissioned a lieutenant, and served in Japan's Guandong Army until the end of World War II. After liberation and the division of Korea in 1945, he returned to southern Korea in May 1946 and became an officer in the South Korean Constabulary during the U.S. occupation of Korea. In early October 1946, while suppressing a riot in Taegu, the police, under the direction of the U.S. Military Government, killed his closest brother, a regional leader of the Left. This spurred Park to join the South Korean Workers Party. Immediately after the Yŏsu-Sunch'ŏn Rebellion collapsed, the Syngman Rhee government arrested Park, then a major, in November 1948 on charges that he led a communist cell in the army. Some U.S. intelligence documents also described him as a communist. Park was sentenced to life imprisonment by a military court, but later President Rhee commuted his sentence to ten years in prison at the urging of several high-ranking South Korean military officers, and after Park's active assistance in the arrest of other SKWP members in the army. In the end, he never served the sentence. During the Korean War Park returned to active service. During the late 1950s he gained the loyalty of a group of young officers, who helped him seize power in the 16 May 1961 coup. After the Park regime was established in 1961, new elites, who were raised and educated in and around Taegu and North Kyŏngsang province, the "T-K group," became prominent in South Korean politics. Park held power for more than 18 years, until 26 October 1979, when he was shot and killed in an American movie–style shootout by his own chief of the Korean Central Intelligence Agency (KCIA), an organization he created to help keep him in power.

As with others who usurped power, Park invoked a "reign of terror and virtue." On 18 May 1961 he forced the general resignation of the Chang Myŏn cabinet and reorganized his junta into the all-powerful Supreme Council for National Reconstruction (SCNR) through which he would rule the country. The regular administration was placed under this omnipotent organ. All political organizations were disbanded and political activity prohibited. Hundreds of former civilian political leaders, including Chang Myŏn, were forbidden to participate in any political activities for several years. After retiring from politics, Chang Myŏn concentrated on religious activities. He died of hepatitis on 4 June 1966. "Corrupt" and politically suspicious individuals were all purged from the bureaucracy and the army on a large scale. Approximately 17,000 civil servants and 2,000 military officers were dismissed. The press was strictly censored, and an estimated two-thirds of all publications were shut down. On 3 July 1961 the Anticommunist Law, as part of the National Security Law, was promulgated to suppress and punish communist activity, but it was used mainly to suppress the political opposition in the name of anticommunism.

To gain popular support, the military regime, along with its reign of terror, also pursued a "reign of virtue," making a clean sweep of the "old evil." It enforced vigorously and harshly the summary roundup of " antisocial elements," of hoodlums and petty criminals. Gangsters, in particular, were paraded on the streets and sentenced to death and executed.

Under the law promulgated on 10 June 1961, the powerful Korean Central Intelligence Agency was created to place all citizens under surveillance. Political offenses were referred to a special revolutionary tribunal. Specifically some 3,000 progressive politicians and students, as well as labor union leaders, were arrested by the military regime under the pretext of searching out pro-communists and went before this tribunal. Through the reign of terror the military regime succeeded in bringing order and stability to South Korean society. At the same time it firmly assumed the reigns of government. As time went on, however, South Koreans increasingly turned against the unrelenting military rule. Even as political repression incurred popular resentment, the regime's rash economic measures failed to revitalize the stagnant economy, and, as a result, the United States exerted continual and increasing pressure on the military leadership to restore civilian rule. In the beginning the United States had cooperated with the military regime to stabilize the economy and finance the First Five-Year Economic Development Plan (1962–1966), but with the military regime's unwillingness to return to civilian government, the United States utilized its economic and military assistance as leverage to bring about change.

Park Chung-hee and other military leaders had always realized that, sooner or later, a return to civilian politics was inevitable. Thus they pledged to transfer power to civilian government at the earliest possible moment. On 12 August 1961 Park Chung-hee announced that he would restore civilian rule by May 1963. He acted to ensure his continued power in a new civilian government by taking three steps: first, he eliminated the older generation of civilian politicians under the pretext of "purifying politics"; second, he amended the constitution to create a strong presidency and a weak legislature; and, third, he established a new political party.

The Political Activity Purification Law of March 1962 banned several thousand persons from political activity on the grounds that they were corrupt, incompetent, indolent, impure, degenerate, and factional. In December 1962 a new constitution was drafted to establish the Third Republic, characterized by a strong presidency and a weak legislature, and providing for the direct election of the president who would appoint cabinet ministers and, above all, was authorized to declare a national emergency by decree whenever he saw fit. On the other hand, the unicameral legislature was greatly weakened by losing its control over the cabinet. The new constitution was put to popular referendum on 17 December 1962 and was approved by a wide majority, receiving 78.8 percent of the vote. In February 1963 the military leaders formed the Democratic Republican Party (DRP) to establish their political power base in the restored civilian government. In August 1963 Park Chung-hee was endorsed as the DRP candidate for the presidency.

The restoration of civilian rule had to overcome a final hurdle: Park Chung-hee's hesitation to surrender power to civilians. Between February and April 1963 he vacillated over the decision to transfer power, and on 16 March he even proposed the extension of military rule for four more years. But intense public denunciation and U.S. pressure forced him to return to his original pledge. Finally, on 19 April 1963, he announced that both presidential and National Assembly elections would be held by the end of the year.

In the presidential election of 15 October 1963, Park Chung-hee won narrowly against Yun Po-sŏn, with only 46.6 percent of the popular vote against Yun's 45.1 percent. A crowded field of opposition candidates contributed to Park's razor-thin victory. Indeed, the combined popular vote for opposition candidates was greater than the vote for Park, but the factionalism of the opposition made it lose the opportunity to remove Park from power. Although Park won the election overwhelmingly in the rural areas, Yun had a large edge in the cities, particularly Seoul. In the National Assembly elections of 26 November 1963, the Democratic Republican Party won a clear majority of seats in the legislature. Mirroring the presidential election, the ruling party won 110 of 175 seats in the Assembly, 7 seats short of a two-thirds majority, but it garnered only one-third of the popular vote. The tremendous discrepancy between elected seats and the popular vote occurred because many districts were flooded with opposition candidates. Without a second round of voting between the two largest vote getters, the failure of the opposition to unite against the DRP resulted in a majority of successful candidates from the government party.[7] The opposition therefore needed to form a united party, which it finally did on 3 May 1965, with the merger of two main opposition parties, the Democratic Politics Party led by Yun Po-sŏn and the Democratic Party headed by Pak Sun-ch'ŏn, into the Democratic People's Party. This new opposition party was renamed the New Democratic Party on 11 February 1967.

With Park Chung-hee sworn in as president on 17 December 1963, an elected civilian government finally took office. Now the Third Republic was formally inaugurated, ending several years of military rule. By mid-October 1972, however, Park Chung-hee once again revised the constitutional structure, this time much more drastically, to create a truly autocratic regime.

The Third Republic

From the start Park Chung-hee was an absolute ruler with an aversion to representative government. Under his leadership the executive became ever more powerful, and the legislature was reduced to impotence. As time went on, the Third Republic became a one-person dictatorship ruled by Park Chung-hee, who controlled the political and economic life of the South Korean population through such administrative agencies as the Presidential Secretariat, the Korean Central Intelligence Agency, the police, the prosecution, the Economic Planning Board, and the Office of National Taxation.

In the decade of the Third Republic Park skillfully used national goals and policy, particularly industrial development, to build up his political power. In the 1960s he concentrated his energies on economic growth. In strengthening his power, economic development was his most powerful political tool as it appealed to the poverty-stricken population. Economic planning had already begun during the period of military rule, but it failed to realize the anticipated results until 1965–1966. Thereafter a useful political tool for Park was the impressive rise in the percentage of annual increase in the gross national product.

Despite Park's high-handed rule, the South Korean population generally appeared content with the country's remarkable economic development. Although in the presidential election held on 3 May 1967 the opposition was more united than in 1963, Park handily defeated his principal opponent, Yun Po-sŏn. He won 51.5 percent of the popular vote while Yun obtained only 40.9 percent. Again, as in the previous election, Park was overwhelmingly supported by the rural population including petty landowners who were politically conservative as long as their standard of living was maintained at subsistence levels.

Park's increased popularity contributed to another victory for the Democratic Republican Party in the National Assembly elections, held on 8 June 1967. The DRP again won a two-thirds majority, taking 129 of 175 seats, and held enough parliamentary seats to pass constitutional amendments. As the DRP heavily rigged the election, however, the main opposition New Democratic Party obtained only 45 seats and boycotted the assembly to protest the election fraud, causing the suspension of normal legislative activity for more than 140 days.

Encouraged by increased popular support, Park sought a third term. In 1969 he devoted himself to drafting a constitutional amendment that would permit him another presidency. Despite some intraparty opposition, the ruling Democratic Republican Party laboriously struggled to put the amendment to a national referendum and, on 17 October 1969, 65.1 percent of the compliant electorate voted for the amendment.

The 1969 constitutional amendment campaign demonstrated that Park's autocratic rule met with strong opposition. While college and even high school students protested in the streets, the opposition party also offered stiff resistance to the revision of the constitution. In the early 1970s the first signs of a significant dissident movement appeared, and, as a result, the atmosphere of the 1971 presidential election was quite different from that in 1967. Nevertheless, Park defeated his opponent, Kim Dae-jung, of the New Democratic Party in the heavily rigged election, held on 27 April 1971, winning 53.2 percent of the vote against Kim's 45.2 percent. Drawing little comfort from the election result, Park feared and hated Kim as his potential rival thereafter.

Following the presidential election, the National Assembly elections were held on 25 May 1971. Despite intense infighting, the opposition New Democratic Party won enough seats in the elections to destroy the governing party's two-thirds majority in the legislature. While the Democratic Republican Party won 113 of 204 seats, the main opposition party obtained 89 seats, with big wins reported in major cities including Seoul, Pusan, and Taegu. As the opposition grew in strength and intellectual awareness increased, the broader public consensus that had backed Park's policies in the 1960s frayed. The parliamentary election, in particular, made it more difficult for Park to manipulate the legislature for his own political purposes. To retain his rule, Park ultimately resorted to unconstitutional measures.

Once elected for a third term, Park further tightened his control over the country, strenuously and stubbornly clamping down on the press, antigovernment students and intellectuals, and suspected subversives. Under the Park regime, the press was not only censored from above but often censored itself to avoid criticizing the government.

Park, in severely suppressing the student movement, adopted a more skillful approach than Rhee had used to cope with the antigovernment activity of university students. He did not try to control student demonstrators on the streets, which could arouse public sympathy for the activists, but instead used the mobile riot police to prevent students from reaching the downtown area in the first place. These tactical squads of police, and sometimes armed troops, were stationed outside campus gates to keep students in. Spies disguised as students infiltrated classrooms to keep students and professors under close surveillance. Whenever martial law was declared, the campuses were occupied by armed troops and student leaders were arrested at will. While such maneuvers against the students were encouraged, students who collaborated with the government won "KCIA scholarships." These skillful and efficient tactics against the student movement continued into the Fourth and Fifth Republics.

Park's repression of the students and intellectuals was evident in a number of spy incidents and trials. On 8 July 1967, the Korean Central Intelligence Agency, after having kidnapped Korean students and intellectuals who had been living in West Germany and the United Kingdom and secretly repatriating them to South Korea, accused them of spying for North Korea. The suspects, numbering 315, were illegally arrested, tortured, and subject to improper trial procedures and severe punishment.

On 27 December 1971, facing violent resistance from the opposition, Park pressured the National Assembly to pass the Law Concerning Special Measures for Safeguarding National Security, which granted him absolute power to mobilize the nation and its people, and to regulate and control all activities in the country, including the press and the economy. He then engineered the so-called *Yushin*, or Revitalization, constitutional coup on 17 October 1972, which brought the Third Republic to an end.

THE SOUTH KOREAN ECONOMY AND SOCIETY

The South Korean Economy before 1961

After the Korean War the landlord class that had been the backbone of traditional Korean society for centuries was deeply hurt economically mainly as a result of farmland reform. The National Assembly passed the Farmland Reform Act Bill on 21 June 1949 (amended in final form on 10 March 1950) which allowed the South Korean government to purchase 331,766 chŏngbo, or 829,415 acres, of farmland from Korean landlords and distribute the land to 918,548 farm households by 1952. The farmers' compensation to the government and the government's repayment to the landlords were set, respectively, at 150 percent and 125 percent of the annual crop. The period for both redemption and repayment was five years.[8] Landlords also sold a considerable amount of farmland directly to their tenants. The Farmland Reform Act Bill, which provided both landlords and tenants with a powerful incentive to make their own separate deals, attained to a considerable extent its principal objective of equal distribution of farmland. From March to May 1950, immediately before the Korean War, 70 to 80 percent of farmland formerly owned by landlords was distributed to tenants on credit, and the amount of tenant land decreased to 12 percent. When the Korean War broke out, North Korea conducted a propaganda campaign in the occupied areas about new land reform and class struggle, but many South Korean farmers who had already owned their farmland were not greatly impressed by this and remained committed to the Republic of Korea. Had the farmland redistribution been delayed, the situation would have turned out quite differently.

The land reform, however, also brought about the fragmentation of landholdings so that even the many tenant farmers who were elevated to the status of landowners still had to struggle to make a living. The government's meager compensation to landlords was almost eliminated, moreover, by rampant wartime and postwar inflation and losses. All but the largest and most flexible landowners were reduced to poverty.

Meanwhile, the war had destroyed some three-fourths of the industrial plants. Rehabilitation programs under both the United States and the United Nations, particularly the U.N. Korean Reconstruction Agency (UNKRA), poured hundreds of millions of dollars into South Korea, making the country heavily dependent on foreign aid, not only for defense but also for other expenditures. Foreign aid constituted one-third of the total budget in 1954, rose to 58.4 percent in 1956, and fell to approximately 38.0 percent of the budget in 1960. Scarcely any enterprise in South Korea had independent, private sources of help, as all the aid came through the South Korean government. After 1956, access to this aid was regulated by the ruling Liberal Party, leading to cozy relations between politics and business. As the United States offered mainly agricultural products in economic aid, there was development in the the consumption industry, aptly named the "three white industries," representing wheat flour, sugar, and cotton. A few entrepreneurs who received preferential treatment from the government monopolized these industries and grew into the *chaebŏl* conglomerates. In return for this special benefit, they offered massive political funds to the Rhee government and the Liberal Party.

Inflation, which had been almost continually on the rise since 1945, remained constant throughout the 1950s. The Rhee government took virtually no effective measures to deal with it. With property destroyed and inflation rampant, the formerly wealthier and middle-class families were severely hurt, in many cases completely ruined. Fortunes were made not in production but in speculation, particularly in foreign exchange, as the legal exchange rate was constantly outstripped by inflation and the government was slow to restore balance. The sale of foreign exchange and the rights for imports became a vast government business, increasingly involving illegal payments to the ruling party and government officials. Because government loans were mainly funneled through the Korean Reconstruction Bank, almost all procurement operations for money or imported goods naturally involved bribery and corruption. In fact, business was no more than an adjunct of the government.

The pre–Korean War economic policies of South Korea were naïve, populist, and undisciplined, and indeed long-range economic planning was not undertaken until Syngman Rhee's fall in 1960. Unfortunately, Syngman Rhee, a seasoned politician, had little understanding of economics, nor did his officials, which left his administration unable to resolve the economic difficulties. Moreover, for nationalist reasons, Rhee tended to act against U.S. advice.

With the Korean War having completely shattered the South Korean economy, reconstruction began immediately after the 1953 armistice but was hampered by the burden of maintaining a huge armed force.[9] Nevertheless, by 1957, the South Korean economy had been boosted by foreign aid and was significantly stabilized. The average annual increase in the GNP was 5.5 percent from 1954 through 1958, with industrial production leading the advance. But then the tightening of fiscal and monetary policies in 1958, coupled with the phasing out of the UNKRA aid program and the reduction in direct U.S. aid in 1957, caused an overall economic decline. From 1958 to 1960, the ever increasing South Korean political crisis worsened the economy, and the situation further deteriorated as a result of poor crops. Popular frustration at the lack of economic progress contributed in part to a political upheaval of 1960.

The ensuing Second Republic did not succeed in stabilizing the economy, but it introduced for the first time a multiyear economic development plan that helped the succeeding military regime implement its own economic programs after 1961. In the Second Republic a new National Reconstruction Program offered great hope of a speedier reconstruction effort, but this long-range economic plan was interrupted by the military coup of 16 May 1961.

South Korean Economic Development since 1961

A government-led economic development policy was necessary during the 1960s and the 1970s, because private entrepreneurs lacked the experience or capital to develop the key industries that were needed for South Korea's economic growth. The new Park military regime undertook the modernization of the country to gain legitimacy with his own people and with other countries, especially the United States; indeed, he firmly believed that economic development was the only way to secure that legitimacy. Thus Park and his coup associates, under the slogans of "modernization of the fatherland" and "economy first," committed themselves to rapid economic progress. Park justified political repression and government corruption under the cloak of economic development; the regime's sole measure of modernization was a high rate of GNP growth.

At first Park embarked on rash and ill-advised economic policies based on naïve populism. Eager for immediate success. his regime failed to realize the anticipated results and, instead of promoting progress, caused further economic confusion. The Park government quickly learned from its initial mistakes, however. Based on the Second Republic's multiyear development planning, on 13 January 1962 it announced the First Five-Year Economic Development Plan (1962–1966). From the start Park tightened government controls over the economic life of the country. For instance, by virtually nationalizing the banks and directly regulating all institutional credit, the Park government extended its command over the business community. It also established an improved foreign-exchange regime and brought the budget under tight control. As a result, the Park regime succeeded in stabilizing the once shaky economy, displaying in the process more energy and effectiveness than any previous ROK government.

Amid increasing stability, the First Five-Year Economic Development Plan progressed toward building a self-sufficient industrial structure, stressing electrification, fertilizers, oil refining, synthetic fibers, and cement. In the absence of domestic financial resources, foreign sources had to supply the capital. Foreign debts were to be repaid with earnings from cheap exports based on cheap labor, South Korea's most abundant natural resource. To attract foreign investments and lower the unit cost of production for exports, the Park regime maintained low wages by every possible means. When South Korea normalized its relations with Japan, the latter supplied an assistance package of $800 million in the form of grants and credits.

As expected, the Park regime's economic development goals and policies worked well. Opportunely a vibrant, booming world economy invited South Korea's exports. A well-organized state under the strong leadership that could deploy an educated, able, and extraordinarily low-wage workforce in a targeted fashion was in a position of strong competitive advantage to enter the global markets. Consequently, exceeding most expectations in achieving the growth of both production and exports, South Korea enjoyed a 4.1 percent increase in GNP in 1962 and 9.3 percent in 1963. Thereafter South Korea consistently maintained an average annual increase of more than 8.0 percent in GNP growth.

The Second Five-Year Economic Development Plan (1967–1971) emphasized modernizing the industrial structure and rapidly building industries that had formerly relied on imports, including steel, machinery, and chemicals. During the First and Second Five-Year Plans, new and basic industries, such as fertilizer plants, oil refineries, cement factories, and power plants, were built. Infrastructure investments were in roads, railways, water and electricity supply, and communication. The Ulsan Oil Refinery Factory, first put into operation in 1964, the Masan Free Export Zone, created in 1969, and the Seoul-Pusan Expressway, opened for traffic in 1970 all symbolized South Korea's rapid economic growth that was often referred to as the "Miracle of the Han River." The annual increase in GNP for 1967–1971 was 10.7 percent. During this period, export grew by an annual average of 33.7 percent. These economic achievements were the pride of the Park Chung-hee government.

The remarkable growth rates in this period revealed the inevitable tendency of modernizing societies to exhibit decline in agriculture while manufacturing expands. The primary industry—agriculture and fishery—grew by an annual average of 4.3 percent during 1962–1969, mining and manufacturing by 17.9 percent, and services by 11.4 percent, but the average GNP growth rate for all industries in this period was 9.9 percent, with the agricultural and fishery sector's share of GNP decreasing from 39.7 percent to 28.4 percent, and manufacturing's share increasing from 15.0 percent to 24.6 percent.The speed and mode of this change in the South Korean industrial structure were conspicuous and carried significant social implications. Rapid industrialization brought about the growth of cities and the subsequent drifting of the population to urban centers. Urban development caused many social problems, particularly the growth of slums resulting from mass migrations of the poverty-stricken rural population to the cities. Another feature of South Korea's rapid economic growth was the striking imbalance that occurred in the geographical distribution of economic development. Major industrial investment was concentrated in Seoul and its neighboring area within the Inch'ŏn-Suwŏn industrial belt, as well as in the cities of Pusan, Ulsan, Masan, and Kumi in the southeast. The Yŏngnam region was the home turf of Park Chung-hee's political power and was comparatively favored in economic development in return for strong electoral support.[10]

Park Chung-hee's economic development programs resembled those that were seen in the Japanese colonial period. Like the former colonial masters, Park fostered and implemented comprehensive economic programs with top-down management and control of the entire economic life of the country. The process led to a close collaboration between government and business leaders and industrial expansion by the major chaebŏl conglomerates.

Rapid Urbanization and the Rise of Urban Values

Until the 1960s South Korean society had been overwhelmingly rural, with most Koreans supporting themselves through farming or fishing, and few ever venturing farther than the nearest market towns, which were not much larger than their home villages. By 1970, however, society had undergone profound changes, especially in rapid urbanization. Park Chung-hee's industrial policies in the 1960s gave rise to mass migrations of rural Koreans to the cities in search of jobs and opportunities. The 1960s thus witnessed the explosive growth of Seoul, as well as Pusan, Taegu, and Inch'ŏn, along with new manufacturing cities including Ulsan and Kumi. In a single generation, South Korea tipped from an agricultural, rural nation to an industrial, urban nation, profoundly modifying social structures and values, as well as behavior. The mass influx of people into cities led to the collapse of traditional values based on life in rural communities matched by the rise of new urban values throughout the nation. Although the shifting of the workforce to urban areas was an engine of economic growth, it drained human capital from the farms, exacerbating poverty in rural areas and permanently decreasing the number of young people in those areas.

The transformation of primarily rural South Korea into an urban society had already begun in the 1950s. The Korean War had brought about the mass movements of refugees and the depletion of the youthful population by military conscription. The war itself exposed South Korean youth to modern society, technologies, and new world outlooks. The war also resulted in the growth of a large officer corps that later became an increasingly significant social group. These changes in urban and rural life continued after the armistice in 1953, as increasing numbers of rural dwellers left their villages for the new urban environment and government price controls on farm products, designed to maintain low food prices and low wages in the large urban labor pools, made it unprofitable to operate small farm plots.

In the 1960s increasing poverty caused a surge in the rural exodus to the cities, with young females, mostly teenagers, seeking to work in light industries such as apparel, textile, shoes, and electronics, and young males, often the eldest or smartest son, seeking a better education. Urbanization increased by an annual rate of more than 4 percent during the 1960s and the 1970s, and continued at a 3 percent rate annually in the 1980s. The population of Seoul more than doubled during the 1960s, from 2.5 million in 1960 to 5.5 million in 1970, and other major cities such as Pusan, Taegu, and Inch'ŏn also grew dramatically. In 1970 the inhabitants of Seoul accounted for some 18 percent of the total Korean population of 31 million.

Distinctive regional features began to emerge in the capital, such as the appearance of numerous restaurants offering regional specialties and the emergence of electoral districts that produced bloc votes for presidential and National Assembly candidates from the same province as many of the district's residents. As urban living standards improved, citizens expressed a strong desire for their children to be educated, particularly at secondary schools and institutions of higher learning. Those with higher education found better job opportunities in the cities, especially Seoul, and were soon absorbed by the rapidly growing industrial and commercial sectors. Joining the ranks of the expanding middle class, a higher portion of better-educated people resided in Seoul, the center of the nation's political, economic, and cultural life. As beneficiaries of the rapidly expanding economy, much of the middle class was content with its situation and was indifferent to Park and his politics. But opposition to the Park regime grew among students, intellectual activists, and highly educated persons dissatisfied with their less well-paid jobs.

Rapid urbanization also further complicated the problems of housing, transportation, sanitation, and pollution inherent in urban life, which, in turn, generated other social problems. Life was hard for most city dwellers, as most of those newly arrived from the countryside were without jobs and would not be able to find work for several months. Most of the newcomers' jobs were the "3D" (dangerous, dirty, and difficult) occupations with low wages. Even though the newcomers assembled in transient squatter settlements and slums, they still appeared to be better off than their rural counterparts, as they had better educational opportunities, which encouraged even more rural citizens to move to the major cities.

The traditional social system was largely preserved throughout South Korea until the early 1970s, but it was increasingly threatened by tha nation's modernization and urbanization. Modern ideas spread from cities to the rural communities, mainly through continuing close family and clan contacts, shaking up the traditional value system. Many city dwellers regularly visited their ancestral villages for family reunions or to perform sacrificial rites, particularly on the Lunar New Year and Ch'usŏk, or Harvest Moon Day, on 15 August (by the lunar calendar). Although some Confucian ethical values declined as a living creed, Confucianism as a whole had a lingering impact on social relations, especially the regulation that members of the same surname and the same family cannot marry, which is a law even today.

Americans also contributed considerably to the transformation of South Korean society. As political and economic ties between South Korea and the United States strengthened during the 1950s and the 1960s, so, too, did certain social and cultural ties. Ever since the late 1940s a sizable presence of American citizens remained in South Korea. Missionaries had been replaced by soldiers as the most obvious presence and influence, and "G.I. culture" altered Korean values and living customs.

The New Village Movement

By the end of the 1960s, with agriculture and rural development consistently neglected and the urban population growing, the stagnant rural economy could not cope with higher food consumption, and thus large amounts of foreign exchange were required for grain imports. The rampant rural exodus imposed great burdens on municipal administrations, particularly in Seoul, and raised the chances of social and political unrest. Cities were terribly overcrowded, rural areas had lost the most youthful and productive members of their labor force, and the 1971 presidential election demonstrated that a substantial erosion of support for the Park regime had occurred in the predominantly rural areas of the southwestern Chŏlla provinces.[11] In April 1970 Park responded to these challenges by advocating the Saemaŭl undong, or New Village Movement (NVM), to increase rural productivity and income. The next year, the movement was launched throughout the country to upgrade the quality of village life by promoting "diligence, self-help, and cooperation." Although actual government investments in the NVM projects were a small proportion of the total budget, the administrative and propaganda effort at both local and national levels was intense. From the start, the highly organized, centrally directed movement had strong political overtones. As the rural areas formed Park's political power base, he had to take action. He backed the movement with the full weight and prestige of his office and, from 1972 to 1975, its momentum was not only sustained but even intensified. Park termed the New Village Movement a "spiritual revolution" and stressed the transformation of values and attitudes in the rural community. Thus his government sought to mobilize rural villagers to improve their material lives and discard their backward ways. An agency was created in the central government to oversee the NVM, and local officials were instructed to mobilize villagers to actively participate.

Initially the NVM targeted improvements in the villages' physical environments, and in many areas local villagers worked together to improve local roads, bridges, water supplies, washing facilities, and toilets. Many thatched roofs were replaced with more permanent materials such as tile. After 1973 the emphasis gradually moved to increasing agricultural productivity and rural incomes. Cash crops, including certain vegetables, were planted, particularly in new plastic hothouses; boundaries between tiny plots were readjusted; extensive irrigation and flood-control projects were undertaken; and advancements in agricultural science and technology included the planting of "green revolution" rice strains and the mechanization of farm work.

The NVM had far-reaching positive effects in rural life, reinforcing the rising expectations of the rural populace. By the mid-1970s rural family incomes had been brought up to the level of urban family incomes, but soon farm incomes fell behind again. The New Village Movement continued into the 1980s, and whatever the Park government's motive had been for starting the program, it certainly benefited the rural communities. Still, however, the merits of the NVM remain controversial.

SOUTH KOREA'S RELATIONS WITH THE UNITED STATES AND JAPAN

The ROK–U.S. Mutual Defense Treaty

The most important diplomatic action to result from the Korean War was the ROK–U.S. Mutual Defense Treaty. Current U.S. security arrangements with South Korea are based formally on this mutual defense treaty, signed in Washington on 1 October 1953 and entered into force on 17 November 1954. The bilateral treaty was created in response to the strong demands of President Syngman Rhee for a U.S. commitment to South Korea's security after the Korean War. Rhee had been uneasy about the end of Korean hostilities, and at the last moment, before the armistice agreement, he threatened to disrupt the peace talks unless the United States made a formal commitment to guarantee South Korea's future security. Eager to end the war as quickly as possible, the

Eisenhower administration reluctantly met Rhee's demand, and, in return, Rhee promised not to undermine the armistice agreement.

The six articles of the ROK–U.S. Mutual Defense Treaty affirmed that the signatories would regard an armed attack on the other as "dangerous to its own peace and safety and declares that it would act to meet the common danger in accordance with its constitutional processes." With this treaty, the United States assumed responsibility for defending the political and territorial integrity of South Korea. As part of that defense, significant numbers of U.S. ground, air, and naval forces would be stationed in South Korea for decades to come. Backed by the continued presence of U.S. forces in South Korea, and given the tense, even dangerous, situation along the demilitarized zone, the wisdom of the treaty was initially unquestioned in both South Korea and the United States.

The treaty not only helped secure the continued existence of the Republic of Korea, but it also helped ensure that the Korean peninsula would remain divided into two hostile camps. For just as South Korea would turn to the United States for assistance and protection, North Korea would depend largely on the Soviet Union and China to rebuild its economic and military structure, at least in the immediate years ahead.

The Syngman Rhee regime was assisted by the introduction of large amounts of U.S. aid in the 1950s. Between 1954 and 1960 roughly $2.6 billion of economic grants-in-aid poured into South Korea, amounting to some 8.6 percent of South Korea's total GNP during that period. Along with this economic aid, the United States also provided $1.2 billion in military assistance, or 76 percent of South Korea's total military budget. Although the purpose of the military aid was obvious, much of the economic aid was used to rebuild the country's badly damaged infrastructure and temporarily feed much of the hungry South Korean population. This U.S. assistance helped create a strong bond between the Korean and American peoples in the years immediately following the war. It also allowed the U.S. government to gain a considerable degree of leverage over the South Korean government.

The Normalization of South Korean–Japanese Relations

The United States played a significant behind-the-scenes mediation role in ROK–Japan normalization. To achieve its goal in East Asia, the United States pressed South Korea and Japan to open trade and investment contacts, as U.S. officials believed that a rapprochement between the two nations would strengthen the anticommunist camp in East Asia by forming "maritime civilizations." Moreover, with growing concerns for its own balance-of-payments problems since the late 1950s, the United States wanted Japan to share the financial burden of assisting South Korea.

During the 1950s, however, little progress was made toward normalization because of President Rhee's staunch anti-Japanese stance and the Japanese government's lack of serious motivation in this regard. The Japanese viewed reparations to the ROK for Japan's colonial rule as the most difficult stumbling block. South Korea claimed much larger reparations than Japan was prepared to pay. The South Korean nationalists, whom Rhee represented, still had vivid memories of Japan's brutal occupation of their country, and they refused to consider normalization of relations. Because any Korean suggestion of normalization talks might cause fierce antigovernment demonstrations that would threaten the government's existence, Rhee suppressed such efforts throughout his years in power.

During the early 1960s, however, several factors contributed to progress in normalization negotiations. The Park Chung-hee regime, which had come to power in May 1961, was eager to obtain Japanese capital to finance its economic development. Beginning in 1964 the Sato Eisaku government was more enthusiastic than any previous Japanese government to pursue a regional anticommunist alliance as envisaged by the United States. Meanwhile, with its escalating military involvement in Vietnam, the United States increased its efforts to establish a rapprochement between South Korea and Japan. In 1964, when South Korean domestic opposition against "humiliating diplomacy with Japan" seriously challenged the Park government's negotiations with Japan, the United States exerted pressure on the Japanese government to formally apologize for its "past regrettable history" with Korea and its people.[12] Many South Koreans expressed their desire that normalization be preceded by Japan's sincere apology for its past colonial rule.

Finally, on 22 June 1965, South Korea and Japan established formal diplomatic relations by signing the Treaty on Basic Relations, opening a new era of mutual economic cooperation. The treaty confirmed that past treaties for the Japanese annexation of Korea in 1910 were void and that the ROK was the only legitimate government on the Korean peninsula. By signing four related agreements, the two governments also settled disputes over the boundary line for fishing in the East Sea, the legal status of Korean residents in Japan, the status of Korean cultural treasures that Japan had appropriated, and Korea's property claims.

Regarding the last issue, Japan was to pay South Korea $45 million. Japan was also to offer, as noted earlier, another assistance package of $800 million in grants and loans as a "gesture of goodwill."[13]

To attain normalization of relations with Japan, Park Chung-hee ignored the political opposition in the National Assembly, suppressed student dissent on the streets, and stifled newspaper criticism. On 12 August 1965 lawmakers from the opposition Democratic People's Party resigned their Assembly seats in protest of the normalization treaty. The next day the ruling Democratic Republican Party approved the treaty in the absence of opposition party members in the Assembly. Although this action was technically legal, it clearly demonstrated Park's disregard and disdain for parliamentary government.[14]

Normalization of South Korean–Japanese relations did not, however, result in a tripartite alliance between the United States, South Korea, and Japan. Normalization also did not resolve the thorny issues that had originated in the "past history" of Japanese colonialism in Korea and were therefore nearly unsolvable. Despite its inherent weaknesses, normalization was characterized as an epochal event in South Korea's foreign relations, as it opened the way for the future economic relations between the two nations.

South Korean–U.S. Relations in the 1960s

Ever since South Korea became a sovereign state in August 1948, the Republic of Korea and the United States have had friendly relations. The United States has assisted South Korea fully in protecting its fragile security and rehabilitating its poverty-stricken economy. Although nominally bilateral, the relationship was actually unilateral: Tthe United States, as the patron, made all the decisions, and South Korea, the client nation, lived with those decisions in terms of military support and economic assistance. After publicly supporting President Syngman Rhee throughout the 1950s, the United States provided him sanctuary in Hawaii when he was removed from power in late April 1960.

When the Second Republic was established shortly after Rhee's fall in 1960, the United States strongly supported the new government of Prime Minister Chang Myŏn, and U.S. officials applauded the growth of democratic institutions, as well as the government's efforts to initiate long-term economic planning. But after a bloodless coup, led by Major General Park Chung-hee, toppled the Chang Myŏn government in 1961, the United States also publicly supported Park Chung-hee's new military regime. When Park displayed unwillingness to return to a civilian government and expressed his intention to extend the

military regime, however, the United States pressured him to transfer power
to a civilian government. Eventually Park yielded to this pressure, and in late
1962 a new constitution was promulgated. In December 1963 the Third Republic
was inaugurated, and Park gave up his generalship in the army, created his own
political party, and successfully ran for the presidency in late 1963. Four years
later, in 1967, he was reelected to a second term.

At this time South Korean–U.S. relations entered a positive period. Perhaps
the most important elements leading to cooperation between the two countries
stemmed from external sources. On 21 January 1968 North Korean commandos
carried out an attack on the Blue House, the South Korean presidential mansion, in an effort to assassinate President Park. Although the assault failed,
the two nations were shocked that North Korean agents had been within one
mile of the Blue House. Then, two days later, four North Korean naval ships
captured the U.S. naval intelligence vessel, the USS *Pueblo,* an electronic "spy
ship," off the country's eastern coast (more on this below), reinforcing the view
in South Korea and the United States that North Korea was still menacing, and
thus further strengthening South Korean–U.S. cooperation.

Another important factor cementing ROK–U.S. ties in the mid-1960s was
the Vietnam War. By 1965 the United States had built up its military forces in
Vietnam, and in order to show that the United States had broad international
support in waging war in Vietnam, President Lyndon B. Johnson sought to recruit other foreign forces to the U.S. cause. In this U.S. campaign, the president
could find only one ally—South Korea—willing to send large combat troops
to Vietnam. President Park wanted to send ROK forces to South Vietnam for a
number of reasons. If South Vietnam was to fall to communism, he was certain
that this would pose a grave threat to the security of Southeast Asia and South
Korea itself. Moreover, he wanted to prevent the United States from pulling its
forces out of South Korea to send to South Vietnam. Another reason is that, at
the time, a significant number of Koreans saw the dispatch of ROK troops as a
way to repay the United States for the sacrifices it had made on behalf of South
Korea during the Korean War. Still another reason was that the troop dispatch
would bring enormous economic benefits to South Korea. This was brought
out when, on 4 March 1966, South Korea and the United States had entered
into a secret agreement, known as the Brown Memorandum, whereby the
United States would provide all the financing for South Korean forces in Vietnam and also send new military equipment to South Korea worth billions
of dollars.

During 1965 and 1973 South Korea sent more than 47,000 troops, two infantry divisions, to Vietnam. Because the tour of duty in Vietnam was one year, the total number of soldiers sent to Vietnam in that period amounted to 312,853. This was the largest contingent of foreign troops sent to Vietnam, second only to U.S. forces. The United States provided offset payments, including soldiers' salaries, for South Koreans in Vietnam, who gained invaluable combat experience and also became proficient in the use of advanced U.S. weaponry.

The vast sums of money earned by South Korean soldiers and businesses from the war in Vietnam had a significant effect on South Korea's economic development, as it supplied urgently needed capital to promote the country's industrial development. South Korea shed a great deal of blood and made many sacrifices to lay the foundation for economic prosperity. Some 4,600 soldiers were killed and 17,000 seriously wounded in that faraway country.

President Park's every effort to lay the groundwork for his country's future economic growth was motivated by the belief that a flourishing economy would legitimize his dictatorship. Since 1965 South Korea's economic growth was primarily a product of the blood, sweat, tears, and self-sacrifice of South Koreans themselves, but the United States also made a great contribution. It provided research and academic facilities for South Korean talent, and many of South Korea's most influential economists and planners studied and were trained at U.S. universities and employed by U.S. firms and agencies before returning to their country. The U.S.-led Vietnam War also provided South Koreans with financing and experience. The hard currency South Korea obtained by participating in the war was a key financial source for industrial investment. The United States further aided South Korea's economic improvement just by providing a market for South Korea's industrial and consumer products.

By the early 1970s significant changes that occurred not only in South Korea but also in East Asia had important, sometimes troubling, impacts on South Korean–U.S. relations. After his reelection for a third term in April 1971, Park Chung-hee proceeded to tighten his control over his country. On 6 December 1971 Park declared a state of national emergency, justifying his action as necessary for national security.[15] This step fit conveniently into the so-called Nixon Doctrine, which resulted in the subsequent reduction of U.S. forces in South Korea.

On 15 July 1969 U.S. President Richard M. Nixon, at a news conference on Guam, explained what the press would call the "Nixon Doctrine." Prompted by the great economic costs of the ongoing Vietnam War, along with opposition from war-weary Americans, the doctrine marked a step back from the Truman Doctrine of 1947. Nixon declared that the United States had a stake in Asian affairs, and when requested by Asian allies who were under threat, would furnish military and economic aid but that the manpower would come from the allies

With the Nixon Doctrine in place, on 27 March 1971 the United States announced the withdrawal from South Korea of the U.S. Army's 7th Infantry Division, which had been stationed there since 1950, decreasing the U.S. military presence from some 60,000 to approximately 40,000. Although necessitated by U.S. needs to cope with changing economic and diplomatic circumstances, the withdrawal was a shock to many South Koreans who viewed the U.S. military presence as an indispensable defense against possible North Korean aggression. Many South Koreans considered it a breach of faith on the part of the United States. Taking advantage of this unease among South Koreans, Park further strengthened his grip on power.

In the 1960s South Korea and the United States were faithfully supportive of their defense and economic alliance. Solemnized by the mutual defense treaty, the U.S. commitment to ROK security as a whole did not waver, although the broad foreign policy and strategic justifications for this commitment shifted from time to time.

THE RISE OF THE JUCHE STATE IN NORTH KOREA

Kim Il-sung's Tightening Grip on Power

Following the Korean War, North Korea was faced with massive postwar political and economic challenges. Kim Il-sung's position had been weakened by his failure to achieve his war aims, and he now faced challenges from factions that had been brought together in the Korean Workers Party (KWP). Kim was able to keep his seat only through ruthless purges of rival factions.

The strongest foreign influence on the structure of North Korea's leadership was the Chinese Communist Party model. Like Mao Zedong, Kim Il-sung was very much a mass-based communist party leader. Since the late 1940s some 12 to 14 percent of the North Korean population was enrolled in the KWP, compared to 1 to 3 percent for communist parties in most countries, making it a mass, rather than an elite, party. The vast majority of KWP members, poor peasants and manual workers with no previous political experience, were enrolled because of their class background, not their grasp of ideology. Party membership offered them status, privileges, and a rudimentary form of political participation. Because they owed their new status in North Korean society to Kim Il-sung, they were a powerful support base for Kim within the party.

In the course of the war, the Korean Workers Party lost up to half its prewar membership through battlefield casualties, desertion, and expulsion. But Kim Il-sung quickly reinstated old members and enrolled new ones, greatly increasing the party membership. By 1953, with his authority in the KWP consolidated by the support and loyalty of newly enrolled members, Kim Il-sung had become the central figure of a personality cult.

Immediately after the war major purges gradually eliminated the leaders of Kim Il-sung's rival factions within the Korean Workers Party. The major political casualties here were domestic South Korean communists led by Pak Hŏn-yŏng, as they were blamed for not rising up in protest in South Korea. The evaporation of their geographical support base in South Korea dealt a mortal blow to them. In early 1953 many leading southern communists, among them Pak Hŏn-yŏng, were publicly denounced, and in August of that year Pak was arrested, tried, and convicted of high treason in show trials. Accused by Kim Il-sung of being a "hireling of U.S. imperialism," Pak was executed in December 1955, a scapegoat for Kim Il-sung's failure to unify the Korean peninsula by force. Two other leading cadres were also purged at this time: Mu Chŏng, the Yan'an faction's leading military official who was removed from office in late 1950 on charges of failing to defend Pyongyang that fall and died soon afterward; and Hŏ Ka-i, the Soviet Korean leader whom Kim Il-sung charged with mismanaging the KWP and who allegedly committed suicide on 2 July 1953.

The Korean War caused the near total destruction of North Korea's economic and industrial bases. Sustained U.N. bombing had razed its capital of Pyongyang and demoralized the war-weary population. Agricultural and industrial production fell far below prewar levels. After the armistice, then, North Korea urgently needed to repair its infrastructure. While barely subsisting on massive Soviet bloc aid, North Korea sorely needed relief and rehabilitation.

The KWP leadership was divided on the issue of postwar recovery and how best to direct national development. Kim Il-sung and his "Kapsan faction," following the model of Stalinism, sought heavy industrialization and the restoration of North Korea's war-making capacity. Kim's faction also rejected full integration into the socialist international division of labor and instead maintained the focus of national self-reliance. Kim's program included the complete nationalization of all industry and the collectivization of all agriculture. In contrast, bureaucratic-technocratic elements led by the Soviet Koreans opposed resurrection of a war economy and advocated more gradualist, moderate policies with priority given to agriculture and light industry. They also preferred less self-reliant and more moderate degrees of nationalization and collectivization. This policy debate was closely related to a power struggle within the North Korean leadership and reflected a far more profound ideological struggle—the "red versus expertise," or "ideology versus technology," conflict. A similar debate had occurred in other communist states at the same time in their development, for instance, Mao Zedong versus Liu Shaoqi in China in the early 1960s.

By the time of the April 1955 Korean Workers Party plenum, Kim Il-sung had garnered enough support to announce the acceleration of socialism and to castigate openly Soviet Korean influence within the party. In December 1955 he severely criticized the leading Soviet Korean cadre and leading economic planner, Pak Ch'ang-ok, who was seen as Hŏ Ka-i's successor to lead the Soviet Korean faction. In January 1956 Kim Il-sung removed him as chairman of the State Economic Planning Commission. By 1962 Soviet Koreans had been driven from significant positions, and Kim Il-sung's increasing independence from the de-Stalinized Soviet Union after 1956 made it difficult for the patron state to aid its supporters in North Korea.

The Third Congress of the Korean Workers Party, convened in April 1956, witnessed little sign of intraparty struggle. In June and July Kim visited the Soviet Union, East Germany, Romania, Hungary, Czechoslovakia, Bulgaria, Albania, Poland, and Mongolia, accompanied by 30 compatriots, in an attempt to garner economic and political support. In Kim's absence, his opponents, emboldened by Soviet leader Nikita Khrushchev's recent de-Stalinization move, maneuvered to oust him from power. They criticized Kim for his increasingly dictatorial rule and for encouraging a personality cult, and pressed for relaxation of economic and social control. But by then Kim's opponents were already too weak to defeat him, and when he returned to North Korea, he overwhelmed his opponents in the subsequent showdown at the crucial party plenum of the KWP in August, expelling from the party those who had led the opposition against him. Between 1956 and 1958 the Yan'an faction, headed by several of North Korea's most senior independence leaders, was swept from power. Ch'oe Ch'ang-ik, a vice premier, was banished to work in the mines. By 1958 Kim and his associates had eliminated the last significant source of opposition and was in total control of the KWP and their country.[16] In North Korea serious power struggles took place only during the first decade of the regime. Later, conflicts within the North Korean leadership arose, but they were relatively minor and occurred only within Kim's Kapsan faction. No further challenges were raised to Kim's prestige and power.

The Soviet Union intervened in the August 1956 political crisis more deeply than China did. Indeed, Soviet Deputy Prime Minister Anastas Mikoyan personally intervened. Following a bitter verbal exchange with North Korea, the Soviet Union recalled its ambassador from Pyongyang. In retaliation, North Korea drastically reduced its coverage of Soviet news events as an overt sign of North Korean alienation from the Soviet Union. Previously North Korean media coverage was filled with adulation of the Soviet Union and its institutions. By removing any mention of his Red Army career from North Korea's official history, Kim Il-sung sought to portray himself as an anti-revisionist leader in the international communist movement. Kim also criticized the peaceful coexistence line of the post-Stalin leadership in the Soviet Union. In December 1957 North Korea and the Soviet Union came to agree that dual Soviet–DPRK citizenship for Soviet Koreans would be abolished. Soviet Koreans in North Korea were forced to return to the Soviet Union if they wanted to retain Soviet citizenship. This measure ultimately eliminated the power of the Soviet Korean faction within the North Korean power structure. Kim Il-sung's stance departed from that of the Soviet Union, and North Korea declared its political independence from its communist patron.

By 1958 Kim Il-sung had established complete dominance over the Korean Workers Party and the North Korean state, and he embarked on a new phase of the North Korean "revolution." Regardless of right or wrong, Kim's policy gradually became state policy, and North Korea gave overriding priority to rapid heavy industrialization and the buildup of its war-making capacity. As light industry and agriculture were considered of lesser importance, North Koreans were afflicted with chronic shortages of basic consumer goods.

The Emergence of the Juche Ideology

The wartime experience greatly diluted the Soviet influence in North Korea, because, in North Korean eyes, it was the Chinese who had saved the state from extinction. Moreover, Kim Il-sung, who followed Stalin's example in encouraging a personality cult to bolster his power, was estranged by Khrushchev's policy of de-Stalinization. Further, in the course of power struggles after the Korean War, Kim Il-sung severely criticized the Yan'an and Soviet Korean factions for slavishly following the prescriptions of Marxism-Leninism. Instead, he insisted on developing and adopting a unique Korean version of Marxism-

Leninism that supposedly harmonized with the realities of the Korean situation. Kim elevated the concept of *juche*, commonly referred to as self-reliance, to a philosophical dogma to be strictly followed. This North Korean ideology was a combination of socialist and nationalist ideas and has often been compared to a state religion.

On 28 December 1955 Kim Il-sung formally enunciated the juche ideology for the first time. Thereafter, it has been North Korea's ruling ideology, dominating all sectors of society, ranging from foreign policy to everyday life. Juche has been declared the sole ideological system in the communist nation, and no other system or way of thinking has been deemed acceptable. In fact, all other ideological systems are considered heretical, and anyone espousing them have been severely punished.

Juche, which emanated from North Korea's militant nationalism, comprises four main concepts related to ideology, politics, the economy, and military affairs; these include, respectively, *chagyŏl*, or self-determination; *chaju*, or independence; *charip*, or self-reliance; and *chawi*, or self-defense. Using an explicit analogy to the human body, the juche ideology likened Kim Il-sung, the Great Leader, to the brain that made decisions and commanded action; the Korean Workers Party was the nervous system that mediated and maintained equilibrium between the brain and the body; and the people were the body (bone and muscle) that implemented decisions and channeled feedback to the Great Leader. Juche was also a declaration meant to exhibit political independence from North Korea's two communist sponsors—the Soviet Union and China. The juche philosophy became synonymous with North Korea's famous autarchy called "Our Style Socialism."

Later, the juche ideology evolved into a political philosophy. The KWP replaced references to Marxism-Leninism in the North Korean constitution with juche in 1977. Then, as approved by the North Korean Supreme People's Assembly on 9 April 1992, the revised constitution substituted juche for Marxism-Leninism as a guiding principle of politics.

Kim Il-sung and his son and successor, Kim Jong-il, used the juche ideology as a political tool to justify the North Korean political system, government structure, and personality cult of father and son, and it has played a key role in solidifying the North Korean political power structure and preventing the collapse of the country, especially in the lean times beginning in the late 1980s. Moreover, the juche ideology was used as a tool to prepare the nation for Kim's familial and ideological heir. Originally the communist state in North Korea had been founded on the orthodox communist principle that placed the party above all else, but the juche ideology converted the country into a unique communist state with the Leader reigning supreme over the party and the people.

The State of Kimilsungism

As anti-Kim factions were completely eliminated from the North Korean leadership, the communist nation was virtually transformed into Kim Il-sung's "kingdom." In North Korea Kim's instructions became the absolute laws of the country. Public debate on policy and ideology vanished, and the Korean Workers Party was reduced to an instrument only for carrying out Kim Il-sung's instructions. North Koreans were forced to live by the slogan "Learn from the glorious revolutionary tradition founded by Comrade Kim Il-sung and his anti-Japanese partisans," which, to the North Korean people, was more than a mere slogan; it guided every aspect of North Korean life, public or private.

From the late 1950s, in accordance with Kim Il-sung's mandate, North Korea increasingly isolated itself from the communist bloc where the Stalinist legacy was generally denied. In North Korea, however, Stalinism was still alive, transformed into so-called Kimilsungism, and exerted profound influence on North Korean life, with the mass media, art, literature, and music all pressed into service to produce and praise Kimilsungism.

The most striking feature of Kimilsungism, as in the Stalinist practice, was Kim's forged imagery as the "fatherly leader." Like other totalitarian regimes, the North Korean government attempted to disassemble individual families and clans, replacing them with the notion that the entire society was one family and the head of state was the father figure. According to North Korea's official explanation, human beings received their natural life from their biological parents, but their lives as social beings derived from a parent-type figure, the "Great Leader." This parental "Great Leader" deserved the veneration and devotion of the people, his "children." As the benevolent parent of the North Korean people, the fatherly Great Leader was committed to the needs of his "children"; the people, in return, gave their loyalty, obedience, and gratitude not to their biological parents but to the Great Leader. Kim Il-sung was promoted as the father not only of North Koreans but of ethnic Koreans anywhere outside North Korea. The Korean Workers Party was referred to as the "mother party." To strengthen "blood ties' with his "children," Kim Il-sung frequently made "on-the-spot-guidance" tours, visiting collective farms, factories, and other sites of economic production throughout the country. The visits transformed

Kim from a distant impersonal authority to a close, benign parental figure. The national territory became a harmonious household where the fatherly Great Leader gave benevolent instruction, inspected conditions, and suggested corrections for his "children." In this way, the Great Leader reached out to physically touch and embrace all the nation's people.

Kim Il-sung's political apparatus also portrayed him as a person with godlike qualities. His persona as a demigod was reinforced through the North Star, the Big Dipper, the pine tree, the contour of Paektu-san, and a red hybrid "Kim-ilsungia" begonia. Although the personality cult of Kim resembled the Stalin cult in the Soviet Union in the 1930s and the 1940s, old Confucian values in North Korea, particularly filial piety, required the people, as the "children," to discharge their duties, loyalty, and devotion to the "fatherly leader" in return for him gracing them with new life as social beings.

According to North Korea's theory of the "Great Leader," the fidelity pledged to him does not end with his generation but is transferred to the new leader. In other words, the fidelity devoted to Kim Il-sung was automatically transferred to Kim Jong-il, his heir and successor. Actually, after Kim Il-sung's death on 8 July 1994, North Korea officially adopted the slogan "Kim Il-sung is Kim Jong-il, and Kim Jong-il is Kim Il-sung."

Culture and art in North Korea served only to spread monolithic Kimist ideology through didactic media. Cultural expression was just an instrument for inculcating the juche ideology and the need to continue the struggle to revolutionize and reunify the "fatherland." "Foreign imperialists," specifically Americans and the Japanese, were depicted as heartless monsters; North Korea's revolutionary heroes and heroines were seen as saintly figures who acted from the purest motives. The three most consistent themes of literature and art were martyrdom during the revolutionary struggle, the happiness of the present society, and the genius of the Great Leader.

Kim Il-sung's absolutist state might be compared to a fanatical religious sect, because the state allowed no dissent from or criticism of Kim Il-sung, his tenets or his decisions. In fact, Kim Il-sung (and his son) established a state that actually practiced a peculiar brand of oriental despotism rather than communism. Even after his death, Kim Il-sung has been designated in the constitution as the country's "Eternal President" and the government went so far as to declare that their nation is a new Korean state founded on 15 April 1912, Kim Il-sung's birthday, with Kim as its progenitor, thereby denying the existence of earlier Korean nations.

THE NORTH KOREAN ECONOMY

The Growing North Korean Economy in the 1950s

In the North, as in southern Korea, the sudden withdrawal of the Japanese and the subsequent partition of the peninsula after World War II created economic chaos. Separation of the agricultural south from the industrial north and the absence of Japan meant that northern Korea lost its traditional markets for raw material exports and semi-finished goods as well as its sources of food and manufactured goods. Making matters worse, the withdrawal of Japanese entrepreneurs and engineers negatively affected the economic base. Thus the urgent task facing the fledgling communist regime in North Korea was to develop a viable economy, which it would soon reorient mainly around other communist countries. The economic problems faced by North Korea would be greatly compounded, however, by the destruction of industrial plants during the Korean War. Therefore North Korea's economic development did not begin to tread a new path until after the war ended in 1953.

Because of massive bombing during the Korean War, North Korea suffered much heavier war damage than South Korea. For most of the 1950s, the communist country was absorbed with the urgent tasks of national reconstruction. The tightly centralized system of North Korea brought political and social conformity to the state and enabled a more rapid recovery than did South Korea's decentralized system, at least for the short run. North Korea's economy became one of the world's most highly centralized and planned economies. As in other Soviet-type or command economies, all economic decisions concerning the selection of output, output targets, allocation of raw materials, prices, distribution of national income, investment, and economic development were implemented through the economic plan devised by the Korean Workers Party and the central government. Complete socialization of the economy, including collectivization of agriculture, was accomplished by 1958, when private ownership of the means of production, land, and commercial enterprises had been entirely replaced by state or cooperative (collective) ownership and control.

North Korea's socialist command economy began with the three-year plan for 1954–1956, officially named the Three-Year Postwar Reconstruction Plan of 1954–1956, followed by a five-year plan for 1957–1961, to consolidate the foundation for further industrialization. This First Five-Year Plan for economic development was completed a year ahead of schedule, in 1960 rather than 1961.

To achieve economic development, North Korea employed a military-like mobilization of its people. Beginning with the *Ch'ŏllima,* meaning Thousand-League Horse, movement in 1958, North Korea mounted a series of production campaigns. The Ch'ŏllima movement, the North Korean version of China's Great Leap Forward, was launched to accelerate the pace of collectivization of agriculture and mobilize agriculture in support of further industrialization. Subsequently Kim Il-sung, and later Kim Jong-il, continued to implement various "speed campaigns."

With the benefit of foreign aid, North Korea, for the first few years after the Korean War, made impressive economic gains, far outstripping those of South Korea. By 1961 North Korea had achieved an industrial miracle. For a time annual economic growth reached as high as 20 percent, and the country was already the most industrial economy in the developing world and a model for other emerging nations. Through this rapid economic reconstruction, North Korea was able to improve its international standing, especially in the Third World. North Korea's speedy economic growth caused South Korea to withdraw the argument of "reunification through marching north" and instead to advocate "peaceful reunification." Even, in the late 1950s North Korea had developed a campaign to "help the poor South Korean brethren." But these gains did not necessarily produce a corresponding improvement in general living standards, because the communist economic doctrine placed first priority on heavy industry and neglected consumer benefits. In North Korea, from the beginning, the emphasis was never on meeting basic individual needs.

The Declining North Korean Economy in the 1960s

From the early 1960s on, the North Korean economy began to encounter difficulties. The First Seven-Year Plan (1961–1967) had to be extended three additional years to 1970, as a result of the burden of a massive defense buildup. To build military strength, North Korea increasingly allocated economic resources to military production. In the 1960s, military expenditures rose to 30 percent of the GNP. This new economic policy dramatically transformed the North Korean economy and the nature of the state itself. While the civilian economy gradually stalled, North Korea increasingly became an armed camp. Clearly the continuing economic decline and the economic catastrophe of the 1990s and the 2000s originated in the policies of the 1960s.[17]

Foreign aid in this period declined sharply, both from the Soviet Union under Nikita Khrushchev in the late 1950s and from China during the chaos of the

Cultural Revolution in the 1960s. In addition, North Korea always had to contend with a labor shortage arising from wartime losses and defection, as well as the high proportion of men in arms.

In the mid-1960s, with the economy severely strained, the North Korean leadership split over policy issues. The hard-liners, represented by Kim Il-sung and the military, supported a continuing military buildup, whereas the moderates, mainly technocrats and economic managers, wanted to restrain the buildup. The division finally ended at a Party Conference in October 1966, when Kim Il-sung purged Kapsan faction members including Pak Kŭm-ch'ŏl and Yi Hyo-sun, who had doubted the wisdom of a military buildup. They were replaced in the KWP by Kim's devoted loyalists and kinsmen, including his wife Kim Sŏng-ae, his younger brother Kim Yŏng-ju, and a nephew-in-law, Hwang Chang-yŏp. This was the last significant leadership purge within the KWP, which thereafter unconditionally followed Kim's teachings and guidelines.

North Korea's reliance on a command economy based on the juche philosophy increasingly led to an insular economic development strategy. Priority was assigned to establishing a self-sufficient industrial base, with consumer goods produced primarily to satisfy domestic demand (few products were exported) and private consumption held to very low levels. This approach sharply contrasted with South Korea's outward-oriented strategy which began in the mid-1960s. As a result, the North Korean economy became increasingly isolated from that of the rest of the world, and its industrial development and structure could not compete in international marketplaces. Because of its self-imposed isolation, the North Korean economy experienced chronic inefficiency, poor-quality goods, limited product diversity, and underutilization of manufacturing plants. A catastrophe loomed on the horizon.

NORTH KOREA'S FOREIGN RELATIONS

Economic Reconstruction and Foreign Assistance

As in South Korea, foreign aid was crucially important to North Korea's postwar reconstruction. North Korea accepted the equivalent of an estimated $4.75 billion in aid between 1946 and 1984, with almost 46 percent of this coming from the Soviet Union, about 18 percent from China, and the rest from East European communist countries. Some two-thirds of the aid were loans and the rest outright grants. Understandably grants dominated in the years immediately after the Korean War, but subsequently loans became the major form of aid. In 1954 the aid North Korea received comprised one-third of its national revenues. By 1960, however, foreign assistance had dropped to less than 3 percent of its total revenues. Thereafter North Korea had to work out its salvation alone.

Although it actively sought foreign aid for national reconstruction, North Korea efficiently used foreign assistance as a means of promoting its ultimate economic autonomy. Kim Il-sung aggressively sought reconstruction aid from the entire socialist community. As early as September 1953 he led a delegation to the Soviet Union, followed by a similar trip to China in November of that year. Other North Korean delegations visited the Eastern European states in 1953, including Poland, Hungary, East Germany, Czechoslovakia, Romania, and Bulgaria. In 1953 the communist states responded by adopting a policy that rendered substantial assistance to North Korea. The Soviet Union offered 1 billion rubles in assistance in September, and China vowed to provide 8 trillion yuan over a ten-year period. In the same month Hungary agreed to give North Korea grants in aid for reconstruction. The next month, Romania signed an agreement providing $7.2 million in aid. East Germany also concluded an assistance treaty, and in November Bulgaria and Poland signed similar agreements. Poland promised delivery of mining equipment and assistance in railway reconstruction. Czechoslovakia, the most industrialized nation of the East European communist nations, shipped machine tool industries and industrial factories to North Korea. Because North Korea urgently needed this foreign aid, it fell into a seemingly unavoidable dependent relationship with the communist states and risked becoming an economic satellite of the socialist bloc.

Since 1954 North Korea continued to depend on foreign aid from East European allies for reconstruction, annually entering into trade agreements with East Germany until 1957 and then reaching a long-term agreement for 1958–1961. East Germany provided machinery and equipment for the chemical industry and synthetic textiles in exchange for North Korean minerals and agricultural and marine products. Czechoslovakia signed a long-term agreement for 1954–1960, providing $12.6 million in credits, including technological assistance. Romania agreed to below-market rates of payments in 1954, and Bulgaria provided medical assistance to North Korea. Poland signed an aid agreement for 1954–1957, and both Bulgaria and Mongolia agreed on noncommercial terms of payments in trade with North Korea in 1955. The Eastern European states each provided assistance to specific industrial sectors of North Korea, which proved to be a highly successful approach for transferring technology and technical expertise to North Korea while minimizing political dependence on any specific aid donor.

North Korea was heavily dependent on Soviet assistance for most of this period. The Soviet Union signed an agreement with North Korea, in 1955, to share technological information at a minimal cost. As a result, more than 40 new industrial plants were constructed in North Korea with Soviet technical assistance. The Soviet Union also provided economic aid of some 300 million rubles between 1956 and 1958. The total amount of Soviet grants and credits to North Korea between 1953 and 1959 was 2.8 billion rubles, equivalent to U.S. $690 million.

In the late 1950s, while Kim Il-sung increasingly disagreed with the economic and political revisionism of the Soviet Union under Khrushchev's leadership, North Korea received substantial financial assistance from the Eastern European allies. Romania gave 25 million rubles to North Korea between 1956 and 1958; Bulgaria provided 30 million rubles; and Hungary gave 7.5 million rubles. Albania offered assistance in the form of 10,000 tons of pitch.[18] Because of this large-scale East European assistance, North Korea secured considerable independence in its relationship with the Soviet Union. North Korean relations with other communist states were successfully established on a footing fairly independent of its relationship with the Soviet Union.

North-South Korean Relations

In the 1950s and 1960s the two Koreas had virtually no dialogue, only open hostilities. In the 1950s North Korea had the initiative in North-South Korean relations, as its successful reconstruction put the communist country in a better position to extend the "revolution" to South Korea.

While internally strengthening the "capacity for revolution," North Korea externally declared a soft line on reunification. Between 1954 and 1958 North Korea vigorously offered a series of unification proposals to its southern neighbor, including a North-South Korean conference or a joint session of the Supreme People's Assembly and the ROK National Assembly; a nonaggression pact with troop reductions on both sides; conversion of the Korean Armistice Agreement into a peace treaty; an international conference for peaceful reunification; simultaneous withdrawal of Chinese and American forces; North-South Korean negotiations on economic and cultural relations; and all-Korea elections under the supervision of neutral nations.[19] South Korea, however, viewed all these proposals only as propaganda exercises and rejected them all. It also considered this outreach a Trojan horse. Thereafter North Koreans repeated some of the proposals according to circumstances.

In December 1962 the Central Committee of the Korean Workers Party established four basic military policies: "turning the entire country into a fortress"; "arming the entire population"; "modernizing the entire armed forces"; and "training the entire army as a cadre army." In accordance with these military policies, ambitious military plans were enforced in the mid-1960s by constructing underground airports, harbors, and storage and warehouses, and organizing a militia of 1.2 million men.

In the mid-1960s Kim Il-sung was deeply impressed with Ho Chi Minh's attempts to reunify Vietnam through guerilla warfare, and he believed a similar approach might be possible in Korea. Thus infiltration and subversion efforts were greatly stepped up against South Korea.

A month after holding ten-day military maneuvers in June 1967, North Korea organized a 2,400-man commando unit with specially selected members from the Korean People's Army trained for guerrilla missions in South Korea. In the first ten months of 1967, 423 major and 117 minor incidents occurred involving North Korean intruders in the demilitarized zone. Some 215 armed clashes broke out between South Korean security forces and North Korean guerrillas; 224 North Korean commandos infiltrating South Korea were killed and 50 were captured by South Korean security forces.[20]

North Korea's hostility toward South Korea reached its climax in early 1968. On 21 January 1968 a squad of 31 North Korean commandos disguised in South Korean Army fatigues penetrated the DMZ and reached the northern edge of Seoul with the acknowledged mission of assassinating South Korean President Park Chung-hee. When they were within one mile of the presidential mansion, they were detected by ROK police. In the ensuing gun battle, all but three commandos were killed and one was taken prisoner, and 37 South Korean security forces were killed. This incident traumatized many South Koreans, as they felt that North Korean soldiers could infiltrate South Korea at any time. Unfortunately their fear was well grounded.

In early November 1968 teams of more than 100 North Korean commandos landed on the eastern coast of South Korea, the Ulchin-Samch'ŏk area, apparently to establish a base for guerrilla warfare in the sparsely populated and impoverished hinterland. Most of the North Korean infiltrators were killed by South Korean security forces. Even though such armed infiltrations brought the two Koreas to the brink of open conflict, the results disappointed the North

Korean leadership. By 1969 the number and scale of infiltration incidents declined as North Korea reconsidered its options.

The North Korean commando incursions had enormous repercussions in South Korea. On 1 April 1968 the South Korean government organized the Homeland Reserve Force, comprised of all discharged soldiers under age 35. Under the "Seoul fortification plan," shelters that could accommodate 300,000 to 400,000 citizens in an emergency were built by 1970. Simply put, sustained tensions between the two Koreas in the two decades following the Korean War seriously threatened South Korea's survival.

North Korean–U.S. Relations

Unpredictability and hostility have generally characterized North Korea's relationship with the United States. Throughout most of the post–Korean War period, North Korea sought a peace treaty with the United States and the withdrawal of U.S. troops from South Korea, and to achieve its goals it pursued a contradictory policy of mixing provocations with the occasional olive branch. But it failed to achieve its goals mainly because of the firm U.S. commitment to South Korean security.

The Berlin meeting of foreign ministers from the United States, the United Kingdom, France, and the Soviet Union, in February 1954, produced an agreement that the countries involved in the Korean War, including China and the Soviet Union, should meet in Geneva to discuss questions regarding the future of Korea. There, the ministers also agreed to settle issues related to Indochina. The Geneva Conference, convened on 26 April 1954, was attended by North and South Korea, 16 U.N. member nations that had troops fighting in the Korean War—except for South Africa—and China and the Soviet Union. This international conference was a chance for the international community to influence the Korean problem. As expected, however, the conference became a hot debating match between the two opposing sides and failed to produce any meaningful result.

After the Geneva Conference, which came to a close on 21 July 1954, the only contact between North Korea and the United States took place at P'anmunjŏm, a so-called truce village designated as a neutral area in the DMZ. There U.S. military personnel representing the U.N. Command faced their counterparts from North Korea and China at the Military Armistice Commission meetings. The Commission dealt mainly with violations of the Korean Armistice Agreement, mostly perpetrated by North Koreans.

In the 1950s and 1960s the North Koreans demonstrated an extremely hostile attitude toward the United States in harsh verbal attacks, occasionally accompanied by military provocations, always demanding the withdrawal of U.S. troops from South Korea and the end of U.N. intervention in Korea's internal affairs. The U.S. military presence in South Korea and U.N. intervention, they argued, obstructed peaceful reunification of the Korean peninsula by the Korean people themselves.

When relations between the United States and South Korea became strained following the military coup on 16 May 1961, North Korea saw a chance to drive a wedge between the two allies. In the early 1960s, at the same time that North Korea strongly demanded the withdrawal of U.S. forces from South Korea, it made conciliatory gestures to establish direct contacts with the United States that would split the United States from South Korea. North Korea's efforts failed, however, as South Korea and the United States restored positive relations again.[21]

During 1966–1969, emboldened by the U.S. preoccupation with Vietnam, North Korea waged another Korean conflict, with numerous border clashes along the DMZ. In those clashes, U.S. casualties numbered 82 killed and 114 wounded. During that same period, on 23 January 1968, just two days after the attempted assassination of the South Korean president, four North Korean naval vessels seized the USS *Pueblo* off the country's eastern coast, igniting a major confrontation with the United States. The *Pueblo*, with its crew of 82 men under Commander Lloyd M. Bucher, was an intelligence-gathering ship, which North Korea claimed had entered its territorial waters in Wŏnsan Bay. The United States insisted that the *Pueblo* had been at sea, at least 13 miles beyond the 12-mile limit imposed by North Korea. During the ship's seizure one crewman was killed and several others, including Bucher, were wounded. Bucher, along with his 81 surviving crew members, were taken prisoner. Already facing an untenable situation in Vietnam, the United States did not want to settle the *Pueblo* case by military force. Thus the United States initiated secret talks with North Korea at P'anmunjŏm in February 1968. Ten months of negotiations finally led to the release, on 22 December 1968, of Commander Bucher and his crew after the United States issued a statement of apology on 21 December acknowledging that the *Pueblo* "had illegally intruded into North Korean territorial waters." Americans also pledged that no U.S. ships would enter North Korea's territorial waters in the future. North Korea claimed a great moral as well as diplomatic victory over this incident. Moreover, North Koreans never returned the ship.

On 15 April 1969 North Korea clashed again with the United States, when two North Korean MiG interceptors shot down a U.S. Navy EC-121 electronic reconnaissance aircraft with 31 men aboard over the East Sea. When downed, the EC-121, operating from a base in Japan, was engaging in electronic surveillance in international air space, some 90 miles off the North Korean coast. All aboard the aircraft were lost. As in the *Pueblo* incident, no U.S. retaliatory action was taken. The emboldened North Koreans became more adventurous and created an increasing number of border clashes along the DMZ. In this "second Korean conflict," North Korea was able to claim several diplomatic victories over the United States.

When the 1960s drew to a close, North Korea and the United States still maintained mutually hostile relations. With the cumulative weight of North Korea's provocations, their relations would have a gloomy outlook in the years to come.

After the Korean War, both Koreas engaged in postwar reconstruction in very different ways. Each of the two belonged to one of the mutually opposing blocs that keenly conflicted with each other: North Korea to "continental civilizations" and South Korea to "maritime civilizations." Thereafter the two Koreas took diametrically opposed paths that would decisively influence their future fortunes. In their cutthroat competition and rivalry, by the end of the 1960s North Korea held the upper hand both economically and militarily over its southern neighbor.

11

REVERSAL OF FORTUNES
(1972–1992)

The Fourth Republic

PRIOR TO THE EARLY 1970S North Korea's economic and political institutions were more stable than those of its southern counterpart. Then, perhaps beginning in 1971, a dramatic reversal began in their relative economic and political strengths, and by the early 1990s South Korea was the much stronger of the two. In the new environment accompanying the end of the Cold War, South Korea had a prosperous economy with fully democratic institutions, whereas North Korea was left behind economically and politically.

On 17 October 1972 President Park Chung-hee staged a "palace coup d'état," establishing a new and more autocratic regime, the Fourth Republic, under the so-called Yushin Constitution. That day Park declared a state of emergency, and imposed martial law on South Korea. He dissolved the National Assembly, closed universities throughout the country, and strictly censored the media. Soon Park set about revising the constitution, after first studying the "generalissimo constitution" of Taiwan. In a national referendum, held on 21 November 1972, the South Korean electorate, under a frightened atmosphere, overwhelmingly approved the new constitution. The Yushin Constitution granted the president emergency powers, empowered him to appoint one-third of the members of the National Assembly, and guaranteed the president indefinite tenure in office. The all-powerful president was to be elected by a rubber-stamp electoral college, the National Conference for Unification, which had some 2,300 locally elected delegates. On 23 December 1972 Park was elected president, with a six-year tenure, without one dissenting vote. Six years later, on 6 July 1978, he won another term in the same manner. Now the period of the Fourth Republic, more commonly referred to as the Yushin era, was fully under way.

Park justified his unconstitutional move on the grounds of the necessity of the times. He argued that he established the new "Yushin system" to eliminate waste in national security programs and to cope with the rapidly changing international situation. Under a more efficient system, he would build national strength continuously, promote economic growth, strengthen national defense, and achieve reunification of the fatherland. He also claimed to be seeking a "Korean-style democracy," one that was right for Korea's situation and would solve its inherent problems. In fact, he did not "Koreanize" democracy; he only created an even more autocratic rule than was seen in the Third Republic.

In accordance with the new constitution, the National Assembly elections were held on 27 February 1973. The ruling Democratic Republican Party gained 73 of 146 locally elected seats. The main opposition New Democratic Party (NDP) won 52 seats. Each of 73 local constituencies elected two assemblymen, and this election system continued into the Fifth Republic (1981–1988). One-third of the total 219 seats were appointed by President Park, giving him a two-thirds majority in the legislature. The National Assembly, along with its political party representation, could be dissolved by Park at any time.

With all powers vested in the presidency and the president literally able to rule by decree, the Yushin regime was hardly challenged by other institutions. Park frequently used his power to completely control all political activity and the entire population, severely punishing any criticism, even of the Yushin Constitution itself. One of Park's most important power bases was the Korean Central Intelligence Agency, which had the entire population under surveillance and routinely engaged in harassing the regime's opponents. These power abuses caused a serious political crisis in relations with Japan on 8 August 1973, when KCIA operatives abducted the self-exiled opposition leader Kim Dae-jung from a hotel in Tokyo five days before he was to establish an anti-Park organization of overseas Koreans. The KCIA agents attempted to assassinate Kim by dumping him at sea, but last-minute U.S. diplomatic intervention forced Kim's release, allowing him to return home. On 13 August 1973 Kim was put under strict house arrest in Seoul, and the Park government, as one would expect, made no effort to identify or penalize his abductors.[1]

Although the Park regime claimed that the Yushin system was "Korean-style democracy," many Koreans did not believe it was, and the Yushin system soon provoked intense opposition from many quarters, including the opposition parties, university students, and dissident intellectuals. The parliamentary opposition was neither strong nor effective, however, as the main opposition, the New Democratic Party, remained divided between the major factions of Kim Dae-jung, Kim Young-sam, and Yi Ch'ŏl-sŭng, and susceptible to government manipulation and intimidation. As a result of government maneuvers, on 25 May 1976 the Kim Young-sam faction and Yi Ch'ŏl-sŭng faction held separate national conventions and each used violence against the other.

After Kim Dae-jung's was repatriated and placed under house arrest, he was banned from political activity and under strict surveillance. Aided by his faction, Kim Young-sam was elected leader of the New Democratic Party in August 1974. Under his leadership, the main opposition party sharply challenged the Park government on fundamental issues of democracy and human rights. In September 1976, however, he lost his leadership and was replaced by Yi Ch'ŏl-sŭng, who did not seriously confront the Park government and thus became increasingly unpopular. As a result, in May 1979, Kim Young-sam was restored to leadership and adopted a hard line against Park's Yushin system. Although Kim had always been outspoken against Park, he had been shielded from the red-baiting commonly used against Park's enemies because, in 1960, his mother had been murdered by North Korean agents. Now, however, Kim Dae-jung was subjected to a sustained red hunt under the Park and Chun Doo-hwan governments.

Meanwhile, universities stubbornly opposed the Yushin system. From early 1974 university students staged anti-Yushin protests, and campus demonstrations became the order of the day during the Yushin years. The Park government responded with brutal suppression and the closing of campuses.

During the Yushin era, many important figures developed a dissident movement, hoping to abolish the Yushin system through a constitutional amendment that would bring back presidential elections by direct popular vote. Leaders of the dissident movement were antigovernment university faculties and Protestant clergymen, along with prominent politicians such as former president Yun Po-sŏn and Kim Dae-jung. All were subjected to sustained surveillance, brutal harassment, and occasional arrest, torture, and imprisonment by the KCIA. In the fabricated "People's Revolutionary Party Reconstruction Committee Incident," on 8 April 1975, eight dissident activists were executed only 18 hours after they were sentenced to death. The order to execute them appears to have come directly from Park.

At the time the population at large accepted the Yushin system as an accomplished fact, first of all because under Park's "reign of terror" South Koreans were constantly in fear of punishment. Continuing economic growth also helped secure popular support for Park's rule. In any case, most South Koreans were touched only indirectly by political repression and actually benefited from what many at the time termed "hothouse" economic development. A difficult international situation also helped Park maintain a strong, repressive leadership. The fall of South Vietnam in late April 1975 caused apprehension among South Koreans about the ROK–U.S. alliance. The Jimmy Carter administration in the United States further aroused South Korean uncertainties about national security, when Carter announced his plan to withdraw the U.S. Army's 2nd Infantry Division from South Korea in 1977. Most South Koreans expressed their fear that this action would prompt North Korea to invade, and they hoped Americans would not support the withdrawal. Indeed, the planned withdrawal caused a major political crisis, even public panic, in South Korea, and eventually Carter reluctantly dropped the idea. Park had found another convenient excuse for his repressive rule in South Koreans' increasing sense of insecurity.

Making efficient use of the KCIA, the Military Security Command, and his growing contingent of bodyguards, Park continued his previous pattern of silencing anyone who interfered or disagreed with his policies through temporary detention, arrest, imprisonment, and brutal torture. His security apparatus continued to stifle the press; all newspapers and broadcast systems were strictly censored. Government-controlled broadcast stations, in particular, became Park's personal propaganda media. His picture and daily activities dominated everyday news.

Beginning in December 1973 dissident activists, mainly university students and intellectuals, launched a national campaign to revise the Yushin Constitution. As their movement gathered momentum, Park issued an emergency decree in January 1974 outlawing all such campaigns. Violators faced trial by secret military courts. As a result, Park's regime was thrown into a vicious cycle of repression followed by dissidence which only further incited repression and harsher protests, and this continued until his death in October 1979. As time went on, Park became more and more uncompromising, especially after an attempted assassination by a Korean resident of Japan on 15 August 1974, the 29th anniversary of Korea's liberation from Japan. The Independence Day shooting missed Park but killed his wife, who was seated behind him.

From January 1974 to May 1975, Park issued nine emergency measures to tighten his grip on power. The most severe and sweeping of all was Emergency Measure Number Nine, issued on 13 May 1975, shortly after the fall of South Vietnam, which made it a crime not only to criticize the Yushin Constitution but also to provide press coverage of such activity, subject to a penalty of more than one year in prison. In early March 1976, however, prominent dissident leaders, including Yun Po-sŏn and Kim Dae-jung, issued the Democratic Declaration demanding the restoration of democracy. Park arrested them on charges of government subversion and sentenced them to prison for five to eight years.

Much of Park's mandate for harsh rule under the Yushin Constitution depended on sustained economic growth. When the South Korean economy underwent a sharp downturn in early 1979, the Park regime faced mounting pressure from the opposition. After a long period of rapid growth, South Korea's economy was slowed by worldwide inflation and recession caused by spiking oil prices after the Iranian revolution in early 1979. An unprecedented wave of bankruptcies and strikes swept the country. The altered sociopolitical situation emboldened Park's critics, especially the opposition New Democratic Party leader Kim Young-sam, who bitterly denounced the Park government.

The South Korean political situation had already undergone profound changes. Although the New Democratic Party obtained 61 of 146 locally elected seats against the ruling Democratic Republican Party's 68 seats in the National Assembly elections held on 12 December 1978, the former won 32.8 percent of the popular vote against the government party's 31.7 percent. The opposition was greatly encouraged to find its voice.

On 9 August 1979 some 190 female employees of the Y. H. Industrial Company, which had gone bankrupt, staged a sit-in at the New Democratic Party headquarters to enlist public sympathy. Two days later the Park government sent 1,000 riot police to drag them out and, in the process, killed a female laborer. The "Y. H. Incident" triggered fierce antigovernment movements as labor unions, university students, and dissident intellectuals united with the New Democratic Party. In retrospect, the event contributed partly to the fall of the Park regime late that year.

A month later, as part of a continuing political struggle, Kim Young-sam publicly appealed to the United States in a *New York Times* interview to end its support for Park's dictatorial regime. In retaliation, Park expelled Kim from the National Assembly on 4 October, plunging South Korea into a political crisis. On 16 October student demonstrations calling for the end of Park's autocratic rule and the Yushin system erupted in Kim's home district of Pusan that spread to the nearby industrial cities of Masan and Ch'angwŏn. Local citizens sympathized with the student demonstrators and joined the struggle against the Yushin system. With the people growing increasingly restless, Park declared martial law on 18 October. Mounting popular unrest triggered a sense of urgency in the Park regime and appeared to crack the armor of the ruling elite.

Amid mounting tension and uncertainty, Park's long and harsh rule abruptly ended on 26 October 1979, when his own KCIA chief, Kim Chae-gyu, shot and killed Park and his politically powerful chief bodyguard, Ch'a Chi-ch'ŏl, in a restaurant gunfight within the presidential compound. Park's assassination was sparked by a conflict within his inner circle over the measures required to cope with the popular unrest. Kim's demand that Park moderate his repressive rule was ridiculed and rejected by Park and Ch'a. After some hours of confusion following the shooting, Kim was taken into custody and later executed. Park's death ended the Yushin system and opened a new era of transition and uncertainty in South Korea.

Today Park Chung-hee is remembered less as the ruthless dictator who retarded South Korea's political development than as the father of the country's remarkable economic progress. Harsh in his methods and unforgiving of his opponents, he is regarded as the leader who successfully industrialized South Korea. Indeed, in his 18 years in power, Park enthusiastically sought South Korea's industrialization and modernization, and achieved considerable results. Having been trained under the Japanese, he clearly patterned his development strategies after those of Japan, where a feudal society had been rapidly transformed into a modern nation between the 1860s and 1930s. Thanks to South Korea's industrial and economic growth under Park's presidency, his reputation, since the mid-1990s, has greatly risen among the South Korean populace. He has been cited as the country's greatest president, commanding unparalleled popularity. In a 2008 *Han'guk ilbo* (Korea Daily) opinion poll, he was considered the greatest president of the nation, winning 56.0 percent of the poll. He was followed by Kim Dae-jung (15.9%), Roh Moo-hyun (12.4%), Chun Doo-hwan (2.8%), Syngman Rhee (1.9%), and Kim Young-sam (0.8%).[2] Another 2008 opinion survey, conducted by KBS I Radio, also found Park to be the greatest president, taking 60.1 percent of the poll, followed by Kim Dae-jung (12.1%)

and Roh Moo-hyun (10.9%).[3] According to a 2008 poll taken in the major daily newspaper *Tonga ilbo,* Park was cited as the political leader with the greatest achievements (56.0%) and the spiritual leader who most influenced the destiny of Korea throughout Korean history (37.0%). Further, 78.2 percent of South Koreans rated the Park administration as contributing most to their nation's economic development.[4] A 2011 *Chosŏn ilbo* poll found 82.6 percent of those polled to rate Park's leadership in South Korea's overall national development affirmatively. Only 13.1 percent viewed his leadership negatively. In particular, a surprising 92.1 percent believed that he had influenced the nation's economic development in a positive way, whereas just 5.3 percent viewed his influence negatively.[5] His high reputation and popularity have created "nostalgia for the Park Chung-hee era" in South Korea, making his daughter, Park Geun-hye, one of the most popular politicians in the 2000s.

His critics, on the other hand, have severely condemned the brutality of his dictatorship, deploring the widespread human rights abuses perpetrated during his rule. For many years thousands of his foes were arrested, imprisoned, tortured, and in many cases killed for criticizing and opposing him. Indeed, he justified his autocratic rule with the quip that dictatorship in affluence was better than democracy in poverty. In sum, although a majority of South Koreans view Park as a leader of unparalleled greatness and remember him as a man who, along with North Korea's Kim Il-sung, left the greatest legacies in modern Korean history, obviously South Koreans exchanged "freedom" for "bread" under his rule.[6]

The Kwangju Incident

With the death of Park Chung-hee, South Korea entered a difficult and uncertain transitional period. Hanging in the balance was progress toward democracy or reversion to the autocratic past. Without a designated successor to Park, a political vacuum was created. Immediately after Park's death, Prime Minister Ch'oe Kyu-ha was made acting president, in accordance with the constitution, whereupon he repealed Park's emergency measures and released prominent opposition leaders, including Kim Dae-jung, and dissident activists from house arrest or prison. In an easily controlled election, Ch'oe became president on 6 December 1979. But having been trained only as a bureaucrat, he had no political backing and was not a forceful leader. Thus he was no more than the head of a caretaker government. The ranks of the parliamentary opposition could offer no clear alternative, as the main opposition, the New Democratic Party, had suffered a chronic, acrimonious leadership split. The release of Kim Dae-jung further complicated the problem of the disunited opposition leadership. The outpouring of ideas as to the nation's future from various civilian sectors only increased the uncertainty, leaving the military leadership as the real power holders.

Although Park was dead, the Yushin Constitution and the government machinery he had created remained intact. Although a South Korean consensus favored an early revision of the constitution and a return to a full democratic order, the military leaders who had trained under Park preferred to return to military-backed authoritarianism. In the absence of a formal mechanism to choose Park's successor, it seemed quite likely that his heir would emerge from among the military leaders.

In a sudden turn of events, Major General Chun Doo-hwan, head of the Military Security Command, was given the responsibility for investigating Park's assassination, which afforded him the opportunity to seize power. He began by dismantling Park's power base by purging the Park government elite. He then proceeded to build his own power base. On 12 December 1979 Chun forcibly deposed the existing military authorities by arresting General Chŏng Sŭng-hwa, the ROK Army chief of staff and martial law commander, and the commanders loyal to him. His justification for this mutinous action was that Chŏng was suspected of having been involved in Park's assassination. On 14 December, two days after his midnight takeover of the military, Chun engineered sweeping changes in the ROK Army, moving his seniors aside and replacing them in sensitive posts with his classmates of the Korean Military Academy and his close friends. For instance, his close friend and successor as president, Roh Tae-woo, became the commanding general of the Capital Security Command. Now Chun could assert complete control over the South Korean armed forces.

During the early months of 1980, while Chun increasingly consolidated his power, aspirations for democracy rapidly gathered momentum among the population. A period that came to be known as the "Seoul Spring," named after Czechoslovakia's "Prague Spring" of 1968, came. The term expressed the public demand for political liberalization and the democratic mood of the day. In the spring of 1980 students took to the streets calling for an end to martial law, abolishment of the Yushin Constitution, and moving toward representative government.

Student demonstration reached a climax in mid-May 1980. On 14 May, with the center of Seoul crowded with demonstrators, the army deployed troops and armored vehicles to guard key buildings. The next day more than 100,000 students swarmed the plaza in front of the Seoul Railway Station, demanding the withdrawal of martial law. On 17 May Chun extended martial law throughout the country, abruptly ending the short-lived democracy movement. At the same time Chun removed all major political leaders and dissident activists from political life. Kim Dae-jung was taken into custody again, Kim Young-sam was placed under house arrest, and Park Chung-hee's former key lieutenants such as Kim Jong-pil and Yi Hu-rak, who had been denounced as corrupt fortune seekers, were also apprehended. The "Seoul Spring" quickly ended, casting the shadow of yet another authoritarian rule.

The following day, on 18 May, in street demonstrations that almost escalated into an armed revolt, students and citizens in Kwangju, the capital city of South Chŏlla province, protested martial law and specifically the arrest of Kim Dae-jung, their favorite opposition leader. The Kwangju uprising, however, ended in severe repression and the slaughter of many people by the ruling military. At first, to quell the demonstrations in Kwangju, Chun's "new military" sent elite troops of the Korean Special Warfare Command (SWC), known as the "Black Berets," and elements of the 7th, 11th, and 3rd Brigades were held responsible for most of the bloodshed between 18 and 20 May. South Korean military officers claimed that the special warfare forces were used because they were mobile and free of the constraint of the U.S.-controlled Combined Forces Command (CFC). Despite their brutal tactics, however, the troops were defeated by the organized efforts of unarmed civilians. On 26 May Chun requested U.S. General John A. Wickham, commander of the U.S. Forces Korea (USFK) and of the CFC, to release the Korean Army's 20th Infantry Division to put down the rebellion. The request was granted, and the next day regular army troops put an end to the resistance. Compared to the early brutal and bloody encounters, the military action was relatively swift and effective. By the time the city was retaken the government estimated that 170 people had been killed, but the official death toll was raised to 240 in 1995 after a reinvestigation. The Kwangju people have claimed, however, that the actual number of casualties was far higher than the earlier official number. Today's estimates range from 500 to 2,000.

The Kwangju incident, officially termed the "Kwangju Democratization Movement" in 1988, fueled a long-lasting and intense opposition to Chun Doo-hwan among South Koreans as well as a deep resentment of the U.S. role in the incident. To opponents of military dictatorship, "Kwangju" became a powerful symbol of popular resistance to authoritarian government. Chun Doo-hwan's name would forever be associated with the tragic Kwangju incident, which many see as a pivotal event in South Korea's struggle for democracy in the long period of dictatorship. As seen in the June Resistance of 1987, memories of "Kwangju" were a decisive restraint on the use of force against any popular movement for democracy. "Kwangju" also greatly damaged the image of the United States; although U.S. approval of Chun's use of military units under the authority of the Combined Forces Command was legal, it linked the United States inseparably to the tragedy. "Kwangju" triggered fervent anti-Americanism among citizens of Chŏlla province and many South Korean students, and became a decisive catalyst for South Korea's ultimate democratization.

The Fifth Republic

After the Kwangju incident, Chun Doo-hwan continued establishing his authoritarian regime. On 31 May, with methodical and speedy actions that clearly revealed a well-laid plan for power, he organized the Special Committee for National Integrity Measures, a military junta. On 7 August Chun promoted his rank to four-star general in preparation for retiring from the army. Then he and his military junta were able to pass their most difficult hurdle—U.S. support and approval. On 8 August General Wickham, in a press interview with American reporters, blessed Chun's coming to power, declaring that the United States would support him if he emerged as president. About a week later, on 16 August, Ch'oe Kyu-ha resigned the presidency, publicly claiming that he was doing so to set a precedent for the peaceful transfer of power. On 27 August, after receiving the endorsement of the ranking commanders of South Korea's armed forces, Chun was elected to the presidency without opposition by the rubber-stamp National Conference for Unification. On 22 October 1980 a national referendum overwhelmingly approved the new Fifth Republic Constitution that established another military-oriented authoritarian rule in South Korea. On 25 February 1981, in accordance with the new constitution, Chun began a new seven-year term as president.

Like his predecessor, Park Chung-hee, Chun placed South Korea under a "reign of terror and virtue." On 4 August 1980, to win support from a population that had lost its freedom, he launched a "purification campaign" known as *Samch'ŏng kyoyuktae,* or Reeducation Corps to Purify the Three Vices. By January 1981 the Chun regime had apprehended 60,755 individuals on suspicion of violating public peace and order. Of these, 3,252 were tried in a military tribunal, 39,786 were sent to purification camps in remote areas and were subjected to military-style physical training for several months, and 17,717 were admonished and then released by the police. A later revelation was that 52 people had died during their "reeducation" and 397 had died from the "aftereffects of reeducation." All the detainees were subjected to harsh living conditions and suffered serious civil rights violations. Many, moreover, were innocent victims picked up by the police. At the same time Chun expelled many senior officials from the civil service as well as others from their positions, or confiscated their property on charges of corruption. By doing so he replaced the existing elite with loyal subordinates and established a new power base for himself.

Like Park Chung-hee, Chun also feared Kim Dae-jung and thus sought to remove him permanently from political life. His attack on Kim, however, raised a serious problem with the United States. Accused of plotting the insurrection in Kwangju, Kim was court-martialed, found guilty, and sentenced to death, but a major diplomatic effort by the United States resulted in a commutation of the sentence and, in December 1982, Kim was released from prison and permitted to take exile in the United States. In return for commuting Kim's sentence, Chun would become the first foreign head of state to visit a U.S. president, the newly inaugurated President Ronald Reagan, in February 1981, which infuriated the South Korean opposition. Reagan's warm reception was a major turning point for Chun, convincing most South Koreans that his takeover was a fait accompli.

By early 1981 Chun's authoritarian regime was modeled after the Yushin system. To justify his military-backed rule, Chun pledged to achieve strong national security, political and social stability, and economic development. Even though he had created an illegitimate regime, thwarted any aspirations toward democracy, and was unpopular among the masses, Chun fancied himself as Korea's Abraham Lincoln.

To prepare for the National Assembly election, Chun formed a new ruling party, the Democratic Justice Party (DJP), in January 1981, which was soon followed by the emergence of a docile opposition party, the Democratic Korea Party (DKP), led by opposition politicians willing to cooperate with the Chun regime. To form the opposition party, Chun lifted the ban on the political activity of certain opposition politicians. The election law provided for two-member elections in each of the local constituencies, guaranteeing two-thirds of the at-large proportional representation seats to whichever party elected the largest number of candidates. In the National Assembly elections, held on 25 March 1981, the DJP won 151 seats in the 276-member Assembly, and the DKP obtained

81 seats. Thus Chun's ruling party secured a clear majority in the legislature. Meanwhile, the more dedicated opposition politicians who were still banned from political activity would soon coalesce around Kim Young-sam.

By 1982 Chun Doo-hwan had a firm grip on power. He consolidated his control by dominating the court system, making efficient use of the state security apparatus to his own advantage, tightening censorship over the media, and appointing his close colleagues such as Roh Tae-woo and loyal subordinates to high positions in the government. Opportunely, after a slump in 1979–1981, the South Korean economy resumed its rapid growth, and this contributed greatly to Chun's iron-fist control. Seeking to win popular support by freeing his country from the austerity enforced by his predecessor, he eased restrictions on overseas travel on 1 August 1981, lifted the midnight-to-four curfew on 5 January 1982, and abolished school uniforms and strict hair regulations in middle schools and high schools on 2 March 1983.[7] Despite these measures, Chun Doo-hwan never gained the trust of the people.

From mid-1982 on, the situation became increasingly unfavorable to Chun. In May 1982 the first of a number of financial scandals involving his in-laws was disclosed. Soon there were revelations of "Fifth Republic irregularities," corruption scandals all deeply associated with influence-peddling by Chun's in-laws, greatly damaging Chun's political and moral legitimacy. Given this opportunity to challenge Chun's power, Kim Young-sam, still under house arrest, went on a hunger strike in May 1983 to protest Chun's repressive rule and urge the opposition to mount an antigovernment struggle. A year later, on 18 May 1984, Kim Young-sam and Kim Dae-jung, the latter still in exile in the United States, organized the Consultative Committee for the Promotion of Democracy (CCPD), a broad coalition of dissidents, to advance the restoration of democracy.

Prepared for the forthcoming National Assembly elections, opposition politicians in the CCPD, who had recently been freed from the ban on their political activity, formed the New Korea Democratic Party (NKDP) on 18 January 1985. The new party stunned the Chun regime by capturing 67 seats in the 276-member National Assembly elections held on 12 February 1985. The ruling Democratic Justice Party won 148 seats, and the existing opposition Democratic Korea Party obtained only 35 seats. Soon most of the elected members from the previous demoralized opposition party joined the new NKDP. Led by the two Kims, the opposition members used this power to aggressively challenge Chun with demands for a constitutional amendment.

In the fierce struggle for democracy, the election process was a key issue. The South Korean population preferred presidential election by direct popular vote, but the constitutional amendment controversy centered not only on direct voting but also on the structure of government—whether it should be presidential (as in the United States), parliamentary (as in Great Britain or Japan), or "dual executive" (as in France).

Chun often repeated his earlier pledge to be the first South Korean president to leave office through a peaceful transfer of power after serving his single seven-year term. As the event drew near, however, Chun increasingly sought to have his longtime associate and friend, Roh Tae-woo, succeed him by any means. The opposition protested, demanding a constitutional amendment establishing an electoral process whereby the president would be chosen by popular vote. The opposition amendment drew wide public support. Yielding to pressure from both the opposition and the general population, Chun, in April 1986, reluctantly allowed a new constitution to be drafted. During the drafting process, the ruling Democratic Justice Party advocated a parliamentary system with a figurehead president, whereas the opposition stood for a directly elected president. Each side's preference for the structure of government reflected its specific strength. The DJP's dominance was in its organization skills and powers of patronage, whereas the opposition was disunited. The DJP, however, lacked a national candidate who, like the opposition's Kim Young-sam and Kim Dae-jung, could command general popularity in a direct election. Therefore the opposition, with its powerful national leaders appealing to the electorate, were more likely to gain power in a direct vote. If it could put up a single candidate in the presidential election, it would be sure of victory. Meanwhile the general population, weary of Chun's authoritarian rule, yearned for a democratic government. In 1986 four university students, in a plea for democratization, took their own lives. In that same year, more than 3,400 protesters were arrested.

The opposition split in the spring of 1987, when New Korea Democratic Party leader Yi Min-u sought to compromise with the ruling party on the constitutional amendment. Seventy-four NKDP lawmakers, under the influence of Kim Young-sam and Kim Dae-jung, left the party on 9 April. On 1 May they inaugurated a new political party, the Reunification Democratic Party (RDP), with Kim Young-sam as the leader, aided by Kim Dae-jung, still formally banned from political activity. Meanwhile, on 13 April 1987, Chun declared an end to all discussion of the constitutional amendment until after the 1988 Seoul Olympics. This meant that the next president would be elected indirectly by the existing electoral college, meaning, specifically, that Chun would select his successor.

It did not take long for Chun to find out he had made a mistake. His announcement to maintain the Fifth Republic constitution gave the opposition major momentum to go on the offensive with immediate and vociferous protests. The ensuing public outcry led to massive demonstrations, with student dissent gathering strength daily. When it was revealed that the police had tortured a Seoul National University student to death, the Chun regime was so damaged politically and morally that, by June 1987, its end was in sight.

The June Resistance

On 10 June 1987 the Democratic Justice Party convention nominated Roh Tae-woo as its presidential candidate. Within hours of the nomination, massive protests against the Chun government erupted in Seoul, soon spreading to more than 30 cities throughout the country. Daily violent clashes pitted student protesters against the riot police, with police tear gas countered by demonstrators throwing stones. To Chun's dismay, the protests drew widespread sympathy and support from conservative white-collar workers as never before.

On 24 June, with street demonstrations still going on, Chun Doo-whan met with opposition leader Kim Young-sam to solve the political crisis but without success. Although Chun expressed his willingness to resume talks on constitutional reform, the antigovernment demonstrations went on unabated. On 26 June more than one million protesters participated in street demonstrations in 37 cities nationwide. In Seoul violent demonstrations, reminiscent of street fighting, continued far into the night. Chun could not crush the protests by force without risking a "second Kwangju." Unable to endure the burden of another major loss of life, Chun had to surrender to the demands of the opposition.

On 29 June, with Chun's encouragement, Roh Tae-woo shocked South Koreans by accepting the direct presidential election, meeting the opposition's central demand. In his "29 June Declaration" Roh also advocated complete amnesty for Kim Dae-jung, as well as freedom of speech, autonomy for universities, and other liberal measures. Amid national jubilation, Roh's dramatic declaration ended the political crisis of June 1987.

As South Korea achieved impressive economic development under authoritarian rule, the discrepancy between economic growth and political backwardness gave rise to public discontent. Toward the end of the Chun regime, South

Koreans demanded an end to military-backed authoritarian rule; to this end, the political upheaval, known as the "June Resistance," became a pivotal moment in South Korean politics, as it aimed to destroy authoritarianism and instead establish a civil, democratic society under the rule of law. South Korea was now on the path to full-fledged democracy.

The Chun Doo-hwan period was filled with many political problems arising from Chun's illegitimate seizure of power and harsh repression. His regime's inherent illegitimacy eclipsed a few achievements, especially continuing economic development, which it had produced. Because his Fifth Republic lacked legitimacy, the Chun regime failed to win public trust and support to the end. The South Korean population generally considered Chun to have stripped the nation of the opportunity to restore democracy. Having devoted himself only to imitating his predecessor, Park Chung-hee, Chun was perhaps a failed president. In a 2008 KBS I Radio opinion poll, Chun was cited as the worst president in the nation's history.[8] Although he ruled his country in an authoritarian manner, however, his power and authority were much weaker than Park's. Despite his nickname, the "slaughterer of Kwangku," he did one thing that gained public favor: he kept his pledge not to seek reelection.

The Roh Tae-woo Administration

Although Chun Doo-hwan remained in office until late February 1988, his Fifth Republic virtually ended on 27 October 1987, when a national referendum overwhelmingly approved the new constitution for the Sixth Republic. The new constitution provided for direct election of the president, with a single five-year term. The presidency was weakened, however, by losing the power to declare a national emergency by decree. The legislature became stronger, with the National Assembly granted new rights to investigate state affairs and approve prime ministerial and Supreme Court appointments. The constitution, a thoroughly democratic document, also guaranteed freedom of political activity, of the press, assembly, and speech.

In the latter part of 1987 South Koreans witnessed a four-way presidential race between Roh Tae-woo, Kim Young-sam, Kim Dae-jung, and Kim Jong-pil. Because Chun and military rule had been so unpopular, it was widely assumed that Roh could not win the presidency by direct popular vote. Both Chun and Roh were confident in a victory, however, because in the 1980s the DJP had won some 35 percent of the popular vote in every election. The two men firmly believed, moreover, that the two most prominent opposition leaders,

Kim Young -sam and Kim Dae-jung, could not reach agreement on a single, unified candidate.

Indeed, the presence of two powerful leaders was a central problem for the opposition. The two Kims were actually lifetime rivals rather than colleagues; their rivalry dated back to the 1960s, when, as promising young politicians, each viewed the other as a predestined contestant, and each had a different geographical and political base. In 1970 the two men, in their forties at that time, contended for the presidential nomination of the New Democratic Party against the incumbent president Park Chung-hee. Kim Dae-jung emerged victorious in the nomination convention, with the support of the Yi Ch'ŏl-sŭng faction from the same Chŏlla region. When the two men united to lead South Korea's struggle for democracy, they were a formidable force, but in their current struggle for power, they were competitive and disunited. As expected, they failed to put up a unified candidate for the forthcoming presidential election. In the end, Roh won the presidency.

On 12 November 1987 Kim Dae-jung started his own political party, the Peace and Democracy Party (PDP), to run for the presidency. With Kim Jong-pil trailing far behind other candidates, the virtually three-way presidential election was held on 16 December 1987. In the absence of a run-off system, Roh won the presidency with only 36.6 percent of the vote. Kim Young-sam obtained 28.0 percent; Kim Dae-jung, 27.0 percent; and Kim Jong-pil, 8.0 percent.

In prior elections, the government party dominated in rural districts, and the opposition party dominated in urban areas. But the 1987 presidential election was characterized by regionalism, with each candidate winning an overwhelming vote from his region of origin—Roh Tae-woo from the Taegu-North Kyŏngsang region, Kim Young-sam from the Pusan-South Kyŏngsang region, Kim Dae-jung from the Kwangju-Chŏlla region, and Kim Jong-pil from the Ch'ungch'ŏng region. This was reminiscent of the rivalry of Chinese warlords occupying their own territories, and it set a precedent for all subsequent presidential, National Assembly, and local elections; each party would secure an absolutely superior position in its own regional stronghold.

Roh's victory in the first truly popular election for the presidency since 1971 gave him the political legitimacy Chun had lacked. When he was sworn in as president of the Sixth Republic and began his five-year term on 25 February 1988, he sought to liberalize all institutions and sectors of South Korea. Thus it was under his administration that the era of true democracy finally began in South Korea.

After their defeat in the presidential election, the major opposition parties soon regained strength and, together, elected more candidates than the government party in the National Assembly elections held on 26 April 1988. In accordance with the new election law, the total seats elected directly from local districts increased from two-thirds to three-fourths. Each local constituency elected one lawmaker rather than the previous two, and the number of election districts more than doubled. Half the at-large proportional representation seats were given to whichever party elected the largest number of candidates, and the remaining seats were distributed to other parties in proportion to their elected numbers.

The new election law worked to the opposition's advantage. Roh's Democratic Justice Party elected 125 of 299 seats, with 34.0 percent of the popular vote; Kim Dae-jung's Peace and Democracy Party won 70 seats, with 19.3 percent of the vote; Kim Young-sam's Reunification Democratic Party won 59 seats, with 23.8 percent of the vote; and Kim Jong-pil's New Democratic Republican Party won 35 seats, with 11.7 percent of the vote. The discrepancy between the elected numbers and the percentages of the popular vote for the two main opposition parties indicated that Kim Dae-jung secured greater regional loyalty in his home district than did Kim Young-sam.

As the three opposition parties combined were a majority, the National Assembly asserted itself as an autonomous legislature. Shortly after the National Assembly went into session, the opposition parties joined forces to elect the Speaker of the National Assembly. They also influenced Roh's appointment of a new Chief Justice. The legislature exercised its restored powers of inspection and investigation without reserve, and in June 1988 it created special panels to review illegal activities that occurred in the Fifth Republic, the Kwangju incident, perceived election fraud, controversial laws, and regional rivalry.

In early 1988, immediately upon Chun's retirement from the presidency, stories of corruption and dictatorial excesses under his regime began surfacing. Many key members of his administration and even members of his family were convicted of criminal charges related to corruption and sentenced to prison terms. On 23 November 1988 Chun officially apologized to the populace for the abuses of his administration and, with his wife, began a two-year, self-imposed exile at the remote Paektam-sa temple in the mountains of Kangwŏn province. The parliamentary opposition held televised legislative hearings on the abuses of the Fifth Republic, which reached its peak on 31 December 1989 when Chun admitted to a degree of responsibility for the scandals in his Fifth Republic.

Meanwhile, South Korea hosted the 24th Summer Olympics from 17 September to 2 October 1988, and it was a great success. For South Koreans, who had been preparing for the event for many years, the Seoul Olympics was far more than a sports festival; it was an opportunity to show the world that their country was no longer a poverty-stricken war victim but a modern, increasingly prosperous nation. The games in Seoul signaled South Korea's rise to prominence and maturity as a regional power in East Asia, especially as they were attended by athletes from the Soviet Union, China, and the communist countries of Central and Eastern Europe, all North Korea's allies, which was a major embarrassment for North Korea. For South Korea, on the other hand, the Olympics provided momentum for the nation to accommodate to the communist world and was also a source of enormous national pride as South Korea took its place on the world stage.

The democratic political system of the Sixth Republic, meanwhile, was faced with the popular demand for more freedom and participation. Professional associations and interest groups, long under the state's domination, began to strive for more autonomy. University teachers, journalists, and lawyers organized their efforts and became increasingly outspoken on political issues. The major business conglomerates, the chaebŏl, sought a greater role in making economic policy. Farmers' associations, which had traditionally been little more than mechanisms for passing along government policies to farmers, began to proliferate and protest the government's liberal trade measures. At the fringes of politics, an extremist wing of the leftist student movement turned to sporadic violence in the late 1980s, including dozens of assaults against government offices, commercial establishments, police stations, and U.S. diplomatic and cultural facilities.

President Roh could not cope with the conflicting demands of newly emerging interest groups, mainly because of structural defects in his presidency. Because the three opposition parties commanded the majority in the National Assembly, Roh was politically powerless. Kim Young-sam was also in a political crisis and needed to join forces with Roh Tae-woo to effectively control the political situation. Kim's Reunification Democratic Party was the third largest party after Roh's Democratic Justice Party and Kim Dae-jung's Peace and Democracy Party. On 22 January 1990 three of the four major political parties announced a merger, creating the Democratic Liberal Party (DLP), which was reminiscent of Japan's ruling Liberal Democratic Party. The DLP was designed to secure a majority (219 seats) of the National Assembly for Roh and to isolate

Kim Dae-jung from other major political forces for Kim Young-sam. Kim Jong-pil dreamed of the first prime minister through a constitutional amendment seeking a parliamentary system. Despite the ostensible justification that it increased political stability, the DLP was the product of a marriage of convenience between the three political leaders. In the end Kim Young-sam turned out to be the biggest winner, as he tirelessly maneuvered himself into the presidency, succeeding Roh in late February 1993.

During the Roh years the movement to local autonomy began, and on 26 March 1991 local elections were held for the second time in 30 years to elect representatives to provincial, city, county, district, and metropolitan area assemblies. The ruling Democratic Liberal Party won a plurality of seats.

The South Korean electorate became increasingly critical of the giant DLP, especially the chronic intraparty rivalry, and in the 24 March 1992 National Assembly elections, the DLP suffered a crushing defeat, losing 71 seats. Candidates from the Kim Young-sam and Kim Jong-pil factions suffered a major blow, with the DLP recovering a bare majority only by absorbing several members who had run as independents. Kim Dae-jung's Peace and Democracy Party greatly enhanced its position, winning 98 seats. The independents obtained 21 seats, and 31 candidates were elected from the newly formed Reunification National Party under the leadership of Chŏng Chu-yŏng, founder and patriarch of the Hyundai Group. Although his support base was seriously eroded, Kim Young-sam was finally endorsed as the DLP presidential candidate, and on 18 December 1992 Kim won the presidency with 42 percent of the vote. His rival, Kim Dae-jung, gained 33.8 percent, and Chŏng Chu-yŏng won 16 percent. With Kim's election to the presidency, the rule by former military strongmen completely ended.

Many South Koreans who preferred strong leadership were tired of Roh's passive guidance. His indecisiveness had earned him the derisive title of "Mul Tae-woo," or Wishy-Washy Tae-woo. In fact, he intentionally assumed a low-profile presidency, explaining that his philosophy of life was to live flexibly, like water. He gained this wisdom, apparently, working as Chun Doo-hwan's number-two man for the previous 40 years. His conclusion, it seems, was that it was better to do nothing than to exercise leadership rashly and make fatal mistakes, especially given that South Korean society was simmering under the heat of democratization. The result was that the government under his presidency drifted aimlessly.

Although it initiated the new Sixth Republic, the Roh Tae-woo presidency was indeed a transitional administration, moving from past military dictatorships toward true democracy. Thus his Sixth Republic was often called the "Fifth-and-a-Half-Republic." A typical Fifth Republic man, Roh was closely identified with the preceding Chun regime. Having seized power after the June resistance that ended military-backed authoritarianism and set South Korea on the path to democracy, Roh was in an awkward position between the two incompatible political ideologies and institutions. He had also been elected to the presidency with less than majority support, and thus he was unable to exercise effective leadership to cope with the volatile situation. Forced to come to terms with seasoned civilian political leaders for his survival, he chose to follow public opinion rather than lead it, and so the public correctly saw him as indecisive and weak.

Still, the achievements of the Roh administration were significant. There was no reversion to authoritarian rule, and the investigation of past abuses of power, though incomplete, eventually resulted, in 1995, in the public humiliation and imprisonment of both Chun and Roh himself. Also notable was his aggressive pursuit of better relations with socialist countries, including the Soviet Union, which recognized the Republic of Korea in 1990, and China, which recognized it in 1992. This policy of *nordpolitik*, the effort to improve relations with communist countries, appeared to move North–South Korean relations into a new phase of negotiations, raising hopes for progress toward reunification.

THE PROSPERING SOUTH KOREAN ECONOMY

The South Korean Economy in the 1970s

In the 1970s the Park Chung-hee government further intensified its industrialization drive, and the Third Five-Year Economic Development Plan (1972–1976) achieved rapid progress in building an export-oriented structure. After the plan was successfully completed, South Korea initiated the Fourth Five-Year Economic Development Plan (1977–1981) to foster the development of industries capable of competing in the world's industrial export market. During the period of the Third and Fourth Five-Year Plans, Park pushed ahead with his ambitious Heavy and Chemical Industries Promotion Plan, a massive program to build six strategic industries—iron and steel, shipbuilding, chemicals, electronics, nonferrous metals, and machinery. Initiated in late 1971 and formally announced in January 1973, the plan was intended to enhance Park's political legitimacy and cope with the perilous security environment on the Korean peninsula. Park viewed the North Korean military buildup with apprehension and had little confidence in U.S. security commitments. The Heavy and Chemical Industries Promotion Plan constituted the core of South Korean economic policy during the 1970s and became the foundation of South Korea's later success in the automobile, shipbuilding, and electronics industries.[9] The completion of the P'ohang Integrated Steel Works in July 1973, the Yŏch'ŏn Petrochemical Industrial Complex in May 1978, and the Kori Atomic Power Plant in July 1978 typified the development of South Korea's heavy and chemical industries in the 1970s.

Also in the 1970s South Korea developed an export-driven economy to the point where exports accounted for as much as one-third of its GDP. Despite the first oil shock in 1973, South Korea established an export record of $10 billion in December 1977. South Korea also sought foreign loans and investment for its economic development, and by the late 1970s the country emerged as one of the largest debtor nations in the world.

The greatly increased GDP and per-capita income in this period rapidly improved material conditions and social stability for a populace that had long suffered from poverty, inflation, stagnation, and uncertainty. Annual per-capita income shot up from $94 in 1960 to more than $1,000 in 1976. This progress far outweighed the burden of authoritarian control in the popular mind. At the same time, however, rapid economic growth produced the rise of the corporate-conglomerate, or chaebŏl, economic structure, widespread corruption resulting from cozy connections between government and business, and increasingly unequal income distribution.

As industrialization speedily progressed, large and ever more diversified business conglomerates, aided by the government, drove the South Korean economy. This cooperative effort between the government and chaebŏl leaders was urgently needed to turn the economy away from consumer goods and light industries and toward heavy, chemical, and import-substitution industries. In return for their responsiveness to regulatory authorities, chaebŏl leaders received various privileges from the government that enabled them to amass great wealth. As time went on, they became involved in an increasingly corrupt system where large sums of money, extracted from big businesses, found their way into the pockets of influential politicians and administrators who often used the money for further influence peddling. The chaebŏl-led industrialization also accelerated the monopolistic and oligopolistic concentration of capital and profits in the hands of a limited number of corporate conglomerates.

Park's policy of partiality for big businesses harmed small- and medium-sized businesses that produced many basic items for daily consumption including food, clothing, and household goods, and also exported soft toys, textiles, garments, wigs, and footwear. Despite their enormous contributions to the national economy, these smaller businesses were disadvantaged by their weak capitalization and continual risk of bankruptcy. They were also vulnerable in their dealings with larger corporations which controlled the national economy. Their fierce competition with one another, moreover, reduced their profit margins to a minimum.[10]

As the South Korean economy rapidly expanded and changed from an agrarian to an industrialized economy, unequal income distribution grew increasingly serious. The Park government attempted to ease the urban-rural gap in income by, for instance, the so-called New Village Movement.

In the 1970s the South Korean economy endured the trials arising from adverse developments in the international economy. The oil shock, in which the price of oil increased fourfold at the end of 1973, struck a severe blow to the South Korean economy which depended heavily on oil imports for energy supply. Specifically the Heavy and Chemical Industries Promotion Plan had to be significantly modified, as the country's industrial emphasis now turned to low-energy consumption industries such as steel, shipbuilding, heavy machinery, electronics, and automobiles. After surviving the crisis, particularly the deep recession and steep inflation, from 1975 on the South Korean economy recovered its earlier momentum, with the annual GDP increasing by 12.3 percent between 1975 and 1979.

In the late 1970s the South Korean economy once again experienced hardships. The economy was hard hit by the second oil shock after the Iranian Revolution in early 1979. Growth in exports and the GNP suddenly slowed. The year 1980 saw its first actual decline in real GDP since 1956.[11] It would take two years for South Korea to emerge from this economic downturn, and the setback contributed in part to the eventual downfall of Park Chung-hee's Yushin regime.

The South Korean Economy in the 1980s

By the early 1980s the South Korean economy had spiraled downward, sparked by the 1979 oil shock, high inflation, large and growing foreign debts, and a poor rice harvest, all resulting in a modest decline in GDP in 1980. In 1981 the South Korean economy slowly began to recover from its worst performance. In the mid-1980s, in an improving economic situation, foreign debt emerged as the most contentious issue, as it was widely seen as a threat to South Korea's political independence and sovereignty. The South Korean government had intentionally undertaken the huge debt to reduce direct foreign investment. The debt became particularly problematic when, between 1980 and 1984, it nearly doubled because of the continuing development of heavy and chemical industries, as well as a vigorous nuclear power program, expansion of the Seoul subway, and construction of a new subway in Pusan.[12] As foreign debt soared to $40.1 billion in mid-1984, South Korea became the fourth largest foreign borrower in the world, only behind Argentina, Brazil, and Mexico. The skyrocketing debt was criticized both by the opposition in the National Assembly and dissident activists, and it was a major campaign issue in the 1985 National Assembly elections.

In late 1985 the South Korean economy began a sharp upturn, as exports rapidly increased. Foreign debt was no longer a major political liability for the Chun Doo-hwan government. Beginning in 1986 South Korea was blessed with the "three lows," three international economic factors that contributed to the rising South Korean economy. The first was the weak U.S. dollar against most major international currencies, particularly a related appreciation of the Japanese yen that raised the prices of Japanese exports. South Korea's enhanced international competitiveness caused an unprecedented boom in exports to the United States. The falling dollar allowed South Korea's new generation of export industries, including automobiles, consumer electronics, ships, and steel, to wrest market shares in the United States from Japanese and European competitors. At the same time strong consumer spending in the United States caused a record-breaking increase in exports of traditional products, notably textiles and clothes. The second factor enhancing the South Korean economy was the falling price of oil, which sharply declined from an average price of $28 a barrel during 1983–1985 to an average of about $16 during 1986–1988, mainly because of overproduction. This substantially reduced South Korea's energy import costs. The third factor was a fall in interest rates, especially the relatively low U.S. prime lending rate, which helped South Korea redeem its foreign debt. These "three lows," or blessings, boosted the South Korean economy and provided a solution to the country's two chronic economic problems—the current account deficit and foreign debt, as the enormous trade surplus that resulted was used to pay off the debt.

Between 1986 and 1988 South Korea experienced an economic boom of unprecedented magnitude. Its GDP grew more than 12 percent annually for three consecutive years. In 1988, as noted, South Korea successfully hosted the biggest Olympics ever, and during this period South Korea emerged as the most powerful of the Asian developing economies, on a par with the other East Asian dynamos, Taiwan, Hong Kong, and Singapore, to form the "Four Dragons of Asia."

As a result of its emphasis on exports, South Korea increased its exports from $17.5 billion to $30.3 billion between 1980 and 1985. In the next three years, from 1986 to 1988, exports doubled to $60.7 billion. The increase in exports in 1988 alone amounted to $13.4 billion, or almost equal to the total exports of $14.7 billion in 1979. South Korea showed its first trade surplus ever in 1986 and achieved an average annual balance of payments surplus of $7.7 billion during 1986–1988.[13]

Since 1988 the situation began to decline. As the Roh Tae-woo administration loosened government control on labor, a steep wage increase followed, causing a considerable loss of international competitiveness. Moreover, South Korea's growing trade surpluses with the United States triggered protectionist responses in the latter nation, on the one hand, and U.S. pressure on South Korea to open its protected domestic markets to U.S. goods, on the other. Under heavy U.S. pressure to liberalize its imports, South Korea instituted sweeping changes that loosened restrictions on imports. As a result, South Korea's trade surpluses with the United States rapidly fell in 1989. The abruptness and magnitude of the changes in exports and the rapid import growth once again plunged South Korea's trade balance into a deficit beginning in the 1990s. Meanwhile, South Korea entered a "bubble" economy, with overheated speculation in real estate and stocks. As the 1990s dawned, the double-digit GDP growth figures of the mid-1980s slowed, and in 1992 the annual GDP growth fell to 4.5 percent.

MILITARISTIC SOUTH KOREAN SOCIETY

Militarization of South Korean Society

The Korean War permanently enhanced the role of the military in South Korean society and politics as well as in national security matters. After Park's coup in May 1961, the military elite tried to create a disciplined, military-style society that was both economically advanced and politically efficient. Later, however, economic modernization caused profound social changes, including the promotion of education and rapid urbanization, all of which corroded the military's authoritarian view of society and encouraged a trend to a more contentious, pluralistic society that displeased many in the military.

The Park Chung-hee regime, as discussed earlier, imposed a nationalistic, militaristic order on every segment of South Korean society that included the mandatory reading of the National Education Charter at every educational rally. The charter, proclaimed on 5 December 1968, was designed to inspire strong national consciousness in the hearts of the populace. Park argued that development of the nation depended on the development of individual citizens and that national revitalization was essential. To inspire nationalism and patriotism, the Park government stressed education in Korean history, and a new subject, "national ethics," became a requirement for a college degree. In 1969 Park required high school and university students to complete the subject "military drills," which, with the downfall of the Park regime, was fated to disappear from the curriculum. After the fall of South Vietnam in April 1975, he further accelerated the militarization of Korean society, transforming the existing student body into the paramilitary Student Defense Corps. First introduced in September 1949 by President Syngman Rhee and dissolved in the aftermath of the April 1960 Student Revolution, the National Student Defense Corps was reorganized by Park in September 1975, and each high school or university was required to establish a unit of the Corps which was organized like the military. With the appearance of these units, campuses were transformed into military camps and students into soldiers. The Corps was abolished in universities in 1980 and in high schools in 1985.

As a result of the prolonged military-oriented rule under Park Chung-hee, military culture pervaded every part of South Korean society. Above all, more than 75 percent of South Korean males served in the regular army and the reserve, and were subjected to harsh military discipline. After establishing the Homeland Reserve Force in April 1968, Park initiated, in September 1975, the Civil Defense Corps system, the South Korean version of North Korea's Worker and Peasant Red Guard, made up of almost all males between the ages of 17 and 50. Already in 1972 civil defense drills had begun on the 15th day of every month.

As the topmost elite of South Korean society in the Third and Fourth Republics, the military occupied positions mainly in powerful organizations such as the Presidential Secretariat, the KCIA, and other military-security offices of the government. Many senior officers retired to go into politics or government service. During the 1970s and the early 1980s nearly half of all senior government officials had a substantial military background. Climbing on the bandwagon, many excellent high school students were admitted to the Korean Military Academy, and although civilians resented the military's ubiquitous presence in every important area of national life, they still gravitated into military life. Civilians were increasingly accustomed to speaking in military parlance and often organized themselves on the model of military organization. Park's efforts to establish uniformity and discipline in society, and discourage free spirits, were represented by his crackdown on men's long hair and women's miniskirts. Long hair, in fact, emerged as a symbol of resistance to the Park regime. In drinking as well, South Koreans enjoyed the *"p'okt'anju,"* or boilermaker, which was in vogue among military officers. Designed to get one drunk quickly, which typified Koreans' *ppalli ppalli,* or "hurry hurry" culture, the boilermaker was comprised of a shot glass filled with whiskey floating in a mug of beer, the whole lot downed in one long swallow, a potent brew that was appropriate for the heavy-drinking Koreans.

South Korean Society in the 1970s

In a rapidly growing economy, technocrats were a distinguished group and became part of the newly emerged elite of South Korean society. Mainly positioned in economics ministries, particularly the Economic Planning Board, they were responsible for the workings of the national economy. Although Park appointed some of them to senior cabinet posts, they were not allowed into the inner circle of Park's regime, which was dominated by the military elite.

In a close government-business nexus, leading businessmen, especially chaebŏl, were allowed access to the topmost people in power, including the president, and formed part of the most powerful elite in the nation. They were always subject to firm government control, however; by removing their special benefits given, the government could drive them into bankruptcy. Despite their enormous wealth, the chaebŏl were not well received and were even disdained by the general population, because of their corruption and greed, harsh attitude toward labor, and insensitivity to social justice and environmental protection.Rapid economic growth increased the size of the middle class, which was comprised of salaried white-collar workers in large private companies and professionals with specialized training such as engineers. This burgeoning strata of society was largely indifferent to politics and exchanged political repression for material prosperity. In the mid-1980s the South Korean middle class was active in politics, but only a small number of dissident groups had opposed Park's autocratic, personal rule in the 1970s.

As South Korea experienced sustained urbanization, many rural residents migrated to expanding cities. Along with the "old" urban poor, they formed the urban lower class, leading subsistence lives as industrial workers, petty merchants, self-employed craftsmen, and service people. Nevertheless, they were materially better off than those who lived in rural areas, and their number was constantly increasing.[14]

Park Chung-hee's "developmental dictatorship" succeeded in achieving re-markable economic development and produced a sense among South Kore-ans of *hamyŏn toenda,* or "We can do anything." Although this attitude made people strongly self-assertive, it also encouraged the "ppalli ppalli disease," noted above, a syndrome that later earned South Korea the label "Republic of Accidents."

South Korean Society in the 1980s

Following Park's precedent, the Fifth Republic under the Chun Doo-hwan presidency preferentially placed retired senior military officers in the civil ser-vice or in state-run corporations. The news media remained strictly restrained in its coverage of political-military issues. Key student antigovernment dem-onstrators were frequently punished by being forcibly drafted into military service, and, while serving in the army, some died under mysterious circum-stances. After the June Resistance of 1987, in the course of democratization, South Koreans demanded complete reformation of these practices.

As industrialization and urbanization continued to grow in the 1980s, South Korea's agricultural sector drifted into a stepchild status, and serious problems arose in rural life. The migration of young people to the cities for education and jobs left behind a smaller and increasingly older farm population. This, along with the accompanying low productivity, irreparably destroyed the farming economy and rural communities.

Meanwhile, in the cities, South Koreans grew increasingly accustomed to urban life, particularly apartment living and the lifestyle of the Western nuclear family. In Seoul and other larger cities, including Pusan, Taegu, and Inch'ŏn, towering high-rise apartments began to replace single homes. In 1990, to solve the extreme housing shortage, President Roh Tae-woo embarked on an ambi-tious project to build two million new housing units, 75 percent of them apart-ments. The new program raised the housing supply rate to 79.1 percent by 1993.[15]

In the 1980s the new industrialized and urbanized social life was also char-acterized by the decline of patriarchal and generational authority. The rapidly changing environments, harsh working conditions, and political repression left people alienated from their traditional ways of life. And as South Korean society became more democratic in the late 1980s, the trends against authoritarianism and traditionalism gathered further momentum. By the late 1980s the rapid democratization of politics and society brought about a more egalitarian, Western-style social life, replacing the prior militaristic, authoritarian lifestyle. This was most remarkable in the urban life led by a majority of South Koreans.

The Minjung Movement

In the 1980s the *minjung* movement actively developed in South Korean society. The term *minjung*, though difficult to define, may be translated as "common people," usually meaning the masses, as opposed to the ruling elite. In other words, although its meaning is vaguely understood, minjung represent a majority of people who are presumably exploited by the numerically smaller ruling elite, particularly the urban proletariat. In the 1970s and 1980s national elites consisted of the military elite, top government officials, and big businesses, and were viewed as serving foreign capitalists, especially Americans. Therefore minjung were antagonistic to military dictatorship, chaebŏl, and foreign powers.

As opportunities for education and employment expanded in the mid-1960s, most university graduates started their new, modern working lives in the cities, seeking material and social success. But a few were committed to radical politics and took the role of critical intellectuals. Though these intellectual dissidents initiated the minjung movement in the 1970s, it did not take off at the time, and they directed their energies instead to resisting Park Chung-hee's autocratic rule.

In the mid-1980s, however, the minjung movement began in earnest. Newly emerged radical student activists and dissident intellectuals, who identified with the Third World, were imbued with Western radical thought, including Marxism, liberation theology, and dependency theory. By the mid-1980s neo-Marxian interpretations dominated much of the student debates concerning South Korean society and South Korean–U.S. relations.

The minjung movement primarily aimed to improve the life of working people, and so student activists and dissident intellectuals tried to align themselves with labor, hoping to politicize them. Since the 1970s some Christian clergy and lay leaders, especially those from the Urban Industrial Mission (UIM), played a pivotal role in the labor movement, raising such issues as low wages, harsh working conditions, and violations of basic labor laws. In the 1980s the "alliance" between the minjung movement and labor took the form of student activists becoming workers themselves.[16]

Although strikes were illegal until late 1987, strikes and sit-ins had occurred, and the student-turned-workers played an important role in the strikes staged by organized labor. South Korea saw an explosion of labor disputes from 1987 through 1989, with more than 3,000 strikes throughout the country during the summer and fall of 1987. In 1988 labor-related laws were amended to make it easier to establish labor unions, and student activists helped workers organize unions and demand improvement in wages and working conditions.

Beyond establishing "labor-intellectual solidarity," student activists tried to realize minjung democracy in which all citizens made decisions on national affairs. They urged radical redistribution of national wealth to benefit poorer classes. They also called for major changes in South Korea's political and economic relationships with the United States and Japan. Their demands represented Marxist revolutionary thought and the ideas of radical Western thinkers such as Herbert Marcuse and the Latin American dependency theorists; to a certain degree, they also were a reflection of North Korean communist ideology. These views were not shared by a majority of South Koreans who saw them as too radical, and so their proponents did not gain wide popular support and were isolated from the mainstream of society.

Since the early 1990s the minjung activists split into two groups: the radicals and moderates. The radicals generally remained in the movement, resorting to violence to dramatize their cause and thus became alienated from the general public. Many moderates, on the other hand, entered the established political world, making a career of politics in both conservative and progressive parties.

SOUTH KOREA'S FOREIGN RELATIONS

Strained Relations with the United States in the 1970s

By the end of the 1970s South Korean–U.S. relations had become considerably strained mainly because South Korea doubted the U.S. commitment to defending the country. Although the United States reaffirmed its commitment to defend South Korea in the event of North Korean aggression, in pursuance of the ROK–U.S. Mutual Defense Treaty, the removal of the U.S. Army's 7th Infantry Division by the end of 1973 led South Koreans to question whether U.S. policy toward South Korea would actually be helpful in the future international or domestic political environment.

In the early 1970s a significant change occurred in U.S.–China relations and in the course of the Vietnam War that deeply affected relations between

South Korea and the United States and between the two Koreas. U.S. President Nixon went to China in 1972, intending to make the most of the Sino-Soviet split then well under way. His visit afforded the United States an opportunity to reduce its security obligations to South Korea. Shocked by a possible U.S.-Chinese détente, the two Koreas attempted to resolve their differences by themselves. The U.S. withdrawal from Vietnam also caused South Koreans uneasiness about the ROK–U.S. alliance. In April 1975, on the eve of the fall of South Vietnam, Kim Il-sung visited China to seek support for an armed invasion of South Korea. Kim's action stunned many South Koreans. The Gerald Ford administration reaffirmed the U.S. determination to remain in South Korea.

At around the same time an influence-peddling scandal known as "Koreagate" was revealed, in which agents employed by the South Korean government illegally developed lobbying activities to win U.S. congressional support for a strong U.S. posture in South Korea. The scheme backfired and severely strained bilateral relations between the two nations. The scandal reflected Seoul's increasing doubts about the U.S. commitment to the security of South Korea.

Under these circumstances President Park strove to make South Korea militarily independent of the United States. As part of achieving self-reliance, the Park government embarked on a nuclear weapons development program. In June 1975 he declared that South Korea would develop its own nuclear weapons if the U.S. nuclear umbrella was withdrawn. The United States strongly opposed South Korea's emergence as a nuclear power, fearing that South Korea's nuclear armament would inevitably cause a nuclear arms race between the two Koreas and also further stimulate Japan's nuclear weapons development, breaking the balance of power in Northeast Asia. Under heavy U.S. pressure, on 29 January 1977, Park stated that he would not develop nuclear weapons.

ROK–U.S. relations were further strained when the Carter administration, inaugurated in January 1977, considered the withdrawal of American ground forces from South Korea. Moreover, Jimmy Carter placed the human rights issue in South Korea on the agenda for South Korean–U.S. ties. Carter's suggestion might be viewed as a natural consequence of the Nixon Doctrine as well as an indication of South Korea's enhanced capability to defend itself. Carter drew immediate criticism in the United States and particularly in South Korea, and his withdrawal plan was seen by many Koreans as an indication that the United States was no longer willing to defend their country against North Korea. The

Carter administration focused on great attention on human rights abuses in South Korea under the Park presidency, and it believed that improvements in human rights would make South Korea internally stronger and more secure, and, to the outside world, provide moral legitimacy to Park's regime. Carter's human rights concerns remained a major irritant in ROK–U.S. relations during the second half of the 1970s.[17]

In the context of soured relations between South Korea and the United States, the Carter administration, in early 1979, reassessed its commitment to withdraw U.S. ground troops from South Korea. In February 1979 Carter announced that further pullout of ground troops would be suspended, and his decision was finally confirmed by a statement issued on 20 July 1979. This provided a major opportunity for fence mending between the two allies, and after Park's assassination on 26 October 1979, the United States reaffirmed its security commitment to South Korea and warned North Korea against any rash action to exploit the unsettled situation.

Return to the Honeymoon in the 1980s

After President Park was assassinated on 26 October 1979, another military strongman, Major General Chun Doo-hwan, emerged as the new authoritarian ruler. As the political crisis in South Korea intensified in the spring of 1980, the United States increasingly saw Chun and another period of military-backed rule as the only alternative for South Korea. After inaugurating the Fifth Republic in October 1980, Chun began his seven-year term as president in late February 1981. A change of political power also occurred in the United States with the 1980 election of President Ronald Reagan, a conservative Republican who won a landslide victory over the more liberal Jimmy Carter. Reagan had committed himself to a determined anticommunist foreign policy and declared that, in the fight against communism, the United States would stand shoulder to shoulder with its allies, whether they were entirely democratic or not. The Reagan administration was a profound gift to the Chun Doo-hwan regime in South Korea, as the new U.S. administration provided Chun unlimited support. As part of establishing strong security ties between the two allies, the Reagan administration ended all talks of U.S. ground troop withdrawal in 1981 and was tolerant of South Korea's human rights abuses. As pointed out previously, in exchange for Chun Doo-hwan's commutation of Kim Dae-jung's death sentence to life imprisonment, Chun gained the honor, in February 1981, of being the first foreign head of state to visit Reagan. As a further sign of closer relations, President Reagan visited South Korea in November 1983 and reaffirmed the U.S. commitment to South Korean security. During his stay in South Korea, Reagan visited U.S. troops in the DMZ and applauded the Chun regime for achieving political stability, economic growth, and a strong security posture.

Critical events such as the tragic downing of the South Korean airliner by a Soviet fighter-interceptor on 1 September 1983 and the "Rangoon bombing," an unsuccessful North Korean attempt to assassinate Chun Doo-hwan, on 9 October 1983 drew strong U.S. support for South Korea and severe U.S. condemnations of the Soviet Union and North Korea. South Korea heartily welcomed Reagan's reelection in the 1984 presidential election. During the South Korean political crisis in the mid-1980s, the United States always sided with the Chun Doo-hwan government. Clearly the United States was more concerned with South Korea's national security and less with its democracy. During the direct presidential election campaign late in 1987 after the June Resistance, the United States betrayed a preference for Roh Tae-woo, Chun's handpicked successor, as shown by Roh's visit to the United States in September 1987.

The George H. W. Bush administration also supported South Korea and reaffirmed the U.S. treaty commitment to the country. The United States also approved South Korea's nordpolitik—its efforts to improve relations with communist countries. Moreover, the United States displayed its friendship with South Korea when it firmly rejected North Korea's demand for bilateral talks, without South Korea's participation, to replace the armistice agreement with a permanent peace treaty.[18]

In short, in the 1980s, official relations between South Korea and the United States could be characterized as "honeymoon ties." The bilateral relationship was based on an intimate friendship between the two governments. Beneath this intimacy, however, anti-Americanism rapidly and increasingly pervaded South Korean society.

The Rise of Anti-Americanism

One of the most dramatic developments in the history of South Korean–U.S. relations was the rise of anti-Americanism in South Korea in the early 1980s. Before the 1980s, the South Korean view of the United States was generally based on "illusions" and "myths" about a virtuous United States and its support for South Korea. The idea of the United States as *Miguk*, the beautiful or virtuous nation, dominated the Korean perception as a "faith." The United States

was more than a friend; it was *the* friend, and the world knew no more enthusiastic allies. From the early 1980s, however, many South Koreans perceived
the United States not as a savior but as a selfish bully. These feelings were deep
enough that South Korean anti-Americanism could not be dismissed as merely
dissent by a small fringe element. Not all South Koreans were anti-American
or unappreciative of what Americans had done for their country, but anti-U.S.
sentiment was common among a significant number of young Koreans, especially university students and young people of university age. This antagonism
toward America also permeated the South Korean military, businesses, and
the government bureaucracy. South Koreans increasingly were voicing their
criticism of the United States over various aspects of South Korean–U.S. relations. The question of how to build a new relationship between the ROK and
the United States was an issue that needed to be settled.

Anti-Americanism was initially the domain of radical students protesting
U.S. imperialism and U.S. support for the South Korean dictatorship by means
of demonstrations and firebombs. Although some protests of this kind still
surface occasionally, anti-Americanism has become more mainstream, fueled
by middle-class anger at the perceived failure of the United States to reward
and respect South Korean accomplishments.

Since the early 1980s, university students voiced the most radical criticism
of the United States. Most students believed that South Korea's military and
economic relations with the United States bred their country's dependence
on U.S. assistance. The large U.S. military presence on South Korean soil was
a major source of intense anti-Americanism among students who saw U.S.
troops in their nation as occupiers, not protectors. The conviction of "U.S. complicity" with South Korean dictatorships became part of the general struggle
against the authoritarian military regime and the democratization movement
in South Korea. The 1980 Kwangju incident particularly inspired much of the
anti-American rhetoric echoing throughout subsequent demonstrations across
the country.

Since 1988 anti-Americanism generated by resentment of U.S. "misbehavior"
in the course of South Korea's democratization has virtually declined. Following the implementation of the 1987 democratic constitution, much public support for the radical student movement has diminished, and for many
middle-class South Koreans, the mass protests of the mid-1980s achieved their
goal. South Korea's political system was democratized, and in 1992, 1997, 2002,
and 2007 politicians without a military background—Kim Young-sam, Kim

Dae-jung, Roh Moo-hyun, and Lee Myung-bak—were elected president consecutively. The more radical aspects of the student movements—the call for redistribution of economic wealth and praise for the North Korean regime—have alienated middle-class Koreans. Even on campuses, true radicals have comprised less than 5 percent of the student body. Still, however, residual anti-Americanism among a small number of student and dissident activists has spread to the mainstream, and charges of "American arrogance" remain a frequent accusation at most anti-U.S. demonstrations.

South Korea's Nordpolitik

During the Cold War period, South Korea's relations with the communist world were characterized by antagonism and hostility, similar to relations between North Korea and the United States. In fact, both Koreas were a "scapegoat" of Cold War politics, as the emergence of the two Koreas made the Korean peninsula into a major battleground in the Cold War.

On 1 September 1983 Korean Air Lines (KAL) Flight 007 was shot down by a Soviet SU-15 interceptor as it strayed over Sakhalin. All aboard, a total of 269, were killed. Outraged, President Reagan denounced the Soviet action as an "act of barbarism," ordered the U.S. forces in South Korea on full alert, and claimed that this was further proof that the Soviet Union was an "evil empire." The Soviets justified the action on the ground that the airliner had been on a spying mission. The incident became a useful propaganda tool for the United States in the Cold War, but it worsened Soviet–U.S. relations at a critical time. It also slowed the pace of improvement in Soviet–South Korean relations. Until the tragic incident occurred, South Korea had cautiously tried to improve relations with the Soviet Union and had enjoyed some progress, but then South Korea bitterly denounced the Russians for their attack, and for a while the warming of relations between the countries was set aside.

In May 1983, when a Chinese airliner was hijacked to South Korea, China officially negotiated with the South Korean government for its return. Thereafter exchanges of visits were frequent, and later bilateral trade steadily increased after China shifted to a free market economy. China's participation in both the 1986 Asian Games held in Seoul and the 1988 Seoul Olympics, despite the North Korean boycott, was a remarkable indication of increasingly improving relations. The Soviet Union also participated in the Seoul Olympiad. As Cold War allies, both China and the Soviet Union, however, constantly supported North Korea's position on inter-Korean relations.

After the successful Seoul Olympics, South Korea increased its efforts to improve relations with communist countries including the Soviet Union and China, although the effort was aimed mainly at North Korea. Named *nordpolitik* after West German Chancellor Willy Brandt's *ostpolitik* of the 1970s, the policy would eventually alter the strategic alignments around the Korean peninsula in a historic fashion.

As the Cold War rapidly thawed in the late 1980s, South Korea seized the opportunity to normalize relations with the communist bloc, first with Hungary in February 1989, then Poland in November 1989, and finally Czechoslovakia, Bulgaria, Mongolia, and Romania, all in March 1990. South Korea also vigorously pushed its nordpolitik to draw closer, in particular, to the Soviet Union and China. In June 1990 President Roh Tae-woo flew to San Francisco to meet briefly with his Soviet counterpart, Mikhail Gorbachev, and on 1 October 1990 the two countries officially normalized relations; South Korean–Soviet economic negotiations soon followed. Finally, South Korea agreed to supply $3 billion in credits to the Soviet Union, which was desperately seeking economic development. Normalization of South Korean–Soviet relations was a product of mutual necessity—healing the breach in their relations for South Korea and securing economic assistance for the Soviet Union.

China was always more sensitive than the Soviet Union to North Korea's reactions, and so it moved more slowly in normalizing political relations with South Korea. Trade between the two countries blossomed, but China remained cautious, insisting on a clear-cut separation of politics from economics. This caution did not last long, however, and from the early 1990s China gathered speed toward normalizing relations with South Korea. In May 1991 China did not veto South Korea's entry into the United Nations, and on 24 August 1992 relations between the two nations were fully normalized. China's determination to establish a formal relationship with South Korea resulted largely from Taiwan's growing diplomatic recognition in the international community at the expense of mainland China. South Korea was the only Asian nation that recognized Taiwan's nationalist regime as China's legitimate government, but to normalize its diplomatic relations with China, South Korea broke off ties with Taiwan.

The ROK's establishment of diplomatic relations with the Soviet Union and China dramatically changed the geopolitical situation on and around the Korean peninsula, especially in that North Korea was left more vulnerable and isolated than before. Although responding to the Soviet action with a bitter denunciation, North Korea coolly accepted China's rapprochement with South

Korea as a fait accompli. The squeezed North Korea then sought to establish relations with the United States and Japan but without success. The new policy of nordpolitik was a great South Korean victory in a fierce zero-sum game of North–South Korean confrontation.

THE TOTALITARIAN STATE IN NORTH KOREA

Consolidation of Kim Il-sung's Autocracy

Since the early 1970s, the destiny of the North Korean state rested wholly on the wisdom and judgment of Kim Il-sung. On 25 December 1972, North Korea promulgated a new constitution that superceded the 1948 constitution. The new constitution reflected many of the changes in the balance of state and party power that had occurred in the 1950s and 1960s, creating a powerful state presidency endowed with the formal functions and powers that Kim Il-sung had already held. Now Kim Il-sung's autocracy was perfected in the totalitarian state of North Korea, and he held that position until his death in July 1994. The new "socialist constitution" moved Korea's national capital from Seoul to Pyongyang, and thereafter North Koreans began to broadcast that Pyongyang was the "heart of all the Korean people."

Since all political power was concentrated in Kim Il-sung and dissent was not tolerated, Kim's decisions and strategies determined the fate of North Korea. Under Kim's absolute leadership, North Korea staked its future on strictly centralized economic planning and rigid ideology. Kim's strategy to inflexibly steer his country was represented by a nationwide ideological campaign known as the Three Revolutions Teams Movement. Officially launched in February 1973 and placed under the leadership of his son, Kim Jong-il, the movement dispatched teams of young "revolutionaries" like those in China's Red Guard, all qualified party cadres and government officials, into mines, factories, and collective farms with the aim of increasing production by reigniting "revolutionary fervor" in three areas: ideology, technology, and culture. Because it depended solely on ideological fervor and neglected technological improvements and efficiency, the campaign failed to attain the desired end but instead accelerated the country's economic stagnation.[19] Indeed, as we have seen earlier on, North Korea's overemphasis on ideology and excessive efforts to build a powerful military force overtaxed North Korean lives as well as the economy, and the adverse effects would later threaten the very survival of the North Korean state.

Kim Jong-il's Rise to Power

After further consolidating his autocracy, Kim Il-sung began to groom his son, Kim Jong-il, as his successor. According to North Korean propagandists, Kim Jong-il was born in a log cabin on the slope of Paektu-san. More objective sources indicate, however, that he was born on 16 February 1942 in a Soviet military camp in the Far East, where his father's guerrilla band hid from Japanese forces. During his youth in the Soviet Union he was known as Yuri Irsenovich Kim, taking his patronymic from his father's Russified name, Irsen. The young Kim graduated from Kimilsung University in 1964 and then worked in the Korean Workers Party organization. In 1973 he emerged as the director of the Three Revolutions Teams Movement, described above, and the following year became a member of the KWP Politburo. Meanwhile, a cult of personality emerged, glorifying the young Kim's accomplishments and urging the people's support with the slogan "Let's give our fealty from generation to generation."

Despite Kim Jong-il's prominence in the party, until 1980 little was said about him publicly. North Korean media referred to him only as the mysterious "party center" that was given credit for wise guidance and great deeds. Throughout this period, Kim Il-sung fully prepared the domestic and foreign public for the first family succession of the communist world. The veil was lifted at the Sixth Korean Workers Party Congress, convened in Pyongyang in October 1980, where Kim Jong-il surfaced as Kim Il-sung's designated successor. He was named to a succession of high-level positions in the KWP hierarchy and was given the title "Dear Leader," similar to his father's moniker, "Great Leader," and he assumed increasing responsibility in broad areas of policy. As for his father's birthday on 15 April, Kim's birthday, on 16 February, was celebrated as a national holiday.

Kim Jong-il completed his rise to power as North Korea began to face difficult, urgent problems. As the number-two man of the North Korean regime, first of all Kim had to help his father struggle with mounting economic failings that had already become North Korea's Achilles' heel. Also, he took almost all the responsibility for solving the problem of North–South Korean relations in a context of the Sino–Japanese and Sino–U.S. entente and China's policy of economic pragmatism. In the 1980s South Koreans believed that Kim was behind much of North Korean terrorism against their country, and he was thought to have masterminded the assassination attempt on South Korean President Chun Doo-hwan while Chun was visiting Burma in October 1983. The younger Kim, therefore, was considered more aggressive and dangerous than his father.

THE NORTH KOREAN ECONOMY

The North Korean Economy in the 1970s

During the 1970s the North Korean economy became increasingly stagnant. This was a predestined consequence, as already discussed, of the rigidity of the juche philosophy. By the early 1970s the centrally planned economy emphasizing heavy and war industries had already reached the limits of its production potential. In the 1970s North Korea implemented various multiyear economic plans to attain economic growth and industrialization. The Six-Year Plan for 1971–1976 was followed by the Second Seven-Year Plan, after a one-year intermission in 1977, for 1978–1984. These plans sought to restructure the industrial composition of North Korea characterized as a typically heavy industry–oriented command socialist economy.

The multiyear economic plans all failed, and in the early 1970s the North Korean economy was already exhausted. The factors that served to stagnate the economy had been experienced for many years: rigid administrative centralization, reliance on ideological rather than financial incentives, and constant mass mobilization of forced labor under the Three Revolutions Teams Movement, which, as noted, was supposed to encourage innovation and eliminate negative bureaucratic attitudes but failed to improve existing, unproductive work methods. Above all, the juche ideology isolated North Korea from the international economy and caused an irreparable technological lag. South Korea, in contrast, had advanced into new phases of technology and economic development.

To resolve these economic difficulties, North Korea tried to induce Western capital investment in the form of credit, enabling it to pay off the debt with the export revenue generated by the newly revitalized industries. But everything went wrong. First, the 1973–1974 oil shock and the resulting global recession derailed North Korean plans. More important, the North Korean economy was unprepared to receive foreign capital and technology. Finally, in 1974, North Korea stopped securing foreign loans and became a chronic debtor nation. Because it could no longer discharge its debt obligations, North Korea became increasingly unable and unwilling to negotiate satisfactory settlements of its debts and was cut off from further access to foreign investment and advanced technology. The North Korean economy essentially stalled at its semi-industrialized stage, and by 1980 economic stagnation set in as a result of the innate weakness of the juche system, with no hope of improvement.

The North Korean Economy in the 1980s

Since 1962 the North Korean leader Kim Il-sung incessantly repeated that North Koreans would soon be able to "eat rice and meat soup, wear silk clothes, and live in a tile-roofed house." But this traditional North Korean goal was not achieved even in the 1980s. From the 1980s on, the general economic situation grew increasingly dire because of inefficient economic strategies.

To solve its growing economic difficulties, the North Korean Supreme People's Assembly approved a policy for organizing joint ventures with foreign governments or corporations by enacting the Joint Venture Law in September 1984. North Korea proceeded to promote trade with Western countries and to stand ready to receive foreign capital. In 1987 it signed a joint-venture agreement with the Soviet Union, and thereafter North Korea attracted foreign investment to the extent that, by 1991, it had more than 100 joint ventures worth approximately $96.5 million, mostly financed by pro–North Korean residents in Japan.[20] But the investment policy trajectory was not followed faithfully and ended in failure. In 1989 North Korea announced that it would develop light industry, long given lower priority, but even this plan stumbled over the lack of technological innovation and structural reform.

NORTH KOREA'S FOREIGN RELATIONS

Relations with the Soviet Union

For three decades between the late 1950s and the late 1980s North Korea dealt with the Soviet Union and China by playing off one against the other and skillfully exploiting the Sino-Soviet rivalry and conflict. North Korea's signing of friendship treaties with both the Soviet Union and China in July 1961 marked the beginning of its balancing act between the two powers.

In the early 1960s North Korea sided with China on a number of foreign policy issues and antagonized the Soviet Union, leading to the point where, by the end of the Khrushchev era in October 1964, a virtual break occurred in their bilateral ties. The Soviet Union withdrew most of its military and economic assistance, seriously damaging North Korea's capabilities, but Kim Il-sung restored relations with Khrushchev's successors and, on the other hand, loosened ties with China which was then experiencing the so-called Cultural Revolution. In the first half of the 1970s, following Chinese Premier Zhou Enlai's visit to North Korea in 1970, North Korea again tilted toward China, and North Korean–Soviet relations were relatively chill.

After China normalized relations with the United States and signed a friendship treaty with Japan in 1978, a new cycle began in North Korean–Soviet relations. The two nations proceeded to warm their ties. The Soviet downing of a South Korean airliner on 1 September 1983 accelerated North Korean–Soviet rapprochement, as it interrupted South Korea's early nordpolitik efforts. Kim Il-sung's visits to the Soviet Union in 1984 and 1986, his first in more than 20 years, further improved North Korean–Soviet ties. Though eroding North Korean–Chinese relations, the visits brought closer security ties with the Soviet Union as well as large shipments of Soviet weapons and various other goods to North Korea.

After coming into power, Mikhail Gorbachev adopted a foreign policy line quite different from that of his predecessors, as he sought a more balanced Soviet posture regarding both North and South Korea, retaining a foothold in North Korea while improving relations with the South. In 1988 the Soviet Union participated in the Seoul Olympics despite North Korea's strong protests, and on 1 October 1990 the Soviet Union normalized relations with South Korea. Gorbachev continued Soviet military assistance to North Korea, but he pressured North Korea to permit inspections by the International Atomic Energy Agency (IAEA) of its nuclear facilities at Yŏngbyŏn. But the collapse of the Soviet Union in late 1991, the fall of Gorbachev, and the rise of Boris Yeltsin cost North Korea its most important strategic patron and most generous and important economic partner. Having lost its patron, North Korea began a steady decline that would increasingly sap the strength of the Kim Il-sung regime.

Relations with China

Until the outbreak of the Korean War, North Korea had been no more than a satellite of the Soviet Union. As summarized above, by 1958, North Korea succeeded in balancing Soviet and Chinese influence on the country, courting one power or the other for its own gains. From 1958 to 1961 North Korea continued to steer a neutral course in the worsening Sino-Soviet relations, but in 1962 it began leaning toward China. By the fall of Nikita Khrushchev in October 1964, North Korea had become China's strongest Asian ally following the Sino-Soviet split. After Khrushchev fell, North Korea moved toward mending the badly deteriorated relations with the Soviet Union and found Khrushchev's successors responding favorably. The internal crisis in China caused by the Cultural Revolution contributed to North Korea's decision to pursue a closer alignment with the Soviet Union, but North Korea's rapprochement with the Soviet Union cooled its relations with China.

As the Cultural Revolution drew to a close at the end of 1969, China moved to improve its relations with North Korea, and in the first half of the 1970s North Korean–Chinese relations were once again cordial. Bilateral ties between the two countries were strengthened when, on 18–26 April 1975, Kim Il-sung visited China, the first visit since 1961, to gain support for invading South Korea. China and the Soviet Union, however, discouraged Kim from any attempt to take advantage of the debacle then unfolding in Indochina.

From 1978 on, relations between North Korea and China were somewhat strained, whereas North Korean–Soviet ties improved. North Korea was unhappy with China's new foreign policy orientation, especially the normalization of Sino–U.S. relations and the signing of the Sino–Japanese peace and friendship treaty, both of which would seriously impact North Korea. The Soviet Union tried to take advantage of this strain in North Korean–Chinese relations.

Amid improving ties between North Korea and the Soviet Union in the early 1980s, North Korea and China also sought to improve their tense relations. China needed North Korea as a political and strategic ally to check Soviet influence, and North Korea needed China to resolve its own growing economic difficulties and problems arising in the leadership succession. In September 1982 Kim Il-sung's trip to China carried significant political implications, as the most important items on the agenda included China's support for a dynastic succession of power, China's economic and military assistance, and North Korea's concern about the increasing South Korean–Chinese contacts.

Kim Il-sung won important concessions from China. The Chinese informally endorsed Kim's son, Kim Jong-il, as his successor and also promised to increase economic and military assistance. China became North Korea's principal source of crude oil, as the trade agreements that concluded in 1982 and 1986 assured that China would ship an average of one million tons of crude oil annually as a "friendship price." On the other hand, North Korea strongly protested China's first official contact with South Korea over the hijacking of a Chinese airliner in May 1983. Chinese officials responded that this was a special case and renewed its pledge that China would not depart from its firm stance against ties with South Korea.

Despite its pledge, as noted earlier, China participated in the Asian Games in Seoul in 1986 and the 1988 Seoul Olympics, as it moved toward improved relations with South Korea. When it normalized its ties with South Korea on

24 August 1992, China promised North Korea that it would establish bilateral relations with South Korea without alienating its communist ally.

Although in the Cold War period China and the Soviet Union were North Korea's most important political, strategic, and economic patrons, China was also a political rival of the Soviet Union in their competition to lead the international communist movement. By the late 1980s, however, the Soviet system was on the verge of collapse, and China no longer faced competition from the Soviet Union as an aid donor. But China remained a reliable patron that North Korea depended on unconditionally for survival.

Relations with Japan

The evolution of North Korean–Japanese relations was determined by three major factors. First, the international Cold War had a deleterious effect on North Korea's relations with Japan. Particularly in the 1950s, Japan gave foreign policy priority to the maintenance of close ties with the United States, North Korea's enemy of long standing. Second, in this context Japan wished to normalize relations with South Korea. Finally, Japan perceived North Korea as a possible threat to its own security.

Immediately after the end of the Korean War, North Korea sought to improve its ties with Japan and thus score a diplomatic triumph over its southern neighbor. But Japan had no intention of promoting its relations with North Korea for fear that this would adversely affect its diplomatic ties with South Korea. Despite Japan's official refusal, however, North Korea continued to seek certain contacts with Japan.

In the 1950s the most remarkable development in bilateral relations between North Korea and Japan was the conclusion of an agreement on the repatriation of Korean residents in Japan. The repatriation of Koreans was a chronic, thorny problem among North Korea, South Korea, and Japan. The signing of the "Calcutta agreement" between the Red Cross Societies of North Korea and Japan in 1959 settled the repatriation problem in North Korea's favor. The Calcutta agreement served Japan's efforts to alleviate the social and economic agony deriving from the Korean minority that was considered a potential threat to the stability of Japanese society and an economic burden on the vanquished Japan. North Korea also profited from the agreement by improving its relations with Japan and solving the manpower shortage necessary for postwar reconstruction.

Normalization of South Korean–Japanese ties in 1965 significantly strained North Korean–Japanese relations. Although North Korea zealously pursued normalization of its diplomatic relations with Japan, Japan adhered to its non-recognition policy toward North Korea. In the late 1960s bilateral relations between the two countries seriously deteriorated, mainly because of the tense situation on the Korean peninsula, notably the attempted assassination of President Park Chung-hee by North Korean commandos, the illegal seizure of the USS *Pueblo,* and the downing of a U.S. EC-121 aircraft.

From the early 1970s, however, North Korea's relations with Japan showed signs of progress. The emerging détente between the major East Asia powers propelled improving relations between the two countries. North Koreans were disappointed, however, when Japan did not seek normalization with their country.

In the 1980s North Korean terrorist activities, notably the Rangoon bombing in 1983 and the blowing up of a South Korean airliner in 1987, hardened Japanese attitudes toward North Korea. On the other hand, since 1988 South Korea's nordpolitik afforded Japan an opportunity to take a more flexible posture toward North Korea. Thus, despite objections from South Korea and the United States, in 1989 Japan began to move toward normalization of its relations with North Korea. But normalization talks ended in failure, mainly over the issue of Japan's reparations to North Korea. During the talks, after Japan expressed "deep regret and repentance" for its colonial rule in Korea, North Korea demanded $11 billion in reparations, but Japan was willing to offer only $5 billion.

In the Cold War period North Korea was generally unfriendly to Japan, which had always rejected North Korean overtures. In the late 1980s North Korea and Japan did engage in normalization talks but without success. Bilateral relations between the two countries remained icy.

Relations with the United States

Apart from the ax murders of two U.S. Army officers in the Joint Security Area of P'anmunjŏm in August 1976, relations between North Korea and the United States were uneventful during the 1970s and 1980s. Despite its hostile verbal and sometimes physical attacks on the United States, North Korea made various conciliatory gestures to establish friendly relations with the United States, but in dealing with the United States, North Korea basically pursued only two goals—the withdrawal of U.S. forces from South Korea and the conclusion of a peace treaty between North Korea and the United States.

Because chances for official channels with the United States were slim, North Korea tried to promote friendly ties with American scholars, academic organizations, journalists, and Congressmen. North Korea frequently invited certain American individuals to visit the country and dispatched some of its scholars to academic conferences in the United States, intending to create better impressions about North Korea there.

The relatively favorable environment in the first half of the 1970s was suddenly shattered by the P'anmunjŏm ax murders on 18 August 1976. The killings occurred when North Korean guards in the Joint Security Area attacked a party of U.S. and South Korean soldiers in a tree-trimming operation on the U.N. side of the area, killing two U.S. Army officers and injuring several other U.N. soldiers. Four hours after the incident, surprised at U.S. and South Korean readiness to punish North Korea, Kim Il-sung expressed his "regret" that the incident had occurred in the DMZ. The United States considered his message a passive acknowledgment that North Korea was wrong.

After the P'anmunjŏm incident, North Korea still sought direct communication with the United States, first resting its hopes on the Carter presidency, inaugurated in January 1977. Kim Il-sung was pleased when, on 9 March 1977, Carter announced his plan to withdraw 33,000 U.S. ground troops from South Korea. Other measures taken by the Carter administration further raised North Korean hopes for direct talks with the United States. On 17 March 1977, in a speech at the U.N. General Assembly, Carter declared that the United States would establish diplomatic relations with former enemy nations. The Carter administration actively sought recognition of North Korea by the United States and Japan, and of South Korea by the Soviet Union and China. But any chance of this was eliminated when the United States refused to have talks with North Korea without South Korea's participation and North Korea insisted on the withdrawal of U.S. troops from South Korea. Meanwhile, North Korea continued making cultural and personal contacts with the United States.

While reaffirming the U.S. security commitment to South Korea, conservative President Ronald Reagan simultaneously tried to improve North Korean–U.S. relations, promoting the cross-recognition scheme but insisting that the United States would not negotiate with North Korea on security issues without South Korea's full participation.

In February 1983 the United States signaled a change in its attitude toward North Korea by allowing U.S. diplomats to make contact with North Koreans in a third country. But the slow improvement in relations between the two countries stalled on 9 October 1983, when North Korean agents attempted to assassinate South Korean President Chun Doo-hwan.

In 1987 the Reagan administration once again allowed U.S. diplomats to contact their North Korean counterparts, and shortly thereafter North Korea and the United States began their councilor-level meeting in Beijing through Chinese mediators. No concrete agreements emerged, however, as North Korea continued to demand that U.S. troops withdraw from South Korea and that a peace treaty replace the existing armistice agreement between North Korea and the United States.

In early May 1990 the United States officially announced that conditions for direct talks with North Korea would include a dialogue between North and South Korea, an end to terrorist attacks and aid to terrorists, and the return of the bodies of American MIAs from the Korean War. On 28 May 1990, for the first time since the end of the Korean War, North Korea returned the bodies of five U.S. soldiers at P'anmunjŏm. By December 1993 a total of 94 bodies of U.S. soldiers had been handed over to the U.N. side at the truce village.

By the early 1990s, to bring a reluctant United States to a bilateral conference table and to continue its production of nuclear weapons, North Korea played the nuclear card and achieved both goals. The nuclear issue would dominate all future negotiations between North Korea and the United States.

At first, the North Koreans denied they were developing nuclear weapons and refused to sign a nuclear safeguard agreement authorizing inspections of their nuclear facilities by the International Atomic Energy Agency. Under heavy pressure from the international community, including the United States and the Soviet Union, in June 1991 North Korea grudgingly notified the IAEA that it would sign the agreement, but it refused to open its nuclear facilities at Yŏngbyŏn to IAEA inspectors.

The new issue of the North Korean nuclear weapons program caused a serious problem for the United States. Fortunately for the United States, on 13 December 1991, the two Koreas concluded the "Basic Agreement on North-South Reconciliation, Nonaggression, Exchange, and Cooperation." The negotiators from both Koreas also initialed, on 31 December 1991, the "Joint Declaration of the Denuclearization of the Korean Peninsula," signed by the prime ministers of the two Korean states on 18 February 1992. North Korea signed the nuclear safeguard agreement on 30 January 1992, at last allowing IAEA inspections of its nuclear facilities in May 1992.[21] Thus certain hopeful signs appeared for improving relations between North Korea and the United States, as well as between both Koreas. But soon the situation deadlocked, as North Korea returned to its earlier uncompromising policy.

NORTH–SOUTH KOREAN RELATIONS

1972–1973 Bilateral Talks

Most of the years before the late 1990s witnessed unremitting hostility between the two Koreas. The people of both Koreas were almost entirely isolated from each other and anxious about their security, but the pattern of total isolation and lack of dialogue was interrupted for three short periods—1972–1973, 1984–1985, and 1991–1992.

From the end of the 1960s to the mid-1970s, dramatic changes took place in the international system, such as the "Nixon Doctrine," U.S. moves toward détente with the Soviet Union and rapprochement with China, and the U.S. withdrawal from Vietnam. This new atmosphere in the international sphere caused the two Koreas to fear that, unless they began resolving their differences on their own initiative, they might lose their own great power patronage. Thus the two Koreas took the path of inter-Korean dialogue.

In August 1971, for the first time since 1953, the two Koreas' Red Cross societies began talks with each other over the plight of families that had been separated when the country was divided. Then, secret contacts between North and South Korea resulted in a surprise Joint Statement on 4 July 1972, simultaneously announced in Seoul and Pyongyang and embodying the basic principles that had been agreed upon for Korean reunification: to solve the problem of reunification independently, with neither foreign interference nor dependence on foreign power, achieve reunification peacefully without the use of armed force, and put the principle of "grand national unity" as a homogeneous Korean people above differences in political or social systems and ideology. The two sides agreed not to vilify each other and to cease armed provocations, promote various inter-Korean exchange programs, cooperate with each other for Red Cross talks, create a North-South Coordination Commission with five members on each side, discuss reunification measures, and establish a telephone "hot line" between Seoul and Pyongyang.

The first Red Cross plenary meeting opened in Pyongyang in August 1972 but deadlocked in July 1973 over the issue of reuniting separated families. The first conference of the North-South Coordination Commission was held at P'anmunjŏm in October 1972. But in August 1973, shortly after the kidnapping of Kim Dea-jung by KCIA operatives, the Commission meeting was suspended indefinitely. North Korea used Park Chung-hee's Yushin coup, particularly the abduction of Kim Dae-jung, as an excuse to discontinue the North–South Korean talks and to renew its propaganda offensive against its southern neighbor. Thereafter both sides periodically proposed resuming the inter-Korean dialogue but merely as lip service, for each time the other side naturally objected. The inter-Korean talks of the early 1970s were predestined to end in failure, as Park Chung-hee and Kim Il-sung, each lacking patriotic spirit, intended to gain political capital from the dialogue for reunification in order to consolidate their own power. In fact, while Park was establishing the Yushin regime in October, Kim was instituting the "socialist constitution" and creating his autocracy in December 1972. Both leaders justified their actions as preparing the ground for reunification. Naturally, therefore, inter-Korean talks produced no meaningful agreement.

The 1972–1973 talks between the two Koreas set a precedent for the negotiations that followed in the 1980s and 1990s, in which initially successful negotiations soon came to a deadlock. In the course of imputing failure to the other side, increasing recrimination and confrontation followed and further increased mutual hostility. The agreement signed by both Koreas was usually dead in the water.

Meanwhile, in late 1972, the North Koreans engaged in digging an extensive underground tunnel in the southern part of the DMZ on orders from the highest echelons of the North Korean regime, shortly after the beginning of the first inter-Korean talks. In November 1974 South Korean forces located the precise location of the first tunnel, and in February 1975 they found the second tunnel. "Tunnel number two" was regarded as a masterpiece of North Korean engineering. Two more fully developed tunnels were found in 1978 and 1990.[22] South Korean forces destroyed the tunnels on the South Korean side of the DMZ. The intercepted tunnels were tangible evidence of North Korea's aggressive and deceptive behavior against South Korea. On the other hand, the Park Chung-hee government would proudly repeat that it had saved the country by finding the North Korean tunnels whenever it faced the stiffest resistance from the political opposition and wanted to justify its political suppression.

Developments since the 1980s

In the 1980s North and South Korea slowly moved toward more open relations. On 12 January 1981, to divert public attention from his repressive rule, South Korean President Chun Doo-hwan proposed an exchange of visits between the two Koreas by the "highest responsible person" of each country "without any condition, and free of obligation." This was rejected by North Korea a week later. On 5 June 1981 Chun again suggested a summit meeting, and again North Korea flatly rejected the proposal.

Two years later North Korea reached the zenith of its pressure tactics against South Korea, when, on 9 October 1983, its agents attempted to assassinate Chun during his state visit to Burma. The agents planted a bomb in the superstructure of the Aung San Martyr's Mausoleum in Rangoon, timed to explode as Chun and his entourage were in the building paying respects to the Burmese national hero. Chun's entourage was waiting for him to arrive when the bomb went off, and 17 South Koreans were killed, including several cabinet members and the chief presidential secretary. Because he arrived late, Chun himself escaped injury or death.

In the aftermath of the assassination attempt North Korean tactics changed, and negotiations were once again activated between the two Koreas during 1984–1985. In September 1984, when South Korea was hit by a typhoon that caused devastating floods, North Korea, on its own initiative, delivered relief supplies, including rice, cement, and medicine, to South Korea through Red Cross channels. This goodwill sprung not from altruism but from political calculations, for North Korea anticipated that South Korea would refuse to accept the relief supplies and that the offer itself would serve North Korea's propaganda war at home and abroad. Thus the South Korean decision to accept the aid was completely unexpected in the North. In any event, the outward display of goodwill had positive effects on North–South Korean relations, and the following year, in 1985, ties between the two Koreas markedly improved. In September 1985 the two countries arranged for an exchange visit between Seoul and Pyongyang of members of separated families, journalists, performers, and support personnel, numbering 151 in all, under the auspices of the Red Cross societies from each country. In the two capitals, dramatic meetings occurred between family members after separations of 35 years or longer. Other channels were also opened for dialogue: delegations headed by officials of vice-ministerial rank worked out an agreement on economic cooperation; delegations of legislators from each side sought a joint parliamentary meeting; and the International Olympic Committee arranged a meeting of sports officials from each side to discuss North Korean participation in the Seoul Olympics to be held in 1988.

On 20 January 1986, however, the North Koreans suspended political talks with South Korea, claiming that the atmosphere for dialogue was poisoned by the South Korea–U.S. annual Team Spirit military exercise. Talks on the Olympics continued but also failed to reach agreement. North Korea considered the Team Spirit exercise a grave threat to its national security and denounced it as a dangerous war game intentionally designed to further destroy inter-Korean relations.

On 29 November 1987 the bombing of a South Korean airliner during a flight over the Andaman Sea killed all 115 persons onboard. Two North Korean agents had planted the bomb on the plane before disembarking themselves in Bahrain. One agent committed suicide with poison, and the other was captured and confessed to having been part of a special task force organized personally by Kim Jong-il. The destruction of the plane was part of an effort by the North Korean leadership to destabilize South Korea during its impending presidential election campaign and to increase international anxiety over the forthcoming Seoul Olympics. The bombing was interpreted as a warning to foreigners that a trip to South Korea would not be safe. This incident stamped North Korea as a terrorist state for a long time to come.

Despite the airline bombing, in 1988 delegations from the South Korean National Assembly and the North Korean Supreme People's Assembly met at P'anmunjŏm to discuss arrangements for a joint parliamentary meeting. The joint meeting never occurred, however, because North Korea once again protested the 1989 annual Team Spirit military exercises. Another channel for inter-Korean dialogue opened on 9 February 1989, when delegations headed by vice-minister level officials met at P'anmunjŏm to discuss arrangements for high-level political and military talks by delegations to be headed by the prime ministers of both governments. But the third round of preliminary meetings, scheduled for 26 April 1989, was postponed to 12 July when North Korea protested the South Korean government's arrest of the dissident South Korean Presbyterian minister Mun Ik-hwan, who had visited North Korea in March–April 1989 and met twice with Kim Il-sung without authorization from the South Korean government. Sports officials from the two Koreas opened still another channel for dialogue on 9 March 1989 over the formation of a joint team for the Asian Games to be held in Beijing in September 1990. The two sides agreed on using the song "Arirang," a traditional Korean folk song, as the official anthem for the joint team but failed to agree on the team name or flag. In the end the the two states would participate separately in the sports festival.

The abortive North-South dialogue of 1988–1989 did produce, however, a constructive by-product. As part of its nordpolitik efforts, in January 1990

South Korea opened its first direct trade with North Korea. On 21 January 1990 Chŏng Chu-yŏng, the patriarch of the Hyundai Group, visited his North Korean birthplace and negotiated with the North Koreans on a joint venture to develop tourism in the Kŭmgang-san region. This would have a tremendous impact on future inter-Korean relations.

In 1990–1991, the two Koreas engaged in unprecedented face-to-face talks, with the prime ministers alternating their visits to Seoul and Pyongyang. Because of differences in their approaches, however, little progress was made. While North Koreans stuck to political issues, their southern counterparts emphasized humanitarian and cultural issues.

The fourth round of the prime ministers' meeting resumed in Pyongyang in October 1991 and produced a joint commitment to work toward the "Basic Agreement on North-South Reconciliation, Nonaggression, Exchange, and Cooperation." The document was adopted and initialed on 31 December 1991, when the fifth round of meetings was held in Seoul. With the agreement, both Koreas seemed to come closer than ever before. Each Korea accepted the other's regime as a legitimate government with a right to exist. Both Koreas also signed the six-point "Joint Declaration of the Denuclearization of the Korean Peninsula," in which they pledged to use nuclear power only for peaceful purposes and not to test, manufacture, produce, receive, possess, store, deploy, or use nuclear weapons in any form, and to permit mutual inspection of nuclear facilities.[23] In a further encouraging development, on 30 January 1992 North Korea signed the Nuclear Safeguard Agreement and allowed IAEA inspections of its nuclear facilities during June 1992 to February 1993.

Inter-Korean talks of the 1980s, unfortunately, followed the pattern established in the 1970s. All bilateral negotiations between the two countries soon came to a standstill, and all previous agreements were abandoned. Despite its promising appearance, the prime ministers' meeting did not insure any substantial gains, as North Koreans continued their nuclear weapons program and the denuclearization declaration ended as scrap paper even before the ink on the protocol had dried.

In the early 1970s the fortunes of both Koreas reversed in favor of South Korea. South Korea's continuing economic growth, engineered by President Park Chung-hee's developmental dictatorship, was chiefly responsible for the reversal. In the 1970s and 1980s, while North Korea, shackled by its hallmark doctrine of juche, continuously declined economically, South Korea was on the road of rapid economic development. South Korea's astonishing economic growth inevitably fanned the flames of democratization in the 1980s, and, as a result, South Korea finally embarked on the path to democracy in mid-1987. North Korea, in contrast, was increasingly transformed into an isolated totalitarian state reminiscent of the state in George Orwell's *1984.*

12

BOTH KOREAS IN A NEW PHASE
(1993 to the Present)

SOUTH KOREAN DEMOCRACY IN FULL BLOOM

The Kim Young-sam Administration

PRESIDENT KIM YOUNG-SAM, sworn in on 25 February 1993, was the first civilian president in a country that had been ruled by former military men since 1961, and he proudly named his administration the "civilian government." His successors, Kim Dae-jung and Roh Moo-hyun, followed suit, defining their administrations, respectively, as the "national government" and "participatory government."

Portraying himself as a reformer, Kim Young-sam suggested a new politics that would address the chronic "Korean disease," the corruption that infested every level of society. Indeed, South Koreans derisively called their country the "ROTC," or Republic of Total Corruption. In his inaugural address he vowed to build a "new Korea," pledging to fight corruption in the public sectors and to revitalize the already strained economy. During his first months in office, he forced the disclosure of his own property as well as that of his cabinet, members of the National Assembly, and high-ranking public servants, a practice still in place today. Within a few weeks a number of prominent figures, including the Speaker of the National Assembly, the mayor of Seoul, and three cabinet ministers, resigned because of public allegations of past corruption.

Kim's anti-corruption drive peaked on 12 August 1993, when he enacted the Act on Real Name Financial Transactions, which ended the traditional practice of shielding money in accounts under false names to cover up illegal profiteering. The implementation of a real-name system formed a vital cornerstone of financial reform, and the new institution was well received by a majority of South Koreans.

A representative of the "democratization forces," Kim wanted to end the coexistence with the "Fifth Republic forces" by purging key military officers with close ties to Chun Doo-hwan and Roh Tae-woo. In March 1993 he replaced both the army chief of staff and the commander of the Military Security Command with successors who had no links with the quasi-secret military fraternity called Hanahoe, or One Society, which had been formed by Chun and Roh in the 1960s and monopolized senior military appointments during the Fifth Republic. The purification of the military was followed by a reshuffling of the ruling party. The monopoly of party hegemony by the Kim Young-sam faction prompted the Kim Jong-pil faction to break away from the party on 30 March 1995 to form a new party, the United Liberal Democrats (ULD). The arrest and trial of Chun Doo-hwan and Roh Tae-woo on charges of mutiny, treason, and corruption, in 1995–1996, completely destroyed the influence and power of the Roh Tae-woo faction. The Democratic Liberal Party opened its doors to professionals and moderate dissidents, changing its name to the New Korea Party (NKP) on 5 December 1995. On 5 September 1995 Kim Dae-jung, who had taken an extended break at home and abroad before gradually returning to active political life, formed another opposition party, the National Congress for New Politics (NCNP). This marked the return of the "period of the three Kims" in the mid-1990s.

On 27 October 1995 former president Roh Tae-woo admitted that he amassed a "governing fund" of 500 billon wŏn (U.S.$625 million) during his tenure. This money was originally deposited in accounts under a false name, but the truth was brought to light by the real-name financial transaction system. The same day Kim Dae-jung voluntarily confessed that he had secretly received two billion wŏn (U.S.$2.5 million) from Roh as a "gift" during the 1992 presidential campaign, and he charged the incumbent president, Kim Young-sam, with accepting much more money than he did, but Kim denied receiving any money at all from Roh. Around the same time many South Koreans clamored for a definite resolution of the lingering doubts about Chun Doo-hwan's December 1979 takeover of the military and the May 1980 Kwangju massacre. Some civic groups filed lawsuits against Chun and his colleagues involved in the critical events of 1979–1980, demanding that they be brought to justice. Earlier Kim had argued that a successful coup was not a crime punishable by the court, thus claiming that the 1979 coup and the 1980 killings should be left for history to judge. Kim's reluctance to press the legal case against the Chun-Roh camp was undoubtedly a by-product of his unnatural coalition with the Fifth Republic forces to form the Democratic Liberal Party in early 1990. As the South Korean public increasingly questioned the amount of money he or his party accepted from Roh, however, Kim abruptly reversed his stand. A special law authorizing legal action against those responsible for the 1979 military takeover and the 1980 Kwangju killings was enacted in the National Assembly on 19 December 1995. By its terms, Kim could try Chun and Roh after the statute of limitations expired. Even before the law was passed, on 3 December the prosecution arrested and jailed Chun after he defiantly refused a subpoena to appear for questioning.

Starting in March 1996 Chun and Roh, their former aides, and the heads of leading chaebŏl, including the Samsung Group, stood at the bar in the bribery trial. Along with Chun and Roh, 14 former military officers, 8 of whom had retired from service as four-star generals, stood trial in the insurrection case. On 26 August 1996 the Seoul District Court sentenced Chun to death for the 1979 military mutiny, treason in 1980, the Kwangju massacre, and corruption in office. Roh was sentenced to 22 and a half years in prison. The other defendants were given lesser sentences. On 16 December 1996 the Seoul High Court commuted Chun's sentence to imprisonment for life and reduced Roh's sentence to 17 years. The court also reduced the sentences of all the other military and civilian defendants.[1] A year later, on 22 December 1997, President Kim Young-sam pardoned Chun and Roh, along with 17 other persons, under a special amnesty agreement with president-elect Kim Dae-jung.

In his first few months in office, Kim Young-sam's approval rating was as high as 97 percent, mainly because of his anti-corruption drive. Then he experienced growing unpopularity, largely because of the increasingly aggravated economic conditions. Furthermore, his judicial punishment of Chun and Roh cost him a considerable loss of popular support in the Taegu–North Kyŏngsang (T-K) region, where he had obtained an overwhelming majority of the vote in the 1992 presidential election. Under these circumstances, Kim's ruling party made poor showings in the 1995 local elections and the 1996 National Assembly elections.

Kim's Democratic Liberal Party reeled from its severe losses in the local elections held on 27 June 1995. The ruling party elected only two metropolitan city mayors and three provincial governors, just one-third of such posts. The DLP completely collapsed in the fall of 1995 and was forced to reorganize its remnants as the New Korea Party (NKP) in December 1995. Then the NKP suffered a virtual defeat in the National Assembly elections held on 11 April 1996, securing 139 of 299 seats. Kim Dae-jung's National Congress for New Politics elected 79 seats, and Kim Jong-pil's United Liberal Democrats won 50 seats. A minor party and the independents obtained 31 seats. Just a week before the elections, on 5 April, North Korea announced that it would no longer accept the duties and limitations of the armistice agreement and sent 130 soldiers armed with AK-47 semiautomatic rifles, light machine guns, and antitank recoilless rifles into the Joint Security Area (JSA) at P'anmunjŏm, in deliberate violation of the armistice. The JSA incursions, part of the "North wind," or threat from North Korea, alarmed the electorate and allowed the NKP, which had been expected to lose because of President Kim's growing unpopularity, to do far better than expected. Apparently as a result of the JSA incident, the ruling party obtained 20 to 30 additional seats, particularly in the metropolitan constituencies. The opposition argued that the ruling party had made a secret deal with North Korea to bring about the "North wind," an allegation flatly denied by the government party.

By early 1997 Kim Young-sam's inner circle, his second son in particular, became embroiled in a financial scandal known as the Hanbo case, where Kim's close circle used political influence to prevent the bankruptcy of the Hanbo Iron and Steel Company, the 14th largest business in South Korea that owed an estimated $5 billion to banks.[2] With his son arrested and imprisoned on charges of corruption on 17 May 1997, Kim's popularity plummeted.

Since his inauguration in February 1993, Kim's management of the economy had always been sharply criticized. The Asian financial crisis that spread to South Korea in October 1997 by itself betrayed his incompetence in managing economics. Kim left office amid an unprecedented economic crisis and scandal, with an embarrassingly low approval rating of just 3 percent.

While South Korean political parties prepared for the coming presidential election, Kim's popularity took a nosedive. The ruling New Korea Party elected former prime minister Yi Hoe-ch'ang as its presidential candidate in a free primary on 21 July 1997. After having been defeated by Yi Hoe-ch'ang, however, Yi In-je, governor of Kyŏnggi province, left the party to declare his own candidacy. His running for the presidency would decisively serve Kim Dae-jung's election to the presidency. In contrast to the ruling party that fell into disorder, the opposition formed a coalition for the election. Kim Dae-jung and Kim Jong-pil joined forces and agreed, in October, that Kim Dae-jung would become their presidential candidate. Then the ruling New Korea Party merged with the minor Democratic Party to form the Grand National Party (GNP) on 21 November 1997.

As the South Korean economy was on the verge of collapse in November–December, the ruling party rapidly lost popular support and the electorate wanted a change in government. As a result, on 18 December 1997, Kim Dae-jung was elected to the presidency by a narrow margin, with 40.3 percent of the vote against Yi Hoe-ch'ang's 38.7 percent and Yi In-je' 19.2 percent. This was the first peaceful change of regime ever between a ruling party and an opposition party. Three weeks after his announcement that he was entirely responsible for the economic crisis, on 25 February 1998 President Kim left office.

Kim Young-sam is remembered as a failed president, for both personal and systemic reasons. He is blamed for allowing the collapse of a once prosperous economy during the East Asian financial crisis and, by a majority of South Koreans, for having humiliated the nation when he presided over South Korea's bailout by the International Monetary Fund (IMF). His populist politics, such as his judicial attacks against Chun and Roh, distracted popular attention from the deteriorating economy only for a while. Widely considered a man of limited intellect, he lacked other qualities required for top leadership. He excessively relied on intuition and instinct to make decisions rather than rational consideration and expert knowledge about public policy. An egoist, Kim was obsessed with public opinion and attached importance to superficial display rather than genuine accomplishments. His North Korea policy, which was replete with inconsistency, is a good example. Overly sensitive to public opinion, his confused and conflicting policy making helped lead his presidency to an anticlimactic end.

Though Kim proudly defined his administration as a "civilian government," in practice his government was cohabited by "democratic forces" and former "military influences." Under his presidency the "street fighters" for democratization, who lacked experience in national administration, became merely props of the ruling elite. Although Kim was proud and self-confident at first, and the people placed great hopes in him, such expectations were short-lived. One of his main accomplishments as president was his strong anti-corruption campaign in public service, but when his second son, often called the "little president," and those in his close circle were implicated in a corruption scandal, public confidence in him was fractured. Ultimately he even lost moral legitimacy.

The Kim Dae-jung Administration

Kim Dae-jung defined his administration as the "national government," in which all the nation's people were political participants, masters of the nation. Kim's most urgent task upon taking office was to overcome the economic crisis, considered by many at the time as the greatest national disaster since the Korean War. Already in November 1997, under the Kim Young-sam administration, South Korea had sought assistance from the IMF and secured a bailout totaling $57 billion. The new Kim Dae-jung administration pledged, in return, to carry out drastic economic reforms, including restructuring the corporate and financial sectors. The result was a significant contraction of the economy and a soaring unemployment rate. Large-scale unemployment generated labor disputes and disrupted families. To stimulate the economy, the Kim Dae-jung administration took steps to encourage foreign investment.

Through the united efforts of the government and populace, in 1999 the economy quickly recovered its strength. The economic growth rate that year was as high as 10.7 percent, with unemployment at 6.3 percent. Current account surpluses amounted to some $25 billion, and foreign exchange holdings increased to $70 billion.

Despite the economic recovery, Kim Dae-jung never enjoyed a political honeymoon. Although he came into power through the "DJP coalition (Kim Dae-jung + Kim Jong-pil)," in which the president gained the estimated 7–8 percent of the popular vote anticipated by Kim Jong-pil's United Liberal Democrats in return for ULD participation in his government, the political coalition was still a minority in the National Assembly. Yi Hoe-ch'ang's Grand National Party held a majority in the legislature.

Soon Kim Dae-jung's approval rating declined sharply, not because of his economic policy but owing to a series of corruption scandals involving his inner circle and his sons. Thus Kim Dae-jung followed in the footsteps of his predecessor, Kim Young-sam, and the scandals put his administration on the defensive. The consequences became immediately evident, when Kim Dae-jung's party failed to take the legislature in the National Assembly elections held on 13 April 2000. The opposition Grand National Party won 133 out of 273 seats, and 115 seats were taken by Kim Dae-jung's New Millennium Democratic Party (NMDP), created on 20 January 2000 to succeed the National Congress for New Politics. Kim Jong-pil's United Liberal Democrats obtained roughly the difference of 17 seats.

The parliamentary election proved to be a failure for the Kim Dae-jung administration both qualitatively and quantitatively. The ruling DJP coalition could not win a single seat in the populous Yŏngnam region (Pusan, Taegu, and North and South Kyŏngsang provinces). Unexpectedly, even the approaching North-South summit did not give Kim Dae-jung an advantage. Just three days before the elections, on 10 April 2000, both Koreas announced that the North-South summit would be held in Pyongyang in mid-June. The announcement gave rise to suspicion and charges from the opposition that the North-South summit was intended to influence the elections and domestic politics. As it turned out, it had little effect on the National Assembly elections, indicating the political maturity of the South Korean electorate.

In mid-June 2000 Kim Dae-jung traveled to Pyongyang to meet Kim Jong-il. The North-South summit was held on 13–15 June, and the two leaders signed and promulgated a five-point declaration, promoting national reunification on the Korean people's own initiative; peace and reconciliation; reunions for separated families; the expediting of economic, social, and cultural exchanges; and the necessity of an ongoing dialogue to implement these agreements. In addition, the declaration promised a reciprocal visit to Seoul by Kim Jong-il.

By the end of the year the two Koreas achieved some success on humanitarian and security issues, including the reopening of rail links severed during the Korean War and of liaison offices in the truce village of P'anmunjŏm; stopping, or toning down, each country's harsh propaganda campaigns against the other; exchanging family reunion groups in August; and marching together at the opening ceremony of the Sydney Olympics in September. Thanks to his efforts toward reconciliation with North Korea, Kim Dae-jung was awarded the Nobel Peace Prize in early December 2000, boosting his popularity.

But excitement was soon replaced by disappointment. The actions taken by North Korea regarding the humanitarian exchange of separated families fell well short of South Korean expectations, its military deployments along the DMZ remained highly offensive, and substantial talks on security matters followed the earlier pattern of progressing at a snail's pace. In turn, Kim Dae-jung's public approval once again declined.

Domestic politics were typical of Korean political culture, in which the ruling and opposition parties bickered endlessly over many issues. Eventually internal strife broke up the "DJP coalition." Because the United Liberal Democrats had won 17 seats in the 13 April 2000 National Assembly elections, the party was short three seats of gaining a bargaining position in the legislature. To make up for the shortfall, four lawmakers of the New Millennium Democratic Party changed their party membership to the ULD, helping the splinter party meet the requirements needed to negotiate. The opposition Grand National Party denounced this move as a "lending of lawmakers" that disregarded the will of the electorate.

The ruling and opposition parties also clashed head on over the wisdom of Kim Dae-jung's North Korea policy. The Grand National Party bitterly criticized Kim's approaches, known as the "sunshine policy," as a policy that "gives too much and receives little." With an eye on the upcoming presidential election, the opposition party worried that Kim and his ruling party might play the North Korea card, specifically Kim Jong-il's reciprocal visit to Seoul. Kim's visit would be a black hole absorbing all the people's attention and placing the president in a position to manipulate the domestic political agenda.

Amid bruising bickering with the opposition Grand National Party, the ruling New Millennium Democratic Party lost in all three National Assembly by-elections (two in Seoul and one in Kangwŏn province) on 25 October 2001, with the opposition party falling short by one seat of holding a majority in the legislature. These by-elections were necessary to fill up vacancies left by election-law violators. The NMDP's losses in Seoul were especially damaging, as these districts were long regarded as party strongholds. GNP victories, however, were seen less as expressions of positive support for the opposition party than erosion of popular support for the ruling party and the Kim Dae-jung administration.

The ruling "DJP coalition," meanwhile, finally collapsed in August–September 2001, beginning with the conservative United Liberal Democrats' demand for the dismissal of Unification Minister Im Tong-wŏn, who had been called the "preacher" of Kim Dae-jung's sunshine policy, over his alleged bungling in sending a group of South Koreans to participate in the North Korean Liberation Day event. During their visit to North Korea, some South Korean participants broke earlier promises not to attend North Korean events. Certain radical members even visited Man'gyŏngdae, Kim Il-sung's birthplace, which was considered inappropriate by the general South Korean population. Kim Jong-pil publicly called for Im's voluntary resignation, which both Kim Dae-jung and Im refused. Then both the GNP and the ULD voted to recommend Im's dismissal as unification minister in the National Assembly on 3 September 2001, causing a political showdown that resulted in the breakdown of the NMDP–ULD coalition. On the same day the ULD lost its independent status as a bargaining body, as the four former NMDP lawmakers withdrew from the party. The ULD move was a premeditated action to arrest further erosion of its identity as a conservative party.

As Kim's presidency approached its end, the presidential election, scheduled for 19 December 2002, dominated South Korean politics. Although increasingly losing popular support, the ruling New Millennium Democratic Party sought to regain political power at all costs. The party made a radical change to the rule for selecting its presidential nominee to the same system governing U.S.-style primary elections. It even allowed ordinary citizens to participate in the selection of its presidential nominee. As the primary progressed, candidates withdrew one by one, and finally Roh Moo-hyun, who, as a human rights lawyer, had been active in the labor movement, was nominated for president on 27 April 2002. The NMDP's new method for nominating presidential candidate was a great success, with the opposition Grand National Party electing Yi Hoe-ch'ang as its presidential nominee on 9 May.

Roh Moo-hyun, whose policy views were all radical or progressive, was popular among the younger generation of South Koreans, particularly the "386 generation," people in their thirties in the late 1990s who were born in the 1960s and entered college in the 1980s and enthusiastically participated in the democratization movement of the 1980s. Highly educated but disenchanted with old-style politics, Roh's followers used the Internet to organize a fan club, known as the *Rohsamo*, or Gathering of Those People Loving Roh Moo-hyun, to articulate their political views and recruit public support for Roh. As the "Roh wind" developed into a storm, Roh's popularity skyrocketed.

The "Roh wind" did not last long, however. By early summer Roh's popularity took a sudden downturn, and Yi Hoe-ch'ang's popularity slowly rose. Two primary factors contributed to this reversal of political fortunes. First, Roh's reckless remarks on sensitive issues, such as South Korean–U.S. ties and inter-Korean relations, alarmed a large segment of the South Korean electorate. During his stumping tour, Roh publicly stated that anti-Americanism was acceptable. On another occasion he was quoted as saying that if inter-Korean relations were well managed, it wouldn't matter if all other matters were in total disorder. His radical and unconventional views were always sharply criticized.

Roh's declining popularity was also the result of the scandals involving Kim Dae-jung's sons and inner circle. As in the previous administration, several of Kim's closest colleagues were arrested and sentenced to jail for influence peddling and similar illegal activities. Kim's second son was convicted of receiving money from businessmen as well as from a high-ranking official of the National Security Planning Agency, and was sentenced to four years in prison. The president's youngest son was also implicated in a case of influence peddling and served nearly one year in jail. The president's eldest son, a member of the National Assembly, was featured in the news media for his close ties with gangsters from his hometown and for using his influence to gain favors, further damaging his father's public image. On 21 June 2002 Kim Dae-jung publicly apologized for the scandals involving his three sons.

Kim's diminishing popularity led to disastrous defeats for the ruling party in local elections held on 13 June 2002. The Grand National Party elected 5 metropolitan city mayors and 6 provincial governors, including the mayoralty of Seoul, out of 16 such posts. In by-elections for 13 National Assembly seats, held on 8 August 2002, the GNP won 11 seats and a majority in the legislature. These were the most serious setbacks that any South Korean ruling party had ever experienced. Later the GNP used its enormous political power to reject two of Kim's candidates for the premiership.

As Yi Hoe-ch'ang's popularity soared, concerns grew in the ruling party over whether Roh would be able to defeat him. Some in the party, searching for an alternative to Roh, saw Chŏng Mong-jun, a son of the late Chŏng Chu-yŏng, emerging as a dark horse who could compete with Yi, and they demanded that he replace Roh in the race for president.

Roh and Chŏng negotiated just a few days before the deadline for registering as a presidential candidate. Eventually they agreed to hold one television debate, and the one scoring higher in a public opinion poll would run as the "unified candidate." In the post-debate poll Roh defeated Chŏng by a slim margin (46.8 percent versus 42.2 percent).

As Chŏng Mong-jun withdrew and publicly pledged to support Roh Moo-hyun, Roh's popularity surged once more. But a few hours before the campaign officially ended, Chŏng abruptly withdrew his endorsement. This turnabout gave a boost to Roh, as it alarmed his supporters who instantly flooded the Internet urging younger voters to vote. Eventually Roh won the presidential election by a margin of only 2.3 percent, with Yi obtaining 46.6 percent and Roh 48.9 percent. With his party successfully retaining power, Kim Dae-jung left office on 25 February 2003.

On 25 February 1998, when heading for the Blue House, Kim Dae-jung gave his word that he would become a successful president, declaring that "a triumphal entry into the Blue House is not what is important; five years from now, when I return to my own house, I want to be rated as a great president."[3] His presidency, however, for a number of reasons, was not the success he aspired it to be. He is often blamed for using the narrow, regional interests of the people of Chŏlla (Honam) region to realize his political ambitions. In the December 1997 presidential election, while receiving only 13.4 percent of the vote in the more populous Kyŏngsang (Yŏngnam) region, he obtained 94.2 percent in Chŏlla province and Kwangju, for which he was ridiculed as the "Honam president" of the "Honam republic," marring the legitimacy and prestige of his office. His presidency was also infested with the scandals involving his three sons, for which he had to apologize twice during his tenure. Accused of governing South Korea in pursuit of his own interests, he was also denounced as a captive of his "sunshine policy." It was later revealed, for example, that to realize the North-South summit, he made clandestine dealings with North Koreans, paying them some $200 million. As a result, his close aides were arrested and imprisoned.

The Roh Moo-hyun Administration

On 25 February 2003 Roh was sworn in as president with an ambitious agenda to reform South Korean society. From the beginning, however, he lacked the political skills and wisdom to carry out the reforms. He also exposed his incompetence in conducting state affairs, as his inefficient administration brought about a sharp polarization of South Korean society, irreparably dividing the country into "conservatives" and "progressives." As social conflicts increasingly arose in the form of frequent strikes and organized protests, political forces became ever more fragmented. Corruption and scandal also raged within Roh's inner circle and dominated the political arena. His casual, even reckless remarks on a range of sensitive issues weakened legitimate state authority by causing unnecessary controversies. His ruling party split, eroding his political base. As discussed later, his approval rating declined to such an extent that only a few months into his presidency he had to ask for a national referendum to restore public confidence in his reputation as a champion against corruption.

The Roh Moo-hyun administration defined itself as the "participatory government" in that it would expand opportunities for participation by voiceless and weaker members of society and also meet the needs of socially disadvantaged groups. As Roh raised the expectations of various social groups for their share of the economic pie, an explosion of demands led to labor unrest, disputes, strikes, and social conflicts that erupted uncontrollably throughout the country.

From the outset Roh had difficulties dealing with the National Assembly. Although defeated in the presidential election, the opposition GNP still held a majority in the legislature. Moreover, although he had been elected as the ruling New Millennium Democratic Party's official nominee, the maverick-style Roh could not forge cordial relations with Kim Dae-jung's followers. Relations with Kim were also strained when Roh refused to veto a GNP-supported bill to appoint an independent counsel to investigate illegal funding channeled to North Korea just before Kim's June 2000 visit to Pyongyang. Many leading NMDP members viewed Roh's action as a betrayal of Kim's trust.

Following the conventional South Korean political custom where every president tries to create his own party, Roh and his supporters left the New Millennium Democratic Party to establish a new party. On 1 November 2003, 36 lawmakers from the party, along with 5 dissident lawmakers from the GNP, formed a new ruling party called Our Open Party (OOP). Roh's followers justified their action as a historical necessity to create a new type of political party that would be managed democratically and would be based on nationwide, rather than regional, programs. Those remaining in the NMDP, however, felt that Roh had betrayed their party. With the creation of the OOP, the NMDP was transformed into an opposition party that stood against Roh.

The moral foundation of Roh's administration was suddenly undermined by revelations that the president's personal confidants, known as "Roh's left and right hands," received illegal money from various businesses, including the Samsung, Lotte, T'aegwang, and Sun&Moon groups. Against this background, Roh shocked the nation by announcing, in mid-October 2003, that he would seek a vote of confidence from the populace, either in a national referendum or by some other means. Although deeply disappointed with Roh, the majority of South Koreans did not want him to leave office, as they feared a possible power vacuum followed by even greater chaos in state affairs. Eventually the opposition parties objected to the referendum proposal as possibly unconstitutional, but basically they believed that Roh's offer was a political trick to preempt his responsibility for a political scandal not yet fully investigated. Encouraged by the public's insecurity when he requested a vote of confidence, Roh, relying on similar intimidation, occasionally announced that he was stepping down from the presidency and retiring from politics.

On 12 March 2004, a month before the National Assembly elections, the Assembly voted to impeach Roh for illegal electioneering and general incompetence. The vote was 193 to 2, with Roh's supporters abstaining. Roh used the impeachment as a last resort to break the political deadlock he faced. After the Assembly successfully impeached him, as expected, the South Korean public greatly sympathized with the ousted president and gave a landslide victory for the OOP in the National Assembly elections of 15 April 2004. The elections resulted in a left-of-center parliamentary majority over the conservative camp. In the elections each voter cast two ballots—one for a candidate and the other for a party. The Our Open Party obtained 152 of 299 seats, and the Grand National Party won 121 seats. The Democratic Labor Party, a wing of the radical Korean Confederation of Trade Unions, elected 10 candidates for the first time in Korean history. On the other hand, the New Millennium Democratic Party suffered a crushing defeat, electing only 9 legislators. Roh's electoral victory was followed, on 14 May, by the Constitutional Court's decision to reinstate the impeached president, ending his two-month period out of office.

While the ruling party enjoyed its highest approval rating in the spring of 2004, Roh's approval rating soon plummeted and the OOP also rapidly lost popularity. The ruling party came under a barrage of criticism in 2005, and in the 30 April and 26 October by-elections, it was resoundingly defeated by taking none of the seats available and lost its majority in the National Assembly. Scandals involving Roh's associates played an important role in the results. On the other hand, the GNP won almost all the by-elections. Suffering defeats in both the by-elections and local elections, the ruling party eventually sought to regroup politically and considered merging with the New Millennium Democratic Party or forming a new party.

Roh's fourth year in office, 2006, signaled the beginning of a lame-duck year as he battled record-low approval ratings and an increasingly hostile party. As popular support dwindled for Roh's policies, the GNP won a sweeping victory in the local elections on 31 May 2006, winning 12 of the nation's 16 metropolitan city and provincial contests. The local elections, which determined 7 mayors of the largest cities and 9 provincial governors, 230 chiefs of smaller administrative districts, and 3,621 members of local councils, had been widely seen as a barometer for the 2007 presidential election. The GNP captured 6 metropolitan city mayoral posts, including that in Seoul, and 6 provincial governorships. The main opposition party also won at least 160, or 70 percent, of 230 seats for smaller city mayors, county magistrates, and district chiefs. The ruling OOP suffered a humiliating defeat, winning only one gubernatorial post in its traditional political stronghold of North Chŏlla province. The minor Democratic Party grabbed two major posts in its traditional power turf, Kwangju and South Chŏlla province, and an independent won the gubernatorial post in Cheju province. In June 2005 the New Millennium Democratic Party was renamed the Democratic Party.

The Grand National Party's landslide victory pushed Roh into deeper political trouble caused by political wrangling and a prolonged economic slump. The poor performance of the ruling party was attributed to the Roh administration's policy failures, economic hardship among the populace, and antipathy against the new ruling elite. People had also been fed up with the government's "arrogant" and "intransient" decision-making process, which critics claimed stirred up tension and confrontation among groups with conflicting interests. Public confidence in Roh and his party also dwindled because of the public perception that the president mismanaged foreign affairs. Roh actively took an accommodating approach to North Korea and once said that he would make "many concessions" and provide "unconditional assistance" to the North. The GNP, in contrast, took a much harder line against the Stalinist neighbor. Following its defeat in the local election, the OOP was on the verge of collapse, and the Roh administration faced mounting challenges to its rule from the opposition parties.

The Grand National Party romped to another strong showing in the legislative by-elections held on 27 July 2006, adding three more seats in the National Assembly to their tally. Four seats were contested, and the splinter Democratic Party obtained one additional seat. The ruling party had already lost 6 seats in by-elections in April 2005 and 4 seats in October 2005. After the July victory, the GNP controlled 126 seats in the legislature to the OOP's 142. Neither party had a majority in the National Assembly. In the May local elections and July by-elections in 2006, voters expressed a fervent hope that the GNP could be a real alternative to the Roh government and the ruling OOP, which had nothing more to offer them.

On 13 October 2006 Roh's minister of foreign affairs and trade, Pan Ki-mun, was chosen by the U.N. General Assembly to succeed Kofi Annan as the eighth secretary-general of the international forum, which was good news for South Koreans, coming 15 years after South Korea joined the world body.In late October 2006 the South Korean government investigated an espionage team called the Ilsimhoe, or One Mind Society, and revealed that North Korea had extended its influence to South Korea's pro-North Korean and anti-U.S. movement in a bid to bring communism to South Korea. The espionage group included former and incumbent officials of the left-wing Democratic Labor Party. Ilsimhoe members, mostly student activists from the 1980s, were suspected of having ties with some members of Roh's administration and with the OOP. Following the inter-Korean summit, in June 2000, and throughout the Roh administration, South Korea had loosened the structure of the state and its alliance with the United States. North Korea, meanwhile, had never stopped working to unify South Korea on its own terms.

North Korea had found an opening in a legally established political party, whereas in the past it had concentrated on underground political parties or operations. After the leftist Democratic Labor Party made inroads into politics in the 2004 National Assembly elections, North Korea now tended to use the party as its means of infiltration. Despite the uproar over the Ilsimhoe, key Democratic Labor Party members flew to North Korea for discussions with top North Korean officials on the impact of North Korea's nuclear test conducted in early October 2006. The Unification Ministry gave the green light to the trip despite objections from the National Intelligence Service, the successor to the National Security Planning Agency, and the Justice Ministry.

In late November 2006, with his authority as president declining, Roh declared that it had become increasingly difficult for him to serve as president in the existing climate of stiff political opposition. He made the remark one day after he withdrew his nomination of a female judge as head of the Constitutional Court in the face of the GNP's objections to the nominee. The nomination of the judge, widely regarded as a progressive figure, had been a major contentious issue between the Roh administration and opposition parties for several months. The public reaction to Roh's cave-in was reflected by his December 2006 approval rating, which, according to an opinion poll, had plunged to an all-time low of 5.7 percent.

Roh's low approval ratings took a toll on his ties with the ruling party. His relationship with the OOP deteriorated to the extent that a growing number of party members wanted to sever all ties with the unpopular president and join forces with the Democratic Party. Despite Roh's fierce protests, talks of cooperation with the splinter group were expected to produce a new party. In early February 2007, 23 OOP lawmakers quit the faltering party en masse, demoting the beleaguered party to second place in the National Assembly with 110 seats, and the following May they formed another party, the United New Party for

Centrist Reform. Other lawmakers from the OOP followed suit, and finally, in late July, the ruling party held only 58 legislative seats.

While the OOP was embroiled in internal disputes over its future course, the GNP was witnessing fierce intraparty competition among its presidential candidates. Rifts were evident between Lee Myung-bak, the former mayor of Seoul, and Park Geun-hye, the daughter of former president Park Chung-hee and the former GNP leader. From early 2007 the fight between them escalated. Yi held commanding leads in all opinion polls, and Park trailed in second place. Then, on 19 March 2007, former Kyŏnggi governor Son Hak-kyu, ranking a distant third in the polls and aware of his meager chance of winning the GNP ticket for the presidential race, announced his defection from the main opposition party.

In June 2007 the United New Party for Centrist Reform, led by former OOP lawmakers, and the splinter Democratic Party, united to form the Centrist United Democratic Party (CUDP). Then, on 20 August, the progressive political bloc established the Grand United New Democratic Party (GUNDP), a coalition consisting of four factions: an OOP splinter group, a CUDP breakaway group, progressive-oriented civic leaders, and a group led by Son Hak-kyu, who had left the Grand National Party. Critics said that the new party, which had 143 seats in the 299-member National Assembly, would be no different from the OOP.

After a bitter primary campaign, Lee Myung-bak defeated Park Geun-hye by a narrow margin and was elected, on 20 August, as the GNP presidential candidate. During the primary campaign Lee had been accused of profiting from estate speculations, and Park Geun-hye, often called the "Yushin princess," failed to show anything of substance other than being Park Chung-hee's daughter.

A major policy of Lee's platform was the cross-Korea canal project, which he believed would lead to an economic revival. But his rivals criticized that the project was unrealistic and too costly to be realized. Lee also pledged the "747 plan," which included 7 percent annual growth in GDP, $40,000 per capita, making South Korea the world's seventh largest economy.

Spurred by the GNP's nomination of a presidential candidate, the GUNDP elected its own presidential candidate on 15 October 2007. The long, bitter, and confusing race to find a progressive standard bearer for president ended in victory for former unification minister Chŏng Tong-yŏng. The opposition GNP branded Chŏng as a "sycophant" to Roh Moo-hyun whom the party described as a "failed president."

As the presidential election drew near, the race for the presidency became increasingly fierce. On 7 November 2007 former Grand National Party leader

Yi Hoe-ch'ang injected instability and uncertainty into the presidential race by abandoning the opposition party and launching an independent run for president. His belated entry seemed to reshape the election dramatically into an unpredictable three-way race between two conservatives and one progressive. Yi's presidential bid would be helpful to Chŏng, insofar as it would divide the conservative vote, but it also made the influence of Park Geun-hye a major factor. She held the key in terms of tipping the balance of power between the two conservatives, who badly needed her support to gain conservative votes. In the end, Park reluctantly supported Lee.

After years of slowing economic growth and instability in housing markets, economic issues commanded top voter attention in the presidential election, and Lee basked in the voter confidence that he would be the best manager of the national economy. On the other hand, the continuing suspicions surrounding him became a useful source of attack for other candidates. In particular, questions about Lee's relationship with a company called BBK were raised. The supposed BBK founder, a Korean-American, was investigated for large-scale embezzlement and stock price-fixing schemes, in which many investors lost substantial amounts of money. Lee denied any association with BBK.

On 5 December 2007 the prosecution cleared Lee of almost all allegations linked to the financial scam perpetrated by his former business partner, and to charges of asset concealment. This dealt a blow to other candidates in the race. On 17 December, just two days before the election, anti-Lee parties in the National Assembly passed a bill providing for an independent counsel essentially to investigate Lee's involvement in the scam.

On 19 December 2007 Lee soared to victory in the presidential election, taking 48.7 percent of the vote. Chŏng Tong-yŏng gained just 26.1 percent, and independent Yi Hoe-ch'ang, who would launch a new party, the Liberty Forward Party, on 10 January 2008, won 15.1 percent. Lee's margin of victory was the largest since democratic presidential elections began 20 years earlier. His triumph ushered in an era of new conservatism in South Korea characterized by a more hard-line approach to North Korea, business-friendly policies, and the pursuit of a more competitive environment in schools and labor markets. Lee's victory was considered a "victory of bread-and-butter issues" over ideological visions that had polarized South Korean society under the progressive Roh Moo-hyun administration. As the South Korean electorate supported Lee despite ceaseless allegations that questioned his morality, its priority was on the "capacity" rather than the "morality" of candidates, and so Lee's pledge to revitalize the once prospering economy and redress the misrule of his predecessor led to his overwhelming victory.

With Lee's election, the Roh Moo-hyun era virtually ended. One of the most important virtues required for any ruler is the ability to identify the spirit of the times and reflect this in the government agenda; in this light Roh had no inkling of what the electorate wanted from him, nor did he even try to find out. He completely neglected the motto "the best governance is in economics"; he paid little attention to people's livelihoods, and as a result his popularity evaporated.

Many South Koreans hoped that Roh would reform Korean politics and society, long dominated by the corrupt establishment. Obsessed with ideological bigotry and self-righteousness, however, Roh confused reform with destruction. He directed his energies to denying the establishment and the past, and, although he defined his administration as participatory, Roh interpreted "participation" as "exclusive participation," where his followers were allowed to participate. Under his administration, South Korean society became more keenly polarized into conservatives versus progressives, the older generation versus the younger generation, the Seoul area against the regions outside the capital, the districts on the southern side of the Han River in Seoul opposed to those on the northern side, pro-government media against antigovernment media, and anti-American forces versus pro-American forces. In particular, he divided the South Korean people into the "20 percent" and the "80 percent"; to gain support from the "80 percent," he denounced the "20 percent" as reactionary old-liners. As he divided the people and pitted them against one another, social conflict and disintegration deepened.

As soon as the unpopular Roh slid into a "lame duck" presidency, he was haunted by spiteful backlash politics, not unlike the situation of the mythological Greek figure Cassandra, who had been given the ability to predict the future along with the curse that no one would believe her. As critical news media coined such noxious phrases as the "Roh Moo-hyun discount" or the "Roh Moo-hyun stress," the Cassandra syndrome spread fast among the Korean population, frustrating the president.

A growing portion of the population opposed Roh's policies not because the policies were regarded as inappropriate but simply because they were proposed by the Roh administration. Curtailment of the mandatory military service, often offered by different politicians prior to crucial elections, was seen differently when Roh proposed it in December 2006. Similar situations unfolded over issues such as real estate and specifically the constitutional amendment that Roh proposed in early January 2007 to introduce a U.S.-style, four-year presidential system. The "anything but Roh" phenomenon increasingly deepened, and his plight was largely attributed to his own loss of trust. Roh failed to convey his trustworthiness to the people because of his arrogance and self-righteousness.

Roh Moo-hyun sought to transform South Korean society, but he did not transform himself. He was obstinate and characterized by intransigence. He fought for what he believed was right but did not have the power to persuade and lead the people. He may have aspired to become a great president like Abraham Lincoln, but instead he had much in common with Lincoln's successor, Andrew Johnson, who was impeached by Congress and came within one vote of being removed from office.

The Lee Myung-bak Administration

Lee Myung-bak took office as president on 25 February 2008, vowing to revitalize the economy, strengthen the ROK–U.S. alliance, and implement a tougher policy toward North Korea. A few days before he assumed office, the independent counsel who had investigated his involvement in the BBK case cleared him of all charges of financial misdeeds.

In the early months of 2008 South Korean party politics was shaken from top to bottom. The feud between the Lee and Park factions over the GNP's slate of nominees for the National Assembly elections, scheduled for 9 April 2008, headed into intense fighting. Each side wanted to field more of their candidates, and this conflict seriously threatened party unity. In late March Park lashed out at the GNP leadership regarding the nominees, demanding that party leaders take responsibility for what she called unprincipled and undemocratic nominations that were deception to the people. At the same time a significant number of senior politicians close to Park departed from the GNP to run in the parliamentary elections as independents or to form another party.

On 11 February 2008 the Grand United New Democratic Party and remnants of the minor Democratic Party agreed to merge into the United Democratic Party. They rejoined just short of four and a half years after they had split. The coalition party was formed to prevent the GNP from sweeping the National Assembly elections. The party changed its name to the Democratic Party in early July 2008. Meanwhile the Democratic Labor Party faced chaos, as the party's minority "People's Democracy" faction threatened to leave the party over an ideological feud with the hard-line majority, the "National Liberation" faction.

On 16 March 2008 the former group left the party to form the New Progressive Party.

In the National Assembly elections on 9 April 2008, the Grand National Party won a slim majority, obtaining 153 seats. The main opposition United Democratic Party won 81 seats, and Yi Hoe-ch'ang's Liberty Forward Party gained 18 seats. Fourteen seats were secured by the "Pro-Park Coalition," a group of Park Geun-hye supporters. The Democratic Labor Party and the newly formed Creative Korea Party took 5 and 3 seats, respectively. Remaining seats went to the independent candidates. Although the GNP had a majority in the National Assembly, the Lee Myung-bak government faced considerable limitations. More than 60 candidates supporting Park Geun-hye were elected, and her faction would constitute the third-largest force in the National Assembly to keep the Lee administration in check. In mid-July 2008, 17 lawmakers, made up of independents as well as members of the Pro-Park Coalition, rejoined the GNP. The ruling party then became a "divided house," with two cohabiting factions. The election marked a clear shift in power from the progressives to the conservatives.

By June 2008 Lee's approval rating reached just 17 percent, mortifying him in view of his striving to stimulate economic growth by whipping the country's lax bureaucracy into shape, cajoling the business establishment into making investments, and taking other actions to boost economic growth and create jobs. Even more humiliating was the campaign to impeach him. Weakening popularity and strengthening opposition put Lee's leadership to the test. Behind these unwelcome developments was his mishandling of the controversy over an agreement to restart imports of U.S. beef that might have been tainted by mad cow disease. The mad cow scare became a rallying point for panicky consumers, angry farmers, hostile unions, leftist schoolteachers, opposition parties, and other forces opposed to Lee. His government failed to address the problem adequately when opponents began to ask why it had made concessions to import the beef despite the threat of mad cow disease. The Lee administration was criticized by its opponents for hastily agreeing to resume beef imports ahead of his summit with U.S. President George W. Bush in mid-April 2008. Some radical critics of these beef imports used the issue to organize an online petition to impeach Lee.

The anti-U.S. beef demonstrations began on 2 May 2008, when hundreds of teenagers held a candlelight vigil in Seoul, and it quickly snowballed. By June the uproar became so overpowering that the entire cabinet offered to resign. A two-month demonstration crippled the Lee government, forcing Lee to apologize twice and replace several government ministers. Opposition parties, civic activists, and labor unions stepped up their protests, denouncing Lee's policies as benefiting only the wealthy and powerful. To many South Koreans, the beef dispute was not only about Lee's unpopular decision to lift an import ban on U.S. beef; it tapped into Korean pride and nationalism. It was also the latest test of whether their leader could resist pressure from the superpowers.

With the public backlash over U.S. beef, Lee faced a potential political crisis that could end his reform drive, squandering much of his political capital. The growing furor over the issue could also hurt Lee's efforts to build a stronger ROK–U.S. alliance and might fuel new anti-Americanism in South Korea. There was already a thin line between nationalism and anti-Americanism among South Koreans. Anti-U.S. beef demonstrations were more an expression of the former than the latter, but the divide grew ever more thin.

The Lee Myung-bak administration continued to undergo trials into 2009, this time because of former President Roh Moo-hyun. In early April 2009, following the arrest of a key aide, Roh Moo-hyun admitted that his wife had accepted $1 million from Pak Yŏn-ch'a, a Pusan-based businessman and Roh's longtime financial backer, whose confession to a massive network of bribery had shaken the nation over the past months. Pak had been arrested on charges of extensive bribery and tax evasion. Roh apologized for troubling the country over the bribery issues involving him, his family, and his associates. Roh's family was accused of receiving a total of $6 million in bribes from Pak. Following Roh's statement, in late April the prosecution summoned the former president for questioning over his alleged corruption during his tenure of office. Prosecutors considered indicting him on bribery charges. This scandal showed how corrupt the inner circle of the Roh administration had been. It was also a political time bomb. Several lawmakers, politicians, and bureaucrats were arrested or were investigated for their alleged involvement in the corruption scandal. The corruption charges against Roh dealt a serious blow to the image of him who touted clean politics as a major achievement of his presidency.

In the meantime, legislative by-elections were held on 29 April 2009. In the elections the ruling GNP suffered defeats in all five electoral districts. Victories were celebrated by three independents, one Democratic Party member, and one New Progressive Party member allied with the Democratic Labor Party. The humiliating results sent shockwaves to the GNP leadership and cast a cloud over President Lee's efforts to push for policies to revive the sluggish economy and reform the educational and public sectors. Voters turned their back on the Lee government because of its incompetence, arrogance, and a set of policy blunders.

On 23 May 2009 Roh Moo-hyun committed suicide by jumping off a cliff near his retirement home in Kimhae, South Kyŏngsang province, apparently driven to the desperate act by humiliating bribery allegations. Being the first former president to end his life at his own hands, Roh's death was a shock and tragedy to the country. The subject of Roh's culpability was put aside and overwhelmed by the sadness over his dramatic death. Immediately after his death, the prosecution decided to end investigations into the corruption case. His supporters directed much of their ire at the prosecution and pro-government conservative media who had relentlessly pursued accusations of corruption against Roh and his family. Many accused the incumbent president of having orchestrated the investigation, an allegation that could become a political liability for him. On the other hand, Roh's opponents criticized him for his irresponsibility in taking the bribery scandal to his grave or even committing suicide as a tactical maneuver.

Roh's suicide plunged South Korean politics into deep uncertainty and aroused strong resistance to President Lee. His suicide reignited the fight between two competing political visions. On 10 June 2009, in commemoration of the 1987 pro-democracy movement, tens of thousands of people, defying a police ban, joined a massive rally in central Seoul, criticizing the incumbent administration of backtracking on democracy and demanding an apology over Roh's death.

Meanwhile President Lee's approval ratings soared, mainly thanks to his centrist, worker-friendly policies, a faster than expected economic recovery, and South Korea's hosting of the G20 Summit to be held in 2010. In June 2009 Lee decided to strengthen the ranks of centrists. His centrist policies stressed welfare for low-income people, thereby enhancing the country's social stability. South Korea has probably been the only country among the G20 nations where the outdated left-right standoff continued. Moreover, the "progressives" and "conservatives" did not clash over modern-day policies but over how to view the country's history, most seriously the question of how to deal with North Korea.

Despite Lee's increasing popularity, however, the legislative by-elections, on 28 October 2009, ended in the Grand National Party's defeat. The ruling party won in two electoral districts out of the five that were open. The opposition

Democratic Party took three constituencies, including two fiercely contested constituencies close to Seoul, which attested to voters' desire to keep the powerful ruling party in check. The GNP controlled 169 seats in the 299-seat National Assembly against the Democratic Party's 86 seats. The election results emboldened the opposition to step up its fight against the Lee administration.

Just one day after the by-elections, on 29 October, the Constitutional Court's ruling on the Media Reform Bill was welcomed by the ruling camp. Judges declared as legally valid the National Assembly's passage on 22 July 2009 of a series of bills aimed at providing easier access to broadcast markets by conglomerates and newspaper publishers. The court ruling gave the green light for one of the major reform drives of President Lee and his Grand National Party. But the ruling camp met with much stronger opposition to its remaining key policies, including the revision of the "Sejong administrative city plan" and the refurbishment of four major rivers.

Initiated by former president Roh Moo-hyun as an election campaign pledge in 2002, the Sejong City project, named after the Chosŏn king Sejong (1418–1450), called for moving nine ministries and four government agencies to the newly built administrative town of Sejong, South Ch'ungch'ŏng province, some 160 kilometers south of Seoul. The project was designed outwardly to promote balanced regional development, but in reality it resulted from Roh's political calculation that it would be of great appeal to the Ch'ungch'ŏng people. The National Assembly passed a special bill on the construction of Sejong City in 2005, with the then opposition Grand National Party voting for the bill in a political gesture so as not to lose the support of the "neutral" Ch'ungch'ŏng region.

Since its inauguration in February 2008, however, the Lee administration looked to downsize the relocation project on the grounds that a regional division of the government was inefficient. Lee sought to revise the bill to keep the offices in Seoul and, as an alternative, to transform the envisioned town into a self-sufficient, multifunctional industrial city. On 27 November 2009, in a nationally televised town hall meeting, President Lee apologized for breaking his promise made during the 2007 presidential campaign to support the administrative city project, and he said that he would seek an alternative development plan for the sake of the country's future.

But here Lee faced a crucial test of his leadership. Opposition parties, as well as the Park Geun-hye faction within the ruling party, vowed to block his plan to revise the Sejong City project, and the opposition mounted street demonstrations to block Lee's revision plan. Park had already raised opposition to Lee's proposal, declaring that a revision would hurt public trust in the GNP. Her real intention, however, was to hold onto the support of the Ch'ungch'ŏng region in the next presidential election to be held in 2012. It was practically impossible for the GNP-controlled National Assembly to approve a revision bill without Park's support.

In January 2010 the Lee government officially scrapped the original plan to move government agencies to Sejong City and announced that instead it would turn the new city into a business, science, and education hub in close partnership with the country's leading conglomerates. It planned to submit a bill on the revision for parliamentary approval. Finally, after the ruling party suffered a huge defeat in local elections held on 2 June 2010, in which the Sejong City development was a major issue, President Lee asked the National Assembly to decide on the fate of his alternative plan for Sejong City. In the elections, residents of the Ch'ungch'ŏng provinces, where Sejong City is located, voted against GNP candidates, and, as expected, on 29 June 2010 the legislature voted down the revision bill by a vote of 164 to 105, with 6 abstentions, dealing Lee a major blow. Some 50 Park Geun-hye followers in the governing party cast nay votes, deepening the factional feud within the ruling party. This legislative action ended months of exhausting political wrangling and a serious division of public opinion over Sejong City. The result was a major setback for the Lee government's push for other major projects, such as the four-river refurbishment project; a key item on President Lee's policy agenda, the river plan was expected to become the next big issue on the political scene.

Opposition parties and civic groups regarded the project to clean up the four major rivers—the Han, Yŏngsan, Kŭm, and Naktong—and develop their basin areas as a disguised prelude to President Lee's main campaign pledge to build a cross-country canal, which he had surrendered following objections by a majority of the people. Lee's opponents urged the government to channel the project's budget to other urgent tasks to create jobs and help poor households. Nevertheless, in late November 2009, as part of its green growth campaign, the Lee administration started the contentious project, at an estimated cost of 22.2 trillion wŏn (U.S.$19.1 billion), with plans to complete it in 2012.

Just before the fate of Sejong City was to come to a vote, local elections were held on 2 June 2010. In the elections, the main opposition Democratic Party defeated the ruling Grand National Party, winning seven metropolitan mayoral and gubernatorial posts while the GNP secured six. The splinter Liberty Forward Party captured one metropolitan mayoral post, and two pro–Democratic

Party independents seized two provincial governorships. Democratic Party dominance was also clear in the elections for 228 chiefs of smaller administrative districts; the opposition party won 92 seats, and the GNP secured 82. The independents and candidates from minor parties took 38; the Liberty Forward Party, 13; and the Democratic Labor Party, 3.

Conducted in the second half of the Lee administration, the local elections were seen as a midterm referendum on the performance of the incumbent government. Because the vote in the local elections was largely a warning to Lee to rethink his future policies, he had no choice but to reconsider his agenda and pledge to review his policy priorities and make a fresh start.

Amid President Lee increasingly losing the public's confidence, by-elections were held throughout the country on 26 October 2011. In the Seoul mayoral by-election, pan-opposition candidate, a civic activist, comfortably defeated the ruling party contender. This election for Seoul mayor carried two significant political implications. First, it was the first major poll that the electorate cast ballots by their "economic class." The voters in their 20s to 40s, the nation's demographic pillar, wanted more stable, if not affluent, lives. Bound by anger and angst, they overwhelmingly supported the opposition bloc's sole candidate. Second, the election of the civic activist brought civic groups into the political arena, raising both expectations and concerns. All in all, the by-election reflected the electorate's frustration with the political establishment and hunger for broad political reforms. It also could signal a paradigm shift in South Korean politics, with generational rift tearing down ideological confrontation and regional rivalry.

After the Seoul mayoral by-election, the ruling Grand National Party was put to the test as to whether it would be able to put itself on the path to its former glory or run adrift until shipwrecked. On the other hand, the victorious opposition merged to form the Democratic Unity Party, on 15 January 2012, as the main opposition party with intent to defeat the government party in the upcoming parliamentary and president polls scheduled to be held in 2012.

For the past 20 years, South Korean democracy has been in full bloom to such an extent that public opinion functions as a crucial determinant for major political parties' presidential candidates. The nongovernmental organizations work actively to promote the welfare of the people, including economic justice, anti-corruption in the public sectors, and environmental protection. These civic groups, both conservative and progressive, become a major source for each administration to look out for talent. The two decades witnessed the coming of two conservative and two progressive administrations. Presently, in South Korean society, the conservatives and progressives are well balanced in strength.

THE SOUTH KOREAN ECONOMY AND SOCIETY

The South Korean Economy

Before the financial crisis of 1997–1998, South Korea's annual growth rate in GNP was still high. As of 1994, tertiary industries accounted for 52 percent of the total GNP, secondary industries took up 40 percent, and primary industries amounted to only 8 percent. The South Korean economy had already followed the pattern of the developed nations. Mainly because of import liberalization in the early 1990s, however, the international current account showed an increasing trade deficit. As a result, cumulative foreign debt steadily increased.

As the nation took its place among the world's developed countries, South Korea made a bid for admission to the Organization for Economic Cooperation and Development (OECD), the "club" of the world's advanced economies, in July 1996. Five months later South Korea became a member of the "OECD club."

Although it was one of only two Asian members of the OECD, South Korea was hit by a sudden and severe financial crisis in late 1997. In November the financial crisis that had begun in Thailand and Indonesia spread without warning to South Korea. By the end of the year South Korea's currency, the wŏn, had lost some two-thirds of its value against the U.S. dollar as foreign investors fled the country, and the value of securities on its stock market had also plunged. To save its troubled and insolvent economy, South Korea sought an IMF bailout amounting to $57 billion in loans in return for the implementation of some painful neoliberal economic reform, including restructuring the corporate sector that produced mass unemployment.

The Asian financial crisis was a terrible wake-up call for the South Korean economy, as the "IMF crisis" proved that the old state-led development strategy no longer worked. From 1998 on, the South Korean economy struggled to find the path to recovery. As a result, the GDP continued to grow at an average annual rate of 4.5 percent, exports of manufactured goods more than doubled, and the restructuring of the corporate and banking sectors was rewarded. All these changes caused the South Korean economy to recover from the unprecedented crisis and maintain the pace of its economic growth in the early 2000s.

After the financial and economic crisis, South Koreans underwent drastic changes in their lives. Most South Koreans worried about their jobs, housing, child rearing, education, and retirement. In particular, while the idea of "life-long employment" was ebbing, "self-development" and "personal asset management" emerged as topics of conversation. Feelings of anxiety, mistrust, and helplessness became increasingly prevalent among the populace. The percentage of people who felt that their quality of life had improved in terms of making a living, social security and health services had dropped remarkably. With the income gap ever widening, the proportion of people who identified themselves with the middle class decreased from 41 percent in 1996 to 28 percent in 2007.

In the 2000s the symbolic center of South Korea's economic gravity shifted from heavy manufacturing to high-tech production and innovation, with the development of leading-edge information technology and telecommunication services. South Korea's success story began when the nation was hit by the financial crisis. The South Korean government turned to the high-tech industry as a solution to overcome the crisis. As a result, South Korea has become the most wired nation in the world. Samsung's efforts to supercede Sony's role as a leader in consumer technology highlighted the image of high-tech South Korea, where broadband penetration and mobile phone usage ranked among the world leaders. Indeed, South Korea's large conglomerates, including Samsung, LG, SK, and Hyundai, poured significant resources into ensuring their long-term competitive advantage. South Koreans used their domestic market as a stepping stone into the world. South Korea's information technology sector accounted for exports of $75 billion in 2004. Broadband was a new market with new demand for modems, routers, servers, and computers, as well as a new infrastructure. South Korea has proceeded to change over to wireless broadband, Wi-Bro, and it has also had digital multimedia broadcasting.

The South Korean economy has faced two critical problems—labor disputes and foreign competition. Government effort to make the labor market more flexible, as part of a U.S.-style neoliberal market economy, generated fierce resistance from the strong South Korean labor movement. South Korea has been known in overseas markets as a nation haunted by combatant labor disputes. Frequent strikes and sit-ins also angered domestic customers. Fewer and fewer South Koreans have supported the militant labor movement that was seen in the 1980s and the 1990s.

Phenomenal plans for investment in the development of the high-tech industry have not entirely superseded South Korea's substantive center of economic gravity in heavy manufacturing—automobile production, shipbuilding, steel, chemicals, and consumer electronics. Moreover, the light industries and self-owned businesses, such as textiles and clothing, footwear, and food processing, have still commanded a significant part of employment, trade, and investment. These industries have faced serious foreign competition, especially from China. As the technological gap between South Korea and China narrowed, Chinese exports in steel and shipbuilding have threatened to undermine South Korea's economic strength. There are growing concerns that South Korea, "sandwiched" between high-tech Japan and low-cost China, might quickly lose its competitive edge if it fails to develop new economic growth engines.

The policy mind-set has not yet substantially changed since the 1980s, still emphasizing export-oriented industrialization. Economic regulators have remained vigilant against capital outflows for foreign investment, leading to charges of corporate xenophobia. Furthermore, the persisting problems of big government–big business collusion have put a dark cloud on the economic horizon. Charges of rampant corruption have filled the headlines of South Korean dailies. Public dissatisfaction with corporate power and crony capitalism has also remained very much front and center.

In late November 2007 the National Assembly passed a law appointing an independent counsel to investigate alleged irregularities by the Samsung Group. Corruption allegations against Samsung had been in the media spotlight since late October 2007, when the group's former chief attorney blew the whistle on the nation's largest conglomerate, arguing that he had evidence to prove that it had amassed slush funds in order to bribe everyone wielding political or other influence in South Korea. South Koreans have often called their country the "Republic of Samsung." On 17 April 2008, after a 99-day inquiry, Yi Kŏn-hŭi, chairman of the Samsung Group, was indicted for tax evasion and breach of trust, but he was cleared of charges of bribery and illegal lobbying because of a lack of evidence. Five days later, on 22 April, Yi resigned as Samsung's chairman. Yi was dogged for years by civic groups claiming that Samsung's opaque ownership structure, based on cross-shareholdings by group companies, led to abuses and was meant to ensure that control of the conglomerate passed seamlessly from Yi to his son.

In 2002 and 2003, South Korea was the world's 11th largest economy in terms of GDP. Thereafter, its ranking dropped as the relative size of other emerging economies, including India, Brazil, Russia, and Australia, accelerated their economic growth. In 2005 South Korea's global ranking was 12th; in 2007 the ranking dropped to 13th; and in 2008 it again fell to 15th. The slide was not surprising, as the economy recorded lower than usual growth compared to the global average. Concerns have been raised that South Korea failed to keep up momentum amid rising political and socioeconomic uncertainties.

In the second half of 2008, a sudden global financial crisis and a worldwide market downturn hammered South Korea's export-led economy into its first recession in 11 years. But the country recovered faster than many other major countries as improving exports, domestic consumption, and corporate investment eased jitters over a global recession. By the end of 2011, South Korea became the world's ninth-largest trading nation with its yearly trade exceeding $1 trillion; it stood as the eighth nation to see annual exports more than $500 billion and ranked seventh in the world in terms of outbound shipments.

Although South Korea has developed the high-tech industry and is Asia's fourth largest economy and a member of the G20, the number of its people who feel unhappy with their lives continues to increase, and many South Koreans are weary from their persistent yearning for material wealth. Because South Korea ranks at the bottom in various happiness indexes, the government needs to improve the quality of its people's lives.

A New Society

As the "democratization forces," represented by Kim Young-sam and Kim Daejung and their followers, triumphed over the "modernization forces," symbolized by the military and big business, authoritarianism became increasingly intolerable and virtually disappeared in South Korean society. In the new political climate, the military was afforded no opportunities to perform any significant role in political life and was forced to commit itself to defending the nation.

As democracy came into full bloom, the centuries-old Confucian traditions of hierarchical authoritarianism and collectivism gradually gave way to egalitarianism and individualism in human relations and social organization. As a dominant value system and political ideology, Confucianism had always permeated major institutions and individual life in Korea. But as South Korea increasingly developed into a mature industrial society, Confucian values gave way to such modern economic values as rationality, efficiency, instrumentalism, materialism, and secular success. South Korean culture as a whole became more consumer-oriented, and the country's values and attitudes underwent tremendous change. Even so, Confucian values still loomed large in people's private, if not national, lives. The Confucian values have been most evident in their influence on education, a major factor in South Korea's economic progress. Equally apparent has been the persistence of hierarchical, often authoritarian, modes of human interaction. Although South Koreans today are more likely to live in nuclear families compared to their parents or grandparents doing so, old Confucian ideas of filial piety remain strong. The new urban class has parents and grandparents who were agricultural workers, and therefore it is still bound by family ritual and obligation. Farm villages are still dear to the heart of almost all South Koreans, and more than ten million Koreans continue to visit their hometowns to observe the lunar New Year's Day and Korean Thanksgiving Day, Ch'usŏk.

An affluent society, South Korea has experienced the inevitable backwash of industrialization. The household-income gap between the top and bottom economic brackets has been increasingly broadened. In order to compensate for income polarization, every South Korean administration has been required to expand spending for welfare programs with the funds secured through tax reform. With the widening income gap, moreover, the middle class has shrunk, and an increasing number of South Koreans have fallen to lower rungs of the social ladder.

The transformation of South Korean society, especially the decline of traditionalism, has greatly impacted the very social foundation, the family. The divorce rate has risen nearly three times in the past decade, catapulting the divorce rate in South Korea past that in European Union countries and Japan. Simultaneously, as South Koreans have increasingly become individualistic and pursued a higher quality of life, the fertility rate has consistently declined. This suggests an imminent decline in South Korea's total population. In the 1960s and 1970s South Korea was in the class of high-fertility countries. For instance, in 1960 the total fertility rate (TFR) was 6.0. Therefore, the South Korean government had adopted strong policies to reduce fertility. Thanks to these policies, the TFR declined to 4.53 in 1970 and 2.87 in 1980 and has consistently decreased since then, reaching 1.59 in 1990, 1.47 in 2000, and 1.08 in 2005, the lowest in the world. The TFR in the United States is 2.05, and in France it is 1.90. With more and more married couples facing mounting child-care costs and other financial burdens, South Korea's fertility rate has become far below the rate of 2.2 needed to maintain the nation's current population.

The low fertility rate and rising longevity have thrust into focus the specter of a rapidly aging society, generating concerns among politicians and pundits about the "gray" future. In fact, the number of South Koreans aged 65 or over has continued to climb. With the anticipated fall in future manpower, South Korea's growth potential will fall along with investments and savings, while the burdens of pensions and medical costs will rise. South Korea is expected to become the most aged country in the world, as senior citizens over 65 will account for some 38 percent of the population by 2050, higher than the average 26 percent of other developed countries.

South Korea has become inescapably high-tech. The penetration of cellular phones and the Internet is almost total. The phenomenal popularity of blogs, chat rooms, and online games has generated an alternative reality for many South Koreans, and new online news sites have challenged the conservative mainstream media's monopoly. Press clubs, a Japanese colonial legacy that controlled the flow of news, have become weakened or have been eliminated.

Recently Korea, formerly perceived as an ethnically homogeneous nation, has been increasingly transformed into a multicultural, even multiethnic, society, as the labor shortage has led to the influx of foreign workers and the rise of international marriages. The number of foreign residents surpassed one million in 2007, accounting for over 2 percent of the nation's entire population. The idea of a "multicultural Korea" is evidenced in the growing number of restaurants selling international food. More striking has been the increasing number of international marriages, noted above. Among newly married couples, approximately one out of ten has been interracial. These international marriages have represented the flip side of the South Korean economic miracle. Urbanization and industrialization have depleted the countryside of young women, who have moved to cities to seek better educational and employment opportunities, as well as a more fashionable lifestyle. The grinding, unglamorous life of family farming has repelled many women, and this by itself has caused a shortage of brides in the countryside. Simply put, present-day South Korean society has all the traits of a mature post-industrial society.

The Hwang U-sŏk Scandal

Having experienced rapid industrialization and modernization, South Koreans have grown accustomed to a culture that believes "the faster, the better," with increasing tendencies to ignore ethical considerations and achieve goals more quickly. A striking example is the public furor over South Korean researcher Hwang U-sŏk, who, in December 2005, was revealed to have fabricated data to support his claim that he cloned human embryos and extracted stem cells from them.

Hwang U-sŏk, a Seoul National University (SNU) veterinary professor, first came to international attention in 1999, when he said that he had cloned a cow. But after Roh Moo-hyun's inauguration as president in February 2003, Hwang gained the status of national hero and global stardom by claiming three firsts— the first cloned human embryonic stem cells, the first patient-specific stem cells, and the first dog clone. Stem cells are master cells that can evolve into blood, liver, muscle, and other cells. They show promise for the treatment of medical conditions including Parkinson's disease, Alzheimer's, diabetes, and spinal cord injuries. The South Korean government poured enormous funds into Hwang's research, designated as a "next-generation motor for growth."

Hwang U-sŏk began drawing South Korea's adulation in February 2004, when he became an international celebrity for writing in the leading U.S. scientific journal *Science* that he had succeeded in producing the world's first human embryonic stem cells from cloned human embryos. In May 2005, he claimed to have developed the world's first human embryonic stem cells tailored to match the DNA of individual patients, and he published the results in *Science* again in June. In August 2005 Hwang reported in the journal *Nature* that he had developed Snuppy, the world's first cloned dog. *Time* magazine named the cloned Afghan puppy the invention of the year in 2005.

The national worship of Hwang was rooted in the fierce national pride in the hearts of ordinary Koreans. His rise to international fame was attributed to the eagerness of South Koreans to embrace new technology and their almost obsessive and fiercely nationalistic desire to become the number-one nation in the world, as exemplified by the South Korean computer chip and shipping industries.

In June 2005 an investigative reporting program of MBC, a major broadcaster in South Korea, received a tip that Hwang's research team may have violated ethical codes and that his 2005 paper in *Science* on tailor-made stem cells was fraudulent. Since November 2005, Hwang's research had been questioned publicly. On 13 November Gerald Schatten, a U.S. professor and a partner in Hwang's research, announced that he had cut all ties with Hwang because he suspected unethical research conduct. On 22 November, MBC broadcast a program which included strong evidence that Hwang's research team had used ova extracted from its junior researchers. Two days later Hwang admitted ethical violations and said that he would resign from all public posts.

In December 2005 the scandal heated up further. On 14 December Schatten asked *Science* to remove his name from the list of coauthors of the 2005 paper.

The next day, MBC aired a follow-up program on Hwang's work, questioning the authenticity of the research itself. On 16 December, Hwang stated that he had asked the journal to retract the paper after its coauthors admitted partial data manipulation. Two days later, SNU launched a probe into Hwang's research, and on 23 December 2005 the SNU investigating panel announced that Hwang had fabricated the entire paper that he had published in *Science* in 2005.

In early January 2006, the SNU investigators released their final investigative report, declaring that Hwang's research team was found also to have fabricated data included in the February 2004 *Science* article. The panel found, however, that Snuppy was indeed created from cloned stem cells of the donor dog, Thai. Meanwhile, the South Korean prosecution launched an investigation into the alleged swapping of cloned stem cells in Hwang's research. Editors at *Science* journal retracted the 2004 and 2005 articles after they saw the final report from Seoul. The yearlong scandal ended as a Seoul court handed down a suspended two-year jail term to Hwang on 26 October 2009.

Through Hwang's downfall, South Koreans belatedly learned a lesson that biotechnology was not the forum in which to play out its industrial policy ambitions. In a strategy envied by other developing countries, South Korea became one of the largest economies in the world by focusing national support on target industries and producing quick results. Unlike electronics or information technology, where the country excelled by building upon technology pioneered by others, biotechnology was a cutting-edge sector, teeming with critics and requiring a highly sophisticated regulatory system.

The Hwang U-sŏk scandal was likened in the scientific community to the "Sŏngsu Bridge collapse." The bridge, a jerry-built structure on the Han River in Seoul, collapsed in October 1994, claiming 32 lives. The greatest lesson that the stem cell scandal taught was that scientific research would progress only gradually and would rarely, if ever, generate remarkable results overnight.

A Credential-Fixated Society

In July 2007, the Sin Chŏng-a scandal, in which the academic credentials of the former college professor and up-and-coming art curator nicknamed the "art world's Cinderella," were revealed to be false, sparking a wave of revelations of fake diplomas that seemed to involve South Koreans in all walks of life, including professors, actresses, a cartoonist, and even a Buddhist monk. Sin was accused of fabricating a doctorate degree and other documents from Yale University and using them to secure a position as an art professor at Seoul's

Tongguk University in 2005. The scandal exposed South Korea's obsession with titles rather than merit, especially its serious tendency to excessively emphasize a person's educational background.

A credential-obsessed society prioritizes a person's educational background instead of his or her actual ability and career performance. In South Korea, degrees from top universities at home and abroad have had a profound impact on every aspect of life, from one's career to one's marriage prospects. South Koreans have tended to hold different attitudes toward a person after learning which school he or she attended and to rank schools and categorize them depending on their location and educational ranking. A majority of South Koreans have an inferiority complex regarding their credentials, and those who graduate from lower-tier schools feel much deprived. This has left universities in regional areas with fewer students and has led to less regional development. This tendency dates back to the traditional Confucian attitude in the pre-modern era and was strengthened following liberation in 1945 in the process of nation building and industrialization by a few elite groups.

In this pressured environment, students are forced to make the utmost efforts to get into prominent schools, but they are given only one final opportunity to gain admission to these schools—the national college entrance examination. Because a student's entire life depends on a single examination, school curricula have tended to focus on the subjects included in the College Scholastic Aptitude Test. The subjects that do not appear on the college entrance examination have either disappeared or occupied a shrinking percentage of the curriculum. Also, many parents claim that what their children learned at school is not enough to succeed in the national examination, which forces the parents to spend tens of thousands of dollars for tuition at private institutions. In this way, "education fever" in South Korea has made the private educational market prosper. Some students go to other countries for better educational opportunities, despite the huge costs. In the 2000s, about 2,000 students left South Korea every month, creating a serious invisible trade deficit. A 2007 OECD report showed that 7.2 percent of South Korea's GDP was spent on education.

Overly enthusiastic parents and a subsequent surge in private education costs have been just a small part of the social malady caused by the country's credential-driven society; another negative aspect is that the overall competitiveness of South Korean universities compared to overseas educational institutions has been undermined. Many different proposals have been made for reforming this credential-fixated society, but the most important step would be to change citizens' attitude and move beyond the belief that educational credentials are everything.

Hallyu

The term "hallyu," or "Korean wave," was coined by the Chinese media in 2001 to describe South Korea's export of pop culture products including one of its popular drama series, *A Jewel in the Palace*, as well as its music and popular singers, all starting in the late 1990s. After a while the Korean popular culture, which had affected millions of Chinese, expanded its popularity over other neighboring countries such as Taiwan, Hong Kong, Vietnam, Thailand, Indonesia, the Philippines, and Japan, and became a regional phenomenon. Since 2000 not only television dramas, music, and movies but also Korea's own traditional foods—such as *kimch'i*, a spicy fermented cabbage dish; *koch'ujang,* or hot pepper paste; and ramen, or instant noodles—and even electronic software have become popular in those countries. This regional success has propelled the more energetic introduction and circulation of Korean culture in other parts of the world, including North and South America, Central/West Asia, and Europe and North Africa. Although hallyu as a distinctive cultural phenomenon has seldom occurred in non-East/Southeast Asian regions, the introduction and presence of a growing Korean pop culture in those areas have occurred to an unprecedented degree. In this sense the Korean wave has been an elastic concept, broad in scope and in constant flux.

More amazing than the wave itself was that the people welcoming it were so attracted to Korean culture, as well as singers and individual actors in popular dramas, that they wanted to learn the Korean language and to visit Korea. In the 2000s, the number of foreigners who visited South Korea from Asian countries more than doubled. Travel companies in South Korea started competing for those visitors with a package that included the popular places where TV dramas took place. Hundreds of thousands of people from Japan, China, and other countries have already visited as a result of hallyu.

Historically Korea was thought to have been dominated culturally by China and Japan, but now it has been spreading its own culture abroad and has become a cultural leader in Asia. The transformation began with South Korea's democratization in the late 1980s, which unleashed sweeping domestic changes. As its democracy and economy have matured, its influence on the rest of Asia, negligible until a decade ago, has also grown. Since 1998 the South Korean government has gradually loosened its authoritarian cultural policy and, with transnational flows cultivated by its far-flung diasporic population, South Korea has created a dynamic and syncretic popular culture. The size of South Korea's entertainment industry jumped from $8.5 billion in 1999 to $43.5 billion in 2003. South Korea's export of cultural products exceeded $1 billion in 2005.

In China, South Korean movies and TV dramas about urban professionals in Seoul have presented images of modern lives, centering on individual happiness and sophisticated consumerism. They have also shown enduring Confucian-rooted values in their emphasis on family relations, offering the Chinese both a reminder of what was lost during the Cultural Revolution and the example of an Asian country that has modernized and retained its traditions. *Three Guys and Three Girls"* and *Three Friends* were South Korea's homegrown version of the U.S. TV show *Friends*. As for *Sex and the City*, its South Korean twin *The Marrying Type*, a sitcom about three single professional women in their thirties looking for love in Seoul, was so popular in China that episodes were illegally downloaded or sold on pirated DVDs.

Why did the Korean media industry have a chance to market its pop cultural products to other Asian countries and experience such unexpected success? Relatively free from political and historical burdens, Korean pop culture was considered in some countries a good alternative to the hegemonic and imperialist Western and Japanese pop culture. Moreover, it was sophisticated and interesting enough to appeal to Asian consumers with diverse preferences and tastes, and could provide something new and different to consumers bored with familiar and abundant Western and Japanese pop culture. Another attractive point was that, early on, Korean pop culture was reasonably priced.

This impassioned and rapid favoritism toward Korean culture has moderated previous negative thoughts about South Korea, such as, for example, that the country was male dominated, feudalistic, and conservative, and has also spurred sales of Korean consumer goods, with Korean car sales rising sharply in Taiwan and other countries in the 2000s. Simply put, the Korean wave has brought considerable political and economic benefits to South Korea.

THE FALTERING JUCHE STATE IN NORTH KOREA

The Last Years of the Kim Il-sung Period

With the dawn of the 1990s, North Korea had to struggle with unprecedented adversity. The collapse of global communism and the Soviet Union, in 1989–1991, imperiled the existence of the North Korean state. In this time of national crisis, North Korea staked its fate on the juche ideology; the demise of communism in Eastern Europe and the Soviet Union convinced Kim Il-sung that his independent policy of juche was correct.

Since the late 1970s the North Korean regime had become even more rigid than ever. The origins of North Korea's crisis in the 1990s were embedded in juche socialism itself, which caused a resistance to fundamental economic and political reform. In the early 1990s, Kim Il-sung and his son, Kim Jong-il, flatly refused to move toward Chinese-style economic reform and adhered inflexibly to an economic autarchy. As a result, the North Korean economy drastically worsened. The "socialist paradise" suffered consecutive years of economic decline, and North Korea's GNP, once on a par with that of South Korea, was estimated at one-sixteenth the size of the booming South Korean economy in the early 1990s, and the gap was growing rapidly. Despite such economic difficulties, both Kims exercised absolute authority over the poverty-stricken North Korean population.

In early July 1994 Kim Il-sung was preoccupied with preparing for the unprecedented summit meeting with South Korean President Kim Young-sam, which was scheduled to begin in Pyongyang on 25 July. But he died of a sudden heart attack on 8 July at the age of 82. Kim's sudden death greatly complicated the problems facing North Korea in the second half of the 1990s.

For the past many years, while South Korea has portrayed Kim Il-sung as a demon, a scoundrel, and a fraud, North Korea has glorified him as a demigod. In particular, the communist North continued to argue that Kim was *the* leader of all Korean independence fighters during Japanese colonial rule. Even South Korean high school history books, revised in 2002, credited him for his role in combating Japanese colonialism. Because the prime test of legitimacy for leadership in postwar Korea was one's record as an independence fighter against Japanese rule, Kim was able to secure legitimacy for power in his own way. But he failed in governing North Korea, providing neither "bread" nor freedom to the North Korean people. He never achieved his stated goal that North Koreans would be able to "eat rice and meat soup, wear silk clothes, and live in a tile-roofed house." Obsessed with the juche ideology, he virtually ruined the North Korean economy, and when he died, instead of a "socialist paradise," he left one of the poorest, most repressive countries in the world to his successor, Kim Jong-il. The "socialist paradise" has been widely seen abroad as a despotic regime that starves its own people. Kim Il-sung's greatest fault, perhaps, was that he failed to solve the chronic food shortages in North Korea.

Kim Jong-il's Succession

Kim Il-sung's death was the single most momentous event in North Korean politics in several decades and came at a time when North Korea was facing perilous crises. The very survival of the North Korean state was in question. With Kim Il-sung's death, his son, Kim Jong-il, succeeded him. The younger Kim's rule, in the three-year period of mourning (1994–1997), went smoothly, beginning with pledges of loyalty by the nation's power elite. This atmosphere of stability and continuity is easily explained by the fact that Kim Jong-il's succession had been long in the making. After his initial promotion to the inner circle at the Sixth Party Congress of the Korean Workers Party in October 1980, the next major step to succession came a full decade later, when he was made Supreme Commander of the Korean People's Army on 24 December 1991. Because the army was the real foundation of power in North Korea, this was a vital step. Following his father's death, Kim Jong-il immediately gained control of his country, but this was not officially confirmed until 10 October 1995. Kim Jong-il did not formally assume his father's offices, those of General Secretary of the KWP and President of the DPRK.

During the period of mourning, from 1994 to 1997, the less than charismatic Kim Jong-il ruled North Korea in accordance with the teachings of the departed Great Leader, *yuhun*. Kim Il-sung proved that he was omnipotent in death as well as in life. The younger Kim was determined to follow in his father's footsteps, and thus "Our Style Socialism" continued and was strengthened under his rule.

Kim Il-sung left his son a steeply declining economy. The fundamental cause of the decline was the inefficiencies of North Korea's centrally planned economy, along with extravagant military spending (some 25 percent of the GDP), and droughts and floods that pushed the economy into a full-blown crisis. Disastrous food shortages occurred as a result of the country's Stalinist-style collective agricultural system. From 1995 to 1998 about three million North Koreans, some 12 percent of the population, reportedly died of malnutrition. Major portions of the North Korean population survived primarily through the influx of food and other economic assistance from the international community, particularly from the United States, its "sworn enemy." North Korea has referred to this period of hardship as the "Arduous March," an apparent comparison with the "Long March" that occurred in the Chinese Civil War, when the Chinese communists fled Jiang Jieshi's nationalist forces, covering a distance of some 6,000 kilometers, or 3,700 miles.

The faltering of the juche state was dramatized by Hwang Chang-yŏp's defection to South Korea in early 1997. Hwang Chang-yŏp, known as the architect of the juche ideology, was then one of North Korea's prominent officials, but in the mid-1990s Hwang had been increasingly kept at a distance from Kim Jong-il. On 28 January 1997 Hwang left Pyongyang to make a keynote address at a symposium in Japan held by the pro–North Korean Federation of Korean Residents in Japan. On 11 February he arrived in Beijing for an overnight stop before returning to Pyongyang the following afternoon. There, upon deciding to defect, he took refuge at the South Korean consulate in the Chinese capital. To avoid humiliating North Korea, China forced Hwang to go to a third country rather than going directly from China to South Korea. On 20 April 1997 Hwang arrived in Seoul by way of the Philippines.[4] In a zero-sum struggle between the two Koreas, the defection of Hwang Chang-yŏp, the first high-level insider ever to desert, struck a serious political blow to North Korea.

Under these circumstances, Kim Jong-il finally took office as General Secretary of the Korean Workers Party on 8 October 1997. Four years earlier Kim had assumed the post of chairman of the National Defense Commission (NDC), which had been created in 1972 as an entity subordinate to the Central People's Committee. Initially the NDC included high-level officers empowered to formulate domestic and foreign policy, but later it had full authority to guide the work of national defense and security. By 1998, a constitutional amendment made the NDC "the highest post of the state," and in the same year Kim Jong-il was "reelected" as chairman of the body.

The Kim Jong-il Period

After the mourning period for his father, Kim Jong-il further consolidated his totalitarian grip on power. On 5 September 1998 the Supreme People's Assembly (SPA), in theory the highest legislative authority in North Korea, met for the first time since Kim Il-sung's death. As expected, it named Kim Jong-il chairman of the National Defense Commission, which was declared to be North Korea's supreme policy-making body. This marked Kim's decision to rule North Korea from a military post and suggested to outsiders a further militarization of the country's politics. The "military-first policy," intended to build a "powerful and great state," was officially adopted in North Korea. Kim retained the office of NDC chairman in 2003 and again in 2009. North Korea, under Kim's rule, declared that it would become a great, prosperous, and powerful socialist nation by 2012, the centennial anniversary of Kim Il-sung's birth.

Through the implementation of the military-first policy, Kim Jong-il tried to maintain the existing order, strengthen his regime based on personal authority, and consolidate control of military forces in order to prevent a coup against the state. Kim's military-first policy also increased the role of the Korean People's Army in daily life. Since the start of the Kim Jong-il era in 1997, North Korea's political system remained stable, and its economy also improved, mainly because of large infusions of foreign aid. Economic difficulties, particularly food shortages, however, were still the country's Achilles' heel. Despite strict internal travel restrictions, food shortages drove North Korean citizens from their authorized residences to seek food elsewhere in the country. The North Korean government had no choice but to ignore the illegal traveling that enabled people to eke out a living, and the result was a flow of information among the people about the nationwide crisis.

Amid chronic economic difficulties, since 2002 North Korea allowed some reforms that, in a sense, legitimized what was already occurring following the virtual collapse of the centrally planned economy: the state-managed rationing system was abolished, the foreign exchange rate was adjusted to a realistic level, and currency exchange was freed to strengthen consumers' ability to buy the necessities of life.

On 12 September 2002 the SPA passed a law to establish the Sinŭiju Special District. Because of its geographical proximity to the Chinese border, the Sinŭiju Special District was expected to play a central role in North Korea's bilateral economic ties with China. Contrary to North Korean expectation, however, the Sinŭiju Special District project did not go smoothly. The Chinese recommended to North Koreans that Kaesŏng, located just above the northern side of the DMZ, rather than Sinŭiju, would be an appropriate special district.

On 3 August 2003 North Korea held parliamentary elections to choose 687 deputies for the 11th Session of the Supreme People's Assembly and 26,650 persons for local parliaments who would serve for the next five years. In the first session of the new SPA on 3 September, Kim Jong-il, as noted earlier, was reelected chairman of the National Defense Commission. Kim Yŏng-nam was retained as chairman of the SPA Presidium, the ceremonial head of state. These elections were followed by a major reshuffling of the cabinet marked by a generational change and the infusion of reform-minded technocrats. The SPA appointed technocrat Pak Pong-ju, a former minister of the chemical industry, as premier, replacing the much older Hong Sŏng-nam. Significant changes were made in the economic team, with five of its members newly recruited. These pragmatic technocrats were expected to advance an economic reform program.

North Korea's efforts to reform its crippled economy were reflected most in its push for joint projects with South Korea. On 26 January 2003 military authorities from the two Koreas signed an agreement allowing civilians to travel through the Military Demarcation Line, clearing the first obstacle to inter-Korean programs such as the reconnection of cross-border railways and roads, establishment of an industrial complex at Kaesŏng, and overland travel to Kŭmgang-san. Among the inter-Korean projects, the Kaesŏng Industrial Complex was particularly important. In August 2000, amid a mood of reconciliation and cooperation following the inter-Korean summit in June of that year, the North Korean Asia-Pacific Peace Committee and South Korea's Hyundai Asan Corporation agreed to develop the Kaesŏng Industrial Complex. The development began with a groundbreaking ceremony on 20 June 2003.

In 2004, to cope with the disastrous agricultural economy, the North Korean government formalized an arrangement whereby private "farmers' markets" were allowed to sell a wider range of goods and some private farming was permitted on an experimental basis. Since late 2004, however, for fear of the breakdown of the communist economic system itself, the North Korean leadership worked hard to turn the clock back, reviving the system that had existed until the mid-1990s and then collapsed under the pressures of famine and social disruption.

Finally, in October 2005, the North Korean government announced that it would revive the Public Distribution System (PDS), under which all major food items were distributed by the state. Private trade in grain was prohibited, and the only legitimate way to buy grain was by presenting food coupons in a state-run shop. Private dealing in grain occurred but on a small scale. By December 2005 the North Korean government terminated most international humanitarian assistance operations in the country. Instead, it called for development assistance only and restricted the activities of remaining international and nongovernmental aid organizations, such the World Food Program. External food aid came primarily from South Korea and China in the form of grants and long-term concessional loans. Firm political control remained the overriding concern of the Stalinist government, which inhibited the loosening of economic regulations.

Under these circumstances, on 1 December 2009, the North Korean govern-ment carried out a currency redenomination that replaced its practically worth-less currency at a rate of 1 new wŏn to 100 old wŏn. North Korea had already conducted five currency reforms, the last one in 1992, all of them during tran-sitional periods or when it felt it needed to tighten control. This latest currency reform was intended to tighten control as well as to manage climbing inflation, confiscate the savings of small businesses, and forbid the use of foreign money. The impromptu currency reform, however, caused severe food shortages. As a result, in late May 2010, bowing to grim reality, the North Korean regime, desperate to prevent mass starvation, lifted all restrictions on private markets as a last resort. This policy switch was an acknowledgment that the currency reform was a failure and that only capitalist-style trading could prevent wide-spread famine.

Amid chronically terrible economic conditions, Kim Jong-il chose his young-est son, Kim Jong-un, as heir to the family dynasty to rule the reclusive state. This second consecutive father-to-son succession was unique even among na-tions that called themselves communist. On 7 June 2010 the Supreme People's Assembly promoted Kim Jong-il's brother-in-law Chang Sŏng-t'aek, a key sup-porter of the younger Kim, to vice chairman of the National Defense Commis-sion, making him the number-two man in the North Korean leadership and signaling that the power transfer to Kim Jong-un was well under way. Further, the cabinet underwent a sweeping reshuffle, with premier Kim Yŏng-il, who had succeeded Pak Pong-ju in April 2007, replaced by Ch'oe Yŏng-nim, a close confidant of Kim Il-sung.

In late September 2010 North Korea officially started the dynastic power suc-cession process, making it the first country in modern history to allow power to be transferred to the third generation of the ruling family. On 28 September the Korean Workers Party, which convened its biggest extraordinary congress in 44 years, commissioned Kim Jong-un a four-star general of the Korean People's Army. The young heir-apparent, then in his mid-twenties, was also appointed a member of the Central Committee of the KWP as well as a vice chairman of the party's powerful Central Military Commission headed by his father. The senior military posts were essential to becoming the supreme leader under the country's "military-first" political system.

With his nation at the edge of starvation and collapse, Kim Jong-il died on 17 December 2011 reportedly of a heart attack. As expected, his son Kim Jong-un tipped to be North Korea's next leader. Even with this "Great Successor," as he was called by North Koreans, there was great possibility of a behind-the-scenes power struggle in this crippled and isolated Stalinist nation.

North Korea now stands at a crossroads, facing the danger of regime change or complete collapse from every direction. One of the most centrally planned and isolated economies in the world, the North Korean economy has been barely surviving. In 2006 North Korea's national income per capita in purchasing power parity (PPP) prices was roughly in the range of that of Zimbabwe, Uzbekistan, Bangladesh, and Sudan. Most remarkable is that in the post–Korean War era and into the mid-1970s, living standards were higher in North Korea than either in South Korea or China. Now, however, North Korea is far behind its rapidly growing neighbors.

Although its leadership calls it a "socialist paradise," in a number of obvious ways North Korea is a "failed state." As a truculent little pariah state, North Korea conjures an Orwellian image of grim dystopia depicted in the novel 1984. In the juche state, the repressed population ekes out a scanty existence under dire poverty and rigid dogma.

Because North Korea was identified with Kim Jong-il, it is essential to address his personality and abilities. A wicked tale about Kim Jong-il in recent years was that he sentenced a bodyguard and his family to years of hard labor because the hapless man used the ashtray in the Dear Leader's limousine and left the evidence behind. The media have been replete with scandalous anecdotes about him, describing him as a lover of slasher flicks and a womanizer with a personal nurse who had fashion-model looks. Sporting a retro bouffant hairstyle, he was also known as the world's single largest consumer of Hennessy cognac.[5]

Some foreign commentators and analysts, however, had a more sympathetic appreciation of Kim and his regime, viewing his perceived recalcitrance as a plaintive cry for understanding and help. The bottom line of this new school of thought was that he was a failed leader trying to come in from the cold and join the world. Regarding the North Korean nuclear crisis, for instance, they argued that, lacking normal relations, which from the North Korean perspective meant a continued threat of attack from the United States, Kim believed that he had no choice but to go nuclear.

These favorable comments do not justify the fact that Kim was a failed leader. Belying his caricature image as an eccentric playboy, he was a ruthless ruler who kept North Korea's brutal regime in place despite severe famine and virtual economic collapse. Obsessed with his father's teachings and his own lust for power, Kim failed to provide the North Korean people with material goods, and he had a devastating impact on the North Korean economy, including excessively operating the limited number of machines and wasting manpower by pushing for anti-economic campaigns such as the "Three Revolutions Teams Movement" and the "70-Day campaign." Moreover, he was irresponsible in casting the entire blame for his country's economic difficulties on his unfortunate subordinates. The North Korean system became even more centralized and autocratic under Kim Jong-il than it had been under his father. Kim demanded absolute obedience and agreement, and viewed any deviation from his thinking as a sign of disloyalty.

NORTH KOREA'S WEAPONS OF MASS DESTRUCTION PROBLEM

The First North Korean Nuclear Crisis

North Korea's nuclear weapons program first started under Kim Il-sung as a means to achieve hegemony over South Korea. After the collapse of the Soviet Union and the end of the Cold War in the early 1990s, North Korea shifted its focus to its own survival. When Kim Jong-il came into power, he promptly addressed the need for North Korea's security, which explains his stubbornness to continue the nuclear program that his father started. North Korea had signed the Nuclear Nonproliferation Treaty (NPT) in 1985, and in January 1992 it also signed the Nuclear Safeguard Agreement, allowing the International Atomic Energy Agency to inspect its nuclear facilities. In late 1992, however, the IAEA found evidence that North Korea had reprocessed more plutonium than the 80 grams it had disclosed to the international watchdog. In February 1993 the IAEA called for a "special inspection" of two apparent nuclear waste sites at Yŏngbyŏn, but North Korea rejected the inspection and announced, on 12 March 1993, that it would withdraw from the NPT. At the same time, North Korea made it clear that the nuclear issues could be resolved at a high-level meeting between the United States and North Korea. On 2 June, a few days before North Korea's withdrawal from the NPT was to take effect, Robert Gallucci, U.S. Assistant Secretary of State for Political and Military Affairs, and North Korea's Deputy Foreign Minister Kang Sŏk-chu began the first round of high-level talks in New York. As a result, on 11 June 1993, North Korea announced that it would not withdraw from the NPT.

The United States and North Korea held the second round of high-level talks on 14–19 July 1993 in Geneva. But the meeting produced no tangible results.

Thereafter, North Korea restricted international inspection of its nuclear facilities at Yŏngbyŏn, particularly its two undeclared sites (a fuel fabrication plant and a nuclear fuel storage facility). Frustrated by North Korean intransience, in March 1994 the IAEA presented the North Korean case to the U.N. Security Council. At this critical juncture, on 19 March, North Korea's chief delegate at the eighth North–South Korean talks at P'anmunjŏm threatened that, if war broke out between the two nations, Seoul, not far from the DMZ, would be a "sea of fire."

In May–June 1994 North Korea further aggravated the situation, by declaring that its nuclear facilities would never be opened to IAEA inspections, and it again threatened to withdraw from the NPT. On 15 June former U.S. president Jimmy Carter took on the role of peace mediator and entered North Korea through P'anmunjŏm. His visit to Pyongyang from 15 to 18 June appeared to be a turning point in the North Korean nuclear crisis, as it was reported that Kim Il-sung would not expel the IAEA inspectors from North Korea but would negotiate with the United States on the nuclear issues and have a summit meeting with South Korean President Kim Young-sam. Receiving new signals from Pyongyang, the United States sensed that it would be possible to solve the North Korean nuclear crisis through further negotiations.

The third round of high-level talks was convened on 8 July in Geneva. But the sudden death of Kim Il-sung on that very day caused an indefinite recess of the talks at the North Koreans' request. In the third round of talks, starting on 5 August, the United States concentrated only on settling the North Korean nuclear crisis, whereas North Korea wanted to settle all the issues pending between the two nations. Following a recess on 12 August, talks resumed on 23 September. After many twists and turns, the two sides signed the Agreed Framework on 21 October 1994. The heart of the agreement was a U.S. commitment to provide North Korea with various economic and diplomatic benefits. In return, North Korea would halt the operations and infrastructure development of its nuclear program; freeze all its nuclear activity and open its nuclear facilities to IAEA inspections; terminate its construction plans for 50-megawatt and 200-megawatt nuclear reactors; suspend the replacement of spent fuel rods; seal off a radiochemical experimental laboratory where spent fuel rods were reprocessed into weapons-grade plutonium; and place nuclear sites under IAEA supervision. To compensate North Korea for abandoning its nuclear weapons program, the United States promised to construct two 1,000-megawatt, light-water nuclear reactors under U.S. supervision and provide 500,000 tons of heavy oil annually to provide energy to North Korea until the new reactors were operational. The cost of the two reactors, estimated at $4–5 billion, would be shouldered mostly by South Korea, whereas the total cost for the substitute energy, estimated at $300 million annually, would be paid by the United States.[6]

Although the United States hailed the agreement, critics charged that it did not go far enough and left too many loopholes through which North Korea could clandestinely pursue a nuclear weapons program. The Agreed Framework did, at any rate, enable North Korea to attain its long-cherished desire to establish diplomatic talks with the United States. Emphasizing the importance of establishing normal relations between the two countries, North Koreans expressed their full satisfaction with the Agreed Framework.

"Soft Landing"

As the impending nuclear crisis waned, the North Korean issue became centered on its economic and, possibly, national collapse. U.S. Secretary of Defense William Perry likened North Korea to a disabled airliner rapidly losing altitude, and he called for seeking a "soft landing," a gradual and orderly transformation of the communist country through reform.[7]

In early 1996, to save itself from having to depend on its southern neighbor, North Korea asked the United States for aid, sending a message to the United States and South Korea that said, essentially, "Feed me or I'll kill myself." The United States was prepared to provide food aid to North Korea to ease the famine, as it feared that the prospect of mass starvation might make North Korea desperate, possibly prompting its hard-line war machine to launch a military strike against South Korea and the U.S. troops there.

By 1998 North Korea succeeded in developing a "Nodong" missile with an estimated range of up to 900 miles, capable of reaching all of South Korea and most of Japan. On 31 August 1998 North Korea test-fired a three-stage rocket, apparently the prototype of the Taep'odong I missile, at a launching site on the shores of the East Sea; the third stage was an attempt to launch a satellite. The satellite launch failed, but it raised concerns that North Korea had developed long-range missiles capable of striking Japan, Alaska, Guam, and the Northern Marianas with nuclear, biological, or chemical warheads.

The test launch of the Taep'odong I rocket shocked the United States, as just two weeks before the *New York Times* reported that U.S. intelligence had detected a suspicious site at Kŭmch'ang-ni that might be considered a secret North Korean underground nuclear weapons facility. The possibility that the

Taep'odong I rocket could be given a nuclear warhead convinced the United States that North Korea had secretly continued its quest for nuclear weapons and could now deliver them via long-range missiles. Soon the United States demanded that it be allowed to inspect the underground complex. North Korea demanded an "admission fee," in terms of food aid. After paying a price of 600,000 tons of food, the United States was allowed to inspect the Kŭmch'ang-ni excavation in late May 1999. A month later, on 25 June, the U.S. State Department announced at last that the site at Kŭmch'ang-ni contained no facilities related to nuclear weapons development.[8]

The test launch of the Taep'odong I missile, however, caused the Clinton administration to undertake a comprehensive review of U.S. policy toward North Korea. Known as the Perry Report, named after former secretary of defense William Perry who led the policy review team, the Perry initiative offered to normalize U.S–North Korean relations, end U.S. economic sanctions, and provide other economic benefits in return for North Korean concessions on the missile and nuclear issues.

The United States then pressed North Korea for talks concerning the nation's missile program. In meetings held in 1999, North Korea demanded $1 billion annually in exchange for a promise not to export missiles. The United States rejected North Korea's demand but offered to lift U.S. economic sanctions. This laid the groundwork for the Berlin agreement of September 1999, in which North Korea agreed to a moratorium on further missile tests in return for the lifting of major U.S. economic sanctions.

On 9–12 October 2000 North Korea's Vice-Marshal Cho Myŏng-nok, first vice chairman of the National Defense Commission and number-two man in North Korea, visited the United States, and gave President Bill Clinton a personal letter from Kim Jong-il inviting Clinton to visit North Korea and resolve differences between the two countries. Clinton, who would soon leave office, sent his secretary of state, Madeleine Albright, instead, and she visited Pyongyang on 23–24 October 2000.

During the visits by Cho and Albright to the United States and North Korea, North Korea proposed not to export medium- and long-range missiles and related technologies in return for "in-kind assistance" from the United States. It also offered to permanently ban missile tests and production above a certain range also in exchange for "in-kind assistance," as well as for help in launching commercial satellites. North Korea also promised to cease the deployment of the Nodong and Taep'odong I missiles. The negotiations between two countries stalled over the details of U.S. verification of a missile agreement and the nature and size of a U.S. financial compensation package.

A major problem in these negotiations was that Clinton would soon leave office, and there was insufficient time to expect a meaningful deal. In the final days of his presidency, Clinton could neither sign nor endorse any agreement on such weighty matters as the North Korean missile-related deal, and as North Korea dragged out the negotiations, it lost a rare opportunity for a rapprochement with the United States. The problem of North Korean weapons of mass destruction would further deteriorate in the next decade.

The Second North Korean Nuclear Crisis

The arrival of President George W. Bush on the scene in January 2001 dramatically changed U.S. policy toward North Korea. In a hard-line approach, Bush publicly expressed his distrust of the secretive North Korean regime and demanded "verification" and "strict reciprocity" as conditions for resuming negotiations on the control of weapons of mass destruction and improvement in U.S.–North Korean relations. In particular, the Bush administration stressed that the Agreed Framework, which had been hailed as a major U.S. foreign policy achievement by its predecessor, should be reviewed and possibly renegotiated.

North Korea was one of the countries that had been ostracized, for historical and ideological reasons, from the U.S.-led global economic and political system. Although North Korea often expressed a desire to join the system, though gradually, the Bush administration had only one answer to North Korea's gesture of reconciliation: "Disarm yourself, if you want food."

In February 2001 North Korea defied the Bush administration by threatening to renege on its promise to suspend missile testing and to freeze the nuclear program. Understandably North Korea wanted President Bush to start where his predecessor, Clinton, had left off. Ruled only in accordance with the "will" of its leader, North Korea found it hard to understand how and why an agreement or promise between the two countries should turn into scraps of paper merely because of a change in government.

According to U.S. officials, North Korea admitted having a secret uranium enrichment program when U.S. officials, headed by James Kelly, Assistant Secretary of State for East Asian and Pacific Affairs, visited Pyongyang in early October 2002. North Korea denied having made such an admission, but the United States retaliated by cutting off shipments of heavy oil to North Korea in December 2002. The United States also suspended construction of the light-water reactors, terminating it completely in November 2005. In carefully calibrated steps to force the United States to the negotiating table, North Korea reactivated the plutonium-based nuclear program that had been shut down in 1994 under the Agreed Framework by restarting the five-megawatt nuclear reactor, announcing that it would restart the plutonium reprocessing plant, and removing 8,000 nuclear fuel rods from storage facilities. In late December 2002 North Korea expelled from the country IAEA inspectors who had been monitoring the freeze of the plutonium facilities. In January 2003 North Korea announced its withdrawal from the NPT.

In early 2003 the United States proposed multilateral talks, which became six-party talks hosted by China. Although North Korea stepped up pressure on the United States for direct negotiations, the United States proposed a multilateral approach by countries in the region, based on its past experience which had shown that a bilateral approach did not work. South Korea, Japan, Russia, and China would join the United States and North Korea in the six-party talks.

The talks began in August 2003 in Beijing, and there North Korea reportedly warned the United States that it would prove it had nuclear weapons by carrying out a nuclear test. The United States discounted the warning as a negotiating tactic. When the talks ended with no tangible progress, North Korea blamed the United States for making a one-sided demand that North Korea first dismantle its nuclear weapons in a "complete, verifiable, and irreversible" manner, and it repeatedly vowed to boost its nuclear deterrent force for self-defense unless the United States changed its hostile policy.

The six-party nations began a second round of talks on 25 February 2004 in Beijing, and these also ended without success. Preventing further progress was North Korea's alleged highly enriched uranium (HEU) program, which, it turned out, was based on nuclear technology it had secretly received from top Pakistani nuclear physicist Abdul Qadeer Khan. On 4 February, Khan revealed that he had sold the technology for enriching uranium not only to North Korea but also to Iran and Libya. North Korea continued to deny the existence of its HEU program, while the United States insisted that North Korea's HEU program put bilateral relations more at stake than even North Korea's plutonium-based nuclear program. Indeed, it was North Korea's alleged admission of such a program to the United States in October 2002 that triggered the second nuclear impasse.

The third round of the six-party talks was held on 23–26 June 2004, also in Beijing. The United States proposed a detailed and gradual plan offering North Korea energy aid from South Korea, China, Russia, and Japan, along with a security guarantee and talks to end North Korea's economic and political isolation in exchange for North Korea's complete dismantling of its nuclear weapons program. The United States called for North Korea to abandon all nuclear programs, including the HEU program, and to take initial steps toward dismantlement during the initial three-month preparatory period. In its own proposal, the North countered by asking for substantial energy assistance from the United States and for immediate compensation, including lifting economic sanctions and removing North Korea from the list of countries sponsoring terrorism. North Korea continued to deny the existence of an HEU program. As before, there were no important breakthroughs.

After the third round of talks, both North Korea and the United States reiterated their positions, the former asking the United States to drop its hostile policy and the latter calling on North Korea to follow the path set by Libya, which had relinquished nuclear programs for economic rewards. Mutual animosity brought about strong verbal exchanges, with President Bush, during his presidential campaign in August 2004, calling Kim Jong-il a "tyrant" and North Korea labeling Bush a "political idiot." Under these circumstances the failure to hold a fourth round of talks came as no surprise.

The logjam finally seemed to break when the fourth round of talks was finally held in September 2005. In the Six-Party Statement of 19 September 2005, North Korea agreed to end its nuclear program in return for security and economic and energy benefits. But the statement did not address the core issue regarding the timing of dismantling North Korea's nuclear programs. The United States claimed before and after the statement that the dismantling process should be an early stage in a settlement process. North Korea strongly maintained that it would not dismantle its nuclear facilities until light-water reactors were physically constructed.

After the fifth round of talks, in November 2005, North Korea declared its boycott of the six-party talks, demanding that the United States rescind its punitive measures against the Banco Delta Asia in Macau, including its in-depth investigation of the bank's illegal transactions. The U.S. Treasury Department charged that the Banco Delta Asia was involved in illegal North Korean activities, including counterfeiting U.S. currency and drug trafficking. North Korea also proposed bilateral talks with the United Sates, but the United States would only agree to talks within the strict six-party framework. In short, the new approach of multilateral talks to cope with the North Korean nuclear weapons problem was an utter failure. To accomplish its goals, North Korea decided to raise the stakes in the nuclear poker game.

North Korea's Nuclear Test and Its Aftermath

On 9 October 2006 North Korea announced that it had successfully tested a nuclear weapon. This came six days after its Foreign Ministry issued a statement, on 3 October, declaring that it would conduct a nuclear test in the future. Other governments and private nuclear experts confirmed that a nuclear explosion had occurred somewhere in North Korea, a less than one kiloton plutonium (not a uranium) bomb, with about 3 to 4 percent of the explosive power of the Hiroshima and Nagasaki atomic bombs. A number of experts postulated that the test had been successful and that only a portion of the plutonium in the bomb had been detonated. Some experts speculated that North Korea might have tried to test the prototype of a small nuclear warhead. On 8 December 2006 U.S. President George W. Bush officially announced that North Korea had detonated a nuclear explosive device.

The nuclear test came after North Korea conducted multiple tests of missiles on 4 July 2006, in which a long-range Taep'odong missile failed but short-range Scud and medium-range Nodong missiles were successful. North Korea's missile launchings refocused U.S. attention on that country's missile program and demonstrated the communist country's apparent attempts to develop long-range missiles that could strike U.S. territories. U.S. officials claimed, in September 2003, that North Korea had produced the Taep'odong II missile in order to reach Alaska, Hawaii, and the U.S. West Coast. But the apparent failure of the Taep'odong missile launched in July indicated that North Korea had not succeeded in developing such long-range missiles. Evaluations of all seven of the short-range missiles by U.S. and other government intelligence agencies reportedly concluded, however, that North Korea had increased the accuracy of its Scud and Nodong missiles and had displayed the capability of North Korea's operational command and control systems for coordinating multiple missile launchings at diverse targets. North Korea's nuclear test also came amid its boycott of the six-party talks, which North Korea had justified since November 2005 by demanding that the United States end its pressure against foreign banks that accepted North Korea's money and allowed the country to have accounts.

Experts on North Korea speculated that the communist country probably would have several motives for conducting a nuclear test. The North Korean military might press for both missile and nuclear tests; North Korean leaders might be motivated to conduct a nuclear test to restore their country's "prestige" after the failure of the Taep'odong missile test; and, diplomatically, North Korea might seek to push the United States to accept bilateral talks and end its pressure on banks that, reportedly, was restricting the flow of foreign exchange to North Korean leader Kim Jong-il. North Korea also might attempt to embarrass the Bush administration before the November 2006 U.S. congressional elections.

International reaction to the nuclear test was harsh. Even China, North Korea's main patron and provider of aid, openly criticized the Stalinist country. The United States immediately condemned the nuclear test and called for a swift response from the U.N. Security Council. At the United Nations, the United States pushed for punitive sanctions and drafted a sanctioning resolution that was eventually adopted. On 15 October 2006 the U.N. Security Council passed a resolution that included sanctions and the possibility of coercive action against North Korea.

Following the nuclear test, strenuous Chinese diplomacy produced a meeting in Beijing between the chief U.S. and North Korean negotiators on 31 October 2006. Then the sixth six-party talks resumed on 18 December of that year. The negotiations ended on 22 December, without progress. North Korea refused to negotiate on the nuclear issue until the United States agreed to end financial sanctions.

In January 2007 the chief negotiators of the United States and North Korea held a meeting to resume the six-party talks in Berlin. In late January a meeting took place between U.S. and North Korean working-level negotiators to resolve the problem of the frozen North Korean assets held by the Banco Delta Asia. The two countries made significant progress at the Berlin meeting, raising hopes of further progress in the next six-party talks. The seventh six-party talks, held in February 2007, produced even more progress, and on 13 February the six-party nations reached an agreement on steps for North Korea to end its nuclear weapons development program. North Korea promised to shut down and seal its main nuclear facilities at Yŏngbyŏn within 60 days. For the initial steps, North Korea would receive 50,000 tons of heavy fuel oil or its equivalent in food and other aid. North Korea also had to provide a complete list of its nuclear programs and disable all existing nuclear facilities. In return, it would receive 950,000 tons of heavy fuel oil or the equivalent in food and other assistance. After 60 days, foreign ministers of six countries would meet to confirm the implementation of the agreement and discuss security cooperation in Northeast Asia. Separately the United States pledged to North Korea that it would resolve within 30 days a dispute over U.S. charges that Banco Delta Asia had laundered illicit North Korean money. This represented a retreat for the United States, which had previously insisted that the banking dispute was a law-enforcement matter that had to be treated separately from nuclear diplomacy.

The nuclear agreement was considered the first meaningful step toward North Korea's denuclearization since the six-party talks began in 2003. But doubts were expressed about proclaiming that the nuclear deal was a breakthrough for dismantling the North Korean nuclear weapons program, as the accord had incentives only and there was no punishment if North Korea failed to comply. The agreement left for future negotiations the question of what to do with North Korea's declared nuclear weapons, estimated to be as many as ten bombs for a stockpile of perhaps 50 kilograms of plutonium, plus the nation's suspected HEU program. Concerns were raised that North Korea would not agree to turn over its nuclear weapons, which it considered its main bargaining chip with the United States and Kim Jong-il's only insurance policy against being toppled as the country's leader.

In mid-March 2007 North Korea announced that it would begin shutting down its main nuclear reactor only after the United States lifted sanctions on North Korean funds that had been frozen in Banco Delta Asia since 2005. After concluding a year-and-a-half investigation into the bank, the U.S. Treasury Department returned $25 million in frozen North Korean funds, rumored to be Kim Jong-il's personal money. It was speculated that Kim had used the frozen money to lavish gifts on those in his inner circle. The settlement of the stand-off over the frozen funds seemed to clear the way for talks to focus on putting in place the nuclear disarmament accord concluded on 13 February 2007.

In mid-July 2007 North Korea shut down its main nuclear reactor at Yŏngbyŏn, readmitted a permanent international inspection team, and received the first shipment of 6,200 tons of heavy oil. The North Korean action had positive ramifications for the six-party talks that would determine the nation's second stage for scrapping its nuclear weapons program, held in Beijing on 18 July. As the next steps, North Korea, in return for large shipments of additional fuel oil, was to permanently disable the reactor so that it could no longer produce plutonium for additional nuclear weapons. Before it reached that step, however, it was also supposed to issue a complete declaration of all nuclear assets, including the number of weapons that it might have produced since 2003. At this point, many observers were skeptical about North Korea's commitment to complete denuclearization.

On 3 October 2007, in a joint statement closing the six-party talks, North Korea promised to dismantle all its nuclear facilities and disclose all its past and present nuclear programs by the end of the year, in return for 950,000 tons of fuel oil or its equivalent in economic aid. After the disabling of all nuclear facilities, the disclosure of its nuclear arsenal would be the next stage in a roadmap to make North Korea nuclear-free. As expected, North Korea did not submit a declaration of its nuclear program by that date. This demonstrated the country's penchant for tough bargaining. A sticking point in North Korea's declaration of nuclear capacity appeared to be whether it had an HEU program; North Korea denied that it had a clandestine program, but the United States claimed there was evidence to the contrary. Also disputed was how much weapons-grade plutonium North Korea had managed to accumulate. Furthermore, in late April 2008, the United States disclosed details of suspected cooperation between North Korea and Syria in building a nuclear reactor that was later destroyed by an Israeli air strike in September 2007. North Korea firmly denied any nuclear link between the two countries.

In early May 2008 North Korea conveyed the full details of its weapons-grade plutonium programs to the United States, and, in return, the United States provided more than 500,000 tons of food aid. Then, in late June 2008, North Korea submitted its declaration of nuclear programs. The United States welcomed the declaration and announced that, as promised, it would delete North Korea from the list of states sponsoring terrorism and would terminate North Korea's inclusion in the Trading with the Enemy Act. In a show of commitment to denuclearization, North Korea demolished an outdated cooling tower in its main nuclear site at Yŏngbyŏn on 27 June 2008.

North Korea was six months late filing the declaration of its nuclear programs and omitted much of the information originally demanded. The 60-page declaration did not address three key international concerns—a list of North Korea's nuclear weapons, a possible HEU program, and the suspected sale of nuclear technology to other countries, including Syria. This raised concerns that North Korea was really not on the path of abandoning its nuclear programs. In any case, the six-party nations failed to agree on a detailed inspection program to verify that North Korea had dismantled its plutonium-based program producing fissile material for nuclear weapons. The United States then postponed the removal of North Korea from the list of states sponsoring terrorism, as North Korea did not agree on a verification regime for the declared nuclear programs and stockpiles. On 10 October 2008, however, the United States removed North Korea from the terrorism blacklist in an effort to salvage the stalled six-party talks on ending the communist country's nuclear programs.

In a nuclear showdown, North Korea raised the stakes by conducting a nuclear test. The United States did not respond effectively to this deliberate nuclear gamble, and after North Korea's nuclear test, in October 2006, the United States scaled back its demands in order to keep negotiations going; the Americans returned North Korean funds that were linked to illicit activities, and they minimized concerns about the HEU programs and removed North Korea from the terrorism list.

Another Long-Range Missile and Nuclear Tests

In January 2009, when the Barack Obama administration was inaugurated, North Korea saw an opportunity for much improved relations with the United States. But it maintained tough negotiating positions, which included both a call for normalizing North Korean–U.S. relations before a final agreement to denuclearize and a demand that a final agreement should include elimination of the "U.S. nuclear threat" to North Korea. It was determined, in other words, to remain a nuclear-armed nation until the United States completely abandoned its "hostile policy" toward the Stalinist state. But the United States would not normalize its relations with North Korea until the latter gave up its nuclear weapons.

On 5 April 2009, in a symbolic defiance of the United States, North Korea test-fired a long-range ballistic missile in the guise of a satellite launch. Although North Korea argued that the launch of this three-stage rocket was designed to propel a satellite into orbit, much of the world viewed it as an effort to prove that North Korea had edged toward the capability of shooting a nuclear warhead on a long-range missile, namely, Taep'odong II. The launch did demonstrate North Korea's significant progress in rocket engineering, and Kim Jong-il's motivations for the launch were undoubtedly as much for domestic as for international consumption. He wanted to show his continued virility and defiance to the international community and underscore the atmosphere of crisis that warranted the people's continued sacrifice in the face of an external threat that only he could guard them against.

South Korea, the United States, and Japan were united in criticizing the rocket launch, whereas China and Russia urged restraint. But nine days after North Korea fired the rocket, the U.N. Security Council unanimously adopted a statement accusing the communist country of violating an earlier U.N. resolution barring ballistic missile activity. Responding to the statement, North Korea announced that it would resume its nuclear weapons program, never again participate in the moribund six-party denuclearization talks, and even conduct another nuclear test.

On 25 May 2009 North Korea declared that it had successfully conducted its second nuclear test—reportedly many times larger than the 2006 test—as a major provocation in the escalating international standoff over its rogue nuclear and missile programs. The test clearly informed the international community that the recalcitrant communist state would not give up its nuclear weapons program. Now, using its long-range missiles, North Korea could fire nuclear weapons at major U.S. cities, and although North Korea might be deterred from doing so in peacetime, in a war with its neighbors the regime might believe that a nuclear weapon demonstration would coerce the United States into abandoning its "nuclear umbrella" support for South Korea and Japan. The United States would be reluctant to retaliate with nuclear weapons if the superpower knew that North Korea could also use nuclear weapons against U.S. cities. To justify these risks, North Korea might have perceived that any war with its neighbors and the United States would be a war for regime survival.

The second nuclear test triggered a swifter, stronger, and more uniform wave of international condemnation than the first one had in 2006. Denouncing the U.N. Security Council Resolution 1874, which imposed financial, trade, and military sanctions on North Korea and for the first time called on U.N. member states to seize banned North Korean weapons and technology that were found aboard ships on the high seas, North Korea vowed to go ahead with uranium enrichment—a second track apart from plutonium to develop a nuclear bomb—and weaponize all the new plutonium it had produced. North Korea's announcement that it would process enriched uranium to make more weapons was an extraordinary public admission of active involvement in a program whose existence had been denied.

If and when North Korea actually begins the denuclearization process, there would be a long way to go for its completion. After disablement was complete and a declaration was accepted by the international community, a third phase would be needed to address all aspects of North Korea's nuclear program. Obviously, however, North Korea would not give up its nuclear weapons program without resistance. There are two schools of thought as to why North Korea clings to nuclear weapons development. One holds that North Korea has been trying to create a bargaining chip to induce the United States to offer economic aid and provide formal assurance that it will not attack the country. Another theory is that North Korea has determined that its security is best assured with a potent nuclear arsenal. North Korea's strategy has been a subtle blending of both aims, keeping its nuclear weapons program even as it seeks to improve ties with the United States.

For Kim Jong-il's North Korea, weapons of mass destruction, particularly nuclear weapons, were not only an essential security assurance and a bargaining tool, but they were also an irreplaceable instrument of domestic control and political survival. Therefore, North Korea has had no intention of giving up its nuclear ambitions, missile development, and other weapons of mass destruction. Furthermore, with Kim Jong-il's death on 17 December 2011, theft or the trafficking of North Korean nuclear material has become a source of concern for neighboring countries, specifically the United States.

NORTH–SOUTH KOREAN RELATIONS

Strained Relations

Many South Koreans have viewed North Korea with a complex mix of fear and kinship. While worrying about the North Korean military threat, they also have seen their northern neighbor as inherent to the historic problem of Korean nationalism. Before the 1990s South Koreans usually were fearful of North Korea, but since then the fear has increasingly been replaced by sympathy and kinship in the new environment accompanying the end of the Cold War and the near-collapse of the North Korean economy.

In the early 1990s the South Korean public, with confidence derived from the successful 1988 Seoul Olympics and continued economic growth, put considerable pressure on the government to make progress in inter-Korean dialogue. On the other hand, North Korea felt extremely vulnerable, especially after Kim Il-sung's death in July 1994. Reflecting the popular will, South Korean President Kim Young-sam took a conciliatory posture toward North Korea in his inaugural address on 25 February 1993, when he said that the allied nations could not overwhelm Korean "ethnicity." But since March 1993, as the

North Korean nuclear issue became serious, South Korean opinion of North Korea rapidly deteriorated. In trying to appease the South Korean electorate, President Kim reversed himself in June 1993 and said that he could not shake hands with North Korea if it had nuclear weapons. Like much of the South Korean public, President Kim's views were inconsistent. He alternated between a hard line against North Korea, calculated to bring about its early collapse, and accommodation to bring about a "soft landing" that would gradually lead to reunification. Because he usually pursued the former, relations between the two Koreas were generally acrimonious. He also often collided with the United States which favored accommodation, and so South Korean–U.S. relations were tense during his term of office.

North Korea's eccentric behavior contributed to the deterioration of the relationship between the two Koreas. In mid-1995, to cope with its chronic food shortages, North Korea quietly asked its southern brethren for help. In June of that year the South Korean government announced a donation of 150,000 tons of rice to North Korea in unmarked bags. But the rice aid only caused anger in South Korea, when a North Korean local official required a South Korean rice ship to hoist a North Korean flag when it entered port on 27 June 1995. In another incident, the North Koreans arrested a sailor on a South Korean rice ship for taking photographs of a North Korean port. These two preposterous events cooled South Korean sympathy for their northern neighbor; when his ruling Democratic Liberal Party suffered a crushing defeat in the local elections, held on 27 June 1995, in which he attempted to manipulate the food aid to North Korea for political gain, President Kim Young-sam reversed his posture on inter-Korean relations in favor of a hard-line stance.

Inter-Korean relations were further damaged by the abortive North Korean submarine incursion into South Korean territorial waters in September 1996. When a North Korean Shark-class submarine ran aground on the rocky coast of the East Sea and was abandoned by its passengers and crew on 18 September, South Korea mobilized 40,000 troops in a massive search for the North Korean intruders. When South Korean forces ended their intensive search in early November, almost all the infiltrators were killed in firefights and one was taken alive.

President Kim Young-sam declared that South Korea would freeze all contact with and assistance to North Korea until the communist neighbor apologized for the submarine incident. In an effort to appease conservative voters, he also declared a comprehensive review of all government policies on North

Korea. On 29 December 1996 North Korea issued a statement of "deep regret" for the submarine incursion and pledged that such an incident would not recur.

The Sunshine Policy

Beginning in late February 1998 the Kim Dae-jung administration pursued the "sunshine policy" to actively engage North Korea. Kim Dae-jung frequently invoked the Aesop fable, from which the policy derived its name, explaining that if North Korea felt the warm sun of beneficence from its southern brethren, it would move toward reform and opening. The Kim Dae-jung administration then made a number of conciliatory gestures and also lowered barriers to trade and other official and informal contacts.

As part of Kim's sunshine policy, Chŏng Chu-yŏng, founder of the Hyundai Group, visited North Korea and completed a deal, in October 1998, that would allow South Korean tourists to visit Kŭmgang-san in return for payments totaling $942 million over six years. Although tourism contributed in part to promoting more inter-Korean economic engagement, it was not profitable for Hyundai, which appealed for a bailout from the South Korean government. Moreover, the unrestricted supply of so much cash to North Korea generated severe criticism from South Korean conservatives.

Even as relations between the two Koreas apparently were improving, in June 1999 North Korea provoked a serious naval clash with South Korea in the Yellow Sea. Although officially ignoring the Northern Limitation Line (NLL) in the Yellow Sea, North Korea had tacitly recognized this maritime border. When it wanted to increase tensions with the South for its own purposes, however, its forces deliberately violated the NLL. After declaring its disapproval of the DMZ in April 1996, North Korea's intrusion across the NLL occurred more frequently. In 1999 North Korea claimed a more southerly maritime demarcation line, which would make the five South Korean–controlled islands a part of its territory. Disputes between North and South Korean vessels had often occurred in this area, and the issue of the NLL had periodically arisen during inter-Korean dialogue. In June 1999, a deadly skirmish at sea finally took place.

North Korea had sparked the naval confrontation on 13 June 1999 when it crossed the NLL. The communist country had not intended to wage a war but instead wanted to make the NLL a disputed issue through continuous military confrontation in the zone south of the maritime line. The confrontation, however, did escalate into a mini-war. Threatened by persistent ramming operations by the South Korean Navy, the North Korean patrol boats fired first. They were answered by a hail of fire from more modern and better-armed southern vessels, initiating a 14-minute gun battle. North Korea not only lost the battle and failed to make the NLL a disputed zone but also experienced its first defeat in battle since the Korean War.

In early 2000 Kim Dae-jung was determined to hold a summit meeting with Kim Jong-il at any cost. On 20 January 2000 he publicly proposed a summit with his northern counterpart to discuss issues of mutual cooperation, peaceful coexistence, and peaceful reunification. On 8 April the negotiators from both Koreas secretly agreed in Shanghai that a summit meeting would be held in Pyongyang on 12–14 June 2000.

After a last-minute postponement, Kim Dae-jung and Kim Jong-il began their three-day summit on 13 June. The two leaders discussed a variety of matters and issued a joint declaration, stating their intention to achieve reunification based on the Korean people's initiative, promptly settle humanitarian issues, build mutual confidence by promoting economic cooperation, promote inter-Korean dialogue between relevant authorities from both Koreas, and plan for Kim Jong-il's reciprocal visit to Seoul.[9]

Why did Kim Jong-il accept his southern counterpart's invitation to a summit? First, Kim Dae-jung skillfully prepared the climate for a meeting. Second, North Korea's desperate economic needs made a summit attractive. Third, Kim Jong-il expected that an inter-Korean summit would generate U.S. action to remove economic sanctions. Finally, he secretly received $200 million from the Kim Dae-jung administration. The opposition party protested that the Kim government had "bought" the summit. In mid-February 2002 Kim Dae-jung apologized to the South Korean public over the scandal, saying that he had sought only to promote "peace and the national interest."

After the summit, active inter-Korean contacts produced some tangible results, including exchange visits by separated family members and relatives, an end to propaganda broadcasts attacking each other, and plans to construct a massive industrial complex at Kaesŏng, where South Korean companies would employ North Korean workers. But this rapid rapprochement in inter-Korean relations failed to realize any substantive results. North Korea still posed a grave threat to South Korea's survival. Kim's sunshine policy lacked reciprocity for South Korea's concessions, and disillusionment and impatience with Kim's policy once again mounted.

Tensions between North Korea and both South Korea and the United States had already been raised when George W. Bush entered the White House in early

2001. The Bush administration expressed skepticism about the North Korean regime and demanded verification of North Korea's nuclear and missile development programs as well as reduction of its conventional weapons deployed along the DMZ. Bush also voiced doubts about the possibility of any meaningful engagement with North Korea. His hard-line stance heightened tensions in North Korea's relations with both the United States and South Korea. As a result, North Korea canceled planned talks with South Korea and suspended all cooperative programs. Having expected the summit to improve relations with the United States, North Korea reacted by freezing most North-South contacts in a gesture of protest.

The deadlock in the inter-Korean rapprochement process gave South Korean conservatives a hand in discounting the sunshine policy. Kim Dae-jung suffered a blow in September 2001, when the National Assembly voted to oust his unification minister. Kim's opponents claimed that the minister was trying to appease North Korea by conceding too much and receiving little in return.

North Korea's attitudes toward the United States and South Korea further hardened as the United States started a campaign against terrorism following the 9/11 attacks in New York and Washington in 2001. U.S.–North Korean tension peaked when President Bush labeled North Korea part of the "axis of evil" in January 2002 and condemned its attempt to develop weapons of mass destruction.

Kim Dae-jung's sunshine policy, which had already borne heavy criticism, was further attacked when another serious naval crash erupted in the zone south of the Northern Limitation Line in June 2002. On 29 June, one of the two North Korean patrol boats, which had crossed the NLL, opened fire at a South Korean patrol boat. Two South Korean naval ships returned fire immediately. The gun battle continued for about 20 minutes, until North Korean ships returned to its waters. One of the South Korean Navy speedboats was directly hit and was sunk. Six South Korean sailors were killed and 19 others wounded. The naval clash came on the eve of the closure of the World Cup soccer finals co-hosted by South Korea and Japan, and also at a time when inter-Korean reconciliation had been stalled. North Korea's provocation had been intentional, probably to seek revenge for the 1999 skirmish that had ended in its defeat.

Much of the South Korean public was enraged. The issue became even more politically explosive by the South Korean government's response to the North Korean provocation. News media close to the Kim Dae-jung administration toned down the incident, describing the naval clash as an accident and thus nullifying Kim Jong-il's responsibility, further intensifying criticism of the sunshine policy. Ultimately Kim Dae-jung was forced to issue a warning to North Korea, while pledging no retaliatory action and the continuation of its sunshine policy. The crisis was eventually resolved when North Korea officially expressed its regret over its aggression.

Despite the stalemate in North–South Korean relations, Kim Dae-jung stuck by his sunshine policy. He believed that whoever succeeded him should inherit his engagement policy. But his sunshine policy only made many South Koreans more skeptical of the United States, their longtime ally, than they were of heavily armed North Korea.

Continuing Engagement

Newly elected South Korean President Roh Moo-hyun pledged to continue his predecessor's high-profile efforts to engage North Korea. As a staunch advocate of engagement with the Stalinist regime in the North, Roh was prepared to throw the South Korea–U.S. alliance away and make common cause with North Korea. Because of increasing dissatisfaction with the sunshine policy among the conservative voters, however, he changed its name to the "peace and prosperity policy." Encouraged by South Korea's friendly attitudes toward its northern neighbor, North Korea stubbornly urged South Koreans to abandon their alliance with the United States and pursue national cooperation with their communist brethren.

From the start the Roh administration pledged to continue aid, trade, and reconciliation programs with North Korea, despite the latter's nuclear weapons policies. At the nuclear crisis talks, Roh hoped to soften both North Korea's position, as well as the U.S. hard line toward the Stalinist state; Roh's position was that the Korean peninsula had to be free of nuclear weapons and the crisis had to be settled through peaceful means, but he consistently opposed sanctions or other coercive measures against North Korea.

As the North Korean nuclear issue dragged on, public momentum in South Korea built in favor of moving forward with inter-Korean reconciliation. Many South Koreans were weary of the North Korean nuclear problem and recognized that the nuclear issue interfered with inter-Korean reconciliation; in more than a few cases, they downplayed negative stories about North Korea.

As the Roh Moo-hyun administration continued its engagement policy toward North Korea, South Korean society witnessed some unprecedented developments. The United States, which had publicly accused North Korea of being the world's most inhumane regime, enacted the North Korean Human Rights Act of 2004, which was intended to help North Korean refugees in China and promote human rights in North Korea. It passed by the U.S. House of Representatives in July 2004 and by the Senate in October. In September, before the bill's passage in the Senate, 27 lawmakers from the ruling Our Open Party delivered a letter to the U.S. Embassy in Seoul asking the Senate to vote down the bill. In July of that year, a South Korean Navy ship fired two warning shots at a North Korean patrol boat crossing into South Korean territorial waters. After North Korea angrily canceled inter-Korean military talks, the South Korean defense minister resigned and apologies were sent to North Korea.

Few South Korean overtures were reciprocated. In 2005 South Korea's Defense White Paper removed the term "main enemy," referring North Korea, and several attempts were made to end the National Security Law banning advocacy of North Korea's communist system. None of these moves was met with a wisp of concession from North Korea.

Meanwhile, however, economic cooperation between the two Koreas managed to progress. Opened in December 2004, the Kaesŏng Industrial Complex used South Korean power and telephone service and employed 4,100 North Koreans working for 15 South Korean companies. In the fall of 2005, 25 more South Korean companies built factories in the industrial park and 700 more were on a waiting list in quest of cheap labor. On the east coast, buses took an average of 19,000 South Korean tourists a month across the DMZ to the North Korean Kŭmgang-san special tourism zone. In 2005 inter-Korean trade surpassed $1 billion for the first time in the country's history.

In early May 2006 Roh expressed his eagerness to meet with Kim Jong-il and to propose many concessions, including massive economic aid for North Korea. Acknowledging the difficulty of pursuing its engagement policy toward North Korea while North Korea was confronting the United States over its nuclear weapons program, Roh hoped that a breakthrough could be found when a second inter-Korean summit was held. Clearly his approach contrasted sharply with the U.S. strategy of applying pressure on North Korea, especially as Roh had said that South Korea would place no conditions on its aid to North Korea.

North Korea responded to Roh by canceling scheduled test runs of a cross-border railway. Although the two Koreas agreed to relink a cross-border railway over their heavily fortified border, North Korea abruptly called off the test runs mainly because of resistance from its hard-line military. The rail crossings would have been deeply symbolic of generally warming relations between the two Koreas. The last train ran across the border in 1951, during the Korean War, carrying wounded soldiers and refugees to South Korea.

North Korea triggered an international furor in early July 2006, when it test-fired seven missiles, including a long-range Taep'odong II that plunged into the East Sea. While the United States and Japan led an effort for the United Nations to impose sanctions, South Korea withheld shipments of aid to North Korea. In the inter-Korean ministerial talks held in Pusan in mid-July 2006, South Korea suspended humanitarian aid, including a North Korean request for 500,000 tons of rice and raw materials for light industries, until Kim Jong-il agreed to return to the six-party talks. This suspension of economic aid to North Korea marked the first punitive action taken by Roh against North Korea following sharp public criticism at home for what many viewed as a weak response to the North Korean missile tests.

Despite South Korea's participation in international sanctions against North Korea, in early September 2006 Roh downplayed the threat posed by North Korea's missile tests. He said that the tests were conducted not for any actual military attack but for political purposes and that North Korea was developing nuclear weapons and missiles only as a "deterrent."

After North Korea announced, in early October 2006, that it had successfully conducted an underground nuclear test, the Roh administration decided to continue its two inter-Korean economic projects even though the U.N. Security Council adopted a resolution sanctioning North Korea on its purported nuclear test on 9 October. After reviewing the draft U.N. resolution, the South Korean government concluded that it was not necessary to stop the Kaesŏng Industrial Complex and package tours to Kŭmgang-san. These two huge inter-Korean projects were a major revenue producer for the Kim Jong-il regime, and it was feared that continuing them would take much of the sting out of any U.N. sanctions against the North.

On 13 February 2007, in the six-party talks, North Korea agreed to shut down its main nuclear reactor and eventually disable its nuclear program in exchange for energy assistance and security guarantees. Two days later Roh adopted an optimistic view regarding inter-Korean relations, saying that South Korea's aid to North Korea could produce beneficial effects similar to those of the Marshall Plan. But the two Koreas differed over how to rebuild relations that were badly frayed by North Korea's menacing missile tests and its subsequent nuclear test.

In early August 2007 the two Koreas agreed to hold a summit between Roh Moo-hyun and Kim Jong-il in Pyongyang on 28–30 August. But they postponed the meeting until 2–4 October ostensibly because of the flooding that killed hundreds of people and left more than 300,000 homeless in North Korea. On 2 October Roh walked across the heavily fortified border with North Korea on his way to the summit in Pyongyang, a symbolic gesture intended to demonstrate his enthusiasm for permanent peace on the Korean peninsula. The summit took place amid rare optimism at international talks on the North Korean nuclear programs but was somewhat overshadowed by North Korea's negotiations with other countries, particularly the United States.

Wrapping up the three-day talks, the two Koreas issued an eight-point joint declaration that mainly focused on economic cooperation projects. According to the declaration, the two Koreas agreed to create a "special peace and coopera-tion zone" in the disputed Yellow Sea encompassing Haeju, a port city in south-western North Korea, and its vicinity in a bid to push ahead with the creation of joint fishing, economic, and maritime peace zones, with shared use of Haeju harbor, the passage of civilian vessels via direct routes in Haeju, and joint use of the Han River estuary. They also agreed to open an air route for South Ko-reans to North Korea's Paektu-san, and South Korea pledged to accelerate the development of Kaesŏng and repair a railway connecting Kaesŏng with Sinŭiju, a North Korean town on China's border, as well as a highway between Kaesŏng and Pyongyang. In addition, South Korea would construct a shipbuilding com-plex in Namp'o, a port town southwest of Pyongyang. These economic projects were in keeping with South Korea's long-term goal of reducing the economic gap between the two Koreas, a necessary step toward reunification. Under the joint declaration, the two sides agreed to work toward replacing the Korean War cease-fire with a peace treaty, and pressing for a meeting with the United States and China, the other signatories of the 1953 armistice. This point ap-peared to be a concession by North Korea, which had long argued that South Korea should not be involved in any peace negotiations, as the signatories of the 1953 armistice were North Korea, China, and the United Nations led by the United States. North Korea also agreed to carry out the nuclear agreement reached on 13 February 2007. The joint declaration sought to allay the North Korean leadership's anxieties about the side effects of economic liberalization, stating that the two Koreas would regard each other with mutual respect and confidence, despite their differing ideologies and political systems. Although it paved the way for much more economic cooperation between the two Koreas, the declaration did little to concretely address North Korea's denuclearization pledge. It also omitted sensitive issues such as North Korea's human-rights problem and the disposition of abductees and prisoners of war, both of which prompted criticism that the pledge only served to bring the summit meeting to a smooth conclusion.

On 14–16 November 2007 the prime ministers of both Koreas met in Seoul to discuss implementing the broad agreement reached in the October inter-Korean summit. The two sides came up with comprehensive agreements during their meeting. The two Koreas also held the defense ministers' meeting in Pyongyang on 27–28 November to discuss measures to implement the agreements concluded in the prime misters' talks. In particular, the North and South Korean militaries agreed on ensuring cross-border security to boost business in the Kaesŏng Industrial Complex and tourism to Kŭmgang-san.

Meanwhile, presidential candidates from the conservative and progressive camps suggested sharply different approaches toward North Korea. The front runner Lee Myung-bak of the conservative Grand National Party called for more reciprocity from North Korea, putting top priority on denuclearization before economic aid. But a hard-core advocate of the sunshine policy, Chŏng Tong-yŏng of the pro-government Grand United New Democratic Party, stressed that inter-Korean economic cooperation and the resolution of North Korea's nuclear problem should be handled simultaneously. The election of Lee Myung-bak as president, on 19 December 2007, signaled the strong possibility that North–South Korean relations would enter a new phase.

A New Course in Inter-Korean Relations

The Lee Myung-bak administration determined to end its predecessors' engagement policy toward North Korea. For a decade, that policy had soothed nerves on the Korean peninsula by giving the truculent but poor Kim Jong-il regime large amounts of food, fertilizer, and trade concessions, all without conditions concerning nuclear weapons, missile proliferation, or human-rights abuses. The Lee government emphasized more reciprocity in its relations with North Korea and tied economic aid to North Korea's nuclear disarmament.

North Korea reacted with exceptional harshness. It clearly decided to teach its southern neighbor a lesson, demonstrating that engagement was possible on its own conditions, regardless of any offers of aid or concessions by the South. As a result, chronically hungry North Korea received virtually no food or fertilizer from the Lee government. An angry North Korea called Lee a "national traitor," a "sycophant of the United States," the leader of a "fascist regime," and an "anti-North confrontation advocator." The North Korean response included the expulsion of most South Korean officials from the Kaesŏng Industrial Complex, the launching of short-range missiles into the Yellow Sea, and the deployment of MIGs and army units provocatively close to the DMZ. North Korea also raised the stakes in the escalating tension by threatening to suspend all dialogue. In South Korea, Lee's critics argued that his new strategy would only antagonize the North Korean regime and undermine progress in inter-Korean relations.

In mid-July 2008 a South Korean female tourist was shot dead by a North Korean soldier at the Kŭmgang-san resort. South Korea demanded an official apology and a security guarantee from North Korea, suspending all tours to Kŭmgang-san. North Korea expelled all South Koreans from the mountain resort and imposed additional restrictions on South Korean passage through the Military Demarcation Line. North Korea further antagonized South Korea in mid-November 2008, when it declared that from 1 December it would shut down all overland passage through the Military Demarcation Line, close the Red Cross liaison office and all direct telephone lines between the two Koreas, and refuse nuclear sampling by the inspectors. The gamble could close down the Kaesŏng Industrial Complex entirely and jeopardize the six-party talks. North Korea's severing of inter-Korean relations, which was aimed to pressure the South to alter its conservative policy, stemmed from the belief that it would soon have the upper hand in relations with South Korea, as U.S. president-elect Barack Obama was open to direct talks with the communist regime. In January 2009 North Korea threatened to take an all-out confrontational posture against South Korea by declaring all military and political agreements between the two Koreas to be void.

With nearly all major cooperative projects stopped, the Kaesŏng Industrial Complex became the only surviving North–South Korean economic venture. In late March 2009, however, North Korea protested the 12-day joint South Korean–U.S. Key Resolve and Foal Eagle military exercises by blocking passage to the industrial complex several times. It also detained a South Korean worker in the economic zone for allegedly criticizing the communist regime and encouraging North Korean employees to defect to South Korea.[10] In May North Korea declared all contracts and regulations on the joint economic project invalid and asserted that if South Korea was not willing to accept new rules, then it was free to leave Kaesŏng. North Korean demands included raising wages of North Korean workers to levels paid to workers in China, shortening the lease period for the land from 50 years to 25 years, and requiring South Korean businesses to pay rent starting in 2010, instead of the previously agreed date of 2014. The communist regime, with this act of brinkmanship, used the industrial complex as a bargaining chip to force the Lee Myung-bak administration to make a choice—continue its North Korea policy or risk losing the Kaesŏng industrial project.

Under these circumstances, and angered by North Korea's second nuclear test, South Korea announced, on 26 May 2009, that it would fully participate in the U.S.-led Proliferation Security Initiative (PSI), a multinational effort begun during the George W. Bush administration to intercept shipments of nuclear weapons and other weapons of mass destruction by countries such as North Korea. For nearly six years South Korea had declined a U.S. invitation to take part in the PSI. Condemning South Korea for joining the global anti-proliferation effort, North Korea warned that it was no longer bound by the 1953 Korean War armistice and threatened military action against South Korea. But the Lee administration declared that it would not compromise in the face of North Korea's heightened threats.

In August 2009 North Korea suddenly made a peace offering to South Korea. It lifted the restrictions on overland travel across the border which it had imposed in December 2008, and it sent a delegation to South Korea to pay respects to the late former president Kim Dae-jung, who died on 18 August. These reconciliatory moves came after the Hyundai Group chairwoman's visit to North Korea in mid-August. When he met her, Kim Jong-il agreed to resume stalled inter-Korean projects, including tours to Kŭmgang-san.

Amid this apparent thaw in inter-Korean relations, however, on 10 November 2009 a brief naval skirmish erupted between the two countries, again raising tension on the Korean peninsula. A badly damaged North Korean patrol boat retreated to the north in flames. There were no South Korean casualties. North Korea might have started the skirmish as a message to U.S. President Obama that he should not ignore the communist country during his first visit as president to Northeast Asia.

On 26 March 2010 the South Korean patrol ship *Cheonan (Ch'ŏnan)* split in half after an unexplained explosion, leaving 46 sailors missing in the Yellow Sea off South Korea's west coast. When the stern of the sunken warship was pulled out of the water, the 46 sailors were all found dead. On 20 May South Korea formally announced that a North Korean torpedo had sunk the warship, basing this claim on the report by an international investigative team that studied the wreckage of the ship and other evidence collected from the scene. South Korea's announcement underscored the continuing threat posed by its northern neighbor and the intractable nature of the dispute between the two Koreas. South Korean President Lee Myung-bak vowed to take stern measures against North Korea, saying that his country would no longer tolerate North Korea's provocations and planned to change its military posture from passive defense to proactive deterrence. On 24 May, South Korea requested the U.N. Security Council to take up the issue, and the Council received broad international support for U.N. sanctions against North Korea. The North might have conducted the attack to avenge the apparent defeat of its navy in November 2009, but, as expected, North Korea angrily denied any blame and threatened a "holy war" against South Korea. It said that it would sever all relations with South Korea and would not engage in any inter-Korean dialogue or contact during President Lee's remaining tenure, thus heightening the risk of armed conflict. A month before, on 23 April, North Korea had confiscated real estate held by South Koreans at the Kumgang-san resort and declared that it would look for a new business partner unless South Korea resumed the tourist projects.

South Koreans had still not recovered from the bitter memories of *Cheonan*, when, on 23 November 2010, North Korea launched a deadly artillery bombardment on the South Korean island of Yŏnp'yŏng-do, near the maritime border of the Northern Limitation Line in the Yellow Sea, killing two South Korean marines and two civilians. South Korea immediately responded with artillery fire, bringing the two Koreas to the brink of a major conflagration. This highly calculated and premeditated North Korean provocation was intended to make the NLL a disputed issue and draw the United States to the negotiating table to formulate a peace treaty. It was also designed to pressure the terror-stricken South Koreans into urging their government to alter its hard-line policy toward North Korea. Both the sinking of *Cheonan* and the massive artillery barrage on Yŏnp'yŏng-do by North Korea displayed the stark reality of the Korean peninsula. Despite the death of Kim Jong-il on 17 December 2011, the prospects for improvement in inter-Korean relations seem hardly promising.

THE CHANGING ROK–U.S. ALLIANCE

North Korea's Influence on the ROK–U.S. Alliance

Since the early 2000s the South Korean–U.S. military alliance, which successfully deterred North Korean aggression for more than five decades, has been reassessed in the light of the practicality. The North Korean menace has been the strongest bond between the two countries, and South Korean–U.S. relations have often been dubbed as "blood-forged," referring to the vital U.S. help to the Republic of Korea during the Korean War. For more than half a century since the war, the United States has had no more stalwart ally in Asia than South Korea. Some 25,200 American troops are stationed in South Korea to protect against an invasion from North Korea, thus representing the continued unified purpose shared by the two nations. The traditional South Korean–U.S. allegiance has provided an indispensable security base for South Korea's phenomenal economic growth and democratization over the decades.

As the 2000s dawned, South Korea and the United States increasingly found themselves with divergent perspectives vis-à-vis North Korea and other emerging challenges to Northeast Asian regional security. In particular, the two allies gradually diverged in their respective perceptions of North Korea and the intentions of its leadership, which interfered considerably with the idea of a rock-solid ROK–U.S. alliance and the success in preventing renewed military conflict on the Korean peninsula.

Following the end of the Cold War in the early 1990s, a divergence emerged between the perceptions of South Korea and the United States regarding North Korea's strategic intentions and the prospects for accommodation and reform. In the mid-1990s there was an apparent dispute between South Korea and the United States over aid to North Korea. To drive a wedge between South Korea and the United States, North Korea bullied South Korea and courted the United States. The overall situation on the Korean peninsula made South Korea feel that the United States acted more like a neutral arbiter between the two Koreas rather than a close ally to South Korea. This was a difficult notion for South Korea to accept, as it was accustomed to viewing the United States as a "blood-forged ally."

As the Kim Dae-jung administration initiated its sunshine policy of rapprochement with North Korea starting in February 1998, South Korea did not dispute the Clinton administration's engagement policy toward its northern neighbor. The Bush administration's confrontational approach toward North Korea, however, dramatically changed South Korean perceptions of the United States and caused a policy and perception gap between the two allies over how to deal with North Korea. President Bush's public insults toward Kim Jong-il and his characterization of North Korea as a member of the "axis of evil" came at the very time when South Koreans were poised to advance the cause of inter-

Korean reconciliation. Bush's policy was widely criticized in South Korea and perceived as an obstacle to North–South Korean reconciliation.

South Korea's tenacious pursuit of engagement profoundly transformed South Korean perceptions of North Korea and the United States. With feelings toward North Korea softened, South Korea's affluent and self-confident population looked more in pity than in fear at its northern neighbor and yearned to help North Korea rather than punish it. Many South Koreans also did not view North Korea as a serious threat and believed that the United States exacerbated tensions on the Korean peninsula more often than North Korea did. Young Koreans, in particular, having grown up in an era where school textbooks no longer portrayed North Koreans as devils with horns and tails, voiced strong sympathy for North Korea and questioned the wisdom of their grandparents and parents in supporting close ties with the United States. They believed that North Korea was less of a threat to peace than their closest ally, the United States, which they described as an "evil empire" bent on dividing and weakening Korea.

North Korea observed the changing climate in the South Korean perception of its alliance with the United States, and so it framed the United States as a hostile bully and emphasized the need for both Koreas to cooperate with each other against the United States. North Korea also used the nuclear threat to turn the South Korean public against the ROK–U.S. alliance, often cleverly portraying U.S. policy in a negative light and attempting to show the United States as acting in a purely unilateral and self-interested manner when dealing with North Korea.

The U.S. Military Presence

The United States Forces Korea (USFK), which has symbolized the ROK–U.S. alliance, has two mandates: to protect South Korea from North Korean threats and to protect U.S. strategic interests in the Far East. Koreans with conservative views have tended to emphasize the first mandate, whereas those with progressive views have more likely stressed the second. But U.S. troops have served both functions. There was a time when North Korea was seen as a military power with a strong economy, and American forces were then seen more as protectors of South Korea. With North Korea on the verge of collapse, however, the USFK has been increasingly thought to be primarily focused on protecting U.S. interests rather than South Korea's security.

The U.S. military presence was always predicated on the continuing North Korean military threat to South Korea. If the threat from North Korea was no longer compelling, neither was the rationale for the ROK–U.S. military alliance. The USFK has been very successful in fulfilling its original mission of deterring another North Korean aggression, but, ironically, this success has made the U.S. military presence less necessary to South Korea. In particular, South Korea's engagement policy toward North Korea, pursued by the Kim Dae-jung and Roh Moo-hyun administrations, had the unintended consequence of making U.S. troops seem less important for South Korea's security.

All these factors together contributed to a growing debate in South Korea over the U.S. military presence, which was increasingly seen as a social irritant and a remnant of the almost forgotten Cold War. Given these doubts over the U.S. military presence, in early June 2004 the United States announced that it planned to withdraw 12,500 of the then 37,000 troops stationed in South Korea by the end of 2005. This would force South Korea to shoulder more responsibility for defending itself against North Korean aggression. The United States made it clear, however, that the troop reduction would be matched by more than $11 billion for modernizing U.S. defensive capabilities in South Korea. The cut in U.S. troops would include 3,600 soldiers from the 2nd Brigade of the 2nd Infantry Division already earmarked for redeployment to Iraq in August 2004. In October 2004, under pressure from South Korea, the two allies agreed to withdraw the 12,500 troops more slowly, in phases stretching to September 2008.

The troop reduction plan was geared at lowering the U.S. military's profile in areas where its presence had provoked resentment and become a troublesome political problem. Reducing the number of troops in South Korea, or at least their visibility, could remove a major irritant. The U.S. military presence was controversial among South Koreans for years, and the deaths of two Korean teenage girls run over by a U.S. military vehicle in June 2002 inflamed violent anti-American sentiment in South Korea.

Souring South Korean–U.S. Relations

Since the late 1990s the international and regional context of South Korean–U.S. relations underwent great and possibly fundamental changes at a rate outpacing the ability of officials to deal with them. South Korea's rapid progress in its own economic and political development over the decades resulted in greater national confidence and a desire for a more equal and mutually respectable relationship with the United States. With the emergence of heightened public criticism of the United States, the relationship with the chief ally became politicized in South Korea to an unprecedented degree. A whole range of contradictory developments unfolded to the point where South Koreans and Americans began to take a hard look at the future of their relationship.

The Relocation of U.S. Bases

In early 2003 the United States made an important decision that would alter the U.S. military presence in South Korea—the redeployment of the 2nd Infantry Division of some 14,000 troops from its positions just below the DMZ to "hub bases" about 75 miles south and the relocation of the Yongsan garrison, housing some 8,000 U.S. military personnel in the center of Seoul, away from the city. These U.S. personnel and bases were all to be relocated to the P'yŏngt'aek site, south of the Han River. The relocation of the 2nd Infantry division, scheduled to be completed by the end of 2008, would facilitate the Pentagon's plans to restructure the army's traditional combat divisions into smaller, mobile combat brigades. A 1991 agreement to relocate the Yongsan base had never been implemented. In July 2004 South Korea and the United States agreed to move the Yongsan compound, with South Korea assuming the estimated cost of $5.5 billion to relocate the base, by the end of 2008. In December 2006, however, it was revealed that the relocation of USFK bases to P'yŏngt'aek could fall three to five years behind schedule. The Yongsan garrison was expected to move to the new site by the end of 2011 and the 2nd Infantry Division at the end of 2013. The delay was caused by the failure to obtain all the necessary land for the transfer of the U.S. bases as a result of anti–U.S. protests by local residents and civic activists.

A Regional Balancer

In March 2005, President Roh Moo-hyun surprised neighboring countries, particularly the United States, when he announced a new foreign policy strategy in which South Korea would fulfill "the role of a balancer in Northeast Asia." Regarding the military aspect of this strategy, Roh said that South Korea would not be drawn into conflicts in Northeast Asia against its will. He expressed his determination to develop an independent armed force with its own command authority as a foundation for that goal. This set the policy to retrieve wartime operational control from the United States and enhance South Korea's capability for a self-reliant defense.

Roh's remarks indicated that South Korea as a "balancer," deciding the balance of power in Northeast Asia, would be locked into neither the tripartite "southern alliance" of South Korea, the United States, and Japan nor the opposing "northern alliance" of North Korea, China, and Russia, and that South Korea would take sides on an issue-by-issue basis. The South Korean government argued that the southern alliance, which had been created to counter the northern alliance in the Cold War period, had become an obstacle to peace and security rather than a bulwark, especially as the northern alliance had disintegrated.

Roh's balancing strategy gave the impression that South Korea would in effect break away from the trilateral security alliance with the United States and Japan and lean toward China, suggesting that the gulf between South Korea and the United States was rapidly widening. The United States, meanwhile, appeared to view South Korea's desire to become a balancing influence in Northeast Asia as an attempt to shake itself free of the alliance with its blood-forged ally. Ironically North Korea's Kim Jong-il stated that it was the United States that should provide the balancing power to stabilize Northeast Asia.

OPLAN 5029–05

Although the ROK Constitution stipulates that the nation's territory covers the entire Korean peninsula, the nation's sovereignty has never been exercised in the area north of the Military Demarcation Line, which is now under North Korean control. In the event that North Korea collapses as a result of internal turmoil, its entire area will automatically come under the jurisdiction of the ROK government and military, and reunification will have been achieved. U.S. military authorities, however, have a different idea. In a North Korean collapse, the United States would be concerned primarily about North Korea's weapons of mass destruction. The United States, therefore, would act to stop the shipment of plutonium, highly enriched uranium, or nuclear weapons out of the country, possibly to terrorists. It was imperative, therefore, that the U.S. commander-in-chief of the South Korea–U.S. Combined Forces Command should quickly take control of a North Korea in total collapse.

When U.S. officers at the Combined Forces Command began mapping out a scenario to prepare for the breakdown of the North Korean regime, the contingency plan, code-named "OPLAN (Operation Plan) 5029–05," essentially defined how the U.S. commander would assume command of all South Korean and U.S. forces on the entire Korean peninsula to secure North Korean weapons of mass destruction and establish public safety. In April 2005 South Korea's National Security Council vetoed the joint military plan which laid out military measures corresponding to various levels of internal trouble in North Korea, such as mass defection of refugees or an armed revolt leading to a regime change. South Korean security officials determined that the contingency plan could infringe upon Korean sovereignty and trigger a full-scale war. The South Korean NSC decision was publicly announced without prior consultation with the U.S. side. This unilateral action was seen as yet another sign of strained relations between the two allies.

Strategic Flexibility

In the spring of 2005 the issue of "strategic flexibility" for the U.S. forces in South Korea became a ticking bomb in the ROK–U.S. alliance. Under the program "Global (Defense) Posture Review (GPR)," the United States gave its overseas troops greater strategic flexibility to respond to regional military situations. As envisioned under the GPR, the United States intended to move South Korean–based forces elsewhere in an emergency, but Roh Moo-hyun, in March 2005, resisted the idea of strategic flexibility, saying that South Korea would never become embroiled in conflicts in Northeast Asia against its will. Roh's position was interpreted as a clear objection to turning the USFK into a regional expeditionary force, and the Roh administration even dubbed it the "Roh Moo-hyun doctrine."

The United States claimed that the idea of strategic flexibility resulted from changes in U.S. global military strategy that would also, in an emergency, allow the U.S. forces elsewhere in the region to be moved to the Korean peninsula to honor its security commitments. In other words, strategic flexibility presumably benefited South Korea as well as the United States. The Roh administration, however, highlighted only its objections to deploying the USFK in conflicts in Northeast Asia and did not point out the trade-off that American troops from elsewhere could be shipped to the Korean peninsula if they were needed. The Roh government's position therefore gave the impression that strategic flexibility meant nothing but sacrifices for South Korea to secure U.S. strategic interests. It was contradictory, however, to expect the dispatch of U.S. troops to the Korean peninsula from other regions in an emergency but oppose deployment of the USFK if emergencies happened elsewhere. The Roh administration was criticized for expecting something for nothing.

In January 2006 South Korea and the United States reached an agreement allowing the USFK to be deployed to trouble spots elsewhere but requiring consent from the ROK government if the United States intervened in a regional conflict. Thus, only with South Korean consent could U.S. forces in South Korea intervene in a flare-up between Taiwan and China or patrol near China if necessary. South Korea risked a further reduction of U.S. troops in the country if it refused the concept of strategic flexibility altogether.

The Recovery of Operational Control

Many South Koreans, as we have seen throughout the book, resented the U.S. military presence as a reminder of past dependency on the United States. The command structure, in particular, dating from the Korean War and giving the U.S. commanding general operational control over the bulk of South Korea's military forces, drew most of the public condemnation. Many South Koreans insisted that it was no longer appropriate for the United States to retain full operational control over their forces now that South Korea had evolved into a regional power. In early October 1994 South Korea and the United States agreed to return peacetime operational control of ROK forces to South Korea.

On several occasions, Roh Moo-hyun emphasized South Korea's need for independent operational capability in war or peace. The question of South Korea's recovering wartime operational control over its military forces from the United States was already put on the agenda of the "Future of the Alliance Initiatives" talks between the two allies in 2003, but no substantial discussions occurred. The shift of operational control involved many practical ramifications that could entail questions even about the necessity of the U.N. Command and, most important, the level of U.S. forces in South Korea.

In the summer of 2006, on a Roh administration initiative, South Korea and the United States agreed to work on a roadmap to establish a new joint command structure that would allow South Korea to exercise independent wartime operational control. The target period to complete the process was 2010 to 2012, but in August the United States announced that it planned to hand the control to South Korea at an earlier date, hoping to transfer complete command by 2009. Growing anti-American sentiment in South Korea and the deteriorating ROK–U.S. military alliance were behind the decision. South Korea, however, then proposed making the target year for transferring control flexible based on the security situation on the Korean peninsula. Finally, on 23 February 2007, South Korea and the United States agreed to dissolve the current ROK–U.S. Combined Forces Command and complete the transfer of control to South Korea on 17 April 2012. President Roh hailed the transfer as "regaining South Korea's military sovereignty." The date for the handover carried symbolic meaning, since 4/17, in U.S. parlance, inverted the date 7/14, which was significant because, on 14 July 1950, ROK President Syngman Rhee had sent a letter to

General Douglas MacArthur, UNC commanding general, stating that he would relinquish command authority to ROK forces.

The return of wartime operational control deeply divided South Korea, with progressives claiming that the 2012 date came too late, as South Korea would be unable to lead the process of instituting a peace regime on the Korean peninsula if it did not have full control of its military. The conservatives believed that it came too early, especially as the denuclearization of North Korea had not occurred. The transfer of control had to be viewed realistically, however, and so the agreement was reached because it met the needs of the two allies. It gave the United States the flexibility it needed for the rapid deployment of the USFK around the globe, and it enabled the Roh Moo-hyun administration to realize its goal of a self-reliant military alliance.

The MacArthur Statue

Since the late 1990s South Korea's engagement policy toward its northern neighbor had unleashed the "south-south conflict," deep ideological divisions in South Korean politics over the wisdom of the attempted engagement with North Korea and, inevitably, the alliance with the United States. Progressives wanted to pursue Korean reunification and national unity as a number-one priority in inter-Korean relations, whereas conservatives were cautious about reconciliation with North Korea and attached great importance to the South Korean–U.S. military alliance.

The "south-south conflict" is vividly demonstrated by the dispute over the MacArthur statue at Freedom Park on a hilltop overlooking the port of Inch'ŏn, Seoul's gateway to the Yellow Sea. The bronze statue commemorates General Douglas MacArthur's landing of U.S. forces on Inch'ŏn, on 15 September 1950, which turned the tide in the Korean War. The park was first established in the late nineteenth century as Man'guk, or All Nations, Park, Korea's first modern-style park. The name was changed in 1957 with the placement of the MacArthur statue. The inscription on the statue's pedestal reads: "We shall never forget what he and his valiant officers and men of the U.N. Command did for us and for freedom."

In 2005 the pledge to never forget appeared to be in danger of being undermined. In May pro–North Korean groups began a series of rallies at Freedom Park and other locations in Inch'ŏn, calling for the statue's removal and the withdrawal of U.S. forces from South Korea. Conservative groups immediately responded, holding their own rallies near the statue to oppose its removal. On

17 July 2005, when two large rallies were held at Freedom Park, one supporting
the statue's removal and the other opposing it, the police had to intervene to
prevent a physical confrontation between the two groups. On 11 September a
leftist group, "People's Solidarity," held rallies across South Korea to demand
that the statue be removed, and they clashed with the riot police trying to keep
them apart from conservative groups holding counter rallies. The Roh Moo-
hyun administration responded to those protesters who wanted to remove the
statue by suggesting that they should not press the issue, as it might erode South
Korean relations with the United States. In fact, public opinion polls showed
that only 10 percent of South Koreans supported removing MacArthur's statue.
Still, anti–U.S. sentiment ran high, whereas the tendency of decreasing enmity toward North Korea, which had begun with the June 2000 inter-Korean
summit, continued. Under these circumstances, the MacArthur statue would
remain controversial.

The Free Trade Agreement

The security issue was so dominant in past South Korean relations with the
United States that other crucial items on the legislative agenda often failed to
draw adequate attention from top South Korean policy makers. The Roh Moo-
hyun administration sought to expand cooperative ties with the United States
in other areas, notably in trade. With bilateral trade exceeding $70 billion a year,
building a new trading system with the United States was essential. The Roh
Moo-hyun administration believed that a free trade agreement (FTA), which
would eliminate many of the barriers to trade and investment, should be at the
center of the new trading system. Roh's pro-FTA policy was exceptionally well
received by his conservative opponents.

South Korea and the United States embarked on a quick march, deciding,
on February 2006, to draw up a free trade agreement within one year. The
first of eight formal negotiating rounds took place in June of that year. Working against an April 2007 deadline, South Korean and U.S. negotiators tried
to bind together two economies that ranked 13th and 1st in size, respectively,
worldwide. For Roh, a free trade pact would cement the alliance with the United
States, countering criticism that he had let South Korea drift into China's economic and political orbit. By jumping over China and Japan to win America's
first free trade pact with an Asian powerhouse, the unpopular president would
leave a strong legacy when he stepped down from office.

Finally, South Korea and the United States concluded a free trade agreement on 1 April 2007. The agreement was comprehensive, with calibrated exceptions made in a respectful bow to political reality. Most tariffs on bilateral trade would be removed within three years. Even in agriculture, where South Korean trade barriers were much higher than in other areas, many tariffs would be phased out over time and many quotas would be expanded; only rice would be exempted from some degree of liberalization.

South Korea and the United States still had considerable ground to cover on the issue of goods from the inter-Korean Kaesŏng Industrial Complex. South Korea wanted goods produced in the industrial park to be fully eligible for FTA preferences, whereas the United States wanted no benefits from the FTA to accrue to the Kim Jong-il regime. The two sides bridged their differences in Annex 22–C on "outward processing zones" (OPZS) on the Korean peninsula. The agreement did not accord trade preferences to goods produced in the Kaesŏng Industrial Complex, but it created a process for future consideration of such a development, if the economic and political situation on the Korean peninsula changed as desired by both countries.

After the conclusion of the trade pact, many South Korean activists staged a demonstration in Seoul, carrying large signs reading, "No to Korea–U.S. FTA," and shouting "FTA go away." They called the Roh administration's push for the agreement a "coup d'état," not an act of governance, and they pledged to nullify the bilateral bill and prevent parliamentary ratification of the agreement.

The free trade agreement between South Korea and the United States was generally expected to open a new era of opportunity and challenge that would determine the fate of South Korea's economy. The trade pact would harm the country's service and agricultural sectors, but in the long term the South Korean economy would gain more than it lost.

During the 2000s questions have been raised about the justification for, and sustainability of, a future ROK–U.S. alliance because of the transition in the global and regional strategic environment in Northeast Asia, differences between South Korean and American priorities and perceptions of the North Korean threat, and South Korea's domestic political transformation. Under these circumstances, during the Roh Moo-hyun administration, the alliance between the two nations faced considerable difficulties. It was strained to the extent that the foundation of the bilateral alliance could be threatened. The "blood-forged alliance" was in need of fence mending.

Return to a Strong Alliance

When President Lee Myung-bak took the oath of office, on 25 February 2008, he vowed to restore South Korea's "blood-forged" relationship with the United States by emphasizing free market solutions. In mid-April 2008 Lee, who was widely considered pro-American, took his first official overseas visit to the United States, where he met with U.S. President George W. Bush at the White House and Camp David. But Lee's pro–U.S. policy soon backfired, when concerns over possible public health threats from U.S. beef imports, commodities of central importance to the South Korea–U.S. FTA, caused a growing popular opposition to the Lee administration.[11] The public backlash against U.S. beef imports also complicated Lee's diplomatic attempts to foster a closer alliance with the United States. The popular protests increasingly shifted from their initial focus on public health to broader anti–U.S. and anti-Lee sentiments. Critics charged that the beef import deal was a "gift" from Lee to Bush, hastily arranged as part of Lee's strategy to develop closer ties with the United States. The anti–U.S. beef protest forced the two nations to suspend attempts to resolve several pending issues indefinitely. These sensitive issues included talks over the upkeep of U.S. forces in South Korea, the relocation of U.S. military bases, and the dispatch of the Korean police to Afghanistan.

During President Bush's visit to South Korea, on 5–6 August 2008, officials from both administrations announced that the outlook of the South Korean–U.S. alliance was shifting from its present scope of defending the Korean peninsula to a more "strategic and future-oriented structure" capable of contributing to global peace and prosperity. In the newly established structure, South Korea was expected to play a more central role in the Proliferation Security Initiative aimed at stemming the spread of weapons of mass destruction around the world.

After the Obama administration was inaugurated in January 2009, South Korea looked to bolster its military alliance with the United States, a position that received positive responses from the new U.S. government. At the G20 summit in London in April 2009, Obama hailed South Korea as "one of America's closest allies and greatest friends."[12]

In mid-June 2009 Presidents Lee and Obama held a summit in Washington to coordinate their efforts aimed at resolving North Korea's nuclear and long-range missile capabilities. Following the 16 June summit, the two leaders declared a "joint vision for the ROK–U.S. alliance." The new vision called for a broader "twenty-first-century strategic partnership" in the realms of politics, economics, culture, and other areas outside the security arena, and proclaimed "extended deterrence" in responding to North Korea's increasing nuclear threats. The term "extended deterrence" was intended as a declaration of South Korea's inclusion under the U.S. umbrella for U.S. protection against nuclear threats or attacks from North Korea. It referred to a comprehensive agreement that an attack against an allied nation would be construed as an attack on U.S. soil, justifying a response that would include mobilizing U.S. nuclear and conventional weapons and resources. Under the extended nuclear pledge, the U.S. military could retaliate against an attack on South Korea by deploying tactical nuclear weapons such as B-61 nuclear bombs carried by B-2/52 bombers and F-15E, F-16, and F/A-18 fighters, or Tomahawk cruise missiles launched from nuclear-powered submarines to strike North Korea's nuclear facilities. U.S. and South Korean leaders mainly discussed ways of deterring and countering lingering nuclear and missile threats, as North Korea heightened tensions on the Korean peninsula through a second nuclear test and a series of short-range missile launches.[13]

President Obama, during his visit to the ROK on 18–19 October 2009, confirmed a continuing U.S. commitment to defend South Korea against North Korean military threats. In response to U.S. security guarantees, South Korea pledged to assist U.S. military operations in Afghanistan, dispatching a Provincial Reconstruction Team (PRT), comprised of some 300 police and military forces, to the war-torn nation to protect civilians.

On 26 June 2010, South Korea and the United States agreed to postpone the U.S. transfer of wartime operational control to South Korea until 1 December 2015, given the volatile security situation on the Korean peninsula caused by North Korea's continued military provocations, specifically its long-range missile and nuclear tests in 2009. Tensions further mounted following the sinking of the South Korean Navy corvette *Cheonan*, which also prompted calls from South Korea to delay the handover. The agreement to postpone the transfer of OPCON came during a summit meeting between Presidents Lee and Obama in Canada while they attended a G20 summit. The decision to delay sent an effective message to North Korea about the strength of the ROK–U.S. alliance and the risk of starting war against South Korea.

In early December 2010 South Korea and the United States reached a deal on a revised Free Trade Agreement. Several rounds of talks were slow to overcome disagreements over U.S. demands for easier terms for car exports, but then

South Korea ceded some points in car tariffs in return for benefits for agricultural and pharmaceutical exports. The new FTA pact faced tough scrutiny by legislatures in both countries, as South Korea's main opposition Democratic Party accused the Lee government of making "humiliating" concessions to the United States on American-manufactured automobile imports and vowed to mount a national campaign in opposition.

In late 2011, a showdown between the ruling Grand National Party and opposition parties loomed over the parliamentary ratification of the new FTA agreement, as rival political parties showed little willingness to compromise. Finally, on 22 November 2011, the National Assembly passed the long-pending pact, with the GNP pressing ahead with the ratification process despite intense resistance from opposition parties. The ratification heightened political tension as the opposition decided to boycott all parliamentary sessions and fight back the ratification.

With the coming of the Lee Myung-bak administration in February 2008, South Korea and the United States had reinforced their ties, putting their alliance on a new path. For instance, immediately after North Korea's bombardment of South Korean territory (Yŏnp'yŏng-do) in November 2010, South Korea and the United States responded with joint naval exercises, including a nuclear-powered U.S. aircraft carrier in the Yellow Sea, intended to signal the allies' resolve to react strongly to any future North Korean aggression. During the Lee Myung-bak administration, the ROK–U.S. alliance again became extremely solid.

SOUTH KOREA'S RELATIONS WITH NEIGHBORING COUNTRIES

Relations with Japan

Koreans have described Japan as a nation that is close (in distance) and remote (in feeling), demonstrating that the relationship has never been smooth. Grievances arising from the colonial era and Japan's incomplete efforts to address its past have bred feelings of hostility toward Japan among South Koreans. Moreover, some Japanese, including politicians and intellectuals, have denied Japanese atrocities in Korea.

Wrangling between South Korea and Japan has often been triggered or escalated by several factors embedded in the East Asian context. Those factors, conspiring with sudden changes in the international environment, considerably undermined the very foundation of bilateral relations. First, as the Cold

War ended, the sense of common purpose that had suppressed nationalistic animosities within South Korea's anticommunist camp became increasingly weak. Second, the rise of China in the region eclipsed, in the eyes of South Koreans, the importance of Japan as a diplomatic partner, and vice versa. Third, North Korea's weapons of mass destruction programs and abduction of Japanese citizens elicited fundamentally different responses from South Korea and Japan.

Changes in domestic politics, moreover, have been just as destabilizing as the international factors. In South Korea, as an authoritarian regime gave way to more democratic administrations in the late 1980s, the government could no longer brush aside, in the name of "national interest," the people's demand for a more assertive stance toward Japan. At times the government even actively politicized such demands to its own advantage. Japan's domestic situation became more erratic as well. Muddling through the "lost decade," many segments of Japanese society, in the 1990s, sought to vent frustration through conservative politics. In the realm of foreign relations, this was translated into an "assertive diplomacy" befitting Japan's national stature. Japan's postwar generation of young politicians, in particular, felt uninhibited by its past history of aggressions and strove for a Japan that could proudly exhibit its presence with authority.

It does not suffice, however, to attribute the South Korean–Japanese cacophonous relations to regional settings and domestic politics. Equally important was the human factor; Japanese politicians and commentators frequently made volatile antagonizing comments on South Korean–Japanese relations, and South Korean audiences, for their part, overreacted. Leaders on both sides failed to recognize the importance of bilateral relations and strategically manage thorny issues such as the visit of Japanese Prime Minister Koizumi Junichiro to the Yasukuni shrine, where Japanese war heroes as well as alleged war criminals are honored; the Japanese government's approval of history textbooks which South Korea has claimed justified and glorified Japan's wartime military aggression against its Asian neighbors, including Korea; and disputes over the sovereignty of Tok-to. The Japanese leaders' apparent callousness to Koreans' historical wounds, along with their Korean counterparts' angry responses, ultimately strained relations between the two countries.

During the rule of Chun Doo-hwan and Roh Tae-woo, Korean-Japanese ties were relatively smooth. Then President Kim Young-sam, despite his initial pledge to work closely with Japan, became reckless and vowed to "fix their bad habits" and "teach Japan a lesson."[14] In contrast, his successor, Kim Dae-jung, established a milestone in bilateral relations by announcing a "twenty-first-century partnership with Japan," starting with a pledge to lift the ban against Japanese cultural products and enthusiastically promote civil and economic exchanges. His counterpart, Obuchi Keizo, was the perfect partner for Kim's drive, as the two leaders worked to improve relations, moving unresolved historical issues to the back burner. In October 1998 South Korea finally began its first phase of cultural exchanges with Japan, starting with movies, videos, and comics. The congenial atmosphere, however, drastically changed upon the inauguration of Koizumi Junichiro as Japan's prime minister in 2001. Criticized for his visit to the controversial Yasukuni shrine, noted above, and amid the history textbook imbroglio, Kim took a hard-line stance against Japan.

In the Roh Moo-hyun–Koizumi era, Korean-Japanese relations were especially unpleasant. Koizumi's insistence on paying respects to the spirits of warriors, including war criminals enshrined at Yasukuni, inflamed Korean passions. He also displayed a general insensitivity toward the feelings of Koreans and other Asians. Roh protested Japan's "glossing over" its atrocious colonization, whereas the Japanese believed that Roh was too willing to make concessions to North Korea and was profoundly hostile to Japan.

Like many of his predecessors, President Lee Myung-bak began his office, in February 2008, with energetic ambitions to put the historical row with Japan in the past and prioritize economic cooperation. His pledge to develop bilateral relations based on a "future-oriented" policy had already been stated by most of his predecessors, but before long the vicious cycle of controversy revolved again when Japan asserted its sovereign rights over Tok-to in its disseminated educational guidelines for young students. For Lee, with his vision of "pragmatic diplomacy," Tok-to was too tempting an opportunity to pass up. His chance came when, in late May 2008, a new guideline for schoolteachers issued by the Japanese Ministry of Education, Culture, Sports, Science, and Technology declared that Tok-to, called Takeshima in Japan, was Japanese territory. The guidebook had been widely used as the basic material in compiling textbooks, and whereas previous guidebooks did not mention Tok-to, the description of Tok-to as Japanese territory reflected Japanese right-wing concerns about the disputed islets even as the South Korean and Japanese governments were seeking cooperative ties.

In a revised guidebook for use in 2012 and beyond, however, Tok-to was not directly declared Japanese territory but was described as illegally occupied by

South Korea and should be treated "in a way identical with the Kuril islands." The guidebook indicated that although Kuril islands "are Japan's inherent territory, they are illegally occupied by Russia." [15]

Japan further angered South Korea by renewing its territorial claim over Tok-to in March 2010, when the Japanese ministry approved five elementary school social studies textbooks designating the South Korean islets as Japanese territory. One of the textbooks used by fifth graders in 2011 claimed that South Korea "illegally occupies" the islets. Previously only three of the five Japanese textbooks for elementary students had described Tok-to as Japanese territory, but now all five contained descriptions or maps indicating Japanese ownership of the islets. [16]

The Lee Myung-bak administration answered Japan's fresh claim over Tok-to by insisting that the islets in the East Sea symbolized Korea's national independence and territorial integrity. Given the persistent, deeply rooted friction between the two countries, particularly the clash over the sovereignty of Tok-to, the bilateral relationship has always been unstable.

Relations with China

On 24 August 1992 South Korea and China normalized their diplomatic relations, ending 43 years of antagonism. Over the years of diplomatic normalization, the relationship between the two countries has been "hot in economics but strange in politics." In other words, non-economic dimensions of the relationship have not caught up with the existing cooperation in economic dimensions.

Following normalized relations, the economic partnership between the two countries has grown increasingly strong as a result of geographical proximity and flourishing regional economic cooperation between Northeast Asian countries. Over the last decade China has become a land of opportunity for South Korea, with the vast Chinese market serving as a new direction for Korean companies with declining competitiveness in the U.S. market. Bilateral trade between South Korea and China that totaled a mere $6.3 billion in 1992 stretched 22.7 times, amounting to $145.3 billion by 2007. In 2003, China eclipsed the United States as South Korea's largest export destination. China also outdid Japan to become South Korea's top import market in 2007. The two-way trade made China Korea's top trading partner and biggest source of trade surpluses, and made South Korea China's third-largest trading partner. Investment was another pillar of this increasingly interdependent relationship, as South Korea's cumulative investment in China, amounting to $39 billion, already surpassed its investment in the United States. Tourism between the two countries also surged from 9,000 visitors in 1988 to more than 4.8 million in 2006, with over 300 flights a day, easily outnumbering those between South Korea and the United States.

Listing positive accomplishments alone, however, does not reflect the whole of this crucial yet complex bilateral relationship. China remained North Korea's biggest ally, and it also lost popularity among South Koreans when, recently, it distorted ancient Korean history in order to integrate the ancient Korean kingdoms of Old Chosŏn, Puyŏ, Parhae, and particularly Koguryŏ into its own history. In late May 2008 China ridiculed the South Korean–U.S. alliance as "a historical relic and a leftover of the Cold War," an outdated mechanism hardly relevant to today's international and regional security issues. China also stressed that it would continue to build friendly relations with North Korea. South Koreans replied by pointing out that if the ROK–U.S. alliance was a historical relic, then the China–North Korea relationship was also a relic, as the Treaty of Friendship, Cooperation, and Assistance between China and North Korea calls for automatic military involvement of the two parties in case of war. China's criticism reflected its unease with strengthening ties between South Korea and the United States that were bolstered by the Lee Myung-bak administration. Lee's predecessor, Roh Moo-hyun, had sought closer cooperation with China and looser ties with the United States.

South Korean–Chinese cooperation was mainly limited to the economy, trade, and investment. Whereas North Korea and China were as close as "lips and teeth," as the catchphrase has it, South Korean–Chinese relations were remote both politically and diplomatically. As China unilaterally supported North Korea's provocations against South Korea in 2010, South Koreans became discontent with China's supportive gestures and wished that China would, instead, be curbing its communist ally.

Bilateral relations between South Korea and China would continue to be strained. Although China remains an important trading partner for South Korea and therefore good relations with China are necessary, it is not South Korea's "friend" politically. China's strategic goals for dominance in Northeast Asia would not be fully compatible with South Korea's interests, as China seeks to draw South Korea out of the U.S. orbit and into its own. Under these circumstances, the core of South Korean diplomacy is its relationship with China, not North Korea.

Relations with Russia

After the dissolution of the Soviet Union, under President Boris Yeltsin North Korea was seen in Russia as a persona non grata. During this period Russian policy toward the Korean peninsula was strictly a unilateral rapprochement with South Korea. Russia's self-imposed alienation from North Korea and consequent loss of influence over the communist country harmed the prospects for improvement in North Korean–Russian relations. A change occurred in the second half of the 1990s, as Russia pursued new approaches to the Korean peninsula in order to recover its lost leverage in the region. It sought to improve its relations with North Korea and take a balanced position on the whole Korean peninsula.

At the same time Russia continued to strengthen its ties with South Korea, particularly in economic areas. The two countries worked together on constructing a bilateral industrial complex in the Nakhodka Free Economic Area in Russia's Far East and on the development of gas fields in Irkutsk. The two sides also agreed to cooperate on reconnecting a planned inter-Korean railroad with the Trans-Siberian Railroad. Russia expressed interest in becoming a conduit for South Korean exports to Europe, which now go by ship, by linking the Korean and Trans-Siberian railroads. South Korea and Russia cooperated in the space program as well. South Korea, with Russian assistance, launched its domestic satellites in 2009 and 2010, respectively, both of which resulted in failure. Politically, since 2003, the two countries have been participants in the six-party talks on the North Korean nuclear weapons issue.

South Korea and Russia have had several overlapping interests and considerable capabilities for developing cooperation in the areas of security, economic modernization, and regional stability. Regarding security, the two countries' common interests have included denuclearization of the Korean peninsula. Economically, the two countries have complemented each other as a major energy consumer and producer. On the issue of regional stability, the rise of China has aroused the keen interest of both South Korea and Russia in either preserving the existing power balance or making even more room for their own participation in shaping the region's future institutional architecture.

Following the end of the Korean War, the "maritime civilizations" of South Korea, the United States, and Japan clashed with the "continental civilizations" of North Korea, China, and the Soviet Union. After the U.S.–Soviet confrontation collapsed in the early 1990s, the Cold War structure disintegrated. Since the 2000s, with the rise of China as a global power, the situation has returned to the status quo ante.

PROSPECTS FOR REUNIFICATION

Koreans' Aspiration for Reunification

How, when, and even whether Korea can be reunified has always been the overarching issue confronting both North and South Korea. Deeply ingrained in the Korean psyche has been the idea that Koreans are a homogeneous people with a proud history dating back some 5,000 years, who have inherited the blood of Tan'gun, the mythical founder of the nation. Korea was a unified nation for more than 1,000 years following the unification of the Three Kingdoms by Silla in 676, or at least since the subsequent reunification of the peninsula under the Koryŏ kingdom in 936. Seen from this historical perspective, Japan's annexation of Korea in the first half of the twentieth century and its subsequent division since World War II are abnormalities in Korean history, and there is a strong desire to restore the nation as quickly as possible to its historical norm as a unified nation.

Pushing such sentiments to their logical extreme leads to calls for reunification at any price, creating a situation where words, such as "the people" and "unification," have become sacred and inviolable, and no opposition is allowed. North Korea and the pro–North Korean elements in South Korea have gone to this extreme. When a pro–North Korean professor in South Korea claimed, in 2005, that North Korea had initiated the Korean War in order to unify the peninsula, and he omitted the fact that North Korea wanted unification solely on its own ideological terms, the conservative camp fiercely opposed his statement.

On the origin of Korea's division, both Koreas have had different views. A commonly heard sentiment among South Koreans is that it made sense for Germany to have been divided, because it had fought a war and lost. But what was the justification for dividing Korea? It would have made more sense for Japan to have been divided, as it was also an Axis Power in World War II. Many South Koreans believe that the United States and the Soviet Union are responsible for the division of the Korean peninsula.

In contrast to this prevailing South Korean view, North Korea has placed the blame squarely on the United States, based on its own unique view of history. According to the North Korean view, the division of the Korean people has been the result of the U.S. military occupation of South Korea and its policy of invasion. The Korean people, who have lived as a homogeneous people for thousands of years, have been divided to this day by U.S. interference in Korean affairs. The issue of reunification is therefore an internal problem for the Korean people and a matter of domestic politics. Korea was not a defeated nation in World War II, and therefore no justification exists for the Korean people's right of self-determination to be violated by the United States. Such North Korean claims have been particularly effective in provoking anti-American sentiment in South Korea.

The question of reunification, of course, comes down to a choice between two different ideologies. Whereas South Korea advocates liberal democracy, North Korea wants its own juche ideology to be the leading philosophy of a unified Korea. North Korea has attempted to form a unified front in South Korea by emphasizing "the people" and "unification."

The Unpredictability of Reunification

Several questions arise pertaining to Korean reunification. When will reunification be achieved? What will it look like? Will the transition be relatively smooth, and, if not, what are the potential problems for Korea and its neighboring powers?

On an emotional level, reunification of the two Koreas would be the realization of the Koreans' long-cherished dream and the healing of wounds inflicted by the long division, as Koreans believe that people in both halves of the Korean peninsula share a common ethnicity. On a practical level, however, reunification of the two Koreas is beyond emotional desire and requires overcoming many barriers. Were unification to occur abruptly, South Korea would be unable to sustain the heavy economic burdens caused by a shattered North Korean economy, and this could lead to the collapse of both Koreas. For this reason, primarily, few South Koreans express wholehearted support for immediate reunification.

Peaceful reunification would be difficult even in the near or distant future. To implement significant changes, particularly the reunification of a divided nation, a sufficient period of time is required. The principle "T + 40" (trauma + 40 years) purports that meaningful changes can only be achieved when the generation stricken by the trauma moves on, leaving a new generation, one not directly traumatized by the dramatic changes, to emerge.[17]

Whether reunification comes quickly or is postponed indefinitely, how will it ultimately be achieved? Most likely it will occur through a highly risky process, perhaps by the sudden collapse of the North Korean regime or a war in which South Korean–U.S. forces are ultimately victorious or peaceful integration of the two Koreas. However it occurs, Korean reunification will decisively shape the future of the new nation. It may bring about a resurgence of Korean nationalism and self-confidence commensurate with the nation's growing national strength and increased international prestige. A reunified Korea will likely seek greater independence in its overall relationship with neighboring powers and will also undoubtedly reshape the strategic balance in Northeast Asia. Historically, Korea has been surrounded by great powers and still remains "a shrimp among whales." Almost certainly, the North Korean nuclear issue will finally be resolved only upon reunification.

Since the collapse of the Cold War in the early 1990s, competition between the two Korean states over which political system was superior virtually ended. South Korea deserves its claim to victory, for, in Korea's long history, no state has had stronger national power than the post-1990s Republic of Korea. While South Korea has prospered as a democracy, its northern neighbor remains at a crossroads, seriously threatened by regime collapse. Under these circumstances, no one can predict how and when Korean reunification will be achieved. Indeed, the time and manner of reunification may be determined by reunification itself. Perhaps reunification of both Koreas will resolve, in a single swoop, many inherent problems in Korea, including North Korea's weapons of mass destruction issue.

Chronology

Until 1 January 1896, Korea used the lunar calendar. On 9 September 1895, the Chosŏn kingdom changed the date of 17 November 1895 (by the lunar calendar) to 1 January 1896 (by the solar calendar). All dates since 1391 have been converted to the modern calendar.

700000 BC	Early Paleolithic culture emerges
100000 BC	Middle Paleolithic culture emerges
40000 BC	Late Paleolithic culture emerges
6000 BC	Neolithic culture emerges
2333 BC	Mythological founding of Old Chosŏn by Tan'gun
1122 BC	Mythological founding of Kija Chosŏn
1000 BC	Bronze Age emerges
451 BC	Puyŏ founded
431 BC	State of Chin established
300 BC	Iron Age emerges
194 BC	Wiman Chosŏn established
108 BC	Wiman Chosŏn falls to Chinese Han empire
108–107 BC	Chinese Han empire creates four commanderies (Nangnang, Imdun, Chinbŏn, and Hyŏndo) in northern Korea and southern Manchuria
75 BC	Koguryŏ people expel Hyŏndo Commandery to northwestern Manchuria
57 BC	State of Saro (Sŏrabŏl, later Silla) founded
37 BC	"New Koguryŏ" emerges
18 BC	Paekche emerges
AD 3	Koguryŏ moves capital from Cholbon (Hwanin) to Kungnae-sŏng
42	Six Kaya confederated kingdoms emerge
205	Chinese Gongsun clan takes control of Liadong region, establishes the Taebang Commandery south of Nangnang
244	Koguryŏ invaded by Chinese Wei forces led by Guanqiu Jian

260   King Koi of Paekche shapes national institution by appointing
      six ministries; creates 16 official ranks and prescribes official
      colors for attire
313   Koguryŏ drives out Nangnang Commandery from northern
      Korea and takes control of the former domain of Old Chosŏn
314   Koguryŏ occupies Chinese commandery of Taebang.
369   King Kŭnch'ogo of Paekche destroys Mahan federation,
      acquiring its territory
371   Paekche strikes Koguryŏ, killing its king, Kogukwŏn
372   Koguryŏ adopts Buddhism, establishes the T'aehak
373   Koguryŏ promulgates yulyŏng
375   Kohŭng of Paekche compiles *Sŏgi*, a history of Paekche
384   Buddhism adopted in Paekche
400   Koguryŏ under King Kwanggaet'o crushes an allied force of
      Paekche, Kaya, and Wae Japanese, and rescues Silla
427   King Changsu of Koguryŏ moves capital from Kungnae-sŏng
      to Pyongyang
433   Paekche and Silla forge marital alliance against Koguryŏ
475   Koguryŏ seizes Paekcke capital of Hansŏng, killing its king
      Kaero
475   King Munju of Paekche moves capital to Ungjin
494   Puyŏ surrenders to Koguryŏ
503   Saro renamed Silla
512   Silla general Isabu conquers "state" of Usan on Ullŭng-do in
      the East Sea
520   Silla king Pŏphŭng promulgates yulyŏng and institutes proper
      attire for officialdom
527   Buddhism officially adopted in Silla
532   Silla king Pŏphŭng conquers Kŭmgwan Kaya
538   King Sŏng of Paekche moves capital from Ungjin to Sabi;
      Paekche introduces Buddhism to Japan
545   Kŏch'ilbu of Silla compiles *Kuksa*, a history of Silla
551   King Sŏng of Paekche repossesses lower reaches of the Han
      River
553   King Chinhŭng of Silla drives Paekche out of the lower Han
      region, securing the Han River basin
554   King Chinhŭng kills Paekche king Sŏng at Kwansan-sŏng
562   King Chinhŭng destroys Tae Kaya, completing Silla's
      acquisition of the Naktong River basin
600   Yi Mun-jin of Koguryŏ compiles *Sinjip*, a history of Koguryŏ
612   Massive Chinese Sui forces invade Koguryŏ but suffer defeat
642   King Ŭija of Paekche captures Silla's Taeya-sŏng;
      Yŏn Kae-somun stages coup and emerges as a military
      strongman in Koguryŏ
643   Paekche occupies Tanghang-sŏng, Silla's outlet to China

645	Massive Chinese Tang forces invade Koguryŏ but suffer defeat.
660	Paekche destroyed by forces of Silla and Tang China
668	Koguryŏ destroyed by Silla and Tang.
671–676	Silla and Tang forces clash on Korean peninsula
676	Silla unifies Korean peninsula south of the Taedong River and Wŏnsan Bay
698	Tae Cho-yŏng, a former Koguryŏ general, establishes Chin (later Parhae) in Manchuria
713	Chin renamed Parhae
751	Pulguk-sa temple, Sŏkkuram grotto, and Tabo-t'ap and Sŏkka-t'ap pagodas built in unified Silla
768	Kim Tae-gong plots against King Hyegong of unified Silla, heralding the beginning of a fierce power struggle among the true-bone aristocracy
828	Chang Po-go of unified Silla establishes the Ch'ŏnghae-jin garrison on Wan-do, controlling and monopolizing international trade with China and Japan
846	Chang Po-go assassinated
851	Unified Silla abolishes Ch'ŏnghae-jin
889	First peasant rebellion in unified Silla
892	Kyŏnhwŏn revolts against Silla; proclaims himself king
900	Kyŏnhwŏn founds Later Paekche
901	Kungye establishes Later Koguryŏ
904	Later Koguryŏ renamed Majin
911	Majin renamed T'aebong
918	Kungye's T'aebong overthrown, and Wang Kŏn's Koryŏ founded
926	Parhae falls to Qidan Liao
935	Silla's last king, Kyŏngsun, surrenders to Koryŏ
936	Koryŏ destroys Later Paekche, ending the Later Three Kingdoms period and unifying Korean peninsula again
958	King Kwangjong establishes civil service examination system
976	King Kyŏngjong institutes Chŏnsikwa as a land reform
983	King Sŏngjong dispatches central officials to head the provincial administrative units, mok, for the first time in Koryŏ
993	First Liao invasion; Koryŏ overcomes the crisis through Sŏ Hŭi's diplomatic maneuvers
1010	Second Liao invasion; Koryŏ suffers initial losses but wins some battles
1018	Third Liao invasion
1019	Koryŏ forces, led by Kang Kam-ch'an, almost annihilate Liao forces
1076	Chŏnsikwa is finally completed.
1087	First set of wooden block print editions of Tripitaka completed

1107–1108	Koryŏ forces, led by Yun Kwan, carry out a massive assault against Nuzhens and construct nine forts in the occupied Hamhŭng plain
1109	Koryŏ returns region of the nine forts to Nuzhens
February 1126	Yi Cha-gyŏm revolts against King Injong
March 1126	Koryŏ enters into new suzerain-subject relationship with the Nuzhen Jin empire
1135	Myoch'ŏng rebels at Pyongyang
1136	Myoch'ŏng rebellion suppressed by government forces
1145	Kim Pu-sik compiles *Samguk sagi*, History of the Three Kingdoms.
1170	Military revolt, led by military officer Chŏng Chung-bu, erupts
1172	First popular uprising under military rule
1196	Ch'oe Ch'ung-hŏn seizes power, establishes military dictatorship
1200	Chogye School founded by Buddhist monk Chinul
1219	Ch'oe U succeeds his father, Ch'oe Ch'ung-hŏn
1231	First Mongol invasion
1232	Koryŏ moves capital from Kaesŏng to Kanghwa-do
1251	Second set of 81,137 wooden blocks of Tripitaka completed
March 1258	Kim Chun and Yu Kyŏng assassinate Ch'oe Ŭi, last ruler of Ch'oe house
December 1258	Mongols establish the Ssangsŏng ch'onggwan-bu to administer the territory north of Ch'ŏl-lyŏng pass
1259	Peace concluded with Mongols; Koryŏ accepts Mongol domination
1268	Im Yŏn kills Kim Chun, seizes power
February 1270	Im Yu-mu succeeds his father, Im Yŏn; Mongols establish Tongnyŏng-bu to govern area north of Chabi-ryŏng pass
May 1270	Im Yu-mu executed, ending military rule
June 1270	Rebellion of the Sam-byŏlch'o begins
February 1273	Sam-byŏlch'o rebellion ends
June 1273	Mongols establish T'amna ch'onggwan-bu to direct livestock raising on Cheju-do
1274	First Mongol expedition to Japan
1280	Mongols establish Chŏngdong haengsŏng in Koryŏ to launch second military campaign against Japan
1281	Second Mongol expedition to Japan
1285	Buddhist monk Iryŏn compiles *Samguk yusa*
1290	Territory under administration of Tongnyŏng-bu returned to Koryŏ
1294	Territory under jurisdiction of T'amna ch'onggwan-bu returned to Koryŏ
1356	Koryŏ, by military force, recovers territory under administration of Ssangsŏng Ch'onggwan-bu

1359	Chinese Red Turbans invade Koryŏ
1361	Red Turbans again invade Koryŏ
1364	Mun Ik-jŏm secretly brings cotton seeds to Koryŏ from Yuan
1376	Ch'oe Yŏng demolishes Japanese pirates at Hongsan
1377	Ch'oe Mu-sŏn persuades government to manufacture cannon and gunpowder; oldest extant book printed by movable metal type, *Chikchi simch'e yojŏl*, appears
1380	Yi Sŏng-gye annihilates Japanese pirates at Unbong
March 1388	Chinese Ming demands the "return" of Koryŏ's northeastern territory
April 1388	Koryŏ determines to invade Liaodong region of Manchuria
May 1388	Yi Sŏng-gye, deputy commander of Koryŏ forces, marches troops back from Wihwa-do, seizing power
June 1388	Yi Sŏng-gye deposes King U and enthrones King Ch'ang
February 1389	Pak Wi leads direct assault on Japanese pirates' lair on Tsushima
November 1389	Yi Sŏng-gye deposes King Ch'ang and enthrones King Kongyang
June 1391	Yi Sŏng-gye promulgates Kwajŏngpŏp, basic statute for land reform
August 1392	Yi Sŏng-gye ascends throne as T'aejo, ending Koryŏ dynasty and founding Chosŏn dynasty
November 1394	Chosŏn moves capital to Hanyang
September 1398	Yi Pang-wŏn kills his younger half-brother, the crown prince, and seizes power
October 1398	T'aejo abdicates throne to King Chŏngjong
February 1400	Yi Pang-wŏn defeats his elder brother, Yi Pang-gan, militarily
December 1400	King Chŏngjong abdicates throne to Yi Pang-wŏn who ascends the throne as T'aejong
September 1418	King Sejong ascends the throne
July 1419	Yi Chong-mu attacks Tsushima, den of Japanese pirates.
1426	Chosŏn opens three ports along southeast coast to Japanese, granting limited trade privileges
May 1433	Ch'oe Yun-dŏk and Yi Ch'ŏn establish four outposts along upper Yalu River
November 1437	Kim Chong-sŏ establishes six garrison forts in northeastern part of Korean peninsula.
September 1441	Chang Yŏng-sil and Yi Ch'ŏn invent the world's first pluviometer
October 1446	King Sejong completes han'gŭl, Korea's written alphabet
September 1451	*Koryŏ sa* compiled
March 1452	*Koryŏ sa chŏryo* compiled
July 1456	King Sejo kills six martyred subjects who opposed his usurpation of the throne and plotted to depose him
November 1457	King Sejo kills his young nephew, King Tanjong
November 1470	King Sŏngjong completes *Kyŏngguk taejŏn*

August 1498	"Literati Purge of 1498"
November 1504	"Literati Purge of 1504"
May 1510	Armed uprising by Japanese residing at the three ports of Pusanp'o, Naeip'o, and Yŏmp'o.
July 1517	Pibyŏnsa is established and empowered to deal with all matters of defense and security
December 1519	"Literati Purge of 1519"
December 1543	Chu Se-bung establishes the Paekundong sŏwŏn, the first of its kind, at P'unggi, Kyŏngsang province
September 1545	"Literati Purge of 1545"
September 1575	Factional strife between Easterners and Westerners begins.
May 1592	158,000 Japanese forces launch surprise attack on Chosŏn, heralding the start of war
June 1592	Japanese forces occupy Seoul.
June–October 1592	Yi Sun-sin gains decisive naval victories over Japanese navy, seizing control of the sea and separating Japanese forces in Chosŏn from their homeland
November 1592	Chosŏn forces, commanded by Kim Si-min, defeat major Japanese force at Chinju
January 1593	40,000-strong Ming Chinese relief army arrives in Chosŏn
March 1593	Chosŏn forces, under Kwŏn Yul, defeat major Japanese force at Haengju
September 1593	Japanese and Ming forces withdraw from Chosŏn
February 1597	141,000 Japanese forces again invade Chosŏn
August 1597	Yi Sun-sin dismissed as commander-in-chief of Chosŏn naval forces, replaced by Wŏn Kyun
August 1597	Yi Sun-sin reinstated after Wŏn Kyun's death
October 1597	Yi Sun-sin, with only 12 remaining warships, achieves victory over Japanese flotilla at Myŏngnyang
December 1598	Japanese forces in full-scale retreat, ending the war
February 1627	Later Jin of Manchus invades Chosŏn
April 1627	Chosŏn reaches agreement with Later Jin
January 1637	Qing, formerly Later Jin, invades Chosŏn again
February 1637	King Injo capitulates to Qing emperor Taizong at Samjŏndo
January 1709	Taedongpŏp enforced throughout the country, abolishing tribute tax system
August 1750	Kyunyŏkpŏp enacted, reducing "military cloth tax" from two cotton bolts to one per year
March 1801	"Catholic Persecution of 1801"
February 1805	Kim Cho-sun holds reins of government, heralding royal in-law government by Andong Kim clan
January 1812	Hong Kyŏng-nae rebels
August 1839	"Catholic Persecution of 1839"
May 1860	Ch'oe Che-u founds Tonghak

March 1862	Peasant uprising at Chinju; succession of riots follow in three southern provinces.
January 1864	Taewŏn'gun takes the reins of government, as son ascends the throne as King Kojong
February 1866	"Catholic Persecution of 1866"
August 1866	U.S. schooner *General Sherman* destroyed and crew members killed
October 1866	"Western Disturbance of 1866"; French force invades Kanghwa-do, carrying off gold, silver, and precious books
April 1871	Taewŏn'gun closes all sŏwŏn but 47
May–June 1871	"Western Disturbance of 1871"; U.S. naval expedition joins battle with Chosŏn force on Kanghwa-do
26 February 1876	Chosŏn concludes Treaty of Kanghwa (Friendship Treaty) with Japan, opens doors to outside world
22 May 1882	Chosŏn and the United States conclude Treaty of Peace, Amity, Commerce, and Navigation
19 July 1882	Revolt of old-line soldiers against reformative government
2 August 1882	Chosŏn government requests Chinese troops to suppress military mutiny
10 August 1882	Chinese forces arrive at Inch'ŏn
30 August 1882	Chosŏn and Japan conclude Treaty of Chemulp'o (Inch'ŏn); leaders of military mutiny are punished and Japan stations guards at its legation in Seoul
20 September 1882	Chosŏn sends delegation, headed by Pak Yŏng-hyo, to Japan to formally apologize; Chosŏn delegation takes present-day South Korean national flag, T'aegŭkki
6 March 1883	T'aegŭkki formally adopted as national flag
8 July 1883	Diplomatic mission, led by Min Yŏng-ik, dispatched to United States
26 November 1883	Chosŏn signs trade and commerce treaties with Great Britain and Germany
7 July 1884	Chosŏn signs trade and commerce treaty with Russia
4 December 1884	Members of Kaehwadang, led by Kim Ok-kyun and allied with Japan, stage coup d'état, killing and wounding several Sadaedang senior officials
5 December 1884	Progressive Kaehwadang members form new government, formulate program of reform
6 December 1884	Chinese forces attack and defeat Japanese forces that assisted in Kaehwadang coup
11 December 1884	Kim Ok-kyun and other Kaehwadang members escape to Japan
9 January 1885	Chosŏn and Japan conclude Treaty of Hansŏng (Seoul) for indemnities to Japanese victims of Kaehwadang coup and compensation for rebuilding Japanese legation

15 April 1885	Great Britain occupies Kŏmun-do off south coast of Chŏlla province to use against Russia, names it "Fort Hamilton"
31 May 1885	China and Japan conclude Convention of Tianjin, calling for troops of both countries to be withdrawn from Chosŏn and requiring prior notification when troops are to be dispatched to Chosŏn
4 June 1886	Chosŏn signs a trade and commerce treaty with France
1 March 1887	Great Britain withdraws its forces from Kŏmun-do
15 February 1894	Start of Tonghak peasant war
10–11 May 1894	Tonghak peasant forces defeat government troops at Hwangt'ohyŏn hill
31 May 1894	Tonghak peasant forces occupy Chŏnju, provincial capital of Chŏlla province
1 June 1894	Chosŏn government formally requests Chinese military assistance to suppress Tonghak peasant rebellion
8 June 1894	Chinese and Japanese forces land, respectively, at Asan Bay and Inch'ŏn
10 June 1894	Chosŏn government and Tonghak forces conclude the "Peace of Chŏnju"; Japanese forces enter Seoul
11 July 1894	Japan demands that Chosŏn carry out internal reforms
15 July 1894	Chosŏn refuses to yield to Japanese pressure and demands the withdrawal of Japanese forces
23 July 1894	Japanese troops drive the pro-Chinese faction out of the government
25 July 1894	Japanese warships attack Chinese forces at Asan Bay, initiating the Sino-Japanese War
27 July 1894	The new pro-Japanese government undertakes the Kabo kyŏngjang
15 September 1894	Japanese forces rout Chinese forces at Pyongyang, winning the Sino-Japanese War
16 November 1894	Tonghak forces again take up arms
22 January 1895	The Tonghak peasant war ends
17 April 1895	Japan and China conclude Treaty of Simonoseki, ending the Sino-Japanese War
8 October 1895	Queen Min assassinated by the Japanese
26 October 1895	Chosŏn government formally adopts the solar calendar
30 December 1895	Compulsory order issued for Korean males to cut their traditional Korean topknot
11 February 1896	Kojong and the crown prince make their way to the Russian legation in Seoul; Russia supplants Japan as the dominant power in Chosŏn; new pro-Russian cabinet formed
7 April 1896	Sŏ Chae-p'il (Philip Jaisohn) founds daily newspaper *Tongnip sinmun*
2 July 1896	Sŏ Chae-p'il establishes Independence Club

20 February 1897	Kojong moves out of Russian legation
12 August 1897	Chosŏn government repeals order to cut the Korean males' topknot
11 October 1897	Kojong proclaims establishment of Great Han Empire
29 October 1898	Independence Club convenes mass meeting of officials and citizenry at Chongno intersection
4 November 1898	Kojong orders dissolution of Independence Club
10 February 1904	Japan launches surprise attack on Russian naval forces at Port Arthur in Manchuria, initiating Russo-Japanese War.
23 February 1904	Japan forces Chosŏn to sign a protocol permitting it to intervene in its internal affairs and occupy strategic points throughout the country
18 May 1904	Chosŏn forced to declare all agreements with Russia void
21 August 1904	Chosŏn forced to accept foreign advisers in all important government ministries
22 February 1905	Japan forcibly incorporates Korean island of Tok-to into its territory, renames it Takeshima
29 July 1905	Taft-Katsura Memorandum provides for secret understanding of U.S. recognition of Japan's paramount interests in Chosŏn in return for Japanese recognition of U.S special interests in the Philippines
12 August 1905	Great Britain recognizes Japan's special interests in Chosŏn
5 September 1905	Treaty of Portsmouth officially ends Russo-Japanese War
17 November 1905	Chosŏn signs Treaty of 1905, putting Japan in charge of Chosŏn's foreign affairs
2 March 1906	Ito Hirobumi, chief mastermind of Japan's imperialism in Chosŏn, becomes first resident-general
29 January 1907	Koreans launch campaign to repay national debt incurred by Chosŏn government's borrowing from Japan
22 April 1907	Kojong dispatches secret envoys to Second World Peace Conference, scheduled to be held in The Hague in June
20 July 1907	Kojong abdicates throne to his son, Sunjong
24 July 1907	Chosŏn cedes to Japanese resident-general full authority over all internal matters
31 July 1907	Japan disbands Chosŏn army; widespread rioting and fighting erupts in Chosŏn against Japanese rule
26 October 1909	An Chung-gŭn assassinates Ito Hirobumi at the Harbin railroad station in Manchuria
22 August 1910	Japan and Chosŏn sign Treaty of Annexation
29 August 1910	Chosŏn becomes a Japanese colony
13 August 1912	Japanese Government-General launches land survey of Korean-owned farmlands
5 November 1918	Japanese Government-General completes land survey

8 February 1919	Some 600 Korean students gather at YMCA Hall in Tokyo demanding Korea's independence
1 March 1919	Declaration of Independence proclaimed, initiating March First Movement
13 April 1919	Korean nationalists establish Korean Provisional Government in Shanghai
10 September 1919	Saito Makoto, new governor-general, proclaims "Cultural Policy"
4–7 June 1920	Korean Independence Army, led by Hong Pŏm-do, defeats a Japanese army contingent in a battle at Fengwu-dong, southeastern Manchuria
21–26 October 1920	A Japanese force suffers crushing defeat by Korean independence fighters, led by Kim Chwa-jin, in a battle at Qingshan-li, southeastern Manchuria
17 April 1925	Korean Communist Party established.
10 June 1926	State funeral of the last Chosŏn king Sunjong; Korean students stage massive anti-Japanese demonstrations, initiating the "10 June Manse Movement"
15 February 1927	Right- and left-wing Korean nationalists form a united nationalist organization, the Sin'ganhoe
27 December 1928	Korean Communist Party dissolved
3 November 1929	Kwangju Student Movement erupts
15 May 1931	Sin'ganhoe dissolved
29 April 1932	Yun Pong-gil hurls bomb at high-ranking Japanese military officials at Hungkou Park, Shanghai, killing or wounding more than ten
1 April 1938	National General Mobilization Law promulgated, imposing mandatory Japanese war conditions on Koreans
11 February 1940	Name Order, requiring Koreans to adopt Japanese names, goes into effect
1 December 1943	Cairo Declaration, issued by the United States, Great Britain, and China, proclaims that Korea should become free and independent "in due course"
8 February 1945	At Yalta Conference, United States calls for a trusteeship for Korea of 20 to 30 years
26 July 1945	At Potsdam Conference, United States and Great Britain issue Potsdam Declaration, threatening Japan with "prompt and utter destruction" if it does not surrender
6 August 1945	United States drops atomic bomb on Hiroshima
8 August 1945	Soviet Union declares war on Japan; Soviet armies invade Manchuria
9 August 1945	United States drops atomic bomb on Nagasaki
15 August 1945 (Korea time)	Japan surrenders unconditionally to Allied powers; Korea is liberated; Yŏ Un-hyŏng organizes Committee for the Preparation of Korean Independence in Seoul

17 August 1945	Cho Man-sik establishes South P'yŏngan Province branch of Committee for the Preparation of Korean Independence
22 August 1945	Soviet forces march into Pyongyang and arrange merger of South P'yŏngan and Pyongyang branches of Committee for the Preparation of Korean Independence, forming the People's Political Committee, with Cho Man-sik as chairman
25 August 1945	Local branches of the Committee for the Preparation of Korean Independence authorized to take over administrative powers of Japanese Government-General by the Soviet command in Pyongyang
2 September 1945	Formal Japanese surrender signed
6 September 1945	Yŏ Un-hyŏng proclaims the establishment of Korean People's Republic in Seoul
7 September 1945	General Douglas MacArthur formally establishes U.S. control in Korea south of 38th parallel
8 September 1945	U.S. 24th Corps, commanded by Lieutenant General John R. Hodge, arrives in Korea
9 September 1945	Lieutenant General Hodge accepts formal surrender of Japanese forces in Seoul
11 September 1945	United States announces the creation of the United States Army Military Government in Korea; Pak Hŏn-yŏng reestablishes Korean Communist Party
16 September 1945	Rightists form Korean Democratic Party in Seoul
25 September 1945	Kim Il-sung arrives in Wŏnsan
10 October 1945	Governor-General Archibald Arnold denies legitimacy of Korean People's Republic, declaring that U.S. Military Government is the only lawful government south of the 38th parallel
16 October 1945	Syngman Rhee returns to Korea
25 October 1945	Syngman Rhee founds Central Council for the Rapid Realization of Korean Independence
17 December 1945	Kim Il-sung named first secretary of North Korean Branch Bureau of Korean Communist Party.
16–26 December 1945	Foreign ministers of United States, Great Britain, and Soviet Union meet in Moscow and agree to implement a five-year trusteeship by the three states, plus China; United States and Soviet Union establish joint commission to form an interim Korean administration, in consultation with the Korean people
29 December 1945	News of the Moscow agreement reaches Korea
31 December 1945	Anti-trusteeship strikes and demonstrations staged throughout Korea
2 January 1946	Korean Communist Party alters its stand and supports trusteeship
15 January 1946	South Korean Constabulary established

8 February 1946	North Korean Interim People's Committee established as governing body under the Soviet occupation, with Kim Il-sung as chairman
14 February 1946	U.S. Military Government creates South Korean Representative Democratic Council as advisory body
15 February 1946	Democratic People's Front formed in the U.S. zone
5 March 1946	North Korean Interim People's Committee initiates social and economic reforms, including land reform
20 March 1946	U.S.–Soviet Joint Commission has first meeting in Seoul
8 May 1946	U.S.–Soviet Joint Commission adjourns indefinitely
28 August 1946	North Korean Workers Party established
25 September 1946	South Korean railroad workers strike, initiating the "October People's Resistance"
1 October 1946	Serious rioting in Taegu
7 October 1946	Left-Right Coalition Committee, a moderate coalition, established by Kim Kyu-sik and Yŏ Un-hyŏng in Seoul
23 November 1946	South Korean Workers Party established
12 December 1946	South Korean Interim Legislative Assembly convenes
20 February 1947	North Korean People's Committee, highest executive governing body, created under Kim Il-sung
22 March 1947	Leftist labor union calls for general workers' strike throughout southern Korea
21 May 1947	The U.S.–Soviet Joint Commission reconvenes in Seoul
3 June 1947	In accordance with U.S. "Koreanization" policy, South Korean Interim Government established
10 July 1947	U.S.–Soviet Joint Commission collapses over which Korean political parties and social organizations should be consulted in pursuance of the Moscow agreement to form a provisional Korean government
19 July 1947	Yŏ Un-hyŏng assassinated
29 July 1947	Left-Right Coalition Committee collapses
17 September 1947	United States presents Korean issue before Second Session of the U.N. General Assembly.
14 November 1947	U.N. General Assembly adopts U.S.-sponsored resolution calling for general elections to establish a national government in Korea
23 January 1948	Soviet Union refuses admission into northern Korea by U.N. Temporary Commission on Korea, charged with supervising Korean elections
6 February 1948	U.N. Temporary Commission consults with Interim Committee of U.N. General Assembly
7 February 1948	South Korean leftists carry out sabotage and strikes in opposition to establishment of separate South Korean government
8 February 1948	Korean People's Army established in northern Korea

26 February 1948	Interim Committee of U.N. General Assembly adopts U.S.-sponsored resolution that the Temporary Commission observe elections for representatives to a national assembly in areas of Korea accessible to the Temporary Commission
22 March 1948	U.S. Military Government announces program to sell formerly Japanese-owned farmland
3 April 1948	South Korean communists initiate Cheju-do uprising
19 April 1948	North-South political leaders' conference convenes in Pyongyang
30 April 1948	North-South political leaders' conference calls for withdrawal of all foreign troops, establishment of a provisional all-Korean government, and peaceful unification of Korea by nationwide elections
10 May 1948	First general elections held in southern Korea
14 May 1948	Protesting the general elections, northern Korea cuts off electric power to southern Korea
31 May 1948	National Assembly convenes in Seoul
12 July 1948	First South Korean constitution adopted
24 July 1948	Syngman Rhee sworn in as South Korean president
15 August 1948	Republic of Korea (South Korea) formally established
25 August 1948	Elections in northern and southern Korea to choose representatives of a Supreme People's Assembly
9 September 1948	Democratic People's Republic of Korea (North Korea) formally established, with Kim Il-sung as premier
19 October 1948	ROK 14th Regiment revolts against government, initiating the Yŏsu-Sunch'ŏn rebellion
27 October 1948	ROK government forces suppress Yŏsu-Sunch'ŏn rebellion
20 November 1948	ROK National Assembly passes National Security Law outlawing communism
12 December 1948	ROK recognized by U.N. General Assembly as the only lawfully constituted government on Korean peninsula
27 December 1948	Soviet Union announces complete withdrawal of its troops from North Korea
10 February 1949	Korean Democratic Party renamed Democratic National Party
17 March 1949	North Korea and Soviet Union conclude cultural and economic treaties, and secret military assistance agreement
4 May 1949	North and South Korea commence border fighting along 38th parallel
21 June 1949	South Korean government promulgates land reform bill
25 June 1949	North Korea forms Democratic Front for the Unification of the Fatherland to forge a united front with Syngman Rhee's opponents
29 June 1949	United States withdraws last of its troops from South Korea

30 June 1949	North Korean Workers Party and South Korean Workers Party merge into Korean Workers Party, with Kim Il-sung as chairman
12 January 1950	In National Press Club speech, U.S. Secretary of State Dean Acheson excludes South Korea from America's defense perimeter in East Asia, casting doubts on U.S. security commitment to the ROK
19 January 1950	U.S. House of Representatives defeats Korea aid bill for 1950
30 March–25 April 1950	In visit to the Soviet Union, Kim Il-sung secures Stalin's approval for invasion of South Korea
3 April 1950	Land reform begins in South Korea, with most farmlands distributed in May and June
13–16 May 1950	Kim Il-sung visits China to secure Mao Zedong's approval for planned invasion of South Korea
30 May 1950	Second ROK National Assembly elections produce a majority of legislators hostile to Rhee government
7 June 1950	Central Committee of Democratic Front for the Unification of the Fatherland proposes all-Korean elections in August to elect a unified assembly
19 June 1950	North Korean Supreme People's Assembly proposes merger with South Korean National Assembly
25 June 1950	North Korean forces cross 38th parallel to invade South Korea, initiating the Korean War
27 June 1950	U.N. Security Council proclaims North Korean attack a breach of world peace and asks for South Korea's assistance
28 June 1950	Seoul falls to North Korean forces
30 June 1950	U.S. President Harry S. Truman commits American ground troops to Korea
5 July 1950	Task Force Smith takes action against North Korean forces just north of Osan
7 July 1950	U.N. Command established, with General Douglas MacArthur as commander
14 July 1950	South Korean President Syngman Rhee hands over authority of South Korean forces to General MacArthur
26 July 1950	"Nogŭn-ni railroad bridge incident," in which American soldiers kill several hundred South Korean civilians
15 September 1950	U.N. forces (X Corps) land at Inch'ŏn
28 September 1950	U.N. forces regain Seoul
1 October 1950	South Korean troops cross 38th parallel
7 October 1950	U.N. General Assembly sanctions advance of U.N. forces into North Korea
19 October 1950	U.N. forces take Pyongyang
25 October 1950	U.N. forces confront Chinese forces
24 November 1950	U.N. forces renew offensive toward Yalu River.
11 December 1950	Hŭngnam evacuation begins

4 January 1951	Seoul again falls to communists
14 March 1951	U.N. forces retake Seoul
11 April 1951	U.S. President Truman relieves General MacArthur of his command, replacing him with Lieutenant General Matthew Ridgway
23 June 1951	Jacob Malik, Soviet representative to the United Nations, proposes armistice negotiations
10 July 1951	Armistice talks begin at Kaesŏng
25 October 1951	Armistice talks resume at P'anmunjŏm
23 December 1951	Liberal Party formed as Syngman Rhee's ruling party
18 January 1952	ROK National Assembly rejects constitutional amendments proposed by Syngman Rhee providing for direct presidential election
25 May 1952	Syngman Rhee declares martial law in Pusan and surrounding regions
26 May 1952	More than 50 opposition legislators arrested in protest against Syngman Rhee's declaration of martial law
4 July 1952	ROK National Assembly passes compromise legislation allowing constitutional amendments for direct presidential election
5 August 1952	Syngman Rhee wins direct presidential election
18 June 1953	Syngman Rhee releases 27,000 North Korean prisoners of war
27 July 1953	Korean armistice signed at P'anmunjŏm
1 October 1953	ROK–U.S. Mutual Defense Treaty signed
20 May 1954	Syngman Rhee's Liberal Party obtains majority of seats in National Assembly elections
29 November 1954	In the "rounded-off" constitutional amendment, Rhee's proposal to abolish two-term limitations on the presidency passes in National Assembly
28 December 1955	Kim Il-sung enunciates the juche ideology
15 May 1956	Synagman Rhee reelected president; in separate vice presidential election, opposition candidate Chang Myŏn defeats Rhee's protégé, Yi Ki-bung
2 May 1958	In National Assembly elections, main opposition Democratic Party gains dramatic win, taking 79 of 233 seats
24 December 1958	National Assembly passes new National Security Law, virtually suspending democracy
15 March 1960	Rhee, unopposed, wins another presidential victory; Rhee's Liberal Party rigs vice presidential election to ensure Chang Myŏn's defeat, leading to violent protests
19 April 1960	April Student Revolution erupts
26 April 1960	President Rhee resigns; three days later leaves Korea for exile in Hawaii; First Republic ends
15 June 1960	ROK constitution amended to provide for a cabinet responsible to legislature

29 July 1960	Democratic Party wins overwhelming victory in National Assembly election
23 August 1960	Chang Myŏn elected ROK prime minister, inaugurating Second Republic.
16 May 1961	Major General Park Chung-hee stages coup, ending Second Republic
18 May 1961	Park Chung-hee forces general resignation of Chang Myŏn cabinet and reorganizes his military junta into Supreme Council for National Reconstruction
13 January 1962	South Korea announces First Five-Year Economic Development Plan (1962–1966)
17 December 1962	New constitution resembling that of the First Republic put to popular referendum and approved by a wide margin
15 October 1963	Park Chung-hee elected president by narrow margin
26 November 1963	Park Chung-hee's Democratic Republican Party wins majority of seats in National Assembly elections
17 December 1963	Park Chung-hee sworn in as president, inaugurating Third Republic.
22 June 1965	South Korea and Japan sign Treaty of Basic Relations, establishing formal diplomatic ties
29 July 1966	South Korea announces the Second Five-Year Economic Development Plan (1967–1971)
3 May 1967	Park Chung-hee wins another presidential term
8 June 1967	Democratic Republican Party obtains a two-thirds majority of seats in National Assembly elections, enabling it to pass constitutional amendments
21 January 1968	Squad of 31 North Korean commandos reaches northern edge of Seoul
23 January 1968	North Korean naval forces seize U.S.S. *Pueblo* in international waters off Bay of Wŏnsan
15 April 1969	North Korea shoots down unarmed U.S. plane in East Sea
17 October 1969	Park Chung-hee's proposal to abolish two-term limitations on presidency ratified by national referendum
22 April 1970	Park Chung-hee proposes New Village Movement
9 February 1971	South Korea announces Third Five-Year Economic Development Plan (1972–1976)
27 April 1971	Park Chung-hee wins third term in rigged presidential elections
25 May 1971	Opposition New Democratic Party wins enough seats in National Assembly elections to destroy ruling Democratic Republican Party's two-thirds majority
27 December 1971	National Assembly grants Park Chung-hee emergency powers
4 July 1972	North and South Korea announce "Joint Statement of 4 July" embodying basic principles for reunification of Korea

17 October 1972	Park Chung-hee stages "Yushin coup d'état," ending Third Republic
21 November 1972	Yushin Constitution ratified by national referendum
23 December 1972	Park Chung-hee elected president by National Conference for Unification
25 December 1972	North Korea promulgates new constitution creating state presidency
27 February 1973	National Assembly elections held, resulting in 146 locally elected seats (two-thirds) in the legislature
8 August 1973	Prominent opposition leader Kim Dae-jung kidnapped by Korean Central Intelligence Agency in Tokyo
15 August 1974	Korean resident of Japan attempts to assassinate Park Chung-hee, killing Park's wife
18 August 1976	North Korean guards murder two U.S. Army officers in Joint Security Area of P'anmunjŏm
6 July 1978	President Park Chung-hee wins another term of office as president
12 December 1978	In National Assembly elections, main opposition New Democratic Party wins more popular votes than ruling Democratic Republican Party, dealing a blow to Park regime
16 October 1979	Students and citizens in Pusan and Masan stage demonstration calling for an end to the Yushin system, which escalates into riots
26 October 1979	Park Chung-hee killed by the chief of Park's own Korean Central Intelligence Agency, Kim Chae-gyu
12 December 1979	Major General Chun Doo-hwan seizes control of South Korean armed forces in a bloody nighttime coup
17 May 1980	Chun Doo-hwan extends martial law to all of South Korea
18 May 1980	Students and citizens in Kwangju protest martial law in street demonstrations that escalate into armed revolt
27 May 1980	South Korean armed forces suppress Kwangju uprising
27 August 1980	Chun Doo-hwan elected president by National Conference for Unification
10 October 1980	Kim Jong-il publicly identified as Kim Il-sung's designated successor at Sixth Korean Workers Party Congress
22 October 1980	New constitution for Fifth Republic of South Korea approved by national referendum
25 March 1981	Chun Doo-hwan's Democratic Justice Party wins majority of seats in National Assembly elections
1 September 1983	Korean Air Liners Flight 007 shot down by Soviet su-15 interceptor, killing all 269 persons aboard
9 October 1983	North Korean agents detonate bomb in superstructure of Aung San shrine in Rangoon, Burma, killing 17 South Korean senior officials

12 February 1985	In National Assembly elections, newly created hard-line opposition party, New Korea Democratic Party, captures 67 seats in the 276-member legislature, representing popular aspirations for democracy
10 June 1987	June Resistance begins
29 June 1987	In his eight-point democratization program, ruling party's presidential candidate Roh Tae-woo agrees to direct presidential election
27 October 1987	New constitution for Sixth Republic approved by national referendum
29 November 1987	Bombing of South Korean airliner, conducted by North Korean agents during a flight over Andaman Sea, kills all 115 persons aboard
16 December 1987	Roh Tae-woo defeats two main opposition leaders, Kim Young-sam and Kim Dae-jung, in presidential election
26 April 1988	Ruling Democratic Justice Party fails to obtain majority of seats in National Assembly elections
17 September–2 October 1988	South Korea hosts 24th Summer Olympiad in Seoul
22 January 1990	Roh Tae-woo's Democratic Justice Party, Kim Young-sam's Reunification Democratic Party, and Kim Jong-pil's New Democratic Republican Party merge into Democratic Liberal Party
1 October 1990	South Korea and Soviet Union agree to normalize diplomatic relations
26 March 1991	Local elections held to elect representatives to metropolitan city, provincial, city, county, and district assemblies in South Korea
31 December 1991	North and South Korea adopt and initial "Basic Agreement on North-South Reconciliation, Nonaggression, Exchanges, and Cooperation" and the "Joint Declaration of the Denuclearization of the Korean Peninsula"
24 March 1992	Ruling Democratic Liberal Party suffers crushing defeat in National Assembly elections
24 August 1992	South Korea and China normalize diplomatic relations
18 December 1992	Kim Young-sam wins presidential election
12 March 1993	North Korea announces intention to withdraw from Nuclear Nonproliferation Treaty, sparking an acute international crisis
8 July 1994	North Korean leader Kim Il-sung dies
21 October 1994	United States and North Korea sign Agreed Framework to freeze North Korea's nuclear activity in return for economic and diplomatic benefits
30 March 1995	Kim Jong-pil establishes United Liberal Democrats, an opposition party

27 June 1995	Kim Young-sam's ruling Democratic Liberal Party suffers severe defeat in local elections
5 September 1995	Kim Dae-jung forms new opposition party, National Congress for New Politics
5 December 1995	Kim Young-sam's Democratic Liberal Party renamed New Korea Party
11 April 1996	Ruling New Korea Party fails to elect majority of seats in National Assembly elections
26 August 1996	Seoul District Court sentences former presidents Chun Doo-hwan to death and Roh Tae-woo to 22 and a half years in prison for military mutiny in 1979, treason in 1980, the Kwangju massacre, and corruption in office
8 October 1997	Kim Jong-il becomes General Secretary of Korean Workers Party in North Korea
21 November 1997	New Korea Party renamed Grand National Party
3 December 1997	South Korea receives $57 billion in bailout loans from International Monetary Fund
18 December 1997	Kim Dae-jung elected ROK president
22 December 1997	Chun Doo-hwan and Roh Tae-woo pardoned under special amnesty
31 August 1998	North Korea test-fires three-stage rocket
5 September 1998	North Korean Supreme People's Assembly elects Kim Jong-il chairman of National Defense Commission
13 June 1999	North Korean patrol boats cross Northern Limitation Line, resulting in naval confrontation between North and South Korean navies
20 January 2000	Kim Dae-jung forms another ruling party, New Millennium Democratic Party
13 April 2000	Kim Dae-jung's New Millennium Democratic Party fails in its bid to become the number-one party in the legislature in National Assembly elections
13–15 June 2000	North-South summit held between Kim Dae-jung and Kim Jong-il in Pyongyang
13 June 2002	Kim Dae-jung's New Millennium Democratic Party suffers a heavy defeat in local elections
29 June 2002	North Korean patrol boat crosses Northern Limitation Line and opens fire on South Korean patrol boat, killing six South Korean sailors and wounding 19 others
19 December 2002	Roh Moo-hyun of the New Millennium Democratic Party elected president
1 November 2003	Roh Moo-hyun forms Our Open Party, another ruling party
12 March 2004	National Assembly impeaches Roh Moo-hyun for illegal electioneering and charges of general incompetence
15 April 2004	Roh Moo-hyun's Our Open Party obtains slim majority of seats in National Assembly elections

14 May 2004	Constitutional Court reinstates Roh as president
31 May 2006	Opposition Grand National Party wins overwhelming victory in local elections
4 July 2006	North Korea conducts multiple missile tests
9 October 2006	North Korea announces successful completion of nuclear weapon test
13 February 2007	North Korea agrees to shut down main nuclear reactor and disable nuclear program in exchange for energy assistance and security guarantees
23 February 2007	South Korea and United States agree to complete transfer of full operational control to South Korea on 17 April 2012
2–4 October 2007	Roh Moo-hyun and Kim Jong-il hold summit in Pyongyang
19 December 2007	Lee Myung-bak of the Grand National Party wins sweeping victory in presidential election
11 February 2008	New main opposition party, the United Democratic Party, formed
9 April 2008	Ruling Grand National Party wins slim majority of seats in National Assembly elections
2 May 2008	In candlelight vigil attended by hundreds of teenagers, anti–U.S. beef demonstrations begin and quickly escalate
10 October 2008	United States removes North Korea from list of states sponsoring terrorism
1 December 2008	North Korea closes overland passage through Military Demarcation Line and Red Cross liaison office, as well as all direct telephone lines between the two Koreas; it also rejects nuclear sampling, leading to a sharp deterioration in inter-Korean relations and jeopardizing the six-party nuclear talks
5 April 2009	North Korea test-fires a long-range ballistic missile in the guise of a satellite launch, sparking widespread international criticism
23 May 2009	Former president Roh Moo-hyun commits suicide, plunging South Korean politics into deep uncertainty
25 May 2009	North Korea conducts its second nuclear test in the escalating international standoff over its rogue nuclear and missile programs
26 March 2010	South Korean patrol ship *Cheonan* is sunk in Yellow Sea off South Korean coast, killing 46 sailors; South Korea and United States conclude that North Korea was responsible
23 April 2010	North Korea confiscates real estate held by South Koreans at the Kŭmgang-san resort
26 June 2010	South Korea and the United States agree to postpone U.S. transfer of wartime operational control to South Korea until 1 December 2015

23 November 2010	North Korea conducts artillery attack on South Korea's island of Yŏnp'yŏng-do just below Northern Limitation Line, escalating tensions between North and South Korea
17 December 2011	North Korean leader Kim Jong-il dies.
13 April 2012	North Korea's rocket launch as a disguised test of a long-range missile ends in failure

Notes

INTRODUCTION

1. South Korea's per-capita gross national income (GNI) shot up from a meager $67 in 1953 to $20,045 in 2007. Adjusted for inflation, its per-capita GNI grew 14-fold from 1954 to 2003, while that of the world expanded 2.8 times. The nation's gross domestic product (GDP) grew 746-fold to $969.9 billion in 2007 from $1.3 billion in 1953. Trade volume skyrocketed to $728.3 billion in 2007 from $230 million in 1948.

2. MacDonald, *The Koreans,* 26.

3. Korean Culture and Information Service, "History Being Whitewashed Again-and-Again."

1. DAWN OF THE KOREAN NATION

1. Lee, *A New History of Korea,* 5.

2. Iryŏn, *Samguk yusa,* 35–37; Cumings, *Korea's Place in the Sun,* 23–24.

3. Lee, *A New History of Korea,* 15–16.

4. Ibid., 17.

5. Chumong's real name was Ch'umo. Since good archers were called *chumong* in Puyŏ, it is certain that Chumong, who was skillful in archery, came south from Puyŏ.

6. Han, *Tasi ch'annŭn uri yŏksa,* 93–94.

2. THE PERIOD OF THE THREE KINGDOMS

1. It is said that Paekche was originally named *Sipche,* meaning "rule over ten persons," representing the fact that ten vassals aided Onjo in founding his state. Later the name was changed to *Paekche,* or "rule over 100 people," indicating that many people followed Onjo's leadership.

2. Han, *Tasi ch'annŭn uri yŏksa,* 107.

3. Paekche and Silla took advantage of internal dissension in Koguryŏ. During the reign of King Anwŏn (531–545), factionalism grew fierce among the Koguryŏ aristocracy. Two royal in-law families fought each other to enthrone their own favorite princes, until eight-year-old King Yangwŏn (545–559) was finally crowned. But the power struggle was never definitively resolved, and ceaseless struggles among the aristocracy sapped the nation's strength.

4. The term *Silla* was a shortened word of the sentence *tŏkŏp ilsin, mangna sabang,* or "the virtuous rule undergoes improvement day by day and spreads in all directions."

5. The term *Kaya* originated in the word *Kara,* a Chinese transliteration of a native Korean word meaning "village."

6. After Koguryŏ's downfall, many of its ruling class and soldiers were forcibly sent to Tang or massacred. In 765 the descendants of Yi Chŏng-gi, who had been forced to settle in the Shandong region, founded their own state, Qi (Che in Korean) (765–819), and carried out a total of five raids on Tang's capital, Leyang. On one of these raids, in 783, the Tang emperor was compelled to flee to seek safety.

7. Lee, *A New History of Korea,* 50–51.

8. The term "Mukhoja," meaning "black (*muk*) barbarian (*hoja*)," may be interpreted as referring to an Indian monk. Since Mukhoja was said to stay in Silla for 71–111 years, several Indian Buddhist monks appear to have clandestinely proselytized Buddhism in the kingdom. The term "Ado" also does not indicate a specific person, but several persons, specifically Buddhist monks from India. The monk Marananta was an Indian monk as well.

9. According to legend, one day Ich'adon presented himself to King Pŏphŭng, who dearly wanted to secure the acceptance of Buddhism in the kingdom. But when Ich'adon announced that he had become a Buddhist, the king had him beheaded. When the executioner completed the task, milk poured out of Ich'adon's body instead of blood. As a result, everybody at the court came to believe that the Buddha possessed supernatural powers. Apparently the king and Ich'adon had agreed on this venture of self-sacrifice in advance.

10. Lee, *Korea and East Asia,* 46. Some Korean scholars claim that the Ch'ŏmsŏngdae was a temple to Inanna (or Ishtar), the Mesopotamian goddess of love and war (and possibly of heaven), said to have been worshiped by Queen Sŏndŏk.

11. Lee, *A New History of Korea,* 63.

12. Silla artifacts, including unique gold metalwork, demonstrate a clear influence from those of the northern nomadic steppes but less Chinese influence than those of Koguryŏ and Paekche.

13. Lee, *A New History of Korea,* 64.

14. Lee, *Korea and East Asia,* 28–29.

15. Mural paintings in Japanese royal tombs, many Korean historians believe, suggest that the Japanese imperial house lineage may have had Korean origins.

16. Lee, *Korea and East Asia,* 28.

17. Ibid., 33.

18. *Chosŏn ilbo,* 24 March 2010 (Seoul).

19. In 2007 the Chinese even tried to co-opt Paekche and Silla into Chinese history. Chinese historians wrongly argue that, just like Koguryŏ, a group of people from the Puyŏ tribe, an ethnic minority in an ancient Chinese borderland area, founded Paekche. According to the Chinese argument, because its people were of the same lineage as the people of Koguryŏ, Paekche was a provincial kingdom established by a Chinese ethnic minority. Silla was also founded by exiles from the Chinese Qin dynasty. The argument that both Paekche and Silla were established by Chinese ethnic minorities and maintained vassal relationships with China is a politically far-fetched interpretation of history to deprive Korea of its entire ancient history.

3. PARHAE, UNIFIED SILLA, AND THE LATER THREE KINGDOMS

1. By the ninth century the Silla people had called Parhae the "Northern State." Viewed in this light, it is surmised that the people of Parhae might have called Silla the "Southern State." Parhae was also termed the "Northern State" in the twelfth-century historical work *Samguk sagi*. Yu Tŭk-kong, historian of the eighteenth-century Chosŏn dynasty, advocated the proper study of Parhae as part of Korean history and coined the term "Northern and Southern States Period" to refer to this era.

2. The kyŏl was a unit measuring the area of farmland. One kyŏl equaled the area of land that could produce 10,000 handfuls, or 1,200 *tu*, of grain. These days, 1 tu is equal to 16 kilograms, but at the time it seems to have been equivalent to one-third that amount. As agricultural technology gradually improved, the output per unit area increased, and thus the amount of kyŏl also increased. In short, the kyŏl was a unit of the area of farmland, based on productivity rather than on the size of a parcel of land.

3. Lee, *A New History of Korea*, 78.

4. Ibid., 80.

5. According to legend, Wŏnhyo set off to China with a close friend, Ŭisang, but he did not complete his journey. One night he awoke quite thirsty, discovered a container filled with delicious cool water, drank it, and went back to sleep. The next morning he saw that the vessel he had drunk from was a human skull and the water was rotten rainwater. At that moment he attained enlightenment, suddenly realizing that the mind controlled everything. He therefore had no reason to proceed to China and returned home.

6. Lee, *A New History of Korea*, 85.

7. Ibid., 108–109.

8. Korean historians divide the entire Silla history into three periods—the early period (before unification), the middle period (the time between the reigns of King Munmu and King Hyegong), and the late period (since the reign of King Sŏndŏk).

4. THE FIRST HALF OF THE KORYŎ PERIOD

1. By the end of the Silla period, Pyongyang was outside the kingdom's territory and had been degraded to a hunting ground for the Nuzhen (formerly Malgal) people. T'aejo advanced the status of the old Koguryŏ capital by making it one of the three capitals of Koryŏ, the Western Capital.

2. In the Koryŏ and Chosŏn dynasties, posthumous titles were given to kings in accordance with their lifetime achievements. Usually *cho* (-*jo*) was given to monarchs who performed meritorious deeds such as founding a dynasty, defending the state against foreign invasion, suppressing rebellions, and so forth, whereas *chong* (-*jong*) was given to kings who did not render these distinguished services. The former kings were called "persons of merit" and the latter "persons of virtue." In Koryŏ, T'aejo (Wang Kŏn) was the only king whose title contained the term "cho," although some other kings deserved it. The Chosŏn dynasty, on the other hand, followed in accordance with the pattern more faithfully than the preceding dynasty and thus witnessed several kings whose posthumous titles had the term "cho."

3. Koryŏ set up several togam, or directorates, as nonpermanent organs to carry out specific tasks.

4. Lee, *A New History of Korea*, 113–116.

5. Han, *Tasi ch'annŭn uri yŏksa*, 218–219.

5. THE SECOND HALF OF THE KORYŎ PERIOD

1. Lee, *A New History of Korea*, 145–147.

2. In 1236 Koryŏ began the re-creation of the Tripitaka on Kanghwa-do. This collection of Buddhist scriptures took 15 years to carve on 81,137 woodblocks.

3. Posthumous titles were bestowed in these ways on six Koryŏ kings: Ch'ungnyŏl-wang (1274–1308), Ch'ungsŏn-wang (1298, 1308–1313), Ch'ungsuk-wang (1313–1330, 1332–1339), Ch'unghye-wang (1330–1332, 1339–1344), Ch'ungmok-wang (1344–1348), and Ch'ungjŏng-wang (1348–1351).

4. Lee, *Korea and East Asia*, 97.

6. THE FIRST HALF OF THE CHOSŎN PERIOD

1. King Sejong also frequently declared a national amnesty to release those imprisoned for minor crimes, and he improved the social status of slaves by banning owners from punishing them at will.

2. Whereas Silla was symbolized by "metal," Koryŏ was represented by "water."

3. Lee, *A New History of Korea*, 180–181.

4. Originally, in 1396, the 37-volume *Koryŏ sa* was compiled in chronological format by Chŏng To-jŏn. Because its emphasis was on the role of bureaucrat-officials, the king commanded that a revised version be published that stressed the role of the monarch.

5. According to the ancient Chinese philosophy of Naturalism, the calendar signs consisted of 10 "heavenly stems" and 12 "earthly branches," the latter associated with the signs of the zodiac. When combined in a sequence of pairs of characters, these formed the traditional cycle of 60, used for counting time in periods of 60 days and 60 years.

6. Lee, *A New History of Korea*, 203.

7. THE SECOND HALF OF THE CHOSŎN PERIOD

1. At first copper mining was not well developed, since copper was mainly imported from Japan. In the eighteenth century, however, when the Japanese forbade the export of copper and China demanded it in great supplies, copper mines began operating on a large scale.

2. Swartout, "A History of Korean-American Relations," 8–10.

3. Chung, *Korean Treaties*, 205.

4. Swartout, "A History of Korean-American Relations," 12–13.

5. When the Chosŏn representatives went to Japan in September 1882, they took the present-day South Korean national flag, the *T'aegŭkki*, or Great Absolute Flag, with them, for the first time in the country's history, to demonstrate that Chosŏn was an independent nation. The T'aegŭkki was formally adopted as the national flag on 6 March 1883.

6. The Hongbŏm included 14 stipulations: Chosŏn's independence from China; the exclusion of royalties and royal in-laws from politics; the enactment of a royal ordinance to prescribe royal succession and other norms for the royal family; separation of the palace apparatus from that of the government proper; the establishment of the modern

cabinet system; taxation specified by law; the placement of all fiscal matters under the jurisdiction of the Ministry of Finance; retrenchment of expenditures for the royal household; the establishment of an annual budget system; restructuring of local government; the promotion of advanced civilization by dispatching students to foreign countries; the establishment of a universal conscription system; protection of people's life and property through civil law and criminal law; and the abolishment of class distinctions and the appointment of talented persons to office.

7. On 4 September 1909, Japan signed an agreement with China stipulating that, in return for China's permission to reconstruct the railroad line between Dandong and Shenyang, Japan relinquished Chosŏn's claim to the Jiandao region of southeastern Manchuria.

8. THE PERIOD OF JAPANESE COLONIAL RULE

1. Cumings, *Korea's Place in the Sun*, 152; Buzo, *The Making of Modern Korea*, 16.
2. Buzo, *The Making of Modern Korea*, 20.
3. Cumings, *Korea's Place in the Sun*, 150.
4. Buzo, *The Making of Modern Korea*, 19.
5. Ibid., 23.
6. In September 1919, immediately after his accession to office, Saito was hit by a bomb launched by a Korean, Kang U-gyu, but he survived.
7. Originally, in 1923, a group of Korean educational leaders sought Japanese approval of their plan to establish a private university. The Japanese rejected their request and, instead, established the Kyŏngsŏng Imperial University as a colonial institute in 1924.
8. Grajdanzev, *Modern Korea*, 75, 104.
9. Government-General, Korea, *Annual Report on the Administration of Tyosen [Chosen], 1937–1938*, 218.
10. Lee, *A New History of Korea*, 337–338. In the late nineteenth and early twentieth centuries, the works of Russian, German, French, British, American, and Japanese authors, including John Bunyan's *Pilgrim's Progress*, translated in 1895, were read by the more educated Koreans, and Korean writers increasingly adopted Western ideas and literary forms.
11. Buzo, *The Making of Modern Korea*, 27–28.
12. Henderson, *Korea*, 103.
13. Suh, *The Korean Communist Movement, 1918–1948*, 15.
14. Lee, *Land Utilization and Rural Economy in Korea*, 163.
15. Lee, *A New History of Korea*, 360; Han, *Tasi ch'annŭn uri yŏksa*, 544.
16. Han, *Tasi ch'annŭn uri yŏksa*, 547.
17. Buzo, *The Making of Modern Korea*, 38, 41.
18. In 1905 Chu Si-gyŏng presented a proposal to the government on the study of the Korean language and the compilation of a Korean dictionary. His efforts resulted in the establishment, in 1907, of a Korean-language research institute and a new system for the national script han'gŭl. Under this system, official documents and communications were no longer written exclusively with Chinese characters but also included han'gŭl. Korean-language spelling and usage were also standardized. Newspapers and books used the new writing system to spread knowledge of Western institutions more rapidly among the

general populace. Chu Si-gyŏng also emphasized the importance of language and script as the foundation of Korea's national spirit and culture. His works on Korean grammar and phonology, published in the years from 1908 to 1914, profoundly influenced scientific research on the Korean language.

19. Lee, *Korea and East Asia*, 164.

20. Korean Culture and Information Service, "History Being Whitewashed Again and Again."

21. Ibid.

22. U.S. Department of State, *Foreign Relations of the United States, 1943*, 3:37 (hereafter, FR).

23. Eden, *Memoirs*, 438.

24. U.S. Department of State, FR, *Conferences at Cairo and Tehran, 1943*, 404.

25. Ibid., 869.

26. U.S. Department of State, FR, *1944*, 5:1224–1228.

27. Ibid., 5:1239–1242.

28. U.S. Department of State, FR, *Conferences at Malta and Yalta, 1945*, 360–361.

29. U.S. Department of State, FR, *The Conference of Berlin*, 2 vols., 1:311–313.

30. U.S. Department of State, FR, *Conferences at Malta and Yalta, 1945*, 770.

31. U.S. Department of State, FR, *1945*, 6:887–891.

32. Matray, *The Reluctant Crusade*, 37–43.

33. U.S. Department of State, FR, *1945*, 6:1039.

34. Rusk, *As I Saw It*, 124.

35. Schnabel, *Policy and Direction*, 10–11.

36. U.S. Department of State, FR, *1945*, 6:1039.

37. Matray, *The Reluctant Crusade*, 46–47.

9. LIBERATION, DIVISION, AND WAR

1. My use of the term "leftist" refers to those on the political Left, including communists and socialists, both seeking radical social and economic change in revolutionary Korea. The term "rightist" refers to those with a conservative viewpoint who want to preserve the existing order.

2. Han, *Han'guk chŏngdang sa*, 25–35; Henderson, *Korea*, 114–115.

3. Cumings, *The Origins of the Korean War: Liberation and the Emergence of Separate Regimes*, 191.

4. Ibid., 255–258.

5. Merrill, *Korea*, 59.

6. Cumings, *The Origins of the Korean War: Liberation and the Emergence of Separate Regimes*, 250.

7. Henderson, *Korea*, 146.

8. U.S. Department of State, *Foreign Relations of the United States, 1947*, 6:857–859 (hereafter, FR).

9. U.S. Department of State, *Korea, 1945–1948*, 70–71.

10. Ibid., 13–14.

11. U.S. Congress, *The United States and the Korean Problem*, 18.

12. Merrill, *Korea*, 76.

13. U.S. Congress, *The United States and the Korean Problem*, 20.

14. Merrill, *Korea*, 79.

15. Lee, *Korea and East Asia*, 175.

16. Henderson, *Korea*, 138–139.

17. Ibid., 139.

18. Chosŏn Ŭnhaeng, *Chosŏn kyŏngje yŏnbo*, I-28; Nongnimbu, *Nongji kaehyŏk sa*, 1:358–359.

19. Lee, *Korea and East Asia*, 177.

20. Scalapino and Lee, *Communism in Korea*, 315.

21. Cumings, *The Origins of the Korean War: Liberation and the Emergence of Separate Regimes*, 387–393.

22. Simmons, *The Strained Alliance*, 25.

23. On 24 February 1946 Ch'oe Yong-gŏn was elected chairman of the Chosŏn Democratic Party. Cho Man-sik was reportedly killed by the retreating North Korean communists at a Pyongyang prison on 18 October 1950 during the Korean War.

24. Merrill, *Korea*, 63–64, 68–69, 98–100, 122–123, 131–132; Tucker, *Encyclopedia of the Korean War*, 131–132.

25. Tucker, *Encyclopedia of the Korean War*, 994–995; Merrill, *Korea*, 98–129; Cumings, *The Origins of the Korean War: The Roaring of the Cataract*, 259–276.

26. U.S. Department of State, FR, *1948*, 6:1305–1308.

27. Merrill, *Korea*, 130–165, 174; Tucker, *Encyclopedia of the Korean War*, 93–94.

28. Merrill, *Korea*, 165–166.

29. Tucker, *Encyclopedia of the Korean War*, 8–9.

30. Goncharov, Lewis, and Litai, *Uncertain Partners*, 131–154.

31. Weathersby, "Soviet Aims in Korea and the Origins of the Korean War," 16; idem, "The Soviet Role in the Early Phase of the Korean War," 442.

32. Goncharov, Lewis, and Litai, *Uncertain Partners*, 143–144.

33. U.S. Department of State, FR, *1950*, 7:211.

34. Tucker, *Encyclopedia of the Korean War*, 654–656.

35. Allegedly, on 26 July 1950, a strafing attack by U.S. aircraft killed upward of 100 among some 500 South civilian refugees at the Nogŭn-ni (village) railroad bridge, and, over the next few days, U.S. troops pinned down the remaining refugees under the bridge, fired on them, and killed some 200. The unfortunate accident of war took place in a desperate fighting situation, where U.S. commanders issued orders authorizing their poorly trained soldiers with little combat experience to fire on civilians as a self-defense against disguised North Korean troops. Ibid., 638.

Regarding the "Nogŭn-ni incident," the United States has opposed the use of the term *haksal*, the Korean word for "massacre" or "manslaughter." The U.S. opposition to the term was related to its conclusion that "Nogŭn-ni" was an accidental incident that occurred under the chaotic situation in the early stage of the Korean conflict. Americans preferred the term "killing" to "massacre."

36. Ibid., 707–711.

37. In commemoration of the advance into North Korea, on 14 September 1956, the ROK government declared 1 October as Armed Forces Day.

38. Kepley, *The Collapse of the Middle Way*, 127.

10. THE PERIOD OF POSTWAR RECONSTRUCTION

1. Buzo, *The Making of Modern Korea*, 84.
2. Palais, "'Democracy' in South Korea," 325.
3. Buzo, *The Making of Modern Korea*, 102.
4. Ibid., 103–104.
5. Palais, "'Democracy' in South Korea," 326.
6. The Chang Myŏn government dusted off a five-year economic plan, a concept that had been rejected three years earlier by Syngman Rhee as too "communist," and set about reworking it. The economic plan was to start in the spring of 1961. As it was a long-term project, the government also launched an initiative called the National Construction Service (NCS) to meet the popular demand for jobs and food. Under the NCS, a program designed to counter the political and social unrest, people were to be given food in return for work on reforestation, flood control, small-scale irrigation and road construction projects instead of receiving food in the form of relief. The spirit of self-reliance and hard work that characterized the NCS was the basis of the future New Village Movement launched by the Park Chung-hee government.
7. Palais, "'Democracy' in South Korea," 332–337.
8. Pak, *A Study of the Land Tenure System in Korea*, 76–84.
9. MacDonald, *The Koreans*, 198.
10. Breidenstein, "Capitalism in South Korea," 235–236.
11. Brandt, "Local Government and Rural Development," 275.
12. Some 10,000 protesters, mostly college students, took to the streets in the center of Seoul on 3 June 1964 to oppose normalizing relations with Japan.
13. Matray, *East Asia and the United States*, 266–267.
14. Palais, "'Democracy' in South Korea," 338.
15. Swartout, "A History of Korean-American Relations," 49–55.
16. Buzo, *The Making of Modern Korea*, 94–96.
17. MacDonald, *The Koreans*, 98.
18. Gills, *Korea versus Korea*, 54–59.
19. Ibid., 60–62.
20. Nahm, "The United States and North Korea since 1945," 106.
21. Ibid., 102–104.

11. REVERSAL OF FORTUNES

1. On 24 October 2007 the National Intelligence Service, the KCIA's successor, through its Development Committee for Clarifying the Past, concluded that Park probably ordered or tacitly approved the kidnapping. The committee also made clear that the bombing of KAL 858, which occurred on 29 November 1987, was indeed a terrorist attack masterminded by North Korea. *Korea Times*, 25 October 2007 (Seoul).
2. *Han'guk ilbo*, 15 August 2008 (Seoul).
3. *Tonga ilbo*, 15 August 2008 (Seoul).
4. Ibid.
5. *Chosŏn ilbo*, 16 May 2011 (Seoul).

6. According to a 2011 poll, while 38.3 percent of those polled thought that Park had had an affirmative impact on South Korea's political demonstration, 56.1 percent rated his impact negatively. Ibid.

7. Buzo, *The Making of Modern Korea*, 156.

8. *Tonga ilbo*, 15 August 2008 (Seoul).

9. Oberdorfer, *The Two Koreas*, 36.

10. Buzo, *The Making of Modern Korea*, 135.

11. Ibid., 136.

12. The Fifth Five-Year Economic and Social Development Plan (1982–1986) sought to shift the emphasis from heavy and chemical industries to technology-intensive industries, such as precision machinery, electronics, and information. More attention was to be devoted to building high-tech products in greater demand on the world market. The Sixth Five-Year Economic and Social Development Plan (1987–1991) continued to stress the goals of the previous plan.

13. Clifford, *Troubled Tiger*, 232–241; Buzo, *The Making of Modern Korea*, 164.

14. Buzo, *The Making of Modern Korea*, 138–139.

15. MacDonald, *The Koreans*, 76–77.

16. Lee, *The Making of Minjung*, 215.

17. Kwak and Patterson, "The Security Relationship between Korea and the United States," 85–94; Swartout, "A History of Korean-American Relations," 58–59.

18. Kwak and Patterson, "The Security Relationship between Korea and the United States," 95; Kim, "The United States and South Korea since 1982," 145; Swartout, "A History of Korean-American Relations," 161.

19. Buzo, *The Making of Modern Korea*, 122, 127.

20. Ibid., 149; MacDonald, *The Koreans*, 225.

21. Nahm, "The United States and North Korea since 1945," 110–126.

22. Oberdorfer, *The Two Koreas*, 57–58.

23. MacDonald, *The Koreans*, 286–287.

12. BOTH KOREAS IN A NEW PHASE

1. Oberdorfer, *The Two Koreas*, 376–382.

2. Buzo, *The Making of Modern Korea*, 182.

3. O, *Taet'ongnyŏng ka ŭi saramdŭl*, 129.

4. Oberdorfer, *The Two Koreas*, 399–406.

5. Kim's tastes were reportedly extravagant; he owned 17 palaces and had collections of hundreds of cars and some 20,000 video tapes. He was believed to spend about $650,000 a year on Hennessy VSOP cognac and maintained an entourage of young women known as the "Pleasure Brigade."

6. Nahm, "The United States and North Korea since 1945," 128–141.

7. Oberdorfer, *The Two Koreas*, 369–370.

8. Ibid., 410–414.

9. Ibid., 431.

10. On 13 August 2009 the South Korean worker was freed from a 136-day confinement. His release was followed by the liberation, during former U.S. president Bill Clinton's

visit to Pyongyang on 4 August, of two American female journalists who had been detained on the charge of crossing the border into North Korea.

11. U.S. beef imports were banned by South Korea five years earlier because of the first case of mad cow disease in the United States. Lee's move to lift the ban prompted widespread protests over perceived health risks and the sense that the government had bowed too easily to the United States.

12. McKeeby, "President Obama Vows Strengthened U.S.-South Korea Ties."

13. *Korea Herald,* 17 June 2009 (Seoul); *Korea Times,* 17 June 2009 (Seoul).

14. *Maeil kyŏngje,* 15 November 1995 (Seoul).

15. *Chosŏn ilbo,* 28 December 2009 (Seoul).

16. *Chungang ilbo,* 31 March 2010 (Seoul).

17. Galtung, "The Neutralization Approach to Korean Reunification," 14.

Bibliography

Allen, Richard C. *Korea's Syngman Rhee: An Unauthorized Portrait*. Rutland, VT: Tuttle, 1960.

Brandt, Vincent. "Local Government and Rural Development." In Sung Hwan Ban, Pal Yong Moon, and Dwight H. Perkins, eds., *Rural Development*. Cambridge, MA: Harvard University Press, 1980.

Brazinsky, Gregg. *Nation Building in South Korea: Koreans, Americans, and the Making of a Democracy*. Chapel Hill: University of North Carolina Press, 2007.

Breidenstein, Gerhard. "Capitalism in South Korea." In Frank Baldwin, ed., *Without Parallel: The American-Korean Relationship since 1945*. New York: Random House, 1974.

Buzo, Adrian. *The Making of Modern Korea*. New York: Routledge, 2002.

Chay, Jongsuk. *Unequal Partners: In Peace and War*. Westport, CT: Praeger, 2002.

Cho, Soon Sung. *Korea in World Politics, 1940–1950*. Berkeley: University of California Press, 1967.

Chosŏn ilbo [Morning Calm daily] (Seoul).

Chosŏn Ŭnhaeng. *Chosŏn kyŏngje yŏnbo* [Korean economic statistics yearbook]. Seoul: Chosŏn Ŭnhaeng, 1948.

Chung, Henry, comp. *Korean Treaties*. New York: H. S. Nichols, 1919.

Chungang ilbo [Central daily] (Seoul).

Clifford, Mark L. *Troubled Tiger: Businessmen, Bureaucrats, and Generals in South Korea*. Armonk, NY: M. E. Sharpe, 1994.

Cumings, Bruce. *Korea's Place in the Sun: A Modern History*. New York: Norton, 1997.

———. *The Origins of the Korean War: Liberation and the Emergence of Separate Regimes, 1945–1947*. Princeton, NJ: Princeton University Press, 1981.

———. *The Origins of the Korean War: The Roaring of the Cataract, 1947–1950*. Princeton, NJ: Princeton University Press, 1990.

Eden, Anthony. *Memoirs: The Reckoning*. Boston: Houghton Mifflin, 1965.

Galtung, Johan. "The Neutralization Approach to Korean Reunification." In Michael Haas, ed., *Korean Reunification: Alternative Pathways*. Westport, CT: Praeger, 1989.

Gills, B. K. *Korea versus Korea: A Case of Contested Legitimacy*. New York: Routledge, 1996.

Goncharov, Sergei N., John W. Lewis, and Xue Litai. *Uncertain Partners: Stalin, Mao, and the Korean War*. Stanford, CA: Stanford University Press, 1994.

Government-General, Korea. *Annual Report on the Administration of Tyosen [Chosen]*, *1937–1938*. Keijo [Seoul]: Government-General, 1938.

Grajdanzev, Andrei J. *Modern Korea*. New York: Institute of Pacific Relations, 1944.

Han, T'ae-su. *Han'guk chŏngdang sa* [A history of Korean political parties]. Seoul: Sint'aeyangsa, 1961.

Han, U-gŭn. *Han'guk t'ongsa* [A comprehensive history of Korea]. Rev. ed. Seoul: Ŭlyu Munhwasa, 1990.

Han, Yŏng-u. *Tasi ch'annŭn uri yŏksa* [Our history revisited]. 5th ed. Seoul: Kyŏngsewŏn, 2004.

Han'guk ilbo [Korea daily] (Seoul).

Henderson, Gregory. *Korea: The Politics of the Vortex*. Cambridge, MA: Harvard University Press, 1968.

Iryŏn. *Samguk yusa* [Memorabilia of the Three Kingdoms]. Translated by Wŏn-jung Kim. Seoul: Minŭm-sa, 2007.

Kepley, David R. *The Collapse of the Middle Way: Senate Republicans and the Bipartisan Foreign Policy, 1948–1952*. Westport, CT: Greenwood, 1987.

Kim, Han-gyo. "The United States and South Korea since 1982." In Yur-bok Lee and Wayne Patterson, eds., *Korean-American Relations, 1866–1997*. Albany: State University of New York Press, 1999.

Kim, Pu-sik. *Samguk sagi* [History of the Three Kingdoms]. Translated and edited by Yi U-gyŏng. Seoul: Han'guk Munhwasa, 2007.

Korea Herald (Seoul).

Korea Times (Seoul).

Korean Culture and Information Service. "History Being Whitewashed Again-and-Again." 15 March 2005. Available at http://www.kois.go.kr.

Kwak, Tae-Hwan, and Wayne Patterson. "The Security Relationship between Korea and the United States, 1960–1982." In Yur-bok Lee and Wayne Patterson, eds., *Korean-American Relations, 1866–1997*. Albany: State University of New York Press, 1999.

Lee, Hoon K. *Land Utilization and Rural Economy in Korea*. Shanghai: Kelly & Walsh, 1936.

Lee, Kenneth B. *Korea and East Asia: The Story of a Phoenix*. Westport, CT: Praeger, 1997.

Lee, Ki-baik. *A New History of Korea*. Translated by Edward W. Wagner, with Edward J. Shultz. Cambridge, MA: Harvard University Press, 1984.

Lee, Namhee. *The Making of Minjung: Democracy and the Politics of Representation in South Korea*. Ithaca, NY: Cornell University Press, 2007.

Maeil kyŏngje [MK Business News] (Seoul).

Matray, James I., ed. *East Asia and the United States: An Encyclopedia of Relations since 1784*. Westport, CT: Greenwood, 2002.

———. *The Reluctant Crusade: American Foreign Policy in Korea, 1941–1950*. Honolulu: University of Hawaii Press, 1985.

McDonald, Donald S. *The Koreans: Contemporary Politics and Society*. 3rd ed. Boulder, CO: Westview, 1996.

McKeeby, David. "President Obama Vows Strengthened U.S.–South Korea Ties." Staff Writer, Embassy of the United States, Seoul, Korea, 2 April 2009.

Merrill, John. *Korea: The Peninsula Origins of the War.* Newark: University of Delaware Press, 1989.

Nahm, Andrew C. 1999. "The United States and North Korea since 1945." In Yur-bok Lee and Wayne Patterson, eds., *Korean-American Relations, 1866–1997.* Albany: State University of New York Press.

Nongnim-bu. *Nongji kaehyŏk sa* [History of farmland reform]. 2 vols. Seoul: Nongnim-bu, 1970.

O, Kyŏng-hwan. *Taet'ongnyŏng ka ŭi saramdŭl* [People of the presidential families]. Seoul: Tori, 2003.

Oberdorfer, Don. *The Two Koreas: A Contemporary History.* Rev. ed. New York: Basic Books, 2001.

Pak, Ki-hyuk. *A Study of the Land Tenure System in Korea.* Seoul: Korea Land Economic Research Center, 1966.

Palais, James B. "'Democracy' in South Korea, 1948–1972." In Frank Baldwin, ed., *Without Parallel: The American-Korean Relationship since 1945.* New York: Random House, 1974.

Pratt, Keith. *Everlasting Flower: A History of Korea.* London: Reaktion Books, 2006.

Pyŏn, T'ae-sŏp. *Han'guk sa t'ongnon* [An outline of Korean history]. 5th ed. Seoul: Samyŏngsa, 2006.

Robinson, Michael E. *Korea's Twentieth-Century Odyssey: A Short History.* Honolulu: University of Hawaii Press, 2007.

Rusk, Dean. *As I Saw It.* New York: Norton, 1990.

Scalapino, Robert, and Chong-sik Lee. *Communism in Korea.* Berkeley: University of California Press, 1972.

Schnabel, James F. *Policy and Direction: The First Year.* Washington, DC: Office of the Chief of Military History, 1972.

Simmons, Robert R. *The Strained Alliance: Peking, P'yongyang, Moscow, and the Politics of the Korean Civil War.* New York: Free Press, 1975.

Suh, Dae-sook. *The Korean Communist Movement, 1918–1948.* Princeton, NJ: Princeton University Press, 1967.

Swartout, Robert R., Jr. "A History of Korean-American Relations." In Ray E. Weisenborn, ed., *Korea's Amazing Century: From Kings to Satellites.* Seoul: Korea Fulbright Foundation, 1996.

Tonga ilbo [East Asia daily] (Seoul).

Tucker, Spencer C., ed. *Encyclopedia of the Korean War: A Political, Social, and Military History.* 2nd ed. Santa Barbara: ABC–CLIO, 2010.

U.S. Congress. Senate. Committee on Foreign Relations. *The United States and the Korean Problem: Documents 1943–1953.* 83rd Congress, 1st Session. Washington, DC: Government Printing Office, 1953.

U.S. Department of State. *Foreign Relations of the United States, 1943.* Vol. 3. Washington, DC: Government Printing Office, 1963.

———. *Foreign Relations of the United States, 1944.* Vol. 5. Washington, DC: Government Printing Office, 1969.

———. *Foreign Relations of the United States, 1945.* Vol. 6. Washington, DC: Government Printing Office, 1969.

————. *Foreign Relations of the United States, 1947*. Vol. 6. Washington, DC: Government Printing Office, 1972.

————. *Foreign Relations of the United States, 1948*. Vol. 6. Washington, DC: Government Printing Office, 1974.

————. *Foreign Relations of the United States, 1950*. Vol. 7. Washington, DC: Government Printing Office, 1976.

————. *Foreign Relations of the United States: The Conference of Berlin*. Washington, DC: Government Printing Office, 1960.

————. *Foreign Relations of the United States: Conferences at Cairo and Tehran, 1943*. Washington, DC: Government Printing Office, 1961.

————. *Foreign Relations of the United States: Conferences at Malta and Yalta, 1945*. Washington, DC: Government Printing Office, 1955.

————. *Korea, 1945–1948*. Washington, DC: Government Printing Office, 1948.

Weathersby, Kathryn. "Soviet Aims in Korea and the Origins of the Korean War, 1945–1950: New Evidence from Russian Archives." Cold War International History Project Working Paper 8. Woodrow Wilson International Center for Scholars, 1993.

————. "The Soviet Role in the Early Phase of the Korean War: New Documentary Evidence. *Journal of American–East Asian Relations* 2 (winter 1993).

Index

JINWUNG KIM (Kim, Chin-ung) is Professor of History at Kyungpook National University in Taegu, South Korea. He was a Fulbright Scholar at Rutgers University between 1992 and 1993. In 2002 Virginia Military Institute appointed Kim to the Eugenio Lopez Visiting Chair for Asian Studies in the Department of History and in the Department of International Studies. He has published widely on South Korean–U.S. relations, with a particular focus on South Korean perceptions of the United States.

Printed in the USA
CPSIA information can be obtained
at www.ICGtesting.com
LVHW020958081023
760494LV00005B/239